MILITARY AIRCRAFT MARKINGS 2004

Peter R. March &
Howard J. Curtis

D0766096

Ian Allan
PUBLISHING

Contents

This twenty-fifth edition published 2004

ISBN 0 7110 3004 9

Published by Ian Allan Publishing

an imprint of Ian Allan Publishing Ltd, Hersham, Surrey KT12 4RG.
Printed by Ian Allan Printing Ltd, Hersham, Surrey KT12 4RG
Code: 0403/E3

Front cover: Hawk T1As of the Royal Air Force Aerobatic Team, the *Red Arrows* in a characteristic pose.
Katsuhiko Tokunaga

Back cover: Two-seat Eurofighter Typhoon ZH590 on a test-flight from Warton. *BAE Systems*

Introduction

This twenty-fifth annual edition of the *abc Military Aircraft Markings*, jointly edited by Peter R. March and Howard J. Curtis, lists in alphabetical and numerical order all of the aircraft that carry a United Kingdom military serial, and **which are based, or might be seen, in the UK**. It also includes airworthy and current RAF/RN/Army aircraft that are based permanently or temporarily overseas. The term **aircraft** used here covers powered, manned aeroplanes, helicopters, airships and gliders. Included are all the current Royal Air Force, Royal Navy, Army Air Corps, Defence Procurement Agency, QinetiQ operated, manufacturers' test aircraft and civilian-owned aircraft with military markings.

Aircraft withdrawn from operational use but which are retained in the UK for ground training purposes or otherwise preserved by the Services and in the numerous museums and collections are listed. The serials of some incomplete aircraft have been included, such as the cockpit sections of machines displayed by the RAF, aircraft used by airfield fire sections and for service battle damage repair training (BDRT), together with significant parts of aircraft held by preservation groups and societies. Where only part of the aircraft fuselage remains the abbreviation <ff> for front fuselage/cockpit section or <rf> for rear fuselage is shown after the type. Many of these aircraft are allocated, and sometimes wear, a secondary identity, such as an RAF 'M' maintenance number. These numbers are listed against those aircraft to which they have been allocated.

A serial 'missing' from a sequence is either because it was never issued as it formed part of a 'black-out block' or because the aircraft is written off, scrapped, sold abroad or allocated an alternative marking. Aircraft used as targets on MoD ranges to which access is restricted, and some un-manned target drones, are *generally* omitted, as are UK military aircraft that have been permanently grounded and are based overseas and unlikely to return to Britain.

In the main, the serials listed are those markings presently displayed on the aircraft. Where an aircraft carries a false serial it is quoted in *italic type*. Very often these serials are carried by replicas, that are denoted by <R> after the type. The manufacturer and aircraft type are given, together with recent alternative, previous, secondary or civil identity shown in round brackets. Complete records of multiple previous identities are only included where space permits. The operating unit and its based location, along with any known unit and base code markings in square brackets, are given as accurately as possible. The unit markings are normally carried boldly on the sides of the fuselage or on the aircraft's fin. In the case of RAF and AAC machines currently in service, they are usually one or two letters or numbers, while the RN continues to use a well-established system of three-figure codes between 000 and 999 together with a fin letter code denoting the aircraft's operational base. RN squadrons, units and bases are allocated blocks of numbers from which individual aircraft codes are issued. To help identification of RN bases and landing platforms on ships, a list of tail-letter codes with their appropriate name, helicopter code number, ship pennant number and type of vessel, is included; as is a helicopter code number/ships' tail-letter code grid cross-reference.

Codes changes, for example when aircraft move between units, and therefore the markings currently painted on a particular aircraft might not be those shown in this edition because of subsequent events. Aircraft currently under manufacture or not yet delivered to the Service, such as Eurofighter Typhoons are listed under their allocated serial number. Likewise there are a number of newly built aircraft for overseas air arms that carry British serials for their UK test and delivery flights. The 14 EH101 Merlin 512s ordered by the Danish government have been allocated the UK serials ZJ990-999 and ZK001-004, for example. The airframes which will not appear in the next edition because of sale, accident, etc, have their fates, where known, given in italic type in the *locations* column.

The Irish Army Air Corps fleet is listed, together with the serials of other overseas air arms whose aircraft might be seen visiting the UK from time to time. The serial numbers are as usually presented on the individual machine or as they are normally identified. Where possible, the aircraft's base and operating unit have been shown.

USAF, US Army and US Navy aircraft based in the UK and in Western Europe, and types that regularly visit the UK from the USA, are each listed in separate sections by aircraft type. The serial number actually displayed on the aircraft is shown in full, with additional Fiscal Year (FY) or full serial information also provided. Where appropriate, details of the operating wing, squadron allocation and base are added. The USAF is, like the RAF, in a continuing period of change, resulting in the adoption of new unit titles, squadron and equipment changes and the closure of bases. Only details that concern changes effected by January 2004 are shown.

Veteran and vintage aircraft which carry overseas military markings but which are based in the UK or regularly visit from mainland Europe, have been separately listed showing their principal means of identification. The growing list of aircraft in government or military service, often under contract to private operating companies, that carry civil registrations has again been included at the end of the respective country.

With the use of the Internet now very well established as a rich source of information, the section listing a selection of military aviation 'world wide web' sites, has again been expanded and up-dated this year. Although only a few of these provide details of aircraft serials and markings, they do give interesting insights into air arms and their operating units, aircraft, museums and a broad range of associated topics.

Information shown is believed to be correct at 31 January 2004, and significant changes can be monitored through the monthly 'Military Markings' and 'Vintage Serials' columns in *Aircraft Illustrated*.

Acknowledgements

The compilers wish to thank the many people who have taken trouble to send comments, additions, deletions and other useful information since the publication of the previous edition of *abc Military Aircraft Markings*. In particular the following individuals: Dave Albrecht, Alan Allen, Alan Barley, Lee Barton, Derek Bower, Tim Cheney, Glyn Coney, Dougie Couch, Marco Dijkshoorn, Dale Donovan, John Dyer, Peter Foster, Maurizio Gandin, Wal Gandy, Nigel Hitchman, Andrew Horrex, Lee Howard, Paul Jackson, Mike Jeff, Phil Jones, Tim Jones, Andrew March, Andy Marden, Stuart McDiarmid, Tom McGhee, Martyn Morgan, Keith Parkinson, Dave Peel, Ian Poxon, Graeme Robertson, John Skelton, Kev Slade, Kev Storer, Michael Tafel, Mike Tighe, Michael Tulip, Bob Turner and Hans van der Vlist.

This compilation has also relied heavily on the publications/editors, aviation groups and societies as follows: Aerodata Quantum+, Pacific Database, Air-Britain Information Exchange, 'Air-Britain News', Airfields e-mail group, BIA e-mail group, Graham Gaff/East London Aviation Society, Brian Pickering/'Military Aviation Review', Military Spotter's Forum, NAMAR e-mail group, P-3 Orion Research Group, Mervyn Thomas/St Athan Aviation Group, SAAB Viggen e-mail group, Mark Walton/'Scottish Air News', 'Scramble' and Mick Boulanger/Wolverhampton Aviation Group.

PRM & HJC

January 2004

Bristol Fighter D8096 is flown by the Shuttleworth Collection from Old Warden. *PRM*

Abbreviations

AAC	Army Air Corps
AACS	Airborne Air Control Squadron
AACTS	Airborne Air Control Training Squadron
AAS	Aeromedical Airlift Squadron
ABS	Air Base Squadron
ACC	Air Combat Command
ACCGS	Air Cadets Central Gliding School
ACCS	Airborne Command and Control Squadron
ACW	Airborne Control Wing
AD&StA	Aberdeen, Dundee & St Andrews
AEF	Air Experience Flight
AESS	Air Engineering & Survival School
AEW	Airborne Early Warning
AF	Arméflyget (Army Air Battalion)
AFB	Air Force Base
AFD	Air Fleet Department
AFRC	Air Force Reserve Command
AFSC	Air Force Systems Command
AFSK	Armeflygskolan (Army Flying School)
AFWF	Advanced Fixed Wing Flight
AG	Airlift Group
AGA	Academia General del Aire (General Air Academy)
AkG	Aufklärüngsgeschwader (Reconnaissance Wing)
AMC	Air Mobility Command
AMD-BA	Avions Marcel Dassault-Breguet Aviation
AMF	Aircraft Maintenance Flight
AMG	Aircraft Maintenance Group
AMIF	Aircraft Maintenance Instruction Flight
AMS	Air Movements School
AMW	Air Mobility Wing
ANG	Air National Guard
APS	Aircraft Preservation Society
ARS	Air Refuelling Squadron
ARW	Air Refuelling Wing
ARWS	Advanced Rotary Wing Squadron
AS	Airlift Squadron/Air Squadron
ASCW	Airborne Surveillance Control Wing
ASF	Aircraft Servicing Flight
AS&RU	Aircraft Salvage and Repair Unit
ATC	Air Training Corps
ATCC	Air Traffic Control Centre
AVDEF	Aviation Defence Service
Avn	Aviation
Avn Co	Aviation Company
AW	Airlift Wing/Armstrong Whitworth Aircraft
AWC	Air Warfare Centre
BAC	British Aircraft Corporation
BAe	British Aerospace PLC
BAPC	British Aviation Preservation Council
BATSUB	British Army Training Support Unit Belize
BATUS	British Army Training Unit Suffield
BBMF	Battle of Britain Memorial Flight
BDRF	Battle Damage Repair Flight
BDRT	Battle Damage Repair Training
Be	Beech
Bf	Bayerische Flugzeugwerke
BFWF	Basic Fixed Wing Flight
BG	Bomber Group
BGA	British Gliding & Soaring Association
bk	black (squadron colours and markings)
bl	blue (squadron colours and markings)
BNFL	British Nuclear Fuels Ltd
BnHATk	Helicopter Attack Battalion
BnHLn	Liaison Battalion
BP	Boulton & Paul
br	brown (squadron colours and markings)
BS	Bomber Squadron
B-V	Boeing-Vertol
BW	Bomber Wing
CAARP	Co-operative des Ateliers Air de la Région Parisienne
CAC	Commonwealth Aircraft Corporation
CAM	College of Aviation Medicine
CARG	Cotswold Aircraft Restoration Group
CASA	Construcciones Aeronautics SA
Cav	Cavalry
CC	County Council
CCF	Combined Cadet Force/Canadian Car & Foundry Company
CDE	Chemical Defence Establishment
CEAM	Centre d'Expérimentation Aériennes Militaires (Military Air Experimental Centre)
CEPA	Centre d'Expérimentation Pratique de l'Aéronautique Navale
CEV	Centre d'Essais en Vol (Flight Test Centre)
CFS	Central Flying School
CGMF	Central Glider Maintenance Flight
CIFAS	Centre d'Instruction des Forces Aériennes Stratégiques (Air Strategic Training Centre)
CinC	Commander in Chief
CinCLANT	Commander in Chief Atlantic
CITac	Centre d'Instruction Tactique (Tactical Training Centre)
Co	Company
Comp	Composite with
CT	College of Technology
CTE	Central Training Establishment
CV	Chance-Vought
D-BA	Daimler-Benz Aerospace
D-BD	Dassault-Breguet Dornier
D&G	Dumfries and Galloway
DARA	Defence Aviation Repair Agency
DEFTS	Defence Elementary Flying Training School
DEODS	Defence Explosives Ordnance Disposal School
DERA	Defence Evaluation and Research Agency
Det	Detachment
DH	de Havilland
DHC	de Havilland Canada
DHFS	Defence Helicopter Flying School
DLMW	Dywizjon Lotniczy Marynarki Wojennej
DLO	Defence Logistics Organisation
dlt	dopravni letka (Transport Squadron)
DPA	Defence Procurement Agency
DS&TL	Defence Science & Technology Laboratory
DTI	Department of Trade and Industry
EA	Escadron Aérien (Air Squadron)
EAAT	Escadrille Avions de l'Armée de Terre
EAC	Ecole de l'Aviation de Chasse (Fighter Aviation School)
EAP	European Aircraft Project
EAT	Ecole de l'Aviation de Transport (Transport Aviation School)
EC	Escadre de Chasse (Fighter Wing)
ECM	Electronic Counter Measures
ECS	Electronic Countermeasures Squadron
EDA	Escadre de Detection Aéroportée (Air Detection Wing)
EdC	Escadron de Convoyage
EDCA	Escadron de Détection et de Control Aéroportée (Airborne Detection & Control Sqn)
EE	English Electric/Escadrille Electronique
EET	Escadron Electronique Tactique (Tactical Electronics Flight)
EH	Escadron d'Helicoptères (Helicopter Flight)
EHI	European Helicopter Industries
EKW	Eidgenössiches Konstruktionswerkstätte
EL	Escadre de Liaison (Liaison Wing)
ELT	Eskadra Lotnictwa Taktycznego (Tactical Air Squadron)
ELTR	Eskadra Lotnictwa Transportowego (Air Transport Squadron)
EMA	East Midlands Airport
EMVO	Elementaire Militaire Vlieg Opleiding (Elementary Flying Training)
ENOSA	Ecole des Navigateurs Operationales Systemes d'Armees (Navigation School)
EoN	Elliot's of Newbury

EPAA	Ecole de Pilotage Elementaire de l'Armée de l'Air (Air Force Elementary Flying School)	HCS	Hunting Contract Services
EPE	Ecole de Pilotage Elementaire (Elementary Flying School)	HF	Historic Flying Ltd
EPNER	Ecole du Personnel Navigant d'Essais et de Reception	HFR	Heeresfliegerregiment (Army Air Regiment)
ER	Escadre de Reconnaissance (Reconnaissance Wing)	HFS	Heeresfliegerverbindungs-und Aufklärungsstaffel
ERS	Escadre de Reconnaissance Stratégique (Strategic Reconnaissance Squadron)	HFVS	Heeresfliegerversuchstaffel
ERV	Escadre de Ravitaillement en Vol (Air Refuelling Wing)	HFWS	Heeresflieger Waffenschule (Army Air Weapons School)
ES	Escadrille de Servitude	Hkp.Bat	Helikopter Bataljon (Helicopter Battalion)
Esc	Escuadron (Squadron)	HMA	Helicopter Maritime Attack
Esk	Eskadrille (Squadron)	HMF	Harrier Maintenance Flight/Helicopter Maintenance Flight
Eslla	Escuadrilla (Squadron)	HMS	Her Majesty's Ship
Esq	Esquadra (Squadron)	HOCU	Harrier OCU
ET	Escadre de Transport (Transport Squadron)	HP	Handley-Page
ETE	Escadron de Transport et Entrainment (Transport Training Squadron)	HQ	Headquarters
ETEC	Escadron de Transport d'Entrainement et de Calibration (Transport Training & Calibration Sqn)	HRO	Harcàszati Repülö Ezred
ETL	Escadron de Transport Légère (Light Transport Squadron)	HS	Hawker Siddeley
ETO	Escadron de Transition Operationnelle	HSF	Harrier Servicing Flight
ETOM	Escadron de Transport Outre Mer (Overseas Transport Squadron)	IAF	Israeli Air Force
ETPS	Empire Test Pilots' School	INTA	Instituto Nacional de Tecnica Aerospacial
ETS	Engineering Training School	IOW	Isle Of Wight
FAA	Fleet Air Arm/Federal Aviation Administration	IWM	Imperial War Museum
FACF	Forward Air Control Flight	JATE	Joint Air Transport Establishment
FBS	Flugbereitschaftstaffel	JbG	Jagdbombergeschwader (Fighter Bomber Wing)
FBW	Fly by wire	JFACTSU	Joint Forward Air Control Training & Standards Unit
FC	Forskokcentralen (Flight Centre)	JG	Jagdgeschwader (Fighter Wing)
FE	Further Education	Kridlo	Wing
FETC	Fire and Emergency Training Centre	Letka	Squadron
ff	Front fuselage	ltBVr	letka Bitevnich Vrtulníkù (Attack Helicopter Squadron)
FG	Fighter Group	LTG	Lufttransportgeschwader (Air Transport Wing)
FH	Fairchild-Hiller	LTV	Ling-Temco-Vought
FI	Falkland Islands	LVG	Luftwaffen Versorgungs Geschwader (Air Force Maintenance Wing)/Luft Verkehrs Gesellschaft
FISt	Flieger Staffel (Flight Squadron)		
Flt	Flight	LZO	Letecky Zku ební Odbor (Aviation Test Department)
FMA	Fabrica Militar de Aviones	m	multi-coloured (squadron colours and markings)
FMT	Flotila Militara de Transport (Transport Regiment)	MAPK	Mira Anachestisis Pantos Kerou (All Weather Interception Sqn)
FMV	Forsvarets Materielwerk	MARPAT	Maritime Patrouillegroep (Maritime Patrol Group)
FONA	Flag Officer Naval Aviation	MASU	Mobile Aircraft Support Unit
FRADU	Fleet Requirements and Air Direction Unit	MBB	Messerschmitt Bolkow-Blohm
FRA	FR Aviation	MCAS	Marine Corps Air Station
FS	Fighter Squadron	McD	McDonnell Douglas
FSAIU	Flight Safety & Accident Investigation Unit	Med	Medical
FSCTE	Fire Services Central Training Establishment	MFG	Marine Flieger Geschwader (Naval Air Wing)
FTS	Flying Training School	MH	Max Holste
FTW	Flying Training Wing	MIB	Military Intelligence Battalion
Fw	Focke Wulf	MiG	Mikoyan — Gurevich
FW	Fighter Wing/Foster Wickner	Mod	Modified
FWTS	Fixed Wing Test Squadron	MR	Maritime Reconnaissance
FY	Fiscal Year	MRF	Meteorological Research Flight
F3 OCU	Tornado F3 Operational Conversion Unit	M&RU	Marketing & Recruitment Unit
GAF	Government Aircraft Factory	MS	Morane-Saulnier
GAL	General Aircraft Ltd	MTM	Mira Taktikis Metaforon (Tactical Transport Sqn)
GAM	Groupe Aerien Mixte (Composite Air Group)	MU	Maintenance Unit
gd	gold (squadron colours and markings)	Mus'm	Museum
GD	General Dynamics	NA	North American
GHL	Groupe d'Helicopteres Legeres (Light Helicopter Group)	NACDS	Naval Air Command Driving School
GI	Ground Instruction/Groupement d'Instruction (Instructional Group)	NAEWF	NATO Airborne Early Warning Force
gn	green (squadron colours and markings)	NAF	Naval Air Facility
GRD	Gruppe fur Rustunggdienste (Group for Service Preparation)	NAS	Naval Air Station
GT	Grupo de Transporte (Transport Wing)	NASU	Naval Air Support Unit
GTT	Grupo de Transporte de Tropos (Troop Carrier Wing)	NATO	North Atlantic Treaty Organisation
		NAWC	Naval Air Warfare Center
gy	grey (squadron colours and markings)	NAWC-AD	Naval Air Warfare Center Aircraft Division
H&W	Hereford and Worcester	NBC	Nuclear, Biological and Chemical
		NE	North-East
HAF	Historic Aircraft Flight	NFATS	Naval Force Aircraft Test Squadron
HC	Helicopter Combat Support Squadron	NI	Northern Ireland
		NMSU	Nimrod Major Servicing Unit
		NYARC	North Yorks Aircraft Restoration Centre

OCU	Operational Conversion Unit
OEU	Operation Evaluation Unit
OFMC	Old Flying Machine Company
OGMA	Oficinas Gerais de Material Aeronautico
or	orange (squadron colours and markings)
OSAC	Operational Support Airlift Command
OVH Kmp	Observations-Helicopter Kompagni
PASF	Puma Aircraft Servicing Flight
PAT	Priority Air Transport Detachment
PBN	Pilatus Britten-Norman
PLM	Pulk Lotnictwa Mysliwskiego (Fighter Regiment)
pr	purple (squadron colours and markings)
PRU	Photographic Reconnaissance Unit
PVH Kmp	Panservaerns-Helicopter Kompagni
pzdlt	pruzkumná dopravni letka (Reconnaissance & Transport Squadron)
r	red (squadron colours and markings)
R	Replica
RAeS	Royal Aeronautical Society
RAF	Royal Aircraft Factory/Royal Air Force
RAFC	Royal Air Force College
RAFM	Royal Air Force Museum
RAFGSA	Royal Air Force Gliding and Soaring Association
RCAF	Royal Canadian Air Force
RE	Royal Engineers
Regt	Regiment
REME	Royal Electrical & Mechanical Engineers
rf	Rear fuselage
RFA	Royal Fleet Auxiliary
RJAF	Royal Jordanian Air Force
RM	Royal Marines
RMB	Royal Marines Base
RMC of S	Royal Military College of Science
RN	Royal Navy
RNAS	Royal Naval Air Station
RNAW	Royal Naval Aircraft Workshop
RNAY	Royal Naval Aircraft Yard
RNGSA	Royal Navy Gliding and Soaring Association
ROF	Royal Ordnance Factory
RQS	Rescue Squadron
R-R	Rolls-Royce
RS	Reid & Sigrist/Reconnaissance Squadron
RSV	Reparto Sperimentale Volo (Experimental Flight School)
RW	Reconnaissance Wing
SA	Scottish Aviation
SAAB	Svenska Aeroplan Aktiebolag
SAH	School of Air Handling
SAL	Scottish Aviation Limited
SAOEU	Strike/Attack Operational Evaluation Unit
SAR	Search and Rescue
Saro	Saunders-Roe
SARTU	Search and Rescue Training Unit
SBoLK	Stíhacie Bombardovacie Letecké Kridlo (Fighter Bomber Air Wing)
SCW	Strategic Communications Wing
SEAE	School of Electrical & Aeronautical Engineering
SEPECAT	Société Européenne de Production de l'avion Ecole de Combat et d'Appui Tactique
SFDO	School of Flight Deck Operations
SHAPE	Supreme Headquarters Allied Forces Europe
si	silver (squadron colours and markings)
SIET	Section d'Instruction et d'Etude du Tir
SKTU	Sea King Training Unit
Skv	Skvadron (Squadron)
SLK	Stíhacie Letecké Kridlo (Fighter Air Wing)
slt	stíhací letka (Fighter Squadron)
SLV	School Licht Vliegwezen (Flying School)
Sm	Smaldeel (Squadron)
SNCAN	Société Nationale de Constructions Aéronautiques du Nord
SOES	Station Operations & Engineering Squadron
SOG	Special Operations Group
SOS	Special Operations Squadron
SoTT	School of Technical Training
SOW	Special Operations Wing

SPAD	Société Pour les Appareils Deperdussin
SPP	Strojirny Prvni Petilesky
Sqn	Squadron
SSF	Station Servicing Flight
SWWAPS	Second World War Aircraft Preservation Society
TA	Territorial Army
TAP	Transporten Avio Polk (Air Transport Regiment)
T&EE	Test & Evaluation Establishment
TFC	The Fighter Collection
TGp	Test Groep
TIARA	Tornado Integrated Avionics Research Aircraft
tlt	taktická letka (Tactical Squadron)
TMF	Tornado Maintenance Flight
TMTS	Trade Management Training School
tpzlt	taktická a pruzkumná letka (Tactical & Reconnaissance Squadron)
TS	Test Squadron
TsAGI	Tsentral'ny Aerogidrodinamicheski Instut (Central Aero & Hydrodynamics Institute)
TsLw	Technische Schule der Luftwaffe (Luftwaffe Technical School)
TSW	Tactical Supply Wing
TW	Test Wing
UAS	University Air Squadron
Uberwg	Uberwachunggeschwader (Surveillance Wing)
UK	United Kingdom
UKAEA	United Kingdom Atomic Energy Authority
UNFICYP	United Nations' Forces in Cyprus
US	United States
USAF	United States Air Force
USAFE	United States Air Forces in Europe
USAREUR	US Army Europe
USCGS	US Coast Guard Station
USEUCOM	United States European Command
USMC	United States Marine Corps
USN	United States Navy
NWTSPM	United States Navy Test Pilots School
VAAC	Vectored thrust Advanced Aircraft flight Control
VFW	Vereinigte Flugtechnische Werke
VGS	Volunteer Gliding School
vlt	vycviková letka (Training Squadron)
VMGR	Marine Aerial Refuelling/Transport Squadron
VMGRT	Marine Aerial Refuelling/Transport Training Squadron
VQ	Fleet Air Reconnaissance Squadron
VR	Fleet Logistic Support Squadron
VS	Vickers-Supermarine
VSD	Vegyes Szállitorepülő Dandàr (Aircraft Transport Brigade)
VSL	Vycvikové Stredisko Letectva (Flying Training Centre)
w	white (squadron colours and markings)
Wg	Wing
WHL	Westland Helicopters Ltd
WLT	Weapons Loading Training
WRS	Weather Reconnaissance Squadron
WS	Westland
WSK	Wytwornia Sprzetu Kominikacyjnego
WTD	Wehrtechnische Dienstelle (Technical Support Unit)
WW2	World War II
y	yellow (squadron colours and markings)
zDL	základna Dopravního Letectva (Air Transport Base)
ZmDK	Zmie an? Dopravn? Kridlo (Mixed Transport Wing)
zSL	základna Speciálního Letectva (Training Air Base)
zTL	základna Taktického Letectva (Tactical Air Base)
zVrL	základna Vrtulníkového Letectva (Helicopter Air Base)

A Guide to the Location of Operational Military Bases in the UK

This section is to assist the reader to locate the places in the United Kingdom where operational military aircraft are based. The term *aircraft* also includes helicopters and gliders.

The alphabetical order listing gives each location in relation to its county and to its nearest classified road(s) (*by* means adjoining; *of* means proximate to), together with its approximate direction and mileage from the centre of a nearby major town or city. Some civil airports are included where active military units are also based, but **excluded** are MoD sites with non-operational aircraft (eg *gate guardians*), the bases of privately-owned civil aircraft that wear military markings and museums.

User	Base name	County/Region	Location	Distance/direction from (town)
QinetiQ	Aberporth	Dyfed	N of A487	6m ENE of Cardigan
Army	Abingdon	Oxfordshire	W by B4017, W of A34	5m SSW of Oxford
RAF	Aldergrove/Belfast	Co Antrim Airport	W by A26	13m W of Belfast
RM	Arbroath	Angus	E of A933	2m NW of Arbroath
RAF/HCS	Barkston Heath	Lincolnshire	W by B6404, S of A153	5m NNE of Grantham
RAF	Benson	Oxfordshire	E by A4074	1m NE of Wallingford
QinetiQ/ RAF	Boscombe Down	Wiltshire	S by A303, W of A338	6m N of Salisbury
RAF	Boulmer	Northumberland	E of B1339	4m E of Alnwick
RAF	Brize Norton	Oxfordshire	W of A4095	5m SW of Witney
Marshall	Cambridge Airport/ Teversham	Cambridgeshire	S by A1303	2m E of Cambridge
RM/RAF	Chivenor	Devon	S of A361	4m WNW of Barnstaple
RAF	Church Fenton	Yorkshire North	S of B1223	7m WNW of Selby
RAF	Colerne	Wiltshire	S of A420, E of Fosse Way	5m NE of Bath
RAF	Coltishall	Norfolk	W of B1150	9m NNE of Norwich
RAF	Coningsby	Lincolnshire	S of A153, W by B1192	10m NW of Boston
RAF	Cosford	Shropshire	W of A41, N of A464	9m WNW of Wolverhampton
RAF	Cottesmore	Rutland	W of A1, N of B668	9m NW of Stamford
RAF	Cranwell	Lincolnshire	N by A17, S by B1429	5m WNW of Sleaford
RN	Culdrose	Cornwall	E by A3083	1m SE of Helston
Army	Dishforth	Yorkshire North	E by A1	4m E of Ripon
USAF	Fairford	Gloucestershire	S of A417	9m ESE of Cirencester
RN	Fleetlands	Hampshire	E by A32	2m SE of Fareham
RAF	Glasgow Airport	Strathclyde	N by M8 jn 28	7m W of city
RAF	Halton	Buckinghamshire	N of A4011, S of B4544	4m ESE of Aylesbury
RAF	Henlow	Bedfordshire	E of A600, W of A6001	1m SW of Henlow
RAF	Honington	Suffolk	E of A134, W of A1088	6m S of Thetford
Army	Hullavington	Wiltshire	W of A429	1m N of M4 jn 17
RAF	Kenley	Greater London	W of A22	1m W of Warlingham
RAF	Kinloss	Grampian	E of B9011, N of B9089	3m NE of Forres
RAF	Kirknewton	Lothian	E by B7031, N by A70	8m SW of Edinburgh
USAF	Lakenheath	Suffolk	W by A1065	8m W of Thetford
RAF	Leeming	Yorkshire North	E by A1	5m SW of Northallerton
RAF	Leuchars	Fife	E of A919	7m SE of Dundee
RAF	Linton-on-Ouse	Yorkshire North	E of B6265	10m NW of York
QinetiQ	Llanbedr	Gwynedd	W of A496	7m NNW of Barmouth
RAF	Lossiemouth	Grampian	W of B9135, S of B9040	4m N of Elgin
RAF	Lyneham	Wiltshire	W of A3102, S of A420	10m WSW of Swindon
RAF	Marham	Norfolk	N by A1122	6m W of Swaffham
Army	Middle Wallop	Hampshire	S by A343	6m SW of Andover
USAF	Mildenhall	Suffolk	S by A1101	9m NNE of Newmarket
RAF	Northolt	Greater London	N by A40	3m E of M40 jn 1
RAF	Odiham	Hampshire	E of A32	2m S of M3 jn 5
RN	Predannack	Cornwall	W by A3083	7m S of Helston
RAF	St Athan	South Glamorgan	N of B4265	13m WSW of Cardiff
RAF	St Mawgan/Newquay	Cornwall	N of A3059	4m ENE of Newquay
RAF	Scampton	Lincolnshire	W by A15	6m N of Lincoln
RAF	Sealand	Flint	W by A550	6m WNW of Chester
RAF	Shawbury	Shropshire	W of B5063	7m NNE of Shrewsbury
RAF	Syerston	Nottinghamshire	W by A46	5m SW of Newark
RAF	Ternhill	Shropshire	SW by A41	3m SW of Market Drayton

User	Base name	County/Region	Location	Distance/direction from (town)
RAF/ Army	Topcliffe	Yorkshire North	E of A167, W of A168	3m SW of Thirsk
RAF	Valley	Gwynedd	S of A5 on Anglesey	5m SE of Holyhead
RAF	Waddington	Lincolnshire	E by A607, W by A15	5m S of Lincoln
Army/ RAF	Wattisham	Suffolk	N of B1078	5m SSW of Stowmarket
RAF	Weston-on-the-Green	Oxfordshire	E by A43	9m N of Oxford
RAF	Wittering	Cambridgeshire	W by A1, N of A47	3m S of Stamford
RAF	Woodvale	Merseyside	W by A565	5m SSW of Southport
RAF	Wyton	Cambridgeshire	E of A141, N of B1090	3m NE of Huntingdon
RN	Yeovilton	Somerset	S by B3151, S of A303	5m N of Yeovil

This privately owned Tiger Moth T5879 is painted in its original RAF training colours. *PRM*

V1075 is one of only a handful of Miles M14A Magisters remaining airworthy. *PRM*

British Military Aircraft Serials

The Committee of Imperial Defence through its Air Committee introduced a standardised system of numbering aircraft in November 1912. The Air Department of the Admiralty was allocated the first batch 1-200 and used these to cover aircraft already in use and those on order. The Army was issued with the next block from 201-800, which included the number 304 which was given to the Cody Biplane now preserved in the Science Museum. By the outbreak of World War 1 the Royal Navy was on its second batch of serials 801-1600 and this system continued with alternating allocations between the Army and Navy until 1916 when number 10000, a Royal Flying Corps BE2C, was reached.

It was decided not to continue with five digit numbers but instead to start again from 1, prefixing RFC aircraft with the letter A and RNAS aircraft with the prefix N. The RFC allocations commenced with A1 an FE2D and before the end of the year had reached A9999 an Armstrong Whitworth FK8. The next group commenced with B1 and continued in logical sequence through the C, D, E and F prefixes. G was used on a limited basis to identify captured German aircraft, while H was the last block of wartime-ordered aircraft. To avoid confusion I was not used, so the new postwar machines were allocated serials in the J range. A further minor change was made in the serial numbering system in August 1929 when it was decided to maintain four numerals after the prefix letter, thus omitting numbers 1 to 999. The new K series therefore commenced at K1000, which was allocated to an AW Atlas.

The Naval N prefix was not used in such a logical way. Blocks of numbers were allocated for specific types of aircraft such as seaplanes or flying-boats. By the late 1920s the sequence had largely been used up and a new series using the prefix S was commenced. In 1930 separate naval allocations were stopped and subsequent serials were issued in the 'military' range which had by this time reached the K series. A further change in the pattern of allocations came in the L range. Commencing with L7272 numbers were issued in blocks with smaller blocks of serials between not used. These were known as blackout blocks. As M had already been used as a suffix for Maintenance Command instructional airframes it was not used as a prefix. Although N had previously been used for naval aircraft it was used again for serials allocated from 1937.

With the build-up to World War 2 the rate of allocations quickly accelerated and the prefix R was being used when war was declared. The letters O and Q were not allotted, and nor was S which had been used up to S1865 for naval aircraft before integration into the RAF series. By 1940 the serial Z9999 had been reached, as part of a blackout block, with the letters U and Y not used to avoid confusion. The option to recommence serial allocation at A1000 was not taken up; instead it was decided to use an alphabetical two-letter prefix with three numerals running from 100 to 999. Thus AA100 was allocated to a Blenheim IV.

This two-letter, three-numeral serial system which started in 1940 continues today. The letters C, I, O, Q, U and Y were, with the exception of NC, not used. For various reasons the following letter combinations were not issued: DA, DB, DH, EA, GA to GZ, HA, HT, JE, JH, JJ, KR to KT, MR, NW, NZ, SA to SK, SV, TN, TR and VE. The first postwar serials issued were in the VP range while the end of the WZs had been reached by the Korean War.

In 2004 the new issues are in the ZK range. With the allocation of ZJ999 to an EH101 Merlin 512 for Denmark it was decided to use the numerals 001 to 099 for the first time, hence the appearance of ZK001 to ZK004 for the remainder of the batch of Merlins. A further change in the issue of serials for target drones has also been made. To prevent the high usage of numbers for target drones which are eventually destroyed, a single serial number should be issued relating to a UAV type. The Agency or Service operating these UAVs will be responsible for the identification of each individual UAV by adding a suffix to the serial number. In practise this has meant that some Army drones carry a letter (A, B, C et seq) to a common serial number.

In general there are now no blackout blocks of unallocated serials. This being so, and at the current rate of issue, the Z range will last for many years. Occasionally an 'out-of-sequence' serial is issued to a manufacturer's prototype or development aircraft ZT800. However, a break in the established sequence came with the Boeing C-17 Globemasters leased from Boeing, that carry the serials ZZ171-ZZ174.

Note: The compilers will be pleased to receive comments, corrections and further information for inclusion in subsequent editions of *Military Aircraft Markings* and the monthly up-date of additions and amendments that is published in *Aircraft Illustrated*. Please send your information to Ian Allan Publishing (Military Aircraft Markings) or by fax to: 0117 968 3928 or e-mail to HJCurtis@ntlworld.com.

British Military Aircraft Markings

A serial in *italics* denotes that it is not the genuine marking for that airframe.

Serial	Type (other identity) [code]	Owner/operator, location or fate	Notes
168	Sopwith Tabloid Scout <R> (G-BFDE)	RAF Museum, Hendon	
304	Cody Biplane (BAPC 62)	Science Museum, South Kensington	
687	RAF BE2b <R> (BAPC 181)	RAF Museum, Hendon	
1701	RAF BE2c <R> (BAPC 117)	Privately owned, Orpington	
2345	Vickers FB5 Gunbus <R> (G-ATVP)	RAF Museum, Hendon	
2699	RAF BE2c	Imperial War Museum, Lambeth	
3066	Caudron GIII (G-AETA/9203M)	RAF Museum, Hendon	
5964	DH2 <R> (BAPC 112)	Privately owned, Stretton on Dunsmore	
5964	DH2 <R> (G-BFVH)	Privately owned, Withybush	
6232	RAF BE2c <R> (BAPC 41)	Yorkshire Air Museum, stored Elvington	
8359	Short 184 <ff>	FAA Museum, RNAS Yeovilton	
A301	Morane BB (frame)	RAF Museum Restoration Centre, Cosford	
A1325	RAF BE2e (G-BVGR)	Privately owned, Milden	
A1742	Bristol Scout D <R> (BAPC 38)	Privately owned, Solihull	
A4850	RAF SE5a <R> (BAPC 176)	*Current location not known*	
A7317	Sopwith Pup <R> (BAPC 179)	Midland Air Museum, Coventry	
A8226	Sopwith 1¹/₂ Strutter <R> (G-BIDW)	RAF Museum, Hendon	
B595	RAF SE5a <R> (G-BUOD) [W]	Privately owned, Kemble	
B1807	Sopwith Pup (G-EAVX) [A7]	Privately owned, Keynsham, Avon	
B2458	Sopwith 1F.1 Camel <R> (G-BPOB/*F542*) [R]	Privately owned, Compton Abbas	
B3459	Nieuport Scout 17/23 <R> (G-BWMJ) [21]	Privately owned, Fairoaks	
B5539	Sopwith 1F.1 Camel <R>	Privately owned, Compton Abbas	
B5577	Sopwith 1F.1 Camel <R> (*D3419*/ BAPC 59) [W]	RAF Museum, Cosford	
B6401	Sopwith 1F.1 Camel <R> (G-AWYY/C1701)	FAA Museum, RNAS Yeovilton	
B7270	Sopwith 1F.1 Camel <R> (G-BFCZ)	Brooklands Museum, Weybridge	
C1904	RAF SE5a <R> (G-PFAP) [Z]	Privately owned, Syerston	
C3011	Phoenix Currie Super Wot (G-SWOT) [S]	The Real Aeroplane Company, Breighton	
C4451	Avro 504J <R> (BAPC 210)	Southampton Hall of Aviation	
C4918	Bristol M1C <R> (G-BWJM)	The Shuttleworth Collection, Old Warden	
C4994	Bristol M1C <R> (G-BLWM)	RAF Museum, Hendon	
C9533	RAF SE5a <R> (G-BUWE) [M]	Privately owned, Boscombe Down	
D276	RAF SE5a <R> (BAPC 208) [A]	Prince's Mead Shopping Centre, Farnborough	
D3419	Sopwith 1F.1 Camel <R> (*F1921*/ BAPC 59)	*Repainted as B5577*	
D5329	Sopwith 5F.1 Dolphin	RAF Museum Restoration Centre, Cosford	
D5649	Airco DH9	Aero Vintage, Hatch	
D7560	Avro 504K	Science Museum, South Kensington	
D7889	Bristol F2b Fighter (G-AANM/ BAPC 166)	Privately owned, Old Warden	
D8084	Bristol F2b Fighter (G-ACAA/ F4516) [S]	The Fighter Collection, Duxford	
D8096	Bristol F2b Fighter (G-AEPH) [D]	The Shuttleworth Collection, Old Warden	
E373	Avro 504K <R> (BAPC 178)	Privately owned,	
E449	Avro 504K (G-EBJE/9205M)	RAF Museum, Hendon	
E2466	Bristol F2b Fighter (BAPC 165) [I]	RAF Museum, Hendon	
E2581	Bristol F2b Fighter [13]	Imperial War Museum, Duxford	
F141	RAF SE5a <R> (G-SEVA) [G]	Privately owned, Boscombe Down	
F235	RAF SE5a <R> (G-BMDB) [B]	Privately owned, Boscombe Down	
F904	RAF SE5a (G-EBIA)	The Shuttleworth Collection, Old Warden	
F938	RAF SE5a (G-EBIC/9208M)	RAF Museum, Hendon	
F943	RAF SE5a <R> (G-BIHF) [S]	Museum of Army Flying, Middle Wallop	

Notes	Serial	Type (other identity) [code]	Owner/operator, location or fate
	F943	RAF SE5a <R> (G-BKDT)	Yorkshire Air Museum, Elvington
	F1010	Airco DH9A [C]	RAF Museum, Hendon
	F3556	RAF RE8	Imperial War Museum, Duxford
	F5447	RAF SE5a <R> (G-BKER) [N]	Privately owned, Cumbernauld
	F5459	RAF SE5a <R> (G-INNY) [Y]	Privately owned, Lee-on-Solent
	F5475	RAF SE5a <R> (BAPC 250)	Brooklands Museum, Weybridge
	F6314	Sopwith 1F.1 Camel (9206M) [B]	RAF Museum Restoration Centre, Cosford
	F8010	RAF SE5a <R> (G-BDWJ) [Z]	Privately owned, Graveley
	F8614	Vickers FB27A Vimy IV <R> (G-AWAU)	RAF Museum, Hendon
	H1968	Avro 504K <R> (BAPC 42)	Yorkshire Air Museum, stored Elvington
	H2311	Avro 504K (G-ABAA)	Gr Manchester Mus of Science & Industry
	H3426	Hawker Hurricane <R> (BAPC 68)	NW Aviation Heritage Group, Hooton Park
	H5199	Avro 504K (BK892/3118M/ G-ACNB/G-ADEV)	The Shuttleworth Collection, Old Warden
	J7326	DH53 Humming Bird (G-EBQP)	Mosquito Aircraft Museum, London Colney
	J8067	Westland Pterodactyl 1a	Science Museum, South Kensington
	J9941	Hawker Hart 2 (G-ABMR)	RAF Museum, Hendon
	K1786	Hawker Tomtit (G-AFTA)	The Shuttleworth Collection, Old Warden
	K1930	Hawker Fury <R> (G-BKBB/ OO-HFU)	Privately owned, Wevelgem, Belgium
	K2048	Isaacs Fury II (G-BZNW)	Privately owned, Fishburn
	K2050	Isaacs Fury II (G-ASCM)	Privately owned, Brize Norton
	K2059	Isaacs Fury II (G-PFAR)	Privately owned, Dunkeswell
	K2060	Isaacs Fury II (G-BKZM)	Privately owned, Haverfordwest
	K2075	Isaacs Fury II (G-BEER)	Privately owned, Alderminster
	K2227	Bristol 105 Bulldog IIA (G-ABBB)	RAF Museum, Hendon
	K2567	DH82A Tiger Moth (DE306/7035M/ G-MOTH)	Privately owned, Tadlow
	K2572	DH82A Tiger Moth (NM129/ G-AOZH)	Privately owned, Redhill
	K2572	DH82A Tiger Moth <R>	The Aircraft Restoration Company, Duxford
	K2587	DH82A Tiger Moth <R> (G-BJAP)	Privately owned, Shobdon
	K3215	Avro 621 Tutor (G-AHSA)	The Shuttleworth Collection, Old Warden
	K3661	Hawker Nimrod II (G-BURZ)	Aero Vintage, St Leonards-on-Sea
	K3731	Isaacs Fury <R> (G-RODI)	Privately owned, Hailsham
	K4232	Avro 671 Rota I (SE-AZB)	RAF Museum, Hendon
	K4259	DH82A Tiger Moth (G-ANMO) [71]	Privately owned, White Waltham
	K4672	Hawker Hind (BAPC 82)	RAF Museum, Cosford
	K4972	Hawker Hart Trainer IIA (1764M)	RAF Museum, Hendon
	K5054	Supermarine Spitfire <R> (BAPC 190/EN398)	Privately owned, Sevenoaks, Kent
	K5054	Supermarine Spitfire <R> (BAPC 214)	Tangmere Military Aviation Museum
	K5054	Supermarine Spitfire <R> (G-BRDV)	Southampton Hall of Aviation
	K5054	Supermarine Spitfire <R> (G-BRDV)	Kent Battle of Britain Museum, Hawkinge
	K5414	Hawker Hind (G-AENP/BAPC 78) [XV]	The Shuttleworth Collection, Old Warden
	K5600	Hawker Audax I (2015M/G-BVVI)	Aero Vintage, St Leonards-on-Sea
	K5673	Isaacs Fury II (G-BZAS)	Bournemouth Aviation Museum
	K5673	Hawker Fury I <R> (BAPC 249)	Brooklands Museum, Weybridge
	K6035	Westland Wallace II (2361M)	RAF Museum, Hendon
	K7271	Hawker Fury II <R> (BAPC 148)	Shropshire Wartime Aircraft Recovery Grp Mus, Sleap
	K8042	Gloster Gladiator II (8372M)	RAF Museum, Hendon
	K8203	Hawker Demon I (G-BTVE/2292M)	Demon Displays, Hatch
	K8303	Isaacs Fury II (G-BWWN) [D]	Privately owned, Lower Upham
	K9926	VS300 Spitfire I <R> (BAPC 217) [JH-C]	RAF Bentley Priory, on display
	K9942	VS300 Spitfire I (8383M) [SD-D]	RAF Museum Restoration Centre, Cosford
	K9962	VS300 Spitfire I <R> [JH-C]	Privately owned,
	L1070	VS300 Spitfire I <R> (BAPC 227) [XT-A]	Edinburgh airport, on display
	L1592	Hawker Hurricane I [KW-Z]	Science Museum, South Kensington
	L1679	Hawker Hurricane I <R> (BAPC 241) [JX-G]	Tangmere Military Aviation Museum
	L1710	Hawker Hurricane I <R> (BAPC 219) [AL-D]	RAF Biggin Hill, on display

Serial	Type (other identity) [code]	Owner/operator, location or fate	Notes
L2301	VS Walrus I (G-AIZG)	FAA Museum, RNAS Yeovilton	
L2940	Blackburn Skua I	FAA Museum, RNAS Yeovilton	
L5343	Fairey Battle I [VO-S]	RAF Museum, Hendon	
L6906	Miles M14A Magister I (G-AKKY/ T9841/BAPC 44)	Museum of Berkshire Aviation, Woodley	
L7005	Boulton Paul P82 Defiant I <R> [PS-B]	Boulton Paul Association, Wolverhampton	
L7181	Hawker Hind (G-CBLK)	Aero Vintage, Hatch	
L8756	Bristol 149 Bolingbroke IVT (RCAF 10001) [XD-E]	RAF Museum, Hendon	
N248	Supermarine S6A (S1596)	Southampton Hall of Aviation	
N500	Sopwith LC-1T Triplane <R> (G-PENY/G-BWRA)	Privately owned, Dunkeswell/RNAS Yeovilton	
N546	Wright Quadruplane 1 <R> (BAPC 164)	Southampton Hall of Aviation	
N1671	Boulton Paul P82 Defiant I (8370M) [EW-D]	RAF Museum, Hendon	
N1854	Fairey Fulmar II (G-AIBE)	FAA Museum, RNAS Yeovilton	
N2078	Sopwith Baby (8214/8215)	FAA Museum, RNAS Yeovilton	
N2532	Hawker Hurricane I <R> (BAPC 272) [GZ-H]	Kent Battle of Britain Museum, Hawkinge	
N2980	Vickers Wellington IA [R]	Brooklands Museum, Weybridge	
N3177	RAF BE2e <R>	Barton Aviation Heritage Society, Barton	
N3194	VS300 Spitfire I <R> (BAPC 220) [GR-Z]	RAF Biggin Hill, on display	
N3289	VS300 Spitfire I <R> (BAPC 65) [DW-K]	Kent Battle of Britain Museum, Hawkinge	
N3313	VS300 Spitfire I <R> (MH314/ BAPC 69) [KL-B]	Kent Battle of Britain Museum, Hawkinge	
N3317	VS361 Spitfire IX <R> (BAPC 268)	Privately owned, St Mawgan	
N3320	VS361 Spitfire IX <R>	Privately owned, Wellesbourne Mountford	
N3378	Boulton Paul P82 Defiant I	Boulton Paul Association, Wolverhampton	
N4389	Fairey Albacore (N4172) [4M]	FAA Museum, RNAS Yeovilton	
N4877	Avro 652A Anson I (G-AMDA) [MK-V]	Imperial War Museum, Duxford	
N5177	Sopwith 1½ Strutter <R>	Botany Bay Village, Chorley, Lancs	
N5182	Sopwith Pup <R> (G-APUP/9213M)	RAF Museum, Hendon	
N5195	Sopwith Pup (G-ABOX)	Museum of Army Flying, Middle Wallop	
N5492	Sopwith Triplane <R> (BAPC 111)	FAA Museum, RNAS Yeovilton	
N5518	Gloster Sea Gladiator	FAA Museum, RNAS Yeovilton	
N5628	Gloster Gladiator II	RAF Museum, Hendon	
N5719	Gloster Gladiator II (G-CBHO)	Privately owned, Glos	
N5903	Gloster Gladiator II (N2276/ G-GLAD) [H]	The Fighter Collection, Duxford	
N5912	Sopwith Triplane (8385M)	RAF Museum, Hendon	
N6181	Sopwith Pup (G-EBKY/N5180)	The Shuttleworth Collection, Old Warden	
N6290	Sopwith Triplane <R> (G-BOCK)	The Shuttleworth Collection, Old Warden	
N6452	Sopwith Pup <R> (G-BIAU)	FAA Museum, RNAS Yeovilton	
N6466	DH82A Tiger Moth (G-ANKZ)	Privately owned, Durley, Hants	
N6537	DH82A Tiger Moth (G-AOHY)	AAC Historic Aircraft Flt, Middle Wallop	
N6720	DH82A Tiger Moth (G-BYTN/ 7014M) [RUO-B]	Privately owned, Hatch	
N6797	DH82A Tiger Moth (G-ANEH)	Privately owned, Goodwood	
N6812	Sopwith 2F.1 Camel	Imperial War Museum, Lambeth	
N6847	DH82A Tiger Moth (G-APAL)	Privately owned, Barton	
N6965	DH82A Tiger Moth (G-AJTW) [FL-J] (wreck)	Privately owned, Tibenham	
N7033	Noorduyn AT-16 Harvard IIB (FX442)	Kent Battle of Britain Museum, Hawkinge	
N9191	DH82A Tiger Moth (G-ALND)	Privately owned, Abergavenny	
N9192	DH82A Tiger Moth (G-DHZF) [RCO-N]	Privately owned, Sywell	
N9389	DH82A Tiger Moth (G-ANJA)	Privately owned, Seething	
N9899	Supermarine Southampton I (fuselage)	RAF Museum, Hendon	
P1344	HP52 Hampden I (9175M) [PL-K]	RAF Museum Restoration Centre, Cosford	
P1344	HP52 Hampden I <rf> (parts Hereford L6012)	RAF Museum, Hendon	
P2617	Hawker Hurricane I (8373M) [AF-A]	RAF Museum, Hendon	
P2790	Hawker Hurricane I <R> [US-X]	Battle of Britain Memorial, Capel le Ferne, Kent	

Notes	Serial	Type (other identity) [code]	Owner/operator, location or fate
	P2793	Hawker Hurricane I <R> (BAPC 236) [SD-M]	Eden Camp Theme Park, Malton, North Yorkshire
	P2902	Hawker Hurricane I (G-ROBT)	Privately owned, Milden
	P2921	Hawker Hurricane I <R> (BAPC 273) [GZ-L]	Kent Battle of Britain Museum, Hawkinge
	P3059	Hawker Hurricane I <R> (BAPC 64) [SD-N]	Privately owned, Bassingbourn
	P3175	Hawker Hurricane I (wreck)	RAF Museum, Hendon
	P3208	Hawker Hurricane I <R> (BAPC 63/L1592) [SD-T]	Kent Battle of Britain Museum, Hawkinge
	P3386	Hawker Hurricane I <R> (BAPC 218) [FT-A]	RAF Bentley Priory, on display
	P3395	Hawker Hurricane IV (KX829) [JX-B]	Millennium Discovery Centre, Birmingham
	P3554	Hawker Hurricane I (composite)	The Air Defence Collection, Salisbury
	P3679	Hawker Hurricane I <R> (BAPC 278) [GZ-K]	Kent Battle of Britain Museum, Hawkinge
	P3717	Hawker Hurricane I (composite) (DR348)	Privately owned, Hinckley, Leics
	P3873	Hawker Hurricane I <R> (BAPC 265) [YO-H]	Yorkshire Air Museum, Elvington
	P4139	Fairey Swordfish II (HS618) [5H]	FAA Museum, RNAS Yeovilton
	P6382	Miles M14A Hawk Trainer 3 (G-AJRS) [C]	The Shuttleworth Collection, Old Warden
	P7350	VS329 Spitfire IIA (G-AWIJ) [XT-D]	RAF BBMF, Coningsby
	P7540	VS329 Spitfire IIA [DU-W]	Dumfries & Galloway Avn Mus, Dumfries
	P7966	VS329 Spitfire II <R> [D-B]	Manx Aviation & Military Museum, Ronaldsway
	P8140	VS329 Spitfire II <R> (P9390/ BAPC 71) [ZF-K]	Norfolk & Suffolk Avn Museum, Flixton
	P8448	VS329 Spitfire II <R> (BAPC 225) [UM-D]	RAF Cranwell, on display
	P9374	VS300 Spitfire IA (G-MKIA)	Privately owned, Braintree
	P9444	VS300 Spitfire IA [RN-D]	Science Museum, South Kensington
	R1914	Miles M14A Magister (G-AHUJ)	Privately owned, Strathallan
	R3821	Bristol 149 Bolingbroke IVT (G-BPIV/Z5722) [UX-N]	The Aircraft Restoration Company, Duxford (damaged)
	R4115	Hawker Hurricane I <R> (BAPC 267) [LE-X]	Imperial War Museum, Duxford
	R4118	Hawker Hurricane I (G-HUPW)	Privately owned, Sutton Courtenay
	R4922	DH82A Tiger Moth II (G-APAO)	Privately owned, Duxford
	R4959	DH82A Tiger Moth II (G-ARAZ) [59]	Privately owned, Temple Bruer
	R5136	DH82A Tiger Moth II (G-APAP)	Privately owned, Henlow
	R5172	DH82A Tiger Moth II (G-AOIS) [FIJ-E]	Privately owned, Sherburn-in-Elmet
	R5250	DH82A Tiger Moth II (G-AODT) [PO-S]	Privately owned, Tibenham
	R5868	Avro 683 Lancaster I (7325M)	RAF Museum, Hendon
	R6690	VS300 Spitfire I <R> (BAPC 254) [PR-A]	Yorkshire Air Museum, Elvington
	R6915	VS300 Spitfire I	Imperial War Museum, Lambeth
	R9125	Westland Lysander III (8377M) [LX-L]	RAF Museum, Hendon
	R9371	HP59 Halifax II <ff>	Cotswold Aircraft Rest'n Grp, Innsworth
	S1287	Fairey Flycatcher <R> (G-BEYB)	FAA Museum, RNAS Yeovilton
	S1579	Hawker Nimrod I <R> (G-BBVO) [571]	Privately owned, Basingstoke
	S1581	Hawker Nimrod I (G-BWWK) [573]	The Fighter Collection, Duxford
	S1595	Supermarine S6B	Science Museum, South Kensington
	T5298	Bristol 156 Beaufighter I (4552M) <ff>	Midland Air Museum, Coventry
	T5424	DH82A Tiger Moth II (G-AJOA)	Privately owned, Chiseldon
	T5672	DH82A Tiger Moth II (G-ALRI)	Privately owned, Chalmington
	T5854	DH82A Tiger Moth II (G-ANKK)	Privately owned, Baxterley
	T5879	DH82A Tiger Moth II (G-AXBW) [RUC-W]	Privately owned, Frensham
	T6296	DH82A Tiger Moth II (8387M)	RAF Museum, Hendon
	T6313	DH82A Tiger Moth II (G-AHVU)	Privately owned, West Meon
	T6562	DH82A Tiger Moth II (G-ANTE)	Privately owned, Sywell
	T6818	DH82A Tiger Moth II (G-ANKT) [91]	The Shuttleworth Collection, Old Warden

Serial	Type (other identity) [code]	Owner/operator, location or fate	Notes
T6953	DH82A Tiger Moth II (G-ANNI)	Privately owned, Little Gransden	
T6991	DH82A Tiger Moth II (HB-UPY/ DE694)	Privately owned, Switzerland	
T7230	DH82A Tiger Moth II (G-AFVE)	Privately owned, stored Booker	
T7238	DH82A Tiger Moth II (G-APPN)	Sold to Spain, June 2003	
T7281	DH82A Tiger Moth II (G-ARTL)	Privately owned, Egton, nr Whitby	
T7404	DH82A Tiger Moth II (G-ANMV) [04]	Privately owned, stored Booker	
T7793	DH82A Tiger Moth II (G-ANKV)	Privately owned, Croydon, on display	
T7842	DH82A Tiger Moth II (G-AMTF)	Privately owned, Boughton, Suffolk	
T7909	DH82A Tiger Moth II (G-ANON)	Privately owned, Sherburn-in-Elmet	
T7997	DH82A Tiger Moth II (NL750/ G-AHUF)	Privately owned, Edburton	
T8191	DH82A Tiger Moth II (G-BWMK)	Privately owned, Welshpool	
T9707	Miles M14A Magister I (G-AKKR/ 8378M/T9708)	Museum of Army Flying, Middle Wallop	
T9738	Miles M14A Magister I (G-AKAT)	Privately owned, Breighton	
V1075	Miles M14A Magister I (G-AKPF)	Privately owned, Old Warden	
V3388	Airspeed AS10 Oxford I (G-AHTW)	Imperial War Museum, Duxford	
V6028	Bristol 149 Bolingbroke IVT (G-MKIV) [GB-D] <rf>	The Aircraft Restoration Co, stored Duxford	
V6799	Hawker Hurricane I <R> (BAPC 72/ V7767) [SD-X]	Gloucestershire Avn Coll, stored Gloucester	
V7350	Hawker Hurricane I (fuselage)	Brenzett Aeronautical Museum	
V7467	Hawker Hurricane I <R> (BAPC 223) [LE-D]	RAF Coltishall, on display	
V7467	Hawker Hurricane I <R> [LE-D]	Wonderland Pleasure Park, Farnsfield, Notts	
V7497	Hawker Hurricane I (G-HRLI)	Hawker Restorations, Milden	
V9367	Westland Lysander IIIA (G-AZWT) [MA-B]	The Shuttleworth Collection, Old Warden	
V9673	Westland Lysander IIIA (V9300/ G-LIZY) [MA-J]	Imperial War Museum, Duxford	
V9723	Westland Lysander IIIA (2442/ OO-SOT) [MA-D]	SABENA Old Timers, Brussels, Belgium	
V9312	Westland Lysander IIIA (G-CCOM)	The Aircraft Restoration Co, Duxford	
W1048	HP59 Halifax II (8465M) [TL-S]	RAF Museum, Hendon	
W2068	Avro 652A Anson I (9261M/ VH-ASM) [68]	RAF Museum, Hendon	
W2718	VS Walrus I (G-RNLI)	Dick Melton Aviation, Great Yarmouth	
W4041	Gloster E28/39 [G]	Science Museum, South Kensington	
W4050	DH98 Mosquito	Mosquito Aircraft Museum, London Colney	
W5856	Fairey Swordfish II (G-BMGC) [A2A]	RN Historic Flight, Yeovilton	
W9385	DH87B Hornet Moth (G-ADND) [YG-L,3]	The Shuttleworth Collection, Old Warden	
X4590	VS300 Spitfire I (8384M) [PR-F]	RAF Museum, Hendon	
X7688	Bristol 156 Beaufighter I (3858M/ G-DINT)	Privately owned, Hatch	
Z1206	Vickers Wellington IV (fuselage)	Midland Warplane Museum, Baxterley	
Z2033	Fairey Firefly I (G-ASTL) [275]	FAA museum, stored RNAS Yeovilton	
Z2315	Hawker Hurricane IIA [JU-E]	Imperial War Museum, Duxford	
Z2389	Hawker Hurricane IIA	Brooklands Museum, Weybridge	
Z5207	Hawker Hurricane IIB (G-BYDL)	Privately owned, Dursley, Glos	
Z5252	Hawker Hurricane IIB (G-BWHA/ Z5053) [GO-B]	Privately owned, Milden	
Z7015	Hawker Sea Hurricane IB (G-BKTH) [7-L]	The Shuttleworth Collection, Old Warden	
Z7197	Percival P30 Proctor III (G-AKZN/ 8380M)	RAF Museum, Hendon	
Z7258	DH89A Dragon Rapide (NR786/ G-AHGD)	Privately owned, Membury (wreck)	
Z7381	Hawker Hurricane XIIA (G-HURI) [XR-T]	Historic Aircraft Collection, Duxford	
AA550	VS349 Spitfire VB <R> (BAPC 230/ AA908) [GE-P]	Eden Camp Theme Park, Malton, North Yorkshire	
AB130	VS349 Spitfire VA (parts)	Privately owned,	
AB910	VS349 Spitfire VB (G-AISU) [IR-C]	RAF BBMF, Coningsby	

Notes	Serial	Type (other identity) [code]	Owner/operator, location or fate
	AD540	VS349 Spitfire VB (wreck)	Kennet Aviation, North Weald
	AE436	HP52 Hampden I [PL-J] (parts)	Lincolnshire Avn Heritage Centre, E Kirkby
	AL246	Grumman Martlet I	FAA Museum, RNAS Yeovilton
	AM561	Lockheed Hudson V (parts)	Cornwall Aero Park, Helston
	AP506	Cierva C30A (G-ACWM)	The Helicopter Museum, Weston-super-Mare
	AP507	Cierva C30A (G-ACWP) [KX-P]	Science Museum, South Kensington
	AR213	VS300 Spitfire IA (*K9853*/G-AIST) [PR-D]	Privately owned, Booker
	AR501	VS349 Spitfire LF VC (G-AWII/ *AR4474*) [NN-A]	The Shuttleworth Collection, Old Warden
	BB807	DH82A Tiger Moth (G-ADWO)	Southampton Hall of Aviation
BE417		Hawker Hurricane XIIB (G-HURR) [LK-A]	The Real Aeroplane Company, Breighton
BE421		Hawker Hurricane IIC <R> (BAPC 205) [XP-G]	RAF Museum, Hendon
	BL614	VS349 Spitfire VB (4354M) [ZD-F]	RAF Museum, Hendon
	BL655	VS349 Spitfire VB (wreck)	Lincolnshire Avn Heritage Centre, East Kirkby
BL924		VS349 Spitfire VB <R> (BAPC 242) [AZ-G]	Tangmere Military Aviation Museum
BM361		VS349 Spitfire VB <R> [XR-C]	RAF Lakenheath, on display
	BM597	VS349 Spitfire LF VB (5718M/ G-MKVB) [JH-C]	Historic Aircraft Collection, Duxford
BN230		Hawker Hurricane IIC (LF751/ 5466M) [FT-A]	RAF Manston, Memorial Pavilion
BR600		VS361 Spitfire IX <R> (BAPC 222) [SH-V]	RAF Uxbridge, on display
BR600		VS361 Spitfire IX <R> (fuselage)	Privately owned,
	BW881	Hawker Hurricane XIIA (G-KAMM)	Privately owned, Milden
CB733		SA122 Bulldog (G-BCUV/G-112)	Privately owned, Old Sarum
DD931		Bristol 152 Beaufort VIII (9131M) [L]	RAF Museum, Hendon
	DE208	DH82A Tiger Moth II (G-AGYU)	Privately owned, Ronaldsway
	DE470	DH82A Tiger Moth II (G-ANMY)	Privately owned,
	DE623	DH82A Tiger Moth II (G-ANFI)	Privately owned, Withybush
	DE673	DH82A Tiger Moth II (6948M/ G-ADNZ)	Privately owned, Old Buckenham
	DE992	DH82A Tiger Moth II (G-AXXV)	Privately owned, Upavon
DE998		DH82A Tiger Moth (comp G-APAO & G-APAP) [RCU-T]	Imperial War Museum, Duxford
	DF112	DH82A Tiger Moth II (G-ANRM)	Privately owned, Clacton
	DF128	DH82A Tiger Moth II (G-AOJJ) [RCO-U]	Privately owned, White Waltham
	DF155	DH82A Tiger Moth II (G-ANFV)	Privately owned, Chilbolton
	DF198	DH82A Tiger Moth II (G-BBRB)	Privately owned, Biggin Hill
	DG202	Gloster F9/40 (5758M)	RAF Museum, Cosford
	DG590	Miles M2H Hawk Major (8379M/ G-ADMW)	RAF Museum Restoration Centre, Cosford
	DP872	Fairey Barracuda II (fuselage)	FAA Museum, stored Yeovilton
	DR613	Foster-Wikner GM1 Wicko (G-AFJB)	Privately owned, Southampton
	DV372	Avro 683 Lancaster I <ff>	Imperial War Museum, Lambeth
	EE416	Gloster Meteor F3 <ff>	Martin Baker Aircraft, Chalgrove, fire section
	EE425	Gloster Meteor F3 <ff>	Gloucestershire Avn Coll, stored Gloucester
	EE531	Gloster Meteor F4 (7090M)	Midland Air Museum, Coventry
	EE549	Gloster Meteor F4 (7008M) [A]	Tangmere Military Aviation Museum
	EF545	VS349 Spitfire VC <ff>	Privately owned, High Wycombe
	EJ693	Hawker Tempest V (N7027E) [SA-J]	Privately owned, Booker
	EJ922	Hawker Typhoon IB <ff>	Brooklands Museum, Weybridge
	EM720	DH82A Tiger Moth II (G-AXAN)	Privately owned, Little Gransden
	EM727	DH82A Tiger Moth II (G-AOXN)	Privately owned, Yeovil
	EN224	VS366 Spitfire F XII (G-FXII)	Privately owned, Newport Pagnell
EN343		VS365 Spitfire PR XI <R> (BAPC 226)	RAF Benson, on display
EN398		VS361 Spitfire F IX <R> (BAPC 184) [WO-A]	Shropshire Wartime Aircraft Recovery Grp Mus, Sleap

Serial	Type (other identity) [code]	Owner/operator, location or fate	Notes
EP120	VS349 Spitfire LF VB (5377M/ 8070M/G-LFVB) [AE-A]	The Fighter Collection, Duxford	
EX976	NA AT-6D Harvard III (FAP.1657)	FAA Museum, RNAS Yeovilton	
EZ259	NA AT-6D Harvard III (G-BMJW) <ff>	Privately owned, Wakefield, West Yorkshire	
FB226	Bonsall Mustang <R> (G-BDWM) [MT-A]	Privately owned, Gamston	
FE695	Noorduyn AT-16 Harvard IIB (G-BTXI) [94]	The Fighter Collection, Duxford	
FE905	Noorduyn AT-16 Harvard IIB (LN-BNM)	RAF Museum, Hendon	
FE992	Noorduyn AT-16 Harvard IIB (G-BDAM) [K-T]	Sold to Canada, 2003	
FJ992	Boeing-Stearman PT-17 Kaydet (OO-JEH) [44]	Privately owned, Wevelgem, Belgium	
FL586	Douglas C-47A Dakota C3 (G-DAKS) [D]	Sold as N147DC	
FL586	Douglas C-47B Dakota (OO-SMA) [AI-N] (fuselage)	Privately owned, North Weald	
FM118	Avro 683 Lancaster B X <ff>	Privately owned, Lee-on-Solent, Hants	
FR886	Piper L-4J Cub (G-BDMS)	Privately owned, Old Sarum	
FR887	Piper J-3C Cub 85 (G-BWEZ)	Privately owned, Cumbernauld	
FS628	Fairchild Argus 2 (43-14601/ G-AIZE)	RAF Museum, Cosford	
FS668	Noorduyn AT-16 Harvard IIB (PH-TBR)	Privately owned, Gilze-Rijen, The Netherlands	
FS728	Noorduyn AT-16 Harvard IIB (HB-RCP)	Privately owned, Gelnhausen, Germany	
FT323	NA AT-6D Harvard III (FAP 1513)	Air Engineering Services, Swansea	
FT391	Noorduyn AT-16 Harvard IIB (G-AZBN)	Privately owned, Goodwood	
FX301	NA AT-6D Harvard III (EX915/ G-JUDI) [FD-NQ]	Privately owned, Bryngwyn Bach, Clwyd	
FX360	Noorduyn AT-16 Harvard IIB (KF435)	Booker Aircraft Museum	
FX760	Curtiss P-40N Kittyhawk IV (9150M) [GA-?]	RAF Museum, Hendon	
FZ626	Douglas Dakota III (KN566/ G-AMPO) [YS-DH]	RAF Lyneham, on display	
HB275	Beech C-45 Expeditor II (G-BKGM)	Privately owned, Exeter	
HB751	Fairchild Argus III (G-BCBL)	Privately owned, Little Gransden	
HG691	DH89A Dragon Rapide (G-AIYR)	Privately owned, Duxford	
HH268	GAL48 Hotspur II (HH379/ BAPC 261) [H]	Museum of Army Flying, AAC Middle Wallop	
HJ711	DH98 Mosquito NF II [VI-C]	Night-Fighter Preservation Tm, Elvington	
HM354	Percival P34 Proctor III (G-ANPP)	Privately owned, Stansted	
HM503	Miles M12 Mohawk (G-AEKW)	RAF Museum Restoration Centre, Cosford	
HM580	Cierva C-30A (G-ACUU) [KX-K]	Imperial War Museum, Duxford	
HS503	Fairey Swordfish IV (BAPC 108)	RAF Museum Restoration Centre, Cosford	
JG891	VS349 Spitfire LF VC (A58-178/ G-LFVC)	Historic Flying Ltd, Audley End	
JR505	Hawker Typhoon IB <ff>	Midland Air Museum, Coventry	
JV482	Grumman Wildcat V	Ulster Aviation Society, Langford Lodge	
JV579	Grumman FM-2 Wildcat (N4845V/ G-RUMW) [F]	The Fighter Collection, Duxford	
JV928	Consolidated PBY-5A Catalina (N423RS) [Y]	Super Catalina Restoration, Lee-on-Solent	
KB889	Avro 683 Lancaster B X (G-LANC) [NA-I]	Imperial War Museum, Duxford	
KB976	Avro 683 Lancaster B X (G-BCOH) <rf>	Aeroventure, Doncaster	
KB994	Avro 683 Lancaster B X (G-BVBP) <ff>	Privately owned, North Weald	
KD345	Goodyear FG-1D Corsair (88297/ G-FGID) [130-A]	The Fighter Collection, Duxford	
KD431	CV Corsair IV [E2-M]	FAA Museum, RNAS Yeovilton	
KE209	Grumman Hellcat II	FAA Museum, RNAS Yeovilton	
KE418	Hawker Tempest <rf>	RAF Museum Restoration Centre, Cosford	
KF183	Noorduyn AT-16 Harvard IIB [3]	DPA/AFD/QinetiQ, Boscombe Down	

Notes	Serial	Type (other identity) [code]	Owner/operator, location or fate
	KF435	Noorduyn AT-16 Harvard IIB <ff>	Privately owned, Swindon
	KF488	Noorduyn AT-16 Harvard IIB <ff>	Bournemouth Aviation Museum
	KF532	Noorduyn AT-16 Harvard IIB <ff>	Newark Air Museum, Winthorpe
	KF584	CCF T-6J Texan (FT239/G-BIWX/ G-RAIX) [RAI-X]	Privately owned, Lee-on-Solent
	KF729	CCF T-6J Texan (G-BJST)	Privately owned, Thruxton
	KG374	Douglas Dakota IV (KN645/8355M) [YS]	RAF Museum, Cosford
	KJ351	Airspeed AS58 Horsa II (TL659/ BAPC 80) [23]	Museum of Army Flying, Middle Wallop
	KK995	Sikorsky Hoverfly I [E]	RAF Museum, Hendon
	KL216	Republic P-47D Thunderbolt (45-49295/9212M) [RS-L]	RAF Museum, Cosford
	KN442	Douglas Dakota C4 (G-AMPZ)	Sold as D-CXXX, July 2003
	KN448	Douglas Dakota C4 <ff>	Science Museum, South Kensington
	KN751	Consolidated Liberator C VI (IAF HE807) [F]	RAF Museum, Cosford
	KP208	Douglas Dakota IV [YS]	Airborne Forces Museum, Aldershot
	KZ191	Hawker Hurricane IV (frame only)	Privately owned, East Garston, Bucks
	KZ321	Hawker Hurricane IV (G-HURY) [JV-N]	The Fighter Collection, Duxford
	LA198	VS356 Spitfire F21 (7118M) [RAI-G]	Glasgow Museum of Transport
	LA226	VS356 Spitfire F21 (7119M)	RAF Museum Restoration Centre, Cosford
	LA255	VS356 Spitfire F21 (6490M) [JX-U]	RAF No 1 Sqn, Cottesmore (preserved)
	LB264	Taylorcraft Plus D (G-AIXA)	RAF Museum, Hendon
	LB294	Taylorcraft Plus D (G-AHWJ)	Museum of Army Flying, Whitchurch, Hants
	LB312	Taylorcraft Plus D (HH982/ G-AHXE)	Privately owned, Netheravon
	LB367	Taylorcraft Plus D (G-AHGZ)	Privately owned, Duxford
	LB375	Taylorcraft Plus D (G-AHGW)	Privately owned, Edge Hill
	LF363	Hawker Hurricane IIC [US-C]	RAF BBMF, Coningsby
	LF738	Hawker Hurricane IIC (5405M) [UH-A]	RAF Museum, Cosford
	LF789	DH82 Queen Bee (K3584/ BAPC 186) [R2-K]	Mosquito Aircraft Museum, London Colney
	LF858	DH82 Queen Bee (G-BLUZ)	Privately owned, Rush Green
	LS326	Fairey Swordfish II (G-AJVH) [L2]	RN Historic Flight, Yeovilton
	LV907	HP59 Halifax III (HR792) [NP-F]	Yorkshire Air Museum, Elvington
	LZ551	DH100 Vampire	FAA Museum, RNAS Yeovilton
	LZ766	Percival P34 Proctor III (G-ALCK)	Imperial War Museum, Duxford
	MF628	Vickers Wellington T10 (9210M)	RAF Museum, Hendon
	MH434	VS361 Spitfire LF IXB (G-ASJV) [ZD-B]	The Old Flying Machine Company, Duxford
	MH486	VS361 Spitfire LF IX <R> (BAPC 206) [FF-A]	RAF Museum, Hendon
	MH415	VS361 Spitfire IX <R> (MJ751/ BAPC 209) [DU-V]	The Aircraft Restoration Co, Duxford
	MH777	VS361 Spitfire IX <R> (BAPC 221) [RF-N]	RAF Northolt, on display
	MJ147	VS361 Spitfire LF IX	Privately owned, Kent
	MJ627	VS509 Spitfire T9 (G-BMSB) [9G-P]	Privately owned, East Kirkby
	MJ751	VS361 Spitfire IX <R> (BAPC 209) [DU-V]	Repainted as MH415
	MJ832	VS361 Spitfire IX <R> (L1096/ BAPC 229) [DN-Y]	RAF Digby, on display
	MK178	VS361 Spitfire LF XVIE (TE311/ X4474/7241M) [LZ-V]	RAF BBMF, stored Coningsby
	MK356	VS361 Spitfire LF IXC (5690M) [2I-V]	RAF BBMF, Coningsby
	MK356	VS361 Spitfire LF IXC <R> [2I-V]	Kent Battle of Britain Museum, Hawkinge
	MK356	VS361 Spitfire LF IXC <R>	RAF Cosford, on display
	MK673	VS361 Spitfire LF XVIE (TB382/ X4277/7244M) [SK-E]	RAF BBMF, stored Coningsby
	MK805	VS361 Spitfire LF IX <R> [SH-B]	Sold to Italy
	MK912	VS361 Spitfire LF IXE (G-BRRA) [SH-L]	Sold to Canada, 2003
	ML407	VS509 Spitfire T9 (G-LFIX) [OU-V]	Privately owned, Duxford
	ML411	VS361 Spitfire LF IXE (G-CBNU)	Privately owned, Kent
	ML427	VS361 Spitfire IX (6457M) [HK-A]	Millennium Discovery Centre, Birmingham

Serial	Type (other identity) [code]	Owner/operator, location or fate	Notes
ML796	Short S25 Sunderland V	Imperial War Museum, Duxford	
ML824	Short S25 Sunderland V [NS-Z]	RAF Museum, Hendon	
MN235	Hawker Typhoon IB	RAF Museum, Hendon	
MP425	Airspeed AS10 Oxford I (G-AITB) [G]	RAF Museum, Hendon	
MS902	Miles M25 Martinet TT1 (TF-SHC)	Museum of Berkshire Aviation, Woodley	
MT197	Auster IV (G-ANHS)	Privately owned, Spanhoe	
MT438	Auster III (G-AREI)	Privately owned, Petersfield	
MT847	VS379 Spitfire FR XIVE (6960M) [AX-H]	Gr Manchester Mus of Science & Industry	
MT928	VS359 Spitfire HF VIIIC (G-BKMI/ MV154/*AR654*)[ZX-M]	Privately owned, East Garston, Bucks	
MV262	VS379 Spitfire FR XIV (G-CCVV)	Privately owned, Booker	
MV268	VS379 Spitfire FR XIVE (MV293/ G-SPIT) [JE-J]	The Fighter Collection, Duxford	
MW401	Hawker Tempest II (IAF HA604/ G-PEST)	Privately owned, Hemswell, Lincs	
MW404	Hawker Tempest II (IAF HA557)	*Sold to France*	
MW758	Hawker Tempest II (IAF HA580)	Privately owned, Gamston	
MW763	Hawker Tempest II (IAF HA586/ G-TEMT) [HF-A]	Privately owned, Gamston	
MW810	Hawker Tempest II (IAF HA591)	*Sold to the US*	
NF370	Fairey Swordfish III	Imperial War Museum, Duxford	
NF389	Fairey Swordfish III [D]	RN Historic Flight, Yeovilton	
NJ633	Auster 5D (G-AKXP)	Privately owned, Keevil	
NJ673	Auster 5D (G-AOCR)	Privately owned, Bagby	
NJ695	Auster 4 (G-AJXV)	Privately owned, Newark	
NJ703	Auster 5 (G-AKPI)	Privately owned, Croft, Lincs	
NJ719	Auster 5 (TW385/G-ANFU)	Privately owned, Newcastle	
NL750	DH82A Tiger Moth II (T7997/ G-AOBH)	Privately owned, Thruxton	
NL846	DH82A Tiger Moth II (F-BGEQ)	Brooklands Museum, Hungerford (under restoration)	
NL985	DH82A Tiger Moth I (7015M/ G-BWIK)	Privately owned, Sywell	
NM181	DH82A Tiger Moth I (G-AZGZ)	Privately owned, Dunkeswell	
NP294	Percival P31 Proctor IV [TB-M]	Lincolnshire Avn Heritage Centre, E Kirkby	
NP303	Percival P31 Proctor IV (G-ANZJ)	Privately owned, Byfleet, Surrey	
NV778	Hawker Tempest TT5 (8386M)	RAF Museum, Hendon	
NX534	Auster III (G-BUDL)	Privately owned, Netheravon	
NX611	Avro 683 Lancaster B VII (8375M/ G-ASXX) [DE-C,LE-C]	Lincolnshire Avn Heritage Centre, E Kirkby	
PA474	Avro 683 Lancaster B I [QR-M]	RAF BBMF, Coningsby	
PF179	HS Gnat T1 (XR541/8602M)	Global Aviation, Humberside	
PK624	VS356 Spitfire F22 (8072M) [RAU-T]	The Fighter Collection, Duxford	
PK664	VS356 Spitfire F22 (7759M) [V6-B]	RAF Museum Restoration Centre, Cosford	
PK683	VS356 Spitfire F24 (7150M)	Southampton Hall of Aviation	
PK724	VS356 Spitfire F24 (7288M)	RAF Museum, Hendon	
PM631	VS390 Spitfire PR XIX	RAF BBMF, Coningsby	
PM651	VS390 Spitfire PR XIX (7758M) [X]	RAF Museum Restoration Centre, Cosford	
PN323	HP Halifax VII <ff>	Imperial War Museum, Lambeth	
PP972	VS358 Seafire LF IIIC (G-BUAR)	Flying A Services, Earls Colne	
PR536	Hawker Tempest II (IAF HA457) [OQ-H]	RAF Museum, Hendon	
PS853	VS390 Spitfire PR XIX (G-MXIX/ G-RRGN) [C]	Rolls-Royce, Filton	
PS915	VS390 Spitfire PR XIX (7548M/ 7711M) [UM-G]	RAF BBMF, Coningsby	
PT462	VS509 Spitfire T9 (G-CTIX/ N462JC) [SW-A]	Privately owned, Caernarfon/Duxford	
PZ865	Hawker Hurricane IIC (G-AMAU) [Q]	RAF BBMF, Coningsby	
RA848	Slingsby Cadet TX1	The Aeroplane Collection, stored Wigan	
RA854	Slingsby Cadet TX1	Privately owned, Wigan	
RA897	Slingsby Cadet TX1	Newark Air Museum, Winthorpe	
RA905	Slingsby Cadet TX1 (BGA1143)	Trenchard Museum, RAF Halton	
RD220	Bristol 156 Beaufighter TF X	Royal Scottish Mus'm of Flight, E Fortune	
RD253	Bristol 156 Beaufighter TF X (7931M)	RAF Museum, Hendon	

Notes	Serial	Type (other identity) [code]	Owner/operator, location or fate
	RF342	Avro 694 Lincoln B II (G-29-1/ G-APRJ)	Privately owned, stored Sandtoft
	RF398	Avro 694 Lincoln B II (8376M)	RAF Museum, Cosford
	RG333	Miles M38 Messenger IIA (G-AIEK)	Privately owned, Felton, Bristol
	RH377	Miles M38 Messenger 4A (G-ALAH)	Privately owned, Stretton, Cheshire
	RH746	Bristol 164 Brigand TF1 (fuselage)	Bristol Aero Collection, Kemble
	RL962	DH89A Dominie II (G-AHED)	RAF Museum Restoration Centre, Cosford
	RM221	Percival P31 Proctor IV (G-ANXR)	Privately owned, Biggin Hill
	RM689	VS379 Spitfire F XIV (G-ALGT) (remains)	Rolls-Royce, Derby
	RM694	VS379 Spitfire F XIV (6640M)	Privately owned, High Wycombe
	RM927	VS379 Spitfire F XIV	Privately owned, High Wycombe
	RN201	VS379 Spitfire FR XIV (SG-31/ SG-3/G-BSKP)	Historic Flying Ltd, Duxford
	RN218	Isaacs Spitfire <R> (G-BBJI) [N]	Privately owned, Langham
	RR232	VS361 Spitfire HF IXC (G-BRSF)	Privately owned, Exeter
	RT486	Auster 5 (G-AJGJ) [PF-A]	Bournemouth Aviation Museum
	RT520	Auster 5 (G-ALYB)	Aeroventure, Doncaster
	RT610	Auster 5A-160 (G-AKWS)	Privately owned, Crowfield
	RW388	VS361 Spitfire LF XVIE (6946M) [U4-U]	Stoke-on-Trent City Museum, Hanley
	RW393	VS361 Spitfire LF XVIE (7293M) [XT-A]	RAF Museum, Cosford
	RX168	VS358 Seafire L IIIC (IAC 157/ G-BWEM)	Privately owned, Norwich
	SL611	VS361 Spitfire LF XVIE	Supermarine Aero Engineering, Stoke-on-Trent
	SL674	VS361 Spitfire LF IX (8392M) [RAS-H]	RAF Museum Restoration Centre, Cosford
	SM520	VS361 Spitfire LF IX (G-ILDA/ G-BXHZ)	Privately owned, Ramsbottom
	SM832	VS379 Spitfire F XIVE (G-WWII) [YB-A]	The Fighter Collection, Duxford
	SM845	VS394 Spitfire FR XVIII (G-BUOS) [GZ-J]	Silver Victory Collection, Duxford
	SX137	VS384 Seafire F XVII	FAA Museum, RNAS Yeovilton
	SX336	VS384 Seafire F XVII (G-KASX)	Kennet Aviation, North Weald
	TA122	DH98 Mosquito FB VI [UP-G]	Mosquito Aircraft Museum, London Colney
	TA634	DH98 Mosquito TT35 (G-AWJV) [8K-K]	Mosquito Aircraft Museum, London Colney
	TA639	DH98 Mosquito TT35 (7806M) [AZ-E]	RAF Museum, Cosford
	TA719	DH98 Mosquito TT35 (G-ASKC)	Imperial War Museum, Duxford
	TA805	VS361 Spitfire HF IX (G-PMNF)	Privately owned, Sandown
	TB252	VS361 Spitfire LF XVIE (G-XVIE) [GW-H]	Historic Flying Ltd, Audley End
	TB752	VS361 Spitfire LF XVIE (8086M) [KH-Z]	RAF Manston, Memorial Pavilion
	TD248	VS361 Spitfire LF XVIE (7246M/ G-OXVI) [D]	Silver Victory Collection, Duxford
	TD248	VS361 Spitfire LF XVIE <R> [8Q-T]	Norfolk & Suffolk Avn Mus'm, Flixton
	TD314	VS361 Spitfire LF IX (N601DA)	Privately owned, Norwich
	TE462	VS361 Spitfire LF XVIE (7243M)	Royal Scottish Mus'm of Flight, E Fortune
	TE517	VS361 Spitfire LF IXE (G-CCIX) [HL-K]	Privately owned, stored Booker
	TG263	Saro SR A1 (G-12-1)	Southampton Hall of Aviation
	TG511	HP67 Hastings C1 (8554M)	RAF Museum, Cosford
	TG517	HP67 Hastings T5	Newark Air Museum, Winthorpe
	TG528	HP67 Hastings C1A	Imperial War Museum, Duxford
	TJ118	DH98 Mosquito TT35 <ff>	Mosquito Aircraft Museum, stored London Colney
	TJ138	DH98 Mosquito B35 (7607M) [VO-L]	RAF Museum, Hendon
	TJ343	Auster 5 (G-AJXC)	Privately owned,
	TJ398	Auster AOP6 (BAPC 70)	Aircraft Pres'n Soc of Scotland, E Fortune
	TJ534	Auster 5 (G-AKSY)	Privately owned, Breighton
	TJ569	Auster 5 (G-AKOW)	Museum of Army Flying, Middle Wallop
	TJ652	Auster 5D (G-AMVD)	Privately owned, Hardwick, Norfolk
	TJ672	Auster 5D (G-ANIJ) [TS-D]	Privately owned, Whitchurch, Hants
	TJ704	Beagle A61 Terrier 2 (VW993/ G-ASCD) [JA]	Yorkshire Air Museum, Elvington

Serial	Type (other identity) [code]	Owner/operator, location or fate	Notes
TK718	GAL59 Hamilcar I	National Tank Museum, Bovington	
TK777	GAL59 Hamilcar I (fuselage)	Museum of Army Flying, Middle Wallop	
TS291	Slingsby Cadet TX1 (BGA852)	Royal Scottish Mus'm of Flight, E Fortune	
TS798	Avro 685 York C1 (G-AGNV)	RAF Museum, Cosford	
TV959	DH98 Mosquito T III [AF-V]	The Fighter Collection, stored Duxford	
TV959	DH98 Mosquito T III <R>	*Currently not known*	
TW439	Auster 5 (G-ANRP)	The Real Aeroplane Company, Breighton	
TW467	Auster 5 (G-ANIE) [ROD-F]	Privately owned, Bassingbourn	
TW511	Auster 5 (G-APAF)	Privately owned, Henstridge	
TW536	Auster AOP6 (7704M/G-BNGE) [TS-V]	Privately owned, Netheravon	
TW591	Auster 6A (G-ARIH) [N]	Privately owned, Abbots Bromley	
TW641	Beagle A61 Terrier 2 (G-ATDN)	Privately owned, Biggin Hill	
TX213	Avro 652A Anson C19 (G-AWRS)	North-East Aircraft Museum, Usworth	
TX214	Avro 652A Anson C19 (7817M)	RAF Museum, Cosford	
TX226	Avro 652A Anson C19 (7865M)	Air Atlantique Historic Flight, Coventry	
TX235	Avro 652A Anson C19	Air Atlantique Historic Flight, Coventry	
VF301	DH100 Vampire F1 (7060M) [RAL-G]	Midland Air Museum, Coventry	
VF512	Auster 6A (G-ARRX) [PF-M]	Privately owned, White Waltham	
VF516	Beagle A61 Terrier 2 (G-ASMZ) [T]	Privately owned, Eggesford	
VF526	Auster 6A (G-ARXU) [T]	Privately owned, Netheravon	
VF548	Beagle A61 Terrier 1 (G-ASEG)	Privately owned, Dunkeswell	
VF560	Auster 6A (frame)	Aeroventure, Doncaster	
VF581	Beagle A61 Terrier 1 (G-ARSL)	Privately owned, Eggesford	
VH127	Fairey Firefly TT4 [200/R]	FAA Museum, RNAS Yeovilton	
VL348	Avro 652A Anson C19 (G-AVVO)	Newark Air Museum, Winthorpe	
VL349	Avro 652A Anson C19 (G-AWSA) [V7-Q]	Norfolk & Suffolk Avn Mus'm, Flixton	
VM325	Avro 652A Anson C19	Privately owned, stored Gloucester	
VM360	Avro 652A Anson C19 (G-APHV)	Royal Scottish Mus'm of Flight, E Fortune	
VM791	Slingsby Cadet TX3 (XA312/8876M)	RAF Manston History Museum	
VN148	Grunau Baby IIb (BAPC 33/BGA2400)	*Sold to Denmark, 2003*	
VN485	VS356 Spitfire F24 (7326M)	Imperial War Museum, Duxford	
VN799	EE Canberra T4 (WJ874)	RAF No 39(1 PRU) Sqn, Marham	
VP293	Avro 696 Shackleton T4 [A] <ff>	Newark Air Museum, Winthorpe	
VP519	Avro 652A Anson C19 (G-AVVR) <ff>	Privately owned, Wolverhampton	
VP952	DH104 Devon C2 (8820M)	RAF Museum, Cosford	
VP955	DH104 Devon C2 (G-DVON)	Privately owned, Kemble	
VP957	DH104 Devon C2 (8822M) <ff>	No 1137 Sqn ATC, Belfast	
VP967	DH104 Devon C2 (G-KOOL)	Privately owned, Redhill	
VP975	DH104 Devon C2 [M]	Science Museum, Wroughton	
VP981	DH104 Devon C2 (G-DHDV)	Air Atlantique Historic Flight, Coventry	
VR137	Westland Wyvern TF1	FAA Museum, RNAS Yeovilton	
VR192	Percival P40 Prentice T1 (G-APIT)	SWWAPS, Lasham	
VR249	Percival P40 Prentice T1 (G-APIY) [FA-EL]	Newark Air Museum, Winthorpe	
VR259	Percival P40 Prentice T1 (G-APJB) [M]	Air Atlantique Historic Flight, Coventry	
VR930	Hawker Sea Fury FB11 (8382M) [110/O]	RN Historic Flight, Yeovilton	
VS356	Percival P40 Prentice T1 (G-AOLU)	Privately owned, Montrose	
VS562	Avro 652A Anson T21 (8012M)	Maes Artro Craft Village, Llanbedr	
VS610	Percival P40 Prentice T1 (G-AOKL) [K-L]	The Shuttleworth Collection, Old Warden	
VS623	Percival P40 Prentice T1 (G-AOKZ) [KQ-F]	Midland Air Museum, Coventry	
VT409	Fairey Firefly AS5 <rf>	North-East Aircraft Museum, stored Usworth	
VT812	DH100 Vampire F3 (7200M) [N]	RAF Museum, Hendon	
VT871	DH100 Vampire FB6 (J-1173/LZ551/G-DHXX) [G]	Source Classic Jet Flight, Bournemouth	
VT935	Boulton Paul P111A (VT769)	Midland Air Museum, Coventry	
VT987	Auster AOP6 (G-BKXP)	Privately owned, Thruxton	
VV106	Supermarine 510 (7175M)	FAA Museum, stored RNAS Yeovilton	
VV217	DH100 Vampire FB5 (7323M)	North-East Aircraft Museum, stored Usworth	
VV612	DH112 Venom FB50 (J-1523/WE402/G-VENI)	Source Classic Jet Flight, Bournemouth	

Notes	Serial	Type (other identity) [code]	Owner/operator, location or fate
	VV901	Avro 652A Anson T21	Yorkshire Air Museum, Elvington
	VW453	Gloster Meteor T7 (8703M) [Z]	RAF Innsworth, on display
	VW985	Auster AOP6 (G-ASEF)	*Repainted as G-ASEF*
	VX113	Auster AOP6	Privately owned, Eggesford
	VX118	Auster AOP6 (G-ASNB)	Vliegend Museum, Seppe, The Netherlands
	VX147	Alon A2 Aircoupe (G-AVIL)	Privately owned, Monewden
	VX185	EE Canberra B(I)8 (7631M) <ff>	Royal Scottish Mus'm of Flight, E Fortune
	VX250	DH103 Sea Hornet NF21 [48] <rf>	Mosquito Aircraft Museum, London Colney
	VX272	Hawker P.1052 (7174M)	FAA Museum, stored RNAS Yeovilton
	VX275	Slingsby T21B Sedbergh TX1 (8884M/BGA 572)	RAF Museum Restoration Centre, Cosford
	VX461	DH100 Vampire FB5 (7646M)	RAF Museum Restoration Centre, Cosford
	VX573	Vickers Valetta C2 (8389M)	RAF Museum, stored Cosford
	VX580	Vickers Valetta C2	Norfolk & Suffolk Avn Museum, Flixton
	VX595	WS51 Dragonfly HR1	FAA Museum, stored RNAS Yeovilton
	VX665	Hawker Sea Fury FB11 <rf>	RN Historic Flight, at BAE Systems Brough
	VX926	Auster T7 (G-ASKJ)	Privately owned,
	VZ345	Hawker Sea Fury T20S	RN Historic Flight, stored Yeovilton
	VZ477	Gloster Meteor F8 (7741M) <ff>	Midland Air Museum, Coventry
	VZ608	Gloster Meteor FR9	Newark Air Museum, Winthorpe
	VZ634	Gloster Meteor T7 (8657M)	Newark Air Museum, Winthorpe
	VZ638	Gloster Meteor T7 (G-JETM) [HF]	Gatwick Aviation Museum, Charlwood, Surrey
	VZ728	RS4 Desford Trainer (G-AGOS)	Snibston Discovery Park, stored Coalville
	VZ962	WS51 Dragonfly HR1 [904]	The Helicopter Museum, Weston-super-Mare
	WA473	VS Attacker F1 [102/J]	FAA Museum, RNAS Yeovilton
	WA576	Bristol 171 Sycamore 3 (7900M/ G-ALSS)	Dumfries & Galloway Avn Mus, Dumfries
	WA577	Bristol 171 Sycamore 3 (7718M/ G-ALST)	North-East Aircraft Museum, Usworth
	WA591	Gloster Meteor T7 (7917M/ G-BWMF) [W]	Meteor Flight, Yatesbury
	WA630	Gloster Meteor T7 [69] <ff>	Robertsbridge Aviation Society, Newhaven
	WA634	Gloster Meteor T7/8	RAF Museum, Cosford
	WA638	Gloster Meteor T7(mod)	Martin Baker Aircraft, Chalgrove
	WA662	Gloster Meteor T7	Aeroventure, Doncaster
	WA984	Gloster Meteor F8 (*WA829*) [A]	Tangmere Military Aviation Museum
	WB188	Hawker Hunter F3 (7154M)	Tangmere Military Aviation Museum
	WB188	Hawker Hunter GA11 (WV256/ G-BZPB)	Hunter Flying Club, Exeter (duck egg green)
	WB188	Hawker Hunter GA11 (XF300/ G-BZPC)	Hunter Flying Club, Exeter (red)
	WB271	Fairey Firefly AS5 [204/R]	*Crashed 12 July 2003, Duxford*
	WB440	Fairey Firefly AS6 <ff>	Privately owned, Newton-le-Willows
	WB491	Avro 706 Ashton 2 (TS897/ G-AJJW) <ff>	Newark Air Museum, Winthorpe
	WB556	DHC1 Chipmunk T10	*Currently not known*
	WB560	DHC1 Chipmunk T10 (comp WG403)	Aeroventure, stored Doncaster
	WB565	DHC1 Chipmunk T10 (G-PVET) [X]	Privately owned, Kemble
	WB569	DHC1 Chipmunk T10 (G-BYSJ) [R]	Privately owned, Duxford
	WB584	DHC1 Chipmunk T10 (7706M) <ff>	Royal Scottish Mus'm of Flight,E Fortune
	WB585	DHC1 Chipmunk T10 (G-AOSY) [M]	Privately owned, Seething
	WB588	DHC1 Chipmunk T10 (G-AOTD) [D]	Privately owned, Old Sarum
	WB615	DHC1 Chipmunk T10 (G-BXIA) [E]	Privately owned, Blackpool
	WB624	DHC1 Chipmunk T10 <ff>	Newark Air Museum, Winthorpe
	WB626	DHC1 Chipmunk T10 <ff>	Privately owned, Aylesbury
	WB627	DHC1 Chipmunk T10 (9248M) [N]	Dulwich College CCF
	WB645	DHC1 Chipmunk T10 (8218M)	*Currently not known*
	WB652	DHC1 Chipmunk T10 (G-CHPY) [V]	Privately owned, Staverton
	WB654	DHC1 Chipmunk T10 (G-BXGO) [U]	Privately owned, Booker
	WB657	DHC1 Chipmunk T10 [908]	RN Historic Flight, Yeovilton
	WB660	DHC1 Chipmunk T10 (G-ARMB)	Privately owned, Leicester
	WB670	DHC1 Chipmunk T10 (8361M) <ff>	Privately owned, Currie, Lothian

Serial	Type (other identity) [code]	Owner/operator, location or fate	Notes
WB671	DHC1 Chipmunk T10 (G-BWTG) [910]	Privately owned, Epse, The Netherlands	
WB685	DHC1 Chipmunk T10 <rf>	North-East Aircraft Museum, stored Usworth	
WB697	DHC1 Chipmunk T10 (G-BXCT) [95]	Privately owned, Wickenby	
WB702	DHC1 Chipmunk T10 (G-AOFE)	Privately owned, Goodwood	
WB703	DHC1 Chipmunk T10 (G-ARMC)	Privately owned, White Waltham	
WB711	DHC1 Chipmunk T10 (G-APPM)	Privately owned, Crowfield	
WB726	DHC1 Chipmunk T10 (G-AOSK) [E]	Privately owned, Audley End	
WB733	DHC1 Chipmunk T10 (comp WG422)	Aeroventure, Doncaster	
WB758	DHC1 Chipmunk T10 (7729M) [P]	Privately owned, Torbay	
WB763	DHC1 Chipmunk T10 (G-BBMR) [14]	Privately owned, Camberley, Surrey	
WB922	Slingsby T21B Sedbergh TX1 (BGA 4366)	Privately owned, Gallows Hill, Dorset	
WB924	Slingsby T21B Sedbergh TX1 (BGA 3901)	Privately owned, Dunstable	
WB938	Slingsby T21B Sedbergh TX1	Privately owned, Halton	
WB943	Slingsby T21B Sedbergh TX1 (BGA 2941)	Privately owned, Rufforth	
WB969	Slingsby T21B Sedbergh TX1	Aeroventure, Doncaster	
WB971	Slingsby T21B Sedbergh TX1 (BGA 3324)	Privately owned, Tibenham	
WB975	Slingsby T21B Sedbergh TX1 (BGA 3288)	Privately owned, Drumshade, Fife	
WB981	Slingsby T21B Sedbergh TX1 (BGA 1218)	Privately owned, Keevil	
WD286	DHC1 Chipmunk T10 (G-BBND)	Privately owned, Little Gransden	
WD288	DHC1 Chipmunk T10 (G-AOSO) [38]	Privately owned, Charlton Park, Wilts	
WD292	DHC1 Chipmunk T10 (G-BCRX)	Privately owned, White Waltham	
WD293	DHC1 Chipmunk T10 (7645M) <ff>	No 210 Sqn ATC, Newport, Gwent	
WD305	DHC1 Chipmunk T10 (G-ARGG)	Privately owned, Meppershall	
WD310	DHC1 Chipmunk T10 (G-BWUN) [B]	Privately owned, Booker	
WD318	DHC1 Chipmunk T10 (8207M) <ff>	*Currently not known*	
WD325	DHC1 Chipmunk T10 [N]	AAC Historic Aircraft Flight, Middle Wallop	
WD331	DHC1 Chipmunk T10 (G-BXDH) [J]	Privately owned, Enstone	
WD347	DHC1 Chipmunk T10 (G-BBRV)	Privately owned, Sheffield	
WD355	DHC1 Chipmunk T10 (WD335/ G-CBAJ)	Privately owned, Wellesbourne Mountford	
WD363	DHC1 Chipmunk T10 (G-BCIH) [5]	Privately owned, North Weald	
WD370	DHC1 Chipmunk T10 <ff>	*Currently not known*	
WD373	DHC1 Chipmunk T10 (G-BXDI) [12]	Privately owned, Duxford	
WD377	DHC1 Chipmunk T10 <ff>	RAF Millom Museum, Haverigg	
WD379	DHC1 Chipmunk T10 (WB696/ G-APLO) [K]	Privately owned, Jersey	
WD386	DHC1 Chipmunk T10 (comp WD377)	Dumfries & Galloway Avn Mus, Prestwick	
WD390	DHC1 Chipmunk T10 (G-BWNK) [68]	Privately owned, Breighton	
WD413	Avro 652A Anson T21 (7881M/ G-VROE)	Air Atlantique Historic Flight, Coventry	
WD615	Gloster Meteor TT20 (WD646/ 8189M) [R]	RAF Manston History Museum	
WD686	Gloster Meteor NF11	Muckleburgh Collection, Weybourne	
WD790	Gloster Meteor NF11 (8743M)<ff>	North-East Aircraft Museum, Usworth	
WD889	Fairey Firefly AS5 <ff>	North-East Aircraft Museum, Usworth	
WD931	EE Canberra B2 <ff>	RAF Museum, stored Cosford	
WD935	EE Canberra B2 (8440M) <ff>	Aeroventure, Doncaster	
WD954	EE Canberra B2 <ff>	Privately owned, Rossendale, Lancs	
WE113	EE Canberra B2 <ff>	Privately owned, Woodhurst, Cambridgeshire	
WE122	EE Canberra TT18 [845] <ff>	Blyth Valley Aviation Collection, Walpole, Suffolk	
WE139	EE Canberra PR3 (8369M)	RAF Museum, Hendon	
WE168	EE Canberra PR3 (8049M) <ff>	Privately owned, Colchester	
WE173	EE Canberra PR3 (8740M) <ff>	Robertsbridge Aviation Society, Mayfield	
WE188	EE Canberra T4	Solway Aviation Society, Carlisle	

Notes	Serial	Type (other identity) [code]	Owner/operator, location or fate
	WE192	EE Canberra T4 <ff>	Blyth Valley Aviation Collection, Walpole, Suffolk
	WE275	DH112 Venom FB50 (J-1601/ G-VIDI)	BAE Systems Hawarden, Fire Section
	WE569	Auster T7 (G-ASAJ)	Privately owned, Bassingbourn
	WE591	Auster T7 (G-ASAK) [Y]	Privately owned, Biggin Hill
	WE600	Auster T7 Antarctic (7602M)	RAF Museum, Cosford
	WE724	Hawker Sea Fury FB11 (VX653/ G-BUCM) [062]	The Fighter Collection, Duxford
	WE982	Slingsby T30B Prefect TX1 (8781M)	RAF Museum, stored Cosford
	WE990	Slingsby T30B Prefect TX1 (BGA 2583)	Privately owned, stored Beds
	WF118	Percival P57 Sea Prince T1 (G-DACA)	Gatwick Aviation Museum, Charlwood, Surrey
	WF122	Percival P57 Sea Prince T1 [575/CU]	Aeroventure, Doncaster
	WF128	Percival P57 Sea Prince T1 (8611M)	Norfolk & Suffolk Avn Museum, Flixton
	WF137	Percival P57 Sea Prince C1	SWWAPS, Lasham
	WF145	Hawker Sea Hawk F1 <ff>	Privately owned, Ingatestone, Essex
	WF225	Hawker Sea Hawk F1 [CU]	RNAS Culdrose, at main gate
	WF259	Hawker Sea Hawk F2 [171/A]	Royal Scottish Mus'm of Flight, E Fortune
	WF369	Vickers Varsity T1 [F]	Newark Air Museum, Winthorpe
	WF372	Vickers Varsity T1 [A]	Brooklands Museum, Weybridge
	WF376	Vickers Varsity T1	Bristol Airport Fire Section
	WF408	Vickers Varsity T1 (8395M)	Privately owned, East Grinstead
	WF410	Vickers Varsity T1 [F]	Brunel Technical College, Lulsgate
	WF643	Gloster Meteor F8 [P]	Norfolk & Suffolk Avn Museum, Flixton
	WF714	Gloster Meteor F8 (WK914)	Privately owned, stored Scampton
	WF784	Gloster Meteor T7 (7895M)	Gloucestershire Avn Coll, stored Gloucester
	WF825	Gloster Meteor T7 (8359M) [A]	Meteor Flight, Yatesbury
	WF877	Gloster Meteor T7 (G-BPOA)	Privately owned, Washington, W Sussex
	WF911	EE Canberra B2 [CO] <ff>	The Griffin Trust, Hooton Park, Cheshire
	WF922	EE Canberra PR3	Midland Air Museum, Coventry
	WG300	DHC1 Chipmunk T10 <ff>	*Currently not known*
	WG303	DHC1 Chipmunk T10 (8208M) <ff>	RAFGSA, Bicester
	WG308	DHC1 Chipmunk T10 (G-BYHL) [71]	Privately owned, Newton
	WG316	DHC1 Chipmunk T10 (G-BCAH)	Privately owned, Leicester
	WG321	DHC1 Chipmunk T10 (G-DHCC)	Privately owned, Wevelgem, Belgium
	WG348	DHC1 Chipmunk T10 (G-BBMV)	Privately owned, Sywell
	WG350	DHC1 Chipmunk T10 (G-BPAL)	Privately owned, Cascais, Portugal
	WG362	DHC1 Chipmunk T10 (8437M/ 8630M/*WX643*) <ff>	No 1094 Sqn ATC, Ely
	WG407	DHC1 Chipmunk T10 (G-BWMX)	Privately owned, Croydon, Cambs
	WG418	DHC1 Chipmunk T10 (8209M/ G-ATDY) <ff>	No 1940 Sqn ATC, Levenshulme, Gr Manchester
	WG419	DHC1 Chipmunk T10 (8206M) <ff>	No 1053 Sqn ATC, Armthorpe
	WG422	DHC1 Chipmunk T10 (8394M/ G-BFAX) [116]	Privately owned, Strathaven
	WG432	DHC1 Chipmunk T10 [L]	Museum of Army Flying, Middle Wallop
	WG465	DHC1 Chipmunk T10 (G-BCEY)	Privately owned, White Waltham
	WG469	DHC1 Chipmunk T10 (G-BWJY) [72]	Privately owned, Newtownards
	WG471	DHC1 Chipmunk T10 (8210M) <ff>	Thameside Aviation Museum, East Tilbury
	WG472	DHC1 Chipmunk T10 (G-AOTY)	Privately owned, Bryngwyn Bach, Clwyd
	WG477	DHC1 Chipmunk T10 (8362M/ G-ATDP) <ff>	No 281 Sqn ATC, Birkdale, Merseyside
	WG482	DHC1 Chipmunk T10 (VH-ZOT) [01]	Privately owned
	WG483	DHC1 Chipmunk T10 (WG393/ VH-ZIT)	Privately owned
	WG486	DHC1 Chipmunk T10 [G]	RAF BBMF, Coningsby
	WG498	Slingsby T21B Sedbergh TX1 (BGA 3245)	Privately owned, Aston Down
	WG511	Avro 696 Shackleton T4 (fuselage)	Flambards Village Theme Park, Helston
	WG718	WS51 Dragonfly HR3 [934]	Privately owned, Elvington

Serial	Type (other identity) [code]	Owner/operator, location or fate	Notes
WG719	WS51 Dragonfly HR5 (G-BRMA)	The Helicopter Museum, Weston-super-Mare	
WG724	WS51 Dragonfly HR5 [932]	North-East Aircraft Museum, Usworth	
WG751	WS51 Dragonfly HR5 [710/GJ]	World Naval Base, Chatham	
WG760	EE P1A (7755M)	RAF Museum, Cosford	
WG763	EE P1A (7816M)	Gr Manchester Mus of Science & Industry	
WG768	Short SB5 (8005M)	RAF Museum, Cosford	
WG774	BAC 221	Science Museum, at FAA Museum, RNAS Yeovilton	
WG777	Fairey FD2 (7986M)	RAF Museum, Cosford	
WG789	EE Canberra B2/6 <ff>	Norfolk & Suffolk Avn Museum, Flixton	
WH132	Gloster Meteor T7 (7906M) [J]	No 276 Sqn ATC, Chelmsford	
WH166	Gloster Meteor T7 (8052M) [A]	Privately owned, Birlingham, Worcs	
WH291	Gloster Meteor F8	SWWAPS, Lasham	
WH301	Gloster Meteor F8 (7930M) [T]	RAF Museum, Hendon	
WH364	Gloster Meteor F8 (8169M)	Gloucestershire Avn Coll, stored Gloucester	
WH453	Gloster Meteor D16 [L]	DPA/QinetiQ, stored Llanbedr	
WH646	EE Canberra T17A <ff>	Midland Air Museum, Coventry	
WH657	EE Canberra B2	Brenzett Aeronautical Museum	
WH665	EE Canberra T17 (8763M) [J]	BAE Systems Filton, Fire Section	
WH725	EE Canberra B2	Imperial War Museum, Duxford	
WH734	EE Canberra B2(mod)	DPA/QinetiQ, Llanbedr	
WH739	EE Canberra B2 <ff>	No 2475 Sqn ATC, Ammanford, Dyfed	
WH740	EE Canberra T17 (8762M) [K]	East Midlands Airport Aeropark	
WH773	EE Canberra PR7 (8696M)	Gatwick Aviation Museum, Charlwood, Surrey	
WH775	EE Canberra PR7 (8128M/8868M) <ff>	Privately owned, Welshpool	
WH779	EE Canberra PR7 <ff>	QinetiQ Farnborough	
WH779	EE Canberra PR7 [BP] <rf>	RAF, stored Shawbury	
WH791	EE Canberra PR7 (8165M/8176M/8187M)	Newark Air Museum, Winthorpe	
WH803	EE Canberra T22 <ff>	Privately owned,	
WH840	EE Canberra T4 (8350M)	Privately owned, Flixton	
WH846	EE Canberra T4	Yorkshire Air Museum, Elvington	
WH849	EE Canberra T4	RAF, stored Shawbury	
WH850	EE Canberra T4 <ff>	Aeroventure, Doncaster	
WH863	EE Canberra T17 (8693M) [CP] <ff>	Newark Air Museum, Winthorpe	
WH876	EE Canberra B2(mod) <ff>	Boscombe Down Museum	
WH887	EE Canberra TT18 [847]	DPA/QinetiQ, stored Llanbedr	
WH903	EE Canberra B2 <ff>	Yorkshire Air Museum, Elvington	
WH904	EE Canberra T19	Newark Air Museum, Winthorpe	
WH946	EE Canberra B6(mod) (8185M) <ff>	Privately owned, Tetney, Grimsby	
WH953	EE Canberra B6(mod) <ff>	Blyth Valley Aviation Collection, Walpole, Suffolk	
WH957	EE Canberra E15 (8869M) <ff>	Lincolnshire Avn Heritage Centre, East Kirkby	
WH960	EE Canberra B15 (8344M) <ff>	Rolls-Royce Heritage Trust, Derby	
WH964	EE Canberra E15 (8870M) <ff>	Privately owned, Southampton	
WH984	EE Canberra B15 (8101M) <ff>	RAF Sealand	
WH991	WS51 Dragonfly HR3	Yorkshire Helicopter Preservation Group, Elvington	
WJ231	Hawker Sea Fury FB11 (WE726) [115/O]	FAA Museum, Yeovilton	
WJ306	Slingsby T21B Sedbergh TX1 (BGA3240) [FGB]	Privately owned, Weston-on-the-Green	
WJ358	Auster AOP6 (G-ARYD)	Museum of Army Flying, Middle Wallop	
WJ565	EE Canberra T17 (8871M) <ff>	Aeroventure, Doncaster	
WJ567	EE Canberra B2 <ff>	Privately owned, Houghton, Cambs	
WJ576	EE Canberra T17 <ff>	Boulton Paul Association, Wolverhampton	
WJ581	EE Canberra PR7 <ff>	Privately owned, Canterbury	
WJ633	EE Canberra T17 [EF] <ff>	RAF Wyton	
WJ639	EE Canberra TT18 [39]	North-East Aircraft Museum, Usworth	
WJ640	EE Canberra B2 (8722M) <ff>	Pinewood Studios, Bucks	
WJ676	EE Canberra B2 (7796M) <ff>	North-West Aviation Heritage, Hooton Park, Cheshire	
WJ677	EE Canberra B2 <ff>	Privately owned, Redruth	
WJ717	EE Canberra TT18 (9052M) <ff>	RAF St Athan, Fire Section	

Notes	Serial	Type (other identity) [code]	Owner/operator, location or fate
	WJ721	EE Canberra TT18 [21] <ff>	Privately owned, Oban
	WJ731	EE Canberra B2T [BK] <ff>	Privately owned, Golders Green
	WJ821	EE Canberra PR7 (8668M)	Army, Bassingbourn, on display
	WJ863	EE Canberra T4 <ff>	Cambridge Airport Fire Section
	WJ865	EE Canberra T4	Privately owned, Bromsgrove
	WJ866	EE Canberra T4	RAF No 39(1 PRU) Sqn, Marham
	WJ880	EE Canberra T4 (8491M) <ff>	Dumfries & Galloway Avn Mus, Dumfries
	WJ903	Vickers Varsity T1 <ff>	Aeroventure, Doncaster
	WJ945	Vickers Varsity T1 (G-BEDV) [21]	Imperial War Museum, Duxford
	WJ975	EE Canberra T19 [S]	Bomber County Aviation Museum, Hemswell
	WJ992	EE Canberra T4	Bournemouth Int'l Airport, Fire Section
	WK102	EE Canberra T17 (8780M) <ff>	Privately owned, Welshpool
	WK118	EE Canberra TT18 <ff>	Privately owned, Worcester
	WK122	EE Canberra TT18 <ff>	Phoenix Aviation, Bruntingthorpe
	WK124	EE Canberra TT18 (9093M) [CR]	MoD FSCTE, Manston
	WK126	EE Canberra TT18 (N2138J) [843]	Gloucestershire Avn Coll, stored Gloucester
	WK127	EE Canberra TT18 (8985M) <ff>	No 2484 Sqn ATC, Bassingbourn
	WK128	EE Canberra B2	DPA/QinetiQ, Llanbedr
	WK146	EE Canberra B2 <ff>	Gatwick Aviation Museum, Charlwood, Surrey
	WK163	EE Canberra B2/6 (G-BVWC)	Air Atlantique Historic Flight, Coventry
	WK198	VS Swift F4 (7428M) (fuselage)	North-East Aircraft Museum, Usworth
	WK275	VS Swift F4	Privately owned, Upper Hill, nr Leominster
	WK277	VS Swift FR5 (7719M) [N]	Newark Air Museum, Winthorpe
	WK281	VS Swift FR5 (7712M) [S]	Tangmere Military Aviation Museum
	WK393	DH112 Venom FB1 <ff>	Aeroventure, Doncaster
	WK436	DH112 Venom FB50 (J-1614/ G-VENM)	Kennet Aviation, North Weald
	WK512	DHC1 Chipmunk T10 (G-BXIM) [A]	Privately owned, Brize Norton
	WK514	DHC1 Chipmunk T10 (G-BBMO)	Privately owned, Wellesbourne Mountford
	WK517	DHC1 Chipmunk T10 (G-ULAS) [84]	Privately owned, Denham
	WK518	DHC1 Chipmunk T10 [K]	RAF BBMF, Coningsby
	WK522	DHC1 Chipmunk T10 (G-BCOU)	Privately owned, Duxford
	WK549	DHC1 Chipmunk T10 (G-BTWF)	Privately owned, Breighton
	WK570	DHC1 Chipmunk T10 (8211M) <ff>	No 424 Sqn ATC, Southampton Hall of Aviation
	WK576	DHC1 Chipmunk T10 (8357M) <ff>	No 1206 Sqn ATC, Lichfield
	WK577	DHC1 Chipmunk T10 (G-BCYM)	Privately owned, Kemble
	WK584	DHC1 Chipmunk T10 (7556M) <ff>	No 2008 Sqn ATC, Bawtry
	WK585	DHC1 Chipmunk T10 (9265M/ G-BZGA)	Privately owned, Shoreham
	WK586	DHC1 Chipmunk T10 (G-BXGX) [V]	Privately owned, Slinfold
	WK590	DHC1 Chipmunk T10 (G-BWVZ) [69]	Privately owned, Spanhoe
	WK608	DHC1 Chipmunk T10 [906]	RN Historic Flight, Yeovilton
	WK609	DHC1 Chipmunk T10 (G-BXDN) [B]	Privately owned, Booker
	WK611	DHC1 Chipmunk T10 (G-ARWB)	Privately owned, Thruxton
	WK613	DHC1 Chipmunk T10 [P]	*Scrapped*
	WK620	DHC1 Chipmunk T10 [T] (fuselage)	Privately owned, Twyford, Bucks
	WK622	DHC1 Chipmunk T10 (G-BCZH)	Privately owned, Horsford
	WK624	DHC1 Chipmunk T10 (G-BWHI)	Privately owned, Hawarden
	WK626	DHC1 Chipmunk T10 (8213M) <ff>	Aeroventure, stored Doncaster
	WK628	DHC1 Chipmunk T10 (G-BBMW)	Privately owned, Goodwood
	WK630	DHC1 Chipmunk T10 (G-BXDG) [11]	Privately owned, Felthorpe
	WK633	DHC1 Chipmunk T10 (G-BXEC) [A]	Privately owned, Redhill
	WK640	DHC1 Chipmunk T10 (G-BWUV) [C]	Privately owned, Wombleton
	WK642	DHC1 Chipmunk T10 (G-BXDP) [94]	Privately owned, Kilrush, Eire
	WK654	Gloster Meteor F8 (8092M) [B]	City of Norwich Aviation Museum
	WK800	Gloster Meteor D16 [Z]	DPA/QinetiQ, Llanbedr
	WK864	Gloster Meteor F8 (WL168/7750M [C]	Yorkshire Air Museum, Elvington
	WK935	Gloster Meteor Prone Pilot (7869M)	RAF Museum, Cosford
	WK991	Gloster Meteor F8 (7825M)	Imperial War Museum, Duxford
	WL131	Gloster Meteor F8 (7751M) <ff>	Aeroventure, Doncaster
	WL181	Gloster Meteor F8 [X]	North-East Aircraft Museum, Usworth

Serial	Type (other identity) [code]	Owner/operator, location or fate	Notes
WL332	Gloster Meteor T7 [888]	Privately owned, Long Marston	
WL345	Gloster Meteor T7	St Leonard's Motors, Hollington, E Sussex	
WL349	Gloster Meteor T7 [Z]	Gloucestershire Airport, Staverton, on display	
WL360	Gloster Meteor T7 (7920M) [G]	Meteor Flight, Yatesbury	
WL375	Gloster Meteor T7(mod)	Dumfries & Galloway Avn Mus, Dumfries	
WL405	Gloster Meteor T7	Meteor Flight, Yatesbury	
WL419	Gloster Meteor T7	Martin Baker Aircraft, Chalgrove	
WL505	DH100 Vampire FB9 (7705M/ G-FBIX)	De Havilland Aviation, Bridgend	
WL505	DH100 Vampire FB6 (J-1167/ VZ304/G-MKVI)	De Havilland Aviation, Swansea	
WL626	Vickers Varsity T1 (G-BHDD) [P]	East Midlands Airport Aeropark	
WL627	Vickers Varsity T1 (8488M) [D] <ff>	Privately owned, Preston, E Yorkshire	
WL679	Vickers Varsity T1 (9155M)	RAF Museum, Cosford	
WL732	BP P108 Sea Balliol T21	RAF Museum, Cosford	
WL795	Avro 696 Shackleton MR2C (8753M) [T]	RAF St Mawgan, on display	
WL798	Avro 696 Shackleton MR2C (8114M) <ff>	Privately owned, Elgin	
WL925	Slingsby T31B Cadet TX3 (WV925) <ff>	RAF No 633 VGS, Cosford	
WM145	AW Meteor NF11 <ff>	N Yorks Aircraft Recovery Centre, Chop Gate	
WM167	AW Meteor NF11 (G-LOSM)	Privately owned, Bournemouth	
WM267	Gloster Meteor NF11 <ff>	Blyth Valley Aviation Collection, Walpole, Suffolk	
WM292	AW Meteor TT20 [841]	FAA Museum, stored RNAS Yeovilton	
WM311	AW Meteor TT20 (WM224/8177M)	East Midlands Airport Aeropark	
WM366	AW Meteor NF13 (4X-FNA) (comp VZ462)	SWWAPS, Lasham	
WM367	AW Meteor NF13 <ff>	Jet Avn Preservation Grp, Long Marston	
WM571	DH112 Sea Venom FAW21 [VL]	Southampton Hall of Aviation, stored	
WM729	DH113 Vampire NF10 <ff>	Mosquito Aircraft Museum, London Colney	
WM913	Hawker Sea Hawk FB5 (8162M) [456/J]	Newark Air Museum, Winthorpe	
WM961	Hawker Sea Hawk FB5 [J]	Caernarfon Air World	
WM969	Hawker Sea Hawk FB5 [10/Z]	Imperial War Museum, Duxford	
WN105	Hawker Sea Hawk FB3 (WF299/ 8164M)	Privately owned, Birlingham, Worcs	
WN108	Hawker Sea Hawk FB5 [033]	Ulster Aviation Society, Langford Lodge	
WN149	BP P108 Balliol T2	Boulton Paul Association, Wolverhampton	
WN411	Fairey Gannet AS1 (fuselage)	Privately owned, Sholing, Hants	
WN493	WS51 Dragonfly HR5	FAA Museum, RNAS Yeovilton	
WN499	WS51 Dragonfly HR5 [Y]	Caernarfon Air World	
WN516	BP P108 Balliol T2 <ff>	North-East Aircraft Museum, Usworth	
WN534	BP P108 Balliol T2 <ff>	Boulton Paul Association, Wolverhampton	
WN890	Hawker Hunter F2 <ff>	Aeroventure, Doncaster	
WN904	Hawker Hunter F2 (7544M) [3]	RE 39 Regt, Waterbeach, on display	
WN907	Hawker Hunter F2 (7416M) <ff>	Robertsbridge Aviation Society, Newhaven	
WN957	Hawker Hunter F5 <ff>	Privately owned, Llanbedr	
WP185	Hawker Hunter F5 (7583M)	Privately owned, Great Dunmow, Essex	
WP190	Hawker Hunter F5 (7582M/8473M/ WP180) [K]	Tangmere Military Aviation Museum	
WP250	DH113 Vampire NF10 <ff>	Privately owned,	
WP255	DH113 Vampire NF10 <ff>	Aeroventure, Doncaster	
WP270	EoN Eton TX1 (8598M)	Gr Manchester Mus of Science & Industry, stored	
WP271	EoN Eton TX1	Privately owned, stored Keevil	
WP308	Percival P57 Sea Prince T1 (G-GACA) [572/CU]	Gatwick Aviation Museum, Charlwood, Surrey	
WP313	Percival P57 Sea Prince T1 [568/ CU]	FAA Museum, stored RNAS Yeovilton	
WP314	Percival P57 Sea Prince T1 (8634M) [573/CU]	Privately owned, Carlisle Airport	
WP321	Percival P57 Sea Prince T1 (N7SY)	Bournemouth Aviation Museum	
WP515	EE Canberra B2 <ff>	Privately owned, Welshpool	
WP772	DHC1 Chipmunk T10 [Q] (wreck)	RAF Manston History Museum	
WP784	DHC1 Chipmunk T10 <ff>	Jet Avn Preservation Grp, Long Marston	
WP788	DHC1 Chipmunk T10 (G-BCHL)	Privately owned, Sywell	

Notes	Serial	Type (other identity) [code]	Owner/operator, location or fate
	WP790	DHC1 Chipmunk T10 (G-BBNC) [T]	Mosquito Aircraft Museum, London Colney
	WP795	DHC1 Chipmunk T10 (G-BVZZ) [901]	Privately owned, Lee-on-Solent
	WP800	DHC1 Chipmunk T10 (G-BCXN) [2]	Privately owned, Halton
	WP803	DHC1 Chipmunk T10 (G-HAPY) [G]	Privately owned, Booker
	WP805	DHC1 Chipmunk T10 (G-MAJR) [D]	Privately owned, Lee-on-Solent
	WP808	DHC1 Chipmunk T10 (G-BDEU)	Privately owned, Binham
	WP809	DHC1 Chipmunk T10 (G-BVTX) [78]	Privately owned, Husbands Bosworth
	WP833	DHC1 Chipmunk T10 (G-BZDU) [H]	Privately owned, Blackpool
	WP835	DHC1 Chipmunk T10 (D-ERTY)	Privately owned, The Netherlands
	WP839	DHC1 Chipmunk T10 (G-BZXE) [A]	Privately owned, Perth
	WP840	DHC1 Chipmunk T10 (G-BXDM) [9]	Privately owned, Halton
	WP844	DHC1 Chipmunk T10 (G-BWOX) [85]	Privately owned, Shobdon
	WP856	DHC1 Chipmunk T10 (G-BVWP) [904]	Privately owned, Horsham
	WP857	DHC1 Chipmunk T10 (G-BDRJ) [24]	Privately owned, Elstree
	WP859	DHC1 Chipmunk T10 (G-BXCP) [E]	Privately owned, Spanhoe Lodge
	WP860	DHC1 Chipmunk T10 (G-BXDA) [6]	Privately owned, Perth
	WP863	DHC1 Chipmunk T10 (8360M/ G-ATJI) <ff>	No 1011 Sqn ATC, Boscombe Down
	WP871	DHC1 Chipmunk T10 [W]	AAC, Middle Wallop, for display
	WP896	DHC1 Chipmunk T10 (G-BWVY) [M]	Privately owned, White Waltham
	WP901	DHC1 Chipmunk T10 (G-BWNT) [B]	Privately owned, East Midlands Airport
	WP903	DHC1 Chipmunk T10 (G-BCGC)	Privately owned, Shoreham
	WP912	DHC1 Chipmunk T10 (8467M)	RAF Museum, Cosford
	WP921	DHC1 Chipmunk T10 (G-ATJJ) <ff>	Privately owned, Brooklands
	WP925	DHC1 Chipmunk T10 (G-BXHA) [C]	Privately owned, Camberley
	WP927	DHC1 Chipmunk T10 (8216M/ G-ATJK) <ff>	No 1343 Sqn ATC, Odiham
	WP928	DHC1 Chipmunk T10 (G-BXGM) [D]	Privately owned, Shoreham
	WP929	DHC1 Chipmunk T10 (G-BXCV) [F]	Privately owned, Rush Green
	WP930	DHC1 Chipmunk T10 (G-BXHF) [J]	Privately owned, Redhill
	WP962	DHC1 Chipmunk T10 [C]	RAF Museum, Hendon
	WP964	DHC1 Chipmunk T10 [Y]	AAC Historic Aircraft Flight, Middle Wallop
	WP969	DHC1 Chipmunk T10 (comp WB685/G-ATHC) [C]	North-East Aircraft Museum, Usworth
	WP971	DHC1 Chipmunk T10 (G-ATHD)	Privately owned, Denham
	WP983	DHC1 Chipmunk T10 (G-BXNN) [B]	Privately owned, Eggesford
	WP984	DHC1 Chipmunk T10 (G-BWTO) [H]	Privately owned, Little Gransden
	WR360	DH112 Venom FB50 (J-1626/ G-DHSS) [K]	Source Classic Jet Flight, Bournemouth
	WR410	DH112 Venom FB50 (J-1539/ G-DHUU/WE410)	Source Classic Jet Flight, Bournemouth
	WR410	DH112 Venom FB54 (J-1790/ G-BLKA) [N]	Mosquito Aircraft Museum, London Colney
	WR421	DH112 Venom FB50 (J-1611/ G-DHTT)	Source Classic Jet Flight, Bournemouth
	WR470	DH112 Venom FB50 (J-1542/ G-DHVM)	Air Atlantique Historic Flight, Coventry
	WR539	DH112 Venom FB4 (8399M) <ff>	Mosquito Aircraft Museum, London Colney
	WR960	Avro 696 Shackleton AEW2 (8772M)	Gr Manchester Mus of Science & Industry
	WR963	Avro 696 Shackleton AEW2	Air Atlantique Historic Flight, Coventry
	WR971	Avro 696 Shackleton MR3 (8119M) [Q]	Fenland & W Norfolk Aviation Museum, Wisbech

Serial	Type (other identity) [code]	Owner/operator, location or fate	Notes
WR974	Avro 696 Shackleton MR3 (8117M) [K]	Gatwick Aviation Museum, Charlwood, Surrey	
WR977	Avro 696 Shackleton MR3 (8186M) [B]	Newark Air Museum, Winthorpe	
WR982	Avro 696 Shackleton MR3 (8106M) [J]	Gatwick Aviation Museum, Charlwood, Surrey	
WR985	Avro 696 Shackleton MR3 (8103M) [H]	Privately owned, Long Marston	
WS103	Gloster Meteor T7 [709/VL]	FAA Museum, stored RNAS Yeovilton	
WS692	Gloster Meteor NF12 (7605M) [C]	Newark Air Museum, Winthorpe	
WS726	Gloster Meteor NF14 (7960M) [G]	No 1855 Sqn ATC, Royton, Gr Manchester	
WS739	Gloster Meteor NF14 (7961M)	Newark Air Museum, Winthorpe	
WS760	Gloster Meteor NF14 (7964M)	Meteor Flight, stored Yatesbury	
WS774	Gloster Meteor NF14 (7959M)	Privately owned, Quedgeley, Glos	
WS776	Gloster Meteor NF14 (7716M) [K]	Privately owned, Sandtoft	
WS788	Gloster Meteor NF14 (7967M) [Z]	Yorkshire Air Museum, Elvington	
WS792	Gloster Meteor NF14 (7965M) [K]	Brighouse Bay Caravan Park, Borgue, D&G	
WS807	Gloster Meteor NF14 (7973M) [N]	Gloucestershire Avn Coll, stored Gloucester	
WS832	Gloster Meteor NF14 [W]	Solway Aviation Society, Carlisle	
WS838	Gloster Meteor NF14	Midland Air Museum, Coventry	
WS843	Gloster Meteor NF14 (7937M) [Y]	RAF Museum, stored Cosford	
WT121	Douglas Skyraider AEW1 [415/CU]	FAA Museum, stored RNAS Yeovilton	
WT205	EE Canberra B15	RAF Manston History Museum	
WT308	EE Canberra B(I)6	RN, Predannack Fire School	
WT309	EE Canberra B(I)6 <ff>	Privately owned, Farnborough	
WT319	EE Canberra B(I)6 <ff>	Privately owned, Lavendon, Bucks	
WT333	EE Canberra B6(mod) (G-BVXC)	Privately owned, Bruntingthorpe	
WT339	EE Canberra B(I)8 (8198M)	RAF Barkston Heath Fire Section	
WT480	EE Canberra T4 [AT]	RAF, stored Shawbury	
WT482	EE Canberra T4 <ff>	Privately owned	
WT483	EE Canberra T4 [83]	Privately owned, Long Marston	
WT486	EE Canberra T4 (8102M) <ff>	Flight Experience Workshop, Belfast	
WT507	EE Canberra PR7 (8131M/8548M) [44] <ff>	No 384 Sqn ATC, Mansfield	
WT509	EE Canberra PR7 [BR]	RAF Marham, BDRT	
WT510	EE Canberra T22 <ff>	Privately owned, Stock, Essex	
WT519	EE Canberra PR7 [CH]	RAF Wyton, Fire Section	
WT520	EE Canberra PR7 (8094M/8184M) <ff>	No 967 Sqn ATC, Warton	
WT525	EE Canberra T22 <ff>	Privately owned, South Woodham Ferrers	
WT532	EE Canberra PR7 (8728M/8890M) <ff>	Bournemouth Aviation Museum	
WT534	EE Canberra PR7 (8549M) [43] <ff>	Boscombe Down Museum	
WT536	EE Canberra PR7 (8063M) <ff>	Privately owned, Shirrell Heath, Hants	
WT537	EE Canberra PR7	BAE Systems Samlesbury, on display	
WT569	Hawker Hunter F1 (7491M)	No 2117 Sqn ATC, Kenfig Hill, Mid-Glamorgan	
WT612	Hawker Hunter F1 (7496M)	RAF Wittering	
WT619	Hawker Hunter F1 (7525M)	Gr Manchester Mus of Science & Industry	
WT648	Hawker Hunter F1 (7530M) <ff>	Boscombe Down Museum	
WT651	Hawker Hunter F1 (7532M) [C]	Newark Air Museum, Winthorpe	
WT660	Hawker Hunter F1 (7421M) [C]	Highland Aircraft Preservation Society, Inverness	
WT680	Hawker Hunter F1 (7533M) [J]	No 1429 Sqn ATC, at QinetiQ Aberporth	
WT684	Hawker Hunter F1 (7422M) <ff>	Privately owned, Lavendon, Bucks	
WT694	Hawker Hunter F1 (7510M)	Caernarfon Air World	
WT711	Hawker Hunter GA11 [833/DD]	Air Atlantique, Coventry	
WT720	Hawker Hunter F51 (RDAF E-408/ 8565M) [B]	RAF Sealand, on display	
WT722	Hawker Hunter T8C (G-BWGN) [878/VL]	Hunter Flying Club, Exeter	
WT723	Hawker Hunter PR11 (G-PRII) [866/VL,3]	Privately owned, Exeter	
WT744	Hawker Hunter GA11 [868/VL]	South West Aviation Heritage, Eaglescott	
WT799	Hawker Hunter T8C [879]	Hunter Flying Club, Exeter	
WT804	Hawker Hunter GA11 [831/DD]	FETC, Moreton-in-Marsh, Glos	
WT806	Hawker Hunter GA11	Northbrook College, Shoreham Airport	

Notes	Serial	Type (other identity) [code]	Owner/operator, location or fate
	WT859	Supermarine 544 <ff>	Privately owned, Booker
	WT867	Slingsby T31B Cadet TX3	Privately owned, Eaglescott
	WT877	Slingsby T31B Cadet TX3	Boulton Paul Association, Wolverhampton
	WT898	Slingsby T31B Cadet TX3 (BGA 3284/BGA 4412)	Privately owned, Rufforth
	WT899	Slingsby T31B Cadet TX3	Privately owned, stored Swindon
	WT901	Slingsby T31B Cadet TX3	Sold to Germany
	WT905	Slingsby T31B Cadet TX3	Privately owned, Keevil
	WT908	Slingsby T31B Cadet TX3 (BGA 3487)	Privately owned, Dunstable
	WT910	Slingsby T31B Cadet TX3 (BGA 3953)	Privately owned, Swansea
	WT933	Bristol 171 Sycamore 3 (G-ALSW/7709M)	Newark Air Museum, Winthorpe
	WV106	Douglas Skyraider AEW1 [427/C]	FAA Museum, stored Yeovilton
	WV198	Sikorsky S55 Whirlwind HAR21 (G-BJWY) [K]	Solway Aviation Society, Carlisle
	WV276	Hawker Hunter F4 (7847M) [D]	Privately owned, stored Scampton
	WV318	Hawker Hunter T7B (9236M/G-FFOX)	Delta Jets, Kemble
	WV322	Hawker Hunter T8C (G-BZSE/9096M) [Y]	Privately owned, Kemble
	WV332	Hawker Hunter F4 (7673M) <ff>	Tangmere Military Aircraft Museum
	WV372	Hawker Hunter T7 (G-BXFI) [R]	Privately owned, Kemble
	WV381	Hawker Hunter GA11 [732/VL] (fuselage)	UKAEA, Culham, Oxon
	WV382	Hawker Hunter GA11 [830/VL]	Jet Avn Preservation Grp, Long Marston
	WV383	Hawker Hunter T7	QinetiQ Farnborough, on display
	WV396	Hawker Hunter T8C (9249M) [91]	RAF Valley, at main gate
	WV483	Percival P56 Provost T1 (7693M) [N-E]	Privately owned
	WV486	Percival P56 Provost T1 (7694M) [N-D]	Privately owned, Thatcham, Berks
	WV493	Percival P56 Provost T1 (G-BDYG/7696M) [29]	Royal Scottish Mus'm of Flight, stored É Fortune
	WV499	Percival P56 Provost T1 (G-BZRF/7698M) [P-G]	Privately owned, Sandtoft
	WV562	Percival P56 Provost T1 (7606M) [P-C]	RAF Museum, Cosford
	WV605	Percival P56 Provost T1 [T-B]	Norfolk & Suffolk Avn Museum, Flixton
	WV606	Percival P56 Provost T1 (7622M) [P-B]	Newark Air Museum, Winthorpe
	WV679	Percival P56 Provost T1 (7615M) [O-J]	Wellesbourne Wartime Museum
	WV703	Percival P66 Pembroke C1 (8108M/G-IIIM)	Privately owned, Tattershall Thorpe
	WV705	Percival P66 Pembroke C1 <ff>	Privately owned, Awbridge, Hants
	WV740	Percival P66 Pembroke C1 (G-BNPH)	Privately owned, Bournemouth
	WV746	Percival P66 Pembroke C1 (8938M)	RAF Museum, Cosford
	WV753	Percival P66 Pembroke C1 (8113M)	Cardiff International Airport Fire Section
	WV781	Bristol 171 Sycamore HR12 (G-ALTD/7839M)	Caernarfon Air World
	WV783	Bristol 171 Sycamore HR12 (G-ALSP/7841M)	RAF Museum, Hendon
	WV787	EE Canberra B2/8 (8799M)	Newark Air Museum, Winthorpe
	WV795	Hawker Sea Hawk FGA6 (8151M)	Highland Aircraft Preservation Group, Dalcross
	WV797	Hawker Sea Hawk FGA6 (8155M) [491/J]	Midland Air Museum, Coventry
	WV798	Hawker Sea Hawk FGA6 [026/CU]	SWWAPS, Lasham
	WV838	Hawker Sea Hawk FGA4 <ff>	Privately owned, Liverpool
	WV856	Hawker Sea Hawk FGA6 [163]	FAA Museum, RNAS Yeovilton
	WV903	Hawker Sea Hawk FGA4 (8153M) [128/C]	RNAS Yeovilton Fire Section
	WV908	Hawker Sea Hawk FGA6 (8154M) [188/A]	RN Historic Flight, Yeovilton
	WV910	Hawker Sea Hawk FGA6 <ff>	Boscombe Down Museum
	WV911	Hawker Sea Hawk FGA4 [115/C]	RN Historic Flight, Yeovilton

Serial	Type (other identity) [code]	Owner/operator, location or fate	Notes
WW138	DH112 Sea Venom FAW22 [227/Z]	FAA Museum, stored RNAS Yeovilton	
WW145	DH112 Sea Venom FAW22 [680/LM]	Royal Scottish Mus'm of Flight, E Fortune	
WW217	DH112 Sea Venom FAW22 [351]	Newark Air Museum, Winthorpe	
WW388	Percival P56 Provost T1 (7616M) [O-F]	Bomber County Aviation Museum, Hemswell	
WW421	Percival P56 Provost T1 (G-BZRE/ 7688M) [P-B]	Privately owned, Sandtoft	
WW442	Percival P56 Provost T1 (7618M) [N]	Gatwick Aviation Museum, Charlwood, Surrey	
WW444	Percival P56 Provost T1 [D]	Privately owned, Brownhills, Staffs	
WW447	Percival P56 Provost T1	*Currently not known*	
WW453	Percival P56 Provost T1 (G-TMKI) [W-S]	Privately owned, Clevedon	
WW654	Hawker Hunter GA11 [834/DD]	Privately owned, Ford, W Sussex	
WX788	DH112 Venom NF3	Aeroventure, Doncaster	
WX853	DH112 Venom NF3 (7443M)	Mosquito Aircraft Museum, London Colney	
WX905	DH112 Venom NF3 (7458M)	Newark Air Museum, Winthorpe	
WZ425	DH115 Vampire T11	Privately owned, Birlingham, Worcs	
WZ450	DH115 Vampire T11 <ff>	Lashenden Air Warfare Museum, Headcorn	
WZ464	DH115 Vampire T11 (N62430) [40]	*Scrapped*	
WZ507	DH115 Vampire T11 (G-VTII) [74]	De Havilland Aviation, Bournemouth	
WZ515	DH115 Vampire T11 [60]	Solway Aviation Society, Carlisle	
WZ518	DH115 Vampire T11	North-East Aircraft Museum, Usworth	
WZ549	DH115 Vampire T11 (8118M) [F]	Ulster Aviation Society, Langford Lodge	
WZ553	DH115 Vampire T11 (G-DHYY) [40]	Air Atlantique Historic Flight, Coventry	
WZ557	DH115 Vampire T11	N Yorks Aircraft Recovery Centre, Chop Gate	
WZ572	DH115 Vampire T11 (8124M) [65] <ff>	Privately owned, Sholing, Hants	
WZ581	DH115 Vampire T11 <ff>	The Vampire Collection, Hemel Hempstead	
WZ584	DH115 Vampire T11 (G-BZRC) [K]	Privately owned, Sandtoft	
WZ589	DH115 Vampire T11 [19]	Lashenden Air Warfare Museum, Headcorn	
WZ589	DH115 Vampire T55 (U-1230/ G-DHZZ)	Source Classic Jet Flight, Bournemouth	
WZ590	DH115 Vampire T11 [19]	Imperial War Museum, Duxford	
WZ608	DH115 Vampire T11 [56] <ff>	*Scrapped*	
WZ620	DH115 Vampire T11 [68]	*Currently not known*	
WZ662	Auster AOP9 (G-BKVK)	Privately owned, Eaglescott	
WZ706	Auster AOP9 (7851M/G-BURR)	Privately owned, Middle Wallop	
WZ711	Auster AOP9/Beagle E3 (G-AVHT)	Privately owned, Middle Wallop	
WZ721	Auster AOP9	Museum of Army Flying, Middle Wallop	
WZ724	Auster AOP9 (7432M)	AAC Middle Wallop, at main gate	
WZ729	Auster AOP9 (G-BXON)	Privately owned, Newark-on-Trent	
WZ736	Avro 707A (7868M)	Gr Manchester Mus of Science & Industry	
WZ744	Avro 707C (7932M)	RAF Museum, Cosford	
WZ753	Slingsby T38 Grasshopper TX1	Southampton Hall of Aviation	
WZ755	Slingsby T38 Grasshopper TX1 (BGA 3481)	Boulton Paul Association, Wolverhampton	
WZ767	Slingsby T38 Grasshopper TX1	North-East Aircraft Museum, stored Usworth	
WZ768	Slingsby T38 Grasshopper TX1 (comp XK820)	Privately owned, Kirton-in-Lindsey, Lincs	
WZ769	Slingsby T38 Grasshopper TX1	*Sold to The Netherlands*	
WZ772	Slingsby T38 Grasshopper TX1	Museum of Army Flying, Middle Wallop	
WZ779	Slingsby T38 Grasshopper TX1	Privately owned, Old Sarum	
WZ784	Slingsby T38 Grasshopper TX1	Solway Aviation Society, Carlisle	
WZ791	Slingsby T38 Grasshopper TX1 (8944M)	RAF Museum, Hendon	
WZ792	Slingsby T38 Grasshopper TX1	Privately owned, Sproughton	
WZ793	Slingsby T38 Grasshopper TX1	Whitgift School, Croydon	
WZ796	Slingsby T38 Grasshopper TX1	Privately owned, stored Nympsfield, Glos	
WZ798	Slingsby T38 Grasshopper TX1	Bournemouth Aviation Museum	
WZ816	Slingsby T38 Grasshopper TX1 (BGA 3979)	Privately owned, Redhill	
WZ819	Slingsby T38 Grasshopper TX1 (BGA 3498)	Privately owned, Halton	
WZ820	Slingsby T38 Grasshopper TX1	Sywell Aviation Museum	

Notes	Serial	Type (other identity) [code]	Owner/operator, location or fate
	WZ822	Slingsby T38 Grasshopper TX1	Aeroventure, stored Doncaster
	WZ824	Slingsby T38 Grasshopper TX1	Privately owned, stored Strathaven, Strathclyde
	WZ826	Vickers Valiant B(K)1 (XD826/ 7872M) <ff>	Privately owned, Foulness
	WZ827	Slingsby T38 Grasshopper TX1	RAFGSA, stored Bicester
	WZ828	Slingsby T38 Grasshopper TX1 (BGA 4421)	Privately owned, Bicester
	WZ831	Slingsby T38 Grasshopper TX1	Privately owned, stored Nympsfield, Glos
	WZ846	DHC1 Chipmunk T10 (G-BCSC/ 8439M)	No 1404 Sqn ATC, Chatham
	WZ847	DHC1 Chipmunk T10 (G-CPMK) [F]	Privately owned, Sleap
	WZ872	DHC1 Chipmunk T10 (G-BZGB) [E]	Privately owned, Newcastle
	WZ879	DHC1 Chipmunk T10 (G-BWUT) [X]	Privately owned, Earls Colne
	WZ882	DHC1 Chipmunk T10 (G-BXGP) [K]	Privately owned, Eaglescott
	XA109	DH115 Sea Vampire T22	Royal Scottish Mus'm of Flight, E Fortune
	XA127	DH115 Sea Vampire T22 <ff>	FAA Museum, stored RNAS Yeovilton
	XA129	DH115 Sea Vampire T22	FAA Museum, stored RNAS Yeovilton
	XA225	Slingsby T38 Grasshopper TX1	Privately owned, Upavon
	XA228	Slingsby T38 Grasshopper TX1	Royal Scottish Mus'm of Flight, E Fortune
	XA230	Slingsby T38 Grasshopper TX1 (BGA 4098)	Privately owned, Henlow
	XA231	Slingsby T38 Grasshopper TX1 (8888M)	RAF Manston History Museum
	XA240	Slingsby T38 Grasshopper TX1 (BGA 4556)	Privately owned, Keevil
	XA241	Slingsby T38 Grasshopper TX1	Shuttleworth Collection, Old Warden
	XA243	Slingsby T38 Grasshopper TX1 (8886M)	Privately owned, Gransden Lodge, Cambs
	XA244	Slingsby T38 Grasshopper TX1	Privately owned, Keevil
	XA282	Slingsby T31B Cadet TX3	Caernarfon Air World
	XA286	Slingsby T31B Cadet TX3	Privately owned, stored Rufforth
	XA289	Slingsby T31B Cadet TX3	Privately owned, Eaglescott
	XA290	Slingsby T31B Cadet TX3	Privately owned, stored Rufforth
	XA293	Slingsby T31B Cadet TX3	Privately owned, Breighton
	XA302	Slingsby T31B Cadet TX3 (BGA3786)	Privately owned, Syerston
	XA459	Fairey Gannet ECM6 [E]	Privately owned, Lambourn, Berks
	XA460	Fairey Gannet ECM6 [768/BY]	Aeroventure, Doncaster
	XA466	Fairey Gannet COD4 [777/LM]	FAA Museum, stored Yeovilton
	XA508	Fairey Gannet T2 [627/GN]	FAA Museum, at Midland Air Museum, Coventry
	XA564	Gloster Javelin FAW1 (7464M)	RAF Museum, Cosford
	XA634	Gloster Javelin FAW4 (7641M)	RAF Leeming, on display
	XA699	Gloster Javelin FAW5 (7809M)	Midland Air Museum, Coventry
	XA847	EE P1B (8371M)	Privately owned, Stowmarket, Suffolk
	XA862	WS55 Whirlwind HAR1 (G-AMJT)	The Helicopter Museum, Weston-super-Mare
	XA864	WS55 Whirlwind HAR1	FAA Museum, stored Yeovilton
	XA870	WS55 Whirlwind HAR1 [911]	Aeroventure, Doncaster
	XA880	DH104 Devon C2 (G-BVXR)	Privately owned, Kemble
	XA893	Avro 698 Vulcan B1 (8591M) <ff>	RAF Museum, Cosford
	XA903	Avro 698 Vulcan B1 <ff>	Privately owned, Wellesbourne Mountford
	XA917	HP80 Victor B1 (7827M) <ff>	Privately owned, Pitscottie, Fife
	XB259	Blackburn B101 Beverley C1 (G-AOAI)	Museum of Army Transport, Beverley
	XB261	Blackburn B101 Beverley C1 <ff>	Duxford Aviation Society, Duxford
	XB446	Grumman TBM-3 Avenger ECM6B	FAA Museum, Yeovilton
	XB480	Hiller HT1 [537]	FAA Museum, stored Yeovilton
	XB812	Canadair CL-13 Sabre F4 (9227M) [U]	RAF Museum, Hendon
	XD145	Saro SR53	RAF Museum, Cosford
	XD163	WS55 Whirlwind HAR10 (8645M) [X]	The Helicopter Museum, Weston-super-Mare
	XD165	WS55 Whirlwind HAR10 (8673M) [B]	Yorkshire Helicopter Preservation Group, stored Doncaster

Serial	Type (other identity) [code]	Owner/operator, location or fate	Notes
XD215	VS Scimitar F1 <ff>	Privately owned, Cheltenham	
XD235	VS Scimitar F1 <ff>	Privately owned, Ingatestone, Essex	
XD317	VS Scimitar F1 [112/R]	FAA Museum, RNAS Yeovilton	
XD332	VS Scimitar F1 [194/C]	Southampton Hall of Aviation, stored	
XD377	DH115 Vampire T11 (8203M) <ff>	Aeroventure, stored Doncaster	
XD382	DH115 Vampire T11 (8033M)	East Midlands Airport Aeropark	
XD425	DH115 Vampire T11 <ff>	RAF Millom Museum, Haverigg	
XD434	DH115 Vampire T11 [25]	Fenland & W Norfolk Aviation Museum, Wisbech	
XD445	DH115 Vampire T11	Bomber County Aviation Museum, Hemswell	
XD447	DH115 Vampire T11 [50]	Jet Avn Preservation Grp, Long Marston	
XD452	DH115 Vampire T11 (7990M) [66] <ff>	Privately owned, Chester	
XD459	DH115 Vampire T11 [63] <ff>	Aeroventure, Doncaster	
XD463	DH115 Vampire T11 (8023M)	Scrapped	
XD506	DH115 Vampire T11 (7983M)	Gloucestershire Avn Coll, stored Gloucester	
XD515	DH115 Vampire T11 (7998M/ XM515)	Privately owned, Rugeley, Staffs	
XD525	DH115 Vampire T11 (7882M) <ff>	Campbell College, Belfast	
XD528	DH115 Vampire T11 (8159M) <ff>	Gamston Aerodrome Fire Section	
XD534	DH115 Vampire T11 [41]	Military Aircraft Pres'n Grp, Barton	
XD536	DH115 Vampire T11 (7734M) [H]	Alleyn's School CCF, Northolt	
XD542	DH115 Vampire T11 (7604M) [N]	Montrose Air Station Museum	
XD547	DH115 Vampire T11 [Z] (composite)	Dumfries & Galloway Avn Mus, Dumfries	
XD593	DH115 Vampire T11 [50]	Newark Air Museum, Winthorpe	
XD595	DH115 Vampire T11 <ff>	Privately owned, Glentham, Lincs	
XD596	DH115 Vampire T11 (7939M)	Southampton Hall of Aviation	
XD599	DH115 Vampire T11 [A] <ff>	Privately owned, Ingatestone, Essex	
XD602	DH115 Vampire T11 (7737M) (composite)	Privately owned, Wearside	
XD616	DH115 Vampire T11 [56]	Mosquito Aircraft Museum, stored Gloucester	
XD622	DH115 Vampire T11 (8160M)	No 2214 Sqn ATC, Usworth	
XD624	DH115 Vampire T11 [O]	Manchester Airport, for display	
XD626	DH115 Vampire T11 [Q]	Midland Air Museum, Coventry	
XD674	Hunting Jet Provost T1 (7570M) [T]	RAF Museum, stored Cosford	
XD693	Hunting Jet Provost T1 (XM129/ G-AOBU) [Z-Q]	Kennet Aviation, North Weald	
XD816	Vickers Valiant B(K)1 <ff>	Brooklands Museum, Weybridge	
XD818	Vickers Valiant B(K)1 (7894M)	RAF Museum, Hendon	
XD857	Vickers Valiant B(K)1 <ff>	RAF Manston History Museum	
XD875	Vickers Valiant B(K)1 <ff>	Highland Aircraft Preservation Group, Dalcross	
XE317	Bristol 171 Sycamore HR14 (G-AMWO) [S-N]	Aeroventure, stored Doncaster	
XE339	Hawker Sea Hawk FGA6 (8156M) [149/E]	RNAS Yeovilton Fire Section	
XE340	Hawker Sea Hawk FGA6 [131/Z]	FAA Museum, at Montrose Air Station Museum	
XE368	Hawker Sea Hawk FGA6 [200/J]	Privately owned, Bruntingthorpe	
XE489	Hawker Sea Hawk FGA6 (G-JETH)	Gatwick Aviation Museum, Charlwood, Surrey	
XE521	Fairey Rotodyne Y (parts)	The Helicopter Museum, Weston-super-Mare	
XE584	Hawker Hunter FGA9 <ff>	NW Aviation Heritage Group, Hooton Park	
XE597	Hawker Hunter FGA9 (8874M) <ff>	Privately owned, Bromsgrove	
XE601	Hawker Hunter FGA9	Boscombe Down Museum	
XE606	Hawker Hunter F6A (XJ673/8841M)	RAF Cottesmore, preserved	
XE624	Hawker Hunter FGA9 (8875M) [G]	Phoenix Aviation, Bruntingthorpe	
XE627	Hawker Hunter F6A [T]	Imperial War Museum, Duxford	
XE643	Hawker Hunter FGA9 (8586M) <ff>	RAF M&RU, Aldergrove	
XE664	Hawker Hunter F4 <ff>	Gloucestershire Avn Coll, stored Gloucester	
XE665	Hawker Hunter T8C (G-BWGM) [876/VL]	Hunter Flying Club, Exeter	
XE668	Hawker Hunter GA11 [832/DD]	RN, Predannack Fire School	
XE670	Hawker Hunter F4 (7762M/8585M) <ff>	RAF Museum, Cosford	

Notes	Serial	Type (other identity) [code]	Owner/operator, location or fate
	XE683	Hawker Hunter F51 (RDAF E-409) [G]	City of Norwich Aviation Museum
	XE685	Hawker Hunter GA11 (G-GAII) [861/VL]	Privately owned, Exeter
	XE689	Hawker Hunter GA11 (G-BWGK) [864/VL]	Hunter Flying Club, Exeter
	XE786	Slingsby T31B Cadet TX3	RAF, stored Arbroath
	XE793	Slingsby T31B Cadet TX3 (8666M)	Privately owned, Tamworth
	XE799	Slingsby T31B Cadet TX3 (8943M) [R]	RAFGSA, Syerston
	XE802	Slingsby T31B Cadet TX3	Privately owned, stored Cupar, Fife
	XE807	Slingsby T31B Cadet TX3) (BGA3545	Sold abroad
	XE849	DH115 Vampire T11 (7928M) [V3]	Privately owned, Shobdon
	XE852	DH115 Vampire T11 [H]	No 2247 Sqn ATC, Hawarden
	XE855	DH115 Vampire T11	Midland Air Museum, Coventry
	XE856	DH115 Vampire T11 (G-DUSK)	Privately owned, Henlow
	XE864	DH115 Vampire T11(comp XD435) <ff>	Privately owned, Ingatstone, Essex
	XE872	DH115 Vampire T11 [62]	Midland Air Museum, Coventry
	XE874	DH115 Vampire T11 (8582M)	Montrose Air Station Museum
	XE897	DH115 Vampire T11 (XD403)	Privately owned, Errol, Tayside
	XE897	DH115 Vampire T55 (U-1214/ G-DHVV)	Source Classic Jet Flight, Bournemouth
	XE920	DH115 Vampire T11 (8196M/ G-VMPR) [A]	The Jet Fighter Experience, Swansea
	XE921	DH115 Vampire T11 [64] <ff>	Privately owned, Yarmouth, IoW
	XE935	DH115 Vampire T11	Aeroventure, Doncaster
	XE946	DH115 Vampire T11 (7473M) <ff>	RAF Cranwell Aviation Heritage Centre
	XE956	DH115 Vampire T11 (G-OBLN)	De Havilland Aviation, Bridgend
	XE979	DH115 Vampire T11 [54]	Privately owned, Birlingham, Worcs
	XE982	DH115 Vampire T11 (7564M) [01]	Privately owned, Dunkeswell
	XE985	DH115 Vampire T11 (WZ476)	De Havilland Aviation, Swansea
	XE993	DH115 Vampire T11 (8161M)	Privately owned, Cosford
	XE995	DH115 Vampire T11 [53]	Privately owned, High Halden, Kent
	XE998	DH115 Vampire T11 (U-1215)	Privately owned, Farnborough
	XF113	VS Swift F7 [19] <ff>	Boscombe Down Museum
	XF114	VS Swift F7 (G-SWIF)	Southampton Hall of Aviation, stored
	XF303	Hawker Hunter F58A (J-4105/ G-BWOU) [105,A]	The Old Flying Machine Company, Scampton
	XF314	Hawker Hunter F51 (RDAF E-412) [N]	Privately owned, Booker
	XF321	Hawker Hunter T7	Hunter Flying Club, Exeter (spares use)
	XF324	Hawker Hunter F51 (RDAF E-427) [D]	British Aviation Heritage, Bruntingthorpe
	XF358	Hawker Hunter T8C [870/VL]	DPA/AFD/QinetiQ, stored Boscombe Down
	XF375	Hawker Hunter F6A (8736M/ G-BUEZ) [05]	The Old Flying Machine Co, Duxford
	XF382	Hawker Hunter F6A [15]	Midland Air Museum, Coventry
	XF383	Hawker Hunter F6 (8706M) <ff>	Privately owned, Kidlington
	XF418	Hawker Hunter F51 (RDAF E-430)	Gatwick Aviation Museum, Charlwood, Surrey
	XF506	Hawker Hunter F4 (WT746/7770M) [A]	Dumfries & Galloway Avn Mus, Dumfries
	XF509	Hawker Hunter F6 (8708M)	Humbrol Paints, Marfleet, E Yorkshire
	XF515	Hawker Hunter F6A (8830M/ G-KAXF) [R]	Kennet Aviation, North Weald
	XF516	Hawker Hunter F6A (8685M/ G-BVVC) [19]	Crashed 1 June 2003, Aberdovey
	XF522	Hawker Hunter F6 <ff>	No 2352 Sqn ATC, Milton Keynes
	XF526	Hawker Hunter F6 (8679M) [78/E]	Privately owned, Birlingham, Worcs
	XF527	Hawker Hunter F6 (8680M)	RAF Halton, on display
	XF545	Percival P56 Provost T1 (7957M) [O-K]	Privately owned, Thatcham
	XF597	Percival P56 Provost T1 (G-BKFW) [AH]	Privately owned, Thatcham
	XF603	Percival P56 Provost T1 (G-KAPW)	Kennet Aviation, North Weald
	XF690	Percival P56 Provost T1 (8041M/ G-MOOS)	Kennet Aviation, North Weald
	XF708	Avro 716 Shackleton MR3 [203/C]	Imperial War Museum, Duxford
	XF785	Bristol 173 (7648M/G-ALBN)	Bristol Aero Collection, Kemble

Serial	Type (other identity) [code]	Owner/operator, location or fate	Notes
XF836	Percival P56 Provost T1 (8043M/ G-AWRY) [JG]	Privately owned, Thatcham	
XF844	Percival P56 Provost T1 [70]	British Aviation Heritage, Bruntingthorpe	
XF877	Percival P56 Provost T1 (G-AWVF) [JX]	Privately owned, Brimpton, Berks	
XF926	Bristol 188 (8368M)	RAF Museum, Cosford	
XF994	Hawker Hunter T8C [873/VL]	Boscombe Down Museum	
XF995	Hawker Hunter T8B (G-BZSF/ 9237M) [K]	Delta Jets, Kemble	
XG154	Hawker Hunter FGA9 (8863M) [54]	RAF Museum, Hendon	
XG160	Hawker Hunter F6A (8831M/ G-BWAF) [U]	Bournemouth Aviation Museum	
XG164	Hawker Hunter F6 (8681M)	Privately owned, Wellington, Somerset	
XG172	Hawker Hunter F6A (8832M) [A]	City of Norwich Aviation Museum	
XG190	Hawker Hunter F51 (RDAF E-425) [C]	Midland Air Museum, Coventry	
XG193	Hawker Hunter FGA9 (XG297) (comp with WT741)	Bomber County Aviation Museum, Hemswell	
XG195	Hawker Hunter FGA9 <ff>	Shropshire Wartime Aircraft Recovery Grp Mus, Sleap	
XG196	Hawker Hunter F6A (8702M) [31]	Army, Mytchett, Surrey, on display	
XG209	Hawker Hunter F6 (8709M) <ff>	Privately owned, Chelmsford	
XG210	Hawker Hunter F6	Privately owned, Beck Row, Suffolk	
XG225	Hawker Hunter F6A (8713M) [S]	RAF Museum, Cosford	
XG226	Hawker Hunter F6A (8800M) [28] <ff>	RAF Manston History Museum	
XG252	Hawker Hunter FGA9 (8840M) [U]	Privately owned, Bosbury, Hereford	
XG254	Hawker Hunter FGA9 (8881M)	Norfolk & Suffolk Avn Museum, Flixton	
XG274	Hawker Hunter F6 (8710M) [71]	Privately owned, Newmarket	
XG290	Hawker Hunter F6 (8711M) <ff>	Boscombe Down Museum	
XG297	Hawker Hunter FGA9 <ff>	Privately owned, Whitwell, Derbyshire	
XG325	EE Lightning F1 <ff>	No 1476 Sqn ATC, Southend	
XG329	EE Lightning F1 (8050M)	Privately owned, Flixton	
XG331	EE Lightning F1 <ff>	Gloucestershire Avn Coll, stored Gloucester	
XG337	EE Lightning F1 (8056M) [M]	RAF Museum, Cosford	
XG452	Bristol 192 Belvedere HC1 (7997M/G-BRMB)	The Helicopter Museum, Weston-super-Mare	
XG454	Bristol 192 Belvedere HC1 (8366M)	Gr Manchester Mus of Science & Industry	
XG462	Bristol 192 Belvedere HC1 <ff>	The Helicopter Museum, stored Weston-super-Mare	
XG474	Bristol 192 Belvedere HC1 (8367M) [O]	RAF Museum, Hendon	
XG502	Bristol 171 Sycamore HR14	Museum of Army Flying, Middle Wallop	
XG506	Bristol 171 Sycamore HR14 (7852M) <ff>	Privately owned, South Kirby	
XG518	Bristol 171 Sycamore HR14 (8009M) [S-E]	Norfolk & Suffolk Avn Museum, Flixton	
XG523	Bristol 171 Sycamore HR14 <ff> [K]	Norfolk & Suffolk Avn Museum, Flixton	
XG544	Bristol 171 Sycamore HR14	Privately owned,	
XG547	Bristol 171 Sycamore HR14 (G-HAPR) [S-T]	The Helicopter Museum, Weston-super-Mare	
XG574	WS55 Whirlwind HAR3 [752/PO]	FAA Museum, stored RNAS Yeovilton	
XG577	WS55 Whirlwind HAR3 (9050M)	RAF Leconfield Crash Rescue Training	
XG588	WS55 Whirlwind HAR3 (G-BAMH/ VR-BEP)	East Midlands Airport Aeropark	
XG594	WS55 Whirlwind HAS7 [517/PO]	FAA Museum, stored Yeovilton	
XG596	WS55 Whirlwind HAS7 [66]	The Helicopter Museum, Weston-super-Mare	
XG613	DH112 Sea Venom FAW21	Imperial War Museum, Duxford	
XG629	DH112 Sea Venom FAW22	Privately owned, Stone, Staffs	
XG680	DH112 Sea Venom FAW22 [438]	North-East Aircraft Museum, Usworth	
XG691	DH112 Sea Venom FAW22 [93/J]	Gloucestershire Avn Coll, stored Gloucester	
XG692	DH112 Sea Venom FAW22 [668/ LM]	Privately owned, Stone, Staffs	
XG730	DH112 Sea Venom FAW22 [499/A]	Mosquito Aircraft Museum, London Colney	
XG736	DH112 Sea Venom FAW22	Ulster Aviation Society, Newtownards	
XG737	DH112 Sea Venom FAW22 [220/Z]	Jet Avn Preservation Grp, stored Long Marston	
XG743	DH115 Sea Vampire T22 [597/LM]	Imperial War Museum, Duxford	

Notes	Serial	Type (other identity) [code]	Owner/operator, location or fate
	XG775	DH115 Vampire T55 (U-1219/ G-DHWW) [VL]	Source Classic Jet Flight, Bournemouth
	XG797	Fairey Gannet ECM6 [277]	Imperial War Museum, Duxford
	XG831	Fairey Gannet ECM6 [396]	Flambards Village Theme Park, Helston
	XG882	Fairey Gannet T5 (8754M) [771/LM]	Privately owned, Errol, Tayside
	XG883	Fairey Gannet T5 [773/BY]	FAA Museum, at Museum of Berkshire Aviation, Woodley
	XG900	Short SC1	Science Museum, South Kensington
	XG905	Short SC1	Ulster Folk & Transpt Mus, Holywood, Co Down
	XH131	EE Canberra PR9	RAF No 39(1 PRU) Sqn, Marham
	XH134	EE Canberra PR9	RAF No 39(1 PRU) Sqn, Marham
	XH135	EE Canberra PR9	RAF No 39(1 PRU) Sqn, Marham
	XH136	EE Canberra PR9 (8782M) [W] <ff>	Phoenix Aviation, Bruntingthorpe
	XH165	EE Canberra PR9 <ff>	Blyth Valley Aviation Collection, Walpole
	XH168	EE Canberra PR9	RAF Marham (damaged)
	XH169	EE Canberra PR9	RAF No 39(1 PRU) Sqn, Marham
	XH170	EE Canberra PR9 (8739M)	RAF Wyton, on display
	XH171	EE Canberra PR9 (8746M) [U]	RAF Museum, Cosford
	XH174	EE Canberra PR9 <ff>	RAF, stored Shawbury
	XH175	EE Canberra PR9 <ff>	Privately owned, Stock, Essex
	XH177	EE Canberra PR9 <ff>	Newark Air Museum, Winthorpe
	XH278	DH115 Vampire T11 (8595M/ 7866M) [42]	Yorkshire Air Museum, Elvington
	XH312	DH115 Vampire T11 [18]	Privately owned, Dodleston, Cheshire
	XH313	DH115 Vampire T11 (G-BZRD) [E]	Privately owned, Sandtoft
	XH318	DH115 Vampire T11 (7761M) [64]	Privately owned, Sholing, Hants
	XH328	DH115 Vampire T11 <ff>	Privately owned, Duxford
	XH330	DH115 Vampire T11 [73]	Privately owned, Camberley, Surrey
	XH537	Avro 698 Vulcan B2MRR (8749M) <ff>	Bournemouth Aviation Museum
	XH558	Avro 698 Vulcan B2 (G-VLCN)	British Aviation Heritage, Bruntingthorpe
	XH560	Avro 698 Vulcan K2 <ff>	Privately owned, Foulness
	XH563	Avro 698 Vulcan B2MRR <ff>	Privately owned, Bruntingthorpe
	XH568	EE Canberra B6(mod) (G-BVIC)	Classic Aviation Projects, Bruntingthorpe
	XH584	EE Canberra T4 (G-27-374) <ff>	Aeroventure, Doncaster
	XH592	HP80 Victor K1A (8429M) <ff>	Phoenix Aviation, Bruntingthorpe
	XH648	HP80 Victor K1A	Imperial War Museum, Duxford
	XH669	HP80 Victor K2 (9092M) <ff>	Privately owned, Foulness
	XH670	HP80 Victor SR2 <ff>	Privately owned, Foulness
	XH672	HP80 Victor K2 (9242M)	RAF Museum, Cosford
	XH673	HP80 Victor K2 (8911M)	RAF Marham, on display
	XH767	Gloster Javelin FAW9 (7955M) [A]	Yorkshire Air Museum, Elvington
	XH783	Gloster Javelin FAW7 (7798M) <ff>	Privately owned, Catford
	XH837	Gloster Javelin FAW7 (8032M) <ff>	Caernarfon Air World
	XH892	Gloster Javelin FAW9R (7982M) [J]	Norfolk & Suffolk Avn Museum, Flixton
	XH897	Gloster Javelin FAW9	Imperial War Museum, Duxford
	XH903	Gloster Javelin FAW9 (7938M) [G]	Gloucestershire Avn Coll, stored Gloucester
	XH992	Gloster Javelin FAW8 (7829M) [P]	Newark Air Museum, Winthorpe
	XJ314	RR Thrust Measuring Rig	Science Museum, South Kensington
	XJ380	Bristol 171 Sycamore HR14 (8628M)	Montrose Air Station Museum
	XJ389	Fairey Jet Gyrodyne (XD759/ G-AJJP)	Museum of Berkshire Aviation, Woodley
	XJ398	WS55 Whirlwind HAR10 (XD768/ G-BDBZ)	Aeroventure, stored Doncaster
	XJ409	WS55 Whirlwind HAR10 (XD779)	Maes Artro Craft Village, Llanbedr
	XJ435	WS55 Whirlwind HAR10 (XD804/ 8671M) [V]	RAF Manston History Museum, spares use
	XJ476	DH110 Sea Vixen FAW1 <ff>	No 424 Sqn ATC, Southampton Hall of Avn
	XJ481	DH110 Sea Vixen FAW1 [VL]	FAA Museum, stored RNAS Yeovilton
	XJ482	DH110 Sea Vixen FAW1 [713/VL]	Norfolk & Suffolk Avn Museum, Flixton
	XJ488	DH110 Sea Vixen FAW1 <ff>	Robertsbridge Aviation Society, Mayfield
	XJ494	DH110 Sea Vixen FAW2	Privately owned, Bruntingthorpe
	XJ560	DH110 Sea Vixen FAW2 (8142M) [242]	Newark Air Museum, Winthorpe
	XJ565	DH110 Sea Vixen FAW2 [127/E]	Mosquito Aircraft Museum, London Colney

Serial	Type (other identity) [code]	Owner/operator, location or fate	Notes
XJ571	DH110 Sea Vixen FAW2 (8140M) [242/R]	Southampton Hall of Aviation	
XJ575	DH110 Sea Vixen FAW2 <ff> [SAH-13]	Wellesbourne Wartime Museum	
XJ579	DH110 Sea Vixen FAW2 <ff>	Midland Air Museum, Coventry	
XJ580	DH110 Sea Vixen FAW2 [131/E]	Tangmere Military Aviation Museum	
XJ615	Hawker Hunter T8C(mod) (XF357/ G-BWGL)	Privately owned, Elvington	
XJ639	Hawker Hunter F6A (8687M) [H]	Hunter Flying Club, Exeter	
XJ714	Hawker Hunter FR10 (comp XG226)	Jet Avn Preservation Grp, Long Marston	
XJ723	WS55 Whirlwind HAR10	Montrose Air Station Museum	
XJ726	WS55 Whirlwind HAR10 [F]	Caernarfon Air World	
XJ727	WS55 Whirlwind HAR10 (8661M) [L]	RAF Manston History Museum	
XJ758	WS55 Whirlwind HAR10 (8464M) <ff>	Privately owned, Welshpool	
XJ771	DH115 Vampire T55 (U-1215/ G-HELV)	Privately owned, Bournemouth	
XJ772	DH115 Vampire T11 [H]	Mosquito Aircraft Museum, London Colney	
XJ823	Avro 698 Vulcan B2A	Solway Aviation Society, Carlisle	
XJ824	Avro 698 Vulcan B2A	Imperial War Museum, Duxford	
XJ917	Bristol 171 Sycamore HR14 [H-S]	Bristol Sycamore Group, stored Kemble	
XJ918	Bristol 171 Sycamore HR14 (8190M)	RAF Museum, Cosford	
XK149	Hawker Hunter F6A (8714M) [L]	Privately owned, Bruntingthorpe	
XK416	Auster AOP9 (7855M/G-AYUA)	Currently not known	
XK417	Auster AOP9 (G-AVXY)	Privately owned, Sutton in Ashfield	
XK418	Auster AOP9 (7976M)	SWWAPS, Lasham	
XK421	Auster AOP9 (8365M) (frame)	Aeroventure, stored Doncaster	
XK488	Blackburn NA39 Buccaneer S1	FAA Museum, stored RNAS Yeovilton	
XK526	Blackburn NA39 Buccaneer S2 (8648M)	RAF Honington, at main gate	
XK527	Blackburn NA39 Buccaneer S2D (8818M) <ff>	Privately owned, North Wales	
XK532	Blackburn NA39 Buccaneer S1 (8867M) [632/LM]	Highland Aircraft Preservation Group, Dalcross	
XK533	Blackburn NA39 Buccaneer S1 <ff>	Royal Scottish Mus'm of Flight, E Fortune	
XK590	DH115 Vampire T11 [V]	Wellesbourne Wartime Museum	
XK623	DH115 Vampire T11 (G-VAMP) [56]	Caernarfon Air World	
XK624	DH115 Vampire T11 [32]	Norfolk & Suffolk Avn Museum, Flixton	
XK625	DH115 Vampire T11 [12]	Brenzett Aeronautical Museum	
XK627	DH115 Vampire T11	Privately owned, Lavendon, Bucks	
XK632	DH115 Vampire T11 [67]	No 2370 Sqn ATC, Denham	
XK637	DH115 Vampire T11 [56]	RAF Millom Museum, Haverigg	
XK655	DH106 Comet C2(RC) (G-AMXA) <ff>	Gatwick Airport, on display (BOAC colours)	
XK695	DH106 Comet C2(RC) (G-AMXH/ 9164M) <ff>	Mosquito Aircraft Museum, London Colney	
XK699	DH106 Comet C2 (7971M)	RAF Lyneham on display	
XK724	Folland Gnat F1 (7715M)	RAF Museum, Cosford	
XK740	Folland Gnat F1 (8396M)	Southampton Hall of Aviation	
XK741	Folland Gnat F1 (fuselage)	Midland Air Museum, Coventry	
XK776	ML Utility 1	Museum of Army Flying, Middle Wallop	
XK788	Slingsby T38 Grasshopper TX1	Privately owned, Sproughton	
XK789	Slingsby T38 Grasshopper TX1	Midland Air Museum, stored Coventry	
XK790	Slingsby T38 Grasshopper TX1	Privately owned, stored Husbands Bosworth	
XK819	Slingsby T38 Grasshopper TX1	Privately owned, Selby	
XK822	Slingsby T38 Grasshopper TX1	Privately owned, Kenley	
XK895	DH104 Sea Devon C20 (G-SDEV) [19/CU]	Privately owned, Shoreham	
XK896	DH104 Sea Devon C20 (G-RNAS) (fuselage)	Privately owned, Filton (spares use)	
XK907	WS55 Whirlwind HAS7 [U]	Midland Air Museum, Coventry	
XK911	WS55 Whirlwind HAS7 [519/PO]	Privately owned, Glos	
XK936	WS55 Whirlwind HAS7 [62]	Imperial War Museum, Duxford	
XK940	WS55 Whirlwind HAS7 (G-AYXT) [911]	The Helicopter Museum, Weston-super-Mare	
XK944	WS55 Whirlwind HAS7	No 617 Sqn ATC, Malpas, Cheshire	
XK970	WS55 Whirlwind HAR10 (8789M)	Privately owned, Dunkeswell	

XL149 – XL824

Notes	Serial	Type (other identity) [code]	Owner/operator, location or fate
	XL149	Blackburn B101 Beverley C1 (7988M) <ff>	Newark Air Museum, Winthorpe
	XL160	HP80 Victor K2 (8910M) <ff>	HP Victor Association, Walpole
	XL164	HP80 Victor K2 (9215M) <ff>	Gatwick Aviation Museum, Charlwood, Surrey
	XL188	HP80 Victor K2 (9100M) (fuselage)	RAF Kinloss Fire Section
	XL190	HP80 Victor K2 (9216M) <ff>	RAF Manston History Museum
	XL231	HP80 Victor K2	Yorkshire Air Museum, Elvington
	XL318	Avro 698 Vulcan B2 (8733M)	RAF Museum, Hendon
	XL319	Avro 698 Vulcan B2	North-East Aircraft Museum, Usworth
	XL360	Avro 698 Vulcan B2A	Midland Air Museum, Coventry
	XL388	Avro 698 Vulcan B2 <ff>	Aeroventure, Doncaster
	XL391	Avro 698 Vulcan B2	Privately owned, Blackpool
	XL426	Avro 698 Vulcan B2 (G-VJET)	Vulcan Restoration Trust, Southend
	XL445	Avro 698 Vulcan K2 (8811M) <ff>	Blyth Valley Aviation Collection, Walpole
	XL449	Fairey Gannet AEW3 <ff>	Privately owned, Camberley, Surrey
	XL472	Fairey Gannet AEW3 [044/R]	Gatwick Aviation Museum, Charlwood, Surrey
	XL497	Fairey Gannet AEW3 [041/R]	RN, Prestwick
	XL500	Fairey Gannet AEW3 (G-KAEW)	World Naval Base, Chatham
	XL502	Fairey Gannet AEW3 (8610M/ G-BMYP)	Privately owned, Sandtoft
	XL503	Fairey Gannet AEW3 [070/E]	FAA Museum, RNAS Yeovilton
	XL563	Hawker Hunter T7 (9218M)	Privately owned, Bosbury, Hereford
	XL564	Hawker Hunter T7 (fuselage)	Boscombe Down Museum
	XL565	Hawker Hunter T7 (parts of WT745)	Privately owned, Bruntingthorpe
	XL568	Hawker Hunter T7A (9224M) [C]	RAF Museum, Cosford
	XL569	Hawker Hunter T7 (8833M)	East Midlands Airport Aeropark
XL571		Hawker Hunter T7 (XL572/8834M/ G-HNTR) [V]	Yorkshire Air Museum, Elvington
	XL573	Hawker Hunter T7 (G-BVGH)	Privately owned, Humberside
	XL577	Hawker Hunter T7 (G-BXKF/ 8676M)	Delta Jets, Kemble
	XL578	Hawker Hunter T7 (fuselage) [77]	Privately owned, Kemble
	XL580	Hawker Hunter T8M [723]	FAA Museum, RNAS Yeovilton
	XL586	Hawker Hunter T7 <rf>	Delta Jets, Kemble
	XL587	Hawker Hunter T7 (8807M/ G-HPUX) [Z]	The Old Flying Machine Company, stored Scampton
	XL591	Hawker Hunter T7	Gatwick Aviation Museum, Charlwood, Surrey
	XL592	Hawker Hunter T7 (8836M) [Y]	Hunter Flying Club, Exeter
	XL601	Hawker Hunter T7 (G-BZSR) [874/VL]	Classic Fighters, Brustem, Belgium
	XL602	Hawker Hunter T8M (G-BWFT)	Hunter Flying Club, Exeter
	XL609	Hawker Hunter T7 <ff>	Boscombe Down Museum
	XL612	Hawker Hunter T7 [2]	DPA/AFD/QinetiQ Boscombe Down, wfu
	XL618	Hawker Hunter T7 (8892M) [05]	Caernarfon Air World
	XL621	Hawker Hunter T7 (G-BNCX)	Privately owned, Brooklands Museum
	XL623	Hawker Hunter T7 (8770M)	The Planets Leisure Centre, Woking
	XL629	EE Lightning T4	DPA/QinetiQ Boscombe Down, at main gate
	XL703	SAL Pioneer CC1 (8034M)	RAF Museum, Cosford
	XL714	DH82A Tiger Moth II (T6099/ G-AOGR)	Privately owned, Swanton Morley
	XL716	DH82A Tiger Moth II (T7363/ G-AOIL)	Privately owned, Chandlers Ford
	XL735	Saro Skeeter AOP12	Privately owned, Tattershall Thorpe
	XL738	Saro Skeeter AOP12 (7860M)	Privately owned, Ivybridge, Devon
	XL739	Saro Skeeter AOP12	AAC Wattisham, on display
	XL762	Saro Skeeter AOP12 (8017M)	Royal Scottish Mus'm of Flight, E Fortune
	XL763	Saro Skeeter AOP12	Privately owned, Leeds
	XL764	Saro Skeeter AOP12 (7940M) [J]	Newark Air Museum, Winthorpe
	XL765	Saro Skeeter AOP12	Privately owned, Melksham, Wilts
	XL770	Saro Skeeter AOP12 (8046M)	Southampton Hall of Aviation
	XL809	Saro Skeeter AOP12 (G-BLIX)	Privately owned, Wilden, Beds
	XL811	Saro Skeeter AOP12	The Helicopter Museum, Weston-super-Mare
	XL812	Saro Skeeter AOP12 (G-SARO)	Privately owned, Old Buckenham
	XL813	Saro Skeeter AOP12	Museum of Army Flying, Middle Wallop
	XL814	Saro Skeeter AOP12	AAC Historic Aircraft Flight, Middle Wallop
	XL824	Bristol 171 Sycamore HR14 (8021M)	Gr Manchester Mus of Science & Industry

Serial	Type (other identity) [code]	Owner/operator, location or fate	Notes
XL829	Bristol 171 Sycamore HR14	Bristol Industrial Museum	
XL840	WS55 Whirlwind HAS7	Privately owned, Bawtry	
XL847	WS55 Whirlwind HAS7 [83]	AAC Middle Wallop Fire Section	
XL853	WS55 Whirlwind HAS7 [PO]	FAA Museum, stored RNAS Yeovilton	
XL875	WS55 Whirlwind HAR9	Perth Technical College	
XL929	Percival P66 Pembroke C1 (G-BNPU)	D-Day Museum, Shoreham Airport	
XL954	Percival P66 Pembroke C1 (9042M/N4234C/G-BXES)	Air Atlantique Historic Flight, Coventry	
XL993	SAL Twin Pioneer CC1 (8388M)	RAF Museum, Cosford	
XM135	BAC Lightning F1 [B]	Imperial War Museum, Duxford	
XM144	BAC Lightning F1 (8417M) <ff>	Privately owned, Booker	
XM169	BAC Lightning F1A (8422M) <ff>	N Yorks Aircraft Recovery Centre, Chop Gate	
XM172	BAC Lightning F1A (8427M)	Privately owned, Booker	
XM173	BAC Lightning F1A (8414M) [A]	RAF Bentley Priory, at main gate	
XM191	BAC Lightning F1A (7854M/8590M) <ff>	RAF M&RU, Bottesford	
XM192	BAC Lightning F1A (8413M) [K]	Bomber County Aviation Museum, Hemswell	
XM223	DH104 Devon C2 (G-BWWC) [J]	Air Atlantique, Coventry	
XM279	EE Canberra B(I)8 <ff>	Privately owned, Flixton	
XM300	WS58 Wessex HAS1	Welsh Industrial & Maritime Mus'm, stored Cardiff	
XM328	WS58 Wessex HAS3 [653/PO]	SFDO, RNAS Culdrose	
XM330	WS58 Wessex HAS1	The Helicopter Museum, Weston-super-Mare	
XM349	Hunting Jet Provost T3A (9046M) [T]	Global Aviation, Binbrook	
XM350	Hunting Jet Provost T3A (9036M) [89]	Aeroventure, Doncaster	
XM351	Hunting Jet Provost T3 (8078M) [Y]	RAF Museum, Cosford	
XM355	Hunting Jet Provost T3A (8229M) [D]	Privately owned, Bruntingthorpe	
XM358	Hunting Jet Provost T3A (8987M) [53]	Privately owned, Newbridge, Powys	
XM362	Hunting Jet Provost T3 (8230M)	RAF No 1 SoTT, Cosford	
XM365	Hunting Jet Provost T3A (G-BXBH) [37]	Privately owned, Norwich	
XM369	Hunting Jet Provost T3 (8084M) [C]	Scrapped at Portsmouth by June 2003	
XM370	Hunting Jet Provost T3A (G-BVSP) [10]	Privately owned, Long Marston	
XM372	Hunting Jet Provost T3 (8917M) [55]	Scrapped at Linton-on-Ouse Fire by June 2003	
XM375	Hunting Jet Provost T3 (8231M) [B]	Scrapped at Cottesmore	
XM383	Hunting Jet Provost T3A [90]	Newark Air Museum, Winthorpe	
XM402	Hunting Jet Provost T3 (8055AM) [J]	Fenland & W Norfolk Aviation Museum, Wisbech	
XM404	Hunting Jet Provost T3 (8055BM)	FETC, Moreton-in-Marsh, Glos	
XM409	Hunting Jet Provost T3 (8082M) <rf>	Air Scouts, Guernsey Airport	
XM410	Hunting Jet Provost T3 (8054AM) [B]	DEODS, Chattenden, Kent	
XM411	Hunting Jet Provost T3 (8434M) <ff>	Aeroventure, Doncaster	
XM412	Hunting Jet Provost T3A (9011M) [41]	Privately owned, Kinross, Scotland	
XM414	Hunting Jet Provost T3A (8996M)	Ulster Avn Soc, Langfor Lodge	
XM417	Hunting Jet Provost T3 (8054BM) [D] <ff>	Privately owned, Cannock	
XM419	Hunting Jet Provost T3A (8990M) [102]	DARA Training School, RAF St Athan	
XM424	Hunting Jet Provost T3A (G-BWDS)	Privately owned, North Weald	
XM425	Hunting Jet Provost T3A (8995M) [88]	Privately owned, Longton, Staffs	
XM463	Hunting Jet Provost T3A [38] (fuselage)	RAF Museum, Hendon	
XM468	Hunting Jet Provost T3 (8081M)	Privately owned, Terrington St Clement	
XM470	Hunting Jet Provost T3A (G-BWZZ) [12]	Privately owned, Hawarden	

Notes	Serial	Type (other identity) [code]	Owner/operator, location or fate
	XM473	Hunting Jet Provost T3A (8974M/ G-TINY)	Bedford College, instructional use
	XM474	Hunting Jet Provost T3 (8121M) <ff>	No 2517 Sqn ATC, Buxton
	XM478	Hunting Jet Provost T3A (8983M/ G-BXDL)	Privately owned, Bournemouth
	XM479	Hunting Jet Provost T3A (G-BVEZ) [54]	Privately owned, Newcastle
	XM480	Hunting Jet Provost T3 (8080M)	4x4 Car Centre, Chesterfield
	XM496	Bristol 253 Britannia C1 (EL-WXA)	Britannia Preservation Society, Kemble
	XM529	Saro Skeeter AOP12 (7979M/ G-BDNS)	Privately owned, Handforth
	XM553	Saro Skeeter AOP12 (G-AWSV)	Privately owned, Middle Wallop
	XM555	Saro Skeeter AOP12 (8027M)	RAF Museum, Cosford
	XM561	Saro Skeeter AOP12 (7980M)	Aeroventure, Doncaster
	XM564	Saro Skeeter AOP12	National Tank Museum, Bovington
	XM569	Avro 698 Vulcan B2 <ff>	Gloucestershire Avn Coll, stored Gloucester
	XM575	Avro 698 Vulcan B2A (G-BLMC)	East Midlands Airport Aeropark
	XM594	Avro 698 Vulcan B2	Newark Air Museum, Winthorpe
	XM597	Avro 698 Vulcan B2	Royal Scottish Mus'm of Flight, E Fortune
	XM598	Avro 698 Vulcan B2 (8778M)	RAF Museum, Cosford
	XM602	Avro 698 Vulcan B2 (8771M) <ff>	Avro Aircraft Heritage Society, Woodford
	XM603	Avro 698 Vulcan B2	Avro Aircraft Heritage Society, Woodford
	XM607	Avro 698 Vulcan B2 (8779M)	RAF Waddington, on display
	XM612	Avro 698 Vulcan B2	City of Norwich Aviation Museum
	XM652	Avro 698 Vulcan B2 <ff>	Privately owned, Welshpool
	XM655	Avro 698 Vulcan B2 (G-VULC)	Privately owned, Wellesbourne Mountford
	XM660	WS55 Whirlwind HAS7 [78]	RAF Millom Museum, Haverigg
	XM685	WS55 Whirlwind HAS7 (G-AYZJ) [513/PO]	Newark Air Museum, Winthorpe
	XM692	HS Gnat T1 <ff>	Thameside Aviation Museum, East Tilbury
	XM693	HS Gnat T1 (7891M)	BAE Systems Hamble, on display
	XM693	*HS Gnat T1 (8618M/XP504/ G-TIMM) [04]*	*Repainted as XS111*
	XM697	HS Gnat T1 (G-NAAT)	Privately owned, Exeter
	XM708	HS Gnat T1 (8573M)	Privately owned, Bruntingthorpe
	XM715	HP80 Victor K2	British Aviation Heritage, Bruntingthorpe
	XM717	HP80 Victor K2 <ff>	RAF Museum, Hendon
	XM819	*Lancashire EP9 Prospector (G-APXW)*	*Museum of Army Flying, Middle Wallop*
	XM833	WS58 Wessex HAS3	SWWAPS, Lasham
	XM870	WS58 Wessex HAS3 [PO]	RN, Predannack Fire School
	XM927	WS58 Wessex HAS3 (8814M) [660/PO]	*Scrapped at Shawbury, 9 July 2003*
	XN126	WS55 Whirlwind HAR10 (8655M) [S]	Pinewood Studios, Elstree
	XN157	Slingsby T21B Sedbergh TX1 (BGA 3255)	Privately owned, stored Long Mynd
	XN185	Slingsby T21B Sedbergh TX1 (8942M/BGA 4077)	RAFGSA, Syerston
	XN187	Slingsby T21B Sedbergh TX1 (BGA 3903)	Privately owned, Seighford
	XN198	Slingsby T31B Cadet TX3	Privately owned, Challock Lees
	XN238	Slingsby T31B Cadet TX3 <ff>	Aeroventure, stored Doncaster
	XN239	Slingsby T31B Cadet TX3 (8889M) [G]	Welsh National Museum, Cardiff
	XN243	Slingsby T31B Cadet TX3 (BGA 3145)	Privately owned, Bicester
	XN246	Slingsby T31B Cadet TX3	Southampton Hall of Aviation
	XN258	WS55 Whirlwind HAR9 [589/CU]	North-East Aircraft Museum, Usworth
	XN263	WS55 Whirlwind HAS7	Privately owned, Bosham, W Sussex
	XN297	*WS55 Whirlwind HAR9 (XN311) [12]*	*Privately owned, Hull*
	XN298	WS55 Whirlwind HAR9 [810/LS]	International Fire Training Centre, Chorley
	XN299	WS55 Whirlwind HAS7 [758]	Tangmere Military Aviation Museum
	XN304	WS55 Whirlwind HAS7 [64]	Norfolk & Suffolk Avn Museum, Flixton
	XN332	Saro P531 (G-APNV) [759]	FAA Museum, stored RNAS Yeovilton
	XN334	Saro P531	FAA Museum, stored RNAS Yeovilton
	XN341	Saro Skeeter AOP12 (8022M)	Stondon Transport Mus & Garden Centre, Beds
	XN344	Saro Skeeter AOP12 (8018M)	Science Museum, South Kensington

Serial	Type (other identity) [code]	Owner/operator, location or fate	Notes
XN351	Saro Skeeter AOP12 (G-BKSC)	Privately owned, Ipswich	
XN380	WS55 Whirlwind HAS7	RAF Manston History Museum	
XN385	WS55 Whirlwind HAS7	Privately owned, Wingates, Lancs	
XN386	WS55 Whirlwind HAR9 [435/ED]	Aeroventure, Doncaster	
XN412	Auster AOP9	Auster 9 Group, Melton Mowbray	
XN435	Auster AOP9 (G-BGBU)	Privately owned, Egham	
XN437	Auster AOP9 (G-AXWA)	Privately owned, North Weald	
XN441	Auster AOP9 (G-BGKT)	Privately owned, Eggesford	
XN459	Hunting Jet Provost T3A (G-BWOT)	Transair(UK) Ltd, North Weald	
XN462	Hunting Jet Provost T3A [17]	FAA Museum, stored RNAS Yeovilton	
XN466	Hunting Jet Provost T3A [29] <ff>	No 1005 Sqn ATC, Radcliffe, Gtr Manchester	
XN492	Hunting Jet Provost T3 (8079M) <ff>	Privately owned, Haydock	
XN493	Hunting Jet Provost T3 (XN137) <ff>	Privately owned, Camberley	
XN494	Hunting Jet Provost T3A (9012M) [43]	Crawley Technical College	
XN497	Hunting Jet Provost T3A [52]	Privately owned, Newby Wiske	
XN500	Hunting Jet Provost T3A [48]	Oxford Avn Services Ltd, Oxford, ground instruction	
XN501	Hunting Jet Provost T3A (8958M) [G]	Privately owned, Billockby, Norfolk	
XN503	Hunting Jet Provost T3 <ff>	No 1284 Sqn ATC, Haverfordwest	
XN508	Hunting Jet Provost T3A <ff>	RAF/DARA, St Athan	
XN510	Hunting Jet Provost T3A (G-BXBI) [40]	Privately owned, Sproughton	
XN511	Hunting Jet Provost T3 [64] <ff>	Aeroventure, Doncaster	
XN549	Hunting Jet Provost T3 (8235M) [32,P]	RAF Shawbury Fire Section	
XN550	Hunting Jet Provost T3 <ff>	Privately owned, Stone, Staffs	
XN551	Hunting Jet Provost T3A (8984M)	DARA Training School, RAF St Athan	
XN554	Hunting Jet Provost T3 (8436M) [K]	Privately owned, Sproughton	
XN573	Hunting Jet Provost T3 [E] <ff>	Newark Air Museum, Winthorpe	
XN577	Hunting Jet Provost T3A (8956M) [89,F]	Privately owned, Billockby, Norfolk	
XN579	Hunting Jet Provost T3A (9137M) [14]	Privately owned, Sproughton	
XN582	Hunting Jet Provost T3A (8957M) [95,H]	Arbury College, Cambridge	
XN584	Hunting Jet Provost T3A (9014M) [E]	Phoenix Aviation, Bruntingthorpe	
XN586	Hunting Jet Provost T3A (9039M) [91,S]	Brooklands Technical College	
XN589	Hunting Jet Provost T3A (9143M) [46]	RAF Linton-on-Ouse, on display	
XN592	Hunting Jet Provost T3 <ff>	Scrapped	
XN593	Hunting Jet Provost T3A (8988M) [97,Q]	Privately owned, Billockby, Norfolk	
XN594	Hunting Jet Provost T3 (8234M/ XN458)	Privately owned, Ashington, W Sussex	
XN597	Hunting Jet Provost T3 (7984M) <ff>	RAF Millom Museum, Haverigg	
XN607	Hunting Jet Provost T3 <ff>	N Yorks Aircraft Recovery Centre, Chop Gate	
XN629	Hunting Jet Provost T3A (G-BVEG/ G-KNOT) [49]	Privately owned, Norwich	
XN632	Hunting Jet Provost T3 (8352M)	Privately owned, Birlingham, Worcs	
XN634	Hunting Jet Provost T3A <ff>	Privately owned, Sproughton	
XN634	Hunting Jet Provost T3A [53] <rf>	BAE Systems Warton Fire Section	
XN636	Hunting Jet Provost T3A (9045M) [15]	Privately owned	
XN637	Hunting Jet Provost T3 (G-BKOU) [03]	Privately owned, Cranfield	
XN647	DH110 Sea Vixen FAW2 <ff>	Privately owned, Bicester	
XN650	DH110 Sea Vixen FAW2 <ff>	Privately owned, Newton Abbot	
XN651	DH110 Sea Vixen FAW2 <ff>	Privately owned, stored Lavendon, Bucks	
XN657	DH110 Sea Vixen D3 [TR-1]	Privately owned, Yateley, Hants	
XN685	DH110 Sea Vixen FAW2 (8173M) [03/VL]	Midland Air Museum, Coventry	
XN696	DH110 Sea Vixen FAW2 <ff>	Blyth Valley Aviation Collection, stored Walpole	
XN714	Hunting H126	RAF Museum, Cosford	

Notes	Serial	Type (other identity) [code]	Owner/operator, location or fate
	XN726	EE Lightning F2A (8545M) <ff>	Boscombe Down Museum
	XN728	EE Lightning F2A (8546M) [V]	Privately owned, Balderton, Notts
	XN734	EE Lightning F3A (8346M/ G-BNCA) <ff>	Privately owned, Cranfield
	XN774	EE Lightning F2A (8551M) <ff>	Privately owned, Boston
	XN776	EE Lightning F2A (8535M) [C]	Royal Scottish Mus'm of Flight, E Fortune
	XN795	EE Lightning F2A <ff>	Privately owned, Foulness
	XN817	AW660 Argosy C1	QinetiQ West Freugh Fire Section
	XN819	AW660 Argosy C1 (8205M) <ff>	Newark Air Museum, Winthorpe
	XN923	HS Buccaneer S1 [13]	Gatwick Aviation Museum, Charlwood, Surrey
	XN928	HS Buccaneer S1 (8179M) <ff>	Privately owned, Kent
	XN957	HS Buccaneer S1	FAA Museum, RNAS Yeovilton
	XN964	HS Buccaneer S1 [613/LM]	Newark Air Museum, Winthorpe
	XN967	HS Buccaneer S1 <ff>	Muckleburgh Collection, Weybourne, Norfolk
	XN972	HS Buccaneer S1 (8183M/XN962) <ff>	RAF Museum, Hendon
	XN974	HS Buccaneer S2A	Yorkshire Air Museum, Elvington
	XN981	HS Buccaneer S2B (fuselage)	Privately owned, Errol
	XN983	HS Buccaneer S2B <ff>	Fenland & W Norfolk Aviation Museum, Wisbech
	XP110	WS58 Wessex HAS3 [55/FL]	RN AESS, *HMS Sultan*, Gosport, BDRT
	XP137	WS58 Wessex HAS3 [711/DD]	SFDO, RNAS Culdrose
	XP142	WS58 Wessex HAS3	FAA Museum, Yeovilton
	XP150	WS58 Wessex HAS3 [LS]	FETC, Moreton-in-Marsh, Glos
	XP160	WS58 Wessex HAS1	RN, Predannack Fire School
	XP165	WS Scout AH1	The Helicopter Museum, Weston-super-Mare
	XP166	WS Scout AH1 (G-APVL)	*Repainted as G-APVL*
	XP190	WS Scout AH1	Aeroventure, Doncaster
	XP191	WS Scout AH1	Privately owned, Dunkeswell
	XP226	Fairey Gannet AEW3 [073/E]	Newark Air Museum, Winthorpe
	XP241	Auster AOP9	Privately owned, Eggesford
	XP242	Auster AOP9 (G-BUCI)	AAC Historic Aircraft Flight, Middle Wallop
	XP244	Auster AOP9 (7864M/*M7922*)	Privately owned, Stretton on Dunsmore
	XP248	Auster AOP9 (7863M/WZ679)	Privately owned, Sandy, Beds
	XP254	Auster AOP11 (G-ASCC)	Privately owned, Tollerton
	XP279	Auster AOP9 (G-BWKK)	Privately owned, Popham
	XP280	Auster AOP9	Snibston Discovery Park, Coalville
	XP281	Auster AOP9	Imperial War Museum, Duxford
	XP283	Auster AOP9 (7859M) (frame)	Privately owned,
	XP286	Auster AOP9	Privately owned, Eggesford
	XP299	WS55 Whirlwind HAR10 (8726M)	RAF Museum, Hendon
	XP330	WS55 Whirlwind HAR10	CAA Fire School, Tees-side Airport
	XP344	WS55 Whirlwind HAR10 (8764M) [H723]	RAF North Luffenham Training Area
	XP345	WS55 Whirlwind HAR10 (8792M) [UN]	Yorkshire Helicopter Preservation Group, Doncaster
	XP346	WS55 Whirlwind HAR10 (8793M)	Privately owned, Long Marston
	XP350	WS55 Whirlwind HAR10	Privately owned,
	XP351	WS55 Whirlwind HAR10 (8672M) [Z]	Gatwick Aviation Museum, Charlwood, Surrey
	XP355	WS55 Whirlwind HAR10 (8463M/ G-BEBC)	City of Norwich Aviation Museum
	XP360	WS55 Whirlwind HAR10 [V]	Privately owned, Upper Hill, nr Leominster
	XP398	WS55 Whirlwind HAR10 (8794M)	Gatwick Aviation Museum, Charlwood, Surrey
	XP399	WS55 Whirlwind HAR10	Privately owned, Rettendon, Essex
	XP404	WS55 Whirlwind HAR10 (8682M)	The Helicopter Museum, Weston-super-Mare
	XP411	AW660 Argosy C1 (8442M) [C]	RAF Museum, Cosford
	XP454	Slingsby T38 Grasshopper TX1	Privately owned, Sywell
	XP463	Slingsby T38 Grasshopper TX1 (BGA 4392)	Privately owned, Rufforth
	XP488	Slingsby T38 Grasshopper TX1	Fenland & W Norfolk Aviation Museum, stored Wisbech
	XP492	Slingsby T38 Grasshopper TX1 (BGA 3480)	Privately owned, Gallows Hill, Dorset
	XP493	Slingsby T38 Grasshopper TX1	Privately owned, stored Aston Down
	XP494	Slingsby T38 Grasshopper TX1	Privately owned, Rattlesden, Suffolk
	XP502	HS Gnat T1 (8576M)	Privately owned, Kemble

Serial	Type (other identity) [code]	Owner/operator, location or fate	Notes
XP505	HS Gnat T1	Science Museum, Wroughton	
XP516	HS Gnat T1 (8580M) [16]	QinetiQ Structures Dept, Farnborough	
XP540	HS Gnat T1 (8608M) [62]	Privately owned, North Weald	
XP542	HS Gnat T1 (8575M) [42]	R. Military College of Science, Shrivenham	
XP556	Hunting Jet Provost T4 (9027M) [B]	RAF Cranwell Aviation Heritage Centre	
XP557	Hunting Jet Provost T4 (8494M) [72]	Bomber County Aviation Museum, Hemswell	
XP558	Hunting Jet Provost T4 (8627M)<ff>	Privately owned, Northants	
XP558	Hunting Jet Provost T4 (8627M)<rf>	Privately owned, Sproughton	
XP563	Hunting Jet Provost T4 (9028M) [C]	Privately owned, Sproughton	
XP568	Hunting Jet Provost T4	Jet Avn Preservation Grp, Long Marston	
XP573	Hunting Jet Provost T4 (8236M) [19]	Jersey Airport Fire Section	
XP585	Hunting Jet Provost T4 (8407M) [24]	NE Wales Institute, Wrexham	
XP627	Hunting Jet Provost T4	North-East Aircraft Museum, Usworth	
XP629	Hunting Jet Provost T4 (9026M) [P]	Privately owned, Sproughton	
XP638	Hunting Jet Provost T4 (9034M) [A]	Privately owned, Ystrad Mynach, Mid Glamorgan	
XP640	Hunting Jet Provost T4 (8501M) [27]	Yorkshire Air Museum, Elvington	
XP642	Hunting Jet Provost T4 <ff>	Privately owned, Lavendon, Bucks	
XP672	Hunting Jet Provost T4 (8458M/ G-RAFI) [03]	Privately owned, Sproughton	
XP680	Hunting Jet Provost T4 (8460M)	FETC, Moreton-in-Marsh, Glos	
XP686	Hunting Jet Provost T4 (8401M/ 8502M) [G]	Privately owned, Sproughton	
XP688	Hunting Jet Provost T4 (9031M)	Privately owned, Wingates, Lancs	
XP701	BAC Lightning F3 (8924M) <ff>	Robertsbridge Aviation Society, Mayfield	
XP703	BAC Lightning F3 <ff>	The Cockpit Collection, RAF Coltishall	
XP706	BAC Lightning F3 (8925M)	Aeroventure, Doncaster	
XP743	BAC Lightning F3 <ff>	No 351 Sqn ATC, Burton-upon-Trent	
XP745	BAC Lightning F3 (8453M) <ff>	Greenford Haulage, West London	
XP772	DHC2 Beaver AL1 (G-BUCJ)	AAC Historic Aircraft Flight, stored Duxford	
XP775	DHC2 Beaver AL1	Privately owned	
XP820	DHC2 Beaver AL1	AAC Historic Aircraft Flight, Middle Wallop	
XP821	DHC2 Beaver AL1 [MCO]	Museum of Army Flying, Middle Wallop	
XP822	DHC2 Beaver AL1	Museum of Army Flying, Middle Wallop	
XP831	Hawker P.1127 (8406M)	Science Museum, South Kensington	
XP841	Handley-Page HP115	FAA Museum, RNAS Yeovilton	
XP846	WS Scout AH1 [B,H] (fuselage)	Currently not known	
XP847	WS Scout AH1	Museum of Army Flying, Middle Wallop	
XP848	WS Scout AH1	AAC Arborfield, on display	
XP849	WS Scout AH1 (G-CBUH)	Repainted as G-CBUH	
XP853	WS Scout AH1	Privately owned, Dunkeswell	
XP854	WS Scout AH1 (7898M/TAD043)	Privately owned, Sproughton	
XP855	WS Scout AH1	Army SEAE, Arborfield	
XP856	WS Scout AH1	Privately owned, Dunkeswell	
XP883	WS Scout AH1	Privately owned, Oaksey Park, Wilts	
XP884	WS Scout AH1	AAC Middle Wallop, instructional use	
XP885	WS Scout AH1	AAC Wattisham, instructional use	
XP886	WS Scout AH1	Yeovil College	
XP888	WS Scout AH1	Privately owned, Sproughton	
XP890	WS Scout AH1 [G] (fuselage)	Privately owned, Ipswich	
XP893	WS Scout AH1	AAC Middle Wallop, BDRT	
XP899	WS Scout AH1 [D]	Army SEAE, Arborfield	
XP900	WS Scout AH1	AAC Wattisham, instructional use	
XP902	WS Scout AH1 <ff>	Aeroventure, stored Doncaster	
XP905	WS Scout AH1	Privately owned, Sproughton	
XP907	WS Scout AH1 (G-SROE)	Privately owned, Wattisham	
XP910	WS Scout AH1	Museum of Army Flying, Middle Wallop	
XP919	DH110 Sea Vixen FAW2 (8163M) [706/VL]	Blyth Valley Aviation Collection, Walpole	
XP924	DH110 Sea Vixen D3 (G-CVIX)	Repainted as G-CVIX, April 2003	
XP925	DH110 Sea Vixen FAW2 [752] <ff>	No 1268 Sqn ATC, Haslemere, Surrey	
XP980	Hawker P.1127	FAA Museum, RNAS Yeovilton	
XP984	Hawker P.1127	Brooklands Museum, Weybridge	
XR220	BAC TSR2 (7933M)	RAF Museum, Cosford	
XR222	BAC TSR2	Imperial War Museum, Duxford	
XR232	Sud Alouette AH2 (F-WEIP)	Museum of Army Flying, Middle Wallop	
XR239	Auster AOP9	Privately owned, Stretton on Dunsmore	
XR240	Auster AOP9 (G-BDFH)	Privately owned, Widmerpool	

Notes	Serial	Type (other identity) [code]	Owner/operator, location or fate
	XR241	Auster AOP9 (G-AXRR)	The Aircraft Restoration Co, Duxford
	XR244	Auster AOP9	AAC Historic Aircraft Flight, Middle Wallop
	XR246	Auster AOP9 (7862M/G-AZBU)	Privately owned, North Coates
	XR267	Auster AOP9 (G-BJXR)	Privately owned, Widmerpool
	XR271	Auster AOP9	Royal Artillery Experience, Woolwich
	XR371	SC5 Belfast C1	RAF Museum, Cosford
	XR379	Sud Alouette AH2	AAC Historic Aircraft Flight, Middle Wallop
	XR453	WS55 Whirlwind HAR10 (8873M) [A]	RAF Odiham, on gate
	XR458	WS55 Whirlwind HAR10 (8662M) [H]	Museum of Army Flying, Middle Wallop
	XR485	WS55 Whirlwind HAR10 [Q]	Norfolk & Suffolk Avn Museum, Flixton
	XR486	WS55 Whirlwind HCC12 (8727M/G-RWWW)	The Helicopter Museum, Weston-super-Mare
	XR498	WS58 Wessex HC2 (9342M) [X]	RAF No 1 SoTT, Cosford
	XR499	WS58 Wessex HC2 [W]	RN AESS, HMS Sultan, Gosport
	XR501	WS58 Wessex HC2	Army, Keogh Barracks, Aldershot, instructional use
	XR502	WS58 Wessex HC2 [Z]	Privately owned, Colsterworth
	XR503	WS58 Wessex HC2	MoD FSCTE, Manston
	XR506	WS58 Wessex HC2 (9343M) [V]	RAF No 1 SoTT, Cosford
	XR507	WS58 Wessex HC2	Privately owned, Hixon, Staffs
	XR508	WS58 Wessex HC2 [B]	RN AESS, HMS Sultan, Gosport
	XR511	WS58 Wessex HC2 [L]	RAF, stored Shawbury
	XR516	WS58 Wessex HC2 [V]	RAF Shawbury, on display
	XR517	WS58 Wessex HC2 [N]	Shoreham Airport, on display
	XR518	WS58 Wessex HC2 [J]	RN AESS, HMS Sultan, Gosport
	XR520	WS58 Wessex HC2	RN AESS, HMS Sultan, Gosport
	XR523	WS58 Wessex HC2 [M]	RN HMS Raleigh, Torpoint, instructional use
	XR525	WS58 Wessex HC2 [G]	RAF, stored Shawbury
	XR526	WS58 Wessex HC2 (8147M)	The Helicopter Museum, Weston-super-Mare
	XR528	WS58 Wessex HC2	SFDO, RNAS Culdrose
	XR529	WS58 Wessex HC2 (9268M) [E]	RAF Aldergrove, on display
	XR534	HS Gnat T1 (8578M) [65]	Newark Air Museum, Winthorpe
	XR537	HS Gnat T1 (8642M/G-NATY) [T]	Bournemouth Aviation Museum
	XR538	HS Gnat T1 (8621M/G-RORI) [01]	Privately owned, Kemble
	XR571	HS Gnat T1 (8493M)	RAF Red Arrows, Scampton, on display
	XR574	HS Gnat T1 (8631M) [72]	RAF No 1 SoTT, Cosford
	XR588	WS58 Wessex HC2 [Hearts]	RAF, stored Shawbury
	XR595	WS Scout AH1 (G-BWHU) [M]	Privately owned, Staddon Heights, Devon
	XR597	WS Scout AH1 (fuselage)	Privately owned, Sproughton
	XR601	WS Scout AH1	Army SEAE, Arborfield
	XR627	WS Scout AH1 [X]	Privately owned, Sproughton
	XR628	WS Scout AH1	Privately owned, Ipswich
	XR629	WS Scout AH1 (fuselage)	Privately owned, Ipswich
	XR635	WS Scout AH1	Privately owned, Sproughton
	XR650	Hunting Jet Provost T4 (8459M) [28]	Boscombe Down Museum
	XR654	Hunting Jet Provost T4 <ff>	Privately owned, Chester
	XR658	Hunting Jet Provost T4 (8192M)	Deeside College, Connah's Quay, Clwyd
	XR662	Hunting Jet Provost T4 (8410M) [25]	Boulton Paul Association, Wolverhampton
	XR672	Hunting Jet Provost T4 (8495M) [50]	RAF Halton, Fire Section
	XR673	Hunting Jet Provost T4 (G-BXLO/9032M) [L]	Privately owned, North Weald
	XR681	Hunting Jet Provost T4 (8588M) <ff>	Robertsbridge Aviation Society, Mayfield
	XR700	Hunting Jet Provost T4 (8589M) <ff>	Currently not known
	XR713	BAC Lightning F3 (8935M) [C]	RAF Leuchars, on display
	XR718	BAC Lightning F6 (8932M) [DA]	Blyth Valley Aviation Collection, Walpole
	XR724	BAC Lightning F6 (G-BTSY)	The Lightning Association, Binbrook
	XR725	BAC Lightning F6	Privately owned, Binbrook
	XR726	BAC Lightning F6 <ff>	Privately owned, Harrogate
	XR728	BAC Lightning F6 [JS]	Lightning Preservation Grp, Bruntingthorpe
	XR747	BAC Lightning F6 <ff>	Privately owned, Cubert, Cornwall
	XR749	BAC Lightning F3 (8934M) [DA]	Tees-side Airport, on display
	XR751	BAC Lightning F3	Privately owned, Tremar, Cornwall
	XR753	BAC Lightning F6 (8969M) [BP]	RAF Leeming on display
	XR753	BAC Lightning F53 (really ZF578)	Tangmere Military Aviation Museum

Serial	Type (other identity) [code]	Owner/operator, location or fate	Notes
XR754	BAC Lightning F6 (8972M) <ff>	Aeroventure, Doncaster	
XR755	BAC Lightning F6	Privately owned, Callington, Cornwall	
XR757	BAC Lightning F6 <ff>	Privately owned, Grainthorpe, Lincs	
XR759	BAC Lightning F6 <ff>	Privately owned, Haxey, Lincs	
XR770	BAC Lightning F6 [AA]	Privately owned, Grainthorpe, Lincs	
XR771	BAC Lightning F6 [BM]	Midland Air Museum, Coventry	
XR806	BAC VC10 C1K <ff>	RAF Brize Norton, BDRT	
XR807	BAC VC10 C1K	RAF No 10 Sqn, Brize Norton	
XR808	BAC VC10 C1K	RAF No 10 Sqn, Brize Norton	
XR810	BAC VC10 C1K	RAF No 10 Sqn, Brize Norton	
XR944	Wallis WA116 (G-ATTB)	RAF Museum, Hendon	
XR954	HS Gnat T1 (8570M) [30]	Source Classic Jet Flight, stored Bournemouth	
XR955	HS Gnat T1 [SAH-2]	*Sold as N4367L*	
XR977	HS Gnat T1 (8640M) [3]	RAF Museum, Cosford	
XR991	HS Gnat T1 (8624M/XS102/ G-MOUR)	Delta Jets, Kemble	
XR993	HS Gnat T1 (8620M/XP534/ G-BVPP)	Kennet Aviation, North Weald	
XS100	HS Gnat T1 (8561M) <ff>	Privately owned, London SW3	
XS101	HS Gnat T1 (8638M) (G-GNAT)	*Sold to Australia, October 2003*	
XS111	HS Gnat T1 (8618M/XP504/ G-TIMM)	Kennet Aviation, North Weald	
XS122	WS58 Wessex HAS3 [655/PO]	RN AESS, *HMS Sultan*, Gosport	
XS149	WS58 Wessex HAS3 [661/GL]	The Helicopter Museum, Weston-super-Mare	
XS165	Hiller UH12E (G-ASAZ) [37]	Privately owned, Sherburn-in-Elmet	
XS176	Hunting Jet Provost T4 (8514M) <ff>	Privately owned, Stamford	
XS177	Hunting Jet Provost T4 (9044M) [N]	RAF Cosford	
XS179	Hunting Jet Provost T4 (8237M) [20]	Gr Manchester Mus of Science & Industry	
XS180	Hunting Jet Provost T4 (8238M) [21]	RAF St Athan, Fire Section	
XS181	Hunting Jet Provost T4 (9033M) <ff>	Privately owned, Bruntingthorpe	
XS183	Hunting Jet Provost T4 <ff>	Privately owned, Plymouth	
XS186	Hunting Jet Provost T4 (8408M) [M]	Privately owned, Sproughton	
XS209	Hunting Jet Provost T4 (8409M)	Privately owned, Bruntingthorpe	
XS215	Hunting Jet Provost T4 (8507M) [17]	RAF Halton	
XS216	Hunting Jet Provost T4 <ff>	No 2357 Sqn ATC, Goole	
XS217	Hunting Jet Provost T4 (9029M)	Privately owned, Bruntingthorpe	
XS218	Hunting Jet Provost T4 (8508M) <ff>	No 447 Sqn ATC, Henley-on-Thames, Berks	
XS231	BAC Jet Provost T5 (G-ATAJ)	Privately owned, Barnstaple	
XS235	DH106 Comet 4C (G-CPDA)	British Aviation Heritage, Bruntingthorpe	
XS416	BAC Lightning T5	Privately owned, Grainthorpe, Lincs	
XS417	BAC Lightning T5 [DZ]	Newark Air Museum, Winthorpe	
XS420	BAC Lightning T5	Privately owned, Farnborough	
XS421	BAC Lightning T5 <ff>	Privately owned, Foulness	
XS456	BAC Lightning T5 [DX]	Privately owned, Wainfleet	
XS457	BAC Lightning T5 <ff>	Privately owned, Grainthorpe, Lincs	
XS458	BAC Lightning T5 [T]	T5 Projects, Cranfield	
XS459	BAC Lightning T5 [AW]	Fenland & W Norfolk Aviation Museum, Wisbech	
XS463	WS Wasp HAS1 (comp XT431)	Crawley College, W. Sussex	
XS481	WS58 Wessex HU5	Aeroventure, Doncaster	
XS482	WS58 Wessex HU5	RAF Manston History Museum	
XS485	WS58 Wessex HC5C (comp XR503) [*Hearts*]	*Scrapped at Gosport by October 2002*	
XS486	WS58 Wessex HU5 (9272M) [524/CU,F]	No 93 Sqn ATC, Colerne	
XS488	WS58 Wessex HU5 (9056M) [XK]	RN AESS, *HMS Sultan*, Gosport	
XS489	WS58 Wessex HU5 [R]	RN AESS, *HMS Sultan*, Gosport	
XS492	WS58 Wessex HU5 [623]	*Scrapped at Fleetlands*	
XS493	WS58 Wessex HU5	RN/DARA, stored Fleetlands	
XS496	WS58 Wessex HU5 [625/PO]	RN AESS, *HMS Sultan*, Gosport	
XS498	WS58 Wessex HC5C (comp XS677) [WK]	Privately owned, Hixon, Staffs	
XS507	WS58 Wessex HU5	RN AESS, *HMS Sultan*, Gosport	

Notes	Serial	Type (other identity) [code]	Owner/operator, location or fate
	XS508	WS58 Wessex HU5	FAA Museum, stored RNAS Yeovilton
	XS510	WS58 Wessex HU5 [626/PO]	RN AESS, *HMS Sultan*, Gosport
	XS511	WS58 Wessex HU5 [M]	RN AESS, *HMS Sultan*, Gosport
	XS513	WS58 Wessex HU5 [419/CU]	RN AESS, *HMS Sultan*, Gosport
	XS514	WS58 Wessex HU5 [L]	RN AESS, *HMS Sultan*, Gosport
	XS515	WS58 Wessex HU5 [N]	Army, Keogh Barracks, Aldershot, instructional use
	XS516	WS58 Wessex HU5 [Q]	RN, Predannack Fire School
	XS520	WS58 Wessex HU5 [F]	RN AESS, *HMS Sultan*, Gosport
	XS522	WS58 Wessex HU5 [ZL]	RN, Predannack Fire School
	XS527	WS Wasp HAS1	FAA Museum, stored RNAS Yeovilton
	XS529	WS Wasp HAS1	RN, Predannack Fire School
	XS539	WS Wasp HAS1 [435]	DARA Fleetlands Apprentice School
	XS567	WS Wasp HAS1 [434/E]	Imperial War Museum, Duxford
	XS568	WS Wasp HAS1 [441]	RN AESS, *HMS Sultan*, Gosport
	XS569	WS Wasp HAS1	DARA Fleetlands Apprentice School
	XS570	WS Wasp HAS1 [445/P]	Warship Preservation Trust, Birkenhead
	XS576	DH110 Sea Vixen FAW2 [125/E]	Imperial War Museum, Duxford
	XS587	DH110 Sea Vixen FAW(TT)2 (8828M/G-VIXN)	Gatwick Aviation Museum, Charlwood, Surrey
	XS590	DH110 Sea Vixen FAW2 [131/E]	FAA Museum, RNAS Yeovilton
	XS596	HS Andover C1(PR)	DPA/AFD/*Open Skies*, Boscombe Down
	XS598	HS Andover C1 (fuselage)	FETC, Moreton-in-Marsh, Glos
	XS606	HS Andover C1	DPA/ETPS, Boscombe Down
	XS639	HS Andover E3A (9241M)	RAF Museum, Cosford
	XS641	HS Andover C1(PR) (9198M) [Z]	MoD HQ DLO, Andover, on display
	XS646	HS Andover C1(mod)	DPA/AFD/QinetiQ, Boscombe Down
	XS652	Slingsby T45 Swallow TX1 (BGA 1107)	Privately owned, Rufforth
	XS674	WS58 Wessex HC2 [R]	Privately owned, Sproughton
	XS675	WS58 Wessex HC2 [*Spades*]	RAF, stored Shawbury
	XS695	HS Kestrel FGA1	RAF Museum Restoration Centre, Cosford
	XS709	HS125 Dominie T1 [M]	RAF No 3 FTS/55(R) Sqn, Cranwell
	XS710	HS125 Dominie T1 (9259M) [O]	RAF No 1 SoTT, Cosford
	XS711	HS125 Dominie T1 [L]	RAF No 3 FTS/55(R) Sqn, Cranwell
	XS712	HS125 Dominie T1 [A]	RAF No 3 FTS/55(R) Sqn, Cranwell
	XS713	HS125 Dominie T1 [C]	RAF No 3 FTS/55(R) Sqn, Cranwell
	XS714	HS125 Dominie T1 (9246M) [P]	MoD FSCTE, Manston
	XS726	HS125 Dominie T1 (9273M) [T]	RAF No 1 SoTT, Cosford
	XS727	HS125 Dominie T1 [D]	RAF No 3 FTS/55(R) Sqn, Cranwell
	XS728	HS125 Dominie T1 [E]	RAF No 3 FTS/55(R) Sqn, Cranwell
	XS729	HS125 Dominie T1 (9275M) [G]	RAF No 1 SoTT, Cosford
	XS730	HS125 Dominie T1 [H]	RAF No 3 FTS/55(R) Sqn, Cranwell
	XS731	HS125 Dominie T1 [J]	RAF No 3 FTS/55(R) Sqn, Cranwell
	XS733	HS125 Dominie T1 (9276M) [Q]	RAF No 1 SoTT, Cosford
	XS734	HS125 Dominie T1 (9260M) [N]	RAF No 1 SoTT, Cosford
	XS735	HS125 Dominie T1 (9264M) [R]	DARA Training School, RAF St Athan
	XS736	HS125 Dominie T1 [S]	RAF No 3 FTS/55(R) Sqn, Cranwell
	XS737	HS125 Dominie T1 [K]	RAF No 3 FTS/55(R) Sqn, Cranwell
	XS738	HS125 Dominie T1 (9274M) [U]	RAF No 1 SoTT, Cosford
	XS739	HS125 Dominie T1 [F]	RAF No 3 FTS/55(R) Sqn, Cranwell
	XS743	Beagle B206Z Basset CC1	DPA/ETPS, Boscombe Down
	XS765	Beagle B206Z Basset CC1 (G-BSET)	Privately owned, Cranfield
	XS770	Beagle B206Z Basset CC1 (G-HRHI)	Privately owned, Cranfield
	XS790	HS748 Andover CC2 <ff>	Boscombe Down Museum
	XS791	HS748 Andover CC2 (fuselage)	Privately owned, Ely
	XS862	WS58 Wessex HAS3	Privately owned, Hixon, Staffs
	XS863	WS58 Wessex HAS1	Imperial War Museum, Duxford
	XS866	WS58 Wessex HAS1 [520/CU]	Sea Scouts, South Littleton, Worcs
	XS868	WS58 Wessex HAS1	RN, Predannack Fire School
	XS870	WS58 Wessex HAS1 [PO]	*Scrapped*
	XS871	WS58 Wessex HAS1 (8457M) [265]	Privately owned, Chippenham, Wilts
	XS876	WS58 Wessex HAS1 [523/PO]	SFDO, RNAS Culdrose
	XS881	WS58 Wessex HAS1	RN, Predannack Fire School
	XS885	WS58 Wessex HAS1 [512/DD]	SFDO, RNAS Culdrose
	XS886	WS58 Wessex HAS1 [527/CU]	Sea Scouts, Evesham, Worcs
	XS887	WS58 Wessex HAS1 [403/FI]	Flambards Village Theme Park, Helston
	XS888	WS58 Wessex HAS1 [521]	Guernsey Airport Fire Section
	XS897	BAC Lightning F6	Aeroventure, Doncaster
	XS898	BAC Lightning F6 <ff>	Privately owned, Lavendon, Bucks

Serial	Type (other identity) [code]	Owner/operator, location or fate	Notes
XS899	BAC Lightning F6 <ff>	The Cockpit Collection, RAF Coltishall	
XS903	BAC Lightning F6 [BA]	Yorkshire Air Museum, Elvington	
XS904	BAC Lightning F6 [BQ]	Lightning Preservation Grp, Bruntingthorpe	
XS919	BAC Lightning F6	Wonderland Pleasure Park, Farnsfield, Notts	
XS922	BAC Lightning F6 (8973M) <ff>	The Air Defence Collection, Salisbury	
XS923	BAC Lightning F6 <ff>	Privately owned, Welshpool	
XS925	BAC Lightning F6 (8961M) [BA]	RAF Museum, Hendon	
XS928	BAC Lightning F6 [D]	BAE Systems Warton, on display	
XS932	BAC Lightning F6 <ff>	Privately owned, Farnborough	
XS933	BAC Lightning F6 <ff>	Privately owned, Farnham	
XS936	BAC Lightning F6	Castle Motors, Liskeard, Cornwall	
XT108	Agusta-Bell 47G-3 Sioux AH1 [U]	Museum of Army Flying, Middle Wallop	
XT123	WS Sioux AH1 (XT827) [D]	AAC Middle Wallop, at main gate	
XT131	Agusta-Bell 47G-3 Sioux AH1 [B]	AAC Historic Aircraft Flight, Middle Wallop	
XT133	Agusta-Bell 47G-3 Sioux AH1 (7923M)	Royal Engineers' Museum, stored Chattenden	
XT140	Agusta-Bell 47G-3 Sioux AH1	Perth Technical College	
XT141	Agusta-Bell 47G-3 Sioux AH1	Privately owned, Dunkeswell	
XT148	Agusta-Bell 47G-3 Sioux AH1	Scrapped at Weston-super-Mare, 2003	
XT150	Agusta-Bell 47G-3 Sioux AH1 (7883M) [R]	AAC Netheravon, at main gate	
XT151	WS Sioux AH1 [W]	Museum of Army Flying, stored Middle Wallop	
XT175	WS Sioux AH1 (TAD175)	Privately owned, Cambs	
XT176	WS Sioux AH1 [U]	FAA Museum, stored Yeovilton	
XT190	WS Sioux AH1	The Helicopter Museum, Weston-super-Mare	
XT200	WS Sioux AH1 [F]	Newark Air Museum, Winthorpe	
XT223	WS Sioux AH1 (G-BGZK/G-XTUN)	Privately owned, Sherburn-in-Elmet	
XT236	WS Sioux AH1 (frame only)	North-East Aircraft Museum, stored Usworth	
XT242	WS Sioux AH1 (composite) [12]	Aeroventure, Doncaster	
XT257	WS58 Wessex HAS3 (8719M)	Privately owned, East Grinstead	
XT277	HS Buccaneer S2A (8853M) <ff>	Privately owned, Welshpool	
XT280	HS Buccaneer S2A <ff>	Dumfries & Galloway Avn Mus, Dumfries	
XT284	HS Buccaneer S2A (8855M) <ff>	Privately owned, Felixstowe	
XT288	HS Buccaneer S2B (9134M)	Royal Scottish Museum of Flight, stored E Fortune	
XT420	WS Wasp HAS1 (G-CBUI) [606]	Privately owned, Thruxton	
XT422	WS Wasp HAS1 [324]	Scrapped at Burgess Hill	
XT427	WS Wasp HAS1 [606]	FAA Museum, stored RNAS Yeovilton	
XT434	WS Wasp HAS1 [455]	DARA Fleetlands Apprentice School	
XT435	WS Wasp HAS1 (NZ3907/ G-RIMM) [430]	Privately owned, Cranfield	
XT437	WS Wasp HAS1 [423]	Boscombe Down Museum	
XT439	WS Wasp HAS1 [605]	Privately owned, Hemel Hempstead	
XT443	WS Wasp HAS1 [422/AU]	The Helicopter Museum, Weston-super-Mare	
XT453	WS58 Wessex HU5 [A/B]	RN AESS, HMS Sultan, Gosport	
XT455	WS58 Wessex HU5 [U]	RN AESS, HMS Sultan, Gosport	
XT456	WS58 Wessex HU5 (8941M) [XZ]	RAF Aldergrove, BDRT	
XT458	WS58 Wessex HU5 [622]	RN AESS, HMS Sultan, Gosport	
XT460	WS58 Wessex HU5	RN AESS, HMS Sultan, Gosport, BDRT	
XT463	WS58 Wessex HC5C (comp XR508) [Clubs]	Privately owned, Hixon, Staffs	
XT466	WS58 Wessex HU5 (8921M) [XV]	RN AESS, HMS Sultan, Gosport	
XT467	WS58 Wessex HU5 (8922M) [BF]	Privately owned, Dunkeswell	
XT468	WS58 Wessex HU5 (comp XT460) [628]	RN, Predannack Fire School	
XT469	WS58 Wessex HU5 (8920M)	RAF No 16 MU, Stafford, ground instruction	
XT472	WS58 Wessex HU5 [XC]	The Helicopter Museum, Weston-super-Mare	
XT474	WS58 Wessex HU5 [820]	RN AESS, HMS Sultan, Gosport	
XT480	WS58 Wessex HU5 [468/RG]	RN/DARA, Fleetlands	
XT482	WS58 Wessex HU5 [ZM/VL]	FAA Museum, RNAS Yeovilton	
XT484	WS58 Wessex HU5 [H]	RN AESS, HMS Sultan, Gosport	
XT485	WS58 Wessex HU5	RN AESS, HMS Sultan, Gosport	
XT575	Vickers Viscount 837 <ff>	Brooklands Museum, Weybridge	
XT596	McD F-4K Phantom FG1	FAA Museum, RNAS Yeovilton	
XT597	McD F-4K Phantom FG1	Boscombe Down Museum	

XT601 – XV130

Notes	Serial	Type (other identity) [code]	Owner/operator, location or fate
	XT601	WS58 Wessex HC2 (9277M) (composite)	RAF Odiham, BDRT
	XT604	WS58 Wessex HC2	East Midlands Airport Aeropark
	XT607	WS58 Wessex HC2 [P]	RN AESS, HMS Sultan, Gosport
	XT617	WS Scout AH1	AAC Wattisham, on display
	XT621	WS Scout AH1	R. Military College of Science, Shrivenham
	XT623	WS Scout AH1	Army SEAE, Arborfield
	XT626	WS Scout AH1 [Q]	AAC Historic Aircraft Flt, Middle Wallop
	XT630	WS Scout AH1 (G-BXRL) [X]	Privately owned, Bruntingthorpe
	XT631	WS Scout AH1 [D]	Privately owned, Ipswich
	XT632	WS Scout AH1 (G-BZBD)	Privately owned, Oaksey Park, Wilts (spares use)
	XT633	WS Scout AH1	Army SEAE, Arborfield
	XT634	WS Scout AH1 (G-BYRX) [T]	Privately owned, Humberside
	XT638	WS Scout AH1 [N]	AAC Middle Wallop, at gate
	XT640	WS Scout AH1	Privately owned, Sproughton
	XT643	WS Scout AH1 [Z]	Army, Thetford
	XT645	WS Scout AH1 (fuselage)	Privately owned, Ipswich
	XT668	WS58 Wessex HC2 [S]	Sold to Uruguay, April 2003
	XT670	WS58 Wessex HC2	RN AESS, HMS Sultan, Gosport, BDRT
	XT671	WS58 Wessex HC2 (G-BYRC) [D]	Privately owned, Redhill
	XT672	WS58 Wessex HC2 [WE]	RAF Shawbury, on display
	XT676	WS58 Wessex HC2 [I]	Sold to Uruguay, April 2003
	XT680	WS58 Wessex HC2 [Diamonds]	RAF, stored Shawbury
	XT681	WS58 Wessex HC2 (9279M) [U]	RAF Benson, BDRT
	XT761	WS58 Wessex HU5	RN AESS, HMS Sultan, Gosport
	XT762	WS58 Wessex HU5	RN, Predannack Fire School
	XT765	WS58 Wessex HU5 [J]	RN AESS, HMS Sultan, Gosport
	XT769	WS58 Wessex HU5 [823]	FAA Museum, RNAS Yeovilton
	XT770	WS58 Wessex HU5 (9055M) [P]	Privately owned, Shawell, Leics
	XT771	WS58 Wessex HU5 [620/PO]	RN AESS, HMS Sultan, Gosport
	XT772	WS58 Wessex HU5 (8805M)	SARTU RAF Valley, ground instruction
	XT773	WS58 Wessex HU5 (9123M) [822/CU]	RAF Cranwell, instructional use
	XT778	WS Wasp HAS1 [430]	FAA Museum, stored Yeovilton
	XT780	WS Wasp HAS1 [636]	DARA Fleetlands Apprentice School
	XT781	WS Wasp HAS1 (NZ3908/ G-KAWW) [426]	Privately owned, Swansea
	XT787	WS Wasp HAS1 (NZ3905/G-KAXT)	Kennet Aviation, North Weald
	XT788	WS Wasp HAS1 (G-BMIR) [316] (painted as XT78?)	Privately owned, Dunkeswell
	XT793	WS Wasp HAS1 (G-BZPP) [456]	Privately owned, Otley
	XT803	WS Sioux AH1 [Y]	Privately owned, Panshanger
	XT852	McD YF-4M Phantom FGR2	QinetiQ West Freugh Fire Section
	XT863	McD F-4K Phantom FG1 <ff>	Privately owned, Cowes, IOW
	XT864	McD F-4K Phantom FG1 (8998M/ XT684) [BJ]	RAF Leuchars on display
	XT891	McD F-4M Phantom FGR2 (9136M) [Z]	RAF Coningsby, at main gate
	XT903	McD F-4M Phantom FGR2 <ff>	RAF Museum Restoration Centre, Cosford
	XT905	McD F-4M Phantom FGR2 [P]	RAF North Luffenham Training Area
	XT907	McD F-4M Phantom FGR2 (9151M) [W]	DEODS, Chattenden, Kent
	XT914	McD F-4M Phantom FGR2 (9269M)	RAF Brampton, Cambs, on display
	XV101	BAC VC10 C1K	RAF No 10 Sqn, Brize Norton
	XV102	BAC VC10 C1K	RAF No 10 Sqn, Brize Norton
	XV104	BAC VC10 C1K	RAF No 10 Sqn, Brize Norton
	XV105	BAC VC10 C1K	RAF No 10 Sqn, Brize Norton
	XV106	BAC VC10 C1K	RAF No 10 Sqn, Brize Norton
	XV107	BAC VC10 C1K	RAF No 10 Sqn, Brize Norton
	XV108	BAC VC10 C1K	RAF No 10 Sqn, Brize Norton
	XV109	BAC VC10 C1K	RAF/DARA, St Athan
	XV118	WS Scout AH1 (9141M)	RAF Air Movements School, Brize Norton
	XV121	WS Scout AH1 (G-BYKJ)	Repainted as G-BYKJ
	XV122	WS Scout AH1 [D]	R. Military College of Science, Shrivenham
	XV123	WS Scout AH1	RAF Shawbury, on display
	XV124	WS Scout AH1 [W]	Army SEAE, Arborfield
	XV126	WS Scout AH1 (G-SCTA) [X]	Repainted as G-SCTA
	XV127	WS Scout AH1	Museum of Army Flying, Middle Wallop
	XV130	WS Scout AH1 (G-BWJW) [R]	Privately owned, Redhill

Serial	Type (other identity) [code]	Owner/operator, location or fate	Notes
XV131	WS Scout AH1 [Y]	AAC 70 Aircraft Workshops, Middle Wallop, BDRT	
XV136	WS Scout AH1 [X]	AAC Netheravon, on display	
XV137	WS Scout AH1 (G-CRUM)	Privately owned, Glenrothes	
XV137	WS Scout AH1 (XV139)	Yeovil College	
XV138	WS Scout AH1	Privately owned, East Dereham, Norfolk	
XV140	WS Scout AH1 (G-KAXL) [K]	Kennet Aviation, North Weald	
XV141	WS Scout AH1	REME Museum, Arborfield	
XV147	HS Nimrod MR1(mod) (fuselage)	*Scrapped at Warton, March 2003*	
XV148	HS Nimrod MR1(mod) <ff>	Privately owned, Guildford	
XV161	HS Buccaneer S2B (9117M) <ff>	Privately owned, Strathclyde	
XV165	HS Buccaneer S2B <ff>	Gloucestershire Avn Coll, stored Gloucester	
XV168	HS Buccaneer S2B	BAE Systems Brough, on display	
XV177	Lockheed C-130K Hercules C3A	RAF Lyneham Transport Wing	
XV179	Lockheed C-130K Hercules C1	RAF Lyneham Transport Wing	
XV181	Lockheed C-130K Hercules C1	*To Austria as 8T-CA, March 2003*	
XV184	Lockheed C-130K Hercules C3	RAF Lyneham Transport Wing	
XV188	Lockheed C-130K Hercules C3A	RAF Lyneham Transport Wing	
XV196	Lockheed C-130K Hercules C1	RAF Lyneham Transport Wing	
XV197	Lockheed C-130K Hercules C3	RAF Lyneham Transport Wing	
XV199	Lockheed C-130K Hercules C3	RAF Lyneham Transport Wing	
XV200	Lockheed C-130K Hercules C1	RAF Lyneham Transport Wing	
XV201	Lockheed C-130K Hercules C1K (fuselage)	Marshalls, Cambridge	
XV202	Lockheed C-130K Hercules C3	RAF Lyneham Transport Wing	
XV205	Lockheed C-130K Hercules C1	RAF Lyneham Transport Wing	
XV206	Lockheed C-130K Hercules C1	RAF Lyneham Transport Wing	
XV208	Lockheed C-130K Hercules W2	DPA/AFD/QinetiQ, Boscombe Down	
XV209	Lockheed C-130K Hercules C3A	RAF Lyneham Transport Wing	
XV212	Lockheed C-130K Hercules C3	RAF Lyneham Transport Wing	
XV214	Lockheed C-130K Hercules C3A	RAF Lyneham Transport Wing	
XV217	Lockheed C-130K Hercules C3	RAF Lyneham Transport Wing	
XV220	Lockheed C-130K Hercules C3	RAF Lyneham Transport Wing	
XV221	Lockheed C-130K Hercules C3	RAF Lyneham Transport Wing	
XV226	HS Nimrod MR2	RAF Kinloss MR Wing	
XV227	HS Nimrod MR2	RAF Kinloss MR Wing	
XV228	HS Nimrod MR2	RAF Kinloss MR Wing	
XV229	HS Nimrod MR2	RAF Kinloss MR Wing	
XV230	HS Nimrod MR2	RAF Kinloss MR Wing	
XV231	HS Nimrod MR2	RAF Kinloss MR Wing	
XV232	HS Nimrod MR2	RAF Kinloss MR Wing	
XV235	HS Nimrod MR2	RAF Kinloss MR Wing	
XV236	HS Nimrod MR2	RAF Kinloss MR Wing	
XV237	HS Nimrod MR2 <ff>	Privately owned, St Austell	
XV238	HS Nimrod <R> (parts of G-ALYW)	RAF M&RU, Bottesford	
XV240	HS Nimrod MR2	RAF Kinloss MR Wing	
XV241	HS Nimrod MR2	RAF Kinloss MR Wing	
XV243	HS Nimrod MR2	RAF Kinloss MR Wing	
XV244	HS Nimrod MR2	RAF Kinloss MR Wing	
XV245	HS Nimrod MR2	RAF Kinloss MR Wing	
XV246	HS Nimrod MR2	RAF Kinloss MR Wing	
XV248	HS Nimrod MR2	RAF Kinloss MR Wing	
XV249	HS Nimrod R1	RAF No 51 Sqn, Waddington	
XV250	HS Nimrod MR2	RAF Kinloss MR Wing	
XV252	HS Nimrod MR2	RAF Kinloss MR Wing	
XV253	HS Nimrod MR2 (9118M)	DPA/BAE Systems, Woodford	
XV254	HS Nimrod MR2	RAF Kinloss MR Wing	
XV255	HS Nimrod MR2	RAF Kinloss MR Wing	
XV259	BAe Nimrod AEW3 <ff>	Privately owned, Carlisle	
XV260	HS Nimrod MR2	RAF Kinloss MR Wing	
XV263	BAe Nimrod AEW3P (8967M) <ff>	BAE Systems, Warton, instructional use	
XV263	BAe Nimrod AEW3P (8967M) <rf>	DPA/BAE Systems, Woodford	
XV268	DHC2 Beaver AL1 (G-BVER)	Privately owned, Cumbernauld	
XV277	HS P.1127(RAF)	Royal Scottish Mus'm of Flight, E Fortune	
XV279	HS P.1127(RAF) (8566M)	RAF Harrier Maintenance School, Wittering	
XV280	HS P.1127(RAF) <ff>	RNAS Yeovilton Fire Section	
XV290	Lockheed C-130K Hercules C3	RAF Lyneham Transport Wing	
XV291	Lockheed C-130K Hercules C1	*To Austria as 8T-CB*	
XV292	Lockheed C-130K Hercules C1	*To Austria as 8T-CC, August 2003*	
XV294	Lockheed C-130K Hercules C3	RAF Lyneham Transport Wing	
XV295	Lockheed C-130K Hercules C1	RAF Lyneham Transport Wing	

Notes	Serial	Type (other identity) [code]	Owner/operator, location or fate
	XV296	Lockheed C-130K Hercules C1K (fuselage)	*Scrapped at Cambridge, 23 July 2003*
	XV299	Lockheed C-130K Hercules C3	RAF Lyneham Transport Wing
	XV301	Lockheed C-130K Hercules C3	RAF Lyneham Transport Wing
	XV302	Lockheed C-130K Hercules C3	Marshalls, Cambridge, fatigue test airframe
	XV303	Lockheed C-130K Hercules C3A	RAF Lyneham Transport Wing
	XV304	Lockheed C-130K Hercules C3A	RAF Lyneham Transport Wing
	XV305	Lockheed C-130K Hercules C3	RAF Lyneham Transport Wing
	XV307	Lockheed C-130K Hercules C3	RAF Lyneham Transport Wing
	XV328	BAC Lightning T5 <ff>	Phoenix Aviation, Bruntingthorpe
	XV333	HS Buccaneer S2B [234/H]	FAA Museum, RNAS Yeovilton
	XV337	HS Buccaneer S2C (8852M) <ff>	Privately owned, Diseworth, Leics
	XV344	HS Buccaneer S2C	QinetiQ Farnborough, on display
	XV350	HS Buccaneer S2B	East Midlands Airport Aeropark
	XV352	HS Buccaneer S2B <ff>	RAF Manston History Museum
	XV353	HS Buccaneer S2B (9144M) <ff>	Privately owned, Dalkeith
	XV359	HS Buccaneer S2B [035/R]	RNAS Culdrose, on display
	XV361	HS Buccaneer S2B	Ulster Aviation Society, Langford Lodge
	XV370	Sikorsky SH-3D [260]	RN AESS, *HMS Sultan*, Gosport
	XV371	WS61 Sea King HAS1(DB) [261]	SFDO, RNAS Culdrose
	XV372	WS61 Sea King HAS1	SFDO, RNAS Culdrose
	XV399	McD F-4M Phantom FGR2 <ff>	Privately owned,
	XV401	McD F-4M Phantom FGR2 [I]	Boscombe Down Museum
	XV402	McD F-4M Phantom FGR2 <ff>	Robertsbridge Aviation Society, Mayfield
	XV406	McD F-4M Phantom FGR2 (9098M) [CK]	Solway Aviation Society, Carlisle
	XV408	McD F-4M Phantom FGR2 (9165M) [Z]	*Scrapped, January 2004*
	XV411	McD F-4M Phantom FGR2 (9103M) [L]	MoD FSCTE, Manston
	XV415	McD F-4M Phantom FGR2 (9163M) [E]	RAF Boulmer, on display
	XV420	McD F-4M Phantom FGR2 (9247M) [BT]	RAF Neatishead, at main gate
	XV424	McD F-4M Phantom FGR2 (9152M) [I]	RAF Museum, Hendon
	XV426	McD F-4M Phantom FGR2 <ff>	The Cockpit Collection, RAF Coltishall
	XV426	McD F-4M Phantom FGR2 [P] <rf>	RAF Coningsby, BDRT
	XV435	McD F-4M Phantom FGR2 [R]	QinetiQ Llanbedr Fire Section
	XV460	McD F-4M Phantom FGR2 <ff>	No 2214 Sqn ATC, Usworth
	XV474	McD F-4M Phantom FGR2 [T]	The Old Flying Machine Company, Duxford
	XV490	McD F-4M Phantom FGR2 <ff>	Privately owned, Nantwich
	XV497	McD F-4M Phantom FGR2 [D]	RAF No 23 Sqn Waddington, (preserved)
	XV498	McD F-4M Phantom FGR2 (XV500/9113M) [U]	RAF St Athan, on display
	XV499	McD F-4M Phantom FGR2	RAF Leeming, WLT
	XV581	McD F-4K Phantom FG1 (9070M) <ff>	No 2481 Sqn ATC, Bridge of Don
	XV582	McD F-4K Phantom FG1 (9066M) [M]	RAF Leuchars, on display
	XV586	McD F-4K Phantom FG1 (9067M) [AJ]	RAF Leuchars, on display
	XV591	McD F-4K Phantom FG1 <ff>	RAF Museum, Cosford
	XV625	WS Wasp HAS1 [471]	RN, stored *HMS Sultan*, Gosport
	XV629	WS Wasp HAS1	*Scrapped at Middle Wallop*
	XV631	WS Wasp HAS1 (fuselage)	QinetiQ Acoustics Dept, Farnborough
	XV642	WS61 Sea King HAS2A [259]	RN AESS, *HMS Sultan*, Gosport
	XV643	WS61 Sea King HAS6 [262]	RAF St Athan, BDRT
	XV647	WS61 Sea King HU5SAR [707]	RN No 771 Sqn, Prestwick
	XV648	WS61 Sea King HU5SAR [708/PW]	AMG, Culdrose
	XV649	WS61 Sea King AEW7 [180/CU]	RN No 849 Sqn, HQ Flt, Culdrose
	XV650	WS61 Sea King AEW7 [182/CU]	*Crashed 22 March 2003, Persian Gulf*
	XV651	WS61 Sea King HU5SAR [824/CU]	RN No 771 Sqn, Culdrose
	XV653	WS61 Sea King HAS6 (9326M) [63/CU]	RAF No 1 SoTT, Cosford
	XV654	WS61 Sea King HAS6 [705] (wreck)	SFDO, RNAS Culdrose
	XV655	WS61 Sea King HAS6 [270/N]	RN, stored *HMS Sultan*, Gosport
	XV656	WS61 Sea King AEW7 [185/N]	RN No 849 Sqn, B Flt, Culdrose
	XV657	WS61 Sea King HAS5 (*ZA135*) [32/DD]	SFDO, RNAS Culdrose

Serial	Type (other identity) [code]	Owner/operator, location or fate	Notes
XV659	WS61 Sea King HAS6 (9324M) [62/CU]	RAF No 1 SoTT, Cosford	
XV660	WS61 Sea King HAS6 [69]	RN, stored *HMS Sultan*, Gosport	
XV661	WS61 Sea King HU5SAR [821]	RN No 771 Sqn, Culdrose	
XV663	WS61 Sea King HAS6	RN, stored *HMS Sultan*, Gosport	
XV664	WS61 Sea King AEW7 [187/R]	RN No 849 Sqn, A Flt, Culdrose	
XV665	WS61 Sea King HAS6 [507/CU]	RN, stored *HMS Sultan*, Gosport	
XV666	WS61 Sea King HU5SAR [823]	RN No 771 Sqn, Culdrose	
XV669	WS61 Sea King HAS1 [10]	RN/DARA, Fleetlands	
XV670	WS61 Sea King HU5 [588]	RN/Westland Helicopters, Yeovil	
XV671	WS61 Sea King AEW7 [183/N]	RN No 849 Sqn, B Flt, Culdrose	
XV672	WS61 Sea King AEW7	RN No 849 Sqn, HQ Flt, Culdrose	
XV673	WS61 Sea King HU5SAR [827/CU]	RN No 771 Sqn, Culdrose	
XV674	WS61 Sea King HAS6 [015/L]	RN, stored *HMS Sultan*, Gosport	
XV675	WS61 Sea King HAS6 [701/PW]	RN, stored *HMS Sultan*, Gosport	
XV676	WS61 Sea King HAS6 [506]	RN/DARA, stored Fleetlands	
XV677	WS61 Sea King HAS6 [269]	RN, stored *HMS Sultan*, Gosport	
XV696	WS61 Sea King HAS6 [267/N]	RN, stored *HMS Sultan*, Gosport	
XV697	WS61 Sea King AEW7 [181/CU]	RN No 849 Sqn, A Flt, Culdrose	
XV699	WS61 Sea King HU5SAR [708]	RN/DARA, stored Fleetlands	
XV700	WS61 Sea King HAS6C [ZC]	RN AMG, Yeovilton (conversion)	
XV701	WS61 Sea King HAS6 [268/N]	RN, stored *HMS Sultan*, Gosport	
XV703	WS61 Sea King HAS6C [ZD]	RN AMG, Yeovilton (conversion)	
XV704	WS61 Sea King AEW7 [186]	*Crashed 22 March 2003, Persian Gulf*	
XV705	WS61 Sea King HU5 [821/CU]	RN/DARA, stored Fleetlands	
XV706	WS61 Sea King HAS6 [017/L]	RN ETS, Culdrose	
XV707	WS61 Sea King AEW7 [184/N]	RN No 849 Sqn, B Flt, Culdrose	
XV708	WS61 Sea King HAS6 [501/CU]	RN, stored *HMS Sultan*, Gosport	
XV709	WS61 Sea King HAS6 [263]	RAF St Mawgan, instructional use	
XV710	WS61 Sea King HAS6 (9325M)	RAF No 1 SoTT, Cosford	
XV711	WS61 Sea King HAS6 [515/CW]	RN, stored *HMS Sultan*, Gosport	
XV712	WS61 Sea King HAS6 [269]	RN AESS, *HMS Sultan*, Gosport	
XV713	WS61 Sea King HAS6 [018]	RN, stored *HMS Sultan*, Gosport	
XV714	WS61 Sea King AEW7 [188]	RN No 849 Sqn, A Flt, Culdrose	
XV720	WS58 Wessex HC2	RAF Benson, instructional use	
XV721	WS58 Wessex HC2 [H]	*Sold to Uruguay, April 2003*	
XV722	WS58 Wessex HC2 [WH]	Privately owned, Hixon, Staffs	
XV724	WS58 Wessex HC2	RN AESS, *HMS Sultan*, Gosport	
XV725	WS58 Wessex HC2 [C]	RN AESS, *HMS Sultan*, Gosport	
XV726	WS58 Wessex HC2 [J]	RAF, stored Shawbury	
XV728	WS58 Wessex HC2 [A]	Newark Air Museum, Winthorpe	
XV729	WS58 Wessex HC2 (G-HANA)	*To Ghana as 9G-BOB, September 2003*	
XV730	WS58 Wessex HC2 [*Clubs*]	RAF, stored Shawbury	
XV731	WS58 Wessex HC2 [Y]	Privately owned,	
XV732	WS58 Wessex HCC4	RAF Museum, Hendon	
XV733	WS58 Wessex HCC4	The Helicopter Museum, Weston-super-Mare	
XV741	HS Harrier GR3 [41]	SFDO, RNAS Culdrose	
XV744	HS Harrier GR3 (9167M) [3K]	R. Military College of Science, Shrivenham	
XV748	HS Harrier GR3 [3D]	Yorkshire Air Museum, Elvington	
XV751	HS Harrier GR3	Privately owned, Bruntingthorpe	
XV752	HS Harrier GR3 (9078M) [B,HF]	RAF No 1 SoTT, Cosford	
XV753	HS Harrier GR3 (9075M) [53]	SFDO, RNAS Culdrose	
XV755	HS Harrier GR3 [M]	RNAS Yeovilton Fire Section	
XV759	HS Harrier GR3 [O] <ff>	Privately owned, Luton, Beds	
XV779	HS Harrier GR3 (8931M)	RAF Wittering on display	
XV783	HS Harrier GR3 [83]	SFDO, RNAS Culdrose	
XV784	HS Harrier GR3 (8909M) <ff>	Boscombe Down Museum	
XV786	HS Harrier GR3 <ff>	RNAS Culdrose	
XV786	HS Harrier GR3 [S] <rf>	RN, Predannack Fire School	
XV798	HS Harrier GR1(mod)	Bristol Aero Collection, stored Kemble	
XV804	HS Harrier GR3 (9280M) [O]	RAF North Luffenham Training Area	
XV808	HS Harrier GR3 (9076M) [08]	SFDO, RNAS Culdrose	
XV810	HS Harrier GR3 (9038M) [K]	Privately owned, Bruntingthorpe	
XV814	DH106 Comet 4 (G-APDF) <ff>	Privately owned, Chipping Campden	
XV863	HS Buccaneer S2B (9115M/ 9139M/9145M) [S]	RAF Lossiemouth	
XV864	HS Buccaneer S2B (9234M)	MoD FSCTE, Manston	
XV865	HS Buccaneer S2B (9226M)	Privately owned, Duxford	
XV867	HS Buccaneer S2B <ff>	N Yorks Aircraft Recovery Centre, Chop Gate	
XW175	HS Harrier T4(VAAC)	DPA/AFD/QinetiQ, Boscombe Down	

Notes	Serial	Type (other identity) [code]	Owner/operator, location or fate
	XW198	WS Puma HC1	RAF No 230 Sqn, Aldergrove
	XW199	WS Puma HC1	RAF No 230 Sqn, Aldergrove
	XW200	WS Puma HC1 (wreck)	RAF, stored Shawbury
	XW201	WS Puma HC1	RAF No 230 Sqn, Aldergrove
	XW202	WS Puma HC1	RAF No 230 Sqn, Aldergrove
	XW204	WS Puma HC1	RAF No 230 Sqn, Aldergrove
	XW206	WS Puma HC1	RAF No 230 Sqn, Aldergrove
	XW207	WS Puma HC1	DPA/Eurocopter, Marignane, France (on repair)
	XW208	WS Puma HC1	DPA/Westland Helicopters, Yeovil
	XW209	WS Puma HC1	RAF No 33 Sqn, Benson
	XW210	WS Puma HC1 (comp XW215)	RAF No 230 Sqn, Aldergrove
	XW211	WS Puma HC1	RAF No 33 Sqn, Benson
	XW212	WS Puma HC1	RAF No 230 Sqn, Aldergrove
	XW213	WS Puma HC1	RAF No 230 Sqn, Aldergrove
	XW214	WS Puma HC1	RAF No 230 Sqn, Aldergrove
	XW216	WS Puma HC1	DPA/Westland Helicopters, Yeovil
	XW217	WS Puma HC1	RAF No 33 Sqn, Benson
	XW218	WS Puma HC1	RAF No 33 Sqn, Benson
	XW219	WS Puma HC1	RAF No 230 Sqn, Aldergrove
	XW220	WS Puma HC1	RAF No 230 Sqn, Aldergrove
	XW221	WS Puma HC1	RAF No 230 Sqn, Aldergrove
	XW222	WS Puma HC1	RAF No 33 Sqn, Benson
	XW223	WS Puma HC1	RAF No 33 Sqn, Benson
	XW224	WS Puma HC1	RAF No 230 Sqn, Aldergrove
	XW225	WS Puma HC1	*Scrapped November 2003*
	XW226	WS Puma HC1	RAF No 230 Sqn, Benson
	XW227	WS Puma HC1	RAF PASF, Benson (wreck)
	XW229	WS Puma HC1	RAF No 33 Sqn, Benson
	XW231	WS Puma HC1	RAF No 230 Sqn, Benson
	XW232	WS Puma HC1	RAF No 33 Sqn, Benson
	XW234	WS Puma HC1	RAF PASF, Benson (wreck)
	XW235	WS Puma HC1	RAF No 33 Sqn, Benson
	XW236	WS Puma HC1	RAF No 33 Sqn, Benson
	XW237	WS Puma HC1	RAF No 230 Sqn, Aldergrove
	XW241	Sud SA330E Puma	QinetiQ Avionics & Sensors Dept, Farnborough
	XW264	HS Harrier T2 <ff>	Gloucestershire Avn Coll, stored Gloucester
	XW265	HS Harrier T4A (9258M) <ff>	No 2345 Sqn ATC, RAF Leuchars
	XW265	HS Harrier T4A (9258M) <rf>	DARA, St Athan
	XW267	HS Harrier T4 (9263M) [SA]	Territorial Army, Toton, Notts
	XW269	HS Harrier T4 (9267M)	DPA/QinetiQ, Boscombe Down, BDRT
	XW270	HS Harrier T4 (fuselage)	Phoenix Aviation, Bruntingthorpe
	XW271	HS Harrier T4 [71]	SFDO, RNAS Culdrose
	XW272	HS Harrier T4 (8783M) (fuselage) (comp XV281)	Marsh Lane Technical School, Preston
	XW276	Aérospatiale SA341 Gazelle (F-ZWRI)	Newark Air Museum, Winthorpe
	XW281	WS Scout AH1 (G-BYNZ) [T]	Privately owned, Wembury, Devon
	XW283	WS Scout AH1 [U]	RM, stored Yeovilton
	XW284	WS Scout AH1 [A] (fuselage)	*Currently not known*
	XW289	BAC Jet Provost T5A (G-BVXT/ G-JPVA) [73]	Kennet Aviation, North Weald
	XW290	BAC Jet Provost T5A (9199M) [41,MA]	RAF No 1 SoTT, Cosford
	XW292	BAC Jet Provost T5A (9128M) [32]	RAF No 1 SoTT, Cosford
	XW293	BAC Jet Provost T5 (G-BWCS) [Z]	Privately owned, Bournemouth
	XW294	BAC Jet Provost T5A (9129M) [45]	RAF No 1 SoTT, Cosford
	XW299	BAC Jet Provost T5A (9146M) [60,MB]	RAF No 1 SoTT, Cosford
	XW301	BAC Jet Provost T5A (9147M) [63,MC]	RAF No 1 SoTT, Cosford
	XW303	BAC Jet Provost T5A (9119M) [127]	RAF No 1 SoTT, Cosford
	XW304	BAC Jet Provost T5 (9172M) [MD]	RAF No 1 SoTT, Cosford
	XW309	BAC Jet Provost T5 (9179M) [V,ME]	RAF No 1 SoTT, Cosford
	XW311	BAC Jet Provost T5 (9180M) [W,MF]	RAF No 1 SoTT, Cosford
	XW312	BAC Jet Provost T5A (9109M) [64]	RAF No 1 SoTT, Cosford
	XW315	BAC Jet Provost T5A <ff>	Privately owned, Wolverhampton

Serial	Type (other identity) [code]	Owner/operator, location or fate	Notes
XW318	BAC Jet Provost T5A (9190M) [78,MG]	RAF No 1 SoTT, Cosford	
XW320	BAC Jet Provost T5A (9015M) [71]	RAF No 1 SoTT, Cosford	
XW321	BAC Jet Provost T5A (9154M) [62,MH]	RAF No 1 SoTT, Cosford	
XW323	BAC Jet Provost T5A (9166M) [86]	RAF Museum, Hendon	
XW324	BAC Jet Provost T5 (G-BWSG) [K]	Privately owned, North Weald	
XW325	BAC Jet Provost T5B (G-BWGF) [E]	Privately owned, Blackpool	
XW327	BAC Jet Provost T5A (9130M) [62]	RAF No 1 SoTT, Cosford	
XW328	BAC Jet Provost T5A (9177M) [75,MI]	RAF No 1 SoTT, Cosford	
XW330	BAC Jet Provost T5A (9195M) [82,MJ]	RAF No 1 SoTT, Cosford	
XW333	BAC Jet Provost T5A (G-BVTC)	Global Aviation, Humberside	
XW335	BAC Jet Provost T5A (9061M) [74]	RAF No 1 SoTT, Cosford	
XW351	BAC Jet Provost T5A (9062M) [31]	RAF No 1 SoTT, Cosford	
XW353	BAC Jet Provost T5A (9090M) [3]	RAF Cranwell, on display	
XW354	BAC Jet Provost T5A (XW355/ G-JPTV)	Privately owned, Cranfield	
XW358	BAC Jet Provost T5A (9181M) [59,MK]	RAF No 1 SoTT, Cosford	
XW360	BAC Jet Provost T5A (9153M) [61,ML]	RAF No 1 SoTT, Cosford	
XW361	BAC Jet Provost T5A (9192M) [81,MM]	RAF No 1 SoTT, Cosford	
XW363	BAC Jet Provost T5A [36]	BAE Systems North West Heritage Group, Warton	
XW364	BAC Jet Provost T5A (9188M) [35,MN]	RAF No 1 SoTT, Cosford	
XW365	BAC Jet Provost T5A (9018M) [73]	RAF No 1 SoTT, Cosford	
XW366	BAC Jet Provost T5A (9097M) [75]	RAF No 1 SoTT, Cosford	
XW367	BAC Jet Provost T5A (9193M) [64,MO]	RAF No 1 SoTT, Cosford	
XW370	BAC Jet Provost T5A (9196M) [72,MP]	RAF No 1 SoTT, Cosford	
XW375	BAC Jet Provost T5A (9149M) [52]	RAF No 1 SoTT, Cosford	
XW404	BAC Jet Provost T5A (9049M)	DARA Training School, RAF St Athan	
XW405	BAC Jet Provost T5A (9187M) [J,MQ]	RAF No 1 SoTT, Cosfordl	
XW409	BAC Jet Provost T5A (9047M)	DARA Training School, RAF St Athan	
XW410	BAC Jet Provost T5A (9125M) [80,MR]	RAF No 1 SoTT, Cosford	
XW413	BAC Jet Provost T5A (9126M) [69]	RAF No 1 SoTT, Cosford	
XW416	BAC Jet Provost T5A (9191M) [84,MS]	RAF No 1 SoTT, Cosford	
XW418	BAC Jet Provost T5A (9173M) [MT]	RAF No 1 SoTT, Cosford	
XW419	BAC Jet Provost T5A (9120M) [125]	RAF No 1 SoTT, Cosford	
XW420	BAC Jet Provost T5A (9194M) [83,MU]	RAF No 1 SoTT, Cosford	
XW421	BAC Jet Provost T5A (9111M) [60]	RAF No 1 SoTT, Cosford	
XW422	BAC Jet Provost T5A (G-BWEB) [3]	Privately owned, North Weald	
XW423	BAC Jet Provost T5A (G-BWUW) [14]	Deeside College, Connah's Quay, Clwyd	
XW425	BAC Jet Provost T5A (9200M) [H,MV]	RAF No 1 SoTT, Cosford	
XW427	BAC Jet Provost T5A (9124M) [67]	RAF No 1 SoTT, Cosford	
XW430	BAC Jet Provost T5A (9176M) [77,MW]	RAF No 1 SoTT, Cosford	
XW432	BAC Jet Provost T5A (9127M) [76,MX]	RAF No 1 SoTT, Cosford	
XW433	BAC Jet Provost T5A (G-JPRO)	Global Aviation, Humberside	
XW434	BAC Jet Provost T5A (9091M) [78,MY]	RAF No 1 SoTT, Cosford	
XW436	BAC Jet Provost T5A (9148M) [68]	RAF No 1 SoTT, Cosford	
XW527	HS Buccaneer S2B <ff>	*Sold to Italy*	
XW530	HS Buccaneer S2B	Buccaneer Service Station, Elgin	
XW541	HS Buccaneer S2B (8858M) <ff>	Privately owned, Welshpool	
XW544	HS Buccaneer S2B (8857M) [Y]	Privately owned, Kemble	
XW547	HS Buccaneer S2B (9095M/ 9169M) [R]	RAF Museum, Hendon	

Notes	Serial	Type (other identity) [code]	Owner/operator, location or fate
	XW550	HS Buccaneer S2B <ff>	Privately owned, West Horndon, Essex
	XW563	SEPECAT Jaguar S (XX822/ 8563M)	RAF Coltishall, on display
	XW566	SEPECAT Jaguar B	QinetiQ Avionics & Sensors Dept, Farnborough
	XW613	WS Scout AH1 (G-BXRS) [W]	Repainted as G-BXRS
	XW616	WS Scout AH1	AAC Dishforth, instructional use
	XW630	HS Harrier GR3	RNAS Yeovilton, Fire Section
	XW635	Beagle D5/180 (G-AWSW)	Privately owned, Spanhoe Lodge
	XW664	HS Nimrod R1	RAF No 51 Sqn, Waddington
	XW665	HS Nimrod R1	RAF No 51 Sqn, Waddington
	XW666	HS Nimrod R1 <ff>	Aeroventure, Doncaster
	XW750	HS748 Series 107	DPA/AFD/QinetiQ, Boscombe Down
	XW763	HS Harrier GR3 (9002M/9041M) <ff>	Privately owned, Bruntingthorpe
	XW768	HS Harrier GR3 (9072M) [N]	RAF No 1 SoTT, Cosford
	XW784	Mitchell-Procter Kittiwake I (G-BBRN) [VL]	Privately owned, Henstridge
	XW795	WS Scout AH1	Blessingbourne Museum, Fivemiletown, Co Tyrone, NI
	XW796	WS Scout AH1	Privately owned, Sproughton
	XW835	WS Lynx	Scrapped at Wattisham, January 2003
	XW838	WS Lynx (TAD 009)	Army SEAE, Arborfield
	XW839	WS Lynx	The Helicopter Museum, Weston-super-Mare
	XW844	WS Gazelle AH1	DARA Fleetlands Apprentice School
	XW845	WS Gazelle HT2 (G-CBSA) [47/CU]	Sold as G-ZELE, May 2003
	XW846	WS Gazelle AH1	AAC No 665 Sqn/5 Regt, Aldergrove
	XW847	WS Gazelle AH1 [H]	AAC No 665 Sqn/5 Regt, Aldergrove
	XW848	WS Gazelle AH1 [D]	AAC No 671 Sqn/2 Regt, Middle Wallop
	XW849	WS Gazelle AH1 [G]	RM No 847 Sqn, Yeovilton
	XW851	WS Gazelle AH1	RM No 847 Sqn, Yeovilton
	XW852	WS Gazelle HCC4 (9331M)	RAF No 1 SoTT, Cosford
	XW853	WS Gazelle HT2 [53/CU]	Sold as G-SWWM, May 2003
	XW854	WS Gazelle HT2 (G-CBSD) [46/CU]	Privately owned, Redhill
	XW855	WS Gazelle HCC4	RAF Museum, Hendon
	XW856	WS Gazelle HT2 (G-GAZL) [49/CU]	Privately owned, Kirknewton
	XW857	WS Gazelle HT2 (G-CBSB) [55/CU]	Privately owned
	XW858	WS Gazelle HT3 (G-DMSS) [C]	Privately owned, Kirkham, Lincs
	XW860	WS Gazelle HT2 (TAD021)	Army SEAE, Arborfield
	XW861	WS Gazelle HT2 (G-BZFJ) [52/CU]	Privately owned, Ford, W Sussex
	XW862	WS Gazelle HT3 (G-CBKC) [D]	Privately owned, Stapleford Tawney
	XW863	WS Gazelle HT2 (TAD022) [42/CU]	Army SEAE, Arborfield
	XW864	WS Gazelle HT2 [54/CU]	FAA Museum, stored RNAS Yeovilton
	XW865	WS Gazelle AH1 [5C]	AAC No 29 Flt, BATUS, Suffield, Canada
	XW866	WS Gazelle HT3 (G-BXTH) [E]	Flightline Ltd, Southend
	XW868	WS Gazelle HT2 (G-CBKD) [50/CU]	Repainted as G-CBKD, 2003
	XW870	WS Gazelle HT3 [F]	MoD FSCTE, Manston
	XW871	WS Gazelle HT2 (G-CBSC) [44/CU]	Privately owned, Goodwood
	XW885	WS Gazelle AH1 (G-ZZEL)	Repainted as G-ZZEL
	XW887	WS Gazelle HT2 (G-CBFD) [FL]	Privately owned, East Garston, Bucks
	XW888	WS Gazelle AH1 (TAD017)	Army SEAE, Arborfield
	XW889	WS Gazelle AH1 (TAD018)	Army SEAE, Arborfield
	XW890	WS Gazelle HT2	RNAS Yeovilton, on display
	XW892	WS Gazelle AH1 (9292M) [C]	AAC, stored Shawbury
	XW893	WS Gazelle AH1 <ff>	Privately owned, East Garston, Bucks
	XW895	WS Gazelle HT2 (G-BXZD) [51/CU]	Privately owned, Barnard Castle
	XW897	WS Gazelle AH1 [Y]	AAC No 658 Sqn/7 Regt, Netheravon
	XW898	WS Gazelle HT3 (G-CBXT) [G]	Privately owned, East Garston, Bucks
	XW899	WS Gazelle AH1 [Z]	AAC No 658 Sqn/7 Regt, Netheravon
	XW900	WS Gazelle AH1 (TAD900)	Army SEAE, Arborfield
	XW902	WS Gazelle HT3 [H]	DPA/QinetiQ, Boscombe Down, spares use
	XW903	WS Gazelle AH1 (G-BZYC)	Sold as N341AH, April 2003
	XW904	WS Gazelle AH1 [H]	AAC No 6(V) Flt/7 Regt, Shawbury
	XW906	WS Gazelle HT3 [J]	QinetiQ Boscombe Down, Apprentice School

Serial	Type (other identity) [code]	Owner/operator, location or fate	Notes
XW908	WS Gazelle AH1 [A]	AAC No 666(V) Sqn/7 Regt, Netheravon	
XW909	WS Gazelle AH1	AAC No 672 Sqn/9 Regt, Dishforth	
XW912	WS Gazelle AH1 (TAD019)	Army SEAE, Arborfield	
XW913	WS Gazelle AH1	AAC No 662 Sqn/3 Regt, Wattisham	
XW917	HS Harrier GR3 (8975M)	RAF Cottesmore, at main gate	
XW919	HS Harrier GR3 [W]	R. Military College of Science, Shrivenham	
XW922	HS Harrier GR3 (8885M)	MoD FSCTE, Manston	
XW923	HS Harrier GR3 (8724M) <ff>	RAF Wittering, Fire Section	
XW924	HS Harrier GR3 (9073M) [G]	RAF Cottesmore, preserved	
XW934	HS Harrier T4 [Y]	DPA, QinetiQ Farnborough (wfu)	
XX105	BAC 1-11/201AC (G-ASJD)	DPA, QinetiQ, Boscombe Down (wfu)	
XX108	SEPECAT Jaguar GR3	Imperial War Museum, Duxford	
XX109	SEPECAT Jaguar GR1 (8918M) [US]	RAF Coltishall, ground instruction	
XX110	SEPECAT Jaguar GR1 (8955M) [EP]	RAF No 1 SoTT, Cosford	
XX110	SEPECAT Jaguar GR1 <R> (BAPC 169)	RAF No 1 SoTT, Cosford	
XX112	SEPECAT Jaguar GR3A [EA]	RAF No 6 Sqn, Coltishall	
XX115	SEPECAT Jaguar GR1 (8821M) (fuselage)	RAF No 1 SoTT, Cosford	
XX116	SEPECAT Jaguar GR3A [EO]	RAF No 6 Sqn, Coltishall	
XX117	SEPECAT Jaguar GR3 [PA]	RAF/DARA, St Athan	
XX119	SEPECAT Jaguar GR3A (8898M) [GD]	RAF No 54 Sqn, Coltishall	
XX121	SEPECAT Jaguar GR1 [EQ]	Privately owned, Charlwood, Surrey	
XX139	SEPECAT Jaguar T4 [PT]	RAF No 16(R) Sqn, Coltishall	
XX140	SEPECAT Jaguar T2 (9008M) <ff>	Privately owned, Charlwood, Surrey	
XX141	SEPECAT Jaguar T2A [T]	AMIF, RAFC Cranwell	
XX144	SEPECAT Jaguar T2A [U]	RAF, stored Shawbury	
XX145	SEPECAT Jaguar T2A	DPA/ETPS, Boscombe Down	
XX146	SEPECAT Jaguar T4 [GT]	RAF No 54 Sqn, Coltishall	
XX150	SEPECAT Jaguar T4 [PW]	RAF/DARA, St Athan	
XX153	WS Lynx AH1	Museum of Army Flying, Middle Wallop	
XX154	HS Hawk T1	DPA/ETPS Boscombe Down	
XX156	HS Hawk T1	RAF No 4 FTS/*208(R) Sqn*, Valley	
XX157	HS Hawk T1A	RAF No 4 FTS, Valley	
XX158	HS Hawk T1A	RAF No 4 FTS/*19(R) Sqn*, Valley	
XX159	HS Hawk T1A	RAF No 4 FTS/*208(R) Sqn*, Valley	
XX160	HS Hawk T1 [CP]	RAF No 100 Sqn, Leeming	
XX161	HS Hawk T1W	RAF/DARA, St Athan (damaged)	
XX162	HS Hawk T1	RAF Aviation Medicine Flt, Boscombe Down	
XX165	HS Hawk T1	RN FRADU, Culdrose	
XX167	HS Hawk T1W	RN FRADU, Culdrose	
XX168	HS Hawk T1	RN FRADU, Culdrose	
XX169	HS Hawk T1	RAF No 4 FTS/*208(R) Sqn*, Valley	
XX170	HS Hawk T1	RN FRADU, Culdrose	
XX171	HS Hawk T1	RN FRADU, Culdrose	
XX172	HS Hawk T1	RAF No 4 FTS/*208(R) Sqn*, Valley	
XX173	HS Hawk T1	RN FRADU, Culdrose	
XX174	HS Hawk T1	RAF/DARA, St Athan	
XX175	HS Hawk T1	RAF, stored Shawbury	
XX176	HS Hawk T1W	RAF No 4 FTS/*19(R) Sqn*, Valley	
XX177	HS Hawk T1	RAF No 4 FTS/*208(R) Sqn*, Valley	
XX178	HS Hawk T1W	RN FRADU, Culdrose	
XX179	HS Hawk T1W	RAF *Red Arrows*, Scampton	
XX181	HS Hawk T1W	RAF No 4 FTS/*208(R) Sqn*, Valley	
XX183	HS Hawk T1	*Crashed 23 July 2003, near Pickering, Yorks*	
XX184	HS Hawk T1	RAF/DARA, St Athan	
XX185	HS Hawk T1	RAF/DARA, St Athan	
XX187	HS Hawk T1A	RAF No 4 FTS, Valley	
XX188	HS Hawk T1A [CF]	RAF No 100 Sqn, Leeming	
XX189	HS Hawk T1A	RAF No 4 FTS/*19(R) Sqn*, Valley	
XX190	HS Hawk T1A	RAF No 4 FTS/*19(R) Sqn*, Valley	
XX191	HS Hawk T1A [CC]	RAF No 100 Sqn/JFACTSU, Leeming	
XX194	HS Hawk T1A [CL]	RAF No 100 Sqn, Leeming	
XX195	HS Hawk T1W	RAF No 4 FTS/*208(R) Sqn*, Valley	
XX196	HS Hawk T1A	RAF No 4 FTS/*208(R) Sqn*, Valley	
XX198	HS Hawk T1A	RAF No 4 FTS/*208(R) Sqn*, Valley	

Notes	Serial	Type (other identity) [code]	Owner/operator, location or fate
	XX199	HS Hawk T1A	RAF No 4 FTS/*19(R) Sqn*, Valley
	XX200	HS Hawk T1A [CF]	RAF No 4 FTS/*208(R) Sqn*, Valley
	XX201	HS Hawk T1A	RAF No 4 FTS/*208(R) Sqn*, Valley
	XX202	HS Hawk T1A	RAF No 4 FTS/*19(R) Sqn*, Valley
	XX203	HS Hawk T1A	RAF No 4 FTS, Valley
	XX204	HS Hawk T1A	RAF No 4 FTS/*19(R) Sqn*, Valley
	XX205	HS Hawk T1A	RAF No 4 FTS/*208(R) Sqn*, Valley
	XX217	HS Hawk T1A	RAF No 4 FTS/*208(R) Sqn*, Valley
	XX218	HS Hawk T1A	RAF No 4 FTS/*19(R) Sqn*, Valley
	XX219	HS Hawk T1A	RAF No 4 FTS/*208(R) Sqn*, Valley
	XX220	HS Hawk T1A	RAF No 4 FTS/*19(R) Sqn*, Valley
	XX221	HS Hawk T1A	RAF No 4 FTS/*19(R) Sqn*, Valley
	XX222	HS Hawk T1A [CI]	RAF No 100 Sqn, Leeming
	XX223	HS Hawk T1 <ff>	Privately owned, Charlwood, Surrey
	XX224	HS Hawk T1W	RN FRADU, Culdrose
	XX225	HS Hawk T1	RAF, stored Shawbury
	XX226	HS Hawk T1	RN FRADU, Culdrose
	XX226	HS Hawk T1 <R> (*XX263*/ BAPC 152)	*Repainted as XX227*
	XX227	HS Hawk T1 <R> (*XX226*/ BAPC 152)	RAF M&RU, Bottesford
	XX227	HS Hawk T1A	RAF *Red Arrows*, Scampton
	XX228	HS Hawk T1A [CG]	RAF No 100 Sqn, Leeming
	XX230	HS Hawk T1A	RAF No 4 FTS/*208(R) Sqn*, Valley
	XX231	HS Hawk T1W	RN FRADU, Culdrose
	XX232	HS Hawk T1	RAF No 4 FTS/*208(R) Sqn*, Valley
	XX233	HS Hawk T1	RAF *Red Arrows*, Scampton
	XX234	HS Hawk T1	RN FRADU, Culdrose
	XX235	HS Hawk T1W	RAF No 4 FTS/*208(R) Sqn*, Valley
	XX236	HS Hawk T1W	RAF No 4 FTS/*19(R) Sqn*, Valley
	XX237	HS Hawk T1	RAF *Red Arrows*, Scampton
	XX238	HS Hawk T1	RN FRADU, Culdrose
	XX239	HS Hawk T1W	RAF No 4 FTS/*19(R) Sqn*, Valley
	XX240	HS Hawk T1	RN FRADU, Culdrose
	XX242	HS Hawk T1	RAF *Red Arrows*, Scampton
	XX244	HS Hawk T1	RAF No 4 FTS/*208(R) Sqn*, Valley
	XX245	HS Hawk T1	RAF No 4 FTS/*208(R) Sqn*, Valley
	XX246	HS Hawk T1A	RAF No 4 FTS/*19(R) Sqn*, Valley
	XX246	HS Hawk T1A <rf>	RAF CTTS, St Athan
	XX247	HS Hawk T1A [CM]	RAF No 100 Sqn, Leeming
	XX248	HS Hawk T1A [CJ]	RAF No 100 Sqn, Leeming
	XX250	HS Hawk T1	RAF No 4 FTS/*19(R) Sqn*, Valley
	XX252	HS Hawk T1A (fuselage)	Privately owned, Charlwood, Surrey
	XX253	HS Hawk T1A	RAF *Red Arrows*, Scampton
	XX253	HS Hawk T1 <R> (*XX297*/ BAPC 171)	*Repainted as XX263*
	XX254	HS Hawk T1A <ff>	RAF/DARA, St Athan
	XX254	HS Hawk T1A	DPA/BAE Systems, stored Scampton
	XX254	HS Hawk T1A <R>	Privately owned, Marlow, Bucks
	XX255	HS Hawk T1A	RAF No 4 FTS/*208(R) Sqn*, Valley
	XX256	HS Hawk T1A	RAF No 4 FTS/*208(R) Sqn*, Valley
	XX258	HS Hawk T1A	RAF No 4 FTS/*19(R) Sqn*, Valley
	XX260	HS Hawk T1A	RAF *Red Arrows*, Scampton
	XX261	HS Hawk T1A	RAF No 4 FTS/*208(R) Sqn*, Valley
	XX263	HS Hawk T1A	RAF No 4 FTS/*208(R) Sqn*, Valley
	XX263	HS Hawk T1 <R> (*XX253*/ BAPC 171)	RAF M&RU, Bottesford
	XX264	HS Hawk T1A	RAF *Red Arrows*, Scampton
	XX265	HS Hawk T1A	RN FRADU, Culdrose
	XX266	HS Hawk T1A	RAF *Red Arrows*, Scampton
	XX278	HS Hawk T1A [CD]	RAF No 100 Sqn, Leeming
	XX280	HS Hawk T1A	RAF No 4 FTS/*19(R) Sqn*, Valley
	XX281	HS Hawk T1A	RAF No 4 FTS/*19(R) Sqn*, Valley
	XX283	HS Hawk T1W	RAF No 4 FTS/*19(R) Sqn*, Valley
	XX284	HS Hawk T1A [CA]	RAF No 100 Sqn, Leeming
	XX285	HS Hawk T1A [CB]	RAF No 100 Sqn, Leeming
	XX286	HS Hawk T1A	RAF No 4 FTS/*19(R) Sqn*, Valley
	XX287	HS Hawk T1A	RAF No 4 FTS/*19(R) Sqn*, Valley
	XX289	HS Hawk T1A [CI]	RAF No 4 FTS, Valley
	XX290	HS Hawk T1W	RAF No 4 FTS/*19(R) Sqn*, Valley
	XX292	HS Hawk T1	RAF *Red Arrows*, Scampton
	XX294	HS Hawk T1	RAF *Red Arrows*, Scampton
	XX295	HS Hawk T1W	RAF No 4 FTS/*208(R) Sqn*, Valley

Serial	Type (other identity) [code]	Owner/operator, location or fate	Notes
XX296	HS Hawk T1	RAF No 100 Sqn, Leeming	
XX299	HS Hawk T1W [CS]	RAF No 100 Sqn, Leeming	
XX301	HS Hawk T1A	RAF No 4 FTS/*208(R) Sqn*, Valley	
XX303	HS Hawk T1A	RAF No 4 FTS/*19(R) Sqn*, Valley	
XX304	HS Hawk T1A <ff>	RAF, stored Shawbury	
XX304	HS Hawk T1A <rf>	Cardiff International Airport Fire Section	
XX306	HS Hawk T1A	RAF *Red Arrows*, Scampton	
XX307	HS Hawk T1	RAF No 4 FTS/*208(R) Sqn*, Valley	
XX308	HS Hawk T1	RAF *Red Arrows*, Scampton	
XX309	HS Hawk T1	RAF No 4 FTS/*208(R) Sqn*, Valley	
XX310	HS Hawk T1W	RAF No 4 FTS/*208(R) Sqn*, Valley	
XX311	HS Hawk T1	RAF No 4 FTS/*19(R) Sqn*, Valley	
XX312	HS Hawk T1W [CK]	RAF No 100 Sqn, Leeming	
XX313	HS Hawk T1W [CE]	RAF No 100 Sqn, Leeming	
XX314	HS Hawk T1W [CN]	RAF No 100 Sqn, Leeming	
XX315	HS Hawk T1A	RAF No 4 FTS/*19(R) Sqn*, Valley	
XX316	HS Hawk T1A	RAF No 4 FTS/*19(R) Sqn*, Valley	
XX317	HS Hawk T1A [CH]	RAF No 4 FTS/*19(R) Sqn*, Valley	
XX318	HS Hawk T1A	RAF No 4 FTS/*19(R) Sqn*, Valley	
XX319	HS Hawk T1A	RAF No 4 FTS/*208(R) Sqn*, Valley	
XX320	HS Hawk T1A	RAF No 4 FTS, Valley	
XX321	HS Hawk T1A	RAF No 4 FTS/*19(R) Sqn*, Valley	
XX322	HS Hawk T1A	RAF No 4 FTS/*208(R) Sqn*, Valley	
XX323	HS Hawk T1A	RAF No 4 FTS/*19(R) Sqn*, Valley	
XX324	HS Hawk T1A	RAF No 4 FTS/*19(R) Sqn*, Valley	
XX325	HS Hawk T1A [CT]	RAF No 100 Sqn/JFACTSU, Leeming	
XX326	HS Hawk T1A <ff>	RAF/DARA, St Athan	
XX326	HS Hawk T1A	DPA/BAE Systems, Brough (on rebuild)	
XX327	HS Hawk T1	RAF Aviation Medicine Flt, Boscombe Down	
XX329	HS Hawk T1A	RAF No 4 FTS/*19(R) Sqn*, Valley	
XX330	HS Hawk T1A [CL]	RAF No 4 FTS/*19(R) Sqn*, Valley	
XX331	HS Hawk T1A	RAF No 4 FTS/*19(R) Sqn*, Valley	
XX332	HS Hawk T1A	RAF No 4 FTS/*19(R) Sqn*, Valley	
XX335	HS Hawk T1A [CR]	RAF No 100 Sqn, Leeming	
XX337	HS Hawk T1A	RAF No 4 FTS/*208(R) Sqn*, Valley	
XX338	HS Hawk T1	RAF No 4 FTS/*19(R) Sqn*, Valley	
XX339	HS Hawk T1A	RAF No 4 FTS/*19(R) Sqn*, Valley	
XX341	HS Hawk T1 ASTRA [1]	DPA/ETPS, Boscombe Down	
XX342	HS Hawk T1 [2]	DPA/ETPS, Boscombe Down	
XX343	HS Hawk T1 [3] (wreck)	Boscombe Down Museum	
XX344	HS Hawk T1 (8847M) (fuselage)	QinetiQ Farnborough Fire Section	
XX345	HS Hawk T1A	RAF No 4 FTS/*19(R) Sqn*, Valley	
XX346	HS Hawk T1A	RAF No 4 FTS/*19(R) Sqn*, Valley	
XX348	HS Hawk T1A	RAF No 4 FTS/*19(R) Sqn*, Valley	
XX349	HS Hawk T1W [CO]	RAF No 100 Sqn, Leeming	
XX350	HS Hawk T1A	RAF No 4 FTS/*19(R) Sqn*, Valley	
XX351	HS Hawk T1A [CQ]	RAF No 100 Sqn, Leeming	
XX370	WS Gazelle AH1	AAC/DARA, Fleetlands	
XX371	WS Gazelle AH1	AAC No 12 Flt, Brüggen	
XX372	WS Gazelle AH1	AAC No 3 Regt, Wattisham	
XX375	WS Gazelle AH1	AAC No 8 Flt, Credenhill	
XX378	WS Gazelle AH1 [Q]	AAC No 671 Sqn/2 Regt, Middle Wallop	
XX379	WS Gazelle AH1	AAC No 669 Sqn/4 Regt, Wattisham	
XX380	WS Gazelle AH1 [A]	RM No 847 Sqn, Yeovilton	
XX381	WS Gazelle AH1	AAC No 9 Regt, Dishforth	
XX382	WS Gazelle HT3 (G-BZYB) [M]	Privately owned, Tadcaster	
XX383	WS Gazelle AH1 [D]	AAC No 666(V) Sqn/7 Regt, Netheravon	
XX384	WS Gazelle AH1	AAC/DARA, stored Fleetlands	
XX385	WS Gazelle AH1	RAF No 7 Sqn, Odiham	
XX386	WS Gazelle AH1	AAC No 12 Flt, Brüggen	
XX387	WS Gazelle AH1 (TAD 014)	Army SEAE, Arborfield	
XX388	WS Gazelle AH1 <ff>	Privately owned, East Garston, Bucks	
XX389	WS Gazelle AH1	AAC No 656 Sqn/9 Regt, Dishforth	
XX392	WS Gazelle AH1	AAC No 3(V) Flt/7 Regt, Leuchars	
XX393	WS Gazelle AH1 (fuselage)	Privately owned, East Garston, Bucks	
XX394	WS Gazelle AH1 [X]	AAC No 654 Sqn/4 Regt, Wattisham	
XX396	WS Gazelle HT3 (8718M) [N]	ATF, RAFC Cranwell	
XX398	WS Gazelle AH1	Privately owned, East Garston, Bucks	
XX399	WS Gazelle AH1 [D]	DPA/Westland Helicopters, Yeovil	
XX403	WS Gazelle AH1	AAC No 671 Sqn/2 Regt, Middle Wallop	
XX405	WS Gazelle AH1	AAC No 665 Sqn/5 Regt, Aldergrove	
XX406	WS Gazelle HT3 (G-CBSH) [P]	Privately owned, Redhill	

Notes	Serial	Type (other identity) [code]	Owner/operator, location or fate
	XX409	WS Gazelle AH1	AAC No 672 Sqn/9 Regt, Dishforth
	XX411	WS Gazelle AH1	Aeroventure, Doncaster
	XX411	WS Gazelle AH1 <rf>	FAA Museum, RNAS Yeovilton
	XX412	WS Gazelle AH1 [B]	RM No 847 Sqn, Yeovilton
	XX413	WS Gazelle AH1 <ff>	Privately owned, East Garston, Bucks
	XX414	WS Gazelle AH1	AAC/DARA, stored Fleetlands
	XX416	WS Gazelle AH1	AAC No 9 Regt, Dishforth
	XX417	WS Gazelle AH1	AAC No 665 Sqn/5 Regt, Aldergrove
	XX418	WS Gazelle AH1	Privately owned, East Garston, Bucks
	XX419	WS Gazelle AH1	AAC No 656 Sqn/9 Regt, Dishforth
	XX431	WS Gazelle HT2 (9300M) [43/CU]	RAF Shawbury, for display
	XX432	WS Gazelle AH1	AAC No 665 Sqn/5 Regt, Aldergrove
	XX433	WS Gazelle AH1 <ff>	Privately owned, East Garston, Bucks
	XX435	WS Gazelle AH1 [V]	AAC No 658 Sqn/7 Regt, Netheravon
	XX436	WS Gazelle HT2 (G-CBSE) [39/CU]	Privately owned,
	XX437	WS Gazelle AH1	AAC No 669 Sqn/4 Regt, Wattisham
	XX438	WS Gazelle AH1	AAC No 9 Regt, Dishforth
	XX439	WS Gazelle AH1	AAC No 9 Regt, Dishforth
	XX440	WS Gazelle AH1 (G-BCHN)	DARA Fleetlands Apprentice School
	XX442	WS Gazelle AH1 [E]	AAC No 666(V) Sqn/7 Regt, Netheravon
	XX443	WS Gazelle AH1 [Y]	AAC Stockwell Hall, Middle Wallop, instructional use
	XX444	WS Gazelle AH1	AAC/DARA, stored Fleetlands
	XX445	WS Gazelle AH1 [T]	AAC No 658 Sqn/7 Regt, Netheravon
	XX447	WS Gazelle AH1 [D1]	AAC No 671 Sqn/2 Regt, Middle Wallop
	XX448	WS Gazelle AH1	AAC No 672 Sqn/9 Regt, Dishforth
	XX449	WS Gazelle AH1	AAC No 664 Sqn/9 Regt, Dishforth
	XX450	WS Gazelle AH1 [D]	Privately owned, East Garston, Bucks
	XX453	WS Gazelle AH1	AAC No 3 Regt, Wattisham
	XX454	WS Gazelle AH1 (TAD 023) (fuselage)	Army SEAE, Arborfield
	XX455	WS Gazelle AH1	AAC/DARA, Fleetlands
	XX456	WS Gazelle AH1	AAC No 3(V) Flt/7 Regt, Leuchars
	XX457	WS Gazelle AH1 <ff>	Jet Avn Preservation Grp, Long Marston
	XX460	WS Gazelle AH1	AAC No 672 Sqn/9 Regt, Dishforth
	XX462	WS Gazelle AH1 [W]	AAC No 658 Sqn/7 Regt, Netheravon
	XX467	HS Hunter T66B/T7 (XL605/ G-TVII) [86]	Privately owned, Exeter
	XX475	HP137 Jetstream T2 (N1036S)	DPA/QinetiQ, stored Boscombe Down
	XX476	HP137 Jetstream T2 (N1037S) [561/CU]	RN No 750 Sqn, Culdrose
	XX477	HP137 Jetstream T1 (G-AXXS/ 8462M) <ff>	Privately owned, Askern, Doncaster
	XX478	HP137 Jetstream T2 (G-AXXT) [564/CU]	RN No 750 Sqn, Culdrose
	XX479	HP137 Jetstream T2 (G-AXUR)	RN, Predannack Fire School
	XX481	HP137 Jetstream T2 (G-AXUP) [560/CU]	RN No 750 Sqn, Culdrose
	XX482	SA Jetstream T1 [J]	RAF, stored Shawbury
	XX483	SA Jetstream T2 <ff>	Dumfries & Galloway Avn Mus, Dumfries
	XX484	SA Jetstream T2 [566/CU]	RN No 750 Sqn, Culdrose
	XX486	SA Jetstream T2 [569/CU]	RN No 750 Sqn, Culdrose
	XX487	SA Jetstream T2 [568/CU]	RN No 750 Sqn, Culdrose
	XX488	SA Jetstream T2 [562/CU]	RN No 750 Sqn, Culdrose
	XX491	SA Jetstream T1 [K]	RNAS Culdrose, spares use
	XX492	SA Jetstream T1 [A]	RAF No 3 FTS/45(R) Sqn, Cranwell
	XX493	SA Jetstream T1 [L]	RAF Cranwell, wfu
	XX494	SA Jetstream T1 [B]	RAF No 3 FTS/45(R) Sqn, Cranwell
	XX495	SA Jetstream T1 [C]	RAF No 3 FTS/45(R) Sqn, Cranwell
	XX496	SA Jetstream T1 [D]	RAF No 3 FTS/45(R) Sqn, Cranwell
	XX497	SA Jetstream T1 [E]	RAF, stored Shawbury
	XX498	SA Jetstream T1 [F]	RAF Cranwell, wfu
	XX499	SA Jetstream T1 [G]	RAF No 3 FTS/45(R) Sqn, Cranwell
	XX500	SA Jetstream T1 [H]	RAF No 3 FTS/45(R) Sqn, Cranwell
	XX510	WS Lynx HAS2 [69/DD]	SFDO, RNAS Culdrose
	XX513	SA Bulldog T1 (G-CCMI) [10]	Privately owned, Meppershall
	XX515	SA Bulldog T1 (G-CBBC) [4]	Privately owned, Blackbushe
	XX518	SA Bulldog T1 (G-UDOG) [S]	Privately owned, Sleap
	XX520	SA Bulldog T1 (9288M) [A]	No 172 Sqn ATC, Haywards Heath
	XX521	SA Bulldog T1 (G-CBEH) [H]	Privately owned, East Dereham, Norfolk
	XX522	SA Bulldog T1 (G-DAWG) [06]	Privately owned, Sleap
	XX524	SA Bulldog T1 (G-DDOG) [04]	Privately owned, North Weald
	XX525	SA Bulldog T1 (G-CBJJ) [8]	Privately owned, Norwich

Serial	Type (other identity) [code]	Owner/operator, location or fate	Notes
XX528	SA Bulldog T1 (G-BZON) [D]	Privately owned, Carlisle	
XX530	SA Bulldog T1 (XX637/9197M) [F]	Rolls-Royce, Renfrew	
XX534	SA Bulldog T1 (G-EDAV) [B]	Privately owned, Tollerton	
XX537	SA Bulldog T1 (G-CBCB) [C]	Privately owned, Elstree	
XX538	SA Bulldog T1 (G-TDOG) [O]	Privately owned, Bewdley, Worcs	
XX539	SA Bulldog T1 [L]	Privately owned, Wellesbourne Mountford	
XX543	SA Bulldog T1 (G-CBAB) [F]	Privately owned, Duxford	
XX546	SA Bulldog T1 (G-WINI) [03]	Privately owned, Blackbushe	
XX549	SA Bulldog T1 (G-CBID) [6]	Privately owned, White Waltham	
XX550	SA Bulldog T1 (G-CBBL) [Z]	Privately owned, Fenland	
XX551	SA Bulldog T1 (G-BZDP) [E]	Privately owned, RAF Lyneham	
XX554	SA Bulldog T1 (G-BZMD) [09]	Privately owned, Wellesbourne Mountford	
XX557	SA Bulldog T1	Privately owned, Paull, Yorks	
XX561	SA Bulldog T1 (G-BZEP) [7]	Privately owned, Biggin Hill	
XX611	SA Bulldog T1 (G-CBDK) [7]	Privately owned, Coventry	
XX612	SA Bulldog T1 (G-BZXC) [A,03]	Privately owned, Wellesbourne Mountford	
XX614	SA Bulldog T1 (G-GGRR) [V]	Privately owned, White Waltham	
XX619	SA Bulldog T1 (G-CBBW) [T]	Privately owned, Coventry	
XX621	SA Bulldog T1 (G-CBEF) [H]	Privately owned, Spanhoe Lodge	
XX622	SA Bulldog T1 (G-CBGX) [B]	Privately owned, Findon, Sussex	
XX623	SA Bulldog T1 [M]	Privately owned, Hurstbourne Tarrant	
XX624	SA Bulldog T1 (G-KDOG) [E]	Privately owned, North Weald	
XX625	SA Bulldog T1 (G-CBBR) [01,N]	Privately owned, Norwich	
XX626	SA Bulldog T1 (9290M) [W,02]	DARA Training School, RAF St Athan	
XX628	SA Bulldog T1 (G-CBFU) [9]	Privately owned, Faversham	
XX629	SA Bulldog T1 (G-BZXZ) [V]	Privately owned, Sleap	
XX630	SA Bulldog T1 (G-SIJW) [5]	Privately owned, Shenington	
XX631	SA Bulldog T1 (G-BZXS) [W]	Privately owned, Newport, Ireland	
XX633	SA Bulldog T1 [X]	Privately owned, Mansfield	
XX634	SA Bulldog T1 [T]	Privately owned, Wellesbourne Mountford	
XX635	SA Bulldog T1 (8767M)	DARA Training School, RAF St Athan	
XX636	SA Bulldog T1 (G-CBFP) [Y]	Privately owned, Biggin Hill	
XX638	SA Bulldog T1 (G-DOGG)	Privately owned, Bourne Park, Hants	
XX653	SA Bulldog T1 [E]	DPA/QinetiQ, stored Boscombe Down	
XX654	SA Bulldog T1 [3]	RAF, stored Shawbury	
XX656	SA Bulldog T1 [C]	Privately owned, Wellesbourne Mountford	
XX658	SA Bulldog T1 (G-BZPS) [07]	Privately owned, Wellesbourne Mountford	
XX659	SA Bulldog T1 [E]	Privately owned, Hixon, Staffs	
XX664	SA Bulldog T1 (G-CBCT) [04]	Privately owned, Sleap	
XX665	SA Bulldog T1	No 2409 Sqn ATC, Halton	
XX667	SA Bulldog T1 (G-BZFN) [16]	Privately owned, Staverton	
XX668	SA Bulldog T1 (G-CBAN) [1]	Privately owned, Colerne	
XX669	SA Bulldog T1 (8997M) [B]	No 2409 Sqn ATC, Halton	
XX671	SA Bulldog T1 [D]	Privately owned, Wellesbourne Mountford	
XX672	SA Bulldog T1 [E]	Barry Technical College, Cardiff Airport	
XX686	SA Bulldog T1 (9291M) [5]	DARA Training School, RAF St Athan	
XX687	SA Bulldog T1 [F]	Barry Technical College, Cardiff Airport	
XX690	SA Bulldog T1 [A]	James Watt College, Greenock	
XX692	SA Bulldog T1 (G-BZMH) [A]	Privately owned, Wellesbourne Mountford	
XX693	SA Bulldog T1 (G-BZML) [07]	Repainted as G-BZML, April 2003	
XX694	SA Bulldog T1 (G-CBBS) [E]	Privately owned, Teesside	
XX695	SA Bulldog T1 (G-CBBT) [3]	Privately owned, Egginton	
XX698	SA Bulldog T1 (G-BZME) [9]	Privately owned, Breighton	
XX699	SA Bulldog T1 (G-CBCV) [F]	Privately owned, Egginton	
XX700	SA Bulldog T1 (G-CBEK) [17]	Privately owned, Blackbushe	
XX702	SA Bulldog T1 (G-CBCR) [_]	Privately owned, Egginton	
XX705	SA Bulldog T1 [5]	QinetiQ Boscombe Down, Apprentice School	
XX707	SA Bulldog T1 (G-CBDS) [4]	Privately owned, Sleap	
XX711	SA Bulldog T1 (G-CBBU) [X]	Privately owned, Egginton	
XX713	SA Bulldog T1 (G-CBJK) [2]	Privately owned, Norwich	
XX720	SEPECAT Jaguar GR3A [GB]	RAF No 54 Sqn, Coltishall	
XX722	SEPECAT Jaguar GR1 (fuselage)	RAF St Mawgan, BDRT	
XX723	SEPECAT Jaguar GR3A [GQ]	RAF No 54 Sqn, Coltishall	
XX724	SEPECAT Jaguar GR3A [GC]	RAF No 54 Sqn, Coltishall	
XX725	SEPECAT Jaguar GR3A	RAF AWC/SAOEU, Boscombe Down	
XX725	SEPECAT Jaguar GR1 <R> (BAPC 150/XX718) [GU]	RAF M&RU, Bottesford	
XX726	SEPECAT Jaguar GR1 (8947M) [EB]	RAF No 1 SoTT, Cosford	
XX727	SEPECAT Jaguar GR1 (8951M) [ER]	RAF No 1 SoTT, Cosford	
XX729	SEPECAT Jaguar GR3A [EL]	RAF No 6 Sqn, Coltishall	

Notes	Serial	Type (other identity) [code]	Owner/operator, location or fate
	XX730	SEPECAT Jaguar GR1 (8952M) [EC]	RAF No 1 SoTT, Cosford
	XX734	SEPECAT Jaguar GR1 (8816M) (fuselage)	Gatwick Aviation Museum, Charlwood
	XX736	SEPECAT Jaguar GR1 (9110M) <ff>	BAE Systems Brough
	XX737	SEPECAT Jaguar GR3A [EE]	RAF No 6 Sqn, Coltishall
	XX738	SEPECAT Jaguar GR3A [GG]	RAF No 54 Sqn, Coltishall
	XX739	SEPECAT Jaguar GR1 (8902M) [I]	RAF No 1 SoTT, Cosford
	XX741	SEPECAT Jaguar GR1A [04]	RAF, stored Shawbury
	XX743	SEPECAT Jaguar GR1 (8949M) [EG]	RAF No 1 SoTT, Cosford
	XX744	SEPECAT Jaguar GR1	Privately owned, Sproughton
	XX745	SEPECAT Jaguar GR1A [GV]	RAF, stored Shawbury
	XX746	SEPECAT Jaguar GR1 (8895M/ 9251M) [S]	RAF No 1 SoTT, Cosford
	XX747	SEPECAT Jaguar GR1 (8903M)	ATF, RAFC Cranwell
	XX748	SEPECAT Jaguar GR3A [GK]	RAF No 54 Sqn, Coltishall
	XX751	SEPECAT Jaguar GR1 (8937M) [10]	RAF No 1 SoTT, Cosford
	XX752	SEPECAT Jaguar GR3A [FC]	RAF No 41 Sqn, Coltishall
	XX753	SEPECAT Jaguar GR1 (9087M) <ff>	RAF M&RU, Bottesford
	XX756	SEPECAT Jaguar GR1 (8899M) [AM]	RAF No 1 SoTT, Cosford
	XX757	SEPECAT Jaguar GR1 (8948M) [CU]	RAF No 1 SoTT, Cosford
	XX761	SEPECAT Jaguar GR1 (8600M) <ff>	Boscombe Down Museum
	XX763	SEPECAT Jaguar GR1 (9009M)	DARA Training School, RAF St Athan
	XX764	SEPECAT Jaguar GR1 (9010M)	DARA Training School, RAF St Athan
	XX765	SEPECAT Jaguar ACT	RAF Museum, Cosford
	XX766	SEPECAT Jaguar GR3A [PE]	RAF No 16(R) Sqn, Coltishall
	XX767	SEPECAT Jaguar GR3A [GE]	RAF No 54 Sqn, Coltishall
	XX818	SEPECAT Jaguar GR1 (8945M) [DE]	RAF No 1 SoTT, Cosford
	XX819	SEPECAT Jaguar GR1 (8923M) [CE]	RAF No 1 SoTT, Cosford
	XX821	SEPECAT Jaguar GR1 (8896M) [P]	AMIF, RAFC Cranwell
	XX824	SEPECAT Jaguar GR1 (9019M) [AD]	RAF No 1 SoTT, Cosford
	XX825	SEPECAT Jaguar GR1 (9020M) [BN]	RAF No 1 SoTT, Cosford
	XX826	SEPECAT Jaguar GR1 (9021M) [34,JH]	RAF No 1 SoTT, Cosford
	XX829	SEPECAT Jaguar T2A [GZ]	RAF, stored Shawbury
	XX830	SEPECAT Jaguar T2 <ff>	The Cockpit Collection, RAF Coltishall
	XX832	SEPECAT Jaguar T2A [EZ]	RAF, stored Shawbury
	XX833	SEPECAT Jaguar T2B	RAF AWC/SAOEU, Boscombe Down
	XX835	SEPECAT Jaguar T4 [FY]	RAF No 41 Sqn, Coltishall
	XX836	SEPECAT Jaguar T2A [X]	RAF, stored Shawbury
	XX837	SEPECAT Jaguar T2 (8978M) [I]	RAF No 1 SoTT, Cosford
	XX838	SEPECAT Jaguar T4 [PR]	RAF No 16(R) Sqn, Coltishall
	XX840	SEPECAT Jaguar T4 [PS]	RAF/DARA, St Athan
	XX841	SEPECAT Jaguar T4 [PQ]	RAF No 16(R) Sqn, Coltishall
	XX842	SEPECAT Jaguar T2A [PX]	RAF No 16(R) Sqn, Coltishall
	XX845	SEPECAT Jaguar T4 [ET]	RAF No 6 Sqn, Coltishall
	XX846	SEPECAT Jaguar T4 [PV]	RAF No 16(R) Sqn, Coltishall
	XX847	SEPECAT Jaguar T4 [PY]	RAF No 16(R) Sqn, Coltishall
	XX885	HS Buccaneer S2B (9225M/ G-HHAA)	The Old Flying Machine Company, Scampton
	XX888	HS Buccaneer S2B <ff>	Privately owned, Barnstaple
	XX889	HS Buccaneer S2B [T]	Gloucestershire Avn Coll, stored Gloucester
	XX892	HS Buccaneer S2B <ff>	Privately owned, Perthshire
	XX893	HS Buccaneer S2B <ff>	Privately owned, Desborough, Northants
	XX894	HS Buccaneer S2B [020/R]	Buccaneer Supporters Club, Bruntingthorpe
	XX895	HS Buccaneer S2B <ff>	Privately owned, Bicester
	XX897	HS Buccaneer S2B(mod)	Bournemouth Aviation Museum
	XX899	HS Buccaneer S2B <ff>	Midland Air Museum, Coventry
	XX900	HS Buccaneer S2B	British Aviation Heritage, Bruntingthorpe
	XX901	HS Buccaneer S2B	Yorkshire Air Museum, Elvington

Serial	Type (other identity) [code]	Owner/operator, location or fate	Notes
XX907	WS Lynx AH1	Westland Helicopters, Yeovil, Fire Section	
XX910	WS Lynx HAS2	The Helicopter Museum, Weston-super-Mare	
XX914	BAC VC10/1103 (8777M) <rf>	RAF Air Movements School, Brize Norton	
XX919	BAC 1-11/402AP (PI-C1121) <ff>	Boscombe Down Museum	
XX946	Panavia Tornado (P02) (8883M)	RAF Museum, Cosford	
XX947	Panavia Tornado (P03) (8797M)	Privately owned, Shoreham, on display	
XX948	Panavia Tornado (P06) (8879M) [P]	RAF No 1 SoTT, Cosford	
XX955	SEPECAT Jaguar GR1A [GK]	RAF, stored Shawbury	
XX956	SEPECAT Jaguar GR1 (8950M) [BE]	RAF No 1 SoTT, Cosford	
XX958	SEPECAT Jaguar GR1 (9022M) [BK,JG]	RAF No 1 SoTT, Cosford	
XX959	SEPECAT Jaguar GR1 (8953M) [CJ]	RAF No 1 SoTT, Cosford	
XX962	SEPECAT Jaguar GR1B (9257M) [E]	RAF No 1 SoTT, Cosford	
XX965	SEPECAT Jaguar GR1A (9254M) [C]	AMIF, RAFC Cranwell	
XX966	SEPECAT Jaguar GR1 (8904M) [EL,JJ]	RAF No 1 SoTT, Cosford	
XX967	SEPECAT Jaguar GR1 (9006M) [AC,JD]	RAF No 1 SoTT, Cosford	
XX968	SEPECAT Jaguar GR1 (9007M) [AJ,JE]	RAF No 1 SoTT, Cosford	
XX969	SEPECAT Jaguar GR1 (8897M) [01]	RAF No 1 SoTT, Cosford	
XX970	SEPECAT Jaguar GR3A [EH]	RAF No 6 Sqn, Coltishall	
XX974	SEPECAT Jaguar GR3 [FE]	RAF No 41 Sqn, Coltishall	
XX975	SEPECAT Jaguar GR1 (8905M) [07]	RAF No 1 SoTT, Cosford	
XX976	SEPECAT Jaguar GR1 (8906M) [BD]	RAF No 1 SoTT, Cosford	
XX977	SEPECAT Jaguar GR1 (9132M) [DL,05]	DARA, RAF St Athan, BDRT	
XX979	SEPECAT Jaguar GR1A (9306M) (fuselage)	RAF Coltishall, instructional use	
XZ101	SEPECAT Jaguar GR1A (9282M) [D]	DPA/QinetiQ Boscombe Down, GI use	
XZ103	SEPECAT Jaguar GR3A [FP]	RAF/DARA, St Athan	
XZ104	SEPECAT Jaguar GR3A [FM]	RAF No 41 Sqn, Coltishall	
XZ106	SEPECAT Jaguar GR3A [FR]	RAF No 41 Sqn, Coltishall	
XZ107	SEPECAT Jaguar GR3A [FH]	RAF No 41 Sqn, Coltishall	
XZ109	SEPECAT Jaguar GR3A [EN]	RAF No 6 Sqn, Coltishall	
XZ112	SEPECAT Jaguar GR3A [GA]	RAF No 54 Sqn, Coltishall	
XZ113	SEPECAT Jaguar GR3	RAFAWC/SAOEU, Boscombe Down	
XZ114	SEPECAT Jaguar GR1A [FB]	RAF/DARA, St Athan	
XZ115	SEPECAT Jaguar GR3 [PD]	RAF/DARA, St Athan	
XZ117	SEPECAT Jaguar GR3 [EP]	RAF No 6 Sqn, Coltishall	
XZ118	SEPECAT Jaguar GR3 [FF]	RAF No 41 Sqn, Coltishall	
XZ119	SEPECAT Jaguar GR1A (9266M) [F]	AMIF, RAFC Cranwell	
XZ129	HS Harrier GR3 [ETS]	RN ETS, Yeovilton	
XZ130	HS Harrier GR3 (9079M) [A,HE]	RAF No 1 SoTT, Cosford	
XZ131	HS Harrier GR3 (9174M) <ff>	No 2156 Sqn ATC, Brierley Hill, W Midlands	
XZ132	HS Harrier GR3 (9168M) [C]	ATF, RAFC Cranwell	
XZ133	HS Harrier GR3 [10]	Imperial War Museum, Duxford	
XZ135	HS Harrier GR3 (8848M) <ff>	RAF M&RU, Bottesford	
XZ138	HS Harrier GR3 (9040M) <ff>	RAFC Cranwell, Trenchard Hall	
XZ145	HS Harrier T4 (9270M) [45]	SFDO, RNAS Culdrose	
XZ146	HS Harrier T4 (9281M) [S]	RAF Wittering, for display	
XZ170	WS Lynx AH9	DPA/Westland Helicopters, Yeovil	
XZ171	WS Lynx AH7	AAC No 656 Sqn/9 Regt, Dishforth	
XZ172	WS Lynx AH7	AAC/DARA, Fleetlands	
XZ173	WS Lynx AH7	AAC No 661 Sqn/1 Regt, Brüggen	
XZ174	WS Lynx AH7	AAC/DARA, Fleetlands	
XZ175	WS Lynx AH7	AAC DPA/Westland Helicopters, Yeovil	
XZ176	WS Lynx AH7	AAC/DARA, stored Fleetlands	
XZ177	WS Lynx AH7	AAC/DARA, Fleetlands	
XZ178	WS Lynx AH7	AAC No 661 Sqn/1 Regt, Brüggen	

Notes	Serial	Type (other identity) [code]	Owner/operator, location or fate
	XZ179	WS Lynx AH7	AAC No 655 Sqn/5 Regt, Aldergrove
	XZ180	WS Lynx AH7 [R]	RM No 847 Sqn, Yeovilton
	XZ181	WS Lynx AH1	AAC/DARA, Fleetlands
	XZ182	WS Lynx AH7	RM No 847 Sqn, Yeovilton
	XZ183	WS Lynx AH7	AAC/DARA, stored Fleetlands
	XZ184	WS Lynx AH7 [Z]	AAC No 655 Sqn/5 Regt, Aldergrove
	XZ185	WS Lynx AH7	AAC No 672 Sqn/9 Regt, Dishforth
	XZ187	WS Lynx AH7	AAC/DARA, stored Fleetlands
	XZ188	WS Lynx AH7	Army SEAE, Arborfield
	XZ190	WS Lynx AH7	AAC No 9 Regt, Dishforth
	XZ191	WS Lynx AH7 [A]	AAC No 671 Sqn/2 Regt, Middle Wallop
	XZ192	WS Lynx AH7	DPA/Westland Helicopters, Yeovil (on rebuild)
	XZ193	WS Lynx AH7 [I]	AAC No 671 Sqn/2 Regt, Middle Wallop
	XZ194	WS Lynx AH7	AAC No 672 Sqn/9 Regt, Dishforth
	XZ195	WS Lynx AH7	AAC/DARA, stored Fleetlands
	XZ196	WS Lynx AH7	AAC No 672 Sqn/9 Regt, Dishforth
	XZ197	WS Lynx AH7	AAC/DARA, Fleetlands
	XZ198	WS Lynx AH7	AAC/DARA, Fleetlands
	XZ203	WS Lynx AH7 [L]	AAC No 671 Sqn/2 Regt, Middle Wallop
	XZ205	WS Lynx AH7	AAC/DARA, Fleetlands
	XZ206	WS Lynx AH7	AAC, Middle Wallop
	XZ207	WS Lynx AH7	AAC/DARA, Fleetlands (damaged)
	XZ208	WS Lynx AH7	RM No 847 Sqn, Yeovilton
	XZ209	WS Lynx AH7	AAC No 655 Sqn/5 Regt, Aldergrove
	XZ210	WS Lynx AH7	AAC/DARA, Fleetlands
	XZ211	WS Lynx AH7	AAC No 655 Sqn/5 Regt, Aldergrove
	XZ212	WS Lynx AH7	AAC No 1 Regt, Brüggen
	XZ213	WS Lynx AH1 (TAD 213)	DARA Fleetlands Apprentice School
	XZ214	WS Lynx AH7	AAC No 657 Sqn, Odiham
	XZ215	WS Lynx AH7 [4]	AAC/DARA, Fleetlands
	XZ216	WS Lynx AH7	AAC No 661 Sqn/1 Regt, Brüggen
	XZ217	WS Lynx AH7	AAC No 664 Sqn/9 Regt, Dishforth
	XZ218	WS Lynx AH7	AAC/DARA, Fleetlands
	XZ219	WS Lynx AH7	AAC No 3 Regt, Wattisham
	XZ220	WS Lynx AH7	AAC No 661 Sqn/1 Regt, Brüggen
	XZ221	WS Lynx AH7	AAC No 654 Sqn/4 Regt, Wattisham
	XZ222	WS Lynx AH7	AAC No 657 Sqn, Odiham
	XZ228	WS Lynx HAS3S [425/KT]	RN/DARA, Fleetlands
	XZ229	WS Lynx HAS3S [634]	RN No 702 Sqn, Yeovilton
	XZ230	WS Lynx HAS3S [302]	RN/DARA, stored Fleetlands
	XZ232	WS Lynx HAS3S [334/SN]	RN No 815 Sqn, *Southampton* Flt, Yeovilton
	XZ233	WS Lynx HAS3(ICE) [644]	RN AMG, Yeovilton
	XZ234	WS Lynx HAS3S [633]	RN No 702 Sqn, Yeovilton
	XZ235	WS Lynx HAS3S [304]	RN AMG, Yeovilton
	XZ236	WS Lynx HMA8	DPA/Westland Helicopters, Yeovil
	XZ237	WS Lynx HAS3S [301]	RN No 815 Sqn, HQ Flt, Yeovilton
	XZ238	WS Lynx HAS3S(ICE) [434/EE]	RN No 815 Sqn, *Endurance* Flt, Yeovilton
	XZ239	WS Lynx HAS3S [344/GW]	RN AMG, Yeovilton
	XZ241	WS Lynx HAS3S(ICE) [435/EE]	RN No 815 Sqn, *Endurance* Flt, Yeovilton
	XZ243	WS Lynx HAS3 <ff>	RNAS Culdrose, Fire Section
	XZ245	WS Lynx HAS3S [422/SU]	RN No 815 Sqn, *Sutherland* Flt, Yeovilton
	XZ246	WS Lynx HAS3S(ICE) [434/EE]	RN/DARA, Fleetlands
	XZ248	WS Lynx HAS3S [638]	RN No 702 Sqn, Yeovilton
	XZ250	WS Lynx HAS3S [304]	RN No 702 Sqn, Yeovilton
	XZ252	WS Lynx HAS3S	RN MASU, Yeovilton
	XZ254	WS Lynx HAS3S [303]	RN No 815 Sqn, HQ Flt, Yeovilton
	XZ255	WS Lynx HMA8	RN/DARA, stored Fleetlands
	XZ257	WS Lynx HAS3S [640]	RN No 702 Sqn, Yeovilton
	XZ286	BAe Nimrod AEW3 <rf>	RAF Kinloss Fire Section
	XZ287	BAe Nimrod AEW3 (9140M) (fuselage)	RAF TSW, Stafford
	XZ290	WS Gazelle AH1	AAC No 665 Sqn/5 Regt, Aldergrove
	XZ291	WS Gazelle AH1	AAC No 12 Flt, Brüggen
	XZ292	WS Gazelle AH1	AAC No 9 Regt, Dishforth
	XZ294	WS Gazelle AH1 [X]	AAC No 658 Sqn/7 Regt, Netheravon
	XZ295	WS Gazelle AH1	AAC No 12 Flt, Brüggen
	XZ296	WS Gazelle AH1	RAF No 7 Sqn, Odiham
	XZ298	WS Gazelle AH1	AAC/DARA, Fleetlands
	XZ299	WS Gazelle AH1	AAC/DARA, Fleetlands
	XZ300	WS Gazelle AH1 [L] (wreck)	Army, Bramley, Hants
	XZ301	WS Gazelle AH1 [U]	AAC No 664 Sqn/9 Regt, Dishforth

Serial	Type (other identity) [code]	Owner/operator, location or fate	Notes
XZ303	WS Gazelle AH1	AAC No 663 Sqn/3 Regt, Wattisham	
XZ304	WS Gazelle AH1	AAC No 6(V) Flt/7 Regt, Shawbury	
XZ305	WS Gazelle AH1 (TAD020)	Army SEAE, Arborfield	
XZ307	WS Gazelle AH1	DARA Fleetlands Apprentice School	
XZ308	WS Gazelle AH1	AAC No 4 Regt, Wattisham	
XZ309	WS Gazelle AH1	AAC Middle Wallop, wfu	
XZ311	WS Gazelle AH1	AAC No 6(V) Flt/7 Regt, Shawbury	
XZ312	WS Gazelle AH1	AAC No 9 Regt, Dishforth	
XZ313	WS Gazelle AH1	AAC No 667 Sqn, Middle Wallop	
XZ314	WS Gazelle AH1	AAC No 8 Flt, Credenhill	
XZ315	WS Gazelle AH1	Privately owned, Sproughton	
XZ316	WS Gazelle AH1 [B]	AAC No 666(V) Sqn/7 Regt, Netheravon	
XZ318	WS Gazelle AH1 (fuselage)	AAC/DARA, stored Fleetlands	
XZ320	WS Gazelle AH1	AAC No 665 Sqn/5 Regt, Aldergrove	
XZ321	WS Gazelle AH1	AAC/DARA, stored Fleetlands	
XZ322	WS Gazelle AH1 (9283M) [N]	DARA, RAF St Athan, BDRT	
XZ323	WS Gazelle AH1 [H]	AAC No 666(V) Sqn/7 Regt, Netheravon	
XZ324	WS Gazelle AH1	AAC No 3(V) Flt/7 Regt, Leuchars	
XZ325	WS Gazelle AH1 [T]	Army SEAE, Arborfield	
XZ326	WS Gazelle AH1	AAC No 665 Sqn/5 Regt, Aldergrove	
XZ327	WS Gazelle AH1	AAC No 3(V) Flt/7 Regt, Leuchars	
XZ328	WS Gazelle AH1	AAC No 658 Sqn/7 Regt, Netheravon	
XZ329	WS Gazelle AH1 (G-BZYD) [J]	Privately owned, East Garston, Bucks	
XZ330	WS Gazelle AH1 [Y]	AAC, Middle Wallop (damaged)	
XZ331	WS Gazelle AH1	AAC No 654 Sqn/4 Regt, Wattisham	
XZ332	WS Gazelle AH1 [O]	Army SEAE, Arborfield	
XZ333	WS Gazelle AH1 [A]	Army SEAE, Arborfield	
XZ334	WS Gazelle AH1	AAC No 665 Sqn/5 Regt, Aldergrove	
XZ335	WS Gazelle AH1	AAC No 6(V) Flt/7 Regt, Shawbury	
XZ337	WS Gazelle AH1	AAC No 664 Sqn/9 Regt, Dishforth	
XZ338	WS Gazelle AH1	AAC No 671 Sqn/2 Regt, Middle Wallop	
XZ340	WS Gazelle AH1 [5B]	AAC No 29 Flt, BATUS, Suffield, Canada	
XZ341	WS Gazelle AH1	AAC No 665 Sqn/5 Regt, Aldergrove	
XZ342	WS Gazelle AH1	AAC No 8 Flt, Credenhill	
XZ343	WS Gazelle AH1	DARA, Fleetlands, hack	
XZ344	WS Gazelle AH1 [Y]	AAC No 658 Sqn/7 Regt, Netheravon	
XZ345	WS Gazelle AH1 [M]	AAC No 671 Sqn/2 Regt, Middle Wallop	
XZ346	WS Gazelle AH1	AAC No 665 Sqn/5 Regt, Aldergrove	
XZ347	WS Gazelle AH1	AAC No 3 Regt, Wattisham	
XZ348	WS Gazelle AH1 (wreck)	AAC/DARA, stored Fleetlands	
XZ349	WS Gazelle AH1 [G1]	AAC No 671 Sqn/2 Regt, Middle Wallop	
XZ355	SEPECAT Jaguar GR3A [FJ]	RAF No 41 Sqn, Coltishall	
XZ356	SEPECAT Jaguar GR3A [GF]	RAF No 54 Sqn, Coltishall	
XZ357	SEPECAT Jaguar GR3A [FK]	RAF No 41 Sqn, Coltishall	
XZ358	SEPECAT Jaguar GR1A (9262M) [L]	AMIF, RAFC Cranwell	
XZ360	SEPECAT Jaguar GR3 [FN]	RAF No 41 Sqn, Coltishall	
XZ361	SEPECAT Jaguar GR3 [FT]	RAF, stored Shawbury	
XZ363	SEPECAT Jaguar GR1A <R> (*XX824*/BAPC 151) [A]	RAF M&RU, Bottesford	
XZ364	SEPECAT Jaguar GR3A [GJ]	RAF No 54 Sqn, Coltishall	
XZ366	SEPECAT Jaguar GR3A [FS]	RAF No 41 Sqn, Coltishall	
XZ367	SEPECAT Jaguar GR3 [GP]	RAF Coltishall, instructional use	
XZ368	SEPECAT Jaguar GR1 [8900M] [E]	RAF No 1 SoTT, Cosford	
XZ369	SEPECAT Jaguar GR3A [EF]	RAF No 6 Sqn, Coltishall	
XZ370	SEPECAT Jaguar GR1 (9004M) [JB]	RAF No 1 SoTT, Cosford	
XZ371	SEPECAT Jaguar GR1 (8907M) [AP]	RAF No 1 SoTT, Cosford	
XZ372	SEPECAT Jaguar GR3 [ED]	RAF No 41 Sqn, Coltishall	
XZ374	SEPECAT Jaguar GR1 (9005M) [JC]	RAF No 1 SoTT, Cosford	
XZ375	SEPECAT Jaguar GR1A (9255M) <ff>	RAF Coltishall, instructional use	
XZ377	SEPECAT Jaguar GR3A [EG]	RAF No 6 Sqn, Coltishall	
XZ378	SEPECAT Jaguar GR1A [EP]	RAF, stored Shawbury	
XZ382	SEPECAT Jaguar GR1 (8908M) [AE]	Privately owned, Bruntingthorpe	
XZ383	SEPECAT Jaguar GR1 (8901M) [AF]	RAF No 1 SoTT, Cosford	
XZ384	SEPECAT Jaguar GR1 (8954M) [BC]	RAF No 1 SoTT, Cosford	
XZ385	SEPECAT Jaguar GR3A [PC]	RAF No 16(R) Sqn, Coltishall	

Notes	Serial	Type (other identity) [code]	Owner/operator, location or fate
	XZ389	SEPECAT Jaguar GR1 (8946M) [BL]	RAF No 1 SoTT, Cosford
	XZ390	SEPECAT Jaguar GR1 (9003M) [35,JA]	RAF No 1 SoTT, Cosford
	XZ391	SEPECAT Jaguar GR3A [EB]	RAF No 6 Sqn, Coltishall
	XZ392	SEPECAT Jaguar GR3A [PF]	RAF No 16(R) Sqn, Coltishall
	XZ394	SEPECAT Jaguar GR3 [GN]	RAF No 54 Sqn, Coltishall
	XZ396	SEPECAT Jaguar GR3A [EM]	RAF No 6 Sqn, Coltishall
	XZ398	SEPECAT Jaguar GR3A [FA]	RAF/DARA, St Athan (conversion)
	XZ399	SEPECAT Jaguar GR3A [EJ]	RAF No 6 Sqn, Coltishall
	XZ400	SEPECAT Jaguar GR3A [GR]	RAF No 54 Sqn, Coltishall
	XZ431	HS Buccaneer S2B (9233M) <ff>	Phoenix Aviation, Bruntingthorpe
	XZ439	BAe Sea Harrier FA2	RN/DARA, stored St Athan
	XZ440	BAe Sea Harrier FA2 [N]	RN AMG, Yeovilton
	XZ455	BAe Sea Harrier FA2 [001] (wreck)	RN Yeovilton, Fire Section
	XZ457	BAe Sea Harrier FA2	Boscombe Down Museum
	XZ459	BAe Sea Harrier FA2	RN/DARA, stored St Athan
	XZ493	BAe Sea Harrier FRS1 (comp XV760) [001/N]	FAA Museum, RNAS Yeovilton
	XZ493	BAe Sea Harrier FRS1 <ff>	RN Yeovilton, Fire Section
	XZ494	BAe Sea Harrier FA2	RN/DARA, stored St Athan
	XZ497	BAe Sea Harrier FA2 [001/N]	RN No 801 Sqn, Yeovilton
	XZ499	BAe Sea Harrier FA2 [003]	FAA Museum, stored Yeovilton
	XZ559	Slingsby T61F Venture T2 (G-BUEK)	Privately owned, Tibenham
	XZ570	WS61 Sea King HAS5(mod)	RN, stored HMS Sultan, Gosport
	XZ571	WS61 Sea King HAS6 [016/L]	RN, stored HMS Sultan, Gosport
	XZ574	WS61 Sea King HAS6 [829/CU]	RN No 771 Sqn, Culdrose
	XZ575	WS61 Sea King HU5	DPA/AFD/QinetiQ, Boscombe Down
	XZ576	WS61 Sea King HAS6	DPA/AFD/QinetiQ, Boscombe Down
	XZ578	WS61 Sea King HU5SAR [709/PW]	RN AMG, Culdrose
	XZ579	WS61 Sea King HAS6 [707/PW]	RN, stored HMS Sultan, Gosport
	XZ580	WS61 Sea King HAS6C [704/PW]	RN/DARA, Fleetlands (conversion)
	XZ581	WS61 Sea King HAS6 [69/CU]	RN, stored HMS Sultan, Gosport
	XZ585	WS61 Sea King HAR3 [A]	RAF No 203(R) Sqn, St Mawgan
	XZ586	WS61 Sea King HAR3	RAF No 202 Sqn, D Flt, Lossiemouth
	XZ587	WS61 Sea King HAR3	RAF No 78 Sqn, Mount Pleasant, FI
	XZ588	WS61 Sea King HAR3	RAF No 22 Sqn, C Flt, Valley
	XZ589	WS61 Sea King HAR3	RAF No 22 Sqn, C Flt, Valley
	XZ590	WS61 Sea King HAR3	RAF No 203(R) Sqn, St Mawgan
	XZ591	WS61 Sea King HAR3	RAF HMF, St Mawgan
	XZ592	WS61 Sea King HAR3	RAF No 202 Sqn, A Flt, Boulmer
	XZ593	WS61 Sea King HAR3	RAF No 202 Sqn, A Flt, Boulmer
	XZ594	WS61 Sea King HAR3 [J]	RAF HMF, St Mawgan
	XZ595	WS61 Sea King HAR3	RAF No 203(R) Sqn, St Mawgan
	XZ596	WS61 Sea King HAR3	RAF No 202 Sqn, E Flt, Leconfield
	XZ597	WS61 Sea King HAR3	RAF No 78 Sqn, Mount Pleasant, FI
	XZ598	WS61 Sea King HAR3	RAF No 202 Sqn, E Flt, Leconfield
	XZ599	WS61 Sea King HAR3	RAF HMF, St Mawgan
	XZ605	WS Lynx AH7 [Y]	RM/DARA, Fleetlands
	XZ606	WS Lynx AH7	AAC No 667 Sqn, Middle Wallop
	XZ607	WS Lynx AH7	AAC No 663 Sqn/3 Regt, Wattisham
	XZ608	WS Lynx AH7	AAC No 657 Sqn, Odiham
	XZ609	WS Lynx AH7	AAC No 657 Sqn, Odiham
	XZ611	WS Lynx AH7	AAC No 672 Sqn/9 Regt, Dishforth
	XZ612	WS Lynx AH7 [N]	RM No 847 Sqn, Yeovilton
	XZ613	WS Lynx AH7 [F]	AAC/DARA, Fleetlands
	XZ614	WS Lynx AH7 [X]	RM No 847 Sqn, Yeovilton
	XZ615	WS Lynx AH7	AAC No 667 Sqn, Middle Wallop
	XZ616	WS Lynx AH7	AAC No 657 Sqn, Odiham
	XZ617	WS Lynx AH7	AAC No 656 Sqn/9 Regt, Dishforth
	XZ630	Panavia Tornado GR1 (8976M)	DARA, RAF St Athan, BDRT
	XZ631	Panavia Tornado GR1	DPA/BAE Systems, Warton
	XZ641	WS Lynx AH7	AAC No 655 Sqn/5 Regt, Aldergrove
	XZ642	WS Lynx AH7	AAC No 663 Sqn/3 Regt, Wattisham
	XZ643	WS Lynx AH7	AAC/DARA, Fleetlands
	XZ645	WS Lynx AH7	AAC No 4 Regt, Wattisham
	XZ646	WS Lynx AH7	AAC/DARA, Fleetlands
	XZ646	WS Lynx AH7 (really XZ649)	QinetiQ Structures Dept, Farnborough
	XZ647	WS Lynx AH7	AAC/DARA, Fleetlands
	XZ648	WS Lynx AH7	AAC No 4 Regt, Wattisham
	XZ651	WS Lynx AH7	AAC No 657 Sqn, Odiham
	XZ652	WS Lynx AH7 [T]	AAC No 671 Sqn/2 Regt, Middle Wallop

Serial	Type (other identity) [code]	Owner/operator, location or fate	Notes
XZ653	WS Lynx AH7	AAC No 657 Sqn, Odiham	
XZ654	WS Lynx AH7	AAC No 655 Sqn/5 Regt, Aldergrove	
XZ655	WS Lynx AH7	AAC/DARA, stored Fleetlands	
XZ661	WS Lynx AH1	AAC/DARA, Fleetlands	
XZ663	WS Lynx AH7	AAC/DARA, stored Fleetlands	
XZ665	WS Lynx AH7	*Scrapped*	
XZ666	WS Lynx AH7	Army SEAE, Arborfield	
XZ668	WS Lynx AH7 [UN] (wreckage)	*Scrapped at Middle Wallop*	
XZ669	WS Lynx AH7	AAC/DARA, Fleetlands	
XZ670	WS Lynx AH7	AAC No 656 Sqn/9 Regt, Dishforth	
XZ671	WS Lynx AH7 <ff>	Westland Helicopters, Yeovil, instructional use	
XZ672	WS Lynx AH7	AAC No 655 Sqn/5 Regt, Aldergrove	
XZ673	WS Lynx AH7	AAC No 655 Sqn/5 Regt, Aldergrove	
XZ674	WS Lynx AH7	AAC/DARA, stored Fleetlands	
XZ675	WS Lynx AH7 [E]	AAC No 671 Sqn/2 Regt, Middle Wallop	
XZ676	WS Lynx AH7 [N]	AAC No 671 Sqn/2 Regt, Middle Wallop	
XZ677	WS Lynx AH7	AAC No 655 Sqn/5 Regt, Aldergrove	
XZ678	WS Lynx AH7	AAC No 667 Sqn, Middle Wallop	
XZ679	WS Lynx AH7	AAC No 664 Sqn/9 Regt, Dishforth	
XZ680	WS Lynx AH7	AAC No 661 Sqn/1 Regt, Brüggen	
XZ689	WS Lynx HMA8 [363/MA]	RN No 815 Sqn, *Marlborough* Flt, Yeovilton	
XZ690	WS Lynx HMA8 [375/SM]	RN AMG, Yeovilton	
XZ691	WS Lynx HMA8 [410/GC]	RN No 815 Sqn, *Gloucester* Flt, Yeovilton	
XZ692	WS Lynx HMA8 [306]	RN No 815 Sqn, HQ Flt, Yeovilton	
XZ693	WS Lynx HAS3S [639]	RN No 702 Sqn, Yeovilton	
XZ694	WS Lynx HAS3S [411/EB]	RN No 815 Sqn, *Edinburgh* Flt, Yeovilton	
XZ695	WS Lynx HMA8 [317]	RN AMG, Yeovilton	
XZ696	WS Lynx HAS3S [336/CF]	RN No 815 Sqn, *Cardiff* Flt, Yeovilton	
XZ697	WS Lynx HMA8 [437/GT]	RN/DARA, Fleetlands	
XZ698	WS Lynx HMA8 [427/SB]	RN No 815 Sqn, *St Albans* Flt, Yeovilton	
XZ699	WS Lynx HAS3 [303]	DPA/Westland Helicopters, Yeovil	
XZ719	WS Lynx HMA8 [317]	RN No 815 Sqn OEU, Yeovilton	
XZ720	WS Lynx HAS3S [344/GW]	RN No 815 Sqn, *Glasgow* Flt, Yeovilton	
XZ721	WS Lynx HMA8 [302]	RN No 815 Sqn, HQ Flt, Yeovilton	
XZ722	WS Lynx HMA8 [474/RM]	RN No 815 Sqn, *Richmond* Flt, Yeovilton	
XZ723	WS Lynx HMA8 [671]	RN No 702 Sqn, Yeovilton	
XZ724	WS Lynx HAS3S [426/PD]	RN AMG, Yeovilton	
XZ725	WS Lynx HMA8 [365/AY]	RN No 815 Sqn, *Argyll* Flt, Yeovilton	
XZ726	WS Lynx HMA8	RN No 815 Sqn, HQ Flt, Yeovilton	
XZ727	WS Lynx HAS3S [426/PD]	RN No 815 Sqn, *Portland* Flt, Yeovilton	
XZ728	WS Lynx HMA8 [415/MM]	RN/DARA, stored Fleetlands	
XZ729	WS Lynx HMA8 [318]	RN No 815 Sqn OEU, Yeovilton	
XZ730	WS Lynx HAS3S [632]	RN No 702 Sqn, Yeovilton	
XZ731	WS Lynx HMA8 [307]	RN/DARA, stored Fleetlands	
XZ732	WS Lynx HMA8 [410/GC]	RN AMG, Yeovilton	
XZ733	WS Lynx HAS3S [425/KT]	RN No 815 Sqn, *Kent* Flt, Yeovilton	
XZ735	WS Lynx HAS3S [350/CL]	RN No 815 Sqn, *Cumberland* Flt	
XZ736	WS Lynx HMA8 [437/GTi]	RN No 815 Sqn, *Grafton* Flt, Yeovilton	
XZ920	WS61 Sea King HU5SAR [CU]	RN No 826 Sqn, Culdrose	
XZ921	WS61 Sea King HAS6 [269/N]	RN, stored *HMS Sultan*, Gosport	
XZ922	WS61 Sea King HAS6C [WA]	RN/DARA, Fleetlands	
XZ930	WS Gazelle HT3 [Q]	RN AESS, *HMS Sultan*, Gosport	
XZ933	WS Gazelle HT3 [T]	DPA/QinetiQ, Boscombe Down, spares use	
XZ934	WS Gazelle HT3 (G-CBSI) [U]	Privately owned, Redhill	
XZ935	WS Gazelle HCC4 (9332M)	RAF No 1 SoTT, Cosford	
XZ936	WS Gazelle HT2 [6]	DPA/ETPS, Boscombe Down	
XZ937	WS Gazelle HT2 (G-CBKA) [Y]	Privately owned, Stapleford Tawney	
XZ938	WS Gazelle HT2 [45/CU]	RAF	
XZ939	WS Gazelle HT2 [9]	DPA/ETPS, Boscombe Down	
XZ940	WS Gazelle HT2 (G-CBBV) [O]	Privately owned, Navan, Eire	
XZ941	WS Gazelle HT2 [B]	DARA Training School, RAF St Athan, BDRT	
XZ942	WS Gazelle HT2 [42/CU]	AAC, Middle Wallop, instructional use	
XZ964	BAe Harrier GR3 [D]	Royal Engineers Museum, Chatham	
XZ966	BAe Harrier GR3 (9221M) [G]	MoD FSCTE, Manston	
XZ968	BAe Harrier GR3 (9222M) [3G]	Muckleborough Collection, Weybourne	
XZ969	BAe Harrier GR3 [69]	RN, Predannack Fire School	
XZ971	BAe Harrier GR3 (9219M) [G]	MoD Wellington, Somerset, on display	
XZ987	BAe Harrier GR3 (9185M) [C]	RAF Stafford, at main gate	
XZ990	BAe Harrier GR3 <ff>	No 1220 Sqn ATC, March, Cambs	
XZ990	BAe Harrier GR3 <rf>	RAF Wittering, derelict	

Notes	Serial	Type (other identity) [code]	Owner/operator, location or fate
	XZ991	BAe Harrier GR3 (9162M) [3A]	DARA, RAF St Athan, BDRT
	XZ993	BAe Harrier GR3 (9240M) (fuselage)	DARA, RAF St Athan, fire training
	XZ994	BAe Harrier GR3 (9170M) [U]	RAF Air Movements School, Brize Norton
	XZ995	BAe Harrier GR3 (G-CBGK/9220M) [3G]	Privately owned, Lowestoft
	XZ996	BAe Harrier GR3 [96]	SFDO, RNAS Culdrose
	XZ997	BAe Harrier GR3 (9122M) [V]	RAF Museum, Hendon
	ZA101	BAe Hawk 100 (G-HAWK)	DPA/BAE Systems, Warton
	ZA105	WS61 Sea King HAR3	RAF HMF, St Mawgan
	ZA110	BAe Jetstream T2 (F-BTMI) [563/CU]	RN No 750 Sqn, Culdrose
	ZA111	BAe Jetstream T2 (9Q-CTC) [565/CU]	RN No 750 Sqn, Culdrose
	ZA126	WS61 Sea King HAS6C [504/CU]	RN AMG, Yeovilton (conversion)
	ZA127	WS61 Sea King HAS6 [509/CU]	RN, stored HMS Sultan, Gosport
	ZA128	WS61 Sea King HAS6 [010]	RN, stored HMS Sultan, Gosport
	ZA129	WS61 Sea King HAS6 [502/CU]	Westland Helicopters, Yeovil (spares recovery)
	ZA130	WS61 Sea King HU5SAR [709/PW]	RN No 771 Sqn, Prestwick
	ZA131	WS61 Sea King HAS6 [271/N]	RN, stored HMS Sultan, Gosport
	ZA133	WS61 Sea King HAS6 [013]	RN AMG, Culdrose
	ZA134	WS61 Sea King HU5SAR [825/CU]	RN AMG, Culdrose
	ZA135	WS61 Sea King HAS6 [705/CU]	RN No 849 Sqn, HQ Flt, Culdrose
	ZA136	WS61 Sea King HAS6 [018/L]	RN, AESS, HMS Sultan, Gosport (wreck)
	ZA137	WS61 Sea King HU5SAR [820/CU]	RN No 771 Sqn, Culdrose
	ZA142	BAe VC10 K2 (G-ARVI) [C]	RAF/DARA, St Athan, wfu
	ZA147	BAe VC10 K3 (5H-MMT) [F]	RAF No 101 Sqn, Brize Norton
	ZA148	BAe VC10 K3 (5Y-ADA) [G]	RAF No 101 Sqn, Brize Norton
	ZA149	BAe VC10 K3 (5X-UVJ) [H]	RAF No 101 Sqn, Brize Norton
	ZA150	BAe VC10 K3 (5H-MOG)	RAF No 101 Sqn, Brize Norton
	ZA166	WS61 Sea King HU5SAR [189/CU]	RN/DARA, stored Fleetlands
	ZA167	WS61 Sea King HU5SAR [822/CU]	RN No 771 Sqn, Culdrose
	ZA168	WS61 Sea King HAS6 [830/CU]	RN No 771 Sqn, Culdrose
	ZA169	WS61 Sea King HAS6 [515/CW]	RN No 771 Sqn, Culdrose
	ZA170	WS61 Sea King HAS5	RN, stored HMS Sultan, Gosport
	ZA175	BAe Sea Harrier FA2 [717]	RN No 899 Sqn, Yeovilton
	ZA176	BAe Sea Harrier FA2 [006/R]	RN AMG, Yeovilton, wfu
	ZA195	BAe Sea Harrier FA2	RN, Yeovilton, instructional use
	ZA250	BAe Harrier T52 (G-VTOL)	Brooklands Museum, Weybridge
	ZA254	Panavia Tornado F2 (9253M) (fuselage)	RAF Coningsby, instructional use
	ZA267	Panavia Tornado F2 (9284M)	RAF Marham, instructional use
	ZA291	WS61 Sea King HC4 [WX]	RN No 848 Sqn, Yeovilton
	ZA292	WS61 Sea King HC4 [ZR]	DPA/Westland Helicopters, Weston-super-Mare
	ZA293	WS61 Sea King HC4 [WO]	RN No 848 Sqn, Yeovilton
	ZA295	WS61 Sea King HC4 [WR]	RN No 848 Sqn, Yeovilton
	ZA296	WS61 Sea King HC4 [VO]	RN No 846 Sqn, Yeovilton
	ZA297	WS61 Sea King HC4 [C]	RN No 845 Sqn, Yeovilton
	ZA298	WS61 Sea King HC4 [G]	RN No 845 Sqn, Yeovilton
	ZA299	WS61 Sea King HC4 [VV]	RN No 846 Sqn, Yeovilton
	ZA310	WS61 Sea King HC4 [WY]	RN No 848 Sqn, Yeovilton
	ZA312	WS61 Sea King HC4 [ZS]	RN/DARA, Fleetlands
	ZA313	WS61 Sea King HC4 [M]	RN AMG, Yeovilton
	ZA314	WS61 Sea King HC4 [F]	RN No 845 Sqn, Yeovilton
	ZA319	Panavia Tornado GR1	Army, Bicester, on display
	ZA320	Panavia Tornado GR1 (9314M) [TAW]	RAF No 1 SoTT, Cosford
	ZA322	Panavia Tornado GR1 (9334M) [TAC]	RAF Marham, Fire Section
	ZA323	Panavia Tornado GR1 [TAZ]	RAF No 1 SoTT, Cosford
	ZA324	Panavia Tornado GR1 [TAY]	RAF Lossiemouth, BDRT
	ZA325	Panavia Tornado GR1 [TAX]	RAF No 1 SoTT, Cosford
	ZA326	Panavia Tornado GR1P	DPA/AFD/QinetiQ, Boscombe Down
	ZA327	Panavia Tornado GR1	DPA/BAE Systems, Warton
	ZA328	Panavia Tornado GR1	DPA/BAE Systems, Warton
	ZA352	Panavia Tornado GR1 (fuselage)	Scrapped at Chesterfield, 2003
	ZA353	Panavia Tornado GR1 [B-53]	DPA/AFD/QinetiQ, Boscombe Down
	ZA354	Panavia Tornado GR1	DPA/BAE Systems, Warton
	ZA355	Panavia Tornado GR1 [TAA]	RAF Lossiemouth, WLT
	ZA356	Panavia Tornado GR1 <ff>	RAF Marham, instructional use

Serial	Type (other identity) [code]	Owner/operator, location or fate	Notes
ZA357	Panavia Tornado GR1 [TTV]	RAF No 1 SoTT, Cosford	
ZA358	Panavia Tornado GR1	Privately owned, Chesterfield (for scrapping)	
ZA359	Panavia Tornado GR1	BAE Systems Warton, Overseas Customer Training Centre	
ZA360	Panavia Tornado GR1 <ff>	RAF Marham, instructional use	
ZA361	Panavia Tornado GR1 [TD]	RAF ASF, Marham	
ZA362	Panavia Tornado GR1 [TR]	RAF, Lossiemouth, wfu	
ZA365	Panavia Tornado GR4 [AJ-Y]	RAF No 617 Sqn, Lossiemouth	
ZA367	Panavia Tornado GR4 [FW]	RAF No 12 Sqn, Lossiemouth	
ZA369	Panavia Tornado GR4A [U]	RAF No 2 Sqn, Marham	
ZA370	Panavia Tornado GR4A [DB]	RAF/DARA, stored St Athan	
ZA371	Panavia Tornado GR4A [C]	RAF No 2 Sqn, Marham	
ZA372	Panavia Tornado GR4A [E]	RAF No 2 Sqn, Marham	
ZA373	Panavia Tornado GR4A [H]	RAF No 2 Sqn, Marham	
ZA375	Panavia Tornado GR1 (9335M) [AJ-W]	RAF Marham, Fire Section	
ZA393	Panavia Tornado GR4 [FE]	RAF No 12 Sqn, Lossiemouth	
ZA395	Panavia Tornado GR4A [N]	RAF No 2 Sqn, Marham	
ZA398	Panavia Tornado GR4A [S]	RAF No 2 Sqn, Marham	
ZA399	Panavia Tornado GR1 [AJ-C]	RAF/DARA, St Athan, BDRT	
ZA400	Panavia Tornado GR4A [T]	RAF No 2 Sqn, Marham	
ZA401	Panavia Tornado GR4A [P]	RAF No 13 Sqn, Marham	
ZA402	Panavia Tornado GR4A	DPA/BAE Systems, Warton	
ZA404	Panavia Tornado GR4A [W]	RAF No 2 Sqn, Marham	
ZA405	Panavia Tornado GR4A [Y]	RAF No 2 Sqn, Marham	
ZA406	Panavia Tornado GR4 [FU]	RAF No 12 Sqn, Lossiemouth	
ZA407	Panavia Tornado GR1 (9336M) [AJ-N]	RAF Marham, for display	
ZA409	Panavia Tornado GR1 [VII]	RAF Lossiemouth, wfu	
ZA410	Panavia Tornado GR4 [DX]	RAF No 31 Sqn, Marham	
ZA411	Panavia Tornado GR1 [TT]	RAF/DARA, stored St Athan	
ZA412	Panavia Tornado GR4 [TT]	RAF No 15(R) Sqn, Lossiemouth	
ZA446	Panavia Tornado GR4 [A]	RAF No 2 Sqn, Marham	
ZA447	Panavia Tornado GR4 [DE]	RAF No 31 Sqn, Marham	
ZA449	Panavia Tornado GR4 [AJ-N]	RAF No 617 Sqn, Lossiemouth	
ZA450	Panavia Tornado GR1 (9317M) [TH]	RAF No 1 SoTT, Cosford	
ZA452	Panavia Tornado GR4 [DF]	RAF No 31 Sqn, Marham	
ZA453	Panavia Tornado GR4 [FH]	RAF No 12 Sqn, Lossiemouth	
ZA455	Panavia Tornado GR1 [F]	*Scrapped at Chesterfield, 2003*	
ZA456	Panavia Tornado GR4	DPA/AFD/QinetiQ, Boscombe Down	
ZA457	Panavia Tornado GR1 [AJ-J]	RAF Museum, Hendon	
ZA458	Panavia Tornado GR4 [T]	RAF No 15(R) Sqn, Lossiemouth	
ZA459	Panavia Tornado GR4 [F]	RAF No 15(R) Sqn, Lossiemouth	
ZA461	Panavia Tornado GR4 [AC]	RAF No 9 Sqn, Marham	
ZA462	Panavia Tornado GR4A [AJ-P]	RAF No 617 Sqn, Lossiemouth	
ZA463	Panavia Tornado GR4 [TL]	RAF No 15(R) Sqn, Lossiemouth	
ZA465	Panavia Tornado GR1 [FF]	Imperial War Museum, Duxford	
ZA466	Panavia Tornado GR1 <ff>	Privately owned, Chesterfield (for scrapping)	
ZA469	Panavia Tornado GR4 [TM]	RAF No 15(R) Sqn, Lossiemouth	
ZA470	Panavia Tornado GR4 [BQ]	RAF No 14 Sqn, Lossiemouth	
ZA472	Panavia Tornado GR4 [AE]	RAF No 9 Sqn, Marham	
ZA473	Panavia Tornado GR4 [BH]	RAF No 14 Sqn, Lossiemouth	
ZA474	Panavia Tornado GR1 [AJ-F]	RAF Lossiemouth, wfu	
ZA475	Panavia Tornado GR1	RAF Lossiemouth, on display	
ZA490	Panavia Tornado GR1 (fuselage)	*Scrapped at Chesterfield, 2003*	
ZA491	Panavia Tornado GR4 [DL]	RAF No 31 Sqn, Marham	
ZA492	Panavia Tornado GR4 [BO]	RAF No 14 Sqn, Lossiemouth	
ZA541	Panavia Tornado GR4 [III]	RAF No 2 Sqn, Marham	
ZA542	Panavia Tornado GR4 [DM]	RAF No 31 Sqn, Marham	
ZA543	Panavia Tornado GR4 [FO]	RAF No 12 Sqn, Lossiemouth	
ZA544	Panavia Tornado GR4 [FZ]	RAF No 12 Sqn, Lossiemouth	
ZA546	Panavia Tornado GR4 [AG]	RAF No 9 Sqn, Marham	
ZA547	Panavia Tornado GR4 [FF]	RAF No 12 Sqn, Lossiemouth	
ZA548	Panavia Tornado GR4 [T]	RAF No 15(R) Sqn, Lossiemouth	
ZA549	Panavia Tornado GR4 [AJ-Z]	RAF/DARA, St Athan	
ZA550	Panavia Tornado GR4 [DD]	RAF No 31 Sqn, Marham	
ZA551	Panavia Tornado GR4 [AX]	RAF No 9 Sqn, Marham	
ZA552	Panavia Tornado GR4 [TX]	RAF No 15(R) Sqn, Lossiemouth	
ZA553	Panavia Tornado GR4 [DI]	RAF No 31 Sqn, Marham	
ZA554	Panavia Tornado GR4 [BF]	RAF No 14 Sqn, Lossiemouth	

Notes	Serial	Type (other identity) [code]	Owner/operator, location or fate
	ZA556	Panavia Tornado GR4 [AJ-C]	RAF No 617 Sqn, Lossiemouth
	ZA556	Panavia Tornado GR1 <R> (ZA368/BAPC 155) [Z]	RAF M&RU, Bottesford
	ZA557	Panavia Tornado GR4 [TJ]	RAF No 15(R) Sqn, Lossiemouth
	ZA559	Panavia Tornado GR4 [AD]	RAF/DARA, St Athan
	ZA560	Panavia Tornado GR4 [BC]	RAF No 14 Sqn, Lossiemouth
	ZA562	Panavia Tornado GR4 [TO]	RAF No 15(R) Sqn, Lossiemouth
	ZA563	Panavia Tornado GR4 [AG]	RAF No 9 Sqn, Marham
	ZA564	Panavia Tornado GR4 [DK]	RAF No 31 Sqn, Marham
	ZA585	Panavia Tornado GR4 [AH]	RAF No 9 Sqn, Marham
	ZA587	Panavia Tornado GR4 [AJ-M]	RAF No 617 Sqn, Lossiemouth
	ZA588	Panavia Tornado GR4 [BB]	RAF No 14 Sqn, Lossiemouth
	ZA589	Panavia Tornado GR4 [DN]	RAF No 31 Sqn, Marham
	ZA591	Panavia Tornado GR4 [DJ]	RAF No 31 Sqn, Marham
	ZA592	Panavia Tornado GR4 [BJ]	RAF No 14 Sqn, Lossiemouth
	ZA594	Panavia Tornado GR4 [TS]	RAF No 15(R) Sqn, Lossiemouth
	ZA595	Panavia Tornado GR4 [VIII]	RAF No 13 Sqn, Marham
	ZA596	Panavia Tornado GR4 [BL]	RAF No 14 Sqn, Lossiemouth
	ZA597	Panavia Tornado GR4 [AJ-O]	RAF No 617 Sqn, Lossiemouth
	ZA598	Panavia Tornado GR4	RAF No 15(R) Sqn, Lossiemouth
	ZA600	Panavia Tornado GR4 [AJ-L]	RAF No 617 Sqn, Lossiemouth
	ZA601	Panavia Tornado GR4 [TE]	RAF No 15(R) Sqn, Lossiemouth
	ZA602	Panavia Tornado GR4 [XIII]	RAF No 13 Sqn, Marham
	ZA604	Panavia Tornado GR4 [TY]	RAF No 15(R) Sqn, Lossiemouth
	ZA606	Panavia Tornado GR4 [BD]	RAF No 14 Sqn, Lossiemouth
	ZA607	Panavia Tornado GR4 [AB]	RAF No 9 Sqn, Marham
	ZA608	Panavia Tornado GR4	RAF No 15(R) Sqn, Lossiemouth
	ZA609	Panavia Tornado GR4	RAF AWC/SAOEU, Boscombe Down
	ZA611	Panavia Tornado GR4 [TK]	RAF No 15(R) Sqn, Lossiemouth
	ZA612	Panavia Tornado GR4 [TZ]	RAF No 15(R) Sqn, Lossiemouth
	ZA613	Panavia Tornado GR4 [AN]	RAF No 9 Sqn, Marham
	ZA614	Panavia Tornado GR4 [DO]	RAF No 31 Sqn, Marham
	ZA634	Slingsby T61F Venture T2 (G-BUHA) [C]	Privately owned, Saltby
	ZA670	B-V Chinook HC2 (N37010)	RAF/DARA, Fleetlands
	ZA671	B-V Chinook HC2 (N37011)	RAF No 27 Sqn, Odiham
	ZA673	B-V Chinook HC2 (N37016)	RAF No 27 Sqn, Odiham
	ZA674	B-V Chinook HC2 (N37019)	RAF No 18 Sqn, Odiham
	ZA675	B-V Chinook HC2 (N37020)	RAF No 7 Sqn, Odiham
	ZA676	B-V Chinook HC1 (N37021/9230M) [FG] (wreck)	AAC, Wattisham
	ZA677	B-V Chinook HC2 (N37022) [EG]	RAF No 7 Sqn, Odiham
	ZA678	B-V Chinook HC1 (N37023/9229M) [EZ] (wreck)	RAF Odiham, BDRT
	ZA679	B-V Chinook HC2 (N37025)	RAF No 18 Sqn, Odiham
	ZA680	B-V Chinook HC2 (N37026)	RAF No 27 Sqn, Odiham
	ZA681	B-V Chinook HC2 (N37027)	RAF No 27 Sqn, Odiham
	ZA682	B-V Chinook HC2 (N37029) [BT]	RAF/DARA, Fleetlands
	ZA683	B-V Chinook HC2 (N37030) [BD]	RAF No 18 Sqn, Odiham
	ZA684	B-V Chinook HC2 (N37031) [EL]	RAF No 7 Sqn, Odiham
	ZA704	B-V Chinook HC2 (N37033) [EJ]	RAF/DARA, Fleetlands (wreck)
	ZA705	B-V Chinook HC2 (N37035) [BE]	RAF No 18 Sqn, Odiham
	ZA707	B-V Chinook HC2 (N37040)	RAF No 7 Sqn, Odiham
	ZA708	B-V Chinook HC2 (N37042) [EC]	RAF No 18 Sqn, Odiham
	ZA709	B-V Chinook HC2 (N37043) [EQ]	RAF No 27 Sqn, Odiham
	ZA710	B-V Chinook HC2 (N37044) [NC]	RAF/DARA, Fleetlands
	ZA711	B-V Chinook HC2 (N37046) [BA]	RAF No 18 Sqn, Odiham
	ZA712	B-V Chinook HC2 (N37047)	RAF No 18 Sqn, Odiham
	ZA713	B-V Chinook HC2 (N37048)	RAF No 27 Sqn, Odiham
	ZA714	B-V Chinook HC2 (N37051) [NT]	RAF No 18 Sqn, Odiham
	ZA717	B-V Chinook HC1 (N37056/9238M) (wreck)	Trenchard Hall, RAF Cranwell, instructional use
	ZA718	B-V Chinook HC2 (N37058) [BN]	RAF No 18 Sqn, Odiham
	ZA720	B-V Chinook HC2 (N37060) [BR]	RAF No 27 Sqn, Odiham
	ZA726	WS Gazelle AH1 [F1]	AAC No 671 Sqn/2 Regt, Middle Wallop
	ZA728	WS Gazelle AH1 [E]	RM No 847 Sqn, Yeovilton
	ZA729	WS Gazelle AH1	AAC Wattisham, BDRT
	ZA730	WS Gazelle AH1	Sold as G-FUKM, October 2003
	ZA731	WS Gazelle AH1	AAC No 29 Flt, BATUS, Suffield, Canada
	ZA733	WS Gazelle AH1	DARA Fleetlands Apprentice School
	ZA734	WS Gazelle AH1	AAC Middle Wallop (wfu)
	ZA735	WS Gazelle AH1	Army SEAE, Arborfield
	ZA736	WS Gazelle AH1	AAC No 29 Flt, BATUS, Suffield, Canada

Serial	Type (other identity) [code]	Owner/operator, location or fate	Notes
ZA737	WS Gazelle AH1	Museum of Army Flying, Middle Wallop	
ZA766	WS Gazelle AH1	AAC No 665 Sqn/5 Regt, Aldergrove	
ZA768	WS Gazelle AH1 [F] (wreck)	AAC/DARA, stored Fleetlands	
ZA769	WS Gazelle AH1 [K]	Army SEAE, Arborfield	
ZA771	WS Gazelle AH1	AAC No 664 Sqn/9 Regt, Dishforth	
ZA772	WS Gazelle AH1	AAC No 665 Sqn/5 Regt, Aldergrove	
ZA773	WS Gazelle AH1 [F]	AAC No 666(V) Sqn/7 Regt, Netheravon	
ZA774	WS Gazelle AH1	AAC/DARA, stored Fleetlands	
ZA775	WS Gazelle AH1	AAC No 665 Sqn/5 Regt, Aldergrove	
ZA776	WS Gazelle AH1 [F]	RM No 847 Sqn, Yeovilton	
ZA802	WS Gazelle HT3 (G-CBSJ) [W]	Sold as G-HOBZ, May 2003	
ZA803	WS Gazelle HT3 [X]	Sold as 9Q-CMF, 2003	
ZA804	WS Gazelle HT3 [I]	DPA/QinetiQ Boscombe Down, spares use	
ZA934	WS Puma HC1 [BZ]	RAF No 230 Sqn, Aldergrove	
ZA935	WS Puma HC1	RAF/DARA, Fleetlands	
ZA936	WS Puma HC1	RAF No 33 Sqn, Benson	
ZA937	WS Puma HC1	RAF No 230 Sqn, Aldergrove	
ZA938	WS Puma HC1	RAF No 33 Sqn, Benson	
ZA939	WS Puma HC1	RAF No 33 Sqn, Benson	
ZA940	WS Puma HC1	RAF No 33 Sqn, Benson	
ZA947	Douglas Dakota C3 [AI]	RAF BBMF, Coningsby	
ZB500	WS Lynx 800 (G-LYNX/ZA500)	The Helicopter Museum, Weston-super-Mare	
ZB506	WS61 Sea King Mk 4X	DPA/AFD/QinetiQ, Boscombe Down	
ZB507	WS61 Sea King HC4 [ZN]	RN No 848 Sqn, Yeovilton	
ZB601	BAe Harrier T4 (fuselage)	RNAS Yeovilton, Fire Section	
ZB603	BAe Harrier T8 [724]	RN No 899 Sqn, Yeovilton	
ZB604	BAe Harrier T8 [722]	RN No 899 Sqn, Yeovilton	
ZB615	SEPECAT Jaguar T2A	DPA/AFD/QinetiQ, Boscombe Down	
ZB625	WS Gazelle HT3 [N]	DPA/AFD/QinetiQ, Boscombe Down	
ZB627	WS Gazelle HT3 (G-CBSK) [A]	Repainted as G-CBSK	
ZB629	WS Gazelle HCC4 (G-CBZL)	Crashed 22 November 2003, Mouswald, Dumfries	
ZB646	WS Gazelle HT2 (G-CBGZ) [59/CU]	Privately owned, Knebworth	
ZB647	WS Gazelle HT2 (G-CBSF) [40/CU]	Privately owned, Babcary, Somerset	
ZB649	WS Gazelle HT2 (G-SIVJ) [VL]	Privately owned, Redhill	
ZB665	WS Gazelle AH1	AAC No 665 Sqn/5 Regt, Aldergrove	
ZB667	WS Gazelle AH1	AAC Middle Wallop	
ZB668	WS Gazelle AH1 (TAD 015)	Army SEAE, Arborfield	
ZB669	WS Gazelle AH1	AAC No 665 Sqn/5 Regt, Aldergrove	
ZB670	WS Gazelle AH1	AAC/DARA, Fleetlands	
ZB671	WS Gazelle AH1 [2]	AAC No 29 Flt, BATUS, Suffield, Canada	
ZB672	WS Gazelle AH1	Army Training Regiment, Winchester	
ZB673	WS Gazelle AH1	AAC No 671 Sqn/2 Regt, Middle Wallop	
ZB674	WS Gazelle AH1	AAC No 665 Sqn/5 Regt, Aldergrove	
ZB676	WS Gazelle AH1	Crashed 22 December 2003, Derry	
ZB677	WS Gazelle AH1	AAC No 29 Flt, BATUS, Suffield, Canada	
ZB678	WS Gazelle AH1	Army	
ZB679	WS Gazelle AH1	AAC/DARA, stored Fleetlands	
ZB682	WS Gazelle AH1	AAC/DARA, Felletlands	
ZB683	WS Gazelle AH1	AAC No 665 Sqn/5 Regt, Aldergrove	
ZB684	WS Gazelle AH1	RAF Air Movements School, Brize Norton	
ZB685	WS Gazelle AH1	Privately owned, Sproughton	
ZB686	WS Gazelle AH1 <ff>	AAC Middle Wallop, instructional use	
ZB688	WS Gazelle AH1	AAC No 671 Sqn/2 Regt, Middle Wallop	
ZB689	WS Gazelle AH1	AAC No 665 Sqn/5 Regt, Aldergrove	
ZB690	WS Gazelle AH1	AAC/DARA, stored Fleetlands	
ZB691	WS Gazelle AH1	AAC No 656 Sqn/9 Regt, Dishforth	
ZB692	WS Gazelle AH1	AAC No 9 Regt, Dishforth	
ZB693	WS Gazelle AH1	AAC No 665 Sqn/5 Regt, Aldergrove	
ZD230	BAC Super VC10 K4 (G-ASGA) [K]	RAF No 101 Sqn, Brize Norton	
ZD234	BAC Super VC10 K4 (G-ASGF/8700M)	RAF Brize Norton, tanker simulator	
ZD235	BAC Super VC10 K4 (G-ASGG) [L]	RAF/DARA, wfu St Athan	
ZD240	BAC Super VC10 K4 (G-ASGL) [M]	RAF No 101 Sqn, Brize Norton	
ZD241	BAC Super VC10 K4 (G-ASGM) [N]	RAF No 101 Sqn, Brize Norton	
ZD242	BAC Super VC10 K4 (G-ASGP) [P]	RAF No 101 Sqn, Brize Norton	
ZD249	WS Lynx HAS3S [637]	RN No 702 Sqn, Yeovilton	
ZD250	WS Lynx HAS3S [630]	RN No 702 Sqn, Yeovilton	

Notes	Serial	Type (other identity) [code]	Owner/operator, location or fate
	ZD251	WS Lynx HAS3S [636]	RN/DARA, Fleetlands
	ZD252	WS Lynx HMA8 [671]	RN/DARA, Fleetlands
	ZD254	WS Lynx HAS3S [635]	RN No 702 Sqn, Yeovilton
	ZD255	WS Lynx HAS3S [372/NL]	RN No 815 Sqn, *Northumberland* Flt, Yeovilton
	ZD257	WS Lynx HMA8 [308]	RN No 815 Sqn, HQ Flt, Yeovilton
	ZD258	WS Lynx HMA8 (*XZ258*) [345/NC]	RN No 815 Sqn, *Newcastle* Flt, Yeovilton
	ZD259	WS Lynx HMA8 [407/YK]	RN No 815 Sqn, *York* Flt, Yeovilton
	ZD260	WS Lynx HMA8 [360/MC]	RN No 815 Sqn, *Manchester* Flt, Yeovilton
	ZD261	WS Lynx HMA8 [309]	RN/DARA, Fleetlands
	ZD262	WS Lynx HMA8 [420/EX]	RN No 815 Sqn, *Exeter* Flt, Yeovilton
	ZD263	WS Lynx HAS3S [305]	RN No 815 Sqn, HQ Flt, Yeovilton
	ZD264	WS Lynx HAS3S [332/LP]	RN No 815 Sqn, *Liverpool* Flt, Yeovilton
	ZD265	WS Lynx HMA8 [404/IR]	RN No 815 Sqn, *Iron Duke* Flt, Yeovilton
	ZD266	WS Lynx HMA8	DPA/AFD/QinetiQ, Boscombe Down
	ZD267	WS Lynx HMA8	DPA/Westland Helicopters, Yeovil
	ZD268	WS Lynx HMA8	RN/DARA, Fleetlands
	ZD272	WS Lynx AH7 [H]	AAC No 671 Sqn/2 Regt, Middle Wallop
	ZD273	WS Lynx AH7	AAC No 655 Sqn/5 Regt, Aldergrove
	ZD274	WS Lynx AH7	AAC/DARA, Fleetlands
	ZD276	WS Lynx AH7 [X]	AAC No 671 Sqn/2 Regt, Middle Wallop
	ZD277	WS Lynx AH7	AAC No 1 Regt, Brüggen
	ZD278	WS Lynx AH7 [A]	AAC No 655 Sqn/5 Regt, Aldergrove
	ZD279	WS Lynx AH7	RN/DARA, stored Fleetlands
	ZD280	WS Lynx AH7	AAC No 652 Sqn/1 Regt, Brüggen
	ZD281	WS Lynx AH7 [K]	AAC No 671 Sqn/2 Regt, Middle Wallop
	ZD282	WS Lynx AH7 [L]	RM No 847 Sqn, Yeovilton
	ZD283	WS Lynx AH7	AAC/DARA, Fleetlands
	ZD284	WS Lynx AH7 [H]	AAC No 661 Sqn/1 Regt, Brüggen
	ZD285	WS Lynx AH7	DPA/AFD/QinetiQ, Boscombe Down
	ZD318	BAe Harrier GR7A	DPA/BAE Systems, Warton
	ZD319	BAe Harrier GR7	DPA/BAE Systems, Warton
	ZD320	BAe Harrier GR9	DPA/BAE Systems, Warton
	ZD321	BAe Harrier GR7 [02]	RAF/DARA, St Athan
	ZD322	BAe Harrier GR7 [03]	RAF No 1 Sqn, Cottesmore
	ZD323	BAe Harrier GR7 [04]	RAF No 4 Sqn, Cottesmore
	ZD327	BAe Harrier GR7 [08]	RAF No 4 Sqn, Cottesmore
	ZD328	BAe Harrier GR7 [09]	RAF HOCU/No 20(R) Sqn, Wittering
	ZD329	BAe Harrier GR7 [10]	RAF No 4 Sqn, Cottesmore
	ZD330	BAe Harrier GR7 [11]	RAF HOCU/No 20(R) Sqn, Wittering
	ZD346	BAe Harrier GR7 [13]	RAF No 1 Sqn, Cottesmore
	ZD347	BAe Harrier GR7A [14A]	RAF No 3 Sqn, Cottesmore
	ZD348	BAe Harrier GR7 [15]	RAF No 1 Sqn, Cottesmore
	ZD350	BAe Harrier GR5 (9189M) <ff>	DARA, RAF St Athan, BDRT
	ZD351	BAe Harrier GR7 [18]	RAF HOCU/No 20(R) Sqn, Wittering
	ZD352	BAe Harrier GR7 [19]	RAF No 3 Sqn, Cottesmore
	ZD353	BAe Harrier GR5 (fuselage)	BAE Systems, Brough
	ZD354	BAe Harrier GR7 [21]	RAF HOCU/No 20(R) Sqn, Wittering
	ZD375	BAe Harrier GR7 [23]	RAF No 1 Sqn, Cottesmore
	ZD376	BAe Harrier GR7A [24A]	RAF No 3 Sqn, Cottesmore
	ZD378	BAe Harrier GR7 [26]	RAF No 4 Sqn, Cottesmore
	ZD379	BAe Harrier GR7 [27]	RAF HOCU/No 20(R) Sqn, Wittering
	ZD380	BAe Harrier GR7 [28]	RAF No 4 Sqn, Cottesmore
	ZD401	BAe Harrier GR7 [30]	RAF No 3 Sqn, Cottesmore
	ZD402	BAe Harrier GR7 [31]	RAF HOCU/No 20(R) Sqn, Wittering
	ZD403	BAe Harrier GR7A [32A]	RAF No 3 Sqn, Cottesmore
	ZD404	BAe Harrier GR7A [33A]	RAF HOCU/No 20(R) Sqn, Wittering
	ZD405	BAe Harrier GR7 [34]	RAF No 1 Sqn, Cottesmore
	ZD406	BAe Harrier GR7 [35]	RAF HOCU/No 20(R) Sqn, Wittering
	ZD407	BAe Harrier GR7 [36]	RAF HOCU/No 20(R) Sqn, Wittering
	ZD408	BAe Harrier GR7 [37]	RAF No 4 Sqn, Cottesmore
	ZD409	BAe Harrier GR7 [38]	RAF No 4 Sqn, Cottesmore
	ZD410	BAe Harrier GR7 [39]	RAF No 3 Sqn, Cottesmore
	ZD411	BAe Harrier GR7	RAF/DARA, St Athan
	ZD412	BAe Harrier GR5 (fuselage)	RAF/DARA, St Athan, instructional use
	ZD431	BAe Harrier GR7A [43A]	RAF No 4 Sqn, Cottesmore
	ZD433	BAe Harrier GR7 [45]	RAF/DARA, St Athan
	ZD435	BAe Harrier GR7 [47]	RAF No 1 Sqn, Cottesmore
	ZD436	BAe Harrier GR7A [48A]	RAF HOCU/No 20(R) Sqn, Wittering
	ZD437	BAe Harrier GR7 [49]	RAF/DARA, St Athan (damaged)
	ZD438	BAe Harrier GR7 [50]	RAF No 1 Sqn, Cottesmore
	ZD461	BAe Harrier GR7A [51A]	RAF No 3 Sqn, Cottesmore
	ZD462	BAe Harrier GR7 (9302M) [52]	RAF No 1 SoTT, Cosford

Serial	Type (other identity) [code]	Owner/operator, location or fate	Notes
ZD463	BAe Harrier GR7 [53]	RAF No 1 Sqn, Cottesmore	
ZD465	BAe Harrier GR7A [55A]	RAF No 3 Sqn, Cottesmore	
ZD466	BAe Harrier GR7 [56]	RAF HOCU/No 20(R) Sqn, Wittering	
ZD467	BAe Harrier GR7 [57]	RAF No 1 Sqn, Cottesmore	
ZD468	BAe Harrier GR7 [58]	RAF No 1 Sqn, Cottesmore	
ZD469	BAe Harrier GR7 [59]	RAF/DARA, St Athan	
ZD470	BAe Harrier GR7 [60]	RAF No 3 Sqn, Cottesmore	
ZD476	WS61 Sea King HC4 [WU]	RN No 848 Sqn, Yeovilton	
ZD477	WS61 Sea King HC4 [H]	RN No 845 Sqn, Yeovilton	
ZD478	WS61 Sea King HC4 [VX]	RN No 846 Sqn, Yeovilton	
ZD479	WS61 Sea King HC4 [WV]	RN/DARA, Fleetlands	
ZD480	WS61 Sea King HC4 [E]	RN No 845 Sqn, Yeovilton	
ZD559	WS Lynx AH5X	DPA/AFD/QinetiQ, Boscombe Down	
ZD560	WS Lynx AH7	DPA/ETPS, Boscombe Down	
ZD565	WS Lynx HMA8 [307]	RN No 815 Sqn, HQ Flt, Yeovilton	
ZD566	WS Lynx HMA8 [670]	RN No 702 Sqn, Yeovilton	
ZD574	B-V Chinook HC2 (N37077)	RAF No 27 Sqn, Odiham	
ZD575	B-V Chinook HC2 (N37078)	RAF No 18 Sqn, Odiham	
ZD578	BAe Sea Harrier FA2 [000,122]	RNAS Yeovilton, at main gate	
ZD579	BAe Sea Harrier FA2 [128/R]	RN No 800 Sqn, Yeovilton	
ZD580	BAe Sea Harrier FA2	Privately owned, Sproughton	
ZD581	BAe Sea Harrier FA2	RN/DARA, stored St Athan	
ZD582	BAe Sea Harrier FA2 [124/R]	RN No 800 Sqn, Yeovilton	
ZD607	BAe Sea Harrier FA2	RAF St Athan, BDRT	
ZD608	BAe Sea Harrier FA2 [731]	RN/DARA, St Athan (spares recovery)	
ZD610	BAe Sea Harrier FA2 [126/R]	RN No 800 Sqn, Yeovilton	
ZD611	BAe Sea Harrier FA2	RN/DARA, St Athan	
ZD612	BAe Sea Harrier FA2	RN ETS, Yeovilton	
ZD613	BAe Sea Harrier FA2 [127/R]	RN No 800 Sqn, Yeovilton	
ZD614	BAe Sea Harrier FA2 [122/R]	Privately owned, Sproughton	
ZD615	BAe Sea Harrier FA2	RN/DARA, stored St Athan	
ZD620	BAe 125 CC3	RAF No 32(The Royal) Sqn, Northolt	
ZD621	BAe 125 CC3	RAF No 32(The Royal) Sqn, Northolt	
ZD625	WS61 Sea King HC4 [VZ]	RN AMG, Yeovilton	
ZD626	WS61 Sea King HC4 [ZZ]	RN No 848 Sqn, Yeovilton	
ZD627	WS61 Sea King HC4 [VR]	RN No 846 Sqn, Yeovilton	
ZD630	WS61 Sea King HAS6 [012/L]	RN AMG, Culdrose	
ZD631	WS61 Sea King HAS6 [66] (fuselage)	RN, Predannack Fire School	
ZD633	WS61 Sea King HAS6 [014/L]	RN, stored HMS Sultan, Gosport	
ZD634	WS61 Sea King HAS6 [503]	RN No 771 Sqn, Culdrose	
ZD636	WS61 Sea King AEW7 [183/L]	RN AMG, Culdrose	
ZD637	WS61 Sea King HAS6 [700/PW]	RN, stored HMS Sultan, Gosport	
ZD667	BAe Harrier GR3 (9201M) [67]	SFDO, RNAS Culdrose	
ZD668	BAe Harrier GR3 (G-CBCU) [3E]	Privately owned, Lowestoft	
ZD670	BAe Harrier GR3 [3A]	The Trocadero, Leicester Square, London	
ZD703	BAe 125 CC3	RAF No 32(The Royal) Sqn, Northolt	
ZD704	BAe 125 CC3	RAF No 32(The Royal) Sqn, Northolt	
ZD707	Panavia Tornado GR4 [TB]	RAF No 15(R) Sqn, Lossiemouth	
ZD708	Panavia Tornado GR4	DPA/BAE Systems, Warton	
ZD709	Panavia Tornado GR4 [DH]	RAF No 31 Sqn, Marham	
ZD710	Panavia Tornado GR1 <ff>	Privately owned, Barnstaple	
ZD711	Panavia Tornado GR4 [II]	RAF No 2 Sqn, Marham	
ZD712	Panavia Tornado GR4 [TR]	RAF No 15(R) Sqn, Lossiemouth	
ZD713	Panavia Tornado GR4 [AJ-F]	RAF No 617 Sqn, Lossiemouth	
ZD714	Panavia Tornado GR4	RAF No 617 Sqn, Lossiemouth	
ZD715	Panavia Tornado GR4	RAF AWC/SAOEU, Boscombe Down	
ZD716	Panavia Tornado GR4 [AJ]	RAF No 9 Sqn, Marham	
ZD719	Panavia Tornado GR4 [BS]	RAF No 14 Sqn, Lossiemouth	
ZD720	Panavia Tornado GR4 [TA]	RAF No 15(R) Sqn, Lossiemouth	
ZD739	Panavia Tornado GR4	RAF AWC/SAOEU, Boscombe Down	
ZD740	Panavia Tornado GR4 [DR]	RAF No 14 Sqn, Lossiemouth	
ZD741	Panavia Tornado GR4 [BZ]	RAF No 14 Sqn, Lossiemouth	
ZD742	Panavia Tornado GR4 [FY]	RAF No 15(R) Sqn, Lossiemouth	
ZD743	Panavia Tornado GR4 [TQ]	RAF No 15(R) Sqn, Lossiemouth	
ZD744	Panavia Tornado GR4 [FD]	RAF Lossiemouth, WLT	
ZD745	Panavia Tornado GR4 [DA]	RAF No 31 Sqn, Marham	
ZD746	Panavia Tornado GR4 [TH]	RAF No 15(R) Sqn, Lossiemouth	
ZD747	Panavia Tornado GR4 [AL]	RAF No 9 Sqn, Marham	
ZD748	Panavia Tornado GR4 [FC]	RAF No 12 Sqn, Lossiemouth	
ZD749	Panavia Tornado GR4 [AP]	RAF No 13 Sqn, Marham	
ZD788	Panavia Tornado GR4 [BE]	RAF No 14 Sqn, Lossiemouth	
ZD789	Panavia Tornado GR1 <ff>	RAF, stored Shawbury	

Notes	Serial	Type (other identity) [code]	Owner/operator, location or fate
	ZD790	Panavia Tornado GR4 [FM]	RAF No 12 Sqn, Lossiemouth
	ZD792	Panavia Tornado GR4	RAF/DARA, stored St Athan
	ZD793	Panavia Tornado GR4 [B]	RAF No 15(R) Sqn, Lossiemouth
	ZD810	Panavia Tornado GR4 [TD]	RAF No 15(R) Sqn, Lossiemouth
	ZD811	Panavia Tornado GR4 [BK]	RAF No 14 Sqn, Lossiemouth
	ZD812	Panavia Tornado GR4 [TU]	RAF No 15(R) Sqn, Lossiemouth
	ZD842	Panavia Tornado GR4 [TV]	RAF No 15(R) Sqn, Lossiemouth
	ZD843	Panavia Tornado GR4 [TG]	RAF No 15(R) Sqn, Lossiemouth
	ZD844	Panavia Tornado GR4 [AJ-A]	RAF No 617 Sqn, Lossiemouth
	ZD847	Panavia Tornado GR4 [AA]	RAF No 9 Sqn, Marham
	ZD848	Panavia Tornado GR4 [AE]	DPA/BAE Systems, Warton
	ZD849	Panavia Tornado GR4 [FG]	RAF No 12 Sqn, Lossiemouth
	ZD850	Panavia Tornado GR4 [AJ-T]	RAF No 617 Sqn, Lossiemouth
	ZD851	Panavia Tornado GR4 [FP]	RAF No 12 Sqn, Lossiemouth
	ZD890	Panavia Tornado GR4 [FD]	RAF No 12 Sqn, Lossiemouth
	ZD892	Panavia Tornado GR4 [TG]	RAF, stored St Athan
	ZD895	Panavia Tornado GR4 [TI]	RAF No 15(R) Sqn, Lossiemouth
	ZD899	Panavia Tornado F2	DPA/BAE Systems, Warton
	ZD900	Panavia Tornado F2 (comp ZE343) (fuselage)	Scrapped at Chesterfield, 2003
	ZD902	Panavia Tornado F2A(TIARA)	DPA/AFD/QinetiQ, Boscombe Down
	ZD903	Panavia Tornado F2 (comp ZE728) (fuselage)	RAF St Athan Fire Section
	ZD905	Panavia Tornado F2 (comp ZE258) (fuselage)	Scrapped at Chesterfield, 2003
	ZD906	Panavia Tornado F2 (comp ZE294) <ff>	RAF Leuchars, BDRT
	ZD932	Panavia Tornado F2 (comp ZE255) (fuselage)	RAF St Athan, BDRT
	ZD933	Panavia Tornado F2 (comp ZE729) (fuselage)	Scrapped at Chesterfield, 2003
	ZD934	Panavia Tornado F2 (comp ZE786) <ff>	RAF Leeming, GI use
	ZD935	Panavia Tornado F2 (comp ZE793) <ff>	RAF, stored Shawbury
	ZD936	Panavia Tornado F2 (comp ZE251) <ff>	Boscombe Down Museum
	ZD938	Panavia Tornado F2 (comp ZE295) <ff>	RAF, stored Shawbury
	ZD939	Panavia Tornado F2 (comp ZE292) <ff>	RAF Cosford, instructional use
	ZD940	Panavia Tornado F2 (comp ZE288) (fuselage)	RAF St Athan Fire Section
	ZD948	Lockheed TriStar KC1 (G-BFCA)	RAF No 216 Sqn, Brize Norton
	ZD949	Lockheed TriStar K1 (G-BFCB)	RAF No 216 Sqn, Brize Norton
	ZD950	Lockheed TriStar KC1 (G-BFCC)	RAF No 216 Sqn, Brize Norton
	ZD951	Lockheed TriStar K1 (G-BFCD)	RAF No 216 Sqn, Brize Norton
	ZD952	Lockheed TriStar KC1 (G-BFCE)	RAF No 216 Sqn, Brize Norton
	ZD953	Lockheed TriStar KC1 (G-BFCF)	RAF No 216 Sqn, Brize Norton
	ZD980	B-V Chinook HC2 (N37082)	RAF No 18 Sqn, Odiham
	ZD981	B-V Chinook HC2 (N37083) [BH]	RAF No 18 Sqn, Odiham
	ZD982	B-V Chinook HC2 (N37085) [BI]	RAF No 18 Sqn, Odiham
	ZD983	B-V Chinook HC2 (N37086)	RAF/DARA, Fleetlands
	ZD984	B-V Chinook HC2 (N37088)	RAF No 18 Sqn, Odiham
	ZD990	BAe Harrier T8 [721]	RN No 899 Sqn, Yeovilton
	ZD991	BAe Harrier T8 (9228M) [722/VL]	Privately owned, Sproughton
	ZD993	BAe Harrier T8 [723/VL]	RN/DARA, St Athan
	ZD996	Panavia Tornado GR4A [I]	DPA/AFD/QinetiQ, Boscombe Down
	ZE116	Panavia Tornado GR4A [X]	RAF No 13 Sqn, Marham
	ZE154	Panavia Tornado F3 (comp ZD901) [LT]	RAF No 25 Sqn, Leeming
	ZE155	Panavia Tornado F3	DPA/BAE Systems, Warton
	ZE156	Panavia Tornado F3 [UX]	RAF F3 OCU/No 56(R) Sqn, Leuchars
	ZE157	Panavia Tornado F3 [TY]	RAF No 25 Sqn, Leeming
	ZE158	Panavia Tornado F3 [UW]	RAF/DARA, St Athan
	ZE159	Panavia Tornado F3 [UV]	RAF No 111 Sqn, Leuchars
	ZE160	Panavia Tornado F3 [TX]	RAF F3 OCU/No 56(R) Sqn, Leuchars
	ZE161	Panavia Tornado F3 [UU]	RAF/DARA, St Athan
	ZE162	Panavia Tornado F3 [UR]	RAF No 111 Sqn, Leuchars
	ZE163	Panavia Tornado F3 (comp ZG753) [TW]	RAF No 43 Sqn, Leuchars
	ZE164	Panavia Tornado F3 [UQ]	RAF No 43 Sqn, Leuchars

Serial	Type (other identity) [code]	Owner/operator, location or fate	Notes
ZE165	Panavia Tornado F3 [UP]	RAF No 43 Sqn, Leuchars	
ZE168	Panavia Tornado F3 [UN]	RAF No 11 Sqn, Leeming	
ZE199	Panavia Tornado F3 [TV]	RAF F3 OCU/No 56(R) Sqn, Leuchars	
ZE200	Panavia Tornado F3 [UM]	RAF/DARA, St Athan	
ZE201	Panavia Tornado F3 [UL]	RAF No 25 Sqn, Leeming	
ZE203	Panavia Tornado F3 [UK]	RAF No 11 Sqn, Leeming	
ZE204	Panavia Tornado F3 [UJ]	RAF No 25 Sqn, Leeming	
ZE206	Panavia Tornado F3 [UI]	RAF No 43 Sqn, Leuchars	
ZE207	Panavia Tornado F3 [UH]	RAF F3 OCU/No 56(R) Sqn, Leuchars	
ZE209	Panavia Tornado F3 [AX]	RAF/EADS, Munich, Germany	
ZE250	Panavia Tornado F3 [TR]	RAF F3 OCU/No 56(R) Sqn, Leuchars	
ZE251	Panavia Tornado F3 (comp ZD936) [UF]	RAF No 111 Sqn, Leuchars	
ZE252	Panavia Tornado F3 (MM7225)	RAF/DARA, stored St Athan	
ZE253	Panavia Tornado F3 [AC]	RAF/EADS, Munich, Germany	
ZE254	Panavia Tornado F3 (comp ZD941) [UD]	RAF No 25 Sqn, Leeming	
ZE255	Panavia Tornado F3 (comp ZD932) [UC]	RAF No 25 Sqn, Leeming	
ZE256	Panavia Tornado F3 [TP]	RAF Leuchars, instructional use	
ZE257	Panavia Tornado F3 [UB]	RAF No 43 Sqn, Leuchars	
ZE258	Panavia Tornado F3 (comp ZD905) [UA]	RAF No 1435 Flt, Mount Pleasant, FI	
ZE287	Panavia Tornado F3 [TO]	RAF No 11 Sqn, Leeming	
ZE288	Panavia Tornado F3 (comp ZD940) [VY]	RAF No 111 Sqn, Leuchars	
ZE289	Panavia Tornado F3 [VX]	RAF No 111 Sqn, Leuchars	
ZE290	Panavia Tornado F3	RAF/DARA, stored St Athan	
ZE291	Panavia Tornado F3 [VW]	RAF No 43 Sqn, Leuchars	
ZE292	Panavia Tornado F3 (comp ZD939) [YY]	RAF No 25 Sqn, Leeming	
ZE293	Panavia Tornado F3 [TL]	RAF F3 OCU/No 56(R) Sqn, Leuchars	
ZE294	Panavia Tornado F3 (comp ZD906) [YX]	RAF No 11 Sqn, Leeming	
ZE295	Panavia Tornado F3 (comp ZD938) [DC]	RAF No 11 Sqn, Leeming	
ZE296	Panavia Tornado F3 [AD]	*To EADS, Munich, November 2003*	
ZE338	Panavia Tornado F3 [YV]	RAF No 43 Sqn, Leuchars	
ZE339	Panavia Tornado F3	RAF/DARA, stored St Athan	
ZE340	Panavia Tornado F3 (*ZE758*/ 9298M) [GO]	RAF No 1 SoTT, Cosford	
ZE341	Panavia Tornado F3 [YU]	RAF No 11 Sqn, Leeming	
ZE342	Panavia Tornado F3 [YS]	RAF No 11 Sqn, Leeming	
ZE343	Panavia Tornado F3 (comp ZD900) [TI]	RAF F3 OCU/No 56(R) Sqn, Leuchars	
ZE350	McD F-4J(UK) Phantom (9080M) <ff>	Privately owned, Ingatestone, Essex	
ZE352	McD F-4J(UK) Phantom (9086M) <ff>	Privately owned, Hooton Park, Cheshire	
ZE356	McD F-4J(UK) Phantom (9060M) [Q]	RAF Waddington, BDRT	
ZE360	McD F-4J(UK) Phantom (9059M) [O]	MoD FSCTE, Manston	
ZE368	WS61 Sea King HAR3	RAF No 202 Sqn, A Flt, Boulmer	
ZE369	WS61 Sea King HAR3	RAF No 202 Sqn, D Flt, Lossiemouth	
ZE370	WS61 Sea King HAR3 [T]	RAF No 202 Sqn, D Flt, Lossiemouth	
ZE375	WS Lynx AH9 [2,9]	AAC No 653 Sqn/3 Regt, Wattisham	
ZE376	WS Lynx AH9	AAC No 659 Sqn/4 Regt, Wattisham	
ZE378	WS Lynx AH7	AAC No 4 Regt, Wattisham	
ZE379	WS Lynx AH7	AAC/DARA, stored Fleetlands	
ZE380	WS Lynx AH9	AAC No 662 Sqn/3 Regt, Wattisham	
ZE381	WS Lynx AH7	AAC No 657 Sqn, Odiham	
ZE382	WS Lynx AH9	AAC No 659 Sqn/4 Regt, Wattisham	
ZE395	BAe 125 CC3	RAF No 32(The Royal) Sqn, Northolt	
ZE396	BAe 125 CC3	RAF No 32(The Royal) Sqn, Northolt	
ZE410	Agusta A109A (AE-334)	AAC No 8 Flt, Credenhill	
ZE411	Agusta A109A (AE-331)	AAC No 8 Flt, Credenhill	
ZE412	Agusta A109A	AAC No 8 Flt, Credenhill	
ZE413	Agusta A109A	AAC No 8 Flt, Credenhill	
ZE418	WS61 Sea King AEW7 [185]	RN AMG, Culdrose (conversion)	
ZE420	WS61 Sea King AEW7 [184/L]	RN AMG, Culdrose (conversion)	
ZE422	WS61 Sea King HAS6 [508/CT]	RN No 771 Sqn, Culdrose	
ZE425	WS61 Sea King HC4 [J]	RN No 845 Sqn, Yeovilton	

ZE426 – ZE558

Notes	Serial	Type (other identity) [code]	Owner/operator, location or fate
	ZE426	WS61 Sea King HC4 [WW]	RN No 848 Sqn, Yeovilton
	ZE427	WS61 Sea King HC4 [B]	RN No 845 Sqn, Yeovilton
	ZE428	WS61 Sea King HC4 [VS]	RN No 846 Sqn, Yeovilton
	ZE432	BAC 1-11/479FU (DQ-FBV)	DPA/ETPS, Boscombe Down
	ZE433	BAC 1-11/479FU (DQ-FBQ)	DPA/GEC-Ferranti, Edinburgh
	ZE438	BAe Jetstream T3 [76]	RN FONA/Heron Flight, Yeovilton
	ZE439	BAe Jetstream T3 [77]	RN, stored Shawbury
	ZE440	BAe Jetstream T3 [78]	RN FONA/Heron Flight, Yeovilton
	ZE441	BAe Jetstream T3 [79]	RN FONA/Heron Flight, Yeovilton
	ZE449	SA330L Puma HC1 (9017M/PA-12)	RAF No 33 Sqn, Benson
	ZE477	WS Lynx 3	The Helicopter Museum, Weston-super-Mare
	ZE495	Grob G103 Viking T1 (BGA3000) [VA]	RAF No 622 VGS, Upavon
	ZE496	Grob G103 Viking T1 (BGA3001) [VB]	RAF No 615 VGS, Kenley
	ZE498	Grob G103 Viking T1 (BGA3003) [VC]	RAF No 614 VGS, Wethersfield
	ZE499	Grob G103 Viking T1 (BGA3004) [VD]	RAF No 615 VGS, Kenley
	ZE501	Grob G103 Viking T1 (BGA3006) [VE]	RAF, stored CGMF Syerston
	ZE502	Grob G103 Viking T1 (BGA3007) [VF]	RAF ACCGS, Syerston
	ZE503	Grob G103 Viking T1 (BGA3008) [VG]	RAF No 625 VGS, Hullavington
	ZE504	Grob G103 Viking T1 (BGA3009) [VH]	RAF No 621 VGS, Hullavington
	ZE520	Grob G103 Viking T1 (BGA3010) [VJ]	RAF No 625 VGS, Hullavington
	ZE521	Grob G103 Viking T1 (BGA3011) [VK]	RAF No 626 VGS, Predannack
	ZE522	Grob G103 Viking T1 (BGA3012) [VL]	RAF No 621 VGS, Hullavington
	ZE524	Grob G103 Viking T1 (BGA3014) [VM]	RAF No 625 VGS, Hullavington
	ZE526	Grob G103 Viking T1 (BGA3016) [VN]	RAF No 662 VGS, Arbroath
	ZE527	Grob G103 Viking T1 (BGA3017) [VP]	RAF No 626 VGS, Predannack
	ZE528	Grob G103 Viking T1 (BGA3018) [VQ]	RAF No 614 VGS, Wethersfield
	ZE529	Grob G103 Viking T1 (BGA3019) (comp ZE655) [VR]	RAF CGMF, Syerston
	ZE530	Grob G103 Viking T1 (BGA3020) [VS]	RAF No 611 VGS, Watton
	ZE531	Grob G103 Viking T1 (BGA3021) [VT]	RAF No 615 VGS, Kenley
	ZE532	Grob G103 Viking T1 (BGA3022) [VU]	RAF No 614 VGS, Wethersfield
	ZE533	Grob G103 Viking T1 (BGA3023) [VV]	RAF No 622 VGS, Upavon
	ZE534	Grob G103 Viking T1 (BGA3024) [VW]	RAF CGMF, Syerston
	ZE550	Grob G103 Viking T1 (BGA3025) [VX]	RAF No 614 VGS, Wethersfield
	ZE551	Grob G103 Viking T1 (BGA3026) [VY]	RAF No 614 VGS, Wethersfield
	ZE552	Grob G103 Viking T1 (BGA3027) [VZ]	RAF ACCGS, Syerston
	ZE553	Grob G103 Viking T1 (BGA3028) [WA]	RAF No 611 VGS, Watton
	ZE554	Grob G103 Viking T1 (BGA3029) [WB]	RAF No 611 VGS, Watton
	ZE555	Grob G103 Viking T1 (BGA3030) [WC]	RAF No 625 VGS, Hullavington
	ZE556	Grob G103 Viking T1 (BGA3031) [WD]	RAF CGMF, Syerston (damaged)
	ZE557	Grob G103 Viking T1 (BGA3032) [WE]	RAF No 622 VGS, Upavon
	ZE558	Grob G103 Viking T1 (BGA3033) [WF]	RAF No 615 VGS, Kenley

Serial	Type (other identity) [code]	Owner/operator, location or fate	Notes
ZE559	Grob G103 Viking T1 (BGA3034) [WG]	RAF No 631 VGS, Sealand	
ZE560	Grob G103 Viking T1 (BGA3035) [WH]	RAF No 661 VGS, Kirknewton	
ZE561	Grob G103 Viking T1 (BGA3036) [WJ]	RAF, stored CGMF Syerston	
ZE562	Grob G103 Viking T1 (BGA3037) [WK]	RAF No 626 VGS, Predannack	
ZE563	Grob G103 Viking T1 (BGA3038) [WL]	RAF No 621 VGS, Hullavington	
ZE564	Grob G103 Viking T1 (BGA3039) [WN]	RAF, stored CGMF Syerston	
ZE584	Grob G103 Viking T1 (BGA3040) [WP]	RAF ACCGS, Syerston	
ZE585	Grob G103 Viking T1 (BGA3041) [WQ]	RAF No 626 VGS, Predannack	
ZE586	Grob G103 Viking T1 (BGA3042) [WR]	RAF No 631 VGS, Sealand	
ZE587	Grob G103 Viking T1 (BGA3043) [WS]	RAF No 611 VGS, Watton	
ZE590	Grob G103 Viking T1 (BGA3046) [WT]	RAF No 661 VGS, Kirknewton	
ZE591	Grob G103 Viking T1 (BGA3047) [WU]	RAF No 631 VGS, Sealand	
ZE592	Grob G103 Viking T1 (BGA3048) [WV]	RAF No 621 VGS, Hullavington	
ZE593	Grob G103 Viking T1 (BGA3049) [WW]	RAF, stored CGMF Syerston	
ZE594	Grob G103 Viking T1 (BGA3050) [WX]	RAF No 615 VGS, Kenley	
ZE595	Grob G103 Viking T1 (BGA3051) [WY]	RAF No 622 VGS, Upavon	
ZE600	Grob G103 Viking T1 (BGA3052) [WZ]	RAF No 622 VGS, Upavon	
ZE601	Grob G103 Viking T1 (BGA3053) [XA]	RAF No 611 VGS, Watton	
ZE602	Grob G103 Viking T1 (BGA3054) [XB]	RAF No 621 VGS, Hullavington	
ZE603	Grob G103 Viking T1 (BGA3055) [XC]	RAF CGMF, Syerston	
ZE604	Grob G103 Viking T1 (BGA3056) [XD]	RAF No 615 VGS, Kenley	
ZE605	Grob G103 Viking T1 (BGA3057) [XE]	RAF, stored CGMF Syerston	
ZE606	Grob G103 Viking T1 (BGA3058) [XF]	RAF CGMF, Syerston	
ZE607	Grob G103 Viking T1 (BGA3059) [XG]	RAF, stored CGMF Syerston	
ZE608	Grob G103 Viking T1 (BGA3060) [XH]	RAF, stored CGMF Syerston	
ZE609	Grob G103 Viking T1 (BGA3061) [XJ]	RAF CGMF, Syerston	
ZE610	Grob G103 Viking T1 (BGA3062) [XK]	RAF No 615 VGS, Kenley	
ZE611	Grob G103 Viking T1 (BGA3063) [XL]	RAF No 611 VGS, Watton	
ZE613	Grob G103 Viking T1 (BGA3065) [XM]	RAF No 625 VGS, Hullavington	
ZE614	Grob G103 Viking T1 (BGA3066) [XN]	RAF No 631 VGS, Sealand	
ZE625	Grob G103 Viking T1 (BGA3067) [XP]	RAF No 625 VGS, Hullavington	
ZE626	Grob G103 Viking T1 (BGA3068) [XQ]	RAF No 626 VGS, Predannack	
ZE627	Grob G103 Viking T1 (BGA3069) [XR]	RAF No 631 VGS, Sealand	
ZE628	Grob G103 Viking T1 (BGA3070) [XS]	RAF No 661 VGS, Kirknewton	
ZE629	Grob G103 Viking T1 (BGA3071) [XT]	RAF No 662 VGS, Arbroath	
ZE630	Grob G103 Viking T1 (BGA3072) [XU]	RAF No 662 VGS, Arbroath	

Notes	Serial	Type (other identity) [code]	Owner/operator, location or fate
	ZE631	Grob G103 Viking T1 (BGA3073) [XV]	RAF No 662 VGS, Arbroath
	ZE632	Grob G103 Viking T1 (BGA3074) [XW]	RAF No 621 VGS, Hullavington
	ZE633	Grob G103 Viking T1 (BGA3075) [XX]	RAF No 614 VGS, Wethersfield
	ZE635	Grob G103 Viking T1 (BGA3077) [XY]	RAF, stored CGMF Syerston
	ZE636	Grob G103 Viking T1 (BGA3078) [XZ]	RAF, stored CGMF Syerston
	ZE637	Grob G103 Viking T1 (BGA3079) [YA]	RAF ACCGS, Syerston
	ZE650	Grob G103 Viking T1 (BGA3080) [YB]	RAF No 622 VGS, Upavon
	ZE651	Grob G103 Viking T1 (BGA3081) [YC]	RAF No 661 VGS, Kirknewton
	ZE652	Grob G103 Viking T1 (BGA3082) [YD]	RAF No 625 VGS, Hullavington
	ZE653	Grob G103 Viking T1 (BGA3083) [YE]	RAF No 661 VGS, Kirknewton
	ZE656	Grob G103 Viking T1 (BGA3086) [YH]	RAF No 625 VGS, Hullavington
	ZE657	Grob G103 Viking T1 (BGA3087) [YJ]	RAF No 615 VGS, Kenley
	ZE658	Grob G103 Viking T1 (BGA3088) [YK]	RAF CGMF, Syerston
	ZE659	Grob G103 Viking T1 (BGA3089) [YL]	*To BGA 5069, September 2003*
	ZE677	Grob G103 Viking T1 (BGA3090) [YM]	RAF No 621 VGS, Hullavington
	ZE678	Grob G103 Viking T1 (BGA3091) [YN]	RAF, stored CGMF Syerston
	ZE679	Grob G103 Viking T1 (BGA3092) [YP]	RAF No 622 VGS, Upavon
	ZE680	Grob G103 Viking T1 (BGA3093) [YQ]	RAF No 662 VGS, Arbroath
	ZE681	Grob G103 Viking T1 (BGA3094) [YR]	RAF CGMF, Syerston (damaged)
	ZE682	Grob G103 Viking T1 (BGA3095) [YS]	RAF No 662 VGS, Arbroath
	ZE683	Grob G103 Viking T1 (BGA3096) [YT]	RAF No 661 VGS, Kirknewton
	ZE684	Grob G103 Viking T1 (BGA3097) [YU]	RAF, stored CGMF Syerston
	ZE685	Grob G103 Viking T1 (BGA3098) [YV]	RAF No 631 VGS, Sealand
	ZE686	Grob G103 Viking T1 (BGA3099)	DPA/Slingsby Kirkbymoorside
	ZE690	BAe Sea Harrier FA2 [731]	RN No 899 Sqn, Yeovilton
	ZE691	BAe Sea Harrier FA2	Privately owned, Sproughton
	ZE692	BAe Sea Harrier FA2 [718]	RN Yeovilton, wfu
	ZE693	BAe Sea Harrier FA2 [714]	RN No 899 Sqn, Yeovilton
	ZE694	BAe Sea Harrier FA2 [004/N]	RN No 801 Sqn, Yeovilton
	ZE695	BAe Sea Harrier FA2 [718]	Privately owned, Sproughton
	ZE696	BAe Sea Harrier FA2 [715]	RN No 899 Sqn, Yeovilton
	ZE697	BAe Sea Harrier FA2 [006]	RN, stored St Athan
	ZE698	BAe Sea Harrier FA2 [123/R]	RN No 800 Sqn, Yeovilton
	ZE700	BAe 146 CC2 (G-6-021)	RAF No 32(The Royal) Sqn, Northolt
	ZE701	BAe 146 CC2 (G-6-029)	RAF No 32(The Royal) Sqn, Northolt
	ZE704	Lockheed TriStar C2 (N508PA)	RAF No 216 Sqn, Brize Norton
	ZE705	Lockheed TriStar C2 (N509PA)	RAF No 216 Sqn, Brize Norton
	ZE706	Lockheed TriStar C2A (N503PA)	RAF No 216 Sqn, Brize Norton
	ZE728	Panavia Tornado F3 (comp ZD903) [TH]	RAF No 25 Sqn, Leeming
	ZE729	Panavia Tornado F3 (comp ZD933) [YR]	RAF No 11 Sqn, Leeming
	ZE731	Panavia Tornado F3 [YP]	RAF No 111 Sqn, Leuchars
	ZE734	Panavia Tornado F3 [YO]	RAF No 11 Sqn, Leeming
	ZE735	Panavia Tornado F3 [TG]	RAF F3 OCU/No 56(R) Sqn, Leuchars
	ZE736	Panavia Tornado F3 (comp ZD937) [YN]	RAF/DARA, St Athan
	ZE737	Panavia Tornado F3 [YM]	RAF No 111 Sqn, Leuchars
	ZE755	Panavia Tornado F3 [YL]	RAF No 25 Sqn, Leeming
	ZE756	Panavia Tornado F3	RAF/DARA, stored St Athan

Serial	Type (other identity) [code]	Owner/operator, location or fate	Notes
ZE757	Panavia Tornado F3 [YJ]	RAF No 25 Sqn, Leeming	
ZE758	Panavia Tornado F3 [YI]	RAF No 25 Sqn, Leeming	
ZE760	Panavia Tornado F3 (MM7206) [AP]	RAF Coningsby, on display	
ZE761	Panavia Tornado F3 (MM7203)	DPA/BAe Systems, Warton	
ZE763	Panavia Tornado F3 [DG]	RAF No 11 Sqn, Leeming	
ZE764	Panavia Tornado F3 [YD]	RAF No 111 Sqn, Leuchars	
ZE785	Panavia Tornado F3	RAF AWC/F3 OEU, Waddington	
ZE786	Panavia Tornado F3 (comp ZD934) [TF]	RAF F3 OCU/No 56(R) Sqn, Leuchars	
ZE788	Panavia Tornado F3 [YA]	RAF AMF, Leeming	
ZE790	Panavia Tornado F3 [VU]	RAF No 11 Sqn, Leeming	
ZE791	Panavia Tornado F3 [XY]	RAF No 111 Sqn, Leuchars	
ZE792	Panavia Tornado F3 (MM7211)	RAF/DARA, stored St Athan	
ZE793	Panavia Tornado F3 (comp ZD935) [TE]	RAF No 111 Sqn, Leuchars	
ZE794	Panavia Tornado F3 [XW]	RAF No 25 Sqn, Leeming	
ZE808	Panavia Tornado F3 [XV]	RAF No 111 Sqn, Leuchars	
ZE810	Panavia Tornado F3 [XU]	RAF No 43 Sqn, Leuchars	
ZE811	Panavia Tornado F3 (MM7208)	RAF/DARA, stored St Athan	
ZE812	Panavia Tornado F3 [XR]	RAF F3 OCU/No 56(R) Sqn, Leuchars	
ZE831	Panavia Tornado F3 [XQ]	RAF No 25 Sqn, Leeming	
ZE832	Panavia Tornado F3 (MM7202) [XP]	RAF F3 OCU/No 56(R) Sqn, Leuchars	
ZE834	Panavia Tornado F3 [XO]	RAF/DARA, St Athan	
ZE837	Panavia Tornado F3 (MM55057) [TD]	RAF F3 OCU/No 56(R) Sqn, Leuchars	
ZE838	Panavia Tornado F3 [XL]	RAF No 43 Sqn, Leuchars	
ZE839	Panavia Tornado F3 [XK]	RAF/DARA, St Athan	
ZE887	Panavia Tornado F3 [DJ]	RAF No 11 Sqn, Leeming	
ZE888	Panavia Tornado F3 [TC]	RAF F3 OCU/No 56(R) Sqn, Leuchars	
ZE889	Panavia Tornado F3 [XI]	RAF F3 OCU/No 56(R) Sqn, Leuchars	
ZE907	Panavia Tornado F3 [XH]	RAF/DARA, St Athan	
ZE908	Panavia Tornado F3 [TB]	RAF F3 OCU/No 56(R) Sqn, Leuchars	
ZE934	Panavia Tornado F3 [TA]	RAF F3 OCU/No 56(R) Sqn, Leuchars	
ZE936	Panavia Tornado F3 [XF]	RAF No 111 Sqn, Leuchars	
ZE941	Panavia Tornado F3 [KT]	RAF F3 OCU/No 56(R) Sqn, Leuchars	
ZE942	Panavia Tornado F3 [XE]	RAF AWC/F3 OEU, Waddington	
ZE961	Panavia Tornado F3 [XD]	RAF No 25 Sqn, Leeming	
ZE962	Panavia Tornado F3 [XC]	RAF No 111 Sqn, Leuchars	
ZE963	Panavia Tornado F3 [YT]	RAF No 111 Sqn, Leuchars	
ZE964	Panavia Tornado F3 [XT]	RAF F3 OCU/No 56(R) Sqn, Leuchars	
ZE965	Panavia Tornado F3 [WT]	RAF F3 OCU/No 56(R) Sqn, Leuchars	
ZE966	Panavia Tornado F3 [VT]	RAF F3 OCU/No 56(R) Sqn, Leuchars	
ZE967	Panavia Tornado F3 [UT]	RAF F3 OCU/No 56(R) Sqn, Leuchars	
ZE968	Panavia Tornado F3 [XB]	RAF No 111 Sqn, Leuchars	
ZE969	Panavia Tornado F3 [XA]	RAF No 25 Sqn, Leeming	
ZE982	Panavia Tornado F3 [VV]	RAF No 25 Sqn, Leeming	
ZE983	Panavia Tornado F3 [WY]	RAF No 43 Sqn, Leuchars	
ZF116	WS61 Sea King HC4 [WP]	RN No 848 Sqn, Yeovilton	
ZF117	WS61 Sea King HC4 [VQ]	RN No 846 Sqn, Yeovilton	
ZF118	WS61 Sea King HC4 [VP]	RN No 846 Sqn, Yeovilton	
ZF119	WS61 Sea King HC4 [VW]	RN No 846 Sqn, Yeovilton	
ZF120	WS61 Sea King HC4 [K]	RN No 845 Sqn, Yeovilton	
ZF121	WS61 Sea King HC4 [VT]	RN AMG, Yeovilton	
ZF122	WS61 Sea King HC4 [VU]	RN No 846 Sqn, Yeovilton	
ZF123	WS61 Sea King HC4 [WQ]	RN No 848 Sqn, Yeovilton	
ZF124	WS61 Sea King HC4 [L]	RN No 845 Sqn, Yeovilton	
ZF135	Shorts Tucano T1	RAF No 1 FTS, Linton-on-Ouse	
ZF136	Shorts Tucano T1	RAF No 1 FTS, Linton-on-Ouse	
ZF137	Shorts Tucano T1	RAF No 1 FTS/207(R) Sqn, Linton-on-Ouse	
ZF138	Shorts Tucano T1	RAF No 1 FTS, Linton-on-Ouse	
ZF139	Shorts Tucano T1	RAF No 1 FTS, Linton-on-Ouse	
ZF140	Shorts Tucano T1	RAF No 1 FTS, Linton-on-Ouse	
ZF141	Shorts Tucano T1	RAF, stored Shawbury	
ZF142	Shorts Tucano T1	RAF No 1 FTS, Linton-on-Ouse	
ZF143	Shorts Tucano T1	RAF No 1 FTS, Linton-on-Ouse	
ZF144	Shorts Tucano T1	RAF No 1 FTS, Linton-on-Ouse	
ZF145	Shorts Tucano T1	RAF No 1 FTS, Linton-on-Ouse	
ZF160	Shorts Tucano T1	RAF, stored Shawbury	
ZF161	Shorts Tucano T1	RAF No 1 FTS, Linton-on-Ouse	
ZF162	Shorts Tucano T1	RAF No 1 FTS, Linton-on-Ouse	

Notes	Serial	Type (other identity) [code]	Owner/operator, location or fate
	ZF163	Shorts Tucano T1	RAF, stored Shawbury
	ZF164	Shorts Tucano T1	RAF, stored Shawbury
	ZF165	Shorts Tucano T1	RAF, stored Shawbury
	ZF166	Shorts Tucano T1	RAF, stored Shawbury
	ZF167	Shorts Tucano T1	RAF No 1 FTS, Linton-on-Ouse
	ZF168	Shorts Tucano T1	RAF No 1 FTS, Linton-on-Ouse
	ZF169	Shorts Tucano T1	RAF No 1 FTS/72(R) Sqn, Linton-on-Ouse
	ZF170	Shorts Tucano T1	RAF No 1 FTS, Linton-on-Ouse
	ZF171	Shorts Tucano T1	RAF No 1 FTS, Linton-on-Ouse
	ZF172	Shorts Tucano T1	RAF, stored Shawbury
	ZF200	Shorts Tucano T1	RAF, stored Shawbury
	ZF201	Shorts Tucano T1	RAF, stored Shawbury
	ZF202	Shorts Tucano T1	RAF No 1 FTS/72(R) Sqn, Linton-on-Ouse
	ZF203	Shorts Tucano T1	RAF, stored Shawbury
	ZF204	Shorts Tucano T1	RAF No 1 FTS, Linton-on-Ouse
	ZF205	Shorts Tucano T1	RAF, stored Shawbury
	ZF206	Shorts Tucano T1	RAF, stored Shawbury
	ZF207	Shorts Tucano T1	RAF No 1 FTS/207(R) Sqn, Linton-on-Ouse
	ZF208	Shorts Tucano T1	RAF No 1 FTS, Linton-on-Ouse
	ZF209	Shorts Tucano T1	RAF No 1 FTS, Linton-on-Ouse
	ZF210	Shorts Tucano T1	RAF No 1 FTS, Linton-on-Ouse
	ZF211	Shorts Tucano T1	RAF, stored Shawbury
	ZF212	Shorts Tucano T1	RAF No 1 FTS, Linton-on-Ouse
	ZF238	Shorts Tucano T1	RAF No 1 FTS, Linton-on-Ouse
	ZF239	Shorts Tucano T1	RAF No 1 FTS, Linton-on-Ouse
	ZF240	Shorts Tucano T1	RAF No 1 FTS, Linton-on-Ouse
	ZF241	Shorts Tucano T1	RAF No 1 FTS/72(R) Sqn, Linton-on-Ouse
	ZF242	Shorts Tucano T1	RAF No 1 FTS, Linton-on-Ouse
	ZF243	Shorts Tucano T1	RAF No 1 FTS, Linton-on-Ouse
	ZF244	Shorts Tucano T1	RAF No 1 FTS/72(R) Sqn, Linton-on-Ouse
	ZF245	Shorts Tucano T1	RAF, stored Shawbury
	ZF263	Shorts Tucano T1	RAF, stored Shawbury
	ZF264	Shorts Tucano T1	RAF No 1 FTS, Linton-on-Ouse
	ZF265	Shorts Tucano T1	RAF, stored Shawbury
	ZF266	Shorts Tucano T1	RAF, stored Shawbury
	ZF267	Shorts Tucano T1	RAF, stored Shawbury
	ZF268	Shorts Tucano T1	RAF No 1 FTS, Linton-on-Ouse
	ZF269	Shorts Tucano T1	RAF No 1 FTS/72(R) Sqn, Linton-on-Ouse
	ZF284	Shorts Tucano T1	RAF, stored Shawbury
	ZF285	Shorts Tucano T1	RAF, stored Shawbury
	ZF286	Shorts Tucano T1	RAF No 1 FTS, Linton-on-Ouse
	ZF287	Shorts Tucano T1	RAF No 1 FTS, Linton-on-Ouse
	ZF288	Shorts Tucano T1	RAF, stored Shawbury
	ZF289	Shorts Tucano T1	RAF No 1 FTS, Linton-on-Ouse
	ZF290	Shorts Tucano T1	RAF No 1 FTS, Linton-on-Ouse
	ZF291	Shorts Tucano T1	RAF No 1 FTS, Linton-on-Ouse
	ZF292	Shorts Tucano T1	RAF No 1 FTS/207(R) Sqn, Linton-on-Ouse
	ZF293	Shorts Tucano T1	RAF No 1 FTS/72(R) Sqn, Linton-on-Ouse
	ZF294	Shorts Tucano T1	RAF No 1 FTS, Linton-on-Ouse
	ZF295	Shorts Tucano T1	RAF No 1 FTS, Linton-on-Ouse
	ZF315	Shorts Tucano T1	RAF No 1 FTS, Linton-on-Ouse
	ZF317	Shorts Tucano T1	RAF No 1 FTS, Linton-on-Ouse
	ZF318	Shorts Tucano T1	RAF, stored Shawbury
	ZF319	Shorts Tucano T1	RAF No 1 FTS, Linton-on-Ouse
	ZF320	Shorts Tucano T1	RAF No 1 FTS, Linton-on-Ouse
	ZF338	Shorts Tucano T1	RAF No 1 FTS, Linton-on-Ouse
	ZF339	Shorts Tucano T1	RAF No 1 FTS, Linton-on-Ouse
	ZF340	Shorts Tucano T1	RAF, stored Shawbury
	ZF341	Shorts Tucano T1	RAF No 1 FTS/207(R) Sqn, Linton-on-Ouse
	ZF342	Shorts Tucano T1	RAF No 1 FTS, Linton-on-Ouse
	ZF343	Shorts Tucano T1	RAF No 1 FTS, Linton-on-Ouse
	ZF344	Shorts Tucano T1	RAF, stored Shawbury
	ZF345	Shorts Tucano T1	RAF No 1 FTS/207(R) Sqn, Linton-on-Ouse
	ZF346	Shorts Tucano T1	RAF, stored Shawbury
	ZF347	Shorts Tucano T1	RAF No 1 FTS, Linton-on-Ouse
	ZF348	Shorts Tucano T1	RAF No 1 FTS, Linton-on-Ouse
	ZF349	Shorts Tucano T1	RAF No 1 FTS, Linton-on-Ouse
	ZF350	Shorts Tucano T1	RAF, stored Shawbury
	ZF372	Shorts Tucano T1	RAF, stored Shawbury
	ZF373	Shorts Tucano T1	RAF, stored Shawbury
	ZF374	Shorts Tucano T1	RAF No 1 FTS/72(R) Sqn, Linton-on-Ouse
	ZF375	Shorts Tucano T1	RAF No 1 FTS, Linton-on-Ouse
	ZF376	Shorts Tucano T1	RAF, stored Shawbury

Serial	Type (other identity) [code]	Owner/operator, location or fate	Notes
ZF377	Shorts Tucano T1	RAF No 1 FTS, Linton-on-Ouse	
ZF378	Shorts Tucano T1	RAF No 1 FTS, Linton-on-Ouse	
ZF379	Shorts Tucano T1	RAF No 1 FTS, Linton-on-Ouse	
ZF380	Shorts Tucano T1	RAF, stored Shawbury	
ZF405	Shorts Tucano T1	RAF No 1 FTS, Linton-on-Ouse	
ZF406	Shorts Tucano T1	RAF No 1 FTS, Linton-on-Ouse	
ZF407	Shorts Tucano T1	RAF No 1 FTS, Linton-on-Ouse	
ZF408	Shorts Tucano T1	RAF, stored Shawbury	
ZF409	Shorts Tucano T1	RAF No 1 FTS, Linton-on-Ouse	
ZF410	Shorts Tucano T1	RAF No 1 FTS, Linton-on-Ouse	
ZF411	Shorts Tucano T1	RAF, stored Shawbury	
ZF412	Shorts Tucano T1	RAF, stored Shawbury	
ZF413	Shorts Tucano T1	RAF No 1 FTS, Linton-on-Ouse	
ZF414	Shorts Tucano T1	RAF No 1 FTS, Linton-on-Ouse	
ZF415	Shorts Tucano T1	RAF, stored Shawbury	
ZF416	Shorts Tucano T1	RAF No 1 FTS, Linton-on-Ouse	
ZF417	Shorts Tucano T1	RAF No 1 FTS, Linton-on-Ouse	
ZF418	Shorts Tucano T1	RAF No 1 FTS, Linton-on-Ouse	
ZF445	Shorts Tucano T1	RAF No 1 FTS/*207(R) Sqn*, Linton-on-Ouse	
ZF446	Shorts Tucano T1	RAF No 1 FTS, Linton-on-Ouse	
ZF447	Shorts Tucano T1	RAF No 1 FTS/*72(R) Sqn*, Linton-on-Ouse	
ZF448	Shorts Tucano T1	RAF No 1 FTS, Linton-on-Ouse	
ZF449	Shorts Tucano T1	RAF, stored Shawbury	
ZF450	Shorts Tucano T1	RAF, stored Shawbury	
ZF483	Shorts Tucano T1	RAF No 1 FTS/*72(R) Sqn*, Linton-on-Ouse	
ZF484	Shorts Tucano T1	RAF, stored Shawbury	
ZF485	Shorts Tucano T1 (G-BULU)	RAF No 1 FTS, Linton-on-Ouse	
ZF486	Shorts Tucano T1	RAF, stored Shawbury	
ZF487	Shorts Tucano T1	RAF No 1 FTS, Linton-on-Ouse	
ZF488	Shorts Tucano T1	RAF, stored Shawbury	
ZF489	Shorts Tucano T1	RAF No 1 FTS, Linton-on-Ouse	
ZF490	Shorts Tucano T1	RAF, stored Shawbury	
ZF491	Shorts Tucano T1	RAF No 1 FTS, Linton-on-Ouse	
ZF492	Shorts Tucano T1	RAF No 1 FTS, Linton-on-Ouse	
ZF510	Shorts Tucano T1	DPA/AFD/QinetiQ, Boscombe Down	
ZF511	Shorts Tucano T1	DPA/AFD/QinetiQ, Boscombe Down	
ZF512	Shorts Tucano T1	RAF No 1 FTS, Linton-on-Ouse	
ZF513	Shorts Tucano T1	RAF No 1 FTS, Linton-on-Ouse	
ZF514	Shorts Tucano T1	RAF No 1 FTS/*72(R) Sqn*, Linton-on-Ouse	
ZF515	Shorts Tucano T1	RAF No 1 FTS, Linton-on-Ouse	
ZF516	Shorts Tucano T1	RAF, stored Shawbury	
ZF534	BAe EAP	Loughborough University	
ZF537	WS Lynx AH9	AAC No 653 Sqn/3 Regt, Wattisham	
ZF538	WS Lynx AH9	AAC No 659 Sqn/4 Regt, Wattisham	
ZF539	WS Lynx AH9	AAC No 7 Air Assault Battalion, Wattisham	
ZF540	WS Lynx AH9	AAC/DARA, stored Fleetlands	
ZF557	WS Lynx HMA8 [375/SM]	RN No 815 Sqn, *Somerset* Flt, Yeovilton	
ZF558	WS Lynx HMA8 [307]	RN/DARA, stored Fleetlands	
ZF560	WS Lynx HMA8 [345/NC]	RN/DARA, Fleetlands	
ZF562	WS Lynx HMA8	RN No 815 Sqn, HQ Flt, Yeovilton	
ZF563	WS Lynx HMA8 [338]	RN No 815 Sqn, HQ Flt, Yeovilton	
ZF573	PBN 2T Islander CC2A (G-SRAY)	RAF Northolt Station Flight	
ZF579	BAC Lightning F53	Gatwick Aviation Museum, Charlwood	
ZF580	BAC Lightning F53	BAE Systems Samlesbury, at main gate	
ZF581	BAC Lightning F53	BAE Systems Rochester, on display	
ZF582	BAC Lightning F53 <ff>	Privately owned, Reading	
ZF583	BAC Lightning F53	Solway Aviation Society, Carlisle	
ZF584	BAC Lightning F53	Ferranti Ltd, South Gyle, Edinburgh	
ZF587	BAC Lightning F53 <ff>	Lashenden Air Warfare Museum, Headcorn	
ZF588	BAC Lightning F53 [L]	East Midlands Airport Aeropark	
ZF590	BAC Lightning F53 <rf>	Pontypridd Technical College	
ZF592	BAC Lightning F53	City of Norwich Aviation Museum	
ZF593	BAC Lightning F53 (fuselage)	Pontypridd Technical College	
ZF594	BAC Lightning F53	North-East Aircraft Museum, Usworth	
ZF595	BAC Lightning T55 (fuselage)	Privately owned, Grainthorpe, Lincs	
ZF596	BAC Lightning T55 <ff>	BAe North-West Heritage Group Warton	
ZF622	Piper PA-31 Navajo Chieftain 350 (N3548Y)	DPA/AFD/QinetiQ, Boscombe Down	
ZF641	EHI-101 [PP1]	SFDO, RNAS Culdrose	
ZF649	EHI-101 Merlin [PP5]	RN AESS, *HMS Sultan*, Gosport	

Notes	Serial	Type (other identity) [code]	Owner/operator, location or fate
	ZG101	EHI-101 (mock-up) [GB]	Westland Helicopters/Agusta, Yeovil
	ZG471	BAe Harrier GR7 [61]	RAF No 4 Sqn, Cottesmore
	ZG472	BAe Harrier GR7 [62]	RAF/DARA, St Athan
	ZG474	BAe Harrier GR7 [64]	RAF No 1 Sqn, Cottesmore
	ZG477	BAe Harrier GR7 [67]	RAF No 4 Sqn, Cottesmore
	ZG478	BAe Harrier GR7 [68]	DPA/BAe Systems, Warton
	ZG479	BAe Harrier GR7 [69]	RAF No 4 Sqn, Cottesmore
	ZG480	BAe Harrier GR7 [70]	RAF No 3 Sqn, Cottesmore
	ZG500	BAe Harrier GR7 [71]	RAF HOCU/No 20(R) Sqn, Wittering
	ZG501	BAe Harrier GR7 [72]	DPA/BAe Systems, Warton
	ZG502	BAe Harrier GR7 [73]	RAF No 4 Sqn, Cottesmore
	ZG503	BAe Harrier GR7 [74]	DPA/BAe Systems, Warton
	ZG504	BAe Harrier GR7 [75]	RAF No 1 Sqn, Cottesmore
	ZG505	BAe Harrier GR7 [76]	RAF No 1 Sqn, Cottesmore
	ZG506	BAe Harrier GR7 [77]	RAF No 3 Sqn, Cottesmore
	ZG507	BAe Harrier GR7 [78]	RAF No 1 Sqn, Cottesmore
	ZG508	BAe Harrier GR9 [79]	DPA/BAe Systems, Warton (conversion)
	ZG509	BAe Harrier GR7 [80]	RAF/DARA, St Athan
	ZG510	BAe Harrier GR7 [81]	RAF No 4 Sqn, Cottesmore
	ZG511	BAe Harrier GR7 [82]	RAF No 4 Sqn, Cottesmore
	ZG512	BAe Harrier GR7 [83]	RAF HOCU/No 20(R) Sqn, Wittering
	ZG530	BAe Harrier GR7 [84]	RAF No 4 Sqn, Cottesmore
	ZG531	BAe Harrier GR7 [85]	RAF No 1 Sqn, Cottesmore
	ZG705	Panavia Tornado GR4A [J]	RAF No 13 Sqn, Marham
	ZG706	Panavia Tornado GR1A [E]	RAF/DARA, stored St Athan
	ZG707	Panavia Tornado GR4A [B]	RAF No 13 Sqn, Marham
	ZG709	Panavia Tornado GR4A [V]	RAF No 13 Sqn, Marham
	ZG710	Panavia Tornado GR4A [D]	*Shot down 23 March 2003, Northern Kuwait*
	ZG711	Panavia Tornado GR4A [O]	RAF No 2 Sqn, Marham
	ZG712	Panavia Tornado GR4A [F]	RAF No 13 Sqn, Marham
	ZG713	Panavia Tornado GR4A [G]	RAF No 13 Sqn, Marham
	ZG714	Panavia Tornado GR4A [Q]	RAF No 2 Sqn, Marham
	ZG726	Panavia Tornado GR4A [K]	DPA/AED/QinetiQ, Boscombe Down
	ZG727	Panavia Tornado GR4A [L]	RAF No 617 Sqn, Lossiemouth
	ZG728	Panavia Tornado F3 (MM7229)	RAF/DARA, stored St Athan
	ZG729	Panavia Tornado GR4A [M]	RAF No 13 Sqn, Marham
	ZG731	Panavia Tornado F3 [WV]	RAF AWC/F3 OEU, Waddington
	ZG732	Panavia Tornado F3 (MM7227) [WU]	RAF F3 OCU/No 56(R) Sqn, Leuchars
	ZG733	Panavia Tornado F3 (MM7228)	RAF/DARA, stored St Athan
	ZG734	Panavia Tornado F3 (MM7231)	RAF/DARA, stored St Athan
	ZG750	Panavia Tornado GR4 [DY]	RAF No 13 Sqn, Marham
	ZG751	Panavia Tornado F3 [WP]	RAF/DARA, St Athan (damaged)
	ZG752	Panavia Tornado GR4 [TW]	RAF No 15(R) Sqn, Lossiemouth
	ZG753	Panavia Tornado F3 [WO]	RAF/DARA, St Athan
	ZG754	Panavia Tornado GR4 [TP]	RAF No 15(R) Sqn, Lossiemouth
	ZG755	Panavia Tornado F3 [WN]	RAF No 43 Sqn, Leuchars
	ZG756	Panavia Tornado GR4 [BX]	RAF No 14 Sqn, Lossiemouth
	ZG757	Panavia Tornado F3 [WM]	RAF No 43 Sqn, Leuchars
	ZG769	Panavia Tornado GR4	RAF/DARA, stored St Athan (damaged)
	ZG770	Panavia Tornado F3 [WK]	RAF F3 OCU/No 56(R) Sqn, Leuchars
	ZG771	Panavia Tornado GR4 [AZ]	RAF No 9 Sqn, Marham
	ZG772	Panavia Tornado F3 [WJ]	RAF No 1435 Flt, Mount Pleasant, FI
	ZG773	Panavia Tornado GR4	DPA/BAE Systems, Warton
	ZG774	Panavia Tornado F3 [WI]	RAF No 11 Sqn, Leeming
	ZG775	Panavia Tornado GR4 [FB]	RAF No 12 Sqn, Lossiemouth
	ZG776	Panavia Tornado F3 [WH]	RAF No 111 Sqn, Leuchars
	ZG777	Panavia Tornado GR4 [TC]	RAF No 15(R) Sqn, Lossiemouth
	ZG778	Panavia Tornado F3 [WG]	RAF No 43 Sqn, Leuchars
	ZG779	Panavia Tornado GR4 [FA]	RAF No 12 Sqn, Lossiemouth
	ZG780	Panavia Tornado F3 [WF]	RAF No 11 Sqn, Leeming
	ZG791	Panavia Tornado GR4 [AJ-T]	RAF No 617 Sqn, Lossiemouth
	ZG792	Panavia Tornado GR4 [AJ-G]	RAF No 617 Sqn, Lossiemouth
	ZG793	Panavia Tornado F3 [WE]	RAF No 11 Sqn, Leeming
	ZG794	Panavia Tornado GR4 [TN]	RAF No 15(R) Sqn, Lossiemouth
	ZG795	Panavia Tornado F3 [WD]	RAF No 1435 Flt, Mount Pleasant, FI
	ZG796	Panavia Tornado F3 [WC]	RAF F3 OCU/No 56(R) Sqn, Leuchars
	ZG797	Panavia Tornado F3 [WB]	RAF No 43 Sqn, Leuchars
	ZG798	Panavia Tornado F3 [WA]	RAF/DARA, St Athan
	ZG799	Panavia Tornado F3 [VS]	RAF No 1435 Flt, Mount Pleasant, FI
	ZG816	WS61 Sea King HAS6 [014/L]	RN, stored *HMS Sultan*, Gosport
	ZG817	WS61 Sea King HAS6 [702/PW]	RN AESS, *HMS Sultan*, Gosport
	ZG818	WS61 Sea King HAS6 [707/PW]	RN, stored *HMS Sultan*, Gosport

Serial	Type (other identity) [code]	Owner/operator, location or fate	Notes
ZG819	WS61 Sea King HAS6 [265/N]	RN AESS, *HMS Sultan*, Gosport	
ZG820	WS61 Sea King HC4 [A]	RN No 845 Sqn, Yeovilton	
ZG821	WS61 Sea King HC4 [D]	RN No 845 Sqn, Yeovilton	
ZG822	WS61 Sea King HC4 [VN]	RN No 846 Sqn, Yeovilton	
ZG844	PBN 2T Islander AL1 (G-BLNE)	AAC No 1 Flt/5 Regt, Aldergrove	
ZG845	PBN 2T Islander AL1 (G-BLNT)	AAC No 1 Flt/5 Regt, Aldergrove	
ZG846	PBN 2T Islander AL1 (G-BLNU)	AAC No 1 Flt/5 Regt, Aldergrove	
ZG847	PBN 2T Islander AL1 (G-BLNV)	AAC No 1 Flt/5 Regt, Aldergrove	
ZG848	PBN 2T Islander AL1 (G-BLNY)	AAC No 1 Flt/5 Regt, Aldergrove	
ZG857	BAe Harrier GR7	RAF AWC/SAOEU, Boscombe Down	
ZG858	BAe Harrier GR7	RAF AWC/SAOEU, Boscombe Down	
ZG859	BAe Harrier GR7 [91]	RAF No 3 Sqn, Cottesmore	
ZG860	BAe Harrier GR9	DPA/BAE Systems, Warton (conversion)	
ZG862	BAe Harrier GR7 [94]	RAF AWC/SAOEU, Boscombe Down	
ZG875	WS61 Sea King HAS6 [013/L]	RN, stored *HMS Sultan*, Gosport (damaged)	
ZG879	Powerchute Raider Mk 1	DPA/Powerchute, Hereford	
ZG884	WS Lynx AH9	DPA/Westland Helicopters, Yeovil	
ZG885	WS Lynx AH9 [7]	AAC No 653 Sqn/3 Regt, Wattisham	
ZG886	WS Lynx AH9	AAC No 659 Sqn/4 Regt, Wattisham	
ZG887	WS Lynx AH9	AAC/DARA, Fleetlands	
ZG888	WS Lynx AH9	AAC/DARA, Fleetlands	
ZG889	WS Lynx AH9	AAC/DARA, stored Fleetlands	
ZG914	WS Lynx AH9	AAC/DARA, Fleetlands	
ZG915	WS Lynx AH9 [7]	AAC/DARA, Fleetlands	
ZG916	WS Lynx AH9 [8]	AAC No 653 Sqn/3 Regt, Wattisham	
ZG917	WS Lynx AH9	AAC No 659 Sqn/4 Regt, Wattisham	
ZG918	WS Lynx AH9	AAC No 659 Sqn/4 Regt, Wattisham	
ZG919	WS Lynx AH9	AAC No 659 Sqn/4 Regt, Wattisham	
ZG920	WS Lynx AH9	AAC No 659 Sqn/4 Regt, Wattisham	
ZG921	WS Lynx AH9	AAC No 653 Sqn/3 Regt, Wattisham	
ZG922	WS Lynx AH9	AAC/DARA, Fleetlands	
ZG923	WS Lynx AH9	AAC No 653 Sqn/3 Regt, Wattisham	
ZG969	Pilatus PC-9 (HB-HQE)	BAE Systems Warton	
ZG989	PBN 2T Islander ASTOR (G-DLRA)	DPA/PBN, Bembridge	
ZG993	PBN 2T Islander AL1 (G-BOMD)	AAC No 1 Flight/5 Regt, Aldergrove	
ZG994	PBN 2T Islander AL1 (G-BPLN) (fuselage)	Britten-Norman, stored Bembridge	
ZH101	Boeing E-3D Sentry AEW1	RAF No 8 Sqn/No 23 Sqn, Waddington	
ZH102	Boeing E-3D Sentry AEW1	RAF No 8 Sqn/No 23 Sqn, Waddington	
ZH103	Boeing E-3D Sentry AEW1	RAF No 8 Sqn/No 23 Sqn, Waddington	
ZH104	Boeing E-3D Sentry AEW1	RAF No 8 Sqn/No 23 Sqn, Waddington	
ZH105	Boeing E-3D Sentry AEW1	RAF No 8 Sqn/No 23 Sqn, Waddington	
ZH106	Boeing E-3D Sentry AEW1	RAF No 8 Sqn/No 23 Sqn, Waddington	
ZH107	Boeing E-3D Sentry AEW1	RAF No 8 Sqn/No 23 Sqn, Waddington	
ZH115	Grob G109B Vigilant T1 [TA]	RAF, stored CGMF Syerston	
ZH116	Grob G109B Vigilant T1 [TB]	RAF No 618 VGS, Odiham	
ZH117	Grob G109B Vigilant T1 [TC]	RAF No 642 VGS, Linton-on-Ouse	
ZH118	Grob G109B Vigilant T1 [TD]	RAF No 612 VGS, Abingdon	
ZH119	Grob G109B Vigilant T1 [TE]	RAF No 632 VGS, Ternhill	
ZH120	Grob G109B Vigilant T1 [TF]	RAF ACCGS/No 644 VGS, Syerston	
ZH121	Grob G109B Vigilant T1 [TG]	RAF No 633 VGS, Cosford	
ZH122	Grob G109B Vigilant T1 [TH]	RAF No 664 VGS, Newtownards	
ZH123	Grob G109B Vigilant T1 [TJ]	RAF No 637 VGS, Little Rissington	
ZH124	Grob G109B Vigilant T1 [TK]	RAF No 642 VGS, Linton-on-Ouse	
ZH125	Grob G109B Vigilant T1 [TL]	RAF CGMF, Syerston	
ZH126	Grob G109B Vigilant T1 (D-KGRA) [TM]	RAF No 612 VGS, Abingdon	
ZH127	Grob G109B Vigilant T1 (D-KEEC) [TN]	RAF No 642 VGS, Linton-on-Ouse	
ZH128	Grob G109B Vigilant T1 [TP]	RAF No 624 VGS, Chivenor RMB	
ZH129	Grob G109B Vigilant T1 [TQ]	RAF No 635 VGS, Samlesbury	
ZH139	BAe Harrier GR7 <R> (BAPC 191/ ZD472)	RAF M&RU, Bottesford	
ZH141	AS355F-1 Twin Squirrel HCC1 (G-OILX)	RAF No 32(The Royal) Sqn, Northolt	
ZH144	Grob G109B Vigilant T1 [TR]	RAF No 636 VGS, Swansea	
ZH145	Grob G109B Vigilant T1 [TS]	RAF No 636 VGS, Swansea	
ZH146	Grob G109B Vigilant T1 [TT]	RAF No 664 VGS, Newtownards	
ZH147	Grob G109B Vigilant T1 [TU]	RAF ACCGS/No 644 VGS, Syerston	
ZH148	Grob G109B Vigilant T1 [TV]	RAF No 613 VGS, Halton	
ZH184	Grob G109B Vigilant T1 [TW]	RAF No 632 VGS, Ternhill	

Notes	Serial	Type (other identity) [code]	Owner/operator, location or fate
	ZH185	Grob G109B Vigilant T1 [TX]	RAF No 663 VGS, Kinloss
	ZH186	Grob G109B Vigilant T1 [TY]	RAF No 613 VGS, Halton
	ZH187	Grob G109B Vigilant T1 [TZ]	RAF No 633 VGS, Cosford
	ZH188	Grob G109B Vigilant T1 [UA]	RAF No 612 VGS, Abingdon
	ZH189	Grob G109B Vigilant T1 [UB]	RAF No 624 VGS, Chivenor RMB
	ZH190	Grob G109B Vigilant T1 [UC]	RAF No 663 VGS, Kinloss
	ZH191	Grob G109B Vigilant T1 [UD]	RAF No 616 VGS, Henlow
	ZH192	Grob G109B Vigilant T1 [UE]	RAF No 635 VGS, Samlesbury
	ZH193	Grob G109B Vigilant T1 [UF]	RAF No 612 VGS, Abingdon
	ZH194	Grob G109B Vigilant T1 [UG]	RAF No 624 VGS, Chivenor RMB
	ZH195	Grob G109B Vigilant T1 [UH]	RAF No 642 VGS, Linton-on-Ouse
	ZH196	Grob G109B Vigilant T1 [UJ]	RAF No 618 VGS, Odiham
	ZH197	Grob G109B Vigilant T1 [UK]	RAF No 618 VGS, Odiham
	ZH200	BAe Hawk 200	BAE Systems Warton, Overseas Customer Training Centre
	ZH205	Grob G109B Vigilant T1 [UL]	RAF No 634 VGS, St Athan
	ZH206	Grob G109B Vigilant T1 [UM]	RAF No 635 VGS, Samlesbury
	ZH207	Grob G109B Vigilant T1 [UN]	RAF No 632 VGS, Ternhill
	ZH208	Grob G109B Vigilant T1 [UP]	RAF No 645 VGS, Topcliffe
	ZH209	Grob G109B Vigilant T1 [UQ]	RAF No 634 VGS, St Athan
	ZH211	Grob G109B Vigilant T1 [UR]	RAF ACCGS/No 644 VGS, Syerston
	ZH247	Grob G109B Vigilant T1 [US]	RAF No 618 VGS, Odiham
	ZH248	Grob G109B Vigilant T1 [UT]	RAF No 637 VGS, Little Rissington
	ZH249	Grob G109B Vigilant T1 [UU]	RAF No 633 VGS, Cosford
	ZH257	B-V CH-47C Chinook (AE-520/ 9217M)	RAF/DARA, Fleetlands
	ZH263	Grob G109B Vigilant T1 [UV]	RAF No 632 VGS, Ternhill
	ZH264	Grob G109B Vigilant T1 [UW]	RAF No 616 VGS, Henlow
	ZH265	Grob G109B Vigilant T1 [UX]	RAF No 645 VGS, Topcliffe
	ZH266	Grob G109B Vigilant T1 [UY]	RAF No 635 VGS, Samlesbury
	ZH267	Grob G109B Vigilant T1 [UZ]	RAF No 645 VGS, Topcliffe
	ZH268	Grob G109B Vigilant T1 [SA]	RAF No 613 VGS, Halton
	ZH269	Grob G109B Vigilant T1 [SB]	RAF No 645 VGS, Topcliffe
	ZH270	Grob G109B Vigilant T1 [SC]	RAF No 616 VGS, Henlow
	ZH271	Grob G109B Vigilant T1 [SD]	RAF No 613 VGS, Halton
	ZH278	Grob G109B Vigilant T1 (D-KAIS) [SF]	RAF No 633 VGS, Cosford
	ZH279	Grob G109B Vigilant T1 (D-KNPS) [SG]	RAF ACCGS/No 644 VGS, Syerston
	ZH536	PBN 2T Islander CC2 (G-BSAH)	RAF Northolt Station Flight
	ZH540	WS61 Sea King HAR3A	RAF No 22 Sqn, A Flt, Chivenor RMB
	ZH541	WS61 Sea King HAR3A [V]	RAF No 22 Sqn, A Flt, Chivenor RMB
	ZH542	WS61 Sea King HAR3A	RAF HMF, St Mawgan
	ZH543	WS61 Sea King HAR3A	RAF No 22 Sqn, B Flt, Wattisham
	ZH544	WS61 Sea King HAR3A	RAF No 22 Sqn, B Flt, Wattisham
	ZH545	WS61 Sea King HAR3A	RAF No 22 Sqn, A Flt, Chivenor RMB
	ZH552	Panavia Tornado F3 [ST]	RAF No 11 Sqn, Leeming
	ZH553	Panavia Tornado F3 [RT]	RAF No 11 Sqn, Leeming
	ZH554	Panavia Tornado F3	RAF/DARA, St Athan
	ZH555	Panavia Tornado F3 [PT]	RAF F3 OCU/No 56(R) Sqn, Leuchars
	ZH556	Panavia Tornado F3 [OT]	RAF No 111 Sqn, Leuchars
	ZH557	Panavia Tornado F3 [NT]	RAF No 11 Sqn, Leeming
	ZH559	Panavia Tornado F3 [MT]	RAF No 43 Sqn, Leuchars
	ZH588	Eurofighter Typhoon (DA2)	DPA/BAE Systems, Warton
	ZH590	Eurofighter Typhoon (DA4)	DPA/BAE Systems, Warton
	ZH653	BAe Harrier T10	DPA/BAE Systems, Warton
	ZH654	BAe Harrier T10	DPA/QinetiQ, stored Boscombe Down (wreck)
	ZH655	BAe Harrier T10 [Q]	RAF/DARA, St Athan
	ZH656	BAe Harrier T10 [104]	DPA/BAE Systems, Warton
	ZH657	BAe Harrier T10 [105]	RAF No 3 Sqn, Cottesmore
	ZH658	BAe Harrier T10 [106]	RAF Wittering (damaged)
	ZH659	BAe Harrier T10 [107]	RAF HOCU/No 20(R) Sqn, Wittering
	ZH660	BAe Harrier T10 [108]	RAF HOCU/No 20(R) Sqn, Wittering
	ZH661	BAe Harrier T10 [109]	RAF HOCU/No 20(R) Sqn, Wittering
	ZH662	BAe Harrier T10 [110]	RAF HOCU/No 20(R) Sqn, Wittering
	ZH663	BAe Harrier T10 [111]	RAF HOCU/No 20(R) Sqn, Wittering
	ZH664	BAe Harrier T10 [112]	RAF No 4 Sqn, Cottesmore
	ZH665	BAe Harrier T10 [113]	RAF HOCU/No 20(R) Sqn, Wittering
	ZH763	BAC 1-11/539GL (G-BGKE)	DPA/AFD/QinetiQ, Boscombe Down
	ZH775	B-V Chinook HC2 (N7424J)	RAF No 18 Sqn, Odiham
	ZH776	B-V Chinook HC2 (N7424L) [ES]	RAF/DARA, Fleetlands
	ZH777	B-V Chinook HC2 (N7424M)	RAF No 78 Sqn, Mount Pleasant, FI

Serial	Type (other identity) [code]	Owner/operator, location or fate	Notes
ZH796	BAe Sea Harrier FA2 [712]	RN No 899 Sqn, Yeovilton	
ZH797	BAe Sea Harrier FA2 [000/N]	RN No 801 Sqn, Yeovilton	
ZH798	BAe Sea Harrier FA2 [002]	RN No 801 Sqn, Yeovilton	
ZH799	BAe Sea Harrier FA2 [730]	RN/DARA, stored St Athan	
ZH800	BAe Sea Harrier FA2 [719]	RN No 899 Sqn, Yeovilton	
ZH801	BAe Sea Harrier FA2 [125/R]	RN No 800 Sqn, Yeovilton	
ZH802	BAe Sea Harrier FA2 [711]	RN No 899 Sqn, Yeovilton	
ZH803	BAe Sea Harrier FA2 [004/N]	RN No 801 Sqn, Yeovilton	
ZH804	BAe Sea Harrier FA2 [730/R]	RN AMG, Yeovilton	
ZH805	BAe Sea Harrier FA2	*Crashed 11 June 2003, Lee Bay, Devon*	
ZH806	BAe Sea Harrier FA2 [122/R]	RN No 800 Sqn, Yeovilton	
ZH807	BAe Sea Harrier FA2 [711]	RN, Predannack Fire School	
ZH808	BAe Sea Harrier FA2 [003]	RN No 801 Sqn, Yeovilton	
ZH809	BAe Sea Harrier FA2 [710/N]	RN No 899 Sqn, Yeovilton	
ZH810	BAe Sea Harrier FA2 [716]	RN No 899 Sqn, Yeovilton	
ZH811	BAe Sea Harrier FA2 [005]	RN No 801 Sqn, Yeovilton	
ZH812	BAe Sea Harrier FA2	RN No 899 Sqn, Yeovilton	
ZH813	BAe Sea Harrier FA2 [006]	RN No 801 Sqn, Yeovilton	
ZH814	Bell 212HP (G-BGMH)	AAC No 7 Flt, Brunei	
ZH815	Bell 212HP (G-BGCZ)	AAC No 7 Flt, Brunei	
ZH816	Bell 212HP (G-BGMG)	AAC No 7 Flt, Brunei	
ZH821	EHI-101 Merlin HM1	DPA/Westland Helicopters, Yeovil	
ZH822	EHI-101 Merlin HM1	DPA/Westland Helicopters, Yeovil	
ZH823	EHI-101 Merlin HM1	DPA/Westland Helicopters, Yeovil	
ZH824	EHI-101 Merlin HM1	DPA/AFD/QinetiQ, Boscombe Down	
ZH825	EHI-101 Merlin HM1	RN/DARA, Fleetlands	
ZH826	EHI-101 Merlin HM1	RN/DARA, stored Fleetlands	
ZH827	EHI-101 Merlin HM1	RN/DARA, stored Fleetlands	
ZH828	EHI-101 Merlin HM1	RN AMG, Culdrose	
ZH829	EHI-101 Merlin HM1	RN/DARA, stored Fleetlands	
ZH830	EHI-101 Merlin HM1	DPA/AFD/QinetiQ, Boscombe Down	
ZH831	EHI-101 Merlin HM1	RN AMG, Culdrose	
ZH832	EHI-101 Merlin HM1	DPA/AFD/QinetiQ, Boscombe Down	
ZH833	EHI-101 Merlin HM1	RN AMG, Culdrose	
ZH834	EHI-101 Merlin HM1 [538/CU]	RN No 700M OEU, Culdrose	
ZH835	EHI-101 Merlin HM1	DPA/Westland Helicopters, Yeovil	
ZH836	EHI-101 Merlin HM1 [582/CU]	RN AMG, Culdrose	
ZH837	EHI-101 Merlin HM1 [587]	RN AMG, Culdrose	
ZH838	EHI-101 Merlin HM1	DPA/Westland Helicopters, Yeovil	
ZH839	EHI-101 Merlin HM1 [539/CU]	RN No 700M OEU, Culdrose	
ZH840	EHI-101 Merlin HM1 [537/CU]	RN No 700M OEU, Culdrose	
ZH841	EHI-101 Merlin HM1 [012]	RN No 820 Sqn, Culdrose	
ZH842	EHI-101 Merlin HM1	DPA/Westland Helicopters, Yeovil	
ZH843	EHI-101 Merlin HM1 [533/CU]	DPA/Westland Helicopters, Yeovil	
ZH844	EHI-101 Merlin HM1	RN FSAIU, Yeovilton (damaged)	
ZH845	EHI-101 Merlin HM1 [535/CU]	DPA/Westland Helicopters, Yeovil	
ZH846	EHI-101 Merlin HM1 [535]	DPA/Westland Helicopters, Yeovil	
ZH847	EHI-101 Merlin HM1	RN No 824 Sqn, Culdrose	
ZH848	EHI-101 Merlin HM1 [457/LA]	RN No 824 Sqn, *Lancaster* Flt, Culdrose	
ZH849	EHI-101 Merlin HM1 [265/R]	RN AMG, Culdrose	
ZH850	EHI-101 Merlin HM1	RN AMG, Culdrose	
ZH851	EHI-101 Merlin HM1 [267]	RN No 824 Sqn, Culdrose	
ZH852	EHI-101 Merlin HM1 [583/CU]	RN No 824 Sqn, Culdrose	
ZH853	EHI-101 Merlin HM1	RN No 824 Sqn, Culdrose	
ZH854	EHI-101 Merlin HM1 [580/CU]	RN No 824 Sqn, Culdrose	
ZH855	EHI-101 Merlin HM1 [587/CU]	RN No 824 Sqn, Culdrose	
ZH856	EHI-101 Merlin HM1 [267/R]	RN No 814 Sqn, Culdrose	
ZH857	EHI-101 Merlin HM1 [268/R]	RN No 814 Sqn, Culdrose	
ZH858	EHI-101 Merlin HM1 [457/LA]	RN No 824 Sqn, Culdrose	
ZH859	EHI-101 Merlin HM1	RN No 824 Sqn, Culdrose	
ZH860	EHI-101 Merlin HM1 [269/R]	RN No 814 Sqn, Culdrose	
ZH861	EHI-101 Merlin HM1 [586]	RN No 824 Sqn, Culdrose	
ZH862	EHI-101 Merlin HM1 [010]	RN No 820 Sqn, Culdrose	
ZH863	EHI-101 Merlin HM1	RN No 814 Sqn, Culdrose	
ZH864	EHI-101 Merlin HM1 [011/CU]	RN No 820 Sqn, Culdrose	
ZH865	Lockheed C-130J-30 Hercules C4 (N130JA)	DPA/AFD/QinetiQ, Boscombe Down	
ZH866	Lockheed C-130J-30 Hercules C4 (N130JE)	RAF Lyneham Transport Wing	
ZH867	Lockheed C-130J-30 Hercules C4 (N130JJ)	RAF Lyneham Transport Wing	
ZH868	Lockheed C-130J-30 Hercules C4 (N130JN)	RAF Lyneham Transport Wing	

Notes	Serial	Type (other identity) [code]	Owner/operator, location or fate
	ZH869	Lockheed C-130J-30 Hercules C4 (N130JV)	RAF Lyneham Transport Wing
	ZH870	Lockheed C-130J-30 Hercules C4 (N73235/N78235)	RAF Lyneham Transport Wing
	ZH871	Lockheed C-130J-30 Hercules C4 (N73238)	DPA/AFD/QinetiQ, Boscombe Down
	ZH872	Lockheed C-130J-30 Hercules C4 (N4249Y)	RAF Lyneham Transport Wing
	ZH873	Lockheed C-130J-30 Hercules C4 (N4242N)	RAF Lyneham Transport Wing
	ZH874	Lockheed C-130J-30 Hercules C4 (N41030)	RAF Lyneham Transport Wing
	ZH875	Lockheed C-130J-30 Hercules C4 (N4099R)	RAF Lyneham Transport Wing
	ZH876	Lockheed C-130J-30 Hercules C4 (N4080M)	RAF Lyneham Transport Wing
	ZH877	Lockheed C-130J-30 Hercules C4 (N4081M)	RAF Lyneham Transport Wing
	ZH878	Lockheed C-130J-30 Hercules C4 (N73232)	RAF Lyneham Transport Wing
	ZH879	Lockheed C-130J-30 Hercules C4 (N4080M)	RAF Lyneham Transport Wing
	ZH880	Lockheed C-130J Hercules C5 (N73238)	DPA/AFD/QinetiQ, Boscombe Down
	ZH881	Lockheed C-130J Hercules C5 (N4081M)	RAF Lyneham Transport Wing
	ZH882	Lockheed C-130J Hercules C5 (N4099R)	RAF Lyneham Transport Wing
	ZH883	Lockheed C-130J Hercules C5 (N4242N)	RAF Lyneham Transport Wing
	ZH884	Lockheed C-130J Hercules C5 (N4249Y)	RAF Lyneham Transport Wing
	ZH885	Lockheed C-130J Hercules C5) (N41030	RAF Lyneham Transport Wing
	ZH886	Lockheed C-130J Hercules C5 (N73235)	RAF Lyneham Transport Wing
	ZH887	Lockheed C-130J Hercules C5 (N4187W)	RAF Lyneham Transport Wing
	ZH888	Lockheed C-130J Hercules C5 (N4187)	RAF Lyneham Transport Wing
	ZH889	Lockheed C-130J Hercules C5 (N4099R)	RAF Lyneham Transport Wing
	ZH890	Grob G109B Vigilant T1 [SE]	RAF ACCGS/No 644 VGS, Syerston
	ZH891	B-V Chinook HC2A (N20075)	RAF No 78 Sqn, Mount Pleasant, FI
	ZH892	B-V Chinook HC2A (N2019V) [BL]	RAF No 18 Sqn, Odiham
	ZH893	B-V Chinook HC2A (N2025L) [BM]	RAF No 18 Sqn, Odiham
	ZH894	B-V Chinook HC2A (N2026E) [BO]	RAF No 18 Sqn, Odiham
	ZH895	B-V Chinook HC2A (N2034K) [BP]	RAF No 18 Sqn, Odiham
	ZH896	B-V Chinook HC2A (N2038G)	DPA/AFD/QinetiQ, Boscombe Down
	ZH897	B-V Chinook HC3 (N2045G)	DPA, stored Boscombe Down
	ZH898	B-V Chinook HC3 (N2057Q)	DPA, stored Boscombe Down
	ZH899	B-V Chinook HC3 (N2057R)	DPA, stored Boscombe Down
	ZH900	B-V Chinook HC3 (N2060H)	DPA, stored Boscombe Down
	ZH901	B-V Chinook HC3 (N2060M)	DPA, stored Boscombe Down
	ZH902	B-V Chinook HC3 (N2064W)	DPA, stored Boscombe Down
	ZH903	B-V Chinook HC3 (N20671)	DPA, stored Boscombe Down
	ZH904	B-V Chinook HC3 (N2083K)	Boeing, Philadelphia, for RAF
	ZJ100	BAe Hawk 102D	BAE Systems Warton
	ZJ117	EHI-101 Merlin HC3	DPA/AFD/QinetiQ, Boscombe Down
	ZJ118	EHI-101 Merlin HC3 [B]	DPA/Westland Helicopters, Yeovil
	ZJ119	EHI-101 Merlin HC3 [C]	DPA/AFD/QinetiQ, Boscombe Down
	ZJ120	EHI-101 Merlin HC3 [D]	RAF No 28 Sqn, Benson
	ZJ121	EHI-101 Merlin HC3 [E]	RAF No 28 Sqn, Benson
	ZJ122	EHI-101 Merlin HC3 [F]	RAF No 28 Sqn, Benson
	ZJ123	EHI-101 Merlin HC3 [G]	RAF No 28 Sqn, Benson
	ZJ124	EHI-101 Merlin HC3 [H]	RAF No 28 Sqn, Benson
	ZJ125	EHI-101 Merlin HC3 [J]	RAF No 28 Sqn, Benson
	ZJ126	EHI-101 Merlin HC3 [K]	RAF No 28 Sqn, Benson
	ZJ127	EHI-101 Merlin HC3 [L]	RAF No 28 Sqn, Benson
	ZJ128	EHI-101 Merlin HC3 [M]	RAF No 28 Sqn, Benson
	ZJ129	EHI-101 Merlin HC3 [N]	RAF No 28 Sqn, Benson
	ZJ130	EHI-101 Merlin HC3 [O]	RAF No 28 Sqn, Benson

Serial	Type (other identity) [code]	Owner/operator, location or fate	Notes
ZJ131	EHI-101 Merlin HC3 [P]	RAF No 28 Sqn, Benson	
ZJ132	EHI-101 Merlin HC3 [Q]	RAF No 28 Sqn, Benson	
ZJ133	EHI-101 Merlin HC3 [R]	RAF No 28 Sqn, Benson	
ZJ134	EHI-101 Merlin HC3 [S]	RAF No 28 Sqn, Benson	
ZJ135	EHI-101 Merlin HC3 [T]	RAF No 28 Sqn, Benson	
ZJ136	EHI-101 Merlin HC3 [U]	RAF No 28 Sqn, Benson	
ZJ137	EHI-101 Merlin HC3 [W]	RAF No 28 Sqn, Benson	
ZJ138	EHI-101 Merlin HC3 [X]	RAF No 28 Sqn, Benson	
ZJ139	AS355F-1 Twin Squirrel HCC1 (G-NUTZ)	RAF No 32(The Royal) Sqn, Northolt	
ZJ140	AS355F-1 Twin Squirrel HCC1 (G-FFHI)	RAF No 32(The Royal) Sqn, Northolt	
ZJ164	AS365N-2 Dauphin 2 (G-BTLC)	RN/Bond Helicopters, Plymouth	
ZJ165	AS365N-2 Dauphin 2 (G-NTOO)	RN/Bond Helicopters, Plymouth	
ZJ166	WAH-64 Apache AH1 (N9219G)	DPA/Westland Helicopters, Yeovil	
ZJ167	WAH-64 Apache AH1 (N3266B)	AAC, stored Shawbury	
ZJ168	WAH-64 Apache AH1 (N3123T)	AAC, stored Shawbury	
ZJ169	WAH-64 Apache AH1 (N3114H)	AAC, stored Shawbury	
ZJ170	WAH-64 Apache AH1 (N3065U)	DPA/Westland Helicopters, Yeovil	
ZJ171	WAH-64 Apache AH1 (N3266T)	DPA/AFD/QinetiQ, Boscombe Down	
ZJ172	WAH-64 Apache AH1	AAC, stored Shawbury	
ZJ173	WAH-64 Apache AH1 (N3266W)	AAC No 656 Sqn/9 Regt, Dishforth	
ZJ174	WAH-64 Apache AH1	AAC, stored Shawbury	
ZJ175	WAH-64 Apache AH1 (N3218V)	AAC, stored Shawbury	
ZJ176	WAH-64 Apache AH1	AAC, stored Shawbury	
ZJ177	WAH-64 Apache AH1	AAC, stored Shawbury	
ZJ178	WAH-64 Apache AH1	AAC, stored Shawbury	
ZJ179	WAH-64 Apache AH1	AAC, stored Shawbury	
ZJ180	WAH-64 Apache AH1	AAC, stored Shawbury	
ZJ181	WAH-64 Apache AH1	AAC, stored Shawbury	
ZJ182	WAH-64 Apache AH1	DPA/Westland Helicopters, Yeovil	
ZJ183	WAH-64 Apache AH1	DPA/Westland Helicopters, Yeovil	
ZJ184	WAH-64 Apache AH1	DPA/Westland Helicopters, Yeovil	
ZJ185	WAH-64 Apache AH1	DPA/AFD/QinetiQ, Boscombe Down	
ZJ186	WAH-64 Apache AH1	DPA/Westland Helicopters, Yeovil	
ZJ187	WAH-64 Apache AH1	AAC, stored Shawbury	
ZJ188	WAH-64 Apache AH1	DPA/Westland Helicopters, Yeovil	
ZJ189	WAH-64 Apache AH1	DPA/Westland Helicopters, Yeovil	
ZJ190	WAH-64 Apache AH1	AAC, stored Shawbury	
ZJ191	WAH-64 Apache AH1	AAC, stored Shawbury	
ZJ192	WAH-64 Apache AH1	AAC, stored Shawbury	
ZJ193	WAH-64 Apache AH1	AAC, stored Shawbury	
ZJ194	WAH-64 Apache AH1	AAC, stored Shawbury	
ZJ195	WAH-64 Apache AH1	DPA/Westland Helicopters, Yeovil	
ZJ196	WAH-64 Apache AH1	DPA/Westland Helicopters, Yeovil	
ZJ197	WAH-64 Apache AH1	AAC, stored Shawbury	
ZJ198	WAH-64 Apache AH1	AAC, stored Shawbury	
ZJ199	WAH-64 Apache AH1	AAC, stored Shawbury	
ZJ200	WAH-64 Apache AH1	AAC, stored Shawbury	
ZJ202	WAH-64 Apache AH1	AAC, stored Shawbury	
ZJ203	WAH-64 Apache AH1	AAC, stored Shawbury	
ZJ204	WAH-64 Apache AH1	DPA/Westland Helicopters, Yeovil	
ZJ205	WAH-64 Apache AH1	DPA/AFD/QinetiQ, Boscombe Down	
ZJ206	WAH-64 Apache AH1	AAC No 673 Sqn/2 Regt, Middle Wallop	
ZJ207	WAH-64 Apache AH1	DPA/Westland Helicopters, Yeovil	
ZJ208	WAH-64 Apache AH1	AAC No 656 Sqn/9 Regt, Dishforth	
ZJ209	WAH-64 Apache AH1	DPA/Westland Helicopters, Yeovil	
ZJ210	WAH-64 Apache AH1	DPA/Westland Helicopters, Yeovil	
ZJ211	WAH-64 Apache AH1	AAC No 673 Sqn/2 Regt, Middle Wallop	
ZJ212	WAH-64 Apache AH1	AAC No 673 Sqn/2 Regt, Middle Wallop	
ZJ213	WAH-64 Apache AH1	AAC No 673 Sqn/2 Regt, Middle Wallop	
ZJ214	WAH-64 Apache AH1	AAC No 673 Sqn/2 Regt, Middle Wallop	
ZJ215	WAH-64 Apache AH1	AAC No 673 Sqn/2 Regt, Middle Wallop	
ZJ216	WAH-64 Apache AH1	AAC No 673 Sqn/2 Regt, Middle Wallop	
ZJ217	WAH-64 Apache AH1	AAC No 673 Sqn/2 Regt, Middle Wallop	
ZJ218	WAH-64 Apache AH1	AAC No 673 Sqn/2 Regt, Middle Wallop	
ZJ219	WAH-64 Apache AH1	AAC No 673 Sqn/2 Regt, Middle Wallop	
ZJ220	WAH-64 Apache AH1	AAC No 673 Sqn/2 Regt, Middle Wallop	
ZJ221	WAH-64 Apache AH1	AAC No 673 Sqn/2 Regt, Middle Wallop	
ZJ222	WAH-64 Apache AH1	AAC, stored Shawbury	
ZJ223	WAH-64 Apache AH1	AAC No 656 Sqn/9 Regt, Dishforth	
ZJ224	WAH-64 Apache AH1	AAC No 656 Sqn/9 Regt, Dishforth	
ZJ225	WAH-64 Apache AH1	AAC No 656 Sqn/9 Regt, Dishforth	

Notes	Serial	Type (other identity) [code]	Owner/operator, location or fate
	ZJ226	WAH-64 Apache AH1	DPA/Westland Helicopters, Yeovil
	ZJ227	WAH-64 Apache AH1	AAC No 656 Sqn/9 Regt, Dishforth
	ZJ228	WAH-64 Apache AH1	AAC No 656 Sqn/9 Regt, Dishforth
	ZJ229	WAH-64 Apache AH1	AAC No 656 Sqn/9 Regt, Dishforth
	ZJ230	WAH-64 Apache AH1	DPA/Westland Helicopters, Yeovil
	ZJ231	WAH-64 Apache AH1	DPA/Westland Helicopters, Yeovil
	ZJ232	WAH-64 Apache AH1	DPA/Westland Helicopters, Yeovil
	ZJ233	WAH-64 Apache AH1	DPA/Westland Helicopters, Yeovil
	ZJ234	Bell 412EP Griffin HT1 (G-BWZR) [S]	DHFS No 60(R) Sqn, RAF Shawbury
	ZJ235	Bell 412EP Griffin HT1 (G-BXBF) [I]	DHFS No 60(R) Sqn, RAF Shawbury
	ZJ236	Bell 412EP Griffin HT1 (G-BXBE) [X]	DHFS No 60(R) Sqn, RAF Shawbury
	ZJ237	Bell 412EP Griffin HT1 (G-BXFF) [T]	DHFS No 60(R) Sqn, RAF Shawbury
	ZJ238	Bell 412EP Griffin HT1 (G-BXHC) [Y]	DHFS No 60(R) Sqn, RAF Shawbury
	ZJ239	Bell 412EP Griffin HT1 (G-BXFH) [R]	DHFS No 60(R) Sqn, RAF Shawbury
	ZJ240	Bell 412EP Griffin HT1 (G-BXIR) [U]	DHFS No 60(R) Sqn/SARTU, RAF Valley
	ZJ241	Bell 412EP Griffin HT1 (G-BXIS) [L]	DHFS No 60(R) Sqn/SARTU, RAF Valley
	ZJ242	Bell 412EP Griffin HT1 (G-BXDK) [E]	DHFS No 60(R) Sqn, RAF Shawbury
	ZJ243	AS350BA Squirrel HT2 (G-BWZS)	School of Army Aviation/No 670 Sqn, Middle Wallop
	ZJ244	AS350BA Squirrel HT2 (G-BXMD)	School of Army Aviation/No 670 Sqn, Middle Wallop
	ZJ245	AS350BA Squirrel HT2 (G-BXME)	School of Army Aviation/No 670 Sqn, Middle Wallop
	ZJ246	AS350BA Squirrel HT2 (G-BXMJ)	School of Army Aviation/No 670 Sqn, Middle Wallop
	ZJ247	AS350BA Squirrel HT2 (G-BXNB)	School of Army Aviation/No 670 Sqn, Middle Wallop
	ZJ248	AS350BA Squirrel HT2 (G-BXNE)	School of Army Aviation/No 670 Sqn, Middle Wallop
	ZJ249	AS350BA Squirrel HT2 (G-BXNJ)	School of Army Aviation/No 670 Sqn, Middle Wallop
	ZJ250	AS350BA Squirrel HT2 (G-BXNY)	School of Army Aviation/No 670 Sqn, Middle Wallop
	ZJ251	AS350BA Squirrel HT2 (G-BXOG)	School of Army Aviation/No 670 Sqn, Middle Wallop
	ZJ252	AS350BA Squirrel HT2 (G-BXOK)	School of Army Aviation/No 670 Sqn, Middle Wallop
	ZJ253	AS350BA Squirrel HT2 (G-BXPG)	School of Army Aviation/No 670 Sqn, Middle Wallop
	ZJ254	AS350BA Squirrel HT2 (G-BXPJ)	School of Army Aviation/No 670 Sqn, Middle Wallop
	ZJ255	AS350BB Squirrel HT1 (G-BXAG)	DHFS, RAF Shawbury
	ZJ256	AS350BB Squirrel HT1 (G-BXCE)	DHFS, RAF Shawbury
	ZJ257	AS350BB Squirrel HT1 (G-BXDJ)	DHFS, RAF Shawbury
	ZJ258	AS350BB Squirrel HT1 (G-BXEO)	DHFS, RAF Shawbury
	ZJ259	AS350BB Squirrel HT1 (G-BXFJ)	DHFS, RAF Shawbury
	ZJ260	AS350BB Squirrel HT1 (G-BXGB)	DHFS, RAF Shawbury
	ZJ261	AS350BB Squirrel HT1 (G-BXGJ)	DHFS, RAF Shawbury
	ZJ262	AS350BB Squirrel HT1 (G-BXHB)	DHFS, RAF Shawbury
	ZJ263	AS350BB Squirrel HT1 (G-BXHK)	DHFS, RAF Shawbury
	ZJ264	AS350BB Squirrel HT1 (G-BXHW)	DHFS, RAF Shawbury
	ZJ265	AS350BB Squirrel HT1 (G-BXHX)	DHFS, RAF Shawbury
	ZJ266	AS350BB Squirrel HT1 (G-BXIL)	DHFS, RAF Shawbury
	ZJ267	AS350BB Squirrel HT1 (G-BXIP)	DHFS, RAF Shawbury
	ZJ268	AS350BB Squirrel HT1 (G-BXJE)	DHFS, RAF Shawbury
	ZJ269	AS350BB Squirrel HT1 (G-BXJN)	DHFS, RAF Shawbury
	ZJ270	AS350BB Squirrel HT1 (G-BXJR)	DHFS, RAF Shawbury
	ZJ271	AS350BB Squirrel HT1 (G-BXKE)	DHFS, RAF Shawbury
	ZJ272	AS350BB Squirrel HT1 (G-BXKN)	DHFS, RAF Shawbury
	ZJ273	AS350BB Squirrel HT1 (G-BXKP)	DHFS, RAF Shawbury
	ZJ274	AS350BB Squirrel HT1 (G-BXKR)	DHFS, RAF Shawbury
	ZJ275	AS350BB Squirrel HT1 (G-BXLB)	DHFS, RAF Shawbury
	ZJ276	AS350BB Squirrel HT1 (G-BXLE)	DHFS, RAF Shawbury
	ZJ277	AS350BB Squirrel HT1 (G-BXLH)	DHFS, RAF Shawbury
	ZJ278	AS350BB Squirrel HT1 (G-BXMB)	DHFS, RAF Shawbury

Serial	Type (other identity) [code]	Owner/operator, location or fate	Notes
ZJ279	AS350BB Squirrel HT1 (G-BXMC)	DHFS, RAF Shawbury	
ZJ280	AS350BB Squirrel HT1 (G-BXMI)	DHFS, RAF Shawbury	
ZJ514	BAE Systems Nimrod MRA4 (XV251) [PA-4]	DPA/BAE Systems, Woodford (conversion)	
ZJ515	BAE Systems Nimrod MRA4 (XV258) [PA-5]	DPA/BAE Systems, Woodford (conversion)	
ZJ516	BAE Systems Nimrod MRA4 (XV247) [PA-1]	DPA/BAE Systems, Woodford (conversion)	
ZJ517	BAE Systems Nimrod MRA4 (XV242) [PA-3]	DPA/BAE Systems, Woodford (conversion)	
ZJ518	BAE Systems Nimrod MRA4 (XV234) [PA-2]	DPA/BAE Systems, Woodford (conversion)	
ZJ519	BAE Systems Nimrod MRA4 (XZ284) [PA-6]	DPA/BAE Systems, Woodford (conversion)	
ZJ520	BAE Systems Nimrod MRA4 (XV247) [PA-7]	DPA/BAE Systems, Woodford (conversion)	
ZJ521	BAE Systems Nimrod MRA4 [PA-8]	BAE Systems, for RAF	
ZJ522	BAE Systems Nimrod MRA4 [PA-9]	BAE Systems, for RAF	
ZJ523	BAE Systems Nimrod MRA4 [PA-10]	BAE Systems, for RAF	
ZJ524	BAE Systems Nimrod MRA4 [PA-11]	BAE Systems, for RAF	
ZJ525	BAE Systems Nimrod MRA4 [PA-12]	BAE Systems, for RAF	
ZJ526	BAE Systems Nimrod MRA4 [PA-13]	BAE Systems, for RAF	
ZJ527	BAE Systems Nimrod MRA4 [PA-14]	BAE Systems, for RAF	
ZJ528	BAE Systems Nimrod MRA4 [PA-15]	BAE Systems, for RAF	
ZJ529	BAE Systems Nimrod MRA4 [PA-16]	BAE Systems, for RAF	
ZJ530	BAE Systems Nimrod MRA4 [PA-17]	BAE Systems, for RAF	
ZJ531	BAE Systems Nimrod MRA4 [PA-18]	BAE Systems, for RAF	
ZJ635	AS355F-1 Twin Squirrel (G-NEXT)	DPA/ETPS, Boscombe Down	
ZJ645	D-BD Alpha Jet (98+62)	DPA/ETPS, Boscombe Down	
ZJ646	D-BD Alpha Jet (98+55)	DPA/AFD/QinetiQ, Llanbedr	
ZJ647	D-BD Alpha Jet (98+71)	DPA/ETPS, Boscombe Down	
ZJ648	D-BD Alpha Jet (98+09)	DPA/AFD/QinetiQ, Boscombe Down	
ZJ649	D-BD Alpha Jet (98+73)	DPA/AFD/QinetiQ, Llanbedr	
ZJ650	D-BD Alpha Jet (98+35)	DPA/AFD/QinetiQ, Boscombe Down	
ZJ651	D-BD Alpha Jet (41+42)	DPA/QinetiQ Boscombe Down, spares use	
ZJ652	D-BD Alpha Jet (41+09)	DPA/QinetiQ Boscombe Down, spares use	
ZJ653	D-BD Alpha Jet (40+22)	DPA/QinetiQ Boscombe Down, spares use	
ZJ654	D-BD Alpha Jet (41+02)	DPA/QinetiQ Boscombe Down, spares use	
ZJ655	D-BD Alpha Jet (41+19)	DPA/QinetiQ Boscombe Down, spares use	
ZJ656	D-BD Alpha Jet (41+40)	DPA/QinetiQ Boscombe Down, spares use	
ZJ690	Bombardier Sentinel R1 (C-GJRG)	Bombardier, for RAF	
ZJ691	Bombardier Sentinel R1 (C-FZVM)	DPA/BAE Systems, Chester	
ZJ692	Bombardier Sentinel R1 (C-FZWW)	DPA/BAE Systems, Chester	
ZJ693	Bombardier Sentinel R1 (C-FZXC)	DPA/BAE Systems, Chester	
ZJ694	Bombardier Sentinel R1	DPA/BAE Systems, Chester	
ZJ695	Eurofighter Training Rig	RAF No 1 SoTT, Cosford	
ZJ696	Eurofighter Training Rig	RAF No 1 SoTT, Cosford	
ZJ697	Eurofighter Training Rig	RAF No 1 SoTT, Cosford	
ZJ698	Eurofighter Training Rig	RAF No 1 SoTT, Cosford	
ZJ699	Eurofighter Typhoon (PT001)	DPA/BAE Systems, Warton	
ZJ700	Eurofighter Typhoon (PS002)	DPA/BAE Systems, Warton	
ZJ702	FR Falconet	For Army	
ZJ703	Bell 412EP Griffin HAR2 (G-CBST) [Spades,3]	RAF No 84 Sqn, Akrotiri	
ZJ704	Bell 412EP Griffin HAR2 (G-CBWT) [Clubs,4]	RAF No 84 Sqn, Akrotiri	
ZJ705	Bell 412EP Griffin HAR2 (G-CBXL) [Hearts, 5]	RAF No 84 Sqn, Akrotiri	
ZJ706	Bell 412EP Griffin HAR2 (G-CBYR) [Diamonds, 6]	RAF No 84 Sqn, Akrotiri	
ZJ707	Bell 412EP Griffin HT1 (G-CBUB) [O]	DHFS No 60(R) Sqn, RAF Shawbury	

Notes	Serial	Type (other identity) [code]	Owner/operator, location or fate
	ZJ708	Bell 412EP Griffin HT1 (G-CBVP) [K]	Bell Helicopters, for RAF
	ZJ800	Eurofighter Typhoon T1 (BT001)	DPA/AFD/QinetiQ, Boscombe Down
	ZJ801	Eurofighter Typhoon T1 (BT002)	DPA/BAE Systems, for RAF
	ZJ802	Eurofighter Typhoon T1 (BT003) [AB]	RAF No 17(R) Sqn, Warton
	ZJ803	Eurofighter Typhoon T1 (BT004) [AA]	RAF No 17(R) Sqn, Warton
	ZJ804	Eurofighter Typhoon T1 (BT005)	DPA/BAE Systems, for RAF
	ZJ805	Eurofighter Typhoon T1 (BT006)	DPA/BAE Systems, for RAF
	ZJ806	Eurofighter Typhoon T1 (BT007)	DPA/BAE Systems, for RAF
	ZJ807	Eurofighter Typhoon T1 (BT008)	DPA/BAE Systems, for RAF
	ZJ808	Eurofighter Typhoon T1 (BT009)	DPA/BAE Systems, for RAF
	ZJ809	Eurofighter Typhoon T1 (BT010)	DPA/BAE Systems, for RAF
	ZJ810	Eurofighter Typhoon T1 (BT011)	DPA/BAE Systems, for RAF
	ZJ811	Eurofighter Typhoon T1 (BT012)	DPA/BAE Systems, for RAF
	ZJ812	Eurofighter Typhoon T1 (BT013)	DPA/BAE Systems, for RAF
	ZJ813	Eurofighter Typhoon T1 (BT014)	DPA/BAE Systems, for RAF
	ZJ814	Eurofighter Typhoon T1 (BT015)	DPA/BAE Systems, for RAF
	ZJ815	Eurofighter Typhoon T1 (BT016)	DPA/BAE Systems, for RAF
	ZJ904	WS Lynx 100	*To R Malaysian Navy as M501-1, June 2003*
	ZJ905	WS Lynx 100	*To R Malaysian Navy as M501-2, 2003*
	ZJ906	WS Lynx 100	*To R Malaysian Navy as M501-3, 2004*
	ZJ907	WS Lynx 100	*To R Malaysian Navy as M501-4, 2003*
	ZJ908	WS Lynx 100	*To R Malaysian Navy as M501-5, July 2003*
	ZJ909	WS Lynx 100	*To R Malaysian Navy as M501-6, 2003*
	ZJ910	Eurofighter Typhoon F2 (BS0001)	DPA/BAE Systems, for RAF
	ZJ911	Eurofighter Typhoon F2 (BS0002)	DPA/BAE Systems, for RAF
	ZJ912	Eurofighter Typhoon F2 (BS0003)	DPA/BAE Systems, for RAF
	ZJ913	Eurofighter Typhoon F2 (BS0004)	DPA/BAE Systems, for RAF
	ZJ914	Eurofighter Typhoon F2 (BS0005)	DPA/BAE Systems, for RAF
	ZJ915	Eurofighter Typhoon F2 (BS0006)	DPA/BAE Systems, for RAF
	ZJ916	Eurofighter Typhoon F2 (BS0007)	DPA/BAE Systems, for RAF
	ZJ917	Eurofighter Typhoon F2 (BS0008)	DPA/BAE Systems, for RAF
	ZJ918	Eurofighter Typhoon F2 (BS0009)	DPA/BAE Systems, for RAF
	ZJ919	Eurofighter Typhoon F2 (BS0010)	DPA/BAE Systems, for RAF
	ZJ920	Eurofighter Typhoon F2 (BS0011)	DPA/BAE Systems, for RAF
	ZJ921	Eurofighter Typhoon F2 (BS0012)	DPA/BAE Systems, for RAF
	ZJ922	Eurofighter Typhoon F2 (BS0013)	DPA/BAE Systems, for RAF
	ZJ923	Eurofighter Typhoon F2 (BS0014)	DPA/BAE Systems, for RAF
	ZJ924	Eurofighter Typhoon F2 (BS0015)	DPA/BAE Systems, for RAF
	ZJ925	Eurofighter Typhoon F2 (BS0016)	DPA/BAE Systems, for RAF
	ZJ926	Eurofighter Typhoon F2 (BS0017)	DPA/BAE Systems, for RAF
	ZJ927	Eurofighter Typhoon F2 (BS0018)	DPA/BAE Systems, for RAF
	ZJ928	Eurofighter Typhoon F2 (BS0019)	DPA/BAE Systems, for RAF
	ZJ929	Eurofighter Typhoon F2 (BS0020)	DPA/BAE Systems, for RAF
	ZJ930	Eurofighter Typhoon F2 (BS0021)	DPA/BAE Systems, for RAF
	ZJ931	Eurofighter Typhoon F2 (BS0022)	DPA/BAE Systems, for RAF
	ZJ932	Eurofighter Typhoon F2 (BS0023)	DPA/BAE Systems, for RAF
	ZJ933	Eurofighter Typhoon F2 (BS0024)	DPA/BAE Systems, for RAF
	ZJ934	Eurofighter Typhoon F2 (BS0025)	DPA/BAE Systems, for RAF
	ZJ935	Eurofighter Typhoon F2 (BS0026)	DPA/BAE Systems, for RAF
	ZJ936	Eurofighter Typhoon F2 (BS0027)	DPA/BAE Systems, for RAF
	ZJ937	Eurofighter Typhoon F2 (BS0028)	DPA/BAE Systems, for RAF
	ZJ938	Eurofighter Typhoon F2 (BS0029)	DPA/BAE Systems, for RAF
	ZJ939	Eurofighter Typhoon F2 (BS0030)	DPA/BAE Systems, for RAF
	ZJ940	Eurofighter Typhoon F2 (BS0031)	DPA/BAE Systems, for RAF
	ZJ941	Eurofighter Typhoon F2 (BS0032)	DPA/BAE Systems, for RAF
	ZJ942	Eurofighter Typhoon F2 (BS0033)	DPA/BAE Systems, for RAF
	ZJ943	Eurofighter Typhoon F2 (BS0034)	DPA/BAE Systems, for RAF
	ZJ944	Eurofighter Typhoon F2 (BS0035)	DPA/BAE Systems, for RAF
	ZJ945	Eurofighter Typhoon F2 (BS0036)	DPA/BAE Systems, for RAF
	ZJ951	BAE Systems Hawk 120D	BAE Systems, Warton
	ZJ954	SA330H Puma HC1	DPA/Eurocopter, for RAF
	ZJ955	SA330H Puma HC1	DPA/Eurocopter, for RAF
	ZJ956	SA330H Puma HC1	DPA/Eurocopter, for RAF
	ZJ957	SA330H Puma HC1	DPA/Eurocopter, for RAF
	ZJ958	SA330H Puma HC1	DPA/Eurocopter, for RAF
	ZJ959	SA330H Puma HC1	DPA/Eurocopter, for RAF
	ZJ960	Grob G109B Vigilant T1 (D-KSMU) [SH]	RAF ACCGS/No 644 VGS, Syerston

Serial	Type (other identity) [code]	Owner/operator, location or fate	Notes
ZJ961	Grob G109B Vigilant T1 (D-KLCW) [SJ]	RAF ACCGS/No 644 VGS, Syerston	
ZJ962	Grob G109B Vigilant T1 (D-KBEU) [SK]	RAF ACCGS/No 644 VGS, Syerston	
ZJ963	Grob G109B Vigilant T1 (D-KMSN) [SL]	RAF No 616 VGS, Henlow	
ZJ964	Bell 212HP (G-BJGV) [A]	AAC No 25 Flt, Belize	
ZJ965	Bell 212HP (G-BJGU) [B]	AAC No 25 Flt, Belize	
ZJ966	Bell 212HP (G-BJJO) [C]	AAC No 25 Flt, Belize	
ZJ967	Grob G109B Vigilant T1 (G-DEWS) [SM]	RAF ACCGS/No 644 VGS, Syerston	
ZJ968	Grob G109B Vigilant T1 (N109BT) [SN]	RAF CGMF, Syerston	
ZJ969	Bell 212 (G-BGLJ)	*Restored as G-BGLJ*	
ZJ970	BAE Systems Hawk 120	*To South African AF as 250, 17 October 2003*	
ZJ971	WS Lynx 120	Westland Helicopters, for Oman	
ZJ972	WS Lynx 120	Westland Helicopters, for Oman	
ZJ973	WS Lynx 120	Westland Helicopters, for Oman	
ZJ974	WS Lynx 120	Westland Helicopters, for Oman	
ZJ975	WS Lynx 120	Westland Helicopters, for Oman	
ZJ976	WS Lynx 120	Westland Helicopters, for Oman	
ZJ977	WS Lynx 120	Westland Helicopters, for Oman	
ZJ978	WS Lynx 120	Westland Helicopters, for Oman	
ZJ979	WS Lynx 120	Westland Helicopters, for Oman	
ZJ980	WS Lynx 120	Westland Helicopters, for Oman	
ZJ981	WS Lynx 120	Westland Helicopters, for Oman	
ZJ982	WS Lynx 120	Westland Helicopters, for Oman	
ZJ983	WS Lynx 120	Westland Helicopters, for Oman	
ZJ984	WS Lynx 120	Westland Helicopters, for Oman	
ZJ985	WS Lynx 120	Westland Helicopters, for Oman	
ZJ986	WS Lynx 120	Westland Helicopters, for Oman	
ZJ987	WS Lynx 110	Westland Helicopters, for Thailand	
ZJ988	WS Lynx 110	Westland Helicopters, for Thailand	
ZJ989	EADS Eagle O	DPA/BAE Systems, Warton	
ZJ990	EH101 Merlin 512	Westland Helicopters for Denmark as M-501	
ZJ991	EH101 Merlin 512	Westland Helicopters for Denmark as M-502	
ZJ992	EH101 Merlin 512	Westland Helicopters for Denmark as M-503	
ZJ993	EH101 Merlin 512	Westland Helicopters for Denmark as M-504	
ZJ994	EH101 Merlin 512	Westland Helicopters for Denmark as M-505	
ZJ995	EH101 Merlin 512	Westland Helicopters for Denmark as M-506	
ZJ996	EH101 Merlin 512	Westland Helicopters for Denmark as M-507	
ZJ997	EH101 Merlin 512	Westland Helicopters for Denmark as M-508	
ZJ998	EH101 Merlin 512	Westland Helicopters for Denmark as M-509	
ZJ999	EH101 Merlin 512	Westland Helicopters for Denmark as M-510	
ZK001	EH101 Merlin 512	Westland Helicopters for Denmark as M-511	
ZK002	EH101 Merlin 512	Westland Helicopters for Denmark as M-512	
ZK003	EH101 Merlin 512	Westland Helicopters for Denmark as M-513	
ZK004	EH101 Merlin 512	Westland Helicopters for Denmark as M-514	
ZK102	Lockheed Martin DesertHawk	Lockheed Martin/DPA	
ZK201	Meggitt Banshee	For Army	
ZK202	Meggitt Banshee	For Army	
ZK203	Meggitt Banshee	For Army	
ZK204	Meggitt Banshee	For Army	
ZK531	BAe Hawk T53 (LL-5306)	DPA/BAE Systems, Warton	
ZK532	BAe Hawk T53 (LL-5315)	DPA/BAE Systems, Warton	
ZK533	BAe Hawk T53 (LL-5317)	DPA/BAE Systems, Warton	
ZK534	BAe Hawk T53 (LL-5319)	DPA/BAE Systems, Brough	
ZK535	BAe Hawk T53 (LL-5320)	DPA/BAE Systems, Warton	
ZT800	WS Super Lynx Mk 300	DPA/Westland Helicopters, Yeovil	
ZZ171	Boeing C-17A Globemaster III (00-201/N171UK)	RAF No 99 Sqn, Brize Norton	
ZZ172	Boeing C-17A Globemaster III (00-202/N172UK)	RAF No 99 Sqn, Brize Norton	
ZZ173	Boeing C-17A Globemaster III (00-203/N173UK)	RAF No 99 Sqn, Brize Norton	
ZZ174	Boeing C-17A Globemaster III (00-204/N174UK)	RAF No 99 Sqn, Brize Norton	
ZZ175	Boeing C-17A Globemaster III	Boeing, Long Beach, for RAF	

The Shuttleworth Collection's Westland Lysander V9367 is painted to represent an aircraft used to drop agents at night in occupied Europe. *PRM*

A rare formation flypast by Shuttleworth's Sea Hurricane Z7015 and Spitfire VC AR501 at Old Warden. *PRM*

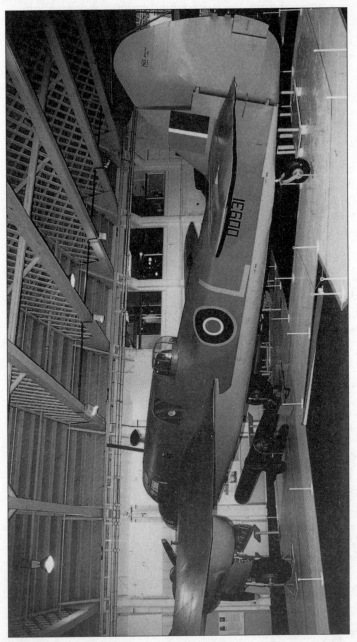

Bristol Beaufort VIII DD931 on display at the RAF Museum, Hendon. *PRM*

Air Atlantique Historic Flight operates Anson T21 WD413 from Coventry. *PRM*

Another of Air Atlantique Historic Flight's classic aircraft is this Canberra B2/6 WK163. *PRM*

Based at Wellesbourne Mountford, this smart Chipmunk T10 WK514 is privately owned. *PRM*

Former Swiss Air Force Venom FB50 WR470 flies from Coventry. *PRM*

Phantom FGR2 XT914 on the gate at RAF Brampton, Huntingdon. *PRM*

Former Army Air Corps Scout AH1 XV140 now flown by Kennet Aviation from North Weald. *PRM*

Lynx HMA8 XZ697 whilst operating with the HMS *Grafton* Flight of No 815 Squadron in 2003. *PRM*

Leuchars-based Tornado F3 ZE207 of No 56 Squadron 'Firebirds'. *PRM*

RN Sea Harrier FA2 ZE693 here operating with 899 Squadron at RNAS Yeovilton. *PRM*

Highly visible black-painted Tucano T1 ZF406 of No 1 FTS, Linton-on-Ouse. *PRM*

BAE Systems Hawk 102D demonstrator ZJ100 touching down at RAF Fairford. *PRM*.

Serial	Type (other identity) [code]	Owner/operator, location or fate	Notes
G-BLVI	Slingsby T.67M Firefly 2	HCS/CFS, Cranwell	
G-BNSO	Slingsby T.67M Firefly 2	HCS/DEFTS, Barkston Heath	
G-BNSP	Slingsby T.67M Firefly 2	HCS/CFS, Cranwell	
G-BNSR	Slingsby T.67M Firefly 2	HCS/CFS, Cranwell	
G-BONT	Slingsby T.67M Firefly 2	HCS/CFS, Cranwell	
G-BUUA	Slingsby T.67M Firefly 2	HCS/DEFTS, Barkston Heath	
G-BUUB	Slingsby T.67M Firefly 2	HCS/DEFTS, Barkston Heath	
G-BUUC	Slingsby T.67M Firefly 2	HCS/DEFTS, Barkston Heath	
G-BUUD	Slingsby T.67M Firefly 2	HCS/DEFTS, Barkston Heath	
G-BUUE	Slingsby T.67M Firefly 2	HCS/DEFTS, Barkston Heath	
G-BUUF	Slingsby T.67M Firefly 2	HCS/DEFTS, Barkston Heath	
G-BUUG	Slingsby T.67M Firefly 2	HCS/DEFTS, Barkston Heath	
G-BUUI	Slingsby T.67M Firefly 2	HCS/DEFTS, Barkston Heath	
G-BUUJ	Slingsby T.67M Firefly 2	HCS/DEFTS, Barkston Heath	
G-BUUK	Slingsby T.67M Firefly 2	HCS/DEFTS, Barkston Heath	
G-BUUL	Slingsby T.67M Firefly 2	HCS/DEFTS, Barkston Heath	
G-BVHC	Grob G.115D-2 Heron	Shorts Bros/RN No 727 Sqn, Plymouth	
G-BVHD	Grob G.115D-2 Heron	Shorts Bros/RN No 727 Sqn, Plymouth	
G-BVHE	Grob G.115D-2 Heron	Shorts Bros/RN No 727 Sqn, Plymouth	
G-BVHF	Grob G.115D-2 Heron	Shorts Bros/RN No 727 Sqn, Plymouth	
G-BVHG	Grob G.115D-2 Heron	Shorts Bros/RN No 727 Sqn, Plymouth	
G-BWXC	Slingsby T.67M Firefly 260	HCS/DEFTS, Barkston Heath	
G-BWXD	Slingsby T.67M Firefly 260	HCS/DEFTS, Barkston Heath	
G-BWXF	Slingsby T.67M Firefly 260	HCS/DEFTS, Barkston Heath	
G-BWXI	Slingsby T.67M Firefly 260	HCS/DEFTS, Barkston Heath	
G-BWXJ	Slingsby T.67M Firefly 260	HCS/DEFTS, Barkston Heath	
G-BWXO	Slingsby T.67M Firefly 260	HCS/DEFTS, Barkston Heath	
G-BWXR	Slingsby T.67M Firefly 260	HCS/DEFTS, Barkston Heath	
G-BWXS	Slingsby T.67M Firefly 260	HCS/DEFTS, Barkston Heath	
G-BWXT	Slingsby T.67M Firefly 260	HCS/DEFTS, Barkston Heath	
G-BWXY	Slingsby T.67M Firefly 260	HCS/DEFTS, Barkston Heath	
G-BYUA	Grob G.115E Tutor (D-EUKB)	Bombardier/Cambridge UAS, Wyton	
G-BYUB	Grob G.115E Tutor	Bombardier/University of Wales AS, St Athan	
G-BYUC	Grob G.115E Tutor	Bombardier/CFS/East Midlands Universities AS, Cranwell	
G-BYUD	Grob G.115E Tutor	Bombardier/Northumbrian Universities AS, Leeming	
G-BYUE	Grob G.115E Tutor	Bombardier/CFS/East Midlands Universities AS, Cranwell	
G-BYUF	Grob G.115E Tutor	Bombardier/Cambridge UAS/University of London AS, Wyton	
G-BYUG	Grob G.115E Tutor	Bombardier/Universities of Glasgow & Strathclyde AS, Glasgow	
G-BYUH	Grob G.115E Tutor	Bombardier/Bristol UAS, Colerne	
G-BYUI	Grob G.115E Tutor	Bombardier/Liverpool UAS/Manchester and Salford Universities AS, Woodvale	
G-BYUJ	Grob G.115E Tutor	Bombardier/Southampton UAS, Boscombe Down	
G-BYUK	Grob G.115E Tutor	Bombardier/CFS/East Midlands Universities AS, Cranwell	
G-BYUL	Grob G.115E Tutor	Bombardier/University of London AS, Wyton	
G-BYUM	Grob G.115E Tutor	Bombardier/Southampton UAS, Boscombe Down	
G-BYUN	Grob G.115E Tutor	Bombardier/University of Wales AS, St Athan	
G-BYUO	Grob G.115E Tutor	Bombardier/University of London AS, Wyton	
G-BYUP	Grob G.115E Tutor	Bombardier/Oxford UAS, Benson	
G-BYUR	Grob G.115E Tutor	Bombardier/East Lowlands UAS/ Aberdeen, Dundee & St Andrews UAS, Leuchars	
G-BYUS	Grob G.115E Tutor	Bombardier/Oxford UAS, Benson	
G-BYUT	Grob G.115E Tutor	Bombardier/University of Wales AS, St Athan	

Civil Registered Aircraft in UK Military Service

Notes	Serial	Type (other identity) [code]	Owner/operator, location or fate
	G-BYUU	Grob G.115E Tutor	Bombardier/Universities of Glasgow & Strathclyde AS, Glasgow
	G-BYUV	Grob G.115E Tutor	Bombardier/Oxford UAS, Benson
	G-BYUW	Grob G.115E Tutor	Bombardier/East Lowlands UAS/ Aberdeen, Dundee & St Andrews UAS, Leuchars
	G-BYUX	Grob G.115E Tutor	Bombardier/Liverpool UAS/Manchester and Salford Universities AS, Woodvale
	G-BYUY	Grob G.115E Tutor	Bombardier/East Lowlands UAS/ Aberdeen, Dundee & St Andrews UAS, Leuchars
	G-BYUZ	Grob G.115E Tutor	Bombardier/Liverpool UAS/Manchester and Salford Universities AS, Woodvale
	G-BYVA	Grob G.115E Tutor	Bombardier/CFS/East Midlands Universities AS, Cranwell
	G-BYVB	Grob G.115E Tutor	Bombardier/Universities of Glasgow & Strathclyde AS, Glasgow
	G-BYVC	Grob G.115E Tutor	Bombardier/Bristol UAS, Colerne
	G-BYVD	Grob G.115E Tutor	Bombardier/Cambridge UAS/University of London AS, Wyton
	G-BYVE	Grob G.115E Tutor	Bombardier/Southampton UAS, Boscombe Down
	G-BYVF	Grob G.115E Tutor	Bombardier/Universities of Glasgow & Strathclyde AS, Glasgow
	G-BYVG	Grob G.115E Tutor	Bombardier/CFS/East Midlands Universities AS, Cranwell
	G-BYVH	Grob G.115E Tutor	Bombardier/East Lowlands UAS/ Aberdeen, Dundee & St Andrews UAS, Leuchars
	G-BYVI	Grob G.115E Tutor	Bombardier/East Lowlands UAS/ Aberdeen, Dundee & St Andrews UAS, Leuchars
	G-BYVJ	Grob G.115E Tutor	Bombardier/Cambridge UAS/University of London AS, Wyton
	G-BYVK	Grob G.115E Tutor	Bombardier/Southampton UAS, Boscombe Down
	G-BYVL	Grob G.115E Tutor	Bombardier/Oxford UAS, Benson
	G-BYVM	Grob G.115E Tutor	Bombardier/East Lowlands UAS/ Aberdeen, Dundee & St Andrews UAS, Leuchars
	G-BYVN	Grob G.115E Tutor	Bombardier/Bristol UAS, Colerne
	G-BYVO	Grob G.115E Tutor	Bombardier/University of Birmingham AS, Cosford
	G-BYVP	Grob G.115E Tutor	Bombardier/Oxford UAS, Benson
	G-BYVR	Grob G.115E Tutor	Bombardier/CFS/East Midlands Universities AS, Cranwell
	G-BYVS	Grob G.115E Tutor	Bombardier/Cambridge UAS/University of London AS, Wyton
	G-BYVT	Grob G.115E Tutor	Bombardier/Cambridge UAS/University of London AS, Wyton
	G-BYVU	Grob G.115E Tutor	Bombardier/Oxford UAS, Benson
	G-BYVV	Grob G.115E Tutor	Bombardier/Yorkshire Universities AS, Church Fenton
	G-BYVW	Grob G.115E Tutor	Bombardier/Yorkshire Universities AS, Church Fenton
	G-BYVX	Grob G.115E Tutor	Bombardier/Yorkshire Universities AS, Church Fenton
	G-BYVY	Grob G.115E Tutor	Bombardier/Yorkshire Universities AS, Church Fenton
	G-BYVZ	Grob G.115E Tutor	Bombardier/Yorkshire Universities AS, Church Fenton
	G-BYWA	Grob G.115E Tutor	Bombardier/University of Wales AS, St Athan
	G-BYWB	Grob G.115E Tutor	Bombardier/Bristol UAS, Colerne
	G-BYWC	Grob G.115E Tutor	Bombardier/Bristol UAS, Colerne
	G-BYWD	Grob G.115E Tutor	Bombardier/Liverpool UAS/Manchester and Salford Universities AS, Woodvale
	G-BYWE	Grob G.115E Tutor	Bombardier/Bristol UAS, Colerne
	G-BYWF	Grob G.115E Tutor	Bombardier/CFS/East Midlands Universities AS, Cranwell
	G-BYWG	Grob G.115E Tutor	Bombardier/Bristol UAS, Colerne
	G-BYWH	Grob G.115E Tutor	Bombardier/Northumbrian Universities AS, Leeming

Serial	Type (other identity) [code]	Owner/operator, location or fate	Notes
G-BYWI	Grob G.115E Tutor	Bombardier/Bristol UAS, Colerne	
G-BYWJ	Grob G.115E Tutor	Bombardier/Liverpool UAS/Manchester and Salford Universities AS, Woodvale	
G-BYWK	Grob G.115E Tutor	Bombardier/CFS/East Midlands Universities AS, Cranwell	
G-BYWL	Grob G.115E Tutor	Bombardier/Liverpool UAS/Manchester and Salford Universities AS, Woodvale	
G-BYWM	Grob G.115E Tutor	Bombardier/CFS/East Midlands Universities AS, Cranwell	
G-BYWN	Grob G.115E Tutor	Bombardier/Liverpool UAS/Manchester and Salford Universities AS, Woodvale	
G-BYWO	Grob G.115E Tutor	Bombardier/University of Birmingham AS, Cosford	
G-BYWP	Grob G.115E Tutor	Bombardier/Yorkshire Universities AS, Church Fenton	
G-BYWR	Grob G.115E Tutor	Bombardier/Cambridge UAS/University of London AS, Wyton	
G-BYWS	Grob G.115E Tutor	Bombardier/Northumbrian Universities AS, Leeming	
G-BYWT	Grob G.115E Tutor	Bombardier/Northumbrian Universities AS, Leeming	
G-BYWU	Grob G.115E Tutor	Bombardier/Cambridge UAS/University of London AS, Wyton	
G-BYWV	Grob G.115E Tutor	Bombardier/University of Birmingham AS, Cosford	
G-BYWW	Grob G.115E Tutor	Bombardier/CFS/East Midlands Universities AS, Cranwell	
G-BYWX	Grob G.115E Tutor	Bombardier/Cambridge UAS/University of London AS, Wyton	
G-BYWY	Grob G.115E Tutor	Bombardier/CFS/East Midlands Universities AS, Cranwell	
G-BYWZ	Grob G.115E Tutor	Bombardier/CFS/East Midlands Universities AS, Cranwell	
G-BYXA	Grob G.115E Tutor	Bombardier/Liverpool UAS/Manchester and Salford Universities AS, Woodvale	
G-BYXB	Grob G.115E Tutor	Bombardier/Southampton UAS, Boscombe Down	
G-BYXC	Grob G.115E Tutor	Bombardier/CFS/East Midlands Universities AS, Cranwell	
G-BYXD	Grob G.115E Tutor	Bombardier/CFS/East Midlands Universities AS, Cranwell	
G-BYXE	Grob G.115E Tutor	Bombardier/Yorkshire Universities AS, Church Fenton	
G-BYXF	Grob G.115E Tutor	Bombardier/University of Birmingham AS, Cosford	
G-BYXG	Grob G.115E Tutor	Bombardier/University of Birmingham AS, Cosford	
G-BYXH	Grob G.115E Tutor	Bombardier/Cambridge UAS/University of London AS, Wyton	
G-BYXI	Grob G.115E Tutor	Bombardier/Liverpool UAS/Manchester and Salford Universities AS, Woodvale	
G-BYXJ	Grob G.115E Tutor	Bombardier/Southampton UAS, Boscombe Down	
G-BYXK	Grob G.115E Tutor	Bombardier/Cambridge UAS/University of London AS, Wyton	
G-BYXL	Grob G.115E Tutor	Bombardier/University of Birmingham AS, Cosford	
G-BYXM	Grob G.115E Tutor	Bombardier/Southampton UAS, Boscombe Down	
G-BYXN	Grob G.115E Tutor	Bombardier/CFS/East Midlands Universities AS, Cranwell	
G-BYXO	Grob G.115E Tutor	Bombardier/University of Birmingham AS, Cosford	
G-BYXP	Grob G.115E Tutor	Bombardier/Cambridge UAS/University of London AS, Wyton	
G-BYXR	Grob G.115E Tutor	Bombardier/Oxford UAS, Benson	
G-BYXS	Grob G.115E Tutor	Bombardier/Oxford UAS, Benson	
G-BYXT	Grob G.115E Tutor	Bombardier/Southampton UAS, Boscombe Down	
G-BYXX	Grob G.115E Tutor	Bombardier/Liverpool UAS/Manchester and Salford Universities AS, Woodvale	
G-BYXY	Grob G.115E Tutor	Bombardier/Northumbrian Universities AS, Leeming	

Civil Registered Aircraft in UK Military Service

Notes	Serial	Type (other identity) [code]	Owner/operator, location or fate
	G-BYXZ	Grob G.115E Tutor	Bombardier/CFS/East Midlands Universities AS, Cranwell
	G-BYYA	Grob G.115E Tutor	Bombardier/Northumbrian Universities AS, Leeming
	G-BYYB	Grob G.115E Tutor	Bombardier/CFS/East Midlands Universities AS, Cranwell
	G-FFRA	Dassault Falcon 20DC (N902FR)	FR Aviation, Teesside
	G-FRAE	Dassault Falcon 20E (N910FR)	FR Aviation, Bournemouth
	G-FRAF	Dassault Falcon 20E (N911FR)	FR Aviation, Bournemouth
	G-FRAH	Dassault Falcon 20DC (N900FR)	FR Aviation, Teesside
	G-FRAI	Dassault Falcon 20E (N901FR)	FR Aviation, Teesside
	G-FRAJ	Dassault Falcon 20E (N903FR)	FR Aviation, Teesside
	G-FRAK	Dassault Falcon 20DC (N905FR)	FR Aviation, Bournemouth
	G-FRAL	Dassault Falcon 20DC (N904FR)	FR Aviation, Teesside
	G-FRAM	Dassault Falcon 20DC (N907FR)	FR Aviation, Bournemouth
	G-FRAO	Dassault Falcon 20DC (N906FR)	FR Aviation, Bournemouth
	G-FRAP	Dassault Falcon 20DC (N908FR)	FR Aviation, Bournemouth
	G-FRAR	Dassault Falcon 20DC (N909FR)	FR Aviation, Bournemouth
	G-FRAS	Dassault Falcon 20C (117501)	FR Aviation, Teesside
	G-FRAT	Dassault Falcon 20C (117502)	FR Aviation, Teesside
	G-FRAU	Dassault Falcon 20C (117504)	FR Aviation, Teesside
	G-FRAW	Dassault Falcon 20ECM (117507)	FR Aviation, Teesside
	G-FRBA	Dassault Falcon 20C	FR Aviation, Bournemouth
	G-HONG	Slingsby T.67M Firefly 2	HCS/DEFTS, Barkston Heath
	G-KONG	Slingsby T.67M Firefly 2	HCS/DEFTS, Barkston Heath
	G-RAFJ	Beech King Air B200 (N6129N)	SERCO/RAF No 3 FTS/45 (R) Sqn, Cranwell
	G-RAFK	Beech King Air B200 (N5013O)	SERCO/RAF No 3 FTS/45 (R) Sqn, Cranwell
	G-RAFL	Beech King Air B200 (N5032K)	SERCO/RAF No 3 FTS/45 (R) Sqn, Cranwell
	G-RAFM	Beech King Air B200 (N51283)	SERCO/RAF No 3 FTS/45 (R) Sqn, Cranwell
	G-RAFN	Beech King Air B200 (N60275)	SERCO/RAF No 3 FTS/45 (R) Sqn, Cranwell
	G-RAFO	Beech King Air B200 (N60476)	SERCO/RAF No 3 FTS/45 (R) Sqn, Cranwell
	G-RAFP	Beech King Air B200 (N61037)	SERCO/RAF No 3 FTS/45 (R) Sqn, Cranwell
	G-XXEA	Sikorsky S-76C+	Air Hanson/The Royal Flight, Blackbushe

One of FR Aviation's fleet of Teesside-based Falcon 20Cs. *PRM*

1764M/K4972	7525M/WT619	7829M/XH992	8012M/VS562
2015M/K5600	7530M/WT648	7839M/WV781	8017M/XL762
2292M/K8203	7532M/WT651	7841M/WV783	8018M/XN344
2361M/K6035	7533M/WT680	7851M/WZ706	8021M/XL824
3118M/H5199/(BK892)	7544M/WN904	7852M/XG506	8022M/XN341
3858M/X7688	7548M/PS915	7854M/XM191	8027M/XM555
4354M/BL614	7556M/WK584	7855M/XK416	8032M/XH837
4552M/T5298	7564M/XE982	7859M/XP283	8033M/XD382
5377M/EP120	7570M/XD674	7860M/XL738	8034M/XL703
5405M/LF738	7582M/WP190	7862M/XR246	8041M/XF690
5466M/*BN230*/(LF751)	7583M/WP185	7863M/*XP248*	8043M/XF836
5690M/MK356	7602M/WE600	7864M/XP244	8046M/XL770
5718M/BM597	7605M/WS692	7865M/TX226	8049M/WE168
5758M/DG202	7606M/WV562	7866M/XH278	8050M/XG329
6457M/ML427	7607M/TJ138	7868M/WZ736	8052M/WH166
6490M/LA255	7615M/WV679	7869M/WK935	8054AM/XM410
6640M/RM694	7616M/WW388	7872M/*WZ826*/(XD826)	8054BM/XN417
6850M/TE184	7618M/WW442	7881M/WD413	8055AM/XM402
6946M/RW388	7622M/WV606	7882M/XD525	8055BM/XM404
6948M/DE673	7631M/VX185	7883M/XT150	8056M/XG337
6960M/MT847	7641M/XA634	7891M/XM693	8057M/XR243
7008M/EE549	7645M/WD293	7894M/XD818	8063M/WT536
7014M/N6720	7646M/VX461	7895M/WF784	8070M/EP120
7015M/NL985	7648M/XF785	7898M/XP854	8072M/PK624
7035M/*K2567*/(DE306)	7673M/WV332	7900M/WA576	8073M/TB252
7060M/VF301	7688M/WW421	7906M/WH132	8078M/XM351
7090M/EE531	7693M/WV483	7917M/WA591	8079M/XN492
7118M/LA198	7694M/WV486	7920M/WL360	8080M/XM480
7119M/LA226	7696M/WV493	7923M/XT133	8081M/XM468
7150M/PK683	7698M/WV499	7928M/XE849	8082M/XM409
7154M/WB188	7704M/TW536	7930M/WH301	8086M/TB752
7174M/VX272	7705M/WL505	7931M/RD253	8092M/WK654
7175M/VV106	7706M/WB584	7932M/WZ744	8094M/WT520
7200M/VT812	7709M/WT933	7933M/XR220	8101M/WH984
7241M/*MK178*(TE311)	7711M/PS915	7937M/WS843	8102M/WT486
7243M/TE462	7712M/WK281	7938M/XH903	8103M/WR985
7244M/*MK673*(TB382)	7715M/XK724	7939M/XD596	8106M/WR982
7246M/TD248	7716M/WS776	7940M/XL764	8108M/WV703
7256M/TB752	7718M/WA577	7955M/XH767	8113M/WV753
7257M/TB252	7719M/WK277	7957M/XF545	8114M/WL798
7279M/TB752	7729M/WB758	7959M/WS774	8117M/WR974
7281M/TB252	7734M/XD536	7960M/WS726	8118M/WZ549
7288M/PK724	7737M/XD602	7961M/WS739	8119M/WR971
7293M/RW393	7741M/VZ477	7964M/WS760	8121M/XM474
7323M/VV217	7750M/*WK864*/(WL168)	7965M/WS792	8124M/WZ572
7325M/R5868	7751M/WL131	7967M/WS788	8128M/WH775
7326M/VN485	7755M/WG760	7971M/XK699	8131M/WT507
7362M/475081/(VP546)	7758M/PM651	7973M/WS807	8140M/XJ571
7416M/WN907	7759M/PK664	7976M/XK418	8142M/XJ560
7421M/WT660	7761M/XH318	7979M/XM529	8147M/XR526
7422M/WT684	7762M/XE670	7980M/XM561	8151M/WV795
7428M/WK198	7764M/XH318	7982M/XH892	8153M/WV903
7432M/WZ724	7770M/*XF506*/(WT746)	7983M/XD506	8154M/WV908
7438M/*18671*/(WP905)	7793M/XG523	7984M/XN597	8155M/WV797
7443M/WX853	7796M/WJ676	7986M/WG777	8156M/XE339
7458M/WX905	7798M/XH783	7988M/XL149	8158M/XE369
7464M/XA564	7806M/TA639	7990M/XD452	8159M/XD528
7470M/XA553	7809M/XA699	7997M/XG452	8160M/XD622
7473M/XE946	7816M/WG763	7998M/*XM515*/(XD515)	8161M/XE993
7491M/WT569	7817M/TX214	8005M/WG768	8162M/WM913
7496M/WT612	7825M/WK991	8009M/XG518	8163M/XP919
7510M/WT694	7827M/XA917	8010M/XG547	8164M/*WN105*/(WF299)

RAF Maintenance Cross-reference

8165M/WH791	8396M/XK740	8565M/*WT720*/(E-408)	8724M/XW923
8169M/WH364	8399M/WR539	8566M/XV279	8726M/XP299
8173M/XN685	8401M/XP686	8570M/XR954	8727M/XR486
8176M/WH791	8406M/XP831	8573M/XM708	8728M/WT532
8177M/*WM311*/(WM224)	8407M/XP585	8575M/XP542	8729M/WJ815
8179M/XN928	8408M/XS186	8576M/XP502	8733M/XL318
8183M/*XN972*/(XN962)	8409M/XS209	8578M/XR534	8736M/XF375
8184M/WT520	8410M/XR662	8582M/XE874	8739M/XH170
8185M/WH946	8413M/XM192	8583M/BAPC 94	8740M/WE173
8186M/WR977	8414M/XM173	8585M/XE670	8741M/XW329
8187M/WH791	8417M/XM144	8586M/XE643	8743M/WD790
8189M/*WD615* (WD646)	8422M/XM169	8588M/XR681	8746M/XH171
8190M/XJ918	8427M/XM172	8589M/XR700	8749M/XH537
8192M/XR658	8429M/XH592	8590M/XM191	8751M/XT255
8196M/XE920	8434M/XM411	8591M/XA813	8753M/WL795
8198M/WT339	8436M/XN554	8595M/XH278	8762M/WH740
8203M/XD377	8437M/WG362	8598M/WP270	8763M/WH665
8205M/XN819	8439M/WZ846	8600M/XX761	8764M/XP344
8206M/WG419	8440M/WD935	8602M/*PF179*/(XR541)	8767M/XX635
8207M/WD318	8442M/XP411	8606M/XP530	8768M/A-522
8208M/WG303	8453M/XP745	8608M/XP540	8769M/A-528
8209M/WG418	8457M/XS871	8610M/XL502	8770M/XL623
8210M/WG471	8458M/XP672	8611M/WF128	8771M/XM602
8211M/WK570	8459M/XR650	8618M/*XS111*/(XP504)	8772M/WR960
8213M/WK626	8460M/XP680	8620M/XP534	8777M/XX914
8216M/WP927	8462M/XX477	8621M/XR538	8778M/XM598
8218M/WB645	8463M/XP355	8624M/*XR991*/(XS102)	8779M/XM607
8229M/XM355	8464M/XJ758	8627M/XP558	8780M/WK102
8230M/XM362	8465M/W1048	8628M/XJ380	8781M/WE982
8234M/XN458	8466M/L-866	8630M/WG362	8782M/XH136
8235M/XN549	8467M/WP912	8631M/XR574	8783M/XW272
8236M/XP573	8468M/MM5701/(BT474)	8633M/3W-17/MK732	8785M/XS642
8237M/XS179	8470M/584219	8634M/WP314	8789M/XK970
8238M/XS180	8471M/701152	8640M/XR977	8792M/XP345
8344M/WH960	8472M/120227/(VN679)	8642M/XR537	8793M/XP346
8350M/WH840	8473M/WP190	8645M/XD163	8794M/XP398
8352M/XN632	8474M/494083	8648M/XK526	8796M/XK943
8355M/*KG374*/(KN645)	8475M/360043/(PJ876)	8653M/XS120	8797M/XX947
8357M/WK576	8476M/24	8655M/XN126	8799M/WV787
8359M/WF825	8477M/4101/(DG200)	8656M/XP405	8800M/XG226
8361M/WB670	8478M/10639	8657M/VZ634	8805M/XT772
8362M/WG477	8479M/730301	8661M/XJ727	8807M/XL587
8364M/WG464	8481M/191614	8662M/XR458	8810M/XJ825
8365M/XK421	8482M/112372/(VK893)	8666M/XE793	8816M/XX734
8366M/XG454	8483M/420430	8668M/WJ821	8818M/XK527
8367M/XG474	8484M/5439	8671M/XJ435	8820M/VP952
8368M/XF926	8485M/997	8672M/XP351	8821M/XX115
8369M/WE139	8486M/BAPC 99	8673M/XD165	8822M/VP957
8370M/N1671	8487M/J-1172	8676M/XL577	8828M/XS587
8371M/XA847	8488M/WL627	8679M/XF526	8830M/XF515
8372M/K8042	8491M/WJ880	8680M/XF527	8831M/XG160
8373M/P2617	8493M/XR571	8681M/XG164	8832M/XG172
8375M/NX611	8494M/XP557	8682M/XP404	8833M/XL569
8376M/RF398	8495M/XR672	8687M/XJ639	8834M/*XL571*
8377M/R9125	8501M/XP640	8693M/WH863	8836M/XL592
8378M/*T9707*	8502M/XP686	8696M/WH773	8838M/*34037*/(429356)
8379M/DG590	8507M/XS215	8700M/ZD234	8839M/*69*/(XG194)
8380M/Z7197	8508M/XS218	8702M/XG196	8840M/XG252
8382M/VR930	8509M/XT141	8703M/VW453	8841M/XE606
8383M/K9942	8514M/XS176	8706M/XF383	8847M/XX344
8384M/X4590	8535M/XN776	8708M/XF509	8848M/XZ135
8385M/N5912	8538M/XN781	8709M/XG209	8852M/XV337
8386M/NV778	8545M/XN726	8710M/XG274	8853M/XT277
8387M/T6296	8546M/XN728	8711M/XG290	8855M/XT284
8388M/XL993	8548M/WT507	8713M/XG225	8857M/XW544
8389M/VX573	8549M/WT534	8714M/XK149	8858M/XW541
8392M/SL674	8554M/TG511	8718M/XX396	8863M/XG154
8394M/WG422	8561M/XS100	8719M/XT257	8867M/XK532
8395M/WF408	8563M/*XX822*/(XW563)	8722M/WJ640	8868M/WH775

8869M/WH957	8972M/XR754	9075M/XV753	9177M/XW328
8870M/WH964	8973M/XS922	9076M/XV808	9179M/XW309
8871M/WJ565	8974M/XM473	9078M/XV752	9180M/XW311
8873M/XR453	8975M/XW917	9079M/XZ130	9181M/XW358
8874M/XE597	8976M/XZ630	9080M/ZE350	9185M/XZ987
8875M/XE624	8978M/XK837	9086M/ZE352	9187M/XW405
8876M/ *VM791/*(XA312)	8983M/XM478	9087M/XX753	9188M/XW364
8879M/XX948	8984M/XN551	9090M/XW353	9189M/ZD350
8880M/XF435	8985M/WK127	9091M/XW434	9190M/XW318
8881M/XG254	8986M/XV261	9092M/XH669	9191M/XW416
8883M/XX946	8987M/XM358	9093M/WK124	9192M/XW361
8884M/VX275	8988M/XN593	9095M/XW547	9193M/XW367
8885M/XW922	8990M/XM419	9096M/WV322	9194M/XW420
8886M/XA243	8995M/XM425	9097M/XW366	9195M/XW330
8888M/XA231	8996M/XM414	9098M/XV406	9196M/XW370
8889M/XN239	8997M/XX669	9100M/XL188	9197M/*XX530/*(XX637)
8890M/WT532	8998M/XT864	9103M/XV411	9198M/XS641
8892M/XL618	9002M/XW763	9109M/XW312	9199M/XW290
8895M/XX746	9003M/XZ390	9110M/XX736	9200M/XW425
8896M/XX821	9004M/XZ370	9111M/XW421	9201M/ZD667
8897M/XX969	9005M/XZ374	9113M/*XV498*	9203M/*3066*
8898M/XX119	9006M/XX967	9115M/XV863	9205M/*E449*
8899M/XX756	9007M/XX968	9117M/XV161	9206M/F6314
8900M/XZ368	9008M/XX140	9118M/XV253	9207M/8417/18
8901M/XZ383	9009M/XX763	9119M/XW303	9208M/F938
8902M/XX739	9010M/XX764	9120M/XW419	9210M/MF628
8903M/XX747	9011M/XM412	9122M/XZ997	9211M/733682
8904M/XX966	9012M/XN494	9123M/XT773	9212M/*KL216/*(45-49295)
8905M/XX975	9014M/XN584	9124M/XW427	9213M/N5182
8906M/XX976	9015M/XW320	9125M/XW410	9215M/XL164
8907M/XZ371	9017M/ZE449	9126M/XW413	9216M/XL190
8908M/XZ382	9018M/XW365	9127M/XW432	9217M/ZH257
8909M/XV784	9019M/XX824	9128M/XW292	9218M/XL563
8910M/XL160	9020M/XX825	9129M/XW294	9219M/XZ971
8911M/XH673	9021M/XX826	9130M/XW327	9220M/XZ995
8918M/XX109	9022M/XX958	9131M/*DD931*	9221M/XZ966
8920M/XT469	9026M/XP629	9132M/XX977	9222M/XZ968
8921M/XT466	9027M/XP556	9133M/*413573*	9224M/XL568
8922M/XT467	9028M/XP563	9134M/XT288	9225M/XX885
8923M/XX819	9029M/XS217	9136M/XT891	9226M/XV865
8924M/XP701	9031M/XP688	9137M/XN579	9227M/XB812
8925M/XP706	9032M/XR673	9139M/XV863	9229M/ZA678
8931M/XV779	9033M/XS181	9140M/XZ287	9230M/ZA676
8932M/XR718	9034M/XP638	9141M/XV118	9233M/XZ431
8934M/XR749	9036M/XM350	9143M/XN589	9234M/XV864
8935M/XR713	9038M/XV810	9144M/XV353	9236M/WV318
8937M/XX751	9039M/XN586	9145M/XV863	9237M/XF445
8938M/WV746	9040M/XZ138	9146M/XW299	9238M/ZA717
8941M/XT456	9041M/XW763	9147M/XW301	9239M/7198/18
8942M/XN185	9042M/XL954	9148M/XW436	9241M/XS639
8943M/XE799	9044M/XS177	9149M/XW375	9242M/XH672
8944M/WZ791	9045M/XN636	9150M/*FX760*	9246M/XS714
8945M/XX818	9046M/XM349	9151M/XT907	9247M/XV420
8946M/XZ389	9047M/XW409	9152M/XV424	9248M/WB627
8947M/XX726	9048M/XM403	9153M/XW360	9249M/WV396
8948M/XX757	9049M/XW404	9154M/XW321	9250M/162068
8949M/XX743	9050M/XG577	9155M/WL679	9251M/XX746
8950M/XX956	9052M/WJ717	9162M/XZ991	9253M/ZA254
8951M/XX727	9055M/XT770	9163M/XV415	9254M/XX965
8952M/XX730	9056M/XS488	9166M/XW323	9255M/XZ375
8953M/XX959	9059M/ZE360	9167M/XV744	9257M/XV962
8954M/XZ384	9060M/ZE356	9168M/XZ132	9258M/XW265
8955M/XX110	9061M/XW335	9169M/XW547	9259M/XS710
8956M/XN577	9062M/XW351	9170M/XZ994	9260M/XS734
8957M/XN582	9066M/XW582	9172M/XW304	9261M/*W2068*
8958M/XN501	9067M/XV586	9173M/XW418	9262M/XZ358
8961M/XS925	9070M/XV581	9174M/XZ131	9263M/XW267
8967M/XV263	9072M/XW768	9175M/P1344	9264M/XS735
8969M/XR753	9073M/XW924	9176M/XW430	9265M/WK585

RAF Maintenance Cross-reference

9266M/XZ119	9277M/XT601	9292M/XW892	9331M/XW852
9267M/XW269	9279M/XT681	9298M/ZE340	9332M/XZ935
9268M/XR529	9280M/XV804	9300M/XX431	9334M/ZA322
9269M/XT914	9281M/XZ146	9302M/ZD462	9335M/ZA375
9270M/XZ145	9282M/XZ101	9306M/XX979	9336M/ZA407
9272M/XS486	9283M/XZ322	9314M/ZA320	9342M/XR498
9273M/XS726	9284M/ZA267	9317M/ZA450	9343M/XR506
9274M/XS738	9288M/XX520	9324M/XV659	
9275M/XS729	9290M/XX626	9325M/XV710	
9276M/XS733	9291M/XX686	9326M/XV653	

Displayed in the RAF Museum, Tempest TT5 NV778 is also allocated the 'M' number 8386M. *PRM*

Another Hendon exhibit is Canberra PR3 WE139/8369M. *PRM*

RN Landing Platform and Shore Station Code-letters

Code	Deck Letters	Vessel Name & Pennant No	Vessel Type & Unit
—	AB	HMS *Albion* (L14)	Assault
—	AS	RFA *Argus* (A135)	Aviation Training ship
365/6	AY	HMS *Argyll* (F231)	Type 23 (815 Sqn)
—	BD	RFA *Sir Bedivere* (L3004)	Landing ship
—	BV	RFA *Black Rover* (A273)	Fleet tanker
335	CF	HMS *Cardiff* (D108)	Type 42 (815 Sqn)
350/1	CL	HMS *Cumberland* (F85)	Type 22 (815 Sqn)
348	CM	HMS *Chatham* (F87)	Type 22 (815 Sqn)
388	CT	HMS *Campbeltown* (F86)	Type 22 (815 Sqn)
—	CU	RNAS Culdrose (HMS *Seahawk*)	
412/3	CW	HMS *Cornwall* (F99)	Type 22 (815 Sqn)
—	DC	HMS *Dumbarton Castle* (P265)	Fishery protection
—	DG	RFA *Diligence* (A132)	Maintenance
411	EB	HMS *Edinburgh* (D97)	Type 42 (815 Sqn)
434/5	EE	HMS *Endurance* (A171)	Ice Patrol (815 Sqn)
420	EX	HMS *Exeter* (D89)	Type 42 (815 Sqn)
—	FA	RFA *Fort Austin* (A386)	Support ship
—	FE	RFA *Fort Rosalie* (A385)	Support ship
—	FL	DARA Fleetlands	
—	FS	HMS *Fearless* (L10)	Assault
410	GC	HMS *Gloucester* (D96)	Type 42 (815 Sqn)
—	GD	RFA *Sir Galahad* (L3005)	Landing ship
437	GT	HMS *Grafton* (F80)	Type 23 (815 Sqn)
—	GV	RFA *Gold Rover* (A271)	Fleet tanker
344	GW	HMS *Glasgow* (D88)	Type 42 (815 Sqn)
—	GY	RFA *Grey Rover* (A269)	Fleet tanker
404	IR	HMS *Iron Duke* (F234)	Type 23 (815 Sqn)
425	KT	HMS *Kent* (F78)	Type 23 (815 Sqn)
—	L	HMS *Illustrious* (R06)	Carrier
457	LA	HMS *Lancaster* (F229)	Type 23 (824 Sqn)
—	LC	HMS *Leeds Castle* (P258)	Fishery protection
332	LP	HMS *Liverpool* (D92)	Type 42 (815 Sqn)
363/4	MA	HMS *Marlborough* (F233)	Type 23 (815 Sqn)
360	MC	HMS *Manchester* (D95)	Type 42 (815 Sqn)
415	MM	HMS *Monmouth* (F235)	Type 23 (824 Sqn)
444	MR	HMS *Montrose* (F236)	Type 23 (815 Sqn)
—	N	HMS *Invincible* (R05)	Carrier
345	NC	HMS *Newcastle* (D87)	Type 42 (815 Sqn)
361/2	NF	HMS *Norfolk* (F230)	Type 23 (815 Sqn)
372	NL	HMS *Northumberland* (F238)	Type 23 (815 Sqn)
417	NM	HMS *Nottingham* (D91)	Type 42 (815 Sqn)
—	O	HMS *Ocean* (L12)	Helicopter carrier
426	PD	HMS *Portland* (F79)	Type 23 (815 Sqn)
—	PV	RFA *Sir Percivale* (L3036)	Landing ship
—	R	HMS *Ark Royal* (R07)	Carrier
474	RM	HMS *Richmond* (F239)	Type 23 (815 Sqn)
427	SB	HMS *St Albans* (F83)	Type 23 (815 Sqn)
355	SM	HMS *Somerset* (F82)	Type 23 (815 Sqn)
334	SN	HMS *Southampton* (D90)	Type 42 (815 Sqn)
422	SU	HMS *Sutherland* (F81)	Type 23 (815 Sqn)
—	TM	RFA *Sir Tristram* (L3505)	Landing ship
—	VL	RNAS Yeovilton (HMS *Heron*)	
462	WM	HMS *Westminster* (F237)	Type 23 (815 Sqn)
407	YK	HMS *York* (D98)	Type 42 (815 Sqn)
—	—	HMS *Bulwark* (L15)	Assault
—	—	HMS *Daring*	Type 45
—	—	HMS *Dauntless*	Type 45
—	—	HMS *Diamond*	Type 45
—	—	RFA *Cardigan Bay*	Landing ship
—	—	RFA *Fort Victoria* (A387)	Auxiliary Oiler

RN Landing Platforms

Code	Deck Letters	Vessel Name & Pennant No	Vessel Type & Unit
—	—	RFA *Fort George* (A388)	Auxiliary Oiler
—	—	RFA *Largs Bay*	Landing ship
—	—	RFA *Lyme Bay*	Landing ship
—	—	RFA *Mounts Bay*	Landing ship
—	—	RFA *Wave Knight* (A389)	Fleet tanker
—	—	RFA *Wave Ruler* (A390)	Fleet tanker

No 845 Squadron Sea King HC4 ZF124 in a winter paint scheme. *PRM*

The code 583/CU identifies Merlin HM1 ZH852 as operating with No 824 Squadron at RNAS Culdrose. *PRM*

Ships' Numeric Code – Deck Letters Analysis

	0	1	2	3	4	5	6	7	8	9
33			LP		SN	CF				
34					GW	NC			CM	
35	CL	CL				SM				
36	MC	NF	NF	MA	MA	AY	AY			
37			NL							
38									CT	
40					IR			YK		
41	GC	EB	CW	CW		MM		NM		
42	EX		SU			KT	PD	SB		
43					EE	EE		GT		
44					MR					
45								LA		
46			WM							
47					RM					

RN Code – Squadron – Base – Aircraft Cross-check

Deck/Base Code Numbers	Letters	Unit	Location	Aircraft Type(s)
000 — 006	L	801 Sqn	Yeovilton	Sea Harrier FA2
000 — 006	L	801 Sqn	Yeovilton	Sea Harrier FA2
010 — 020	CU	820 Sqn	Culdrose	Merlin HM1
122 — 129	R	800 Sqn	Yeovilton	Sea Harrier FA2
180 — 182	CU	849 Sqn HQ Flt	Culdrose	Sea King AEW7
183 — 185	L	849 Sqn B Flt	Culdrose	Sea King AEW7
186 — 188	R	849 Sqn A Flt	Culdrose	Sea King AEW7
264 — 274	R	814 Sqn	Culdrose	Merlin HM1
300 — 308	PO	815 Sqn	Yeovilton	Lynx HAS3/HMA8
318 — 319	PO	815 Sqn OEU	Yeovilton	Lynx HMA8
332 — 479	*	815 Sqn	Yeovilton	Lynx HAS3/HMA8
535 — 541	CU	700M OEU	Culdrose	Merlin HM1
560 — 573	CU	750 Sqn	Culdrose	Jetstream T2
576 — 579	-	FONA	Yeovilton	Jetstream T3
580 — 585	CU	824 Sqn	Culdrose	Merlin HM1
630 — 648	PO	702 Sqn	Yeovilton	Lynx HAS3
670 — 676	PO	702 Sqn	Yeovilton	Lynx HMA8
700 — 709	PW	771 Sqn	Prestwick	Sea King HAS6
710 — 719	VL	899 Sqn	Yeovilton	Sea Harrier FA2
720 — 724	VL	899 Sqn	Yeovilton	Harrier T8
730 — 731	VL	899 Sqn	Yeovilton	Sea Harrier FA2
820 — 827	CU	771 Sqn	Culdrose	Sea King HU5

*See foregoing separate ships' Deck Letters Analysis
Note that only the 'last two' digits of the Code are worn by some aircraft types, especially helicopters.

Royal Air Force Squadron Markings

This table gives brief details of the markings worn by aircraft of RAF squadrons. While this may help to identify the operator of a particular machine, it may not always give the true picture. For example, from time to time aircraft are loaned to other units while others (such as those with No 4 FTS at Valley) wear squadron marks but are actually operated on a pool basis. Squadron badges are usually located on the front fuselage.

Squadron	Type(s) operated	Base(s)	Distinguishing marks & other comments
No 1 Sqn	Harrier GR7/T10	RAF Cottesmore	Badge: A red & white winged number 1 on a white diamond. Tail fin has a red stripe with the badge repeated on it.
No 2 Sqn	Tornado GR4A	RAF Marham	Badge: A wake knot on a white circular background flanked on either side by black and white triangles. Tail fin has a black stripe with white triangles and the badge repeated on it. Codes are single letters inside a white triangle on the tail.
No 3 Sqn	Harrier GR7/7A/T10	RAF Cottesmore	Badge: A blue cockatrice on a white circular background flanked by two green bars edged with yellow. Tail fin has a green stripe edged with yellow.
No 4 Sqn	Harrier GR7/T10	RAF Cottesmore	Badge: A yellow lightning flash inside a red and black circle flanked by bars on either side repeating this design. Tail fin has a yellow lightning flash on a red and black stripe.
No 6 Sqn	Jaguar GR3/T2A	RAF Coltishall	Badge: A red winged can opener inside a circle edged in red. Tail has a light blue bar with red diagonal lines. Aircraft are coded E*.
No 7 Sqn	Chinook HC2/ Gazelle HT3	RAF Odiham	Badge (on tail): A blue badge containing the seven stars of Ursa Major ('The Plough') in yellow. Aircraft are coded E*. Aircraft pooled with No 18 Sqn and No 27 Sqn.
No 8 Sqn	Sentry AEW1	RAF Waddington	Badge (on tail): A grey, sheathed, Arabian dagger. Aircraft pooled with No 23 Sqn.
No 9 Sqn	Tornado GR4	RAF Marham	Badge: A green bat on a black circular background, flanked by yellow and green horizontal stripes. The green bat also appears on the tail, edged in yellow. Aircraft are coded A*.
No 10 Sqn	VC10 C1K	RAF Brize Norton	Badge (on tail): A yellow arrow with red wings.
No 11 Sqn	Tornado F3	RAF Leeming	Roundel is superimposed over a yellow diamond on a black background. Badge (on tail): Two black eagles in flight.
No 12 Sqn	Tornado GR4	RAF Lossiemouth	Roundel is superimposed on a green chevron. Tail fin has a black & white horizontal stripe with the squadron badge, a fox's head on a white circle, in the middle. Aircraft are coded F*.

Squadron	Type(s) operated	Base(s)	Distinguishing marks & other comments
No 13 Sqn	Tornado GR4/GR4A	RAF Marham	A yellow lightning flash on a green and blue background on the nose. Badge (on tail): A lynx's head over a dagger on a white shield.
No 14 Sqn	Tornado GR4	RAF Lossiemouth	Badge: A red cross on a white circle, with wings either side, flanked by blue diamonds on a white background. The blue diamonds are repeated horizontally across the tail. Aircraft are coded B*.
No 15(R) Sqn	Tornado GR4	RAF Lossiemouth	Roman numerals XV appear in white on the tail. Aircraft are either coded T* or TA*.
No 16(R) Sqn	Jaguar GR3/T2A/T4	RAF Coltishall	Badge: Two keys crossed on a black circle. On the tail is a black circle containing the 'Saint' emblem from the 60's TV series.
No 17(R) Sqn	Typhoon T1/F2	Warton	Badge (on tail): A gauntlet on a black and white shield. Roundel is flanked by two white bars which have a pair of jagged black lines running along them horizontally. Aircraft are coded A*.
No 18 Sqn	Chinook HC2	RAF Odiham	Badge (on tail): A red winged horse on a black circle. Aircraft are coded B*. Aircraft pooled with No 7 Sqn and No 27 Sqn.
No 19(R) Sqn	Hawk T1/T1A/T1W	RAF Valley	Badge (on tail): A fish flanked by two wings on a yellow circle. Aircraft also carry black and white checks either side of the roundel on the fuselage. Aircraft pooled with No 208(R) Sqn; part of No 4 FTS.
No 20(R) Sqn [HOCU]	Harrier GR7/7A/T10	RAF Wittering	Badge: An eagle in a white circle flanked by a white stripe on a blue background. On the tail is a stripe made up of black, yellow, green and red triangles.
No 22 Sqn	Sea King HAR3/HAR3A	A Flt: RMB Chivenor B Flt: Wattisham C Flt: RAF Valley	Badge: A black pi symbol in front of a white Maltese cross on a red circle.
No 23 Sqn	Sentry AEW1	RAF Waddington	Badge (on tail): A red eagle preying on a yellow falcon. Aircraft pooled with No 8 Sqn.
No 24 Sqn	Hercules C1/C3/C4/C5	RAF Lyneham	No squadron markings carried. Aircraft pooled with No 30 Sqn, No 47 Sqn, No 57(R) Sqn and No 70 Sqn.
No 25 Sqn	Tornado F3	RAF Leeming	Badge (on tail): A hawk on a gauntlet.
No 27 Sqn	Chinook HC2	RAF Odiham	Badge (on tail): An dark green elephant on a green circle, flanked by green and dark green stripes. Aircraft pooled with No 7 Sqn and No 18 Sqn.
No 28 Sqn	Merlin HC3	RAF Benson	Badge: A winged horse above white two crosses on a red shield.
No 30 Sqn	Hercules C1/C3	RAF Lyneham	No squadron markings carried. Aircraft pooled with No 24 Sqn, No 47 Sqn, No 57(R) Sqn and No 70 Sqn.

RAF Squadron Markings

Squadron	Type(s) operated	Base(s)	Distinguishing marks & other comments
No 31 Sqn	Tornado GR4	RAF Marham	Badge: A gold, five-pointed star on a yellow circle flanked by yellow and green checks. The star is repeated on the tail. Aircraft are coded D*.
No 32 (The Royal) Sqn	125 CC3/146 CC2/ Twin Squirrel HCC1	RAF Northolt	No squadron markings carried but aircraft carry a distinctive livery with a blue flash along the middle of the fuselage and a red tail.
No 33 Sqn	Puma HC1	RAF Benson	Badge: A stag's head.
No 39 (1 PRU) Sqn	Canberra PR9/T4	RAF Marham	Badge (on tail): A winged bomb on a light blue circle. Aircraft are coded A*.
No 41 Sqn	Jaguar GR3/T4	RAF Coltishall	Badge: A red, double armed cross, flanked by red and white horizontal stipes. Stripes repeated on tail. Aircraft are coded F*.
No 42(R) Sqn	Nimrod MR2	RAF Kinloss	No squadron markings usually carried. Aircraft pooled with No 120 Sqn, No 201 Sqn and No 206 Sqn.
No 43 Sqn	Tornado F3	RAF Leuchars	Badge (on tail): A black and red gamecock in a band of black and white squares.
No 45(R) Sqn	King Air B200	RAF Cranwell	No squadron markings usually carried. Part of No 3 FTS.
No 47 Sqn	Hercules C1/C3	RAF Lyneham	No squadron markings usually carried. Aircraft pooled with No 24 Sqn, 30 Sqn, No 57(R) Sqn and No 70 Sqn.
No 51 Sqn	Nimrod R1	RAF Waddington	Badge (on tail): A red goose in flight.
No 54 Sqn	Jaguar GR3/GR3A/T2/T4	RAF Coltishall	Badge: A blue lion on a yellow shield, flanked by blue and yellow checks. A stripe of blue and yellow checks also appears on the tail. Aircraft are coded G*.
No 55(R) Sqn	Dominie T1	RAF Cranwell	Badge (on tail): A blue fist holding an arrow on a white circle.
No 56(R) Sqn [F3OCU]	Tornado F3	RAF Leuchars	Badge (on tail): A gold phoenix rising from red flames. The tail fin has a stripe made up of red and white checks.
No 60(R) Sqn	Griffin HT1	RAF Shawbury [DHFS] & RAF Valley [SARTU]	No squadron markings usually carried.
No 70 Sqn	Hercules C1/C3/C4/C5	RAF Lyneham	No squadron markings usually carried. Aircraft pooled with No 24 Sqn, No 30 Sqn, No 47 Sqn and No 57(R) Sqn.
No 72(R) Sqn	Tucano T1	RAF Linton-on-Ouse	Badge: A black swift in flight on a red disk, flanked by blue bars edged with red. The blue bars edged with red also flank the roundel on the fuselage; part of No 1 FTS.
No 78 Sqn	Chinook HC2/ Sea King HAR3	RAF Mount Pleasant	Badge: A yellow, heraldic tiger with two tails, on a black circle. The badge appears on the tail of the Chinook and by the cockpit on the Sea King.

Squadron	Type(s) operated	Base(s)	Distinguishing marks & other comments
No 84 Sqn	Griffin HAR2	RAF Akrotiri	Badge (on tail): A scorpion on a playing card symbol (diamonds, clubs etc.). Aircraft carry a vertical blue stripe through the roundel on the fuselage.
No 99 Sqn	Globemaster III	RAF Brize Norton	Badge (on tail): A black puma leaping.
No 100 Sqn	Hawk T1/T1A	RAF Leeming	Badge (on tail): A skull in front of two bones crossed. Aircraft are usually coded C*.
No 101 Sqn	VC10 K3/K4	RAF Brize Norton	Badge (on tail): A lion behind a castle turret.
No 111 Sqn	Tornado F3	RAF Leuchars	Badge (on tail): A cross in front of crossed swords on a light grey circle, flanked by a stripe of darker grey.
No 120 Sqn	Nimrod MR2	RAF Kinloss	No squadron markings usually carried. Aircraft pooled with No 42(R) Sqn, No 201 Sqn and No 206 Sqn.
No 201 Sqn	Nimrod MR2	RAF Kinloss	No squadron markings usually carried. Aircraft pooled with No 42(R) Sqn, No 120 Sqn and No 206 Sqn.
No 202 Sqn	Sea King HAR3	A Flt: RAF Boulmer D Flt: RAF Lossiemouth E Flt: RAF Leconfield	Badge: A mallard alighting on a white circle.
No 203(R) Sqn	Sea King HAR3	RAF St Mawgan	Badge: A green sea horse on a white circle.
No 206 Sqn	Nimrod MR2	RAF Kinloss	No squadron markings usually carried. Aircraft pooled with No 42(R) Sqn, No 120 Sqn and No 201 Sqn.
No 207(R) Sqn	Tucano T1	RAF Linton-on-Ouse	Badge: A red winged lion on a white disk. The roundel on the fuselage is flanked by red bars edged with yellow; part of No 1 FTS.
No 208(R) Sqn	Hawk T1/T1A/T1W	RAF Valley	Badge (on tail): A Sphinx inside a white circle, flanked by flashes of yellow. Aircraft also carry blue and yellow bars either side of the roundel on the fuselage and a blue and yellow chevron on the nose. Aircraft pooled with No 19(R) Sqn; part of No 4 FTS.
No 216 Sqn	TriStar K1/KC1/C2/C2A	RAF Brize Norton	Badge (on tail): An eagle in flight with a bomb in its claws.
No 230 Sqn	Puma HC1	RAF Aldergrove	Badge: A tiger in front of a palm tree on a black pentagon.
No 617 Sqn	Tornado GR4	RAF Lossiemouth	Badge: Dam breached, flanked on either side by red lightning flashes on a black background. Tail fin is black with a red lightning flash. Aircraft are coded AJ-*.
No 1435 Flt	Tornado F3	RAF Mount Pleasant	Badge (on tail): A red Maltese cross on a white circle, flanked by red and white horizontal bars.

University Air Squadrons/ Air Experience Flights

Now that the conversion to the Tutor has taken place, UAS aircraft often carry squadron badges and markings, usually on the tail. Squadron crests all consist of a white circle surrounded by a blue circle, topped with a red crown and having a yellow scroll beneath. Each differs by the motto on the scroll, the UAS name running around the blue circle & by the contents at the centre and it is the latter which are described below. From April 1996 all AEFs have come under the administration of local UASs and these are listed here.

UAS	Base(s)	Marks
Aberdeen, Dundee & St Andrews UAS	RAF Leuchars	A red lion holding a stone turret between its paws above a crown.
University of Birmingham AS/No 8 AEF	RAF Cosford	A blue griffon with two heads.
Bristol UAS/No 3 AEF	RAF Colerne	A sailing ship on water.
Cambridge UAS/No 5 AEF	RAF Wyton	A heraldic lion in front of a red badge.
East Lowlands UAS/No 12 AEF	RAF Leuchars	An open book in front of a white diagonal cross edged in blue.
East Midlands Universities AS/No 7 AEF	RAF Cranwell	A yellow quiver, full of arrows.
Universities of Glasgow and and Strathclyde AS/No 4 AEF	Glasgow	A bird of prey in flight, holding a branch in its beak, in front of an upright sword.
Liverpool UAS	RAF Woodvale	A bird atop an open book, holding a branch in its beak.
University of London AS/No 6 AEF	RAF Wyton	A globe superimposed over an open book.
Manchester and Salford Universities AS/ No 10 AEF	RAF Woodvale	A bird of prey with a green snake in its beak.
Northumbrian Universities AS/ No 11 AEF	RAF Leeming	A white cross on a blue background.
Oxford UAS	RAF Benson	An open book in front of crossed swords.
Southampton UAS/No 2 AEF	Boscombe Down	A red stag in front of a stone pillar.
University of Wales AS/No 1 AEF	DARA St Athan	A red Welsh dragon in front of an open book, clasping a sword. Some aircraft have the dragon in front of white and green squares.
Yorkshire Universities AS/No 9 AEF	RAF Church Fenton	An open book in front of a Yorkshire rose with leaves.

Fleet Air Arm Squadron Markings

This table gives brief details of the markings worn by aircraft of FAA squadrons. Squadron badges, when worn, are usually located on the front fuselage. All FAA squadron badges comprise a crown atop a circle edged in gold braid and so the badge details below list only what appears in the circular part.

Squadron	Type(s) operated	Base(s)	Distinguishing marks & other comments
No 700M OEU	Merlin HM1	RNAS Culdrose	Badge: A pair of gold scales on a background of blue and white waves, flanked by two bees.
No 702 Sqn	Lynx HAS3/HMA8	RNAS Yeovilton	Badge: A Lynx rearing up in front of a circle comprising alternate dark blue and white sectors.
No 727 Sqn	Heron	Plymouth	Badge: The head of Britannia wearing a gold helmet on a background of blue and white waves.
No 750 Sqn	Jetstream T2	RNAS Culdrose	Badge: A Greek runner bearing a torch & sword on a background of blue and white waves.
No 771 Sqn	Sea King HU5/HAS6	RNAS Culdrose & Prestwick	Badge: Three bees on a background of blue and white waves.
No 800 Sqn	Sea Harrier FA2	RNAS Yeovilton	Badge: A trident and two crossed swords on a blue background. On the tail is a red triangle with the trident and two crossed swords upon it.
No 801 Sqn	Sea Harrier FA2	RNAS Yeovilton	Badge: A winged trident on a white background. On the tail is a white winged trident and there are black & white checks upon the rudder.
No 814 Sqn	Merlin HM1	RNAS Culdrose	Badge: A winged tiger mask on a background of dark blue and white waves.
No 815 Sqn	Lynx HAS3/HMA8	RNAS Yeovilton	Badge: A winged, gold harpoon on a background of blue and white waves.
No 820 Sqn	Merlin HM1	RNAS Culdrose	Badge: A flying fish on a background of blue and white waves.
No 824 Sqn	Merlin HM1	RNAS Culdrose	Badge: A heron on a background of blue and white waves.
No 845 Sqn	Sea King HC4	RNAS Yeovilton	Badge: A dragonfly on a background of blue and white waves.
No 846 Sqn	Sea King HC4	RNAS Yeovilton	Badge: A swordsman riding a winged horse whilst attacking a serpent on a background of blue and white waves. Aircraft are usually coded V*.
No 847 Sqn	Gazelle AH1 & Lynx AH7	RNAS Yeovilton	Badge: A gold sea lion on a blue background.
No 848 Sqn	Sea King HC4	RNAS Yeovilton	Badge: Inside a red circle, a hawk in flight with a torpedo in its claws above white and blue waves. Aircraft are usually coded W*.
No 849 Sqn	Sea King AEW7	RNAS Culdrose	Badge: A winged streak of lightning with an eye in front on a background of blue and white waves.
No 899 Sqn	Harrier T8 & Sea Harrier FA2	RNAS Yeovilton	Badge: A winged gauntlet on a background of blue and white waves beneath a cloudy sky. On the tail is a winged gauntlet edged in black.

Historic Aircraft in Overseas Markings

Some *historic, classic and warbird* aircraft carry the markings of overseas air arms and can be seen in the UK, mainly preserved in museums and collections or taking part in air shows.

Notes	Serial	Type (other identity)	Owner/operator, location
	ARGENTINA		
	-	Bell UH-IH Iroquois (AE-406) [Z]	RAF Valley, instructional use
	0729	Beech T-34C Turbo Mentor	FAA Museum, stored RNAS Yeovilton
	0767	Aermacchi MB339AA	Rolls-Royce Heritage Trust, stored Derby
	A-515	FMA IA58 Pucara (ZD485)	RAF Museum, Cosford
	A-517	FMA IA58 Pucara (G-BLRP)	Privately owned, Channel Islands
	A-522	FMA IA58 Pucara (8768M)	FAA Museum, at NE Aircraft Museum, Usworth
	A-528	FMA IA58 Pucara (8769M)	Norfolk & Suffolk Avn Museum, Flixton
	A-533	FMA IA58 Pucara (ZD486) <ff>	Boscombe Down Museum
	A-549	FMA IA58 Pucara (ZD487)	Imperial War Museum, Duxford
	AE-409	Bell UH-1H Iroquois [656]	Museum of Army Flying, Middle Wallop
	AE-422	Bell UH-1H Iroquois	FAA Museum, stored RNAS Yeovilton
	AUSTRALIA		
	A2-4	Supermarine Seagull V (VH-ALB)	RAF Museum, Hendon
	A16-199	Lockheed Hudson IIIA (G-BEOX) [SF-R]	RAF Museum, Hendon
	A17-48	DH82A Tiger Moth (G-BPHR)	Privately owned, Swindon
	A19-144	Bristol 156 Beaufighter XIc (JM135/A8-324)	The Fighter Collection, Duxford
	A79-808	DH115 Vampire T33	De Havilland Aviation, Swansea
	A92-480	GAF Jindivik 4A (A92-LLAN-1)	QinetiQ Llanbedr, on display
	A92-664	GAF Jindivik 4A	Privately owned, Llanbedr
	A92-708	GAF Jindivik 4A	Bristol Aero Collection, stored Kemble
	N6-766	DH115 Sea Vampire T22 (XG766/ G-SPDR)	De Havilland Aviation, Swansea
	BELGIUM		
	FT-36	Lockheed T-33A	Dumfries & Galloway Avn Mus, Dumfries
	H-50	Noorduyn AT-16 Harvard IIB (OO-DAF)	Privately owned, Brasschaat, Belgium
	HD-75	Hanriot HD1 (G-AFDX)	RAF Museum, Hendon
	IF-68	Hawker Hunter F6 <ff>	Privately owned, Welshpool
	K-16	Douglas C-53D Skytrooper (OT-CWG/N49G)	Air Dakota, Brussels, Belgium
	L-44	Piper L-18C Super Cub (OO-SPQ)	BSD Aeroclub FBA, Bierset, Belgium
	L-47	Piper L-18C Super Cub (OO-SPG)	BSD Aeroclub FBA, Bierset, Belgium
	L-57	Piper L-18C Super Cub (OO-GDH)	BSD Aeroclub FBA, Bierset, Belgium
	L-156	Piper L-18C Super Cub (OO-LGB)	BSD Aeroclub FBA, Bierset, Belgium
	V-18	Stampe SV-4B (OO-GWD)	Antwerp Stampe Centre, Antwerp-Deurne, Belgium
	V-29	Stampe SV-4B (OO-GWB)	Antwerp Stampe Centre, Antwerp-Deurne, Belgium
	BOLIVIA		
	FAB184	SIAI-Marchetti SF.260W (G-SIAI)	Privately owned, Booker
	BOTSWANA		
	OJ1	BAC Strikemaster 83 (ZG805/ G-BXFU)	Global Aviation, Humberside
	BRAZIL		
	1317	Embraer T-27 Tucano	Shorts, Belfast (engine test bed)
	BURKINA FASO		
	BF-8431	SIAI-Marchetti SF.260 (G-NRRA) [31]	Privately owned, Elstree
	CANADA		
	622	Piasecki HUP-3 Retriever (51-16622/N6699D)	The Helicopter Museum, Weston-super-Mare
	920	VS Stranraer (CF-BXO) [Q-N]	RAF Museum, Hendon

Serial	Type (other identity)	Owner/operator, location	Notes
3349	NA64 Yale (G-BYNF)	Privately owned, Duxford	
5450	Hawker Hurricane XII (G-TDTW)	Hawker Restorations Ltd, Milden	
5487	Hawker Hurricane II (G-CBOE)	Privately owned, Thruxton	
9754	Consolidated PBY-5A Catalina (VP-BPS) [P]	Privately owned, Lee-on-Solent	
9893	Bristol 149 Bolingbroke IVT	Imperial War Museum store, Duxford	
9940	Bristol 149 Bolingbroke IVT	Royal Scottish Mus'm of Flight, E Fortune	
15195	Fairchild PT-19A Cornell	RAF Museum Restoration Centre, Cosford	
16693	Auster J/1N Alpha (G-BLPG) [693]	Privately owned, Headcorn	
18013	DHC1 Chipmunk 22 (G-TRIC) [013]	The Shuttleworth Collection, Old Warden	
18393	Avro Canada CF-100 Canuck 4B (G-BCYK)	Imperial War Museum, Duxford	
18671	DHC1 Chipmunk 22 (WP905/ 7438M/G-BNZC) [671]	Privately owned, Wombleton	
20310	CCF T-6J Harvard IV (G-BSBG) [310]	Privately owned, Liverpool	
21261	Lockheed T-33A-N Silver Star (G-TBRD)	Golden Apple Operations/OFMC, Duxford	
21417	Canadair CT-133 Silver Star	Yorkshire Air Museum, Elvington	
23140	Canadair CL-13 Sabre [AX] <rf>	Midland Air Museum, Coventry	
23380	Canadair CL-13 Sabre <rf>	RAF Millom Museum, Haverigg	
FJ777	Boeing-Stearman PT-13D Kaydet (42-17786/G-BRTK)	Privately owned, Swanton Morley	

CHINA

2632016	Nanchang CJ-6A Chujiao (G-BXZB) (also wears 2632019)	Privately owned, Hibaldstow	
2751219	Nanchang CJ-6A Chujiao (G-BVVG) [China 1219]	Privately owned, Breighton	

CZECH REPUBLIC

3677	Letov S-102 (MiG-15) (613677)	Royal Scottish Mus'm of Flight, E Fortune	
3794	Letov S-102 (MiG-15) (623794)	Imperial War Museum, stored Duxford	
9147	Mil Mi-4	The Helicopter Museum, Weston-super-Mare	

DENMARK

A-011	SAAB A-35XD Draken	Privately owned, Grainthorpe, Lincs	
AR-107	SAAB S-35XD Draken	Newark Air Museum, Winthorpe	
E-402	Hawker Hunter F51	Privately owned, Farnborough	
E-419	Hawker Hunter F51	North-East Aircraft Museum, Usworth	
E-420	Hawker Hunter F51 (G-9-442)	Privately owned, Walton-on-Thames	
E-421	Hawker Hunter F51	Brooklands Museum, Weybridge	
E-423	Hawker Hunter F51 (G-9-444)	SWWAPS, Lasham	
E-424	Hawker Hunter F51 (G-9-445)	Aeroventure, Doncaster	
ET-272	Hawker Hunter T7 <ff>	Boulton Paul Association, Wolverhampton	
ET-273	Hawker Hunter T7 <ff>	Aeroventure, Doncaster	
K-682	Douglas C-47A Skytrain (OY-BPB)	Foreningen For Flyvende Mus, Vaerløse, Denmark	
L-866	Consolidated PBY-6A Catalina (8466M)	RAF Museum, Cosford	
R-756	Lockheed F-104G Starfighter	Midland Air Museum, Coventry	
S-881	Sikorsky S-55C	The Helicopter Museum, Weston-super-Mare	
S-882	Sikorsky S-55C	Paintball Adventure West, Lulsgate	
S-887	Sikorsky S-55C	Privately owned, Marksbury, Somerset	

ECUADOR

FAE259	BAC Strikemaster 80 (G-UPPI) [T59]	Privately owned, Duxford	

EGYPT

0446	Mikoyan MiG-21UM <ff>	Thameside Aviation Museum, Tilbury	
7907	Sukhoi Su-7 <ff>	Robertsbridge Aviation Society, Mayfield	

FINLAND

VI-3	Valtion Viima 2 (OO-EBL)	Privately owned, Brasschaat, Belgium	

FRANCE

3	Mudry/CAARP CAP-10B (G-BXRA)	Privately owned, Sedlescombe, Sussex	
06	Dewoitine D27 (290/F-AZJD)	The Old Flying Machine Company, Duxford	

Historic Aircraft

Notes	Serial	Type (other identity)	Owner/operator, location
	20	MH1521C1 Broussard (G-BWGG) [315-SQ]	Privately owned, Rednal
	37	Nord 3400 (G-ZARA) [MAB]	Privately owned, Boston
	57	Dassault Mystère IVA [8-MT]	Imperial War Museum, Duxford
	67	SNCAN 1101 Noralpha (F-GMCY) [CY]	Privately owned, la Ferté-Alais, France
	68	Nord 3400 [MHA]	Privately owned,
	70	Dassault Mystère IVA	Midland Air Museum, Coventry
	78	Nord 3202 (G-BIZK)	Privately owned, Swanton Morley
	79	Dassault Mystère IVA [2-EG]	Norfolk & Suffolk Avn Museum, Flixton
	83	Dassault Mystère IVA [8-MS]	Newark Air Museum, Winthorpe
	83	Morane-Saulnier MS.733 Alcyon (F-AZKS)	Privately owned, Montlucon, France
	84	Dassault Mystère IVA [8-NF]	Lashenden Air Warfare Museum, Headcorn
	85	Dassault Mystère IVA [8-MV]	British Aviation Heritage, Bruntingthorpe
	100	Mudry/CAARP CAP-10B (G-BXRB)	Privately owned, Sedlescombe, Sussex
	101	Dassault Mystère IVA [8-MN]	Bomber County Aviation Museum, Hemswell
	104	MH1521M Broussard (F-GHFG) [307-FG]	Privately owned, France
	105	Nord N2501F Noratlas (F-AZVM) [62-SI]	Le Noratlas de Provence, Aix les Milles, France
	120	SNCAN Stampe SV4C (G-AZGC)	Privately owned, Reading
	121	Dassault Mystère IVA	City of Norwich Aviation Museum
	128	Morane-Saulnier MS.733 Alcyon (F-BMMY)	Privately owned, St Cyr, France
	134	Mudry/CAARP CAP-10B (G-BXRC)	Privately owned, Sedlescombe, Sussex
	135	Mudry/CAARP CAP-10B (G-BXFE)	Privately owned, Sedlescombe, Sussex
	143	Morane-Saulnier MS733 Alcyon (G-MSAL)	The Squadron, North Weald
	FR145	SO1221 Djinn [CDL]	Privately owned, Luton
	146	Dassault Mystère IVA [8-MC]	North-East Aircraft Museum, Usworth
	185	MH1521M Broussard (G-BWLR)	Privately owned, Longhope
	282	Dassault MD311 Flamant (F-AZFX) [316-KY]	Memorial Flt Association, la Ferté-Alais, France
	316	MH1521M Broussard (F-GGKR) [315-SN]	The Old Flying Machine Company, Duxford
	318	Dassault Mystère IVA [8-NY]	Dumfries & Galloway Avn Mus, Dumfries
	319	Dassault Mystère IVA [8-ND]	Rebel Air Museum, Andrewsfield
	396	Stampe SV4A (G-BWRE)	Privately owned, stored Sandown
	538	Dassault Mirage IIIE [3-QH]	Yorkshire Air Museum, Elvington
	1058	SO1221 Djinn (FR108) [CDL]	The Helicopter Museum, Weston-super-Mare
	1417	SA.341G Gazelle I (G-BXJK)	Privately owned, Stapleford Tawney
	17473	Lockheed T-33A	Midland Air Museum, Coventry
	42157	NA F-100D Super Sabre [11-ML]	North-East Aviation Museum, Usworth
	63938	NA F-100F Super Sabre [11-MU]	Lashenden Air Warfare Museum, Headcorn
	121748	Grumman F8F-2P Bearcat (F-AZRJ) [5834/P]	Privately owned, Anemasse, France
	125716	Douglas AD-4N Skyraider (F-AZFN) [22-DG]	Privately owned, Etampes, France
	126965	Douglas AD-4NA Skyraider (OO-FOR)	Privately owned, Braaschaat, Belgium
	133704	CV F4U-7 Corsair (125541/ F-AZYS) [14.F.6]	Privately owned, Le Castellet, France
	517545	NA T-28S Fennec (N14113) [CD-113]	Privately owned, Duxford
	517692	NA T-28S Fennec (F-AZFV/ G-TROY) [142]	Privately owned, Duxford
	56-5395	Piper L-18C Super Cub (52-2436/ G-CUBJ) [CDG]	Privately owned, Breighton
	C850	Salmson 2A2 <R>	Barton Aviation Heritage Society, Barton
	MS824	Morane-Saulnier Type N <R> (G-AWBU)	Privately owned, Compton Abbas
	TE184	VS361 Spitfire LF XVIE (6850M/ G-MXVI) [D]	De Cadenet Motor Racing, Halton

GERMANY

Notes	Serial	Type (other identity)	Owner/operator, location
	-	Fieseler Fi103R-IV (V-1) (BAPC 91)	Lashenden Air Warfare Museum, Headcorn
	-	Focke-Achgelis Fa330A-1 (8469M)	RAF Museum, Cosford

Serial	Type (other identity)	Owner/operator, location	Notes
-	Fokker Dr1 Dreidekker <R> (G-BVGZ)	Privately owned, Breighton	
-	Fokker Dr1 Dreidekker <R> (BAPC 88)	FAA Museum, RNAS Yeovilton	
3	SNCAN 1101 Noralpha (G-BAYV)	Barton Aviation Heritage Society, Barton	
6	Messerschmitt Bf109G-2/Trop (10639/8478M/G-USTV)	RAF Museum, Hendon	
8	Focke Wulf Fw190 <R> (G-WULF)	The Real Aeroplane Company, Breighton	
14	Messerschmitt Bf109 <R> (BAPC 67)	Kent Battle of Britain Museum, Hawkinge	
14	SNCAN 1101 Noralpha (G-BSMD)	Privately owned, North Weald	
152/17	Fokker Dr1 Dreidekker <R> (G-ATJM)	Privately owned, East Garston, Bucks	
210/16	Fokker EIII (BAPC 56)	Science Museum, South Kensington	
214	SPP Yak C-11 (G-DYAK)	Classic Aviation Company, Hannover, Germany	
422/15	Fokker EIII <R> (G-AVJO)	Privately owned, Compton Abbas	
425/17	Fokker Dr1 Dreidekker <R> (BAPC 133)	Kent Battle of Britain Museum, Hawkinge	
626/8	Fokker DVII <R> (N6268)	Blue Max Movie Aircraft Museum, Booker	
764	Mikoyan MiG-21SPS <ff>	Privately owned, Booker	
959	Mikoyan MiG-21SPS	Midland Air Museum, Coventry	
1190	Messerschmitt Bf109E-3 [4]	Imperial War Museum, Duxford	
1480	Messerschmitt Bf109 <R> (BAPC 66) [6]	Kent Battle of Britain Museum, Hawkinge	
1983	Messerschmitt Bf109E-3 (G-EMIL)	Privately owned, Sussex	
2088	Fieseler Fi156A Storch (G-STCH)	Privately owned, Sussex	
2100	Focke-Wulf Fw189A-1 (G-BZKY) [V7+1H]	Privately owned, W Sussex	
4101	Messerschmitt Bf109E-3 (DG200/ 8477M) [12]	RAF Museum, Hendon	
6357	Messerschmitt Bf109 <R> (BAPC 74) [6]	Kent Battle of Britain Museum, Hawkinge	
7198/18	LVG CVI (G-AANJ/9239M)	RAF Museum, Hendon	
7485	Messerschmitt Bf109F-4	Charleston Aviation Services, Colchester	
8147	Messerschmitt Bf109F-4	Charleston Aviation Services, Colchester	
8417/18	Fokker DVII (9207M)	RAF Museum, Hendon	
12802	Antonov An-2T (D-FOFM)	Privately owned, Lahr, Germany	
15458	Messerschmitt Bf109F-4	Charleston Aviation Services, Colchester	
100143	Focke-Achgelis Fa330A-1	Imperial War Museum, Duxford	
100502	Focke-Achgelis Fa330A-1	The Real Aeroplane Company, Breighton	
100509	Focke-Achgelis Fa330A-1	Science Museum, stored Wroughton	
100545	Focke-Achgelis Fa330A-1	Fleet Air Arm Museum, stored RNAS Yeovilton	
100549	Focke-Achgelis Fa330A-1	Lashenden Air Warfare Museum, Headcorn	
110451	Fieseler Fi156D Storch (G-STOR)	Privately owned, Sussex	
112372	Messerschmitt Me262A-2a (AM.51/VK893/8482M) [4]	RAF Museum, Hendon	
120227	Heinkel He162A-2 Salamander (VN679/AM.65/8472M) [2]	RAF Museum, Hendon	
120235	Heinkel He162A-1 Salamander (AM.68)	Imperial War Museum, Lambeth	
191316	Messerschmitt Me163B Komet	Science Museum, South Kensington	
191454	Messerschmitt Me163B Komet <R> (BAPC 271)	The Shuttleworth Collection, Old Warden	
191614	Messerschmitt Me163B Komet (8481M)	RAF Museum Restoration Centre, Cosford	
191659	Messerschmitt Me163B Komet (8480M) [15]	Royal Scottish Mus'm of Flight, E Fortune	
191660	Messerschmitt Me163B Komet (AM.214) [3]	Imperial War Museum, Duxford	
211028	Focke Wulf Fw190D-9 (G-DORA)	Privately owned, Sussex	
280020	Flettner Fl282/B-V20 Kolibri (frame only)	Midland Air Museum, Coventry	
360043	Junkers Ju88R-1 (PJ876/8475M) [D5+EV]	RAF Museum, Hendon	
420430	Messerschmitt Me410A-1/U2 (AM.72/8483M) [3U+CC]	RAF Museum, Cosford	
475081	Fieseler Fi156C-7 Storch (VP546/ AM.101/7362M)[GM+AK]	RAF Museum, Cosford	
494083	Junkers Ju87D-3 (8474M) [RI+JK]	RAF Museum, Hendon	

Historic Aircraft

Notes	Serial	Type (other identity)	Owner/operator, location
	584219	Focke Wulf Fw190F-8/U1 (AM.29/8470M) [38]	RAF Museum, Hendon
	701152	Heinkel He111H-23 (8471M) [NT+SL]	RAF Museum, Hendon
	730301	Messerschmitt Bf110G-4 (AM.34/8479M) [D5+RL]	RAF Museum, Hendon
	733682	Focke Wulf Fw190A-8/R7 (AM.75/ 9211M)	Imperial War Museum, Lambeth
	2+1	Focke Wulf Fw190 <R> (G-SYFW) [7334]	Privately owned, Guernsey, CI
	2E+RA	Fieseler Fi-156C-2 Storch (NX436FS)	Privately owned, North Weald
	4+1	Focke Wulf Fw190 <R> (G-BSLX)	Privately owned, Riseley
	4V+GH	Amiot AAC1/Ju52 (Port.AF 6316) [9]	Imperial War Museum, Duxford
	22+35	Lockheed F-104G Starfighter	SWWAPS, Lasham
	22+57	Lockheed F-104G Starfighter	Privately owned, Grainthorpe, Lincs
	58+89	Dornier Do28D-2 Skyservant (D-ICDY)	Moosreiner Consulting, Hamburg, Germany
	96+21	Mil Mi-24D (406)	Imperial War Museum, Duxford
	96+26	Mil Mi-24D (429)	The Helicopter Museum, Weston-super-Mare
	97+04	Putzer Elster B (G-APVF)	Privately owned, Breighton
	98+14	Sukhoi Su-22M-4	The Old Flying Machine Company, stored Scampton
	99+24	NA OV-10B Bronco (F-AZKM)	Privately owned, Montelimar, France
	99+26	NA OV-10B Bronco (G-BZGL)	Privately owned, Duxford
	99+32	NA OV-10B Bronco (G-BZGK)	Privately owned, Duxford
	AZ+JU	CASA 3.52L (F-AZJU)	Amicale J-B Salis, la Ferté-Alais, France
	BU+CC	CASA 1.131E Jungmann (G-BUCC)	Privately owned, Goodwood
	BU+CK	CASA 1.131E Jungmann (G-BUCK)	Privately owned, White Waltham
	CC+43	Pilatus P-2 (G-CJCI)	Privately owned, Norwich
	CF+HF	Morane-Saulnier MS502 (EI-AUY)	Imperial War Museum, Duxford
	CW+BG	CASA 1.131E Jungmann (G-BXBD) [483]	Privately owned, Kemble
	D5397/17	Albatros DVA <R> (G-BFXL)	FAA Museum, RNAS Yeovilton
	ES+BH	Messerschmitt Bf108B-2 (D-ESBH)	Messerschmitt Stiftung, Germany
	FI+S	Morane-Saulnier MS505 (G-BIRW)	Royal Scottish Mus'm of Flight, E Fortune
	FM+BB	Messerschmitt Bf109G-6 (D-FMBB)	Messerschmitt Stiftung, Germany
	JA+120	Canadair CL-13 Sabre 4 (MM19607)	Privately owned
	KG+EM	Nord 1002 (G-ETME)	Privately owned, Booker
	LG+03	Bücker Bü133C Jungmeister (G-AEZX)	Privately owned, Milden
	LG+OI	Bücker Bü133C Jungmeister (G-AYSJ)	The Fighter Collection, Duxford
	NJ+C11	Nord 1002 (G-ATBG)	Privately owned, Sutton Bridge
	S4+A07	CASA 1.131E Jungmann (G-BWHP)	Privately owned, Yarcombe, Devon
	S5+B06	CASA 1.131E Jungmann 2000 (G-BSFB)	Privately owned, Stretton, Cheshire
	TA+RC	Morane-Saulnier MS505 (G-BPHZ)	Historic Aircraft Collection, Duxford

GHANA

Notes	Serial	Type (other identity)	Owner/operator, location
	G-102	SA122 Bulldog	Privately owned, Hurstbourne Tarrant
	G-108	SA122 Bulldog (G-BCUP)	Privately owned, Hurstbourne Tarrant

GREECE

Notes	Serial	Type (other identity)	Owner/operator, location
	51-6171	NA F-86D Sabre	North-East Aircraft Museum, Usworth
	52-6541	Republic F-84F Thunderflash [541]	North-East Aircraft Museum, Usworth
	63-8418	Northrop F-5A	Martin-Baker Ltd, Chalgrove, Fire Section

HONG KONG

Notes	Serial	Type (other identity)	Owner/operator, location
	HKG-5	SA128 Bulldog (G-BULL)	Privately owned, Slinfold
	HKG-6	SA128 Bulldog (G-BPCL)	Privately owned, Elstree
	HKG-11	Slingsby T.67M Firefly 200 (G-BYRY)	Privately owned, Tibenham
	HKG-13	Slingsby T.67M Firefly 200 (G-BXKW)	Privately owned, Tibenham

Historic Aircraft

Serial	Type (other identity)	Owner/operator, location	Notes
HUNGARY			
501	Mikoyan MiG-21PF	Imperial War Museum, Duxford	
INDIA			
Q497	EE Canberra T4 (WE191) (fuselage)	Dumfries & Galloway Avn Mus, Dumfries	
INDONESIA			
LL-5313	BAe Hawk T53	BAE Systems, Brough	
IRAQ			
333	DH115 Vampire T55 <ff>	Aeroventure, Doncaster	
ITALY			
MM5701	Fiat CR42 (BT474/8468M) [13-95]	RAF Museum, Hendon	
MM52801	Fiat G46-3B (G-BBII) [4-97]	Privately owned, Sandown	
MM53692	CCF T-6G Texan	RAeS Medway Branch, Rochester	
MM53774	Fiat G59-4B (I-MRSV) [181]	Privately owned, Parma, Italy	
MM54099	NA T-6G Texan (G-BRBC) [RR-56]	Privately owned, Chigwell	
MM54-2372	Piper L-21B Super Cub	Privately owned, Kesgrave, Suffolk	
W7	Avia FL3 (G-AGFT)	Privately owned, Sandtoft	
JAPAN			
-	Yokosuka MXY 7 Ohka II (BAPC 159)	Defence School, Chattenden	
24	Kawasaki Ki100-1B (8476M/ BAPC 83)	RAF Museum, Hendon	
3685	Mitsubishi A6M3-2 Zero	Imperial War Museum, Duxford	
5439	Mitsubishi Ki46-III (8484M/ BAPC 84)	RAF Museum, Cosford	
15-1585	Yokosuka MXY 7 Ohka II (BAPC 58)	Science Museum, at FAA Museum, RNAS Yeovilton	
997	Yokosuka MXY 7 Ohka II (8485M/ BAPC 98)	Gr Manchester Mus of Science & Industry	
I-13	Yokosuka MXY 7 Ohka II (8486M/ BAPC 99)	RAF Museum, Cosford	
JORDAN			
408	SA125 Bulldog	Privately owned, RAF Wittering	
417	SA125A Bulldog	Privately owned, RAF Wittering	
418	SA125A Bulldog	Privately owned, RAF Wittering	
420	SA125A Bulldog	Privately owned, RAF Wittering	
MEXICO			
52	Mudry/CAARP CAP-10B (EPC-152/N4238C)	Privately owned, Hatch	
MYANMAR			
UB424	VS361 Spitfire IX (UB425)	Historic Flying Ltd, Duxford	
UB441	VS361 Spitfire IX (ML119)	Privately owned, Rochester	
NETHERLANDS			
174	Fokker S-11 Instructor (E-31/ G-BEPV)	Privately owned, Elstree	
204	Lockheed SP-2H Neptune [V]	RAF Museum, Cosford	
A-12	DH82A Tiger Moth (PH-TYG)	Privately owned, Gilze-Rijen, The Netherlands	
B-64	Noorduyn AT-16 Harvard IIB (PH-LSK)	Privately owned, Gilze-Rijen, The Netherlands	
B-71	Noorduyn AT-16 Harvard IIB (PH-MLM)	Privately owned, Gilze-Rijen, The Netherlands	
B-118	Noorduyn AT-16 Harvard IIB (PH-IIB)	Privately owned, Gilze-Rijen, The Netherlands	
E-14	Fokker S-11 Instructor (PH-AFS)	Privately owned, Lelystad, The Netherlands	
E-15	Fokker S-11 Instructor (G-BIYU)	Privately owned, White Waltham	
E-18	Fokker S-11 Instructor (PH-HTC)	Dukes of Brabant AF, Eindhoven, The Netherlands	
E-20	Fokker S-11 Instructor (PH-GRB)	Privately owned, Gilze-Rijen, The Netherlands	
E-27	Fokker S-11 Instructor (PH-HOL)	Privately owned, Lelystad, The Netherlands	

Historic Aircraft

Notes	Serial	Type (other identity)	Owner/operator, location
	E-32	Fokker S-11 Instructor (PH-HOI)	Privately owned, Gilze-Rijen, The Netherlands
	E-36	Fokker S-11 Instructor (PH-ACG)	Privately owned, Lelystad, The Netherlands
	E-39	Fokker S-11 Instructor (PH-HOG)	Privately owned, Lelystad, The Netherlands
	G-29	Beech D18S (N5369X)	KLu Historic Flt, Gilze-Rijen, The Netherlands
	MK732	VS 361 Spitfire LF IXC (8633M/ PH-OUQ) [3W-17]	KLu Historic Flight, Lelystad, The Netherlands
	N-202	Hawker Hunter F6 [10] <ff>	Privately owned, Eaglescott
	N-250	Hawker Hunter F6 (G-9-185) <ff>	Imperial War Museum, Duxford
	N-268	Hawker Hunter FGA78 (Qatar QA-10)	Yorkshire Air Museum, Elvington
	N-315	Hawker Hunter T7 (XM121)	Jet Avn Preservation Grp, Long Marston
	N5-149	NA B-25J Mitchell (44-29507/ *HD346*/N320SQ) [232511]	Duke of Brabant AF, Eindhoven, The Netherlands
	R-55	Piper L-18C Super Cub (52-2466/ G-BLMI)	Privately owned, White Waltham
	R-109	Piper L-21B Super Cub (54-2337/ PH-GAZ)	Privately owned, Gilze-Rijen, The Netherlands
	R-122	Piper L-21B Super Cub (54-2412/ PH-PPW)	Privately owned, Gilze-Rijen, The Netherlands
	R-137	Piper L-21B Super Cub (54-2427/ PH-PSC)	Privately owned, Gilze-Rijen, The Netherlands
	R-151	Piper L-21B Super Cub (54-2441/ G-BIYR)	Privately owned, Dunkeswell
	R-156	Piper L-21B Super Cub (54-2446/ G-ROVE)	Privately owned, Headcorn
	R-163	Piper L-21B Super Cub (54-2453/ G-BIRH)	Privately owned, Lee-on-Solent
	R-167	Piper L-21B Super Cub (54-2457/ G-LION)	Privately owned, Turweston, Bucks
	R-177	Piper L-21B Super Cub (54-2467/ PH-KNR)	Privately owned, Gilze-Rijen, The Netherlands
	R-181	Piper L-21B Super Cub (54-2471/ PH-GAU)	Privately owned, Gilze-Rijen, The Netherlands
	R-345	Piper J-3C Cub (PH-UCS)	Privately owned, The Netherlands
	S-9	DHC2 L-20A Beaver (PH-DHC)	KLu Historic Flt, Gilze-Rijen, The Netherlands
	Y-74	Consolidated PBY-5A Catalina (2459/PH-PBY)	Neptune Association, Valkenburg, The Netherlands
	NEW ZEALAND		
	NZ3909	WS Wasp HAS1 (XT782)	Kennet Aviation, North Weald, spares use
	NZ6361	BAC Strikemaster 87 (OJ5/ G-BXFP)	Privately owned, Chalgrove
	NORTH KOREA		
	-	WSK Lim-2 (MiG-15) (01420/ G-BMZF)	FAA Museum, RNAS Yeovilton
	NORTH VIETNAM		
	1211	WSK Lim-5 (MiG-17F) (G-MIGG)	Privately owned, Bournemouth
	NORWAY		
	423/427	Gloster Gladiator I (L8032/ G-AMRK/*N2308*)	The Shuttleworth Collection, Old Warden
	848	Piper L-18C Super Cub (LN-ACL) [FA-N]	Privately owned, Norway
	56321	SAAB S91B Safir (G-BKPY) [U-AB]	Newark Air Museum, Winthorpe
	OMAN		
	853	Hawker Hunter FR10 (XF426)	RAF Museum, Hendon
	POLAND		
	05	WSK SM-2 (Mi-2) (1005)	The Helicopter Museum, Weston-super-Mare
	309	WSK SBLim-2A (MiG-15UTI) <ff>	Royal Scottish Mus'm of Flight, E Fortune
	408	WSK-PZL Mielec TS-11 Iskra (1H-0408)	Privately owned, Coventry

Serial	Type (other identity)	Owner/operator, location	Notes
1018	WSK-PZL Mielec TS-11 Iskra (1H-1018/G-ISKA)	Privately owned, Bruntingthorpe	
1120	WSK Lim-2 (MiG-15bis)	RAF Museum, Cosford	

PORTUGAL

Serial	Type (other identity)	Owner/operator, location	Notes
85	Isaacs Fury II (G-BTPZ)	Privately owned, Ormskirk	
1360	OGMA/DHC1 Chipmunk T20 (fuselage) (G-BYYU)	Privately owned, Little Staughton	
1365	OGMA/DHC1 Chipmunk T20 (G-DHPM)	Privately owned, Spanhoe Lodge	
1372	OGMA/DHC1 Chipmunk T20 (HB-TUM)	Privately owned, Switzerland	
1377	DHC1 Chipmunk 22 (G-BARS)	Privately owned, Yeovilton	
1741	CCF Harvard IV (G-HRVD)	Air Atlantique Historic Flight, Coventry	
1747	CCF T-6J Harvard IV (20385/ G-BGPB)	The Aircraft Restoration Co, Duxford	

QATAR

Serial	Type (other identity)	Owner/operator, location	Notes
QA12	Hawker Hunter FGA78 <ff>	Privately owned, South Wales	
QP30	WS Lynx Mk 28 (G-BFDV/TD 013)	Army SEAE, Arborfield	
QP31	WS Lynx Mk 28	DARA Fleetlands Apprentice School	
QP32	WS Lynx Mk 28 (TD 016)	AAC Stockwell Hall, Middle Wallop	

RUSSIA (& FORMER SOVIET UNION)

Serial	Type (other identity)	Owner/operator, location	Notes
-	Mil Mi-24V (3532424810853)	Privately owned, Hawarden	
-	Mil Mi-24D (3532464505029)	BAE Systems, Rochester	
1	SPP Yak C-11 (G-BZMY)	Privately owned, North Weald	
01	Yakovlev Yak-52 (9311709/ G-YKSZ)	Privately owned, Old Buckenham	
02	Yakovlev Yak-52 (888615/G-CBLJ)	Privately owned, North Weald	
2	Yakovlev Yak-18T (RA-02933)	Privately owned, Wickenby	
2	Yakovlev Yak-52 (9311708/ G-YAKS)	Privately owned, North Weald	
03	Mil Mi-24D (3532461715415)	Privately owned, Hawarden	
03	Yakovlev Yak-9UM (0470403/ F-AZYJ)	Privately owned, Dijon, France	
03	Yakovlev Yak-52 (899803/ G-YAKR)	Privately owned, North Weald	
04	Mikoyan MiG-23ML (024003607)	Newark Air Museum, Winthorpe	
04	Yakovlev Yak-52 (9211612/ RA-22521)	Privately owned, Wellesbourne Mountford	
05	Yakovlev Yak-50 (832507/YL-CBH)	Privately owned, Hawarden	
07	WSK SM-1 (Mi-1) (Czech. 2007)	The Helicopter Museum, Weston-super-Mare	
07	Yakovlev Yak-18M (G-BMJY)	Privately owned, East Garston, Bucks	
09	Yakovlev Yak-52 (9411809/ G-BVMU)	Privately owned, Sandy, Beds	
9	Polikarpov Po-2 (ZK-POZ)	The Shuttleworth Collection, Old Warden	
10	Yakovlev Yak-52 (9110580)	Privately owned, White Waltham	
11	SPP Yak C-11 (G-YCII)	Privately owned, North Weald	
12	LET L-29 Delfin (194555/ES-YLM/ G-DELF)	Privately owned, Manston	
14	Yakovlev Yak-52 (899404/ G-CCCP)	Privately owned, North Wealdl	
18	LET L-29S Delfin (591771/YL-PAF)	Privately owned, Hawarden	
19	Yakovlev Yak-52 (811202/YL-CBI)	Privately owned, Hawarden	
20	Lavochkin La-11	The Fighter Collection, Duxford	
20	Yakovlev Yak-52 (790404/YL-CBJ)	Privately owned, Hawarden	
23	Mikoyan MiG-27D (83712515040)	Privately owned, Hawarden	
26	Yakovlev Yak-52 (9111306/ G-BVXK)	Privately owned, White Waltham	
27	SPP Yak C-11 (G-OYAK)	Privately owned, North Weald	
31	Yakovlev Yak-52 (9111311/ G-YAKV)	Privately owned, Rendcomb	
35	Sukhoi Su-17M-3 (25102)	Privately owned, Hawarden	
35	Yakovlev Yak-52 (9010508/ RA-02080)	Privately owned, White Waltham	
36	LET/Yak C-11 (G-KYAK)	Privately owned, North Weald	
36	SPP Yak C-11 (G-IYAK)	Privately owned, Sleap	
42	Yakovlev Yak-52 (833901/ G-LENA)	Privately owned, North Weald	

Historic Aircraft

Notes	Serial	Type (other identity)	Owner/operator, location
	49	Yakovlev Yak-55M (880606/ RA-44526)	Privately owned, White Waltham
	50	Mikoyan MiG-23MF (023003508)	Privately owned, Hawarden
50	Yakovlev Yak-50 (812101/ G-CBPM)	Privately owned, North Weald
50	Yakovlev Yak-50 (822305/ G-BXNO)	Privately owned, Denham
	50	Yakovlev Yak-52 (9111415/ G-CBRW)	Privately owned, White Waltham
	51	LET L-29S Delfin (491273/ YL-PAG)	Privately owned, Hawarden
	52	Yakovlev Yak-52 (800708/ G-CBMP)	Privately owned, Sherburn-in-Elmet
	52	Yakovlev Yak-52 (878202/ G-BWVR)	Privately owned, Barton
	54	Sukhoi Su-17M (69004)	Privately owned, Hawarden
	55	Yakovlev Yak-52 (9111505/ G-BVOK)	Intrepid Aviation, North Weald
	56	Yakovlev Yak-52 (811504)	Privately owned, Hawarden
	56	Yakovlev Yak-52 (9111506/ RA-44516)	Privately owned, White Waltham
69	Hawker Hunter FGA9 (8839M/ XG194)	RAF North Luffenham Training Area
69	Yakovlev Yak-50 (801810/G-BTZB)	Privately owned, Audley End
69	Yakovlev Yak-52 (855509/LY-ALS)	Privately owned, Little Gransden
69	Yakovlev Yak-52 (899413/ G-XYAK)	Privately owned, Compton Abbas
	71	Mikoyan MiG-27M (61912507006)	Newark Air Museum, Winthorpe
72	Yakovlev Yak-52 (9111608/ G-BXAV)	Privately owned, North Weald
	74	Yakovlev Yak-52 (877404/ G-LAOK) [JA-74, IV-62]	Privately owned, Tollerton
	74	Yakovlev Yak-52 (888802/G-BXID)	Privately owned, Wellesbourne Mountford
	96	Yakovlev Yak-55M (901103/ G-YKSS)	Privately owned, Headcorn
	98	Yakovlev Yak-52 (888911/ G-CBRU)	Privately owned, White Waltham
	100	Yakovlev Yak-52 (866904/G-YAKI)	Privately owned, Popham
101	Yakovlev Yak-52 (866915/ RA-02705)	Privately owned, Rochester
111	Aero L-39ZO Albatros (*28+02*/ G-OTAF)	The Old Flying Machine Company, Duxford
	112	Yakovlev Yak-52 (822610/LY-AFB)	Privately owned, Little Gransden
	139	Yakovlev Yak-52 (833810/ G-BWOD)	Privately owned, Sywell
503	Mikoyan MiG-21SMT (G-BRAM)	Privately owned, Farnborough
	1342	Yakovlev Yak-1 (G-BTZD)	Privately owned, Milden
1-12	Yakovlev Yak-52 (9011013/ RA-02293)	Privately owned, Halfpenny Green
	1870710	Ilyushin Il-2 (G-BZVW)	Privately owned, Sandtoft
	1878576	Ilyushin Il-2 (G-BZVX)	Privately owned, Sandtoft
	44-4315	Bell P63-C Kingcobra	Privately owned, Sussex
	44-4368	Bell P63-C Kingcobra	Privately owned, Sussex
	BH328	Hawker Hurricane IIb	Privately owned, Isle of Wight
	PT879	VS361 Spitfire LF IX (G-BYDE)	Privately owned, Isle of Wight
	(RK858)	VS361 Spitfire LF IX	The Fighter Collection, Duxford
	(SM639)	VS361 Spitfire LF IX	Privately owned, Catfield

SAUDI ARABIA

	1104	BAC Strikemaster 80	Global Aviation, Humberside
	1107	BAC Strikemaster 80	Global Aviation, Humberside
	1112	BAC Strikemaster 80 (G-FLYY)	Privately owned, Hawarden
	1114	BAC Strikemaster 80A (G-BZYH)	Privately owned, Sproughton
	1115	BAC Strikemaster 80A	Global Aviation, Humberside
	1120	BAC Strikemaster 80A	Global Aviation, Humberside
	1125	BAC Strikemaster 80A	Privately owned, Bentwaters
	1129	BAC Strikemaster 80A	Global Aviation, Humberside
	1130	BAC Strikemaster 80A	Global Aviation, Humberside
	1133	BAC Strikemaster 80A (G-BESY)	Imperial War Museum, Duxford
	55-713	BAC Lightning T55 (ZF598)	Midland Air Museum, Coventry

Serial	Type (other identity)	Owner/operator, location	Notes
SLOVAKIA			
7708	Mikoyan MiG-21MF	Boscombe Down Museum	
SOUTH AFRICA			
92	Westland Wasp HAS1 (G-BYCX)	Privately owned, Bournemouth	
221	DH115 Vampire T55 <ff>	Privately owned, Hemel Mempstead	
6130	Lockheed Ventura II (AJ469)	RAF Museum, Cosford	
7429	NA AT-6D Harvard III (D-FASS)	Privately owned, Germany	
SOUTH VIETNAM			
24550	Cessna L-19E Bird Dog (G-PDOG) [GP]	Privately owned, Lincs	
SPAIN			
B.2I-27	CASA 2.111B (He111H-16) (B.2I-103)	Imperial War Museum, stored Duxford	
C.4E-88	Messerschmitt Bf109E	Privately owned, East Garston, Bucks	
C.4K-102	Hispano HA 1.112M1L Buchon (G-BWUE)	Privately owned, Breighton	
E.3B-114	CASA 1.131E Jungmann (G-BJAL)	Privately owned, Breighton	
E.3B-143	CASA 1.131E Jungmann (G-JUNG)	Privately owned, White Waltham	
E.3B-153	CASA 1.131E Jungmann (G-BPTS) [781-75]	Privately owned, Duxford	
E.3B-336	CASA 1.131E Jungmann (G-BUTA)	Privately owned, Breighton	
E.3B-350	CASA 1.131E Jungmann (G-BHPL) [05-97]	Privately owned, Kemble	
(E.3B-369)	CASA 1.131E Jungmann (G-BPDM) [781-32]	Privately owned, Chilbolton	
E.3B-521	CASA 1.131E Jungmann [781-3]	RAF Museum, Hendon	
EM-01	DH60G Moth (G-AAOR)	Privately owned, Rendcomb	
ES.1-16	CASA 1.133L Jungmeister	Privately owned, Stretton, Cheshire	
SWEDEN			
081	CFM 01 Tummelisa <R> (SE-XIL)	Privately owned, Karlstad, Sweden	
05108	DH60 Moth	Privately owned, Langham	
17239	SAAB B-17A (SE-BYH) [7-J]	Flygvapenmuseum, Linköping, Sweden	
28693	DH100 Vampire FB6 (J-1184/SE-DXY) [9-G]	Scandinavian Historic Flight, North Weald	
29640	SAAB J-29F [20-08]	Midland Air Museum, Coventry	
29670	SAAB J-29F (SE-DXB) [10-R]	Flygvapenmuseum/F10 Wing, Angelholm, Sweden	
32028	SAAB 32A Lansen (G-BMSG)	Privately owned, Cranfield	
34066	Hawker Hunter F58 (J-4089/SE-DXA) [9-G]	Scandinavian Historic Flight, North Weald	
35075	SAAB J-35J Draken [40]	Imperial War Museum, Duxford	
A14	Thulin A/Bleriot XI (SE-XMC)	Privately owned, Karlstad, Sweden	
SWITZERLAND			
A-10	CASA 1.131E Jungmann (G-BECW)	Privately owned, Denham	
A-12	Bücker Bu131B Jungmann (G-CCHY)	Privately owned, Booker	
A-50	CASA 1.131E Jungmann (G-CBCE)	Privately owned, Breighton	
A-57	CASA 1.131E Jungmann (G-BECT)	Privately owned, Goodwood	
A-125	Pilatus P-2 (G-BLKZ)	Privately owned, North Weald	
A-701	Junkers Ju52/3m (HB-HOS)	Ju-Air, Dubendorf, Switzerland	
A-702	Junkers Ju52/3m (HB-HOT)	Ju-Air, Dubendorf, Switzerland	
A-703	Junkers Ju52/3m (HB-HOP)	Ju-Air, Dubendorf, Switzerland	
A-806	Pilatus P3-03 (G-BTLL)	Privately owned, stored Headcorn	
C-552	EKW C-3605 (G-DORN)	Privately owned, Bournemouth	
C-558	EKW C-3605	Privately owned, Spanhoe	
J-1008	DH100 Vampire FB6	Mosquito Aircraft Museum, London Colney	
J-1149	DH100 Vampire FB6 (G-SWIS)	Privately owned, Bournemouth	
J-1172	DH100 Vampire FB6 (8487M)	RAF Museum Restoration Centre, Cosford	
J-1573	DH112 Venom FB50 (G-VICI)	Source Classic Jet Flight, Bournemouth	
J-1605	DH112 Venom FB50 (G-BLID)	Gatwick Aviation Museum, Charlwood, Surrey	
J-1629	DH112 Venom FB50	Air Atlantique, Coventry	
J-1632	DH112 Venom FB50 (G-VNOM)	Kennet Aviation, North Weald	

Historic Aircraft

Notes	Serial	Type (other identity)	Owner/operator, location
	J-1649	DH112 Venom FB50	Air Atlantique, Coventry
	J-1704	DH112 Venom FB54	RAF Museum, Cosford
	J-1712	DH112 Venom FB54 <ff>	Botany Bay Village, Chorley, Lancs
	J-1758	DH112 Venom FB54 (N203DM)	Privately owned, stored North Weald
	J-4015	Hawker Hunter F58 (J-4040/ HB-RVS)	Privately owned, Altenrhein, Switzerland
	J-4021	Hawker Hunter F58 (G-HHAC)	Historic Flying Ltd/OFMC, Scampton
	J-4031	Hawker Hunter F58 (G-BWFR)	The Old Flying Machine Company, Scampton
	J-4058	Hawker Hunter F58 (G-HHAD)	The Old Flying Machine Company, Scampton
	J-4066	Hawker Hunter F58 (G-HHAE)	The Old Flying Machine Company, Scampton
	J-4072	Hawker Hunter F58 (G-HHAB)	The Old Flying Machine Company, Scampton
	J-4081	Hawker Hunter F58 (G-HHAF)	The Old Flying Machine Company, Scampton
	J-4083	Hawker Hunter F58 (G-EGHH)	Privately owned, Bournemouth
	J-4086	Hawker Hunter F58 (HB-RVU)	Privately owned, Altenrhein, Switzerland
	J-4090	Hawker Hunter F58 (G-SIAL)	The Old Flying Machine Company, Scampton
	J-4091	Hawker Hunter F58	British Aviation Heritage, Bruntingthorpe
	J-4201	Hawker Hunter T68 (HB-RVR)	Privately owned, Altenrhein, Switzerland
	J-4205	Hawker Hunter T68 (HB-RVP)	Privately owned, Altenrhein, Switzerland
	U-80	Bücker Bü133D Jungmeister (G-BUKK)	Privately owned, White Waltham
	U-99	Bücker Bü133C Jungmeister (G-AXMT)	Privately owned, Breighton
	U-110	Pilatus P-2 (G-PTWO)	Privately owned, Earls Colne
	U-142	Pilatus P-2 (G-BONE)	Privately owned, Hibaldstow
	V-54	SE3130 Alouette II (G-BVSD)	Privately owned, Staverton

USA

Notes	Serial	Type (other identity)	Owner/operator, location
	-	Noorduyn AT-16 Harvard IIB (KLu B-168)	American Air Museum, Duxford
	001	Ryan ST-3KR Recruit (G-BYPY)	Privately owned, Breighton
	1	Spad XIII <R> (G-BFYO/*S3398*)	American Air Museum, Duxford
	14	Boeing-Stearman A75N-1 Kaydet (G-ISDN)	Privately owned, Rendcomb
	23	Fairchild PT-23 (N49272)	Privately owned, Halfpenny Green
	26	Boeing-Stearman A75N-1 Kaydet (G-BAVO)	Privately owned, Old Buckenham
	27	NA SNJ-7 Texan (90678/G-BRVG)	Privately owned, Goodwood
	43	Noorduyn AT-16 Harvard IIB (43-13064/G-AZSC) [SC]	Privately owned, North Weald
	44	Boeing-Stearman D75N-1 Kaydet (42-15852/G-RJAH)	Privately owned, Rendcomb
	49	Curtiss P-40M Kittyhawk (43-5802/ G-KITT/*P8196*)	The Fighter Collection, Duxford
	57	WS55 Whirlwind HAS7 (XG592)	*Task Force* Adventure Park, Cowbridge, S Glam
	85	WAR P-47 Thunderbolt <R> (G-BTBI)	Privately owned, Carlisle
	112	Boeing-Stearman PT-13D Kaydet (42-17397/G-BSWC)	Privately owned, Staverton
	118	Boeing-Stearman PT-13A Kaydet (38-470/G-BSDS)	Privately owned, Swanton Morley
	379	Boeing-Stearman PT-13D Kaydet (42-14865/G-ILLE)	Privately owned, Oaksey Park
	441	Boeing-Stearman N2S-4 Kaydet (30010/G-BTFG)	Privately owned, Perth
	540	Piper L-4H Grasshopper (43-29877/G-BCNX)	Privately owned, Monewden
	578	Boeing-Stearman N2S-5 Kaydet (N1364V)	Privately owned, North Weald
	628	Beech D17S (44-67761/N18V)	Privately owned, stored North Weald
	718	Boeing-Stearman PT-13D Kaydet (42-17555/N5345N)	Privately owned, Tibenham
	744	Boeing-Stearman A75N-1 Kaydet (42-16532/OO-USN)	Privately owned, Wevelgem, Belgium
	817	Boeing-Stearman PT-17 Kaydet (N59269)	Privately owned, North Weald

Serial	Type (other identity)	Owner/operator, location	Notes
854	Ryan PT-22 Recruit (42-17378/ G-BTBH)	Privately owned, Wellesbourne Mountford	
855	Ryan PT-22 Recruit (41-15510/ N56421)	Privately owned, Halfpenny Green	
897	Aeronca 11AC Chief (G-BJEV) [E]	Privately owned, English Bicknor, Glos	
1102	Boeing-Stearman N2S-5 Kaydet (G-AZLE)	Privately owned, Tongham	
1164	Beech D18S (G-BKGL)	The Aircraft Restoration Co, Duxford	
1180	Boeing-Stearman N2S-3 Kaydet (3403/G-BRSK)	Privately owned, Tibenham	
2807	NA T-6G Texan (49-3072/ G-BHTH) [V-103]	Northbrook College, Shoreham	
6136	Boeing-Stearman A75N-1 Kaydet (42-16136/G-BRUJ) [205]	Privately owned, Liverpool	
6771	Republic F-84F Thunderstreak (BAF FU-6)	RAF Museum, stored Cosford	
7797	Aeronca L-16A (47-0797/G-BFAF)	Privately owned, Finmere	
8084	NA AT-6D Harvard III (42-85068/ LN-AMY)	The Old Flying Machine Company, Duxford	
8178	NA F-86A Sabre (48-0178/ G-SABR) [FU-178]	Golden Apple Operations/ARC, Duxford	
8242	NA F-86A Sabre (48-0242) [FU-242]	American Air Museum, Duxford	
01532	Northrop F-5E Tiger II <R>	RAF Alconbury on display	
02538	Fairchild PT-19B (N33870)	Privately owned, North Weald	
07539	Boeing-Stearman N2S-3 Kaydet (N63590) [143]	Privately owned, Tibenham	
14286	Lockheed T-33A (51-4286)	American Air Museum, Duxford	
O-14419	Lockheed T-33A (51-4419)	Midland Air Museum, Coventry	
14863	NA AT-6D Harvard III (41-33908/ G-BGOR)	Privately owned, Goudhurst, Kent	
15154	Bell OH-58A Kiowa (70-15154)	R. Military College of Science, Shrivenham	
15445	Piper L-18C Super Cub (51-15445/ G-BLGT)	Privately owned, Dunkeswell	
15990	Bell AH-1F Hueycobra (67-19590)	Museum of Army Flying, Middle Wallop	
16445	Bell AH-1F Hueycobra (69-16445)	R. Military College of Science, Shrivenham	
16506	Hughes OH-6A Cayuse (67-16506)	The Helicopter Museum, Weston-super-Mare	
16579	Bell UH-1H Iroquois (66-16579)	The Helicopter Museum, Weston-super-Mare	
16718	Lockheed T-33A (51-6718)	City of Norwich Aviation Museum	
17962	Lockheed SR-71A (64-17962)	American Air Museum, Duxford	
18263	Boeing-Stearman PT-17 Kaydet (41-8263/N38940) [822]	Privately owned, Tibenham	
19252	Lockheed T-33A (51-9252)	Tangmere Military Aviation Museum	
20249	Noorduyn AT-16 Harvard IIB (PH-KLU) [XS-249]	Privately owned, Lelystad, The Netherlands	
21605	Bell UH-1H Iroquois (72-21605)	American Air Museum, Duxford	
21714	Grumman F8F-2P Bearcat (121714/G-RUMM) [201-B]	The Fighter Collection, Duxford	
24538	Kaman HH-43F Huskie (62-4535)	Midland Air Museum, Coventry	
24541	Cessna L-19E Bird Dog (F-GFVE)	Privately owned, Redhill	
24568	Cessna L-19E Bird Dog (LN-WNO)	Army Aviation Norway, Kjeller, Norway	
28521	CCF Harvard IV (G-TVIJ) [TA-521]	Privately owned, Woodchurch, Kent	
30274	Piper AE-12 (N203SA)	Privately owned, Henstridge	
30861	NA TB-25J Mitchell (44-30861/ N9089Z)	Privately owned, North Weald	
31145	Piper L-4B Grasshopper (43-1145/ G-BBLH) [26-G]	Privately owned, Biggin Hill	
31171	NA B-25J Mitchell (44-31171/ N7614C)	American Air Museum, Duxford	
31952	Aeronca O-58B Defender (G-BRPR)	Privately owned, Earls Colne	
34037	NA TB-25N Mitchell (44-29366/ N9115Z/8838M)	RAF Museum, Hendon	
37414	McD F-4C Phantom (63-7414)	Midland Air Museum, Coventry	
39624	Wag Aero Sport Trainer (G-BVMH) [39-D]	Privately owned, Lincoln	
40467	Grumman F6F-5K Hellcat (80141/ G-BTCC) [19]	The Fighter Collection, Duxford	
41386	Thomas-Morse S4 Scout <R> (G-MJTD)	Privately owned, Hitchin	

Historic Aircraft

Notes	Serial	Type (other identity)	Owner/operator, location
	42165	NA F-100D Super Sabre (54-2165) [VM]	American Air Museum, Duxford
	42174	NA F-100D Super Sabre (54-2174) [UH]	Midland Air Museum, Coventry
	42196	NA F-100D Super Sabre (54-2196) [LT]	Norfolk & Suffolk Avn Museum, Flixton
	46214	Grumman TBM-3E Avenger (69327/CF-KCG) [X-3]	American Air Museum, Duxford
	46867	Grumman FM-2 Wildcat (N909WJ)	Flying A Services, North Weald
	48846	Boeing B-17G Fortress (44-8846/ F-AZDX) [DS-M]	Assoc Fortresse Toujours Volant, Paris, France
	53319	Grumman TBM-3R Avenger (G-BTDP) [319-RB]	Privately owned, North Weald
	54137	CCF Harvard IV (MM54137/ G-CTKL) [69]	Privately owned, North Weald
	54433	Lockheed T-33A (55-4433)	Norfolk & Suffolk Avn Museum, Flixton
	54439	Lockheed T-33A (55-4439)	North-East Aircraft Museum, Usworth
	58811	NA B-25J Mitchell (45-8811/ F-AZID) [HD]	Privately owned, Athens, Greece
	60312	McD F-101F Voodoo (56-0312)	Midland Air Museum, Coventry
	60689	Boeing B-52D Stratofortress (56-0689)	American Air Museum, Duxford
	63000	NA F-100D Super Sabre (54-2212) [FW-000]	USAF Croughton, Oxon, at gate
	63319	NA F-100D Super Sabre (54-2269) [FW-319]	RAF Lakenheath, on display
	63428	Republic F-105G Thunderchief (62-4428)	USAF Croughton, Oxon, at gate
	66692	Lockheed U-2CT (56-6692)	American Air Museum, Duxford
	70270	McD F-101B Voodoo (57-270) (fuselage)	Midland Air Museum, Coventry
	80425	Grumman F7F-3P Tigercat (N7235C/G-RUMT) [WT-14]	The Fighter Collection, Duxford
	82062	DHC U-6A Beaver (58-2062)	Midland Air Museum, Coventry
	91822	Republic F-105D Thunderchief (59-1822)	American Air Museum, Duxford
	93542	CCF Harvard IV (G-BRLV) [LTA-542]	Privately owned, North Weald
	96995	CV F4U-4 Corsair (OE-EAS) [BR-37]	Tyrolean Jet Services, Innsbruck, Austria
	97264	CV F4U-4 Corsair (F-AZVJ) [403]	Flying Legend, Dijon, France
	111836	NA AT-6C Harvard IIA (41-33262/ G-TSIX) [JZ-6]	The Real Aeroplane Company, Breighton
	111989	Cessna L-19A Bird Dog (51-11989/ N33600)	Museum of Army Flying, Middle Wallop
	115042	NA T-6G Texan (51-15042/ G-BGHU) [TA-042]	Privately owned, Headcorn
	115227	NA T-6G Texan (51-15227/ G-BKRA)	Privately owned, Staverton
	115302	Piper L-18C Super Cub (51-15302/ G-BJTP) [TP]	Privately owned, Bidford
	115684	Piper L-21A Super Cub (51-15684/ G-BKVM) [DC]	Privately owned, North Coates
	124143	Douglas AD-4NA Skyraider (F-AZDP) [205-RM]	Amicale J-B Salis, la Ferté-Alais, France
	124485	Boeing B-17G Fortress (44-85784/ G-BEDF) [DF-A]	B-17 Preservation Ltd, Duxford
	124724	CV F4U-5NL Corsair (F-AZEG) [22]	Amicale J-B Salis, la Ferté-Alais, France
	126922	Douglas AD-4NA Skyraider (G-RADR) [402-AK]	Kennet Aviation, North Weald
	126956	Douglas AD-4NA Skyraider (F-AZDQ) [3-RM]	Aéro Retro, St Rambert d'Albon, France
	127002	Douglas AD-4NA Skyraider (F-AZHK) [618-G]	Privately owned, Cuers, France
	133704	CV F4U-5NL Corsair (124541/ F-AZYS) [14.F.6]	Privately owned, Le Castellet, France
	134076	NA AT-6D Harvard III (41-34671/ F-AZSC) [TA076]	Privately owned, Cean, France
	138179	NA T-28A Trojan (OE-ESA) [BA]	Tyrolean Jet Services, Innsbruck, Austria
	140547	NA T-28C Trojan (N2800Q)	Privately owned
	146289	NA T-28C Trojan (N99153) [2W]	Norfolk & Suffolk Aviation Museum, Flixton
	150225	WS58 Wessex 60 (G-AWOX) [123]	Privately owned, Lulsgate

134

Serial	Type (other identity)	Owner/operator, location	Notes
151632	NA TB-25N Mitchell (44-30925/ G-BWGR)	Privately owned, Sandtoft	
155529	McD F-4S Phantom (ZE359) [AJ-114]	American Air Museum, Duxford	
155848	McD F-4S Phantom [WT-11]	Royal Scottish Mus'm of Flight, E Fortune	
159233	HS AV-8A Harrier [CG-33]	Imperial War Museum North, Salford Quays	
162068	McD AV-8B Harrier II (9250M) (fuselage)	RAF Cottesmore BDRT	
162071	McD AV-8B Harrier II (fuselage)	Rolls-Royce, Filton	
162730	McD AV-8B Harrier II (fuselage)	RAF, St Athan	
162958	McD AV-8B Harrier II (fuselage)	QinetiQ, Boscombe Down	
211072	Boeing-Stearman PT-17 Kaydet (N50755)	Privately owned, Swanton Morley	
217786	Boeing-Stearman PT-17 Kaydet (41-8169/CF-EQS) [25]	American Air Museum, Duxford	
219993	Bell P-39Q Airacobra (42-19993/ N139DP)	The Fighter Collection	
226413	Republic P-47D Thunderbolt (45-49192/N47DD) [ZU-N]	American Air Museum, Duxford	
226671	Republic P-47M Thunderbolt (G-THUN) [MX-X]	The Fighter Collection, Duxford	
231983	Boeing B-17G Fortress (44-83735/ F-BDRS) [IY-G]	American Air Museum, Duxford	
234539	Fairchild PT-19B Cornell (42-34539/N50429) [63]	Privately owned, Dunkeswell	
236657	Piper L-4A Grasshopper (42-36657/G-BGSJ) [44-A]	Privately owned, Dunkeswell	
237123	Waco CG-4A Hadrian (BAPC 157) (fuselage)	Yorkshire Air Museum, Elvington	
238410	Piper L-4A Grasshopper (42-38410/G-BHPK) [44-A]	Privately owned, Tibenham	
243809	Waco CG-4A Hadrian (BAPC 185)	Museum of Army Flying, Middle Wallop	
252983	Schweizer TG-3A (42-52983/ N66630)	American Air Museum, Duxford	
314887	Fairchild Argus III (43-14887/ G-AJPI)	Privately owned, Felthorpe	
315211	Douglas C-47A (43-15211/ N1944A) [J8-Z]	Privately owned, Booker	
315509	Douglas C-47A (43-15509/ G-BHUB) [W7-S]	American Air Museum, Duxford	
329405	Piper L-4H Grasshopper (43-29405/G-BCOB) [23-A]	Privately owned, South Walsham	
329417	Piper L-4A Grasshopper (42-38400/G-BDHK)	Privately owned, Coleford	
329471	Piper L-4H Grasshopper (43-29471/G-BGXA) [44-F]	Privately owned, Martley, Worcs	
329601	Piper L-4H Grasshopper (43-29601/G-AXHR) [44-D]	Privately owned, Nayland	
329854	Piper L-4H Grasshopper (43-29854/G-BMKC) [44-R]	Privately owned, Newtownards	
329934	Piper L-4H Grasshopper (43-29934/G-BCPH) [72-B]	Privately owned, White Waltham	
330238	Piper L-4H Grasshopper (43-30238/G-LIVH) [24-A]	Privately owned, Barton	
330485	Piper L-4H Grasshopper (43-30485/G-AJES) [44-C]	Privately owned, Shifnal	
343251	Boeing-Stearman N2S-5 Kaydet (43517/G-NZSS) [27]	Privately owned, Swanton Morley	
411622	NA P-51D Mustang (44-74427/ F-AZSB) [G4-C]	Privately owned, Nimes, France	
413317	NA P-51D Mustang (44-74409/ N51RT) [VF-B]	RAF Museum, Hendon	
413573	NA P-51D Mustang (44-73415/ 9133M/N6526D) [B6-V]	RAF Museum, Cosford	
413704	NA P-51D Mustang (44-73149/ G-BTCD) [B7-H]	The Old Flying Machine Company, Duxford	
414151	NA P-51D Mustang (44-73140/ NL314BG) [HO-M]	Flying A Services, North Weald	
414419	NA P-51D Mustang (45-15118/ G-MSTG) [LH-F]	Privately owned, Norwich	
414450	NA P-51D Mustang (44-73877/ N167F) [B6-S]	Scandinavian Historic Flight, North Weald	

Historic Aircraft

Notes	Serial	Type (other identity)	Owner/operator, location
	434602	Douglas A-26B Invader (44-34602/ N167B) [BC-602]	Scandinavian Historic Flight, North Weald
	435710	Douglas A-26C Invader (44-35710/ OO-INV)	Historic Invader Avn, Schiphol, The Netherlands
442268		Noorduyn AT-16 Harvard IIB (KF568/LN-TEX) [TA-268]	Scandinavian Historic Flight, Oslo, Norway
	454467	Piper L-4J Grasshopper (45-4467/ G-BILI) [44-J]	Privately owned, White Waltham
	454537	Piper L-4J Grasshopper (45-4537/ G-BFDL) [04-J]	Privately owned, Shempston Farm, Lossiemouth
	461748	Boeing B-29A Superfortress (44-61748/G-BHDK) [Y]	American Air Museum, Duxford
463209		NA P-51D Mustang <R> (BAPC 255) [WZ-S]	American Air Museum, Duxford
	463864	NA P-51D Mustang (44-63864/ G-CBNM) [HL-W]	The Fighter Collection, Duxford
	472035	NA P-51D Mustang (44-72035/ G-SIJJ)	Privately owned, North Weald
	472216	NA P-51D Mustang (44-72216/ G-BIXL) [HO-M]	Privately owned, East Garston, Bucks
472218		CAC-18 Mustang 22 (A68-192/ G-HAEC) [WZ-I]	Privately owned, Woodchurch, Kent
472218		NA P-51D Mustang (44-73979) [WZ-I]	Imperial War Museum, Lambeth
	472773	NA P-51D Mustang (44-72773/ G-SUSY) [QP-M]	Privately owned, Sywell
	474425	NA P-51D Mustang (44-74425/ NL11T) [OC-G]	Dutch Mustang Flt, Lelystad, The Netherlands
	474923	NA P-51D Mustang (44-74923/ N6395)	Privately owned, Lelystad, The Netherlands
	479744	Piper L-4H Grasshopper (44-79744/G-BGPD) [49-M]	Privately owned, Marsh, Bucks
	479766	Piper L-4H Grasshopper (44-79766/G-BKHG) [63-D]	Privately owned, Goldcliff, Gwent
	480015	Piper L-4H Grasshopper (44-80015/G-AKIB) [44-M]	Privately owned, Bodmin
	480133	Piper L-4J Grasshopper (44-80133/G-BDCD) [44-B]	Privately owned, Slinfold
	480321	Piper L-4J Grasshopper (44-80321/G-FRAN) [44-H]	Privately owned, Rayne, Essex
	480480	Piper L-4J Grasshopper (44-80480/G-BECN) [44-E]	Privately owned, Kersey, Suffolk
	480551	Piper L-4J Grasshopper (44-80551/LN-KLT) [43-S]	Scandinavian Historic Flight, Oslo, Norway
	480636	Piper L-4J Grasshopper (44-80636/G-AXHP) [58-A]	Privately owned, Southend
	480723	Piper L-4J Grasshopper (44-80723/G-BFZB) [E5-J]	Privately owned, Egginton
	480752	Piper L-4J Grasshopper (44-80752/G-BCXJ) [39-E]	Privately owned, Old Sarum
	483868	Boeing B-17G Fortress (44-83868/ N5237V) [A-N]	RAF Museum, Hendon
	486893	NA B-25J Mitchell (N6123C)	Tyrolean Jet Services, Innsbruck, Austria
	493209	NA T-6G Texan (49-3209/ G-DDMV/*41*)	Privately owned, Gloucester
	511701A	Beech C-45H (51-11701/G-BSZC) [AF258]	Privately owned, Bryngwyn Bach
607327		PA-18 Super Cub 95 (G-ARAO) [09-L]	Privately owned, Denham
2106449		NA P-51C Mustang (43-25147 /N51PR/G-PSIC) [HO-W]	The Fighter Collection, Duxford
2-134		NA T-6G Texan (114700)	Privately owned, North Weald
	3-1923	Aeronca O-58B Defender (43-1923/G-BRHP)	Privately owned, Chiseldon
18-2001		Piper L-18C Super Cub (52-2401/ G-BIZV)	Privately owned, Oxenhope
	39-139	Beech YC-43 Traveler (N295BS)	Dukes of Brabant AF, Eindhoven, The Netherlands
	40-1766	Boeing-Stearman PT-17 Kaydet	Privately owned, Swanton Morley
	41-24216	Consolidated B-24D Liberator <ff>	American Air Museum, Duxford
	41-33275	NA AT-6C Texan (G-BICE) [CE]	Privately owned, Ipswich
	42-12417	Noorduyn AT-16 Harvard IIB (Klu. B-163)	Covert Forces Museum, Harrington, Northants

Serial	Type (other identity)	Owner/operator, location	Notes
42-35870	Talyorcraft DCO-65 (G-BWLJ) [129]	Privately owned, Nayland	
42-58678	Taylorcraft DF-65 (G-BRIY) [IY]	Privately owned, North Weald	
42-78044	Aeronca 11AC Chief (G-BRXL)	Privately owned, High Cross, Herts	
42-84555	NA AT-6D Harvard III (FAP.1662/ G-ELMH) [EP-H]	Privately owned, Hardwick, Norfolk	
42-93510	Douglas C-47A Skytrain [CM] <ff>	Privately owned, Kew	
43-9628	Douglas A-20G Havoc <ff>	Privately owned, Hinckley, Leics	
43-35943	Beech 3N Expeditor (G-BKRG) [943]	Privately owned, Bruntingthorpe	
44-13954	NA P-51D Mustang	Privately owned, Coventry	
44-14574	NA P-51D Mustang (fuselage)	East Essex Aviation Museum, Clacton	
44-51228	Consolidated B-24M Liberator [RE-N]	American Air Museum, Duxford	
44-79609	Piper L-4H Grasshopper (G-BHXY) [PR]	Privately owned, Bodmin	
44-80594	Piper L-4J Grasshopper (G-BEDJ)	Privately owned, White Waltham	
44-80647	Piper L-4J Grasshopper (D-EGAF)	The Vintage Aircraft Co, Fürstenwalde, Germany	
44-83184	Fairchild UC-61K Argus III (G-RGUS)	Privately owned, Sturgate, Lincs	
51-9036	Lockheed T-33A	Newark Air Museum, Winthorpe	
54-005	NA F-100D Super Sabre (54-2163)	Dumfries & Galloway Avn Mus, Dumfries	
54-223	NA F-100D Super Sabre (54-2223)	Newark Air Museum, Winthorpe	
54-2447	Piper L-21B Super Cub (G-SCUB)	Privately owned, Anwick	
63-699	McD F-4C Phantom (63-7699) [CG]	Midland Air Museum, Coventry	
64-17657	Douglas A-26A Invader (N99218) <ff>	Tower Museum, Ludham, Norfolk	
65-777	McD F-4C Phantom (63-7419) [LN]	RAF Lakenheath, on display	
67-120	GD F-111E Aardvark (67-0120) [UH]	American Air Museum, Duxford	
68-0060	GD F-111E Aardvark <ff>	Dumfries & Galloway Avn Mus, Dumfries	
72-1447	GD F-111F Aardvark <ff>	American Air Museum, Duxford	
72-448	GD F-111E Aardvark (68-0011) [LN]	RAF Lakenheath, on display	
76-020	McD F-15A Eagle (76-0020) [BT]	American Air Museum, Duxford	
76-124	McD F-15B Eagle (76-0124) [LN]	RAF Lakenheath, instructional use	
77-259	Fairchild A-10A Thunderbolt (77-0259) [AR]	American Air Museum, Duxford	
80-219	Fairchild GA-10A Thunderbolt (80-0219) [AR]	RAF Alconbury, on display	
92-048	McD F-15A Eagle (74-0131) [LN]	RAF Lakenheath, on display	
146-11042	Wolf WII <R> (G-BMZX) [7]	Privately owned, Haverfordwest	
146-11083	Wolf WII <R> (G-BNAI) [5]	Privately owned, Haverfordwest	
H-57	Piper L-4A Grasshopper (42-36375/G-AKAZ)	Privately owned, Duxford	

YUGOSLAVIA

23194	Soko G-2A Galeb (YU-YAG)	Privately owned, Biggin Hill	
23196	Soko G-2A Galeb (YU-YAC)	Privately owned, Biggin Hill	
30139	Soko P-2 Kraguj [139]	Privately owned, Biggin Hill	
30140	Soko P-2 Kraguj (G-RADA) [140]	Privately owned, Biggin Hill	
30146	Soko P-2 Kraguj (G-BSXD) [146]	Privately owned, Elstree	
30149	Soko P-2 Kraguj (G-SOKO) [149]	Privately owned, Bournemouth	
30151	Soko P-2 Kraguj [151]	D-Day Aviation Museum, Shoreham	

This privately owned Strikemaster (G-UPPI) is painted in Ecuadorian AF colours as FAE259. *PRM*

F-86A Sabre 8178/G-SABR is owned by Golden Apple Operations and flown from Duxford. *PRM*

Irish Military Aircraft Markings

Serial	Type (other identity)	Owner/operator, location	Notes
34	Miles M14A Magister (N5392)	IAC stored, Baldonnel	
141	Avro 652A Anson C19	IAC stored, Baldonnel	
161	VS509 Spitfire T9 (G-CCCA)	Historic Flying Ltd, Duxford	
164	DHC1 Chipmunk T20	IAC stored, Baldonnel	
168	DHC1 Chipmunk T20	IAC No 1 Operations Wing, Baldonnel	
172	DHC1 Chipmunk T20	IAC stored, Baldonnel	
173	DHC1 Chipmunk T20	South East Aviation Enthusiasts, Dromod	
176	DH104 Dove 4 (VP-YKF)	South East Aviation Enthusiasts, Waterford	
177	Percival P56 Provost T51 (G-BLIW)	Privately owned, Shoreham	
181	Percival P56 Provost T51	Privately owned, Thatcham	
183	Percival P56 Provost T51	IAC stored, Baldonnel	
184	Percival P56 Provost T51	South East Aviation Enthusiasts, Waterford	
187	DH115 Vampire T55	South East Aviation Enthusiasts, Waterford	
189	Percival P56 Provost T51 (comp XF846)	IAC Baldonnel Fire Section	
191	DH115 Vampire T55	IAC Museum, Baldonnel	
192	DH115 Vampire T55	South East Aviation Enthusiasts, Waterford	
195	Sud SA316 Alouette III	IAC No 302 Sqn/3 Operations Wing, Baldonnel	
196	Sud SA316 Alouette III	IAC No 302 Sqn/3 Operations Wing, Baldonnel	
197	Sud SA316 Alouette III	IAC No 302 Sqn/3 Operations Wing, Baldonnel	
198	DH115 Vampire T11 (XE977)	IAC stored, Baldonnel	
199	DHC1 Chipmunk T22	IAC stored, Baldonnel	
203	Reims-Cessna FR172H	IAC No 104 Sqn/1 Operations Wing, Baldonnel	
205	Reims-Cessna FR172H	IAC No 104 Sqn/1 Operations Wing, Baldonnel	
206	Reims-Cessna FR172H	IAC No 104 Sqn/1 Operations Wing, Baldonnel	
207	Reims-Cessna FR172H	IAC, stored, Waterford	
208	Reims-Cessna FR172H	IAC No 104 Sqn/1 Operations Wing, Baldonnel	
210	Reims-Cessna FR172H	IAC No 104 Sqn/1 Operations Wing, Baldonnel	
211	Sud SA316 Alouette III	IAC No 302 Sqn/3 Operations Wing, Baldonnel	
212	Sud SA316 Alouette III	IAC No 302 Sqn/3 Operations Wing, Baldonnel	
213	Sud SA316 Alouette III	IAC No 302 Sqn/3 Operations Wing, Baldonnel	
214	Sud SA316 Alouette III	IAC No 302 Sqn/3 Operations Wing, Baldonnel	
215	Fouga CM170 Super Magister	IAC, stored Baldonnel	
216	Fouga CM170 Super Magister	Carlow Institute of Technology, instructional use	
217	Fouga CM170 Super Magister	IAC 3 Operations Wing, Baldonnel	
218	Fouga CM170 Super Magister	IAC, stored Baldonnel	
219	Fouga CM170 Super Magister	IAC, stored Baldonnel	
220	Fouga CM170 Super Magister	Cork University, instructional use	
222	SIAI SF-260WE Warrior	IAC Flying Training School, Baldonnel	
225	SIAI SF-260WE Warrior	IAC Flying Training School, Baldonnel	
226	SIAI SF-260WE Warrior	IAC Flying Training School, Baldonnel	
227	SIAI SF-260WE Warrior	IAC Flying Training School, Baldonnel	
229	SIAI SF-260WE Warrior	IAC Flying Training School, Baldonnel	
230	SIAI SF-260WE Warrior	IAC Flying Training School, Baldonnel	
231	SIAI SF-260WE Warrior	IAC Flying Training School, Baldonnel	
240	Beech Super King Air 200MR	IAC No 102 Sqn/1 Operations Wing, Baldonnel	
241	Aérospatiale SA342L Gazelle	IAC No 303 Sqn/3 Operations Wing, Baldonnel	
243	Reims-Cessna FR172K	IAC No 104 Sqn/1 Operations Wing, Baldonnel	
244	Aérospatiale SA365F Dauphin II	IAC No 301 Sqn/3 Operations Wing,	

Irish Military Aircraft Markings

Notes	Serial	Type (other identity)	Owner/operator, location
			Baldonnel
	245	Aérospatiale SA365F Dauphin II	IAC No 301 Sqn/3 Operations Wing, Baldonnel
	246	Aérospatiale SA365F Dauphin II	IAC No 301 Sqn/3 Operations Wing, Baldonnel
	247	Aérospatiale SA365F Dauphin II	IAC No 301 Sqn/3 Operations Wing, Baldonnel
	251	Grumman G1159C Gulfstream IV	IAC No 102 Sqn/1 Operations Wing, Baldonnel
	252	Airtech CN.235 MPA Persuader	IAC No 101 Sqn/1 Operations Wing, Baldonnel
	253	Airtech CN.235 MPA Persuader	IAC No 101 Sqn/1 Operations Wing Baldonnel
	254	PBN-2T Defender 4000 (G-BWPN)	IAC No 106 Sqn/1 Operations Wing, Baldonnel
	255	AS355N Twin Squirrel (G-BXEV)	IAC No 106 Sqn/1 Operations Wing, Baldonnel
	256	Eurocopter EC135T-1	IAC No 106 Sqn/1 Operations Wing, Baldonnel
	257	Sikorsky S.61N	IAC No 301 Sqn/3 Operations Wing, Sligo
	258	Bombardier Learjet 45	IAC No 102 Sqn/1 Operations Wing, Baldonnel
	260	Pilatus PC-9	Pilatus for IAC
	261	Pilatus PC-9	Pilatus for IAC
	262	Pilatus PC-9	Pilatus for IAC
	263	Pilatus PC-9	Pilatus for IAC
	264	Pilatus PC-9	Pilatus for IAC
	265	Pilatus PC-9	Pilatus for IAC
	266	Pilatus PC-9	Pilatus for IAC
	267	Pilatus PC-9	Pilatus for IAC
	268	Pilatus PC-9	Pilatus for IAC
	269	Pilatus PC-9	Pilatus for IAC

Baldonnel-based CN.235 MPA Persuader 253 is operated by 106 Squadron, Irish Air Corps. *PRM*

Overseas Military Aircraft Markings

Aircraft included in this section are a selection of those likely to be seen visiting UK civil and military airfields on transport flights, exchange visits, exercises and for air shows. It is not a comprehensive list of *all* aircraft operated by the air arms concerned.

ALGERIA
Force Aérienne Algérienne/ Al Quwwat al Jawwiya al Jaza'eriya

Lockheed C-130H Hercules

7T-WHE	(4935)
7T-WHF	(4934)
7T-WHI	(4930)
7T-WHJ	(4928)
7T-WHQ	(4926)
7T-WHR	(4924)
7T-WHS	(4912)
7T-WHT	(4911)
7T-WHY	(4913)
7T-WHZ	(4914)

Lockheed C-130H-30 Hercules

7T-WHA	(4997)
7T-WHB	(5224)
7T-WHD	(4987)
7T-WHL	(4989)
7T-WHM	(4919)
7T-WHN	(4894)
7T-WHO	(4897)
7T-WHP	(4921)

Grumman G.1159A Gulfstream III/ G.1159C Gulfstream IV/ G.1159C Gulfstream IVSP
Ministry of Defence, Boufarik

7T-VPC	(1418)	
		Gulfstream IV
7T-VPM	(1421)	
		Gulfstream IV
7T-VPR	(1288)	
		Gulfstream IVSP
7T-VPS	(1291)	
		Gulfstream IVSP
7T-VRD	(399)	
		Gulfstream III

Gulfstream Aerospace Gulfstream V
Ministry of Defence, Boufarik

7T-VPG	(617)

AUSTRALIA
Royal Australian Air Force

Boeing 707-338C/368C*
33 Sqn, Amberley
A20-261*
A20-623
A20-624
A20-629

Boeing 737-7DT
34 Sqn, Canberra
A36-001
A36-002

Canadair CL.604 Challenger
34 Sqn, Canberra
A37-001
A37-002
A37-003

Lockheed C-130H Hercules
36 Sqn, Richmond, NSW
A97-001
A97-002
A97-003
A97-004
A97-005
A97-006
A97-007
A97-008
A97-009
A97-010
A97-011
A97-012

Lockheed C-130J-30 Hercules II
37 Sqn, Richmond, NSW
A97-440
A97-441
A97-442
A97-447
A97-448
A97-449
A97-450
A97-464
A97-465
A97-466
A97-467

Lockheed P-3 Orion
10/11 Sqns, Maritime Patrol Group, Edinburgh, NSW

A9-656	AP-3C	11 Sqn
A9-657	P-3W	11 Sqn
A9-658	P-3W	10 Sqn
A9-659	P-3W	11 Sqn
A9-660	AP-3C	10 Sqn
A9-661	AP-3C	10 Sqn
A9-662	P-3W	11 Sqn
A9-663	P-3W	11 Sqn
A9-664	P-3W	11 Sqn
A9-665	AP-3C	10 Sqn
A9-751	P-3C	11 Sqn
A9-752	AP-3C	10 Sqn
A9-753	P-3C	10 Sqn
A9-755	P-3C	10 Sqn
A9-756	P-3C	11 Sqn
A9-757	P-3C	10 Sqn
A9-758	P-3C	10 Sqn
A9-759	AP-3C	10 Sqn
A9-760	AP-3C	10 Sqn

AUSTRIA
Öesterreichische Luftstreitkräfte

Airtech CN.235-300
Fliegerregiment I
 Flachenstaffel, Tulln
6T-AA

Lockheed C-130K Hercules
Fliegerregiment III
 Transportstaffel, Linz
8T-CA
8T-CB
8T-CC

SAAB 35ÖE Draken
Fliegerregiment II
 1 Staffel/Uberwg, Zeltweg;
 2 Staffel/Uberwg, Graz

01	(351401)	1 Staffel
02	(351402)	1 Staffel
03	(351403)	1 Staffel
04	(351404)	1 Staffel
05	(351405)	1 Staffel
06	(351406)	1 Staffel
07	(351407)	1 Staffel
08	(351408)	1 Staffel
09	(351409)	1 Staffel
10	(351410)	1 Staffel
11	(351411)	1 Staffel
12	(351412)	1 Staffel
13	(351413)	2 Staffel
14	(351414)	2 Staffel
15	(351415)	2 Staffel
16	(351416)	2 Staffel
18	(351418)	2 Staffel
19	(351419)	2 Staffel
20	(351420)	2 Staffel
21	(351421)	2 Staffel
22	(351422)	2 Staffel
23	(351423)	2 Staffel
24	(351424)	2 Staffel

SAAB 105ÖE
Fliegerregiment III
 Dusenstaffel, Linz

(yellow)

B	(105402)
D	(105404)
E	(105405)
F	(105406)
G	(105407)
I	(105409)
J	(105410)

(green)

B	(105412)
D	(105414)

GF-16 (105416)
GG-17 (105417)
(red)
B (105422)
C (105423)
D (105424)
E (105425)
F (105426)
G (105427)
H (105428)
I (105429)
J (105430)
(blue)
A (105431)
B (105432)
C (105433)
D (105434)
E (105435)
F (105436)
G (105437)
I (105439)
J (105440)

Short SC7 Skyvan 3M
Fliegerregiment I
  Flachenstaffel, Tulln
5S-TA
5S-TB

BAHRAIN
BAE RJ.100
Bahrain Defence Force
A9C-BDF

Boeing 747SP-21
Bahrain Amiri Flt
A9C-HMH

Boeing 747-4P8
Bahrain Amiri Flt
A9C-HMK

Grumman G.1159
Gulfstream IITT/G.1159C
Gulfstream IV-SP
Govt of Bahrain
A9C-BAH Gulfstream IV-SP
A9C-BG Gulfstream IITT

BELGIUM
Belgische Luchtmacht
D-BD Alpha Jet E
7/11 Smaldeel (1 Wg),
  Bevekom
AT-01
AT-02
AT-03
AT-05
AT-06
AT-08
AT-10
AT-11
AT-12
AT-13
AT-14
AT-15
AT-17
AT-18
AT-19
AT-20
AT-21
AT-22
AT-23
AT-24

AT-25
AT-26
AT-27
AT-28
AT-29
AT-30
AT-31
AT-32
AT-33

Airbus A.310-322
21 Smaldeel (15 Wg),
  Melsbroek
CA-01
CA-02

Dassault Falcon 900B
21 Smaldeel (15 Wg),
  Melsbroek
CD-01

**Embraer ERJ.135LR/
ERJ.145LR***
21 Smaldeel (15 Wg),
  Melsbroek
CE-01
CE-02
CE-03*
CE-04*

Lockheed C-130H Hercules
20 Smaldeel (15 Wg),
  Melsbroek
CH-01
CH-02
CH-03
CH-04
CH-05
CH-07
CH-08
CH-09
CH-10
CH-11
CH-12

Dassault Falcon 20E
21 Smaldeel (15 Wg),
  Melsbroek
CM-01
CM-02

General Dynamics F-16
(MLU aircraft are marked
with a *)
1,350 Smaldeel (2 Wg),
  Florennes [FS];
31,349 Smaldeel, OCU
  (10 Wg), Kleine-Brogel
  [BL]

FA-46	F-16A	2 Wg
FA-47	F-16A	2 Wg
FA-48	F-16A*	2 Wg
FA-50	F-16A(R)	2 Wg
FA-56	F-16A*	10 Wg
FA-57	F-16A*	2 Wg
FA-58	F-16A*	2 Wg
FA-60	F-16A*	10 Wg
FA-61	F-16A*	10 Wg
FA-65	F-16A*	10 Wg
FA-66	F-16A*	2 Wg
FA-67	F-16A*	2 Wg
FA-68	F-16A*	12 Wg
FA-69	F-16A*	2 Wg
FA-70	F-16A*	10 Wg
FA-71	F-16A*	2 Wg
FA-72	F-16A*	2 Wg
FA-73	F-16A*	10 Wg
FA-74	F-16A*	10 Wg
FA-75	F-16A*	2 Wg
FA-76	F-16A*	10 Wg
FA-77	F-16A*	10 Wg
FA-78	F-16A*	10 Wg
FA-81	F-16A*	10 Wg
FA-82	F-16A*	10 Wg
FA-83	F-16A*	2 Wg
FA-84	F-16A*	10 Wg
FA-86	F-16A*	10 Wg
FA-87	F-16A*	10 Wg
FA-88	F-16A*	2 Wg
FA-89	F-16A*	2 Wg
FA-90	F-16A*	10 Wg
FA-91	F-16A*	2 Wg
FA-92	F-16A*	2 Wg
FA-94	F-16A*	2 Wg
FA-95	F-16A*	10 Wg
FA-97	F-16A*	2 Wg
FA-98	F-16A*	10 Wg
FA-99	F-16A*	10 Wg
FA-100	F-16A*	10 Wg
FA-101	F-16A*	2 Wg
FA-102	F-16A*	2 Wg
FA-103	F-16A	2 Wg
FA-104	F-16A*	2 Wg
FA-106	F-16A*	10 Wg
FA-107	F-16A	2 Wg
FA-108	F-16A*	10 Wg
FA-109	F-16A	10 Wg
FA-110	F-16A*	10 Wg
FA-111	F-16A*	10 Wg
FA-112	F-16A*	10 Wg
FA-114	F-16A*	10 Wg
FA-115	F-16A*	2 Wg
FA-116	F-16A*	10 Wg
FA-117	F-16A*	2 Wg
FA-118	F-16A	2 Wg
FA-119	F-16A*	10 Wg
FA-120	F-16A*	10 Wg
FA-121	F-16A*	2 Wg
FA-123	F-16A*	10 Wg
FA-124	F-16A*	10 Wg
FA-125	F-16A*	2 Wg
FA-126	F-16A*	2 Wg
FA-127	F-16A	2 Wg
FA-128	F-16A	2 Wg
FA-129	F-16A*	10 Wg
FA-130	F-16A*	10 Wg
FA-131	F-16A	2 Wg
FA-132	F-16A*	2 Wg
FA-133	F-16A	2 Wg
FA-134	F-16A*	10 Wg
FA-135	F-16A*	2 Wg
FA-136	F-16A*	10 Wg
FB-01	F-16B*	2 Wg
FB-02	F-16B	OCU
FB-04	F-16B	2 Wg
FB-05	F-16B*	2 Wg
FB-08	F-16B*	10 Wg
FB-09	F-16B	2 Wg
FB-10	F-16B	2 Wg
FB-12	F-16B	2 Wg
FB-14	F-16B*	10 Wg
FB-15	F-16B*	OCU
FB-17	F-16B*	OCU
FB-18	F-16B*	2 Wg
FB-20	F-16B*	2 Wg
FB-21	F-16B*	2 Wg
FB-22	F-16B*	OCU
FB-23	F-16B*	10 Wg

FB-24   F-16B*   OCU

Fouga CM170 Magister
Fouga Flight/7 Smaldeel
(1 Wg), Bevekom
MT-04
MT-13
MT-14
MT-26
MT-34
MT-35
MT-37
MT-40
MT-44
MT-48

**Westland Sea King
Mk48/48A***
40 Smaldeel, Koksijde
RS-01
RS-02
RS-03*
RS-04
RS-05

**SIAI Marchetti
SF260M/SF260D***
Ecole de Pilotage
  Elementaire (5 Sm/1 Wg),
  Bevekom
ST-02
ST-03
ST-04
ST-06
ST-10
ST-12
ST-15
ST-16
ST-17
ST-18
ST-19
ST-20
ST-22
ST-23
ST-24
ST-25
ST-26
ST-27
ST-30
ST-31
ST-32
ST-34
ST-35
ST-36
ST-40*
ST-41*
ST-42*
ST-43*
ST-44*
ST-45*
ST-46*
ST-47*
ST-48*

**Aviation Légère de la
Force Terrestre/Belgische
Landmacht**
  Sud SA318C/SE3130*
  Alouette II
16 BnHLn, Bierset;
SLV, Brasschaat

A-22*	16 BnHLn
A-40	SLV
A-41	SLV

A-43	SLV	
A-44	SLV	
A-46	SLV	
A-47	16 BnHLn	
A-49	16 BnHLn	
A-50	SLV	
A-53	16 BnHLn	
A-54	16 BnHLn	
A-55	SLV	
A-57	16 BnHLn	
A-59	16 BnHLn	
A-61	SLV	
A-62	SLV	
A-64	SLV	
A-65	SLV	
A-66	SLV	
A-68	16 BnHLn	
A-69	16 BnHLn	
A-70	SLV	
A-72	16 BnHLn	
A-73	16 BnHLn	
A-74	16 BnHLn	
A-75	16 BnHLn	
A-77	16 BnHLn	
A-78	16 BnHLn	
A-79	SLV	
A-80	SLV	

**Britten-Norman BN-2A/
BN-2B-21* Islander**
16 BnHLn, Bierset;
SLV, Brasschaat

B-01	LA	16 BnHLn	
B-02*	LB	16 BnHLn	
B-04*	LD	SLV	
B-07*	LG	16 BnHLn	
B-08*	LH	SLV	
B-09*	LI	SLV	
B-10*	LJ	SLV	
B-11*	LK	SLV	
B-12	LL	SLV	

Agusta A109HA/HO*
17 BnHATk, Bierset;
18 BnHATk, Bierset;
SLV, Brasschaat

H-01*	SLV
H-02*	SLV
H-03*	SLV
H-04*	SLV
H-05*	18 BnHATk
H-06*	17 BnHATk
H-07*	17 BnHATk
H-08*	18 BnHATk
H-09*	18 BnHATk
H-10*	18 BnHATk
H-11*	17 BnHATk
H-12*	17 BnHATk
H-13*	17 BnHATk
H-14*	17 BnHATk
H-15*	SLV
H-17*	17 BnHATk
H-18*	18 BnHATk
H-20	18 BnHATk
H-21	18 BnHATk
H-22	17 BnHATk
H-23	17 BnHATk
H-24	17 BnHATk
H-25	18 BnHATk
H-26	18 BnHATk
H-27	18 BnHATk
H-28	17 BnHATk
H-29	18 BnHATk
H-30	17 BnHATk

H-31	18 BnHATk
H-32	18 BnHATk
H-33	18 BnHATk
H-34	SLV
H-35	18 BnHATk
H-36	17 BnHATk
H-37	17 BnHATk
H-38	17 BnHATk
H-39	18 BnHATk
H-40	18 BnHATk
H-41	18 BnHATk
H-42	SLV
H-43	17 BnHATk
H-44	17 BnHATk
H-45	17 BnHATk
H-46	17 BnHATk

**Force Navale Belge/Belgische
Zeemacht**
  Sud SA316B Alouette III
Koksijde Heli Flight

M-1	(OT-ZPA)
M-2	(OT-ZPB)
M-3	(OT-ZPC)

Gendarmerie/Rijkswacht
  Cessna 182 Skylane
Luchsteundetachment,
  Melsbroek

G-01	C.182Q
G-04	C.182R

  MDH MD.520N
Luchsteundetachment,
  Melsbroek
G-14
G-15

  MDH MD.900 Explorer
Luchsteundetachment,
  Melsbroek
G-10
G-11
G-12

**BOTSWANA
Botswana Defence Force**
  **Grumman G.1159C
  Gulfstream IV**
OK-1

  Lockheed C-130B Hercules
OM-1
OM-2
OM-3

**BRAZIL
Força Aérea Brasileira**
  Boeing KC-137
2° GT 2° Esq, Galeão
2401
2402
2403
2404

  Lockheed C-130 Hercules
1° GT, 1° Esq, Galeão;
1° GTT, 1° Esq, Afonsos

2451	C-130E	1° GTT
2453	C-130E	1° GTT
2454	C-130E	1° GTT
2456	C-130E	1° GTT
2458	SC-130E	1° GT
2459	SC-130E	1° GT

2461	KC-130H	1° GT
2462	KC-130H	1° GT
2463	C-130H	1° GT
2464	C-130H	1° GT
2465	C-130H	1° GT
2467	C-130H	1° GT
2470	C-130H	1° GT
2471	C-130H	1° GT
2472	C-130H	1° GT
2473	C-130H	1° GT
2474	C-130H	1° GT
2475	C-130H	1° GT
2476	C-130H	1° GT
2477	C-130H	1° GT
2478	C-130H	1° GT
2479	C-130H	1° GT

BRUNEI
Airbus A.340
Brunei Govt, Bandar Seri
 Bergawan
V8-BKH   A.340-212

Boeing 747-430
Brunei Govt, Bandar Seri
 Bergawan
V8-ALI

Boeing 767-27GER
Brunei Govt, Bandar Seri
 Bergawan
V8-MHB

Gulfstream Aerospace
Gulfstream V
Brunei Govt, Bandar Seri
 Bergawan
V8-001

BULGARIA
Bulgarsky Voenno-Vazdushni
Sily
 Antonov An-30
 16 TAP, Sofia/Dobroslavtzi
 055

Bulgarian Govt
 Dassault Falcon 2000
 Bulgarian Govt, Sofia
 LZ-OOI

 Tupolev Tu-134A-3
 Bulgarian Govt, Sofia
 LZ-TUG

 Tupolev Tu-154M
 Bulgarian Govt, Sofia
 LZ-BTQ
 LZ-BTZ

BURKINA FASO
 Boeing 727-14
 Govt of Burkina Faso,
  Ouagadougou
 XT-BBE

CAMEROON
 Grumman G.1159A
 Gulfstream III
 Govt of Cameroon, Yaounde
 TJ-AAW

CANADA
Canadian Forces
 Lockheed CC-130 Hercules
 CC-130E/CC-130E(SAR)*
 413 Sqn, Greenwood (SAR)
  (14 Wing);
 424 Sqn, Trenton (SAR)
  (8 Wing);
 426 Sqn, Trenton (8 Wing);
 429 Sqn, Trenton (8 Wing);
 435 Sqn, Winnipeg (17 Wing);
 436 Sqn, Trenton (8 Wing)

130305*	8 Wing
130306*	14 Wing
130307	8 Wing
130308*	8 Wing
130310*	8 Wing
130311*	8 Wing
130313	8 Wing
130314*	14 Wing
130315*	14 Wing
130316	8 Wing
130317	8 Wing
130319	8 Wing
130320	8 Wing
130323	8 Wing
130324*	8 Wing
130325	8 Wing
130326	8 Wing
130327	8 Wing
130328	8 Wing

CC-130H/CC-130H(T)*

130332	17 Wing
130333	17 Wing
130334	8 Wing
130335	8 Wing
130336	17 Wing
130337	8 Wing
130338*	17 Wing
130339*	17 Wing
130340*	17 Wing
130341*	17 Wing
130342*	17 Wing

CC-130H-30

130343	8 Wing
130344	8 Wing

Lockheed CP-140 Aurora/
CP-140A Arcturus*
404/405/415 Sqns,
 Greenwood (14 Wing);
407 Sqn, Comox (19 Wing)

140101	407 Sqn
140102	14 Wing
140103	407 Sqn
140104	14 Wing
140105	407 Sqn
140106	14 Wing
140107	14 Wing
140108	14 Wing
140109	14 Wing
140110	14 Wing
140111	14 Wing
140112	14 Wing
140113	407 Sqn
140114	14 Wing
140115	14 Wing
140116	407 Sqn
140117	14 Wing
140118	14 Wing
140119*	14 Wing
140120*	14 Wing
140121*	14 Wing

De Havilland Canada CT-142
402 Sqn, Winnipeg (17 Wing)

142803	CT-142
142804	CT-142
142805	CT-142
142806	CT-142

Canadair CC-144 Challenger
412 Sqn, Ottawa (8 Wing)

144601	CC-144A
144602	CC-144A
144604	CC-144A
144614	CC-144B
144615	CC-144B
144616	CC-144B
144617	CC-144C
144618	CC-144C

Airbus CC-150 Polaris
(A310-304/A310-304F*)
437 Sqn, Trenton (8 Wing)

15001	216
15002*	212
15003*	202
15004*	205
15005*	204

CHILE
Fuerza Aérea de Chile
 Boeing 707
 Grupo 10, Santiago

902	707-351C
903	707-330B
904	707-358C

 Boeing 737
 Grupo 10, Santiago

921	737-58N
922	737-330

 Extra EA-300L
 Los Halcones

145	[2]
146	[3]
147	[4]
148	[5]
149	[1]

 Grumman G.1159C
 Gulfstream IV
 Grupo 10, Santiago
 911

 Lockheed C-130B/H
 Hercules
 Grupo 10, Santiago

994	C-130B
995	C-130H
996	C-130H
997	C-130B
998	C-130B

CROATIA
 Canadair CL.601 Challenger
 Croatian Govt, Zagreb
 9A-CRO
 9A-CRT

CZECH REPUBLIC
Ceske Vojenske Letectvo
Aero L-39/L-59 Albatros
42 slt/4 zTL, Cáslav;
321 tpzlt & 322 tlt/32 zTL,
  Náměšt;
341 vlt/34 zSL, Pardubice;
LZO, Praha/Kbely
0001 L-39MS LZO
0103 L-39C 341 vlt/34 zSL
0105 L-39C 341 vlt/34 zSL
0106 L-39C 341 vlt/34 zSL
0107 L-39C 341 vlt/34 zSL
0108 L-39C 341 vlt/34 zSL
0113 L-39C 32 zTL
0115 L-39C 341 vlt/34 ZSL
0440 L-39C 341 vlt/34 zSL
0441 L-39C 341 vlt/34 zSL
0444 L-39C 32 zTL
0445 L-39C 341 vlt/34 zSL
0448 L-39C 341 vlt/34 zSL
2341 L-39ZA 32 zTL
2344 L-39ZA 42 slt/4 zTL
2347 L-39ZA 42 slt/4 zTL
2350 L-39ZA 42 slt/4 zTL
2415 L-39ZA 42 slt/4 zTL
2418 L-39ZA 32 zTL
2421 L-39ZA 42 slt/4 zTL
2424 L-39ZA 32 zTL
2427 L-39ZA 42 slt/4 zTL
2430 L-39ZA 42 slt/4 zTL
2433 L-39ZA 42 slt/4 zTL
2436 L-39ZA 32 zTL
3903 L-39ZA 32 zTL
4605 L-39C 341 vlt/34 ZSL
4606 L-39C 341 vlt/34 ZSL
5013 L-39ZA 32 zTL
5015 L-39ZA 42 slt/4 zTL
5017 L-39ZA 42 slt/4 zTL
5019 L-39ZA 32 zTL

Aero L-159 ALCA/L-159T*
42 slt/4 zTL, Cáslav;
322 tlt/32 zTL, Náměšt;
LZO, Praha/Kbely
5831* LZO
5832 LZO
6001 4 zTL
6002 4 zTL
6003 4 zTL
6004
6005 4 zTL
6006 4 zTL
6007 4 zTL
6008 4 zTL
6009 4 zTL
6010 4 zTL
6011 4 zTL
6012 4 zTL
6013 4 zTL
6014 4 zTL
6015 4 zTL
6016 4 zTL
6017 4 zTL
6018 4 zTL
6019 32 zTL
6020 32 zTL
6021 32 zTL
6022 32 zTL
6023 32 zTL
6024 32 zTL
6025 32 zTL
6026 4 zTL
6027 4 zTL

6028 32 zTL
6029 32 zTL
6030 32 zTL
6031 32 zTL
6032 32 zTL
6033 32 zTL
6034 32 zTL
6035 32 zTL
6036 32 zTL
6037 32 zTL
6038 32 zTL
6039 32 zTL
6040 32 zTL
6041 32 zTL
6042 32 zTL
6043
6044
6045
6046
6047
6048 32 zTL
6049 32 zTL
6050 32 zTL
6051 32 zTL
6052 32 zTL
6053 32 zTL
6054
6055
6057
6058 4 zTL
6059 4 zTL
6060 4 zTL
6061 4 zTL
6062 4 zTL

Antonov An-24V
61 dlt/6 zDL, Praha/Kbely
7109
7110

Antonov An-26/An-26Z-1M*
61 dlt/6 zDL, Praha/Kbely
2408
2409
2507
3209*
4201

Antonov An-30FG
344 pzdlt/34 zSL, Pardubice
1107

Canadair CL.601-3A
Challenger
61 dlt/6 zDL, Praha/Kbely
5105

LET 410 Turbolet
61 dlt/6 zDL, Praha/Kbely;
344 pzdlt/34 zSL, Pardubice
0503 L-410MA
          344 pzdlt/34 zSL
0712 L-410UVP-S
          344 pzdlt/34 zSL
0731 L-410UVP
          61 dlt/6 zDL
0926 L-410UVP-T
          61 dlt/6 zDL [4]
0928 L-410UVP-T
          61 dlt/6 zDL
0929 L-410UVP-T
          61 dlt/6 zDL [2]
1132 L-410UVP-T
          61 dlt/6 zDL [3]

1134 L-410UVP
          61 dlt/6 zDL
1504 L-410UVP
          61 dlt/6 zDL
1523 L-410FG
          344 pzdlt/34 zSL
1525 L-410FG
          344 pzdlt/34 zSL
1526 L-410FG
          344 pzdlt/34 zSL
2312 L-410UVP-E
          61 dlt/6 zDL
2601 L-410UVP-E
          61 dlt/6 zDL
2602 L-410UVP-E
          61 dlt/6 zDL
2710 L-410UVP-E
          61 dlt/6 zDL

LET 610M
61 dlt/6 zDL, Praha/Kbely;
LZO, Praha/Kbely
0003 61 dlt/6 zDL
0005 LZO

Mikoyan MiG-21MF/
MiG-21UM*
41 slt/4 zTL, Cáslav;
LZO, Ceske Budejovice
2205 41 slt/4 zTL
2500 41 slt/4 zTL
2614 41 slt/4 zTL
3186* 41 slt/4 zTL
3746* 41 slt/4 zTL
4003 41 slt/4 zTL
4017 41 slt/4 zTL
4175 41 slt/4 zTL
4307 LZO
4405 41 slt/4 zTL
5031* 41 slt/4 zTL
5201 41 slt/4 zTL
5203 LZO
5210 41 slt/4 zTL
5212 41 slt/4 zTL
5213 41 slt/4 zTL
5214 41 slt/4 zTL
5301 41 slt/4 zTL
5302 41 slt/4 zTL
5303 41 slt/4 zTL
5304 41 slt/4 zTL
5305 41 slt/4 zTL
5508 41 slt/4 zTL
5512 41 slt/4 zTL
5581 41 slt/4 zTL
5603 41 slt/4 zTL
7701 41 slt/4 zTL
7802 41 slt/4 zTL
9011* 41 slt/4 zTL
9332* 41 slt/4 zTL
9333* 41 slt/4 zTL
9341* 41 slt/4 zTL
9399* 41 slt/4 zTL
9410 41 slt/4 zTL
9414 41 slt/4 zTL
9707 41 slt/4 zTL
9711 41 slt/4 zTL
9801 41 slt/4 zTL
9802 LZO
9804 41 slt/4 zTL
9805 41 slt/4 zTL

Mil Mi-24
331 ltBVr/33 zVrL, Přerov
0103 Mi-24D

0140	Mi-24D
0142	Mi-24D
0146	Mi-24D
0151	Mi-24D
0214	Mi-24D
0216	Mi-24D
0217	Mi-24D
0218	Mi-24D
0219	Mi-24D
0220	Mi-24D
0701	Mi-24V1
0702	Mi-24V1
0703	Mi-24V1
0705	Mi-24V1
0709	Mi-24V1
0710	Mi-24V1
0788	Mi-24V1
0789	Mi-24V1
0790	Mi-24V1
0812	Mi-24V1
0815	Mi-24V1
0816	Mi-24V1
0834	Mi-24V2
0835	Mi-24V2
0836	Mi-24V2
0837	Mi-24V2
0838	Mi-24V2
0839	Mi-24V2
4010	Mi-24D
4011	Mi-24D
6050	Mi-24DU
7353	Mi-24V
7354	Mi-24V
7355	Mi-24V

Tupolev Tu-154
61 dlt/6 zDL, Praha/Kbely

0601	Tu-154B-2
1003	Tu-154M
1016	Tu-154M

Yakovlev Yak-40
61 dlt/6 zDL, Praha/Kbely

0260	Yak-40
1257	Yak-40K

DENMARK
Flyvevåbnet

Lockheed C-130H Hercules/ C-130J-30 Hercules II
Eskadrille 721, Aalborg

B-536	C-130J-30
B-537	C-130J-30
B-538	C-130J-30
B-678	C-130H
B-679	C-130H
B-680	C-130H

Canadair CL.604 Challenger
Eskadrille 721, Aalborg
C-080
C-168
C-172

General Dynamics F-16
(MLU aircraft are marked with a *)
Eskadrille 726, Aalborg;
Eskadrille 727, Skrydstrup;
Eskadrille 730, Skrydstrup

E-004	F-16A*	Esk 726
E-005	F-16A*	Esk 726
E-007	F-16A*	Esk 726
E-008	F-16A*	Esk 726
E-011	F-16A	Esk 726
E-016	F-16A*	Esk 726
E-017	F-16A*	Esk 730
E-018	F-16A*	Esk 726
E-024	F-16A	Esk 730
E-070	F-16A*	Esk 730
E-074	F-16A	Esk 730
E-075	F-16A	Esk 730
E-107	F-16A*	Esk 726
E-180	F-16A	Esk 730
E-182	F-16A	Esk 730
E-184	F-16A	Esk 727
E-187	F-16A*	Esk 730
E-188	F-16A*	Esk 730
E-189	F-16A*	Esk 730
E-190	F-16A*	Esk 730
E-191	F-16A	Esk 730
E-192	F-16A*	Esk 730
E-193	F-16A*	Esk 730
E-194	F-16A*	Esk 730
E-195	F-16A	Esk 730
E-196	F-16A	Esk 727
E-197	F-16A*	Esk 730
E-198	F-16A*	Esk 726
E-199	F-16A*	Esk 730
E-200	F-16A	Esk 727
E-202	F-16A*	Esk 730
E-203	F-16A*	Esk 730
E-596	F-16A*	Esk 730
E-597	F-16A*	Esk 730
E-598	F-16A*	Esk 726
E-599	F-16A*	Esk 727
E-600	F-16A*	Esk 730
E-601	F-16A*	Esk 730
E-602	F-16A*	Esk 730
E-603	F-16A*	Esk 730
E-604	F-16A*	Esk 726
E-605	F-16A*	Esk 730
E-606	F-16A*	Esk 730
E-607	F-16A*	Esk 730
E-608	F-16A*	Esk 726
E-609	F-16A*	Esk 726
E-610	F-16A*	Esk 730
E-611	F-16A	Esk 726
ET-022	F-16B	Esk 727
ET-197	F-16B	Esk 727
ET-198	F-16B*	Esk 727
ET-199	F-16B*	Esk 730
ET-204	F-16B*	Esk 726
ET-206	F-16B*	Esk 730
ET-207	F-16B*	Esk 730
ET-208	F-16B	Esk 730
ET-210	F-16B	Esk 727
ET-612	F-16B*	Esk 726
ET-613	F-16B*	Esk 726
ET-614	F-16B*	Esk 726
ET-615	F-16B*	Esk 726

Grumman G.1159A Gulfstream III
Eskadrille 721, Aalborg
F-249
F-313

SAAB T-17 Supporter
Eskadrille 721, Aalborg;
Flyveskolen, Karup (FLSK)

T-401	FLSK
T-402	Esk 721
T-403	FLSK
T-404	FLSK
T-405	FLSK
T-407	Esk 721
T-408	FLSK
T-409	FLSK
T-410	FLSK
T-411	FLSK
T-412	FLSK
T-413	FLSK
T-414	Esk 721
T-415	FLSK
T-417	FLSK
T-418	Esk 721
T-419	FLSK
T-420	Esk 721
T-421	FLSK
T-423	FLSK
T-425	FLSK
T-426	FLSK
T-427	FLSK
T-428	FLSK
T-429	FLSK
T-430	FLSK
T-431	Esk 721
T-432	FLSK

Sikorsky S-61A Sea King
Eskadrille 722, Vaerløse
Detachments at:
Aalborg, Ronne, Skrydstrup
U-240
U-275
U-276
U-277
U-278
U-279
U-280
U-481

Søvaernets Flyvetjaeneste (Navy)
Westland Lynx Mk 80/90/90B
Eskadrille 728, Karup

S-134	Mk 90B
S-142	Mk 90B
S-170	Mk 90B
S-175	Mk 80
S-181	Mk 90B
S-191	Mk 90B
S-249	Mk 90
S-256	Mk 90

Haerens Flyvetjaeneste (Army)
Hughes 500M
Eskadrille 724, Vandel
H-201
H-202
H-203
H-205
H-206
H-207
H-209
H-211
H-213
H-244
H-245
H-246

Aérospatiale AS.550C-2 Fennec
Eskadrille 724, Vandel
P-090
P-234
P-254
P-275
P-276
P-287

P-288		Jyväskylä/Tikkakoski;			HN-462	HavLLv 21		
P-319		Tukilentolaivue (Det.),			HN-463	HavLLv 21		
P-320		Kuopio/Rissala*			HN-464	HavLLv 11		
P-339		LJ-1*			HN-465	HavLLv 21		
P-352		LJ-2			HN-466	HavLLv 11		
P-369		LJ-3			HN-467	HavLLv 31		

EGYPT
Al Quwwat al-Jawwiya il Misriya
  Lockheed C-130H/ C-130H-30* Hercules
  16 Sqn, Cairo West
  1271/SU-BAB
  1272/SU-BAC
  1273/SU-BAD
  1274/SU-BAE
  1275/SU-BAF
  1277/SU-BAI
  1278/SU-BAJ
  1279/SU-BAK
  1280/SU-BAL
  1281/SU-BAM
  1282/SU-BAN
  1283/SU-BAP
  1284/SU-BAQ
  1285/SU-BAR
  1286/SU-BAS
  1287/SU-BAT
  1288/SU-BAU
  1289/SU-BAV
  1290/SU-BEW
  1291/SU-BEX
  1292/SU-BEY
  1293/SU-BKS*
  1294/SU-BKT*
  1295/SU-BKU*

Egyptian Govt
  Airbus A.340-211
  Egyptian Govt, Cairo
  SU-GGG

  Boeing 707-366C
  Egyptian Govt, Cairo
  SU-AXJ

  Grumman G.1159A Gulfstream III/ G.1159C Gulfstream IV/ G.1159C Gulfstream IV-SP/ Gulfstream 400
  Egyptian Air Force/Govt, Cairo
  SU-BGM Gulfstream IV
  SU-BGU Gulfstream III
  SU-BGV Gulfstream III
  SU-BNC Gulfstream IV
  SU-BND Gulfstream IV
  SU-BNO Gulfstream IV-SP
  SU-BNP Gulfstream IV-SP
  SU-BPE Gulfstream 400

FINLAND
Suomen Ilmavoimat
  Fokker F.27 Friendship
  Tukilentolaivue, Jyväskylä/Tikkakoski
  FF-1 F.27-100
  FF-2 F.27-100
  FF-3 F.27-400M

  Gates Learjet 35A
  Tukilentolaivue,

McDonnell Douglas F-18 Hornet
  Hävittäjälentolaivue 11, Roveniemi;
  Hävittäjälentolaivue 21, Tampere/Pirkkala;
  Hävittäjälentolaivue 31, Kuopio/Rissala;
  Koelentokeskus, Halli

F-18C Hornet

HN-401	HavLLv 31
HN-402	HavLLv 21
HN-403	HavLLv 31
HN-404	HavLLv 11
HN-405	HavLLv 21
HN-406	HavLLv 11
HN-407	HavLLv 21
HN-408	HavLLv 31
HN-409	HavLLv 21
HN-410	KoelntK
HN-411	HavLLv 11
HN-412	HavLLv 21
HN-413	HavLLv 21
HN-414	KoelntK
HN-415	HavLLv 31
HN-416	HavLLv 11
HN-417	HavLLv 21
HN-418	HavLLv 31
HN-419	HavLLv 11
HN-420	HavLLv 11
HN-421	HavLLv 21
HN-422	
HN-423	HavLLv 21
HN-424	HavLLv 11
HN-425	HavLLv 21
HN-426	HavLLv 31
HN-427	HavLLv 21
HN-428	
HN-429	HavLLv 11
HN-431	HavLLv 31
HN-432	HavLLv 11
HN-433	HavLLv 31
HN-434	HavLLv 21
HN-435	HavLLv 31
HN-436	HavLLv 21
HN-437	
HN-438	HavLLv 31
HN-439	HavLLv 21
HN-440	HavLLv 11
HN-441	HavLLv 21
HN-442	HavLLv 31
HN-443	
HN-444	HavLLv 31
HN-445	HavLLv 21
HN-446	HavLLv 31
HN-447	HavLLv 11
HN-448	HavLLv 11
HN-449	HavLLv 21
HN-450	HavLLv 11
HN-451	HavLLv 21
HN-452	HavLLv 21
HN-453	HavLLv 21
HN-454	
HN-455	HavLLv 21
HN-456	HavLLv 21
HN-457	HavLLv 11

F-18D Hornet

HN-461	KoelntK

FRANCE
Armée de l'Air
Aérospatiale
  SN601 Corvette
  CEV, Cazaux
  1 MV
  2 MW
  10 MX

  Aérospatiale TB-30 Epsilon
  Cartouche Dorée,
  (EPAA 00.315) Cognac;
  EPAA 00.315, Cognac;
  SOCATA, Tarbes
  Please note: A large number of these machines are kept in temporary storage at Chateaudun

1	315-UA
2	315-UB
3	FZ SOCATA
4	315-UC
5	315-UD
6	315-UE
7	315-UF
8	315-UG
9	315-UH
10	315-UI
12	315-UK
13	315-UL
14	315-UM
15	315-UN
16	315-UO
17	315-UP
19	315-UR
20	315-US
21	315-UT
23	315-UV
24	315-UW
25	315-UX
26	315-UY
27	315-UZ
28	315-VA
29	315-VB
30	315-VC
31	315-VD
32	315-VE
33	315-VF
34	315-VG
35	315-VH
36	315-VI
37	315-VJ
38	315-VK
39	315-VL
40	315-VM
41	315-VN
42	315-VO
43	315-VP
44	315-VQ
45	315-VR
46	315-VS
47	315-VT
48	315-VU
49	315-VV
50	315-VW
52	315-VX
53	315-VY

54	315-VZ	
56	315-WA	
57	F-ZVLB	
61	315-WD	
62	315-WE	
63	315-WF	
64	315-WG	
65	315-WH	
66	315-WI	
67	315-WJ	
68	315-WK	
69	315-WL	
70	315-WM	
72	315-WO	
73	315-WP	
74	315-WQ	
75	315-WR	
76	315-WS	
77	315-WT	
78	315-WU	
79	315-WV	
80	315-WW	
81	315-WX	
82	315-WY	
83	315-WZ	
84	315-XA	
85	315-XB	
86	315-XC	
87	315-XD	
88	315-XE	
89	315-XF	
90	315-XG	
91	315-XH	
92	F-SEXI [1]*	
93	315-XJ	
94	315-XK	
95	315-XL	
96	315-XM	
97	315-XN	
98	315-XO	
99	315-XP	
100	F-SEXQ [2]*	
101	315-XS	
102	315-XS	
103	315-XT	
104	315-XU	
105	F-SEXV [4]*	
106	315-XW	
107	315-XX	
108	315-XY	
109	315-XZ	
110	315-YA	
111	315-YB	
112	315-YC	
113	315-YD	
114	315-YE	
115	315-YF	
116	315-YG	
117	F-SEYH [3]*	
118	315-YI	
119	315-YJ	
120	315-YK	
121	315-YL	
122	315-YM	
123	315-YN	
124	315-YO	
125	315-YP	
126	315-YQ	
127	315-YR	
128	315-YS	
129	315-YT	
130	315-YU	
131	315-YV	
132	315-YW	

133	315-YX
134	315-YY
135	315-YZ
136	315-ZA
137	315-ZB
138	315-ZC
139	315-ZD
140	315-ZE
141	315-ZF
142	315-ZG
143	315-ZH
144	315-ZI
145	315-ZJ
146	315-ZK
149	315-ZM
150	315-ZN
152	315-ZO
153	315-ZP
154	315-ZQ
155	315-ZR
158	315-ZS
159	315-ZT

Airbus A.310-304
ET 03.060 *Esterel,*
Paris/Charles de Gaulle

418	F-RADC
421	F-RADA
422	F-RADB

Airbus A.319CJ-115
ETEC 00.065, Villacoublay

1485	F-RBFA
1556	F-RBFB

Airbus A.340-311
ET 03.060 *Esterel,*
Paris/Charles de Gaulle

013	
058	

Airtech CN-235M-200
ET 00.042 *Ventoux,*
Mont-de-Marsan;
ETL 01.062 *Vercours,* Creil;
ETOM 00.052 *La Tontouta,*
Noumea;
ETOM 00.082 *Maine,*
Faaa-Tahiti

045	62-IB	01.062
065	82-IC	00.082
066	52-ID	00.052
071	62-IE	01.062
072	82-IF	00.082
105	52-IG	00.052
107	52-IH	00.052
111	62-II	01.062
114	62-IJ	01.062
123	62-IM	00.042
128	62-IK	00.042
129	62-IL	01.062
137	62-IN	01.062
141	62-IO	01.062
152	62-IP	01.062
156	62-IQ	01.062
158	62-IR	01.062
160	62-IS	01.062
165	62-IT	01.062

Boeing C-135 Stratotanker
ERV 00.093 *Bretagne,*
Istres

470	C-135FR	93-CA
471	C-135FR	93-CB

472	C-135FR	93-CC
474	C-135FR	93-CE
475	C-135FR	93-CF
497	KC-135R	93-CM
525	KC-135R	93-CN
574	KC-135R	93-CP
735	C-135FR	93-CG
736	C-135FR	93-CH
737	C-135FR	93-CI
738	C-135FR	93-CJ
739	C-135FR	93-CK
740	C-135FR	93-CL

Boeing E-3F Sentry
EDCA 00.036, Avord

201	36-CA
202	36-CB
203	36-CC
204	36-CD

CASA 212-300 Aviocar
CEV, Cazaux & Istres

377	MO
378	MP
386	MQ
388	MS

Cessna 310
CEV, Cazaux & Istres

187	310N	BJ
188	310N	BK
190	310N	BL
192	310N	BM
193	310N	BG
194	310N	BH
242	310K	AW
244	310K	AX
513	310N	BE
693	310N	BI
820	310Q	CL
981	310Q	BF

D-BD Alpha Jet
AMD-BA, Istres;
CEAM (EC 02.330),
Mont-de-Marsan;
CEV, Cazaux & Istres;
CITac 00.339 *Aquitaine,*
Luxeuil;
EAC 00.314, Tours;
EC 01.002 *Cicogne,* Dijon;
EC 01.007 *Provence* &
EC 02.007 *Argonne,*
St Dizier;
EPNER, Istres;
ERS 01.091 *Gascogne,*
Mont-de-Marsan;
ETO 01.008 *Saintonge* &
ETO 02.008 *Nice,* Cazaux;
GI 00.312, Salon de Provence;
Patrouille de France (PDF)
(EPAA 20.300),
Salon de Provence

01	F-ZJTS	CEV
E1		CEV
E3	314-LV	00.314
E4		CEV
E5	339-WH	00.339
E7	314-LJ	00.314
E8		CEV
E9	8-MJ	01.008
E10	314-LK	00.314
E11	314-LD	00.314
E12		CEV

E13	8-NM	02.008
E14	8-NX	02.008
E15	8-NO	02.008
E17	7-PY	02.007
E18	8-NN	02.008
E19	330-AH	CEAM
E20	339-DI	00.339
E21	330-AL	CEAM
E22	314-UB	00.314
E23	314-UG	00.314
E24	314-TJ	00.314
E25		
E26	314-LS	00.314
E28	8-NK	02.008
E29	314-TM	00.314
E30	314-TD	00.314
E31	F-TERK	PDF [4]
E32	314-LF	00.314
E33	8-MZ	01.008
E34	8-MF	01.008
E35	314-UF	00.314
E36	7-PV	02.007
E37	8-NI	02.008
E38	339-DG	00.339
E41	F-TERA	PDF
E42	7-PX	02.007
E43	314-LI	00.314
E44	314-LP	00.314
E45	314-TF	00.314
E46	8-NL	02.008
E47	7-PJ	02.007
E48	8-MH	01.008
E49	314-TA	00.314
E51	314-TH	00.314
E52		
E53	314-TC	00.314
E55	314-UC	00.314
E58		
E59	314-LY	00.314
E60		EPNER
E61		
E63	314-LN	00.314
E64	314-TL	00.314
E65	8-MD	01.008
E66	8-ME	01.008
E67	314-TB	00.314
E68	339-DK	00.339
E69	314-TO	00.314
E72	314-LA	00.314
E73	8-ND	02.008
E74	8-MS	01.008
E75	F-TERW	PDF [2]
E76	8-MR	01.008
E79	330-AH	CEAM
E80		CEV
E81	314-LX	00.314
E82	8-NB	02.008
E83	7-PU	02.007
E84	314-UK	00.314
E85	339-DM	00.339
E86	8-NS	02.008
E87		
E88	314-LL	00.314
E89		
E90		
E91	2-EL	01.002
E92	330-AK	CEAM
E93		
E94	F-TERH	PDF [3]
E95		
E96	314-LC	00.314
E97	339-DL	00.339
E98	314-TT	00.314
E99	8-NF	02.008

E100		EPNER
E101	8-NQ	02.008
E102	8-NY	02.008
E103	314-UA	00.314
E104		
E105	314-LE	00.314
E106	8-NA	02.008
E107	312-RT	00.312
E108		
E109	8-NJ	02.008
E110	8-NG	02.008
E112	DA	01.091
E113	312-RU	00.312
E114	314-TU	00.314
E115	8-NW	02.008
E116		
E117	F-TERI	PDF
E118	314-LM	00.314
E119	8-MI	01.008
E120	F-TERG	PDF [1]
E121	8-NE	02.008
E122	F-TERD	PDF [6]
E123	8-ML	01.008
E124	312-RS	00.312
E125	314-LG	00.314
E126	314-LU	00.314
E127		
E128	F-TERN	PDF
E129		
E130	314-LQ	00.314
E131	312-RV	00.312
E132	314-LZ	00.314
E133	8-MN	01.008
E134	F-TERM	PDF [5]
E135	F-TERX	PDF [7]
E136	314-TN	00.314
E137	339-DE	00.339
E138	314-LT	00.314
E139	330-AH	CEAM
E140	314-UD	00.314
E141		
E142	314-LB	00.314
E143	314-TQ	00.314
E144	314-LO	00.314
E145		
E146	7-PW	02.007
E147	8-NH	02.008
E148	8-MG	01.008
E149	8-MO	01.008
E150	8-NC	02.008
E151	8-MC	01.008
E152	339-DH	00.339
E153	314-TG	00.314
E154	339-DF	00.339
E155	314-TP	00.314
E156	314-TI	00.314
E157		
E158		
E159	7-PP	02.007
E160	F-TERC	PDF
E161	8-MK	01.008
E162	314-TZ	00.314
E163	F-TERB	PDF [9]
E164	8-MB	01.008
E165	F-TERE	PDF [0]
E166	314-TX	00.314
E167		
E168	314-TS	00.314
E169	F-TERQ	PDF [8]
E170	7-PQ	02.007
E171	314-LR	00.314
E173	314-LH	00.314
E176	8-MA	01.008

Dassault Falcon 20
CEV, Cazaux & Istres;
CITac 00.339 Aquitaine,
Luxeuil;
ETEC 00.065, Villacoublay

22	CS	CEV
79	CT	CEV
86	CG	CEV
93	F-RAED	00.065
96	CB	CEV
104	CW	CEV
124	CC	CEV
131	CD	CEV
138	CR	CEV
167	(F-RAEB)	00.065
182	339-JA	00.339
188	CX	CEV
252	CA	CEV
263	CY	CEV
288	CV	CEV
291	65-EG	00.065
342	F-RAEC	00.065
375	CZ	CEV
422	F-RAEH	00.065
451	339-JC	00.339
483	339-JI	00.339

Dassault Falcon 50
ETEC 00.065, Villacoublay

5	F-RAFI	
27	(F-RAFK)	
34	(F-RAFL)	
78	F-RAFJ	

Dassault Falcon 900
ETEC 00.065, Villacoublay

| 2 | (F-RAFP) | |
| 4 | (F-RAFQ) | |

Dassault Mirage IVP
ERS 01.091 Gascogne,
Mont-de-Marsan

25	AX	
36	BI	
53	BZ	
59	CF	
61	CH	

Dassault Mirage F.1
CEAM (EC 02.330),
Mont-de-Marsan;
CEV, Cazaux & Istres;
EC 01.030 Alsace &
EC 02.030 Normandie
Niemen, Colmar;
ER 01.033 Belfort,
ER 02.033 Savoie
& EC 03.033 Lorraine,
Reims;
Mirage F.1CT

207	330-AO	CEAM
219	30-SN	01.030
220		
221	30-SY	01.030
223	30-QX	02.030
225	330-AJ	CEAM
226		
227	330-AP	CEAM
228	30-QT	02.030
229	30-QC	02.030
230	33-FH	03.033
231	30-SA	01.030
232	33-FK	02.033
233	30-QG	02.030

France

234	30-SI	01.030
235	30-SK	01.030
236	30-SB	01.030
237	30-SM	01.030
238	33-FN	03.033
239	30-QD	02.030
241	30-QA	02.030
242	30-QV	02.030
243	30-QJ	02.030
244	30-QH	02.030
245	30-SX	01.030
246	33-FX	03.033
248	330-AI	CEAM
251	33-FM	03.033
252	30-QO	02.030
253	30-SJ	01.030
254		
255		
256	30-SL	01.030
257	30-SF	01.030
258	33-FO	03.033
259	30-QZ	02.030
260		
261	30-SY	01.030
262	30-SE	01.030
264	30-SW	01.030
265	33-FQ	03.033
267	30-QU	02.030
268	30-SR	01.030
271	30-QQ	02.030
272	30-QL	02.030
273	33-FG	03.033
274		
275	33-FY	03.033
278	30-QU	02.030
279	30-SC	01.030
280	30-SD	01.030
281	33-FI	03.033
283	30-SV	01.030

Mirage F.1B

501		
502	33-FR	03.033
504	33-FV	03.033
505		
507		
509		
510		
511	33-FT	03.033
512	33-FL	03.033
513	33-FA	03.033
514	33-FZ	03.033
516	330-AC	CEAM
517	33-FB	03.033
518	33-FF	03.033
519	33-FC	03.033
520	33-FJ	03.033

Mirage F.1CR

602		CEV
603	33-CB	01.033
604	33-NU	02.033
605	33-CO	01.033
606	33-NP	02.033
607	33-ND	02.033
608	33-NG	02.033
610	33-NQ	02.033
611	33-NN	02.033
612	33-NJ	02.033
613	33-CC	01.033
614	33-CN	01.033
615	33-NZ	02.033
616	33-NM	02.033
617	33-NO	02.033
620	33-CT	01.033
622	33-NH	02.033

623	33-CM	01.033
624	33-NY	02.033
627	33-CF	01.033
628	33-NB	02.033
630	33-CU	01.033
631	33-NS	02.033
632	33-CL	01.033
634	33-CK	01.033
635	33-NX	02.033
636	33-CG	01.033
637	33-CP	01.033
638	33-CI	01.033
640	33-CH	01.033
641	33-CD	01.033
642	33-NC	02.033
643	33-CK	01.033
645	33-CC	01.033
646	33-NW	02.033
647	33-CQ	01.033
648	33-CE	01.033
649	33-NI	02.033
650	33-CJ	01.033
651	33-NB	02.033
653	33-NV	02.033
654	33-CS	01.033
655	330-AT	CEAM
656	33-NK	02.033
657	33-CV	01.033
658	33-CW	01.033
659		
660	33-CY	01.033
661	33-NE	02.033
662	33-NA	02.033

Dassault Mirage 2000B

AMD-BA, Istres;
CEAM (EC 02.330),
 Mont-de-Marsan;
CEV, Cazaux & Istres;
EC 02.002 *Côte d'Or*, Dijon;
EC 01.005 *Vendée* &
 EC 02.005 *Ile de France*,
 Orange;
EC 01.012 *Cambrésis* &
 EC 02.012 *Picardie*,
 Cambrai

501	(BX1)	CEV
502	5-OH	02.005
504		CEV
505	5-OY	02.005
506	5-OD	02.005
507	5-OX	02.005
508	5-OT	02.005
509	5-OP	02.005
510	5-OQ	02.005
512	5-OU	02.005
513	5-OI	02.005
514	5-OE	02.005
515	5-OG	02.005
516	5-OL	02.005
518	5-OM	02.005
519	5-OW	02.005
520	5-OS	02.005
521	5-ON	02.005
522	5-OV	02.005
523	12-KA	02.012
524	330-AZ	CEAM
525	12-YP	01.012
526	12-KO	02.012
527	12-KM	02.012
528	12-YQ	01.012
529	12-KJ	02.012
530	12-YM	01.012

Dassault Mirage 2000C/ 2000-5F*

CEAM (EC 02.330),
 Mont-de-Marsan;
CEV, Istres;
EC 01.002 *Cigognes* &
 EC 02.002 *Côte d'Or*, Dijon;
EC 01.005 *Vendée* &
 EC 02.005 *Ile de France*,
 Orange;
EC 01.012 *Cambrésis* &
 EC 02.012 *Picardie*,
 Cambrai;
EC 04.033 *Vexin*, Djibouti

1	5-NC	01.005
2		CEV
3	5-OR	02.005
4	5-NB	01.005
5	5-NI	01.005
8	5-OA	02.005
9	5-OJ	02.005
11	5-NJ	01.005
12	5-NV	01.005
13	5-NM	01.005
14	5-NW	01.005
15	5-NA	01.005
16	5-NE	01.005
17	5-NR	01.005
18	5-NP	01.005
19	5-OB	02.005
20	5-OF	02.005
21	5-OZ	02.005
22	5-ND	01.005
25	5-NU	01.005
27	5-NT	01.005
28	5-NN	01.005
29	5-NO	01.005
30	5-NQ	01.005
32	5-NS	01.005
34	5-NH	01.005
35	5-NL	01.005
36	5-OC	02.005
37	5-OO	02.005
38*	2-FK	02.002
40*	2-FG	02.002
41*	2-EJ	01.002
42*	2-EF	01.002
43*	330-AA	CEAM
44*	2-EQ	01.002
45*		
46*	2-EN	01.002
47*	2-EP	01.002
48*	2-ER	01.002
49*	2-FF	02.002
51*	330-AS	CEAM
52*	2-FC	02.002
53*		
54*	2-FY	02.002
55*	2-FA	02.002
56*	2-EG	01.002
57*	2-ET	01.002
58*	2-FO	02.002
59*	2-EV	01.002
61*	2-EM	01.002
62*	2-ED	01.002
63*	2-FQ	02.002
64	330-AQ	CEAM
65*	2-EK	01.002
66*	2-FD	02.002
67*	2-FL	02.002
68*	2-FM	02.002
69*	2-FE	02.002
70*	2-EC	01.002
71*	2-EH	01.002

72*	2-FR	02.002
73*	2-ES	01.002
74*	2-EU	01.002
76*	2-EB	01.002
77*	330-AX	CEAM
78*	2-FZ	02.002
79	12-YF	01.012
80	12-YJ	01.012
81	12-KP	02.012
82	12-KS	02.012
83	12-YL	01.012
85	12-KE	02.012
86	33-LE	04.033
87	12-KN	02.012
88	12-KI	02.012
89	12-YQ	02.012
90	12-YS	01.012
91		
92	330-AW	CEAM
93	12-KK	02.012
94	12-YI	01.012
95	12-KM	02.012
96		
97	12-YT	01.012
98	12-YU	01.012
99	12-YH	01.012
100	12-YG	01.012
101		
102	12-KR	02.012
103	12-YN	01.012
104	12-KG	02.012
105	12-YF	01.012
106		
107	12-KQ	02.012
108	12-YD	01.012
109	12-KF	02.012
111		
112	12-YC	01.012
113	12-YO	01.012
114	12-YK	01.012
115	12-KH	02.012
116		
117	12-KC	02.012
118	12-YE	01.012
119	12-KD	02.012
120	12-KU	02.012
121		
122		
123	12-YA	01.012
124	12-KB	02.012
X7		CEV

Dassault Mirage 2000D
AMD-BA, Istres;
CEAM (EC 02.330),
   Mont-de-Marsan;
CEV, Istres;
EC 01.003 *Navarre*,
   EC 02.003 *Champagne* &
   EC 03.003 *Ardennes*,
   Nancy;
EC 04.033 *Vexin*, Djibouti

601	3-IA	01.003
602	3-JY	02.003
603	330-AA	CEAM
604	3-IN	01.003
605		
606	3-XX	03.003
607		CEV
609	3-JP	02.003
610	3-II	01.003
611		
612	3-JK	02.003
613	3-XU	03.003
614	3-ID	01.003
615	3-JA	02.003
616	3-JS	02.003
617	3-XA	03.003
618	3-JF	02.003
619	3-JE	02.003
620	3-IM	01.003
621	3-JG	02.003
622		
623	3-IB	01.003
624	3-IW	01.003
625	3-JC	02.003
626	3-XH	03.003
627		
628	3-XF	03.003
629	3-XO	03.003
630	3-XD	03.003
631	3-XI	03.003
632	3-XJ	03.003
634	3-IL	01.003
635	3-XP	03.003
636	3-JJ	02.003
637	3-XC	03.003
638	3-IJ	01.003
639	3-XQ	03.003
640	3-IR	01.003
641	3-XG	03.003
642	3-JB	02.003
643		
644	3-IU	01.003
645	3-XL	03.003
646	3-IC	01.003
647	3-IO	01.003
648	3-XT	03.003
649	3-JW	02.003
650	3-IA	01.003
651	3-JV	02.003
652	3-XN	03.003
653	3-IE	01.003
654	3-IT	01.003
655	3-XE	03.003
657	3-JM	02.003
658	3-JN	02.003
659	3-XR	03.003
660		
661	3-IH	01.003
662	3-IP	01.003
663	3-XS	03.003
664	3-JU	02.003
665	3-XV	03.003
666	3-IK	01.003
667	3-JX	02.003
668	330-AR	CEAM
669	3-JZ	02.003
670	3-IQ	01.003
671	3-XK	03.003
672		CEV
673		
674	3-XL	03.003
675	3-JI	02.003
676		CEV
677	3-XY	03.003
678	330-AG	CEAM
679	330-AM	CEAM
680	3-XM	03.003
681	3-IG	01.003
682	3-JR	02.003
683	3-JT	02.003
684	3-IF	01.003
685	3-XZ	03.003
686	3-JH	02.003

Dassault Mirage 2000N
CEAM (EC 02.330),
   Mont-de-Marsan;
CEV, Istres;
EC 01.004 *Dauphiné* &
   EC 02.004 *Lafayette*,
   Luxeuil;
EC 03.004 *Limousin*, Istres

301		CEV
303	4-CL	03.004
304	4-CK	03.004
305	4-CS	03.004
306	4-BL	02.004
307	4-CH	03.004
309	4-AO	01.004
310	4-CE	03.004
311	4-BT	02.004
312	4-CN	03.004
313	4-CR	03.004
314	4-AX	01.004
315	4-BF	02.004
316	4-BH	02.004
317	4-CR	03.004
318	4-BP	02.004
319	4-AC	01.004
320	4-CD	03.004
322	4-CP	03.004
323	4-CV	03.004
324	4-CX	03.004
325	4-CC	03.004
326	4-CM	03.004
327	4-CJ	03.004
329	4-AU	01.004
330	4-AT	01.004
331	4-BO	02.004
332	4-BN	02.004
333	4-AB	01.004
334	330-AV	CEAM
335	4-CI	03.004
336	4-BI	02.004
337	4-AK	01.004
338	4-CG	03.004
339	4-AD	01.004
340	4-AA	01.004
341	4-AF	01.004
342	4-BA	02.004
343	4-AH	01.004
344	4-BV	02.004
345	4-BU	02.004
348	4-AL	01.004
349	4-BM	02.004
350	4-AJ	01.004
351	4-AQ	01.004
353	4-BD	02.004
354	4-BJ	02.004
355	4-AE	01.004
356	4-BX	02.004
357	4-CO	03.004
358	4-BQ	02.004
359	4-BG	02.004
360	4-CB	03.004
361	4-CL	03.004
362	4-CU	03.004
363	4-BK	02.004
364	4-BB	02.004
365	4-BE	02.004
366		
367	4-AS	01.004
368	4-AR	01.004
369	4-AG	01.004
370	4-CA	03.004
371	4-AV	01.004
372	4-BR	02.004
373	4-CF	03.004
374	4-BS	02.004
375	4-BC	02.004

France

Dassault Rafale-B
AMD-BA, Istres;
CEV, Istres
301	CEV
302	CEV
B01	CEV

Dassault Rafale-C
AMD-BA, Istres;
CEV, Istres
101	AMD-BA
C01	CEV

DHC-6 Twin Otter 200/300*
ET 00.042 *Ventoux*,
  Mont-de-Marsan;
GAM 00.056 *Vaucluse*,
  Evreux
292	CC	00.056
298	CD	00.056
300	CE	00.056
730*	CA	00.042
742*	CB	00.042
745*	CV	00.042
790*	CW	00.042

Douglas DC-8-72CF
EE 00.051 *Aubrac*, Evreux;
ET 03.060 *Esterel*, Paris/
Charles de Gaulle
46013	F-RAFG	03.060
46043		00.051
46130	F-RAFF	03.060

Embraer EMB.121AA/AN* Xingu
EAT 00.319, Avord
054	YX
055*	YZ
064	YY
66*	
69*	ZB
70*	ZC
072	YA
073	YB
075	YC
076	YD
77*	ZD
078	YE
080	YF
082	YG
083*	ZE
084	YH
086	YI
089	YJ
090*	ZF
091	YK
092	YL
095	YM
096	YN
098	YO
099	YP
101	YR
102	YS
103	YT
105	YU
107	YV
108	YW
111	YQ

Embraer EMB.312F Tucano
GI 00.312, Salon de
  Provence
438	312-UW

439	312-UY
456	312-JA
457	312-JB
458	312-JC
459	312-JD
460	312-JE
461	312-JF
462	312-JG
463	312-JH
464	312-JI
466	312-JK
467	312-JL
468	312-JM
469	312-JN
470	312-JO
471	312-JP
472	312-JQ
473	312-JR
474	312-JS
475	312-JT
477	312-JU
478	312-JV
479	312-JX
480	312-JY
481	312-JZ
483	312-UB
484	312-UC
485	312-UD
486	312-UE
487	312-UF
488	312-UG
489	312-UH
490	312-UI
491	312-UJ
492	312-UK
493	312-UL
494	312-UM
495	312-UN
496	312-UO
497	312-UP
498	312-UQ
499	312-UR
500	312-US
501	312-UT
503	312-UV
504	312-UX

Eurocopter AS.332 Super Puma/AS.532 Cougar
EH 03.067 *Parisis*,
  Villacoublay;
EH 05.067 *Alpilles*,
  Aix-en-Provence;
ETOM 00.082 *Maine*,
  Faaa-Tahiti;
GAM 00.056 *Vaucluse*,
  Evreux;
CEAM, Mont-de-Marsan
2014	AS.332C	PN	
			05.067
2057	AS.332C	PO	
			00.082
2093	AS.332L	F-ZKCM	
2233	AS.332L-1	67-FY	
			03.067
2235	AS.332L-1	67-FZ	
			03.067
2244	AS.332C	PM	
			00.082
2342	AS.532UL	FX	
			00.056
2369	AS.532UL	FW	
			00.056

2375	AS.532UL	FV	
			00.056
2377	AS.332L-1	67-FU	
			03.067
2461	AS.532A-2	IH	CEAM

Lockheed C-130H/C-130H-30* Hercules
ET 02.061 *Franche-Comté*,
  Orléans
4588	61-PM
4589	61-PN
5114	61-PA
5116	61-PB
5119	61-PC
5140	61-PD
5142*	61-PE
5144*	61-PF
5150*	61-PG
5151*	61-PH
5152*	61-PI
5153*	61-PJ
5226*	61-PK
5227*	61-PL

Morane Saulnier MS.760 Paris
CEV, Cazaux & Istres
115	OV
119	NL

Nord 262A/262D* Frégate
CEV, Istres;
EPNER, Istres;
ETE 00.041 *Verdun*, Metz;
ET 00.042 *Ventoux*,
  Mont-de-Marsan;
ETEC 00.065, Villacoublay
58	MJ	EPNER
67	MI	CEV
88*	AL	00.042
89*	AZ	00.041
93*	AP	00.065
95*	AR	00.065
106*	AY	00.041
109*	AM	00.065
110*	AS	00.065

SEPECAT Jaguar
CEV, Cazaux & Istres;
CEAM (EC 02.330),
  Mont-de-Marsan;
CITac 00.339 *Aquitaine*,
  Luxeuil;
EC 01.007 *Provence*,
  St Dizier
Jaguar A
A99	7-HC	01.007
A104	7-HM	01.007
A120	7-HL	01.007
A122	7-HA	01.007
A128	7-HP	01.007
A129	7-HD	01.007
A133	7-HB	01.007
A135	7-HF	01.007
A137	7-HQ	01.007
A138	7-HV	01.007
A140	7-HI	01.007
A 141	7-HU	01.007
A145	7-HG	01.007
A148	7-HN	01.007
A150	7-HE	01.007
A153	7-HK	01.007
A154	7-HO	01.007

A157	7-HH	01.007
A158	7-HT	01.007
A159	7-HJ	01.007
A160	7-HS	01.007

Jaguar E

E3	339-WF	00.339
E6	7-HR	01.007
E10	339-WL	00.339
E12	339-WI	00.339
E19	339-WG	00.339
E22	7-HX	01.007
E29	339-WJ	00.339
E32	7-HW	01.007
E35	7-HY	01.007
E37	7-HZ	01.007

SOCATA TBM 700
CEV, Cazaux & Istres;
ETE 00.041 *Verdun*, Metz;
ETE 00.043 *Médoc*, Bordeaux;
ETE 00.044 *Mistral*, Villacoublay;
ETEC 00.065, Villacoublay;
EdC 00.070, Chateaudun

33	XA	00.043
35	XB	00.043
70	XC	00.043
77	XD	00.041
78	65-XE	00.044
80	41-XF	00.041
93	XL	00.043
94	65-XG	00.070
95	65-XH	00.065
103	41-XI	00.041
104	XJ	00.044
105	65-XK	00.065
106	MN	CEV
110	XP	00.041
111	XM	00.065
117	XN	00.041
125	65-XO	00.065
131	XQ	00.065
146	XR	00.065
147	XS	00.065

Transall C-160F/C-160NG GABRIEL*/C-160R
CEAM (EET 06.330), Mont-de-Marsan;
CEV, Cazaux & Istres;
EET 01.054 *Dunkerque*, Metz;
ET 01.061 *Touraine* & ET 03.061 *Poitou*, Orléans;
ET 01.064 *Bearn* & ET 02.064 *Anjou*, Evreux;
ETOM 00.050 *Réunion*, St Denis;
ETOM 00.055 *Ouessant*, Dakar;
ETOM 00.058 *Guadeloupe*, Pointe-à-Pitre;
ETOM 00.088 *Larzac*, Djibouti

RA02	C-160R	61-MI	01.061
RA04	C-160R	61-MS	01.061
RA06	C-160R	61-ZB	03.061
R1	C-160R	61-MA	01.061
R2	C-160R	61-MB	01.061
R3	C-160R	61-MC	00.058
R4	C-160R	61-MD	01.061
R5	C-160R	61-ME	01.061
R11	C-160R	61-MF	01.061
R12	C-160R	61-MG	01.061
R13	C-160R	61-MH	00.050
R15	C-160R	61-MJ	01.061
R17	C-160R	61-ML	01.061
R18	C-160R	61-MM	01.061
R42	C-160R	61-MN	01.061
R43	C-160R	61-MO	01.061
R44	C-160R	61-MP	01.061
R45	C-160R	61-MQ	01.061
R46	C-160R	61-MR	01.061
R48	C-160R	61-MT	01.061
R49	C-160R	59-MU	CEV
R51	C-160R	61-MW	01.061
R52	C-160R	61-MX	01.061
R53	C-160R	61-MY	01.061
R54	C-160R	61-MZ	01.061
R55	C-160R	61-ZC	03.061
R86	C-160R	61-ZD	03.061
R87	C-160R	61-ZE	00.050
R88	C-160R	61-ZF	03.061
R89	C-160R	61-ZG	03.061
R90	C-160R	61-ZH	03.061
R91	C-160R	61-ZI	03.061
R92	C-160R	61-ZJ	03.061
R93	C-160R	61-ZK	03.061
R94	C-160R	61-ZL	03.061
R95	C-160R	61-ZM	03.061
R96	C-160R	61-ZN	03.061
R97	C-160R	61-ZO	03.061
R98	C-160R	61-ZP	03.061
R99	C-160R	61-ZQ	03.061
R100	C-160R	61-ZR	03.061
R153	C-160R	61-ZS	03.061
R154	C-160R	61-ZT	03.061
R157	C-160R	61-ZW	03.061
R158	C-160R	61-ZX	03.061
R159	C-160R	61-ZY	03.061
R160	C-160R	61-ZZ	03.061
R201	C-160R	64-GA	01.064
R202	C-160R	64-GB	02.064
R203	C-160R	64-GC	01.064
R204	C-160R	64-GD	02.064
R205	C-160R	64-GE	01.064
R206	C-160R	64-GF	02.064
R207	C-160R	64-GG	01.064
R208	C-160R	64-GH	02.064
R210	C-160R	64-GJ	02.064
R211	C-160R	64-GK	01.064
R212	C-160R	64-GL	02.064
R213	C-160R	64-GM	01.064
R214	C-160R	64-GN	02.064
R215	C-160R	64-GO	01.064
F216	C-160NG*	54-GT	01.054
R217	C-160R	64-GQ	01.064
R218	C-160R	64-GR	02.064
F221	C-160NG*	GS	01.054
R223	C-160R	64-GW	01.064
R224	C-160R	64-GX	02.064
R225	C-160R	64-GY	01.064
R226	C-160R	64-GZ	02.064

Aéronavale/Marine Aérospatiale
SA.321G Super Frelon
32 Flottille, Hyères & Lanvéoc/Poulmic

101
106
118
134
137
144
148
160
162
163
165

France

Dassault-Breguet Atlantique 2
21 Flottille, Nimes/Garons;
23 Flottille, Lorient/
  Lann Bihoué

1	21F
2	23F
3	23F
4	21F
5	23F
6	23F
7	21F
8	23F
9	21F
10	23F
11	23F
12	23F
13	23F
14	21F
15	23F
16	21F
17	21F
18	21F
19	23F
20	21F
21	21F
22	23F
23	21F
24	21F
25	21F
26	23F
27	23F
28	21F
29	
30	

Dassault Falcon 10(MER)
ES 57, Landivisiau

32	
101	
129	
133	
143	
185	

Dassault Falcon 20G Guardian
25 Flottille, Papeete &
  Tontouta

48	
65	
72	
77	
80	

Dassault Falcon 50 SURMAR
24 Flottille, Lorient/Lann
  Bihoué

7	
30	
36	
132	

Dassault Rafale-M
12 Flottille, Landivisiau;
AMD-BA, Istres;
CEV, Istres

M01	CEV
M02	CEV
1	CEV
2	12F
3	
4	12F

5	12F
6	12F
7	12F
8	12F
9	12F
10	12F

Dassault Super Etendard
11 Flottille, Landivisiau;
17 Flottille, Landivisiau;
CEV, Cazaux & Istres

1	11F
2	11F
3	11F
4	11F
6	11F
8	17F
10	11F
11	17F
12	17F
13	17F
14	17F
15	17F
16	11F
17	11F
18	17F
19	11F
23	11F
24	11F
25	17F
28	17F
30	11F
31	17F
32	11F
33	11F
35	11F
37	11F
38	11F
39	11F
41	11F
43	17F
44	17F
45	11F
46	17F
47	11F
48	11F
49	17F
50	17F
51	17F
52	17F
55	11F
57	17F
59	11F
61	17F
62	11F
64	11F
65	11F
66	11F
68	CEV
69	11F
71	17F

Embraer EMB.121AN Xingu
24 Flottille, Lorient/
  Lann Bihoué
28 Flottille, Hyères

30	24F
47	24F
65	24F
67	24F
68	28F
71	24F
74	24F
79	24F

81	24F
85	28F
87	28F

Eurocopter SA.365/ AS.565 Panther
35 Flottille, Hyères,
  (with detachments at
  Cherbourg, La Rochelle
  & Le Touquet)
36 Flottille, Hyères

17	SA.365N	35F
19	SA.365N	35F
24	SA.365N	35F
57	SA.365N	35F
81	SA.365N	35F
91	SA.365N	35F
313	SA.365F1	35F
318	SA.365F1	35F
322	SA.365F1	35F
355	AS.565MA	36F
362	AS.565MA	35F
436	AS.565MA	36F
452	AS.565MA	35F
453	AS.565MA	35F
466	AS.565MA	36F
482	AS.565MA	35F
486	AS.565MA	36F
503	AS.565MA	35F
505	AS.565MA	36F
506	AS.565MA	35F
507	AS.565MA	36F
511	AS.565MA	36F
519	AS.565MA	36F
522	AS.565MA	36F

Nord 262E Frégate
28 Flottille, Hyères;
ERCE, Hyères;
ES 10, Hyères;
ES 55, Aspretto

45	28F
46	28F
51	28F
53	28F
60	28F
63	28F
69	28F
70	28F
71	28F
72	28F
73	28F
75	28F
79	10S
100	28F

Northrop Grumman E-2C Hawkeye
4 Flottille, Lorient/Lann
  Bihoué

1	(165455)
2	(165456)

Westland Lynx HAS2(FN)/HAS4(FN)*
31 Flottille, Hyères;
34 Flottille,
  Lanvéoc/Poulmic;
CEPA, Hyères;

260	
262	34F
263	34F
265	34F
266	31F

267	31F
268	
269	34F
270	31F
271	34F
272	31F
273	34F
275	34F
276	34F
620	34F
621	34F
622	34F
623	34F
624	31F
625	31F
627	34F
801*	31F
802*	31F
804*	31F
806*	34F
807*	34F
808*	34F
810*	34F
811*	31F
812*	31F
813*	34F
814*	31F

Aviation Legére de l'Armée de Terre (ALAT)
Cessna F.406 Caravan II
EAAT, Rennes
0008	ABM
0010	ABN

SOCATA TBM 700
EAAT, Rennes
99	ABO
100	ABP
115	ABQ
136	ABR
139	ABS
156	ABT
159	ABU
160	ABV

French Govt
Aérospatiale AS.355F-1 Twin Écureuil
Douanes Francaises
F-ZBAC	(5026)
F-ZBEF	(5236)
F-ZBEJ	(5003)
F-ZBEK	(5298)
F-ZBEL	(5299)

Beech Super King Air B200
Sécurité Civile
F-ZBEM	
F-ZBFJ	98
F-ZBFK	96
F-ZBMB	B97

Cessna F.406 Caravan II
Douanes Francaises
F-ZBAB	(0025)
F-ZBBB	(0039)
F-ZBCE	(0042)
F-ZBCF	(0077)
F-ZBCG	(0066)
F-ZBCH	(0075)
F-ZBCI	(0070)
F-ZBCJ	(0074)

F-ZBEP	(0006)	
F-ZBES	(0017)	
F-ZBFA	(0001)	
F-ZBGA	(0086)	
F-ZBGB	(0090)	

Dassault Falcon 20
AVDEF, Nimes/Garons
F-GPAA	Falcon 20ECM
F-GPAB	Falcon 20E

Fokker F-27-600
Sécurité Civile
F-ZBFF	71	(10432)
F-ZBFG	72	(10440)

GERMANY
Luftwaffe, Marineflieger
Airbus A.310-304/MRTT*
1/FBS, Köln-Bonn
- 10+21
- 10+22
- 10+23
- 10+24*
- 10+25*
- 10+26*
- 10+27*

Canadair CL601-1A Challenger
3/FBS, Köln-Bonn
- 12+02
- 12+03
- 12+04
- 12+05
- 12+06
- 12+07

Eurofighter EF.2000/ EF.2000T* Typhoon
EADS, Manching;
TsLw-1, Kaufbeuren;
WTD-61, Ingolstadt
30+02*	EADS
98+03*	EADS
98+30	WTD-61
98+31*	TsLw-1
98+33*	EADS
98+34*	EADS

McD F-4F Phantom
Flugleherzentrum F-4F, Hopsten;
JG-71 *Richthoven*, Wittmundhaven;
JG-74 *Molders*, Neuburg/ Donau;
TsLw-1, Kaufbeuren;
WTD-61, Ingolstadt
37+01	FIZ F-4F
37+03	JG-71
37+04	TsLw-1
37+09	JG-74
37+10	JG-74
37+11	FIZ F-4F
37+12	FIZ F-4F
37+13	JG-74
37+14	TsLw-1
37+15	WTD-61
37+16	WTD-61
37+17	JG-74
37+22	JG-71
37+26	JG-71
37+28	JG-71

37+29	FIZ F-4F
37+32	JG-71
37+34	FIZ F-4F
37+36	FIZ F-4F
37+37	FIZ F-4F
37+38	FIZ F-4F
37+39	JG-71
37+44	FIZ F-4F
37+45	JG-74
37+48	JG-74
37+55	JG-71
37+61	JG-74
37+63	JG-71
37+65	JG-71
37+71	JG-74
37+75	FIZ F-4F
37+76	JG-71
37+77	JG-71
37+78	JG-71
37+79	JG-71
37+81	JG-74
37+82	JG-71
37+83	JG-71
37+84	JG-74
37+85	JG-71
37+86	JG-71
37+88	FIZ F-4F
37+89	JG-71
37+92	JG-74
37+93	FIZ F-4F
37+94	JG-74
37+96	FIZ F-4F
37+97	JG-74
37+98	JG-71
38+00	JG-74
38+01	JG-71
38+02	JG-74
38+03	FIZ F-4F
38+05	FIZ F-4F
38+06	JG-74
38+07	JG-71
38+09	JG-74
38+10	JG-74
38+12	JG-71
38+13	WTD-61
38+14	JG-71
38+16	JG-74
38+17	JG-74
38+18	JG-74
38+20	FIZ F-4F
38+24	JG-74
38+25	JG-74
38+26	JG-74
38+27	JG-71
38+28	JG-74
38+29	JG-71
38+30	JG-71
38+31	JG-74
38+32	FIZ F-4F
38+33	JG-74
38+36	JG-74
38+37	FIZ F-4F
38+39	JG-74
38+40	JG-71
38+42	JG-71
38+43	FIZ F-4F
38+44	JG-71
38+45	JG-71
38+46	JG-71
38+48	JG-74
38+49	JG-74
38+50	FIZ F-4F
38+53	JG-74
38+54	JG-71

38+55	JG-71	43+65	JbG-38	44+76	JbG-31
38+56	JG-74	43+67	JbG-38	44+78	JbG-31
38+57	JG-74	43+68	JbG-32	44+79	JbG-33
38+58	JG-71	43+69	AkG-51	44+80	JbG-31
38+60	JG-74	43+70	JbG-33	44+83	JbG-33
38+61	JG-71	43+71	JbG-38	44+84	JbG-33
38+62	FIZ F-4F	43+72	JbG-38	44+85	JbG-33
38+64	JG-71	43+73	AkG-51	44+86	AkG-51
38+66	JG-74	43+76	JbG-38	44+87	AkG-51
38+67	JG-74	43+78	TsLw-1	44+88	AkG-51
38+68	JG-74	43+79	AkG-51	44+89	JbG-33
38+69	JG-74	43+80	AkG-51	44+90	JbG-38
38+70	JG-74	43+81	AkG-51	44+91	JbG-33
38+73	FIZ F-4F	43+82	AkG-51	44+92	JbG-31
38+74	JG-74	43+85	JbG-33	44+94	JbG-33
38+75	JG-71	43+86	JbG-33	44+95	JbG-38
		43+87	MFG-2	44+96	JbG-31

Panavia Tornado Strike/Trainer1/ECR2

AkG-51 *Immelmann*, Schleswig/Jagel;
EADS, Manching;
JbG-31 *Boelcke*, Nörvenich;
JbG-32, Lechfeld;
JbG-33, Büchel;
JbG-38 *Ostfriesland*, Jever;
MFG-2, Eggebek;
TsLw-1, Kaufbeuren;
WTD-61, Ingolstadt

		43+90'	JbG-38	44+97	JbG-38
		43+92'	JbG-31	45+00	JbG-38
		43+94'	JbG-38	45+02	MFG-2
		43+96	AkG-51	45+04	JbG-33
		43+98	AkG-51	45+06	AkG-51
		44+00	JbG-31	45+07	JbG-33
		44+04	AkG-51	45+08	JbG-33
		44+06		45+12'	MFG-2
43+01'	JbG-38	44+07	JbG-32	45+13'	MFG-2
43+02'	JbG-38	44+08	JbG-38	45+14'	JbG-38
43+03'	JbG-38	44+09	JbG-33	45+15'	MFG-2
43+04'	JbG-38	44+10'	JbG-32	45+16'	JbG-38
43+05'	JbG-38	44+11	JbG-33	45+17	JbG-33
43+06'	JbG-38	44+13	TsLw-1	45+18	JbG-33
43+07'	JbG-38	44+15	AkG-51	45+19	JbG-33
43+08'	JbG-32	44+16'	JbG-31	45+20	AkG-51
43+10'	JbG-38	44+17	AkG-51	45+21	JbG-33
43+11'	JbG-38	44+19	JbG-31	45+22	JbG-33
43+13	EADS	44+21	JbG-31	45+23	JbG-31
43+15'	JbG-38	44+23	JbG-33	45+24	JbG-33
43+17'	JbG-38	44+24	AkG-51	45+25	AkG-51
43+20	JbG-31	44+25'	JbG-38	45+28	MFG-2
43+23'	JbG-33	44+26	JbG-33	45+29	WTD-61
43+25	JbG-31	44+27	JbG-33	45+30	MFG-2
43+27	JbG-31	44+29	JbG-31	45+31	MFG-2
43+28	JbG-32	44+30	JbG-31	45+33	MFG-2
43+29'	JbG-31	44+31	JbG-31	45+34	MFG-2
43+31'	JbG-31	44+32	JbG-38	45+35	MFG-2
43+32	JbG-31	44+33	JbG-33	45+36	MFG-2
43+33'	JbG-33	44+34	AkG-51	45+37	MFG-2
43+34	TsLw-1	44+35	JbG-31	45+38	MFG-2
43+35'	AkG-51	44+37'	JbG-38	45+39	MFG-2
43+37'	JbG-32	44+41	JbG-31	45+40	MFG-2
43+38	JbG-31	44+42	AkG-51	45+41	MFG-2
43+40	JbG-33	44+43	JbG-31	45+42	MFG-2
43+41	JbG-31	44+44	JbG-31	45+43	MFG-2
43+43'	AkG-51	44+46	JbG-33	45+44	MFG-2
43+45'		44+48	JbG-33	45+45	MFG-2
43+46	AkG-51	44+50	AkG-51	45+46	MFG-2
43+47	AkG-51	44+52	JbG-31	45+47	MFG-2
43+48	AkG-51	44+53	AkG-51	45+49	MFG-2
43+50	AkG-51	44+54	JbG-33	45+50	MFG-2
43+52	JbG-38	44+55	JbG-38	45+51	AkG-51
43+53	JbG-33	44+57	JbG-31	45+52	MFG-2
43+54	JbG-31	44+58	JbG-31	45+53	MFG-2
43+55	MFG-2	44+61	AkG-51	45+54	MFG-2
43+58	JbG-33	44+62	JbG-32	45+55	MFG-2
43+59	TsLw-1	44+63	JbG-33	45+56	MFG-2
43+60		44+64	AkG-51	45+57	AkG-51
43+61	TsLw-1	44+65	AkG-51	45+59	MFG-2
43+62	JbG-33	44+66		45+60'	AkG-51
43+63	JbG-32	44+68	AkG-51	45+64	TsLw-1
43+64	JbG-33	44+69	AkG-51	45+66	MFG-2
		44+70	JbG-31	45+67	AkG-51
		44+71	JbG-31	45+68	MFG-2
		44+72'	JbG-33	45+69	JbG-31
		44+75'	JbG-31	45+70'	JbG-33

45+71	MFG-2
45+72	MFG-2
45+74	TsLw-1
45+76	JbG-38
45+77[1]	JbG-33
45+78	JbG-33
45+79	JbG-31
45+81	JbG-31
45+82	JbG-31
45+84	AkG-51
45+85	AkG-51
45+86	JbG-33
45+87	JbG-33
45+88	JbG-31
45+89	
45+90	JbG-31
45+91	AkG-51
45+92	JbG-31
45+93	AkG-51
45+94	JbG-33
45+95	JbG-31
45+99[1]	AkG-51
46+02	JbG-33
46+05[1]	MFG-2
46+10	WTD-61
46+11	MFG-2
46+12	MFG-2
46+13	AkG-51
46+14	AkG-51
46+15	MFG-2
46+18	MFG-2
46+19	MFG-2
46+20	MFG-2
46+21	MFG-2
46+22	MFG-2
46+23[2]	JbG-32
46+24[2]	JbG-32
46+25[2]	JbG-32
46+26[2]	JbG-32
46+27[2]	JbG-32
46+28[2]	JbG-32
46+29[2]	JbG-32
46+30[2]	JbG-32
46+31[2]	JbG-32
46+32[2]	JbG-32
46+33[2]	JbG-32
46+34[2]	JbG-32
46+35[2]	JbG-32
46+36[2]	JbG-32
46+37[2]	JbG-32
46+38[2]	JbG-32
46+39[2]	JbG-32
46+40[2]	WTD-61
46+41[2]	JbG-32
46+42[2]	JbG-32
46+43[2]	JbG-32
46+44[2]	JbG-32
46+45[2]	JbG-32
46+46[2]	JbG-32
46+47[2]	JbG-32
46+48[2]	JbG-32
46+49[2]	JbG-32
46+50[2]	JbG-32
46+51[2]	JbG-32
46+52[2]	JbG-32
46+53[2]	JbG-32
46+54[2]	JbG-32
46+55[2]	JbG-32
46+56[2]	JbG-32
46+57[2]	JbG-32
98+59	WTD-61
98+60	WTD-61
98+79[2]	WTD-61

Transall C-160D
LTG-61, Landsberg;
LTG-62, Wunstorf;
LTG-63, Hohn;
WTD-61, Ingolstadt

50+06	LTG-63
50+07	LTG-61
50+08	LTG-63
50+09	LTG-62
50+10	LTG-62
50+17	LTG-62
50+29	LTG-62
50+33	LTG-61
50+34	LTG-63
50+35	LTG-62
50+36	LTG-62
50+37	LTG-62
50+38	LTG-62
50+40	LTG-61
50+41	LTG-62
50+42	LTG-63
50+44	LTG-61
50+45	LTG-63
50+46	LTG-62
50+47	LTG-61
50+48	LTG-61
50+49	LTG-63
50+50	LTG-62
50+51	LTG-61
50+52	LTG-62
50+53	LTG-61
50+54	LTG-63
50+55	LTG-62
50+56	LTG-63
50+57	WTD-61
50+58	LTG-62
50+59	LTG-63
50+60	LTG-62
50+61	LTG-63
50+62	LTG-62
50+64	LTG-61
50+65	LTG-62
50+66	LTG-61
50+67	LTG-63
50+68	LTG-61
50+69	LTG-63
50+70	LTG-63
50+71	LTG-63
50+72	LTG-63
50+73	LTG-63
50+74	LTG-61
50+75	LTG-63
50+76	LTG-63
50+77	LTG-63
50+78	LTG-62
50+79	LTG-63
50+81	LTG-62
50+82	LTG-63
50+83	LTG-62
50+84	LTG-61
50+85	LTG-63
50+86	LTG-61
50+87	LTG-63
50+88	LTG-61
50+89	LTG-62
50+90	LTG-62
50+91	LTG-62
50+92	LTG-61
50+93	LTG-61
50+94	LTG-63
50+95	LTG-63
50+96	LTG-61
50+97	LTG-62
50+98	LTG-61

50+99	LTG-61
51+00	LTG-62
51+01	LTG-62
51+02	LTG-63
51+03	LTG-62
51+04	LTG-61
51+05	LTG-62
51+06	LTG-63
51+07	LTG-62
51+08	WTD-61
51+09	LTG-63
51+10	LTG-61
51+11	LTG-62
51+12	LTG-63
51+13	LTG-61
51+14	LTG-63
51+15	LTG-61

Dornier Do.228/Do.228LM*
MFG-3, Nordholz;
WTD-61, Ingolstadt

57+01*	MFG-3
57+02*	MFG-3
57+03	MFG-3
57+04*	MFG-3
98+78	WTD-61

Breguet Br.1150 Atlantic
*Elint
MFG-3, Nordholz

61+03*
61+04
61+05
61+06*
61+08
61+09
61+10
61+11
61+12
61+13
61+14
61+15
61+16
61+17
61+18*
61+19*
61+20

Eurocopter AS.532U-2 Cougar
3/FBS, Berlin-Tegel

82+01
82+02
82+03

Westland Lynx Mk88/ Super Lynx Mk88A*
MFG-3, Nordholz

83+02*
83+03*
83+04*
83+05*
83+06*
83+07*
83+09*
83+10*
83+11*
83+12*
83+13*
83+15*
83+17
83+18*
83+19*
83+20*

83+21*		
83+22*		
83+23*		
83+24*		
83+25*		
83+26*		

Westland Sea King HAS41
MFG-5, Kiel-Holtenau

89+50		
89+51		
89+52		
89+53		
89+54		
89+55		
89+56		
89+57		
89+58		
89+60		
89+61		
89+62		
89+63		
89+64		
89+65		
89+66		
89+67		
89+68		
89+69		
89+70		
89+71		

NH Industries NH.90
98+90

Heeresfliegertruppe
Eurocopter EC.135P-1
HFWS, Bückeburg

82+51		
82+52		
82+53		
82+54		
82+55		
82+56		
82+57		
82+58		
82+59		
82+60		
82+61		
82+62		
82+63		
82+64		
82+65		

MBB Bo.105
HFR-15, Rheine-Bentlage;
HFR-25, Laupheim;
HFR-26, Roth;
HFR-35, Mendig;
HFS-400, Cottbus;
HFVS-910, Bückeburg;
HFWS, Bückeburg;
KHSR-36, Fritzlar;
TsLw-3, Fassberg;
WTD-61, Ingolstadt

Reg	Type	Unit
80+01	Bo.105M	HFR-35
80+02	Bo.105M	HFWS
80+03	Bo.105M	HFWS
80+05	Bo.105M	HFR-35
80+07	Bo.105M	HFWS
80+08	Bo.105M	HFR-25
80+14	Bo.105M	HFWS
80+15	Bo.105M	HFR-15
80+18	Bo.105M	HFR-15
80+21	Bo.105M	HFR-15
80+22	Bo.105M	HFS-400
80+26	Bo.105M	HFR-35
80+27	Bo.105M	HFR-35
80+33	Bo.105M	HFR-35
80+36	Bo.105M	HFR-25
80+40	Bo.105M	HFR-25
80+42	Bo.105M	HFR-25
80+47	Bo.105M	HFR-26
80+48	Bo.105M	HFR-25
80+49	Bo.105M	HFS-400
80+51	Bo.105M	HFWS
80+54	Bo.105M	HFR-15
80+59	Bo.105M	HFR-35
80+61	Bo.105M	HFS-400
80+66	Bo.105M	HFR-15
80+68	Bo.105M	HFR-15
80+69	Bo.105M	HFR-15
80+73	Bo.105M	HFR-15
80+76	Bo.105M	HFR-15
80+79	Bo.105M	HFR-35
80+82	Bo.105M	HFR-25
80+83	Bo.105M	HFR-25
80+85	Bo.105M	HFR-25
80+86	Bo.105M	HFS-400
80+88	Bo.105M	HFS-400
80+89	Bo.105M	HFS-400
80+90	Bo.105M	HFS-400
80+91	Bo.105M	HFR-35
80+92	Bo.105M	HFR-35
80+93	Bo.105M	HFS-400
80+94	Bo.105M	HFR-25
80+97	Bo.105M	HFR-35
80+98	Bo.105M	HFR-25
86+01	Bo.105P	
86+02	Bo.105P	HFWS
86+03	Bo.105P	HFWS
86+04	Bo.105P	KHSR-36
86+05	Bo.105P	HFWS
86+06	Bo.105P	HFWS
86+07	Bo.105P	HFWS
86+08	Bo.105P	HFWS
86+09	Bo.105P	HFWS
86+10	Bo.105P	
86+11	Bo.105P	KHSR-36
86+12	Bo.105P	HFWS
86+13	Bo.105P	HFWS
86+14	Bo.105P	
86+15	Bo.105P	
86+16	Bo.105P	HFWS
86+17	Bo.105P	HFVS-910
86+18	Bo.105P	HFR-26
86+19	Bo.105P	HFR-26
86+20	Bo.105P	HFWS
86+21	Bo.105P	KHSR-36
86+22	Bo.105P	HFWS
86+23	Bo.105P	HFWS
86+24	Bo.105P	HFVS-910
86+25	Bo.105P	
86+26	Bo.105P	KHSR-36
86+27	Bo.105P	HFR-26
86+28	Bo.105P	HFWS
86+29	Bo.105P	
86+30	Bo.105P	HFR-26
86+31	Bo.105P	
86+32	Bo.105P	HFR-26
86+33	Bo.105P	HFR-26
86+34	Bo.105P	HFR-26
86+35	Bo.105P	HFR-26
86+36	Bo.105P	KHSR-36
86+37	Bo.105P	
86+38	Bo.105P	KHSR-36
86+39	Bo.105P	
86+41	Bo.105P	
86+42	Bo.105P	HFR-26
86+43	Bo.105P	
86+44	Bo.105P	HFR-26
86+45	Bo.105P	KHSR-36
86+46	Bo.105P	HFR-26
86+47	Bo.105P	
86+48	Bo.105P	
86+49	Bo.105P	KHSR-36
86+50	Bo.105P	
86+51	Bo.105P	KHSR-36
86+52	Bo.105P	
86+53	Bo.105P	KHSR-36
86+54	Bo.105P	
86+55	Bo.105P	
86+56	Bo.105P	KHSR-36
86+57	Bo.105P	
86+58	Bo.105P	KHSR-36
86+59	Bo.105P	
86+60	Bo.105P	TsLw-3
86+61	Bo.105P	HFR-26
86+62	Bo.105P	HFVS-910
86+63	Bo.105P	HFR-26
86+64	Bo.105P	HFR-26
86+65	Bo.105P	HFR-26
86+66	Bo.105P	HFVS-910
86+67	Bo.105P	HFR-26
86+68	Bo.105P	KHSR-36
86+69	Bo.105P	HFR-26
86+70	Bo.105P	
86+71	Bo.105P	KHSR-36
86+72	Bo.105P	KHSR-36
86+73	Bo.105P	HFWS
86+74	Bo.105P	KHSR-36
86+75	Bo.105P	KHSR-36
86+76	Bo.105P	HFR-26
86+77	Bo.105P	
86+78	Bo.105P	HFR-26
86+80	Bo.105P	
86+81	Bo.105P	KHSR-36
86+83	Bo.105P	
86+84	Bo.105P	
86+85	Bo.105P	
86+86	Bo.105P	
86+87	Bo.105P	
86+88	Bo.105P	
86+89	Bo.105P	
86+90	Bo.105P	HFR-26
86+91	Bo.105P	HFR-26
86+92	Bo.105P	KHSR-36
86+93	Bo.105P	HFVS-910
86+94	Bo.105P	HFWS
86+95	Bo.105P	
86+96	Bo.105P	HFR-26
86+97	Bo.105P	KHSR-36
86+98	Bo.105P	HFR-35
86+99	Bo.105P	HFR-26
87+00	Bo.105P	HFR-26
87+01	Bo.105P	HFR-26
87+02	Bo.105P	HFR-26
87+03	Bo.105P	TsLw-3
87+04	Bo.105P	KHSR-36
87+05	Bo.105P	HFR-26
87+06	Bo.105P	KHSR-36
87+07	Bo.105P	HFR-26
87+08	Bo.105P	HFWS
87+09	Bo.105P	KHSR-36
87+10	Bo.105P	HFR-26
87+11	Bo.105P	KHSR-36
87+12	Bo.105P	KHSR-36
87+13	Bo.105P	KHSR-36
87+14	Bo.105P	KHSR-36
87+15	Bo.105P	KHSR-36
87+16	Bo.105P	KHSR-36
87+17	Bo.105P	KHSR-36
87+18	Bo.105P	HFWS

87+19	Bo.105P	KHSR-36
87+20	Bo.105P	HFR-26
87+21	Bo.105P	HFWS
87+22	Bo.105P	
87+23	Bo.105P	KHSR-36
87+24	Bo.105P	
87+25	Bo.105P	HFR-26
87+26	Bo.105P	
87+27	Bo.105P	
87+28	Bo.105P	
87+29	Bo.105P	HFVS-910
87+30	Bo.105P	TsLw-3
87+31	Bo.105P	
87+32	Bo.105P	HFWS
87+33	Bo.105P	HFR-26
87+34	Bo.105P	HFR-26
87+35	Bo.105P	HFR-26
87+36	Bo.105P	HFR-26
87+37	Bo.105P	HFR-26
87+38	Bo.105P	KHSR-36
87+39	Bo.105P	KHSR-36
87+41	Bo.105P	KHSR-36
87+42	Bo.105P	KHSR-36
87+43	Bo.105P	KHSR-36
87+44	Bo.105P	KHSR-36
87+45	Bo.105P	HFR-16
87+46	Bo.105P	
87+47	Bo.105P	HFR-15
87+48	Bo.105P	
87+49	Bo.105P	
87+50	Bo.105P	HFR-26
87+51	Bo.105P	
87+52	Bo.105P	
87+53	Bo.105P	HFR-26
87+55	Bo.105P	HFVS-910
87+56	Bo.105P	HFR-26
87+57	Bo.105P	HFR-26
87+58	Bo.105P	HFWS
87+59	Bo.105P	KHSR-36
87+60	Bo.105P	KHSR-36
87+61	Bo.105P	KHSR-36
87+62	Bo.105P	KHSR-36
87+63	Bo.105P	HFWS
87+64	Bo.105P	KHSR-36
87+65	Bo.105P	KHSR-36
87+66	Bo.105P	KHSR-36
87+67	Bo.105P	HFWS
87+68	Bo.105P	HFWS
87+69	Bo.105P	HFR-26
87+70	Bo.105P	HFR-35
87+71	Bo.105P	HFR-26
87+72	Bo.105P	HFR-15
87+73	Bo.105P	HFWS
87+74	Bo.105P	HFVS-910
87+75	Bo.105P	
87+76	Bo.105P	HFR-15
87+77	Bo.105P	
87+78	Bo.105P	
87+79	Bo.105P	
87+80	Bo.105P	
87+81	Bo.105P	
87+82	Bo.105P	
87+83	Bo.105P	
87+84	Bo.105P	HFVS-910
87+85	Bo.105P	HFR-35
87+86	Bo.105P	HFR-26
87+87	Bo.105P	HFR-35
87+88	Bo.105P	HFR-26
87+89	Bo.105P	HFR-26
87+90	Bo.105P	HFWS
87+91	Bo.105P	HFR-35
87+92	Bo.105P	HFR-26
87+93	Bo.105P	HFR-26
87+94	Bo.105P	HFR-26
87+95	Bo.105P	HFR-26
87+96	Bo.105P	HFR-26
87+97	Bo.105P	KHSR-36
87+98	Bo.105P	HFR-26
87+99	Bo.105P	KHSR-36
88+01	Bo.105P	KHSR-36
88+02	Bo.105P	KHSR-36
88+03	Bo.105P	KHSR-36
88+04	Bo.105P	KHSR-36
88+05	Bo.105P	HFVS-910
88+06	Bo.105P	KHSR-36
88+07	Bo.105P	KHSR-36
88+08	Bo.105P	KHSR-36
88+09	Bo.105P	HFR-35
88+10	Bo.105P	HFWS
88+11	Bo.105P	KHSR-36
88+12	Bo.105P	KHSR-36
98+28	Bo.105C	WTD-61

Sikorsky/VFW CH-53G/CH-53GS*
HFR-15, Rheine-Bentlage;
HFR-25, Laupheim;
HFR-35, Mendig;
HFWS, Bückeburg;
TsLw-3, Fassberg;
WTD-61, Ingolstadt

84+01*	WTD-61	
84+02	WTD-61	
84+05	HFWS	
84+06	HFR-15	
84+09	HFR-25	
84+10	HFWS	
84+11	HFWS	
84+12	HFR-15	
84+13	HFWS	
84+14	HFWS	
84+15*	HFR-25	
84+16	HFWS	
84+17	HFR-25	
84+18	HFWS	
84+19	TsLw-3	
84+21	HFWS	
84+22	HFR-15	
84+23	HFR-35	
84+24	HFR-35	
84+25*	HFR-35	
84+26	HFR-35	
84+27	HFWS	
84+28	HFR-25	
84+29	HFR-35	
84+30*	HFR-35	
84+31	HFR-35	
84+32	HFR-35	
84+33	HFR-35	
84+34	HFR-35	
84+35	HFR-35	
84+36	HFR-35	
84+37	HFWS	
84+38	HFR-35	
84+39	HFR-35	
84+40	HFR-25	
84+41	HFWS	
84+42*	HFR-25	
84+43	HFR-25	
84+44	HFR-25	
84+45*	HFR-25	
84+46	HFR-35	
84+47	HFR-25	
84+48	HFR-25	
84+49	HFWS	
84+50	HFR-25	

84+51*	HFR-25
84+52*	HFR-25
84+53	HFR-25
84+54	HFR-25
84+55	HFR-25
84+56	HFR-35
84+57	HFR-35
84+58	HFR-25
84+60	HFR-25
84+62*	HFR-25
84+63	HFR-25
84+64*	HFR-25
84+65	HFR-35
84+66*	HFR-35
84+67*	HFR-15
84+68	HFWS
84+69	HFR-15
84+70	HFR-15
84+71	HFR-15
84+72	HFR-15
84+73	HFR-15
84+74	HFR-15
84+75	HFR-15
84+76	HFWS
84+77	HFR-15
84+78	HFR-15
84+79*	HFR-15
84+80	HFR-15
84+82	HFR-35
84+83	HFR-15
84+84	HFR-15
84+85*	HFR-15
84+86	HFR-15
84+87	HFR-15
84+88	HFR-15
84+89	HFR-35
84+90	HFR-15
84+91*	HFR-15
84+93	HFR-35
84+94	HFR-35
84+95	HFR-25
84+96	HFR-25
84+97	HFR-25
84+98*	HFR-25
84+99	HFR-15
85+00*	HFWS
85+01	HFR-35
85+02	HFR-35
85+03	HFR-35
85+04	HFR-25
85+05	HFR-25
85+06	HFR-25
85+07*	HFWS
85+08	HFR-15
85+10*	HFR-35
85+11	HFR-25
85+12*	HFR-15

Eurocopter AS.665 Tiger
WTD-61, Ingolstadt
98+23
98+25
98+26
98+27

GHANA
Ghana Air Force
Fokker F-28 Fellowship 3000
VIP Flight, Accra
G-530

Grumman G.1159A
Gulfstream III
VIP Flight, Accra
G-540

GREECE
Elliniki Polemiki Aeroporía
Embraer
ERJ.135/145
356 MTM/112 PM, Elefsís;
380 Mira/112 PM, Elefsís
ERJ.135LR
145-209   356 MTM
ERJ.135BJ Legacy
135L-484 356 MTM
ERJ.145 AEW
145-374   380 Mira
145-671   380 Mira
145-729   380 Mira
145-757   380 Mira

Gulfstream Aerospace
Gulfstream V
356 MTM/112 PM, Elefsís
678

Lockheed C-130H Hercules
356 MTM/112 PM, Elefsís
*ECM
741*
742
743
744
745
746
747*
749
751
752

Lockheed F-16C/F-16D*
Fighting Falcon
330 Mira/111 PM,
 Nea Ankhialos;
340 Mira/115PM, Souda
341 Mira/111 PM,
 Nea Ankhialos;
346 MAPK/110 PM, Larissa;
347 Mira/111 PM,
 Nea Ankhialos

046	341 Mira
047	347 Mira
048	341 Mira
049	347 Mira
050	341 Mira
051	347 Mira
052	341 Mira
053	347 Mira
054	341 Mira
055	347 Mira
056	341 Mira
057	347 Mira
058	341 Mira
059	347 Mira
060	341 Mira
061	347 Mira
062	341 Mira
063	347 Mira
064	341 Mira
065	347 Mira
066	341 Mira
067	347 Mira
068	341 Mira
069	347 Mira

070	341 Mira
071	347 Mira
072	341 Mira
073	347 Mira
074	341 Mira
075	341 Mira
076	341 Mira
077*	341 Mira
078*	341 Mira
079*	341 Mira
080*	341 Mira
081*	341 Mira
082*	341 Mira
083*	347 Mira
084*	341 Mira
110	330 Mira
111	330 Mira
112	346 MAPK
113	330 Mira
114	346 MAPK
115	330 Mira
116	330 Mira
117	330 Mira
118	346 MAPK
119	330 Mira
120	330 Mira
121	330 Mira
122	346 MAPK
124	330 Mira
125	330 Mira
126	346 MAPK
127	330 Mira
128	346 MAPK
129	330 Mira
130	346 MAPK
132	346 MAPK
133	330 Mira
134	346 MAPK
136	346 MAPK
138	346 MAPK
139	330 Mira
140	346 MAPK
141	330 Mira
143	346 MAPK
144*	330 Mira
145*	330 Mira
146*	346 MAPK
147*	330 Mira
148*	346 MAPK
149*	330 Mira
500	
501	340 Mira
502	340 Mira
503	340 Mira
504	340 Mira
505	340 Mira
506	340 Mira
507	340 Mira
508	340 Mira
509	340 Mira
510	
511	
512	
513	
514	
515	
516	
517	
518	
519	
520	
521	
522	
523	

524	
525	
526	
527	
528	
529	
529	
530	
531	
532	
533	
534	
535	
536*	340 Mira
537*	340 Mira
538*	
539*	
600*	
601*	
602*	340 Mira
603*	340 Mira
604*	340 Mira
605*	340 Mira
606*	
607*	
608*	340 Mira
609*	340 Mira
610*	
611*	
612*	
613*	
614*	
615*	
616*	
617*	
618*	
619*	

SAAB SF.340AEW&C
380 Mira/112 PM, Elefsis
004

HUNGARY
Magyar Honvédseg Repülö
Csapatai
Antonov An-26
89 VSD, Szolnok

405	(03405)
406	(03406)
407	(03407)
603	(03603)

Mikoyan MiG-29/29UB*
59 HRO, Kecskemét
01
02
03
04
05
06
07
08
09
10
11
12
14
15
16
18
19
20
21
23

24*
25*
26*
27*
28*
29*

ISRAEL
Heyl ha'Avir
  Boeing 707
  120 Sqn, Tel Aviv

120	RC-707
128	RC-707
137	RC-707
140	KC-707
242	KC-707
248	KC-707
250	KC-707
255	EC-707
260	KC-707
264	RC-707
272	VC-707
275	KC-707
290	VC-707

  Lockheed C-130 Hercules
  103 Sqn & 131 Sqn, Tel Aviv

102	C-130H
106	C-130H
208	C-130E
305	C-130E
309	C-130E
310	C-130E
313	C-130E
314	C-130E
316	C-130E
420	KC-130H
427	C-130H
428	C-130H
435	C-130H
436	C-130H
522	KC-130H
545	KC-130H

Israeli Govt
  Hawker 800XP
  Israeli Govt, Tel Aviv
  4X-COV

ITALY
Aeronautica Militare Italiana
  Aeritalia G222/C-27J
  9a Brigata Aerea,
    Pratica di Mare:
      8° Gruppo & 71° Gruppo;
  46a Brigata Aerea, Pisa:
    2° Gruppo & 98° Gruppo;
  RSV, Pratica di Mare
  G222AAA

CSX62144	RS-44	RSV

  G222RM

MM62139	14-20	8
MM62140	14-21	8
MM62141	14-22	8

  G222TCM

MM62111	46-83	98
MM62117	46-25	2
MM62119	46-21	2
MM62124	46-88	98
MM62125	14-24	8
MM62136	46-97	98
MM62137	46-95	98
MM62145	46-50	8
MM62153X	RS-46	RSV

MM62154	46-54	8

G222VS

MM62107		71

C-27J

MMCSX62127		Alenia

Aeritalia-EMB AMX/AMX-T*
  2° Stormo, Rivolto:
    14° Gruppo;
  32° Stormo, Amendola:
    13° Gruppo &
    101° Gruppo;
  51° Stormo, Istrana:
    103° Gruppo &
    132° Gruppo;
  RSV, Pratica di Mare

MMX595		Alenia
MMX596		Alenia
MMX597		Alenia
MMX599		Alenia
MM7089		
MM7090		
MM7091	32-64	101
MM7092	RS-14	RSV
MM7093		
MM7094	3-37	
MM7095		103
MM7096		
MM7097	3-36	
MM7098	3-35	
MM7099		
MM7100	32-66	101
MM7101	51-25	103
MM7102	2-03	14
MM7103		
MM7104	51-26	103
MM7106	3-25	
MM7107		
MM7110		
MM7111		
MM7112		
MM7115	2-12	14
MM7116	32-11	13
MM7117	3-34	
MM7118	2-11	14
MM7119		
MM7120		
MM7122	3-32	
MM7123		
MM7124		
MM7125	RS-11	RSV
MM7126		
MM7127	3-24	
MM7128		
MM7129	66	101
MM7130		
MM7131	2-19	
MM7132	51-12	103
MM7133	2-18	14
MM7134	51-07	103
MM7135		
MM7138		
MM7139		
MM7140	51-26	103
MM7141		
MM7142		
MM7143	51-20	103
MM7144	51-41	132
MM7145	51-44	132
MM7146	51-21	103
MM7147	32-04	13
MM7148	51-15	103
MM7149		
MM7150	32-65	101

MM7151	51-40	132
MM7152	51-03	103
MM7153	32-60	101
MM7154	51-54	132
MM7155	32-05	13
MM7156	32-10	13
MM7157	32-06	13
CSX7158	RS-12	RSV
MM7159	51-11	103
MM7160	32-14	13
MM7161	2-21	14
MM7162	51-01	103
MM7163	2-25	
MM7164	51-37	132
MM7165	51-32	132
MM7166		
MM7167	2-01	14
MM7168	51-30	132
MM7169	32-26	13
MM7170	51-35	132
MM7172	51-37	132
MM7173	2-16	14
MM7174	51-04	103
MM7175	51-42	132
MM7176	2-20	14
MM7177	32-25	13
MM7178	32-24	13
MM7179		
MM7180		
MM7182	51-16	103
MM7183	32-22	13
MM7184	51-33	132
MM7185	32-02	13
MM7186	51-05	103
MM7189		
MM7190	32-17	13
MM7191	32-01	13
MM7192	51-31	132
MM7193		
MM7194	32-03	13
MM7195		
MM7196	32-13	13
MM7197	32-21	13
MM7198		
MM55024*	15	RSV
MM55025*	RS-16	RSV
MM55026*	32-43	101
MM55027*		
MM55029*	32-50	101
MM55030*	32-41	101
MM55031*	32-40	101
MM55034*	18	RSV
MM55035*		
MM55036*	32-51	101
MM55037*	32-64	101
MM55038*	32-53	101
MM55039*	32-54	101
MM55040*	32-52	101
MM55041*	32-55	101
MM55042*	32-56	101
MM55043*	32-65	101
MM55044*	32-57	101
MM55046*	32-47	101
MM55047*	32-45	101
MM55048*	32-44	101
MM55049*	32-46	101
MM55050*	32-43	101
MM55051*	32-42	101

Aermacchi MB339A/
MB339CD*
  61° Stormo, Lecce:
    212° Gruppo &
    213° Gruppo;

Italy

Aermacchi, Venegono;
Frecce Tricolori [FT]
  (313o Gruppo), Rivolto
  (MB339A/PAN);
RSV, Pratica di Mare

MMX606*		RSV
MM54440	61-00	
MM54441	61-71	
MM54442	61-112	
CSX54443	Aermacchi	
MM54445	61-25	
MM54446	61-01	
MM54447	61-02	
MM54450	61-115	
MM54451	61-116	
MM54452		
MM54453	61-05	
MM54455	61-07	
MM54456	61-10	
MM54457	61-11	
MM54458	61-12	
MM54459	61-13	
MM54460	61-14	
MM54462	61-16	
MM54463	61-17	
MM54467	61-23	
MM54468	61-24	
MM54471	61-27	
MM54472	61-30	
MM54473		[FT]
MM54475	10	[FT]
MM54477	9	[FT]
MM54478	6	[FT]
MM54479		[FT]
MM54480	7	[FT]
MM54482	8	[FT]
MM54483	61-102	
MM54484	61-101	
MM54485	12	[FT]
MM54486	3	[FT]
MM54487	61-31	
MM54488	61-32	
MM54489	61-33	
MM54490	61-34	
MM54491	61-35	
MM54492	61-36	
MM54493	61-37	
MM54494	61-40	
MM54496	61-42	
MM54498	61-44	
MM54499	61-45	
MM54500		[FT]
MM54503	61-51	
MM54504	61-52	
MM54505	0	[FT]
MM54506	61-54	
MM54507	61-55	
MM54508	61-56	
MM54509	61-57	
MM54510	61-60	
MM54511	61-61	
MM54512	61-62	
MM54513	61-63	
MM54514	61-64	
MM54515	61-65	
MM54516	61-66	
MM54517		[FT]
MM54518	61-70	
MM54532		
MM54533	61-72	
MM54534	61-73	
MM54535	61-74	
MM54536	1	[FT]
MM54537		

MM54538	61-75	
MM54539	61-76	
MM54541	61-100	
MM54542	5	[FT]
MM54543		[FT]
MM54544*	Aermacchi	
MM54545	61-84	
MM54546	2	[FT]
MM54547	4	[FT]
MM54548	61-90	
MM54549	61-107	
MM54550	61-110	
MM54551	2	[FT]
MM55052	61-96	
MM55053	61-97	
MM55054	61-15	
MM55055	61-20	
MM55058	61-41	
MM55059	61-26	
MM55062*	RS-26	RSV
MM55063*	RS-27	RSV
MM55064*	61-130	
MM55065*	61-131	
MM55066*	61-132	
MM55067*	61-133	
MM55068*	61-134	
MM55069*	61-135	
MM55070*	61-136	
MM55072*	61-140	
MM55073*	61-141	
MM55074*	61-142	
MM55075*	61-143	
MM55076*	61-144	
MM55077*		
MM55078*	RS-29	RSV
MM55079*		
MM55080*		
MM55081*		
MM55082*		
MM55083*		
MM55084*		
MM55085*		
MM55086*		
MM55087*		
MM55088*		
MM55089*		
MM55090*		
MM55091*		

Airbus A.319CJ-115
31° Stormo, Roma-
  Ciampino:
  306° Gruppo

MM62173	
MM62174	
MM62209	

Boeing 707-328B/-3F5C*
9ª Brigata Aerea,
  Pratica di Mare:
  8° Gruppo;

MM62148	14-01
MM62149	14-02
MM62150*	14-03
MM62151*	14-04

Breguet Br.1150 Atlantic
41° Stormo, Catania:
  88° Gruppo

MM40108	41-70
MM40109	
MM40110	41-72
MM40111	41-73
MM40112	41-74

MM40113	
MM40114	41-76
MM40115	41-77
MM40116	
MM40117	41-02
MM40118	
MM40119	
MM40120	41-05
MM40121	41-06
MM40122	
MM40123	
MM40124	41-11
MM40125	41-12

Dassault Falcon 50
31° Stormo, Roma-Ciampino:
  93° Gruppo

MM62020	
MM62021	
MM62026	
MM62029	

Dassault Falcon 900EX
31° Stormo, Roma-Ciampino:
  93° Gruppo

MM62171	
MM62172	
MM62210	

Eurofighter EF.2000/
EF.2000T* Typhoon
Alenia, Torino/Caselle;
RSV, Pratica di Mare

MMX602	RS-01	RSV
MMX603		Alenia
MMX614*		Alenia
MM7235		Alenia
CSX55092*		Alenia
CSX55093*		Alenia

Lockheed C-130J/C-130J-30
Hercules II
46a Brigata Aerea, Pisa:
  2° Gruppo & 50° Gruppo
C-130J

MM62175	46-40	2
MM62176	46-41	2
MM62177	46-42	2
MM62178	46-43	2
MM62179	46-44	2
MM62180	46-45	2
MM62181	46-46	50
MM62182	46-47	50
MM62183	46-48	50
MM62184	46-49	50
MM62185	46-50	
MM62186	46-51	

C-130J-30

MM62187	46-53
MM62188	46-54
MM62189	46-55
MM62190	46-56
MM62191	46-57
MM62192	
MM62193	
MM62194	
MM62195	
MM62196	

Lockheed (GD) F-16A-ADF/
F-16B*
5° Stormo, Cervia:
  23° Gruppo

Italy

37° Stormo, Trapani:
18° Gruppo

MM7238	18
MM7239	
MM7240	
MM7241	
MM7242	
MM7243	
MM7244	
MM7245	
MM7246	23
MM7266*	18
MM7267*	18
MM7268*	23
MM7269*	23

Lockheed F-104 Starfighter

4° Stormo, Grosseto:
9° Gruppo & 20° Gruppo;
9° Stormo, Grazzanise:
10° Gruppo;
RSV, Pratica di Mare

F-104S-ASA-M

MM6704	5-31	
MM6717	37-22	
MM6720	9-51	10
MM6731	37-03	
MM6732	37-04	
MM6733	4-51	20
MM6734	9-30	10
MM6739	4-6	9
MM6762	RS-02	RSV
MM6763	9-33	10
MM6764	37-11	
MM6767	37-05	
MM6770	9-35	10
MM6771	4-5	9
MM6787	9-38	10
MM6838	4-58	20
MM6849	4-10	9
MM6850		
MM6872	37-23	
MM6873	4-7	9
MM6876	9-39	10
MM6881	4-59	20
MM6890	4-50	10
MM6912	9-42	10
MM6914	4-1	9
MM6923	4-2	9
MM6926	4-12	9
MM6930	999	10
MM6932	4-20	9
MM6934	9-31	10
MM6935	9-32	10
MM6936	9-41	10
MM6939	4-52	20

TF-104G/TF-104G-M*

MM54226*	4-23	20
MM54232*	4-29	20
MM54233	RS-09	RSV
MM54247*	4-32	20
MM54250*	4-33	20
MM54251*	4-34	20
MM54253*	4-35	20
MM54258*	4-40	20
MM54260*	4-41	20
MM54261*	4-42	20
MM54554*	4-48	20
MM54555*	4-45	20
MM54556*	4-47	20

Panavia Tornado ADV/ Trainer[1]

36° Stormo, Gioia del Colle:
12° Gruppo

MM7204	36-05	(ZE730)
MM7205	36-06	(ZE787)
MM7207	36-27	(ZE762)
MM7209	36-25	(ZE835)
MM7210	36-14	(ZE836)
MM7226	36-21	(ZE911)
MM7230	36-11	(ZG730)
MM7232	36-10	(ZG735)
MM7233	36-23	(ZG768)
MM7234	36-24	(ZE167)
MM55056[1]	36-01	(ZE202)
MM55060[1]	36-30	(ZE208)
MM55061[1]	36-20	(ZE205)

Panavia Tornado Strike/ Trainer1/ECR2

6° Stormo, Ghedi:
102° Gruppo &
154° Gruppo;
50° Stormo, Piacenza:
155° Gruppo;
156° Gruppo Autonomo,
Gioia del Colle;
RSV, Pratica di Mare

MM7002	6-10	154
MM7003	6-23	154
MM7004	36-46	156
MM7005[2]		
MM7006	6-16	154
MM7007	36-37	156
MM7008		
MM7009	6-09	154
MM7011		
MM7013	36-40	156
MM7014		
MM7015	50-53	155
MM7016		
MM7018	6-46	102
MM7019[2]	50-05	155
MM7020[2]	50-21	155
MM7021[2]	50-01	155
MM7022		
MM7023	6-13	154
MM7025	6-43	102
MM7026	6-44	102
MM7027[2]	50-51	155
MM7028		
MM7029	6-22	154
MM7030[2]	50-04	155
MM7031	6-21	154
MM7033	50-50	155
MM7034	6-30	154
MM7035	36-47	156
MM7036[2]	50-..	155
MM7037	6-47	102
MM7038	36-41	156
MM7039	6-02	154
CMX704[0]	RS-01	RSV
MM7041	6-36	102
MM7042	6-31	102
MM7043		
MM7044	6-04	154
MM7046[2]	6-06	154
MM7047[2]	50-43	155
MM7048		Alenia
MM7049	6-34	102
MM7050	36-44	156
MM7051	50-45	155

MM705		
MM7053[2]	50-07	155
MM7054[2]	50-40	155
MM7055	50-42	155
MM7056	36-50	156
MM7057	6-12	154
MM7058		
MM7059	50-47	155
MM7061	6-01	154
MM7062[2]	50-44	155
MM7063	36-42	156
MM7064	6-26	154
MM7065	6-25	154
MM7066		
MM7067	6-36	102
CSX7068[2]		Alenia
MM7070[2]	50-46	155
MM7071	6-35	102
MM7072	36-57	156
MM7073[2]		Alenia
MM7075		
MM7078	50-02	155
CMX7079[2]		Alenia
MM7080	6-33	102
MM7081	6-11	154
MM7082[2]	6-14	154
MM7083	6-37	102
MM7084		
CMX7085	36-50	Alenia
MM7086	36-35	156
MM7087		
MM7088	6-18	154
MM55000[1]	6-51	102
MM55001[1]	6-42	102
MM55002[1]	6-52	102
MM55003[1]	6-..	154
MM55004[1]	6-53	102
MM55005[1]	6-40	102
MM55006[1]	6-44	102
MM55007[1]	36-55	156
MM55008[1]	6-45	102
MM55009[1]	36-56	156
MM55010[1]	6-42	102
MM55011[1]		

Piaggio P-180AM Avanti

9ª Brigata Aerea,
Pratica di Mare:
71° Gruppo;
36° Stormo, Gioia del Colle:
636ª SC;
RSV, Pratica di Mare

MM62159		636
MM62160	54	RSV
MM62161		71
MM62162		71
MM62163		71
CSX62164		RSV
MM62199		71
MM62201		71
MM62202		71
MM62203		71

Guardia di Finanza Aérospatiale ATR.42-400MP

2° Gruppo EM,
Pratica di Mare

MM62165	GF-13
MM62166	GF-14

Marina Militare Italiana
McDonnell Douglas
AV-8B/TAV-8B Harrier II+
Gruppo Aerei Imbarcarti,
Taranto/Grottaglie
AV-8B

MM7199	1-03
MM7200	1-04
MM7201	1-05
MM7212	1-06
MM7213	1-07
MM7214	1-08
MM7215	1-09
MM7217	1-11
MM7218	1-12
MM7219	1-13
MM7220	1-14
MM7221	1-15
MM7222	1-16
MM7223	1-18
MM7224	1-19

TAV-8B

MM55032	1-01
MM55033	1-02

Italian Govt
Dassault Falcon 200
Italian Govt/Soc. CAI,
Roma/Ciampino
I-CNEF
I-SOBE

Dassault Falcon 900
Italian Govt/Soc. CAI,
Roma/Ciampino
I-DIES
I-FICV
I-NUMI

IVORY COAST
Grumman G.1159C
Gulfstream IV
Ivory Coast Govt, Abidjan
TU-VAD

JAPAN
Japan Air Self Defence Force
Boeing 747-47C
701st Flight Sqn, Chitose
20-1101
20-1102

JORDAN
Al Quwwat al Jawwiya
al Malakiya al Urduniya
Extra EA-300S
Royal Jordanian Falcons,
Amman
JY-RNA
JY-RNC
JY-RND
JY-RNE
JY-RNG
JY-RNL

Lockheed C-130H
Hercules
3 Sqn, Al Matar AB/Amman
344
345
346
347

Jordanian Govt
Airbus A.340-211
Jordanian Govt, Amman
JY-ABH

Canadair CL.604
Challenger
Jordanian Govt, Amman
JY-ONE
JY-TWO

Lockheed L.1011 TriStar
500
Jordanian Govt, Amman
JY-HKJ

KAZAKHSTAN
Boeing 757-2M6
Govt of Kazakhstan, Almaty
P4-NSN

Tupolev Tu-134A-3
Govt of Kazakhstan, Almaty
UN-65799

KENYA
Kenyan Air Force
Fokker 70ER
308

KUWAIT
Al Quwwat al Jawwiya
al Kuwaitiya
Lockheed L100-30
Hercules
41 Sqn, Kuwait International
KAF 323
KAF 324
KAF 325

Kuwaiti Govt
Airbus A.300C4-620
Kuwaiti Govt, Safat
9K-AHI

Airbus A.310-308
Kuwaiti Govt, Safat
9K-ALD

Gulfstream Aerospace
Gulfstream V
Kuwaiti Govt/Kuwait
Airways, Safat
9K-AJD
9K-AJE
9K-AJF

KYRGYZSTAN
Tupolev Tu-134A-3
Govt of Kyrgyzstan, Bishkek
EX-65119

Tupolev Tu-154B/Tu-154M
Govt of Kyrgyzstan, Bishkek

EX-85294	Tu-154B
EX-85718	Tu-154M
EX-85762	Tu-154M

LITHUANIA
Karines Oro Pajegos
LET 410 Turbolet
I Transporto Eskadrile,
Zokniai
01
02

Lithuanian Govt
Lockheed L.1329 Jetstar
731
Lithuanian Govt, Vilnius
LY-AMB

LUXEMBOURG
NATO
Boeing 707 TCA/CT-49A
NAEWF, Geilenkirchen
LX-N19997
LX-N19999
LX-N20000
LX-N20199

Boeing E-3A
NAEWF, Geilenkirchen
LX-N90442
LX-N90443
LX-N90444
LX-N90445
LX-N90446
LX-N90447
LX-N90448
LX-N90449
LX-N90450
LX-N90451
LX-N90452
LX-N90453
LX-N90454
LX-N90455
LX-N90456
LX-N90458
LX-N90459

MALAYSIA
Royal Malaysian Air Force/
Tentera Udara Diraja
Malaysia
Boeing 737-7H6
2 Sqn, Simpang
M53–01

Bombardier BD.700-1A10
Global Express
2 Sqn, Simpang
M48-02

Lockheed C-130 Hercules
14 Sqn, Labuan;
20 Sqn, Subang

M30-01 C-130H(MP)	20 Sqn
M30-02 C-130H	14 Sqn
M30-03 C-130H	14 Sqn
M30-04 C-130H-30	20 Sqn
M30-05 C-130H	14 Sqn
M30-06 C-130H	14 Sqn
M30-07 C-130T	20 Sqn
M30-08 C-130H(MP)	20 Sqn
M30-09 C-130H(MP)	20 Sqn
M30-10 C-130H-30	20 Sqn
M30-11 C-130H-30	20 Sqn
M30-12 C-130H-30	20 Sqn
M30-14 C-130H-30	20 Sqn
M30-15 C-130H-30	20 Sqn
M30-16 C-130H-30	20 Sqn

MEXICO
Fuerza Aérea Mexicana
Boeing 757-225
8° Grupo Aéreo, Mexico City
TP-01   (XC-UJM)

MOROCCO
Force Aérienne Royaume
Marocaine/Al Quwwat al
Jawwiya al Malakiya
Marakishiya

Airtech CN.235M-100
Escadrille de Transport,
Rabat

023	CNA-MA
024	CNA-MB
025	CNA-MC
026	CNA-MD
027	CNA-ME
028	CNA-MF
031	CNA-MG

CAP-231/CAP-232
Marche Verte
CAP-231

09	CN-ABL
22	CN-ABM
23	CN-ABN
24	CN-ABO

CAP-232

28	CNA-BP
29	CN-ABQ
31	CN-ABR
36	CNA-BS
37	CNA-BT

Lockheed C-130H
Hercules
Escadrille de Transport, Rabat

4535	CN-AOA
4551	CN-AOC
4575	CN-AOD
4581	CN-AOE
4583	CN-AOF
4713	CN-AOG
4717	CN-AOH
4733	CN-AOI
4738	CN-AOJ
4739	CN-AOK
4742	CN-AOL
4875	CN-AOM
4876	CN-AON
4877	CN-AOO
4888	CN-AOP
4892	CN-AOQ
4907	CN-AOR
4909	CN-AOS
4940	CN-AOT

Govt of Morocco
Boeing 707-138B
Govt of Morocco, Rabat
CNA-NS

Cessna 560 Citation V
Govt of Morocco, Rabat
CNA-NW

Dassault Falcon 50
Govt of Morocco, Rabat
CN-ANO

Grumman
G.1159 Gulfstream IITT/
G.1159A Gulfstream III
Govt of Morocco, Rabat

CNA-NL	Gulfstream IITT
CNA-NU	Gulfstream III
CNA-NV	Gulfstream III

NAMIBIA
Dassault Falcon 900B
Namibian Govt, Windhoek
V5-NAM

NETHERLANDS
Koninklijke Luchtmacht
Agusta-Bell AB.412SP
303 Sqn, Leeuwarden
R-01
R-02
R-03

Boeing-Vertol CH-47D
Chinook
298 Sqn, Soesterberg
D-101
D-102
D-103
D-104
D-105
D-106
D-661
D-662
D-663
D-664
D-665
D-666
D-667

Eurocopter AS.532U-2
Cougar
300 Sqn, Gilze-Rijen
S-400
S-419
S-433
S-438
S-440
S-441
S-442
S-444
S-445
S-447
S-450
S-453
S-454
S-456
S-457
S-458
S-459

Fokker 50
334 Sqn, Eindhoven
U-05
U-06

Fokker 60UTA-N
334 Sqn, Eindhoven
U-01
U-02
U-03
U-04

General Dynamics F-16
TGp/306/311/312 Sqns,
Volkel;
313/315 Sqns, Twenthe;
322/323 Sqns, Leeuwarden

J-001	F-16AM	322 Sqn
J-002	F-16AM	322 Sqn
J-003	F-16AM	322 Sqn
J-004	F-16AM	322 Sqn
J-005	F-16AM	322 Sqn
J-006	F-16AM	322 Sqn
J-008	F-16AM	322 Sqn
J-009	F-16AM	322 Sqn
J-010	F-16AM	322 Sqn
J-011	F-16AM	312 Sqn
J-013	F-16AM	322 Sqn
J-014	F-16AM	322 Sqn
J-015	F-16AM	315 Sqn
J-016	F-16AM	322 Sqn
J-017	F-16AM	312 Sqn
J-018	F-16AM	313 Sqn
J-019	F-16AM	323 Sqn
J-020	F-16AM	315 Sqn
J-021	F-16AM	311 Sqn
J-055	F-16AM	322 Sqn
J-057	F-16AM	323 Sqn
J-058	F-16AM	315 Sqn
J-060	F-16AM	315 Sqn
J-061	F-16AM	322 Sqn
J-062	F-16AM	322 Sqn
J-063	F-16AM	322 Sqn
J-064	F-16BM	322 Sqn
J-065	F-16BM	313 Sqn
J-066	F-16BM	TGp
J-067	F-16BM	315 Sqn
J-068	F-16BM	322 Sqn
J-135	F-16AM	311 Sqn
J-136	F-16AM	315 Sqn
J-137	F-16AM	322 Sqn
J-138	F-16AM	315 Sqn
J-139	F-16AM	323 Sqn
J-141	F-16AM	315 Sqn
J-142	F-16AM	323 Sqn
J-143	F-16AM	315 Sqn
J-144	F-16AM	315 Sqn
J-145	F-16AM	313 Sqn
J-146	F-16AM	313 Sqn
J-192	F-16AM	311 Sqn
J-193	F-16AM	312 Sqn
J-194	F-16AM	312 Sqn
J-196	F-16AM	323 Sqn
J-197	F-16AM	315 Sqn
J-198	F-16AM	315 Sqn
J-199	F-16AM	312 Sqn
J-201	F-16AM	312 Sqn
J-202	F-16AM	312 Sqn
J-203	F-16AM	311 Sqn
J-204	F-16AM	323 Sqn
J-205	F-16AM	322 Sqn
J-207	F-16AM	312 Sqn
J-208	F-16BM	312 Sqn
J-209	F-16BM	315 Sqn
J-210	F-16BM	312 Sqn
J-211	F-16BM	322 Sqn
J-251	F-16AM	306 Sqn
J-253	F-16AM	311 Sqn
J-254	F-16AM	311 Sqn
J-255	F-16AM	306 Sqn
J-257	F-16AM	306 Sqn
J-267	F-16BM	306 Sqn
J-269	F-16BM	306 Sqn
J-270	F-16BM	306 Sqn
J-360	F-16AM	323 Sqn
J-362	F-16AM	315 Sqn
J-363	F-16AM	323 Sqn
J-364	F-16AM	323 Sqn
J-365	F-16AM	313 Sqn
J-366	F-16AM	315 Sqn
J-367	F-16AM	322 Sqn
J-368	F-16BM	311 Sqn
J-369	F-16BM	315 Sqn
J-508	F-16AM	315 Sqn
J-509	F-16AM	315 Sqn
J-510	F-16AM	322 Sqn
J-511	F-16AM	313 Sqn

J-512	F-16AM	313 Sqn
J-513	F-16AM	323 Sqn
J-514	F-16AM	315 Sqn
J-515	F-16AM	322 Sqn
J-516	F-16AM	311 Sqn
J-616	F-16AM	315 Sqn
J-617	F-16AM	313 Sqn
J-619	F-16AM	313 Sqn
J-620	F-16AM	315 Sqn
J-622	F-16AM	323 Sqn
J-623	F-16AM	323 Sqn
J-624	F-16AM	311 Sqn
J-627	F-16AM	311 Sqn
J-628	F-16AM	315 Sqn
J-630	F-16AM	311 Sqn
J-631	F-16AM	311 Sqn
J-632	F-16AM	312 Sqn
J-633	F-16AM	312 Sqn
J-635	F-16AM	312 Sqn
J-636	F-16AM	311 Sqn
J-637	F-16AM	312 Sqn
J-638	F-16AM	312 Sqn
J-640	F-16AM	312 Sqn
J-641	F-16AM	311 Sqn
J-642	F-16AM	312 Sqn
J-643	F-16AM	322 Sqn
J-644	F-16AM	313 Sqn
J-646	F-16AM	306 Sqn
J-647	F-16AM	311 Sqn
J-648	F-16AM	312 Sqn
J-649	F-16BM	306 Sqn
J-650	F-16BM	323 Sqn
J-652	F-16BM	315 Sqn
J-653	F-16BM	312 Sqn
J-654	F-16BM	312 Sqn
J-655	F-16BM	306 Sqn
J-656	F-16BM	313 Sqn
J-657	F-16BM	313 Sqn
J-864	F-16AM	315 Sqn
J-866	F-16AM	312 Sqn
J-867	F-16AM	313 Sqn
J-868	F-16AM	311 Sqn
J-869	F-16AM	311 Sqn
J-870	F-16AM	313 Sqn
J-871	F-16AM	312 Sqn
J-872	F-16AM	312 Sqn
J-873	F-16AM	315 Sqn
J-874	F-16AM	311 Sqn
J-875	F-16AM	313 Sqn
J-876	F-16AM	311 Sqn
J-877	F-16AM	311 Sqn
J-878	F-16AM	311 Sqn
J-879	F-16AM	313 Sqn
J-881	F-16AM	323 Sqn
J-882	F-16BM	306 Sqn
J-884	F-16BM	311 Sqn
J-885	F-16BM	323 Sqn

**Grumman G-1159C
Gulfstream IV**
334 Sqn, Eindhoven
V-11

**Lockheed C-130H-30
Hercules**
334 Sqn, Eindhoven
G-273
G-275

**MBB Bo.105CB/
Bo.105CB-4***
931 Sqn, Gilze-Rijen
B-41*
B-44

B-47
B-68
B-76

**MDH AH-64D Apache
Longbow**
301 Sqn, Gilze-Rijen;
302 Sqn, Gilze-Rijen

Q-01	302 Sqn
Q-02	302 Sqn
Q-03	302 Sqn
Q-04	301 Sqn
Q-05	302 Sqn
Q-06	302 Sqn
Q-07	302 Sqn
Q-08	302 Sqn
Q-09	301 Sqn
Q-10	301 Sqn
Q-11	
Q-12	
Q-13	302 Sqn
Q-14	302 Sqn
Q-15	301 Sqn
Q-16	301 Sqn
Q-17	302 Sqn
Q-18	301 Sqn
Q-19	301 Sqn
Q-20	301 Sqn
Q-21	302 Sqn
Q-22	302 Sqn
Q-23	302 Sqn
Q-24	301 Sqn
Q-25	301 Sqn
Q-26	302 Sqn
Q-27	
Q-28	
Q-29	301 Sqn
Q-30	302 Sqn

**McDonnell Douglas
KDC-10**
334 Sqn, Eindhoven
T-235
T-264

Pilatus PC-7
131 EMVO Sqn,
Woensdrecht
L-01
L-02
L-03
L-04
L-05
L-06
L-07
L-08
L-09
L-10
L-11
L-12
L-13

Sud Alouette III
300 Sqn, Soesterberg
A-247
A-275
A-292
A-301

**Marine Luchtvaart Dienst
Beech Super King Air 200**
OVALK, Valkenburg
PH-SBK

Lockheed P-3C Orion
MARPAT (320 Sqn &
321 Sqn), Valkenburg
and Keflavik
300
301
302
303
304
305
307
308
309
312

Westland SH-14D Lynx
HELIGRP (7 Sqn &
860 Sqn), De Kooij
(7 Sqn operates
860 Sqn aircraft on loan)
261
262
264
265
267
268
269
270
271
276
277
280
281
283

**Netherlands Govt
Fokker 70**
Dutch Royal Flight, Schiphol
PH-KBX

NEW ZEALAND
**Royal New Zealand Air Force
Boeing 757-2K2**
40 Sqn, Whenuapai
NZ7571
NZ7572

**Lockheed C-130H
Hercules**
40 Sqn, Whenuapai
NZ7001
NZ7002
NZ7003
NZ7004
NZ7005

Lockheed P-3K Orion
5 Sqn, Whenuapai
NZ4201
NZ4202
NZ4203
NZ4204
NZ4205
NZ4206

NIGERIA
**Federal Nigerian Air Force
Lockheed C-130H/
C-130H-30* Hercules**
88 MAG, Lagos
NAF-910
NAF-912
NAF-913
NAF-917*

NAF-918*

Nigerian Govt
Boeing 727-2N6
Federal Govt of Nigeria,
Lagos
5N-FGN   [001]

Dassault Falcon 900
Federal Govt of Nigeria,
Lagos
5N-FGE
5N-FGO

Grumman
G.1159 Gulfstream II/
G.1159A Gulfstream III
Federal Govt of Nigeria,
Lagos
5N-AGV   Gulfstream II
5N-FGP   Gulfstream III
Gulfstream Aerospace
Gulfstream V
Federal Govt of Nigeria,
Lagos
5N-FGS

Hawker 1000
Federal Govt of Nigeria,
Lagos
5N-FGR

NORWAY
Luftforsvaret
Bell 412SP
339 Skv, Bardufoss;
720 Skv, Rygge

139	339 Skv
140	720 Skv
141	720 Skv
142	720 Skv
143	339 Skv
144	339 Skv
145	720 Skv
146	339 Skv
147	720 Skv
148	339 Skv
149	339 Skv
161	339 Skv
162	339 Skv
163	720 Skv
164	720 Skv
165	720 Skv
166	720 Skv
167	720 Skv
194	720 Skv

Dassault Falcon 20 ECM
717 Skv, Rygge
041
053
0125

General Dynamics F-16
(MLU aircraft are marked
with a *)
331 Skv, Bodø (r/w/bl);
332 Skv, Rygge (y/bk);
338 Skv, Ørland

272	F-16A*	332 Skv
273	F-16A*	332 Skv
275	F-16A*	332 Skv
276	F-16A	338 Skv
277	F-16A*	332 Skv
279	F-16A*	338 Skv
281	F-16A	332 Skv
282	F-16A*	332 Skv
284	F-16A*	338 Skv
285	F-16A*	338 Skv
286	F-16A*	338 Skv
288	F-16A*	338 Skv
289	F-16A*	332 Skv
291	F-16A*	338 Skv
292	F-16A*	338 Skv
293	F-16A*	332 Skv
295	F-16A*	338 Skv
297	F-16A*	332 Skv
298	F-16A*	331 Skv
299	F-16A*	331 Skv
302	F-16B*	332 Skv
304	F-16B*	338 Skv
305	F-16B*	338 Skv
306	F-16B*	332 Skv
658	F-16A*	338 Skv
659	F-16A*	338 Skv
660	F-16A*	331 Skv
661	F-16A*	338 Skv
662	F-16A*	338 Skv
663	F-16A*	331 Skv
664	F-16A*	331 Skv
665	F-16A*	331 Skv
666	F-16A*	
667	F-16A*	331 Skv
668	F-16A*	331 Skv
669	F-16A*	331 Skv
670	F-16A*	332 Skv
671	F-16A*	338 Skv
672	F-16A	
673	F-16A*	331 Skv
674	F-16A	331 Skv
675	F-16A*	338 Skv
677	F-16A*	331 Skv
678	F-16A*	331 Skv
680	F-16A*	331 Skv
681	F-16A*	331 Skv
682	F-16A*	331 Skv
683	F-16A*	331 Skv
686	F-16A*	331 Skv
687	F-16A*	331 Skv
688	F-16A*	331 Skv
689	F-16B*	332 Skv
690	F-16B*	338 Skv
691	F-16B*	338 Skv
692	F-16B*	332 Skv
693	F-16B*	338 Skv
711	F-16B*	338 Skv

Lockheed C-130H Hercules
335 Skv, Gardermoen
952
953
954
955
956
957

Lockheed P-3C Orion
333 Skv, Andøya
3296
3297
3298
3299

Lockheed P-3N Orion
333 Skv, Andøya
4576
6603

Northrop F-5A
Eye of the Tiger Project,
Rygge
128
130
131
133
134
896
902

Northrop F-5B
Eye of the Tiger Project,
Rygge
136
243
244
387
906
907
908
909

Westland Sea King Mk 43/
Mk 43A/Mk 43B
330 Skv:
A Flt, Bodø;
B Flt, Banak;
C Flt, Ørland;
D Flt, Sola

060	Mk 43
062	Mk 43
066	Mk 43
069	Mk 43
070	Mk 43
071	Mk 43B
072	Mk 43
073	Mk 43
074	Mk 43
189	Mk 43A
322	Mk 43B
329	Mk 43B
330	Mk 43B

Kystvakt (Coast Guard)
Westland Lynx Mk86
337 Skv, Bardufoss
207
216
228
232
237
350

OMAN
Royal Air Force of Oman
BAC 1-11/485GD
4 Sqn, Seeb
551
552
553

Lockheed C-130H
Hercules
4 Sqn, Seeb
501
502
503

Omani Govt
Boeing 747SP-27
Govt of Oman, Seeb
A4O-SO
A4O-SP

Boeing 747-430
Govt of Oman, Seeb
A4O-OMN

Grumman G.1159C
Gulfstream IV
Govt of Oman, Seeb
A4O-AB
A4O-AC

PAKISTAN
Pakistan Fiza'ya
  Boeing 707-340C
  68-19635 12 Sqn
  68-19866 12 Sqn

Pakistani Govt
  Boeing 737-33A
  Govt of Pakistan, Karachi
  AP-BEH

PERU
Fuerza Aérea Peruana
  Douglas DC-8-62AF
  370 (OB-1372)
  371 (OB-1373)

POLAND
Polskie Wojska Lotnicze
  Antonov An-26
  13 ELTR, Krakow/Balice
  1307
  1310
  1402
  1403
  1406
  1407
  1508
  1509
  1602
  1603
  1604

  CASA 295M
  13 ELTR, Krakow/Balice
  011
  012

  Mikoyan MiG-29A/UB*
  1 ELT, Minsk/Mazowiecki;
  41 ELT, Malbork
  01   41 ELT
  02   41 ELT
  04*   41 ELT
  06   41 ELT
  08   41 ELT
  10   41 ELT
  11   41 ELT
  13   41 ELT
  15*   1 ELT
  18   41 ELT
  19   41 ELT
  24   41 ELT
  26*   41 ELT
  28*   1 ELT
  32   41 ELT
  38   1 ELT
  40   1 ELT
  42*   1 ELT
  48*   41 ELT
  54   1 ELT
  56   1 ELT
  59   1 ELT
  64*   1 ELT

65   1 ELT
66   1 ELT
67   1 ELT
70   1 ELT
77   1 ELT
83   1 ELT
86   1 ELT
92   1 ELT
105   1 ELT
108   1 ELT
111   1 ELT
114   1 ELT
115   1 ELT
128   41 ELT
300   41 ELT
310   41 ELT
314   41 ELT
315   41 ELT
408* 41 ELT
800   41 ELT
5115 41 ELT

PZL M28 Bryza
13 ELTR, Balice;
LGPR, Bydgoszcz
0203   M28B-1   13 ELTR
0204   M28B-1   13 ELTR
0723   M28RL   LGPR
1003   M28TD   13 ELTR

Tupolev Tu-154M
36 SPLT, Warszawa
101
102

Yakovlev Yak-40
36 SPLT, Warszawa
032
034
036
037
038
040
041
042
043
044
045
047
048

Lotnictwo Marynarki
Wojennej
  PZL M28 Bryza
  1 DLMW, Gydnia/Babie
    Doly;
  3 DLMW, Cewice/
    Siemirowice
  0404   M28B-E   1 DLMW
  0405   M28B-E   1 DLMW
  0810   M28B-1R   PZL
  1006   M28B-1R   3 DLMW
  1007   M28B-1   1 DLMW
  1008   M28B-1R   3 DLMW
  1017   M28B-1R   3 DLMW
  1022   M28B-1R   3 DLMW
  1114   M28B-1R   3 DLMW
  1115   M28B-1R   3 DLMW
  1116   M28B-1R   3 DLMW
  1117   M28B-1   1 DLMW
  1118   M28B-1   1 DLMW

PORTUGAL
Força Aérea Portuguesa

Aérospatiale
SA.330C Puma
Esq 711, Lajes;
Esq 751, Montijo
19502   Esq 751
19503   Esq 751
19504   Esq 751
19505   Esq 751
19506   Esq 711
19508   Esq 711
19509   Esq 751
19511   Esq 711
19512   Esq 751
19513   Esq 711

CASA 212A/212ECM*
Aviocar
Esq 401, Sintra;
Esq 501, Sintra;
Esq 502, Sintra;
Esq 711, Lajes
16501*   Esq 501
16502*   Esq 501
16503   Esq 501
16504   Esq 501
16505   Esq 502
16506   Esq 502
16507   Esq 502
16508   Esq 502
16509   Esq 501
16510   Esq 401
16511   Esq 502
16512   Esq 401
16513   Esq 711
16514   Esq 711
16515   Esq 711
16517   Esq 711
16519   Esq 401
16520   Esq 711
16521*   Esq 401
16522*   Esq 401
16523*   Esq 401
16524*   Esq 401

CASA 212-300 Aviocar
Esq 401, Sintra
17201
17202

D-BD Alpha Jet
Esq 103, Beja;
Esq 301, Beja
15201
15202
15204
15205
15206
15208
15209
15210
15211
15213
15214
15215
15216
15217
15218
15219
15220
15221
15222
15223
15224
15225

15226
15227
15228
15229
15230
15231
15232
15233
15235
15236
15237
15238
15239
15240
15241
15242
15243
15244
15246
15247
15250

Dassault Falcon 20DC
Esq 504, Lisbon/Montijo
17103

Dassault Falcon 50
Esq 504, Lisbon/Montijo
17401
17402
17403

Lockheed C-130H/
C-130H-30* Hercules
Esq 501, Lisbon/Montijo
16801*
16802*
16803
16804
16805
16806*

Lockheed (GD)
F-16A/F-16B*
Esq 201, Monte Real;
Esq 304, Monte Real
15101   Esq 201
15102   Esq 201
15103   Esq 201
15104   Esq 201
15105   Esq 201
15106   Esq 201
15107   Esq 201
15108   Esq 201
15109   Esq 201
15110   Esq 201
15112   Esq 201
15113   Esq 201
15114   Esq 201
15115   Esq 201
15116   Esq 201
15117   Esq 201
15118*   Esq 201
15119*   Esq 201
15120*   Esq 201
15121   Esq 304
15122   Esq 304
15123   Esq 304
15124   Esq 304
15125   Esq 304
15126   Esq 304
15127   Esq 304
15128   Esq 304
15129   Esq 304

15130   Esq 304
15131   Esq 304
15132   Esq 304
15133   Esq 304
15134   Esq 304
15135   Esq 304
15136   Esq 304
15137   Esq 304
15138   Esq 304
15139*   Esq 304
15140*   Esq 304
15141*   Esq 304

Lockheed P-3P Orion
Esq 601, Lisbon/Montijo
14801
14802
14803
14804
14805
14806

Marinha
Westland Super Lynx Mk 95
Esq de Helicopteros,
   Lisbon/Montijo
19201
19202
19203
19204
19205

QATAR
Airbus A.310-304
Qatari Govt, Doha
A7-AAF

Airbus A.319CJ-133
Qatari Govt, Doha
A7-HHJ

Airbus A.320-232
Qatari Govt, Doha
A7-AAG

Airbus A.340-211/-541*
Qatari Govt, Doha
A7-HHH*
A7-HHK

ROMANIA
Fortele Aeriene Romania
Lockheed C-130B
Hercules
19 FMT, Bucharest/Otapeni
5927
5930
6150
6166

RUSSIA
Voenno-Vozdushniye Sily
Rossioki Federatsii (Russian
Air Force)
Sukhoi Su-27
TsAGI, Gromov Flight
   Institute, Zhukhovsky
595   Su-27P
597   Su-30
598   Su-27P

Russian Govt
Ilyushin Il-62M
Russian Govt, Moscow
RA-86466
RA-86467
RA-86468
RA-86536
RA-86537
RA-86540
RA-86553
RA-86554
RA-86559
RA-86561
RA-86710
RA-86711
RA-86712

Ilyushin Il-96-300
Russian Govt, Moscow
RA-96012
RA-96016

Tupolev Tu-134A
Russian Govt, Moscow
RA-65904

Tupolev Tu-154B-2
Russian Govt, Moscow
RA-85426
RA-85594

Tupolev Tu-154M
Russian Govt, Moscow;
Open Skies*
RA-85629
RA-85630
RA-85631
RA-85645
RA-85651
RA-85653
RA-85655*
RA-85658
RA-85659
RA-85666
RA-85675
RA-85676
RA-85843

SAUDI ARABIA
Al Quwwat al Jawwiya
as Sa'udiya
BAe 125-800/-800B*
1 Sqn, Riyadh
HZ-105
HZ-109*
HZ-110*

Boeing 737-7DP/-8DP*
1 Sqn, Riyadh
HZ-101*
HZ-102

Boeing E-3A/KE-3A/
RE-3A Sentry
18 Sqn, Riyadh;
19 Sqn, Riyadh
1801 E-3A
1802 E-3A
1803 E-3A
1804 E-3A
1805 E-3A
1811 KE-3A
1812 KE-3A
1813 KE-3A

1814 KE-3A
1815 KE-3A
1816 KE-3A
1818 KE-3A
1901 RE-3A

Grumman G.1159A
Gulfstream III/G.1159C
Gulfstream IV
1 Sqn, Riyadh
HZ-108   Gulfstream III

Lockheed C-130/L.100
Hercules
1 Sqn, Prince Sultan AB;
4 Sqn, Jeddah;
16 Sqn, Prince Sultan AB;
32 Sqn, Prince Sultan AB

111	VC-130H	1 Sqn
112	VC-130H	1 Sqn
451	C-130E	4 Sqn
452	C-130E	4 Sqn
455	C-130E	4 Sqn
461	C-130H	4 Sqn
462	C-130H	4 Sqn
463	C-130H	4 Sqn
464	C-130H	4 Sqn
465	C-130H	4 Sqn
466	C-130H	4 Sqn
467	C-130H	4 Sqn
468	C-130H	4 Sqn
471	C-130H-30	4 Sqn
472	C-130H	4 Sqn
473	C-130H	4 Sqn
474	C-130H	4 Sqn
475	C-130H	4 Sqn
476	C-130E	4 Sqn
477	C-130H	4 Sqn
1601	C-130H	16 Sqn
1602	C-130H	16 Sqn
1603	C-130H	16 Sqn
1604	C-130H	16 Sqn
1605	C-130E	16 Sqn
1606	C-130E	16 Sqn
1607	C-130E	16 Sqn
1608	C-130E	16 Sqn
1609	C-130E	16 Sqn
1611	C-130E	16 Sqn
1614	C-130H	16 Sqn
1615	C-130H	16 Sqn
1618	C-130H	16 Sqn
1619	C-130H	16 Sqn
1622	C-130H-30	16 Sqn
1623	C-130H-30	16 Sqn
1624	C-130H	16 Sqn
1625	C-130H	16 Sqn
1626	C-130H	16 Sqn
3201	KC-130H	32 Sqn
3202	KC-130H	32 Sqn
3203	KC-130H	32 Sqn
3204	KC-130H	32 Sqn
3205	KC-130H	32 Sqn
3206	KC-130H	32 Sqn
3207	KC-130H	32 Sqn
HZ-114	VC-130H	1 Sqn
HZ-115	VC-130H	1 Sqn
HZ-116	VC-130H	1 Sqn
HZ-117	L.100-30	1 Sqn
HZ-128	L.100-30	1 Sqn
HZ-129	L.100-30	1 Sqn

Saudi Govt
Airbus A.340-211
Royal Embassy of Saudi
   Arabia, Riyadh
HZ-124

Boeing 737-268
Saudi Royal Flight, Jeddah
HZ-HM4

Boeing 747-3G1
Saudi Royal Flight, Jeddah
HZ-HM1A

Boeing 747SP-68
Saudi Govt, Jeddah;
Saudi Royal Flight, Jeddah
HZ-AIF   Govt
HZ-AIJ   Royal Flight
HZ-HM1B Royal Flight

Boeing MD-11
Saudi Royal Flight, Jeddah
HZ-AFA1
HZ-HM7

Canadair CL.604
Challenger
Saudi Royal Flight, Jeddah
HZ-AFA2

Dassault Falcon 900
Saudi Govt, Jeddah
HZ-AFT
HZ-AFZ

Grumman G.1159A
Gulfstream III
Armed Forces Medical
   Services, Riyadh;
Saudi Govt, Jeddah
HZ-AFN   Govt
HZ-AFR   Govt
HZ-MS3   AFMS

Grumman G.1159C
Gulfstream IV
Armed Forces Medical
   Services, Riyadh;
Saudi Govt, Jeddah
HZ-AFU   Govt
HZ-AFV   Govt
HZ-AFW   Govt
HZ-AFX   Govt
HZ-AFY   Govt
HZ-MS4   AFMS

Gulfstream Aerospace
Gulfstream V
Armed Forces Medical
   Services, Riyadh
HZ-MS5
HZ-MS5A

Lockheed C-130H/
L.100 Hercules
Armed Forces Medical
   Services, Riyadh
HZ-MS6   L.100-30
HZ-MS7   C-130H
HZ-MS8   C-130H-30
HZ-MS09   L.100-30
HZ-MS019   C-130H

Lockheed L.1011 TriStar 500
Saudi Royal Flight, Jeddah
HZ-HM5
HZ-HM6

SINGAPORE
Republic of Singapore Air Force
Boeing KC-135R
Stratotanker
750
751
752
753

Lockheed C-130 Hercules
122 Sqn, Paya Labar

720	KC-130B
721	KC-130B
724	KC-130B
725	KC-130B
730	C-130H
731	C-130H
732	C-130H
733	C-130H
734	KC-130H
735	C-130H

SLOVAKIA
Slovenske Vojenske Letectvo
Aero L-39 Albatros
31 SLK/3 Letka, Sliač [SL];
VSL, Koštice;
White Albatroses,
   Koštice (WA)

0101	L-39C	WA [4]
0102	L-39C	WA [6]
0103	L-39C	VSL
0111	L-39C	WA [5]
0112	L-39C	WA [1]
0442	L-39C	WA [2]
0443	L-39C	WA [7]
0730	L-39V	VSL
0745	L-39V	VSL
1701	L-39ZA	31 SLK
1725	L-39ZA	31 SLK
1730	L-39ZA	31 SLK
4701	L-39ZA	31 SLK
4703	L-39ZA	31 SLK
4707	L-39ZA	31 SLK
4711	L-39ZA	31 SLK

Antonov An-24V
32 ZmDK/1 Letka, Piešťany
2903
5605

Antonov An-26
32 ZmDK/1 Letka, Piešťany
2506
3208

LET 410 Turbolet
31 SLK/4 Letka, Sliač [SL];
32 ZmDK/1 Letka, Piešťany;
VSL, Košice

0730	L-410UVP	32 ZmDK
0927	L-410T	31 SLK
0930	L-410T	32 ZmDK
1133	L-410T	VSL
1203	L-410FG	32 ZmDK
1521	L-410FG	32 ZmDK
2311	L-410UVP	32 ZmDK

Mikoyan MiG-29A/UB*
31 SLK/1 & 2 Letka,
  Sliač [SL]
0619
0820
0921
1303*
2123
3709
3911
4401*
5113
5304*
5515
5817
6124
6425
6526
6627
6728
7501
8003
8605
9308

Sukhoi Su-25K/UBK*
33 SBoLK/2 Letka, Malacky
1006
1007
1008
1027
3237*
5033
5036
6017
6018
8072
8073
8074
8075

Slovak Govt
  Tupolev Tu-154M
  Slovak Govt,
    Bratislava/Ivanka
  OM-BYO
  OM-BYR

  Yakovlev Yak-40
  Slovak Govt,
    Bratislava/Ivanka
  OM-BYE
  OM-BYL

SLOVENIA
Slovene Army
  LET 410UVP-E
  15 Brigada, Ljubljana
  L4-01
  Pilatus PC-9M
  15 Brigada, Ljubljana
  L9-51
  L9-52
  L9-53
  L9-54
  L9-55
  L9-56
  L9-57
  L9-58
  L9-59
  L9-60
  L9-61
  L9-62
  L9-63

L9-64
L9-65
L9-66
L9-67
L9-68
L9-69

Slovenian Govt
  Gates LearJet
  Slovenian Govt, Ljubljana
  S5-BAA   LearJet 35A
  S5-BAB   LearJet 24D

SOUTH AFRICA
South African Air Force/
  Suid Afrikaanse Lugmag
  Boeing 707
  60 Sqn, Waterkloof
  1415   328C
  1417   328C
  1419   328C
  1423   344C

  Boeing 737-7ED
  21 Sqn, Waterkloof
  ZS-RSA

  Dassault Falcon 900
  21 Sqn, Waterkloof
  ZS-NAN

  **Lockheed C-130B/
  C-130BZ* Hercules**
  28 Sqn, Waterkloof
  401
  402*
  403
  404
  405*
  406*
  407*
  408*
  409*

SPAIN
Ejército del Aire
  Airbus A.310-304
  Grupo 45, Torrejón
  T.22-1   45-50
  T.22-2   45-51

  **Airtech
  CN.235M-10 (T.19A)/
  CN.235M-100 (T.19B)**
  Ala 35, Getafe

T.19A-01	35-60	
T.19A-02	35-61	
T.19B-03	35-21	
T.19B-04	35-22	
T.19B-05	35-23	
T.19B-06	35-24	
T.19B-07	35-25	
T.19B-08	35-26	
T.19B-09	35-27	
T.19B-10	35-28	
T.19B-11	35-29	
T.19B-12	35-30	
T.19B-13	35-31	
T.19B-14	35-32	
T.19B-15	35-33	
T.19B-16	35-34	
T.19B-17	35-35	
T.19B-18	35-36	
T.19B-19	35-37	
T.19B-20	35-38	

Boeing 707
408 Esc, Torrejón;
Grupo 45, Torrejón

T.17-1	331B	45-10
T.17-2	331B	45-11
T.17-3	368C	45-12
TM.17-4	351C	408-21

CASA 101EB Aviojet
Grupo 54, Torrejón;
Grupo de Escuelas de
  Matacán (74);
AGA, San Javier (79);
Patrulla Aguila, San Javier*

E.25-01	79-01	
E.25-05	79-05	
E.25-06	79-06	[2]*
E.25-07	79-07	[7]*
E.25-08	79-08	[1]*
E.25-09	79-09	
E.25-10	79-10	
E.25-11	79-11	
E.25-12	79-12	
E.25-13	79-13	
E.25-14	79-14	
E.25-15	79-15	
E.25-16	79-16	
E.25-17	74-40	
E.25-18	74-42	
E.25-19	79-19	
E.25-20	79-20	
E.25-21	79-21	
E.25-22	79-22	
E.25-23	79-23	[4]*
E.25-24	79-24	
E.25-25	79-25	
E.25-26	79-26	[3]*
E.25-27	79-27	
E.25-28	79-28	
E.25-29	74-45	
E.25-31	79-31	
E.25-33	74-02	
E.25-34	79-34	
E.25-35	54-20	
E.25-37	79-37	
E.25-38	79-38	
E.25-40	79-40	
E.25-41	74-41	
E.25-43	74-43	
E.25-44	79-44	
E.25-45	79-45	
E.25-46	79-46	
E.25-47	79-47	
E.25-48	79-48	
E.25-49	79-49	
E.25-50	79-33	
E.25-51	74-07	
E.25-52	79-34	[6]*
E.25-53	74-09	
E.25-54	79-35	
E.25-55	54-21	
E.25-56	74-11	
E.25-57	74-12	
E.25-59	74-13	
E.25-61	54-22	
E.25-62	79-17	
E.25-63	74-17	
E.25-64	79-18	
E.25-65	79-95	
E.25-66	74-20	
E.25-67	74-21	
E.25-68	74-22	

Spain

E.25-69	79-97
E.25-71	74-25
E.25-72	74-26
E.25-73	79-98
E.25-74	74-28
E.25-75	74-29
E.25-76	74-30
E.25-78	79-02
E.25-79	79-39
E.25-80	79-03
E.25-81	74-34
E.25-83	74-35
E.25-84	79-04
E.25-86	79-32 [5]*
E.25-87	79-29
E.25-88	74-39

CASA 212 Aviocar
**212 (XT.12)/
212A (T.12B)/
212B (TR.12A)/
212D (TE.12B)/
212DE (TM.12D)/
212E (T.12C)/
212S (D.3A)/
212S1 (D.3B)/
212-200 (T.12D)/
212-200 (TR.12D)**
Ala 37, Villanubla;
Ala 46, Gando, Las Palmas;
CLAEX, Torrejón (54);
Ala 72, Alcantarilla;
Grupo Esc, Matacán (74);
AGA (Ala 79), San Javier;
403 Esc, Getafe;
408 Esc, Torrejón;
801 Esc, Palma/
Son San Juan;
803 Esc, Cuatro Vientos;
INTA, Torrejón

D.3A-1	(801 Esc)
D.3A-2	(803 Esc)
D.3B-3	(803 Esc)
D.3B-4	(801 Esc)
D.3B-5	(801 Esc)
D.3B-6	(801 Esc)
D.3B-7	(803 Esc)
D.3B-8	(801 Esc)
XT.12A-1	54-10
TR.12A-4	403-02
TR.12A-5	403-03
TR.12A-6	403-04
TR.12A-8	403-06
T.12B-9	74-83
TE.12B-10	79-92
T.12B-12	74-82
T.12B-13	74-70
T.12B-14	37-01
T.12B-15	37-02
T.12B-16	74-71
T.12B-17	37-03
T.12B-18	46-31
T.12B-19	46-32
T.12B-20	37-04
T.12B-21	37-05
T.12B-22	37-06
T.12B-23	72-01
T.12B-24	54-12
T.12B-25	74-72
T.12B-26	72-02
T.12B-27	46-33
T.12B-28	72-03
T.12B-29	37-08
T.12B-30	74-73

T.12B-31	46-34
T.12B-33	72-04
T.12B-34	74-74
T.12B-35	37-09
T.12B-36	37-10
T.12B-37	72-05
T.12B-39	74-75
TE.12B-40	79-93
TE.12B-41	79-94
T.12C-43	46-50
T.12C-44	37-50
T.12B-46	74-76
T.12B-47	72-06
T.12B-48	37-11
T.12B-49	72-07
T.12B-52	46-35
T.12B-53	46-36
T.12B-54	46-37
T.12B-55	46-38
T.12B-56	74-79
T.12B-57	72-08
T.12C-59	37-51
T.12C-60	37-52
T.12C-61	37-53
T.12B-63	37-14
T.12B-64	46-40
T.12B-65	74-80
T.12B-66	72-09
T.12B-67	74-81
T.12B-68	37-15
T.12B-69	37-16
T.12B-70	37-17
T.12B-71	37-18
TM.12D-72	408-01
TM.12D-74	54-11
T.12D-75	403-07
TR.12D-76	37-60
TR.12D-77	37-61
TR.12D-78	37-62
TR.12D-79	37-63
TR.12D-80	37-64
TR.12D-81	37-65

CASA 295
Ala 35, Getafe

T.21-01	35-39
T.21-02	35-40
T.21-03	35-41
T.21-04	35-42
T.21-05	35-43
T.21-06	35-44
T.21-07	35-45
T.21-08	35-46
T.21-09	35-47

Cessna 560 Citation VI
403 Esc, Getafe

TR.20-01	403-11
TR.20-02	403-12

Dassault Falcon 20D/E/F
Grupo 45, Torrejón;
408 Esc, Torrejón

TM.11-1	20E	45-02
TM.11-2	20D	45-03
TM.11-3	20D	408-11
TM.11-4	20E	408-12

Dassault Falcon 900/900B*
Grupo 45, Torrejón

T.18-1	45-40
T.18-2	45-41
T.18-3*	45-42
T.18-4*	45-43

T.18-5*	45-44

Eurofighter EF.2000T Typhoon
Ala 11, Moron
CASA, Getafe

XC.16-02	CASA
XCE.16-01	Ala 11

Fokker F.27M Friendship 400MPA
802 Esc, Gando, Las Palmas

D.2-01	802-10
D.2-02	802-11
D.2-03	802-12

Lockheed C-130H/ C-130H-30/KC-130H Hercules
311 Esc/312 Esc (Ala 31), Zaragoza

TL.10-01	C-130H-30	31-01
T.10-02	C-130H	31-02
T.10-03	C-130H	31-03
T.10-04	C-130H	31-04
TK.10-5	KC-130H	31-50
TK.10-6	KC-130H	31-51
TK.10-7	KC-130H	31-52
T.10-8	C-130H	31-05
T.10-9	C-130H	31-06
T.10-10	C-130H	31-07
TK.10-11	KC-130H	31-53
TK.10-12	KC-130H	31-54

Lockheed P-3A/P-3B/P-3M Orion
Grupo 22, Morón

P.3-01	P-3A	22-21
P.3-03	P-3A	22-22
P.3-08	P-3B	22-31*
P.3-09	P-3M	22-32*
P.3-10	P-3B	22-33*
P.3-11	P-3B	22-34*
P.3-12	P-3B	22-35*

McDonnell Douglas F-18 Hornet
Ala 11, Morón;
Ala 12, Torrejón;
Ala 15, Zaragoza;
Esc 462, Gran Canaria
EF-18A/EF-18B* Hornet

CE.15-1	15-70*
CE.15-2	15-71*
CE.15-3	15-72*
CE.15-4	15-73*
CE.15-5	15-74*
CE.15-6	15-75*
CE.15-7	15-76*
CE.15-8	12-71*
CE.15-9	15-77*
CE.15-10	12-73*
CE.15-11	12-74*
CE.15-12	12-75*
C.15-13	12-01
C.15-14	15-01
C.15-15	15-02
C.15-16	15-03
C.15-18	15-05
C.15-20	15-07
C.15-21	15-08
C.15-22	15-09
C.15-23	15-10

C.15-24	15-11
C.15-25	15-12
C.15-26	15-13
C.15-27	15-14
C.15-28	15-15
C.15-29	15-16
C.15-30	15-17
C.15-31	15-18
C.15-32	15-19
C.15-33	15-20
C.15-34	15-21
C.15-35	15-22
C.15-36	15-23
C.15-37	15-24
C.15-38	15-25
C.15-39	15-26
C.15-40	15-27
C.15-41	15-28
C.15-43	15-30
C.15-44	12-02
C.15-45	12-03
C.15-46	12-04
C.15-47	15-31
C.15-48	12-06
C.15-49	12-07
C.15-50	12-08
C.15-51	12-09
C.15-52	12-10
C.15-53	12-11
C.15-54	12-12
C.15-55	12-13
C.15-56	12-14
C.15-57	12-15
C.15-58	12-16
C.15-59	12-17
C.15-60	12-18
C.15-61	12-19
C.15-62	12-20
C.15-64	12-22
C.15-65	12-23
C.15-66	12-24
C.15-67	15-33
C.15-68	12-26
C.15-69	12-27
C.15-70	12-28
C.15-72	12-30

F/A-18A Hornet

C.15-73	11-01
C.15-74	46-02
C.15-75	46-03
C.15-76	21-04
C.15-77	21-05
C.15-78	46-06
C.15-79	46-07
C.15-80	21-08
C.15-81	11-09
C.15-82	46-10
C.15-83	46-11
C.15-84	46-12
C.15-85	46-13
C.15-86	11-14
C.15-87	46-15
C.15-88	46-16
C.15-89	21-17
C.15-90	46-18
C.15-92	46-20
C.15-93	46-21
C.15-94	46-22
C.15-95	46-23
C.15-96	46-24

**Arma Aérea de l'Armada
Española
BAe/McDonnell Douglas
EAV-8B/EAV-8B+/
TAV-8B Harrier II**
Esc 009, Rota
EAV-8B

VA.1A-15	01-903
VA.1A-18	01-906
VA.1A-19	01-907
VA.1A-21	01-909
VA.1A-22	01-910
VA.1A-23	01-911
VA.1A-24	01-912

EAV-8B+

VA.1B-25	01-914
VA.1B-26	01-915
VA.1B-27	01-916
VA.1B-28	01-917
VA.1B-29	01-918
VA.1B-30	01-919
VA.1B-31	01-920
VA.1B-34	01-923
VA.1B-35	01-924

TAV-8B

VAE.1A-33	01-922

Cessna 550 Citation 2
Esc 004, Rota

U.20-1	01-405
U.20-2	01-406
U.20-3	01-407

**SUDAN
Dassault Falcon 900B**
Sudanese Govt, Khartoum
ST-PSA

**SWEDEN
Svenska Flygvapnet
Beechcraft Super King
Air (Tp.101)**
Flottiljer 7, Såtenäs;
Flottiljer 17, Ronneby/
Kallinge;
Flottiljer 21, Luleå/
Kallax

101002	012	F21
101003	013	F17
101004	014	F7

**Grumman G.1159C
Gulfstream 4
(Tp.102A/S.102B Korpen/
Tp.102C)**
Flottiljer 17M, Stockholm/
Bromma & Uppsala
Tp.102A

102001	021

S.102B Korpen

102002	022
102003	023

Tp.102C

102004	024

**Lockheed C-130 Hercules
(Tp.84)**
Flottiljer 7, Såtenäs

84001	841	C-130E
84002	842	C-130E
84003	843	C-130H
84004	844	C-130H
84005	845	C-130H
84006	846	C-130H

84007	847	C-130H
84008	848	C-130H

**Rockwell Sabreliner-40
(Tp.86)**
FMV, Malmslätt

86001	861
86002	862

SAAB 37 Viggen
Flottiljer 4, Östersund/
Frösön;
Flottiljer 21, Luleå/Kallax;
FMV, Malmslätt
JA 37/JA 37Dᴰ/JA 37DIᴵ

37311	03	F21
37318	58	
37319	59	
37320	60	
37325	25	F4
37326ᴵ	26	FMV
37327	08	
37331	31	F4
37341	41	F4
37343	43	F4
37347ᴰ	43	SAAB
37350	50	F21
37353	33	F21
37357	57	F4
37363	10	F21
37366	13	SAAB
37369	16	F21
37370	17	F21
37371	18	F21
37375	25	
37377	37	F4
37379	15	F21
37380	50	F4
37382	52	F4
37385	55	F4
37386ᴰ	46	F4
37388	58	F4
37390	60	F4
37394	47	
37395	65	
37397ᴵ	20	F4
37398ᴵ	08	F4
37401ᴵ	01	F4
37404ᴰ	24	
37405	25	F21
37406	26	F4
37407	27	F21
37409	29	F21
37412ᴰ	12	F4
37413ᴰ	13	F4
37414ᴵ	14	F4
37415ᴵ	15	
37418ᴰ	18	F4
37421ᴵ	21	F4
37422ᴵ	22	F4
37424ᴵ	24	F4
37426ᴵ	26	
37428ᴵ	28	F4
37429D	29	F4
37433	33	
37434	34	
37436ᴵ	32	F4
37437ᴵ	37	F4
37438ᴰ	38	F4
37439	01	F4
37440ᴵ	40	F4
37442ᴵ	52	
37443ᴰ	43	F4
37444ᴵ	04	F4

Sweden

37445ᴰ	45	F4	39135	135	F10	39802	802	FMV
37446ⁱ	06	F4	39136	36	F17	39803	803	F7
37449ʲ	49	F4	39137	137	F10	39804	804	F7
Sk 37/Sk 37E*			39138	138	F17	39805	805	F7
37801	80	F4	39139	39	F10	39806	806	F7
37807*	70	F21	39140	140	F17	39807	807	F7
37808*	71	F21	39141	41	FMV	39808	808	FMV
37809*	72	F21	39142	42	F7	39809	809	F21
37811*	73	F21	39143	43	F10	39810		
37813*	74	F21	39144	44	F10	39811	811	FMV
37814*	76	F21	39145	45	F17	39812		
37817*	75	F21	39146	46	F17	39813	813	FMV
AJSH 37			39147	147	F17	39814	814	FMV
37901	51	F21	39148	48	F10	**JAS 39C**		
37903	53	F21	39149	149	F7	39-6	6	SAAB
37911	33	F21	39150	50	F10	39208	208	SAAB
37913			39151	51	F7	39209	209	FMV
37916	37	FMV	39152	52	F7	39210	210	SAAB
37918	57	F21	39153	53	F10	39211	211	SAAB
37922	61	F21	39154	54	F7	39212	212	FMV
AJSF 37			39155	55	F7	39213		
37950	48	F21	39157	157	F17	39214		
37951	50	F21	39158	58	F7	39215		
37954	54	F21	39159	59	F7	39216	216	FMV
37957	56	F21	39160	60	F7	39217		
37958	58	F21	39161	61	F7	39218		
37960	60	F21	39162	162	F17	39219		
37971	62	F21	39163	163	F17	39220		
37974	64	F21	39164	64	F17	39221		
37976	66	F21	39165	165	F17	39222		
			39166	66	F7	39223		
SAAB JAS 39 Gripen			39167	167	F17	39224		
Flottiljer 7, Såtenäs [G];			39168	168	F10	39225		
Flottiljer 10, Angelholm;			39169	169	F7	39226		
Flottiljer 17, Ronneby/			39170	170	F17	39227		
Kallinge;			39171	171	F10	39228		
Flottiljer 21, Luleå/			39172	172	F17	39229		
Kallax			39173	173	F17	39230		
FMV, Malmslätt			39174	174	F17	39231		
JAS 39			39175	175	F17	39232		
39-5	55	FMV	39176	176	F17	39233		
JAS 39A			39177	177	F21	39234		
39101	51	FMV	39178	178	F10	39235		
39103	103	FMV	39179	179	F17	39236		
39104	04	F7	39180	180	F10	39237		
39105	105	F10	39181	181	F7	39238		
39106	106	F10	39182	182	F7	39239		
39107	107	F7	39183	183	F17	39240		
39108	108	F7	39184	184	F17			
39109	09	F7	39185	185	FMV	**SAAB SF.340 (OS.100)*/**		
39110	10	F7	39186	186	F7	**SF.340AEW&C (S.100B)**		
39111	11	F7	39187	187	F21	**Argus**		
39112	112	F7	39188	188	F7	Flottiljer 17M, Uppsala		
39113	13	F7	39189	189	FMV	100001	001*	
39114	14	F7	39190	190	F21	100002	002	
39115	15	F7	39191	191	F17	100005	005	
39116	16	SAAB	39192	192	F7	100006	006	
39117	17	F7	39193	193	F21	100007	007	
39118	18	SAAB	39194	194	F21			
39119	19	F7	39195	195	FMV	**Förvarsmaktens**		
39120	120	F7	39196	196	FMV	**Helikopterflottilj**		
39121	21	F7	39197	197	F21	**Aérospatiale AS.332M-1**		
39122	122	F7	39198	198	F21	**Super Puma (Hkp.10)**		
39123	23	F7	39199	199	F21	1.HkpBat, Lycksele &		
39124	124	F17	39200	200	FMV	Östersund/Frösön		
39125	125	F7	39201	201	F21	2.HkpBat, Ronneby/Kallinge,		
39126	26	F17	39202	202	F21	Såtenäs, Sundsvall,		
39127	27	F7	39203	203	F21	Uppsala & Visby;		
39128	28	F7	39204	204	F21	10402	92	2.HkpBat
39129	29	F7	39205	205	F21	10403	93	1.HkpBat
39131	31	F7	39206	206	F21	10405	95	2.HkpBat
39132	132	F21	**JAS 39B**			10406	96	2.HkpBat
39133	133	F7	39800	56	FMV	10407	97	1.HkpBat
39134	134	F7	39801	70	F7	10408	98	2.HkpBat

10410	90	2.HkpBat
10411	88	1.HkpBat
10412	89	1.HkpBat

Agusta-Bell AB.412HP (Hkp.11)
1.HkpBat, Boden;
4.HkpBat, Malmslätt

11331	31	4.HkpBat
11332	32	
11333	33	1.HkpBat
11335	35	1.HkpBat
11336	36	
11337	37	
11338	38	
11339	39	
11340	40	
11341	41	
11342	42	

MBB Bo.105CBS (Hkp.9A)
1.HkpBat, Boden;
4.HkpBat, Malmslätt

09201	01	4.HkpBat
09202	02	1.HkpBat
09203	03	4.HkpBat
09204	04	4.HkpBat
09205	05	1.HkpBat
09206	06	4.HkpBat
09207	07	1.HkpBat
09208	08	1.HkpBat
09209	09	4.HkpBat
09210	10	1.HkpBat
09211	11	1.HkpBat
09212	12	1.HkpBat
09213	13	4.HkpBat
09214	14	4.HkpBat
09215	15	4.HkpBat
09216	16	4.HkpBat
09217	17	4.HkpBat
09218	18	4.HkpBat
09219	19	1.HkpBat
09220	20	4.HkpBat
09221	90	4.HkpBat

Vertol/Kawasaki-Vertol 107
2.HkpBat, Berga,
Goteborg/Säve, &
Ronneby/Kallinge;
FMV (Flygvapnet), Malmslätt
Vertol 107-II-15 (Hkp.4B)

04061	61	2.HkpBat
04063	63	2.HkpBat
04064	64	2.HkpBat

Kawasaki-Vertol KV.107-II-16 (Hkp.4C)

04065	65	2.HkpBat
04067	67	2.HkpBat
04068	68	2.HkpBat
04069	69	2.HkpBat
04070	70	2.HkpBat
04071	71	2.HkpBat
04072	72	FMV

Vertol 107-II-15 (Hkp.4D)

04073	73	2.HkpBat
04074	74	2.HkpBat
04075	75	2.HkpBat
04076	76	2.HkpBat

SWITZERLAND
Schweizerische Flugwaffe
(Most aircraft are pooled
centrally. Some carry unit
badges but these rarely
indicate actual operators.)

**Aérospatiale AS.332M-1/
AS.532UL Super Puma**
Leichte Abteilung 6
(LtSt 6), Alpnach
Detachments at Emmen,
Meiringen, Payerne &
Sion

AS.332M-1

T-311
T-312
T-313
T-314
T-315
T-316
T-317
T-318
T-319
T-320
T-321
T-322
T-323
T-324
T-325

AS.532UL

T-331
T-332
T-333
T-334
T-335
T-336
T-337
T-338
T-339
T-340
T-341
T-342

Beechcraft Super King Air 350C
Flugswaffenbrigade 31,
Dübendorf

T-784

Dassault Falcon 50
VIP Flight, Dübendorf

T-783

Gates Learjet 35A
VIP Flight, Dübendorf

T-781

McDonnell Douglas F/A-18 Hornet
Flieger Staffel 11 (FlSt 11),
Meiringen;
Flieger Staffel 17 (FlSt 17),
Payerne;
Flieger Staffel 18 (FlSt 18),
Payerne

F/A-18C

J-5001
J-5002
J-5003
J-5004
J-5005
J-5006
J-5007
J-5008
J-5009
J-5010
J-5011
J-5012
J-5013
J-5014
J-5015
J-5016
J-5017
J-5018
J-5019
J-5020
J-5021
J-5022
J-5023
J-5024
J-5025
J-5026

F/A-18D

J-5232
J-5233
J-5234
J-5235
J-5236
J-5237
J-5238

Northrop F-5 Tiger II
Flieger Staffel 1 (FlSt 1),
Turtman;
Flieger Staffel 6 (FlSt 6), Sion;
Flieger Staffel 8 (FlSt 8),
Meiringen;
Flieger Staffel 11 (FlSt 11),
Meiringen;
Flieger Staffel 13 (FlSt 13),
Meiringen;
Flieger Staffel 18 (FlSt 18),
Payerne;
Flieger Staffel 19 (FlSt 19),
Mollis;
Gruppe fur Rustunggdienste
(GRD), Emmen;
Instrumentation Flieger Staffel
14 (InstruFlSt 14),
Dübendorf;
Patrouille Suisse, Emmen
(*P. Suisse*)

F-5E

J-3001	
J-3002	
J-3004	
J-3005	
J-3006	
J-3007	
J-3008	InstruFlSt 14
J-3009	
J-3010	
J-3011	
J-3014	
J-3015	
J-3016	
J-3024	
J-3025	
J-3027	
J-3029	
J-3030	
J-3033	
J-3034	
J-3036	
J-3037	
J-3038	
J-3041	
J-3043	
J-3044	
J-3046	
J-3047	
J-3049	

J-3051		00326	86-0066 Öncel Filo
J-3052		23539	86-0068 Öncel Filo
J-3053		23563	86-0069 Öncel Filo
J-3054		23567	86-0070 Öncel Filo
J-3055		72609	86-0071 Öncel Filo
J-3056		80110	86-0072 Öncel Filo
J-3057			86-0191* Öncel Filo
J-3058		**Cessna 650 Citation VII**	86-0192* Öncel Filo
J-3060		224 Filo, Ankara/Etimesğut	86-0193* Öncel Filo
J-3061		004	86-0194* Öncel Filo
J-3062		005	86-0195* Öncel Filo
J-3063			86-0196* Öncel Filo
J-3065		**Grumman G.1159C**	87-0002* Öncel Filo
J-3066		**Gulfstream IV**	87-0003* Öncel Filo
J-3067		224 Filo, Ankara/Etimesğut	87-0009 Öncel Filo
J-3068		003	87-0010 Öncel Filo
J-3069		TC-ATA	87-0011 Öncel Filo
J-3070		TC-GAP	87-0013 Öncel Filo
J-3072			87-0014 Öncel Filo
J-3073		**Lockheed C-130B Hercules**	87-0015 Öncel Filo
J-3074		222 Filo, Erkilet	87-0016 Öncel Filo
J-3075		3496 (23496)	87-0017 Öncel Filo
J-3076		10960	87-0018 Öncel Filo
J-3077		10963	87-0019 Öncel Filo
J-3079		70527	87-0020 Öncel Filo
J-3080	P. Suisse	80736	87-0021 Öncel Filo
J-3081	P. Suisse		88-0013* Öncel Filo
J-3082	P. Suisse	**Lockheed C-130E Hercules**	88-0014* 141 Filo
J-3083	P. Suisse	222 Filo, Erkilet	88-0015* 141 Filo
J-3084	P. Suisse	01468 12-468	88-0019 Öncel Filo
J-3085	P. Suisse	01947	88-0020 Öncel Filo
J-3086	P. Suisse	13186 12-186	88-0021 Öncel Filo
J-3087	P. Suisse	13187	88-0024 142 Filo
J-3088	P. Suisse	13188 12-188	88-0025 141 Filo
J-3089	P. Suisse	13189	88-0026 142 Filo
J-3090	P. Suisse	73-991	88-0027 Öncel Filo
J-3091	P. Suisse		88-0028 142 Filo
J-3092		**Transall C-160D**	88-0029 142 Filo
J-3093		221 Filo, Erkilet	88-0030 191 Filo
J-3094		019	88-0031 Öncel Filo
J-3095		68-020	88-0032 Öncel Filo
J-3096		021	88-0033 141 Filo
J-3097	GRD	022	88-0034 141 Filo
J-3098		023	88-0035 141 Filo
F-5F		024	88-0036 141 Filo
J-3201		025 12-025	88-0037 141 Filo
J-3202		69-026	89-0022 141 Filo
J-3203		027	89-0023 141 Filo
J-3204	GRD	69-028 12-028	89-0024 141 Filo
J-3205		029	89-0025 141 Filo
J-3206		69-031	89-0026 141 Filo
J-3207		032	89-0027 141 Filo
J-3208		69-033	89-0028 141 Filo
J-3209		034	89-0030 141 Filo
J-3210		035	89-0031 141 Filo
J-3211		036	89-0032 141 Filo
J-3212		037 12-037	89-0034 162 Filo
		038	89-0035 162 Filo
SYRIA		039	89-0036 162 Filo
Tupolev Tu-134A		69-040	89-0037 162 Filo
Govt of Syria, Damascus			89-0038 162 Filo
YK-AYA		**TUSAS-GD F-16C/F-16D***	89-0039 162 Filo
		Fighting Falcon	89-0040 162 Filo
TUNISIA		4 AJÜ, Mürted:	89-0041 162 Filo
Boeing 737-7HJ		141 Filo, 142 Filo	89-0042* 141 Filo
Govt of Tunisia, Tunis		& Öncel Filo	89-0043* 162 Filo
TS-IOO		5 AJÜ, Merzifon:	89-0044* 162 Filo
		151 Filo & 152 Filo;	89-0045* 182 Filo
TURKEY		6 AJÜ, Bandirma:	90-0001 162 Filo
Türk Hava Kuvvetleri		161 Filo & 162 Filo;	90-0004 162 Filo
Boeing KC-135R		8 AJÜ, Diyarbakir:	90-0005 162 Filo
Stratotanker		181 Filo & 182 Filo;	90-0006 162 Filo
101 Filo, Incirlik		9 AJÜ, Balikesir:	90-0007 162 Filo
00325		191 Filo & 192 Filo	90-0008 162 Filo

90-0009	162 Filo	93-0014	181 Filo	94-1557*	152 Filo
90-0010	162 Filo	93-0657	141 Filo	94-1558*	Öncel Filo
90-0011	162 Filo	93-0658		94-1559*	152 Filo
90-0012	161 Filo	93-0659		94-1560*	151 Filo
90-0013	161 Filo	93-0660	151 Filo	94-1561*	191 Filo
90-0014	161 Filo	93-0661	151 Filo	94-1562*	192 Filo
90-0015	161 Filo	93-0662	151 Filo	94-1563*	192 Filo
90-0016	161 Filo	93-0663	151 Filo	94-1564*	191 Filo
90-0017	161 Filo	93-0664			
90-0018	161 Filo	93-0665		**TURKMENISTAN**	
90-0019	161 Filo	93-0666		**BAe 1000B**	
90-0020	162 Filo	93-0667	151 Filo	Govt of Turkmenistan,	
90-0021	161 Filo	93-0668		Ashkhabad	
90-0022*	161 Filo	93-0669	152 Filo	EZ-B021	
90-0023*	161 Filo	93-0670			
90-0024*	161 Filo	93-0671		**Boeing 757-23A**	
91-0001	161 Filo	93-0672	152 Filo	Govt of Turkmenistan,	
91-0002	161 Filo	93-0673	Öncel Filo	Ashkhabad	
91-0003	161 Filo	93-0674	192 Filo	EZ-A010	
91-0004	161 Filo	93-0675	192 Filo		
91-0005	161 Filo	93-0676	192 Filo	**UGANDA**	
91-0006	161 Filo	93-0677	192 Filo	**Grumman G.1159C**	
91-0007	161 Filo	93-0678	192 Filo	**Gulfstream IV**	
91-0008	141 Filo	93-0679	192 Filo	Govt of Uganda, Entebbe	
91-0010	141 Filo	93-0680	192 Filo	5X-UEF	
91-0011	141 Filo	93-0681	192 Filo		
91-0012	141 Filo	93-0682	192 Filo	**UKRAINE**	
91-0013	192 Filo	93-0683	192 Filo	**Ukrainian Air Force**	
91-0014	141 Filo	93-0684	192 Filo	**Ilyushin Il-76MD**	
91-0015	182 Filo	93-0685	192 Filo	321 TAP, Uzin	
91-0016	182 Filo	93-0686	192 Filo	78820	
91-0017	182 Filo	93-0687	192 Filo	UR-76413	
91-0018	182 Filo	93-0688	192 Filo	UR-76537	
91-0019	182 Filo	93-0689	Öncel Filo	UR-76624	
91-0020	182 Filo	93-0690	192 Filo	UR-76677	
91-0022*	141 Filo	93-0691*		UR-76687	
91-0024*	141 Filo	93-0692*	152 Filo	UR-76697	
92-0001	182 Filo	93-0693*	Öncel Filo	UR-76699	
92-0002	182 Filo	93-0694*			
92-0003	162 Filo	93-0695*	192 Filo	**Ilyushin Il-62M**	
92-0004	182 Filo	93-0696*	192 Filo	Govt of Ukraine, Kiev	
92-0005	191 Filo	94-0071	192 Filo	UR-86527	
92-0006	182 Filo	94-0072	191 Filo	UR-86528	
92-0007	182 Filo	94-0073	191 Filo		
92-0008	191 Filo	94-0074	191 Filo	**Tupolev Tu-134**	
92-0009	191 Filo	94-0075	191 Filo	Govt of Ukraine, Kiev	
92-0010	182 Filo	94-0076	191 Filo	UR-63982	
92-0011	182 Filo	94-0077	191 Filo		
92-0012	182 Filo	94-0078	191 Filo	**UNITED ARAB EMIRATES**	
92-0013	182 Filo	94-0079	191 Filo	**United Arab Emirates Air Force**	
92-0014	182 Filo	94-0080	191 Filo	*Abu Dhabi*	
92-0015	181 Filo	94-0081	191 Filo	**Lockheed C-130H/**	
92-0016	182 Filo	94-0082	191 Filo	**L.100-30* Hercules**	
92-0017	181 Filo	94-0083	191 Filo	1211	
92-0018	181 Filo	94-0084	191 Filo	1212	
92-0019	181 Filo	94-0085	191 Filo	1213	
92-0020	181 Filo	94-0086	191 Filo	1214	
92-0021	181 Filo	94-0087	191 Filo	1215*	
92-0022*	181 Filo	94-0088		1216*	
92-0023*	181 Filo	94-0089	152 Filo		
92-0024*	182 Filo	94-0090		*Dubai*	
93-0001	181 Filo	94-0091	152 Filo	311*	
93-0003	181 Filo	94-0092		312*	
93-0004	181 Filo	94-0093			
93-0005	181 Filo	94-0094	Öncel Filo	**Airbus A.319CJ-113X**	
93-0006	181 Filo	94-0095	152 Filo	Dubai Air Wing	
93-0007	181 Filo	94-0096	152 Filo	A6-ESH	
93-0008	181 Filo	94-0105*	191 Filo		
93-0009	181 Filo	94-0106*	191 Filo	**Boeing 737-2W8/**	
93-0010	181 Filo	94-0107*	191 Filo	**7F0/7Z5/8EC**	
93-0011	181 Filo	94-0108*	151 Filo	Govt of Abu Dhabi;	
93-0012	181 Filo	94-0109*	152 Filo	Govt of Dubai	
93-0013	181 Filo	94-0110*	152 Filo	A6-AIN 7Z5 Abu Dhabi	

United Arab Emirates – Yugoslavia

A6-AUH	8EX	Dubai
A6-DAS	7Z5	Abu Dhabi
A6-ESJ	2W8	Dubai
A6-HRS	7F0	Dubai
A6-LIW	7Z5	Dubai
A6-MRM	8EC	Dubai

**Boeing 747SP-31/
747SP-Z5***
Govt of Dubai
A6-SMM
A6-SMR
A6-ZSN*

Boeing 747-2B4BF/422/4F6
Dubai Air Wing;
Govt of Abu Dhabi

A6-GDP	2B4BF	Dubai
A6-HRM	422	Dubai
A6-MMM	422	Dubai
A6-YAS	4F6	Abu Dhabi

Boeing 767-341ER
Govt of Abu Dhabi
A6-SUL

Dassault Falcon 900
Govt of Abu Dhabi
A6-AUH

**Grumman G.1159C
Gulfstream IV**
Dubai Air Wing
A6-HHH

YEMEN
Boeing 747SP-27
Govt of Yemen, Sana'a
7O-YMN

YUGOSLAVIA
Dassault Falcon 50
Govt of Yugoslavia,
  Belgrade
YU-BNA

**Gates Learjet 25B/
LearJet 25D***
Govt of Yugoslavia,
  Belgrade
YU-BJG
YU-BKR*

French Navy Rafale-M. *PRM*

Belgian Air Force Falcon 20E from 21 Squadron at Melsbroek. *PRM*

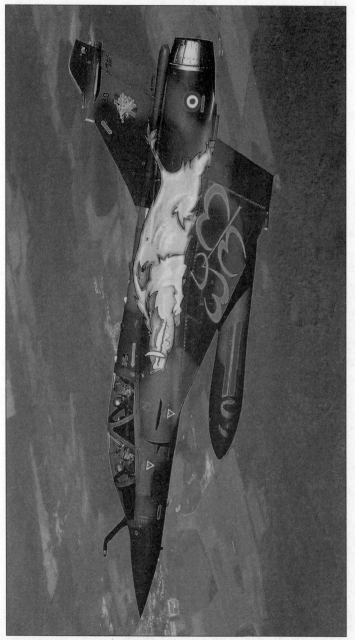

Colourful Mirage 2000D No 630 specially marked to celebrate 60 years of the Nancy-based EC 03.003 'Ardennes'. *via H. J. Curtis*

Royal Malaysian Air Force C-130H-30 Hercules M30-10 of No 20 Squadron. *PRM*

Newly delivered in 2003, RNZAF Boeing 757 NZ7571 replaced a Boeing 727. *PRM*

This JAS 39A Gripen 39192 is flown by F7 (7 Squadron) Swedish Air Force. *PRM*

48th Fighter Wing F-15E Strike Eagle coming in to land at RAF Lakenheath, Suffolk. *PRM*

US Military Aircraft Markings

All USAF aircraft have been allocated a fiscal year (FY) number since 1921. Individual aircraft are given a serial according to the fiscal year in which they are ordered. The numbers commence at 0001 and are prefixed with the year of allocation. For example F-15C Eagle 84-001 (84-0001) was the first aircraft ordered in 1984. The fiscal year (FY) serial is carried on the technical data block which is usually stencilled on the left-hand side of the aircraft just below the cockpit. The number displayed on the fin is a corruption of the FY serial. Most tactical aircraft carry the fiscal year in small figures followed by the last three or four digits of the serial in large figures. Large transport and tanker aircraft such as C-130s and KC-135s sometimes display a five-figure number commencing with the last digit of the appropriate fiscal year and four figures of the production number. An example of this is KC-135R 58-0128 which displays 80128 on its fin.

USN serials follow a straightforward numerical sequence which commenced, for the present series, with the allocation of 00001 to an SB2C Helldiver by the Bureau of Aeronautics in 1940. Numbers in the 165000 series are presently being issued. They are usually carried in full on the rear fuselage of the aircraft.

UK-based USAF Aircraft

The following aircraft are normally based in the UK. They are listed in numerical order of type with individual aircraft in serial number order, as depicted on the aircraft. The number in brackets is either the alternative presentation of the five-figure number commencing with the last digit of the fiscal year, or the fiscal year where a five-figure serial is presented on the aircraft. Where it is possible to identify the allocation of aircraft to individual squadrons by means of colours carried on fin or cockpit edge, this is also provided.

Notes	Type			Notes	Type		
	McDonnell Douglas				86-0166	F-15C	y
	F-15C Eagle/F-15D Eagle/				86-0167	F-15C	y
	F-15E Strike Eagle				86-0171	F-15C	y
	LN: 48th FW, RAF Lakenheath:				86-0172	F-15C	y
	492nd FS blue/white				86-0174	F-15C	y
	493rd FS black/yellow				86-0175	F-15C	y
	494th FS red/white				86-0176	F-15C	y
	00-3000	F-15E	r		86-0178	F-15C	y
	00-3001	F-15E	r		86-0182	F-15D	y
	00-3002	F-15E	r		91-0300	F-15E	r
	00-3003	F-15E	r		91-0301	F-15E	bl
	00-3004	F-15E	r		91-0302	F-15E	bl
	01-2000	F-15E	r		91-0303	F-15E	bl
	83-0018	F-15C	y		91-0304	F-15E	bl
	84-0001	F-15C	y		91-0306	F-15E	r
	84-0004	F-15C	y		91-0307	F-15E	bl
	84-0009	F-15C	y		91-0308	F-15E	bl
	84-0010	F-15C	y		91-0309	F-15E	bl
	84-0014	F-15C	y		91-0310	F-15E	r
	84-0015	F-15C	y		91-0311	F-15E	bl
	84-0019	F-15C	y		91-0312	F-15E	bl
	84-0027	F-15C	y		91-0313	F-15E	m	[48th OG]
	84-0044	F-15D	y	[48th OSS]	91-0314	F-15E	r	[494th FS]
	86-0147	F-15C	y		91-0315	F-15E	r
	86-0154	F-15C	y		91-0316	F-15E	r
	86-0156	F-15C	y		91-0317	F-15E	r
	86-0159	F-15C	y		91-0318	F-15E	r
	86-0160	F-15C	y		91-0320	F-15E	r
	86-0163	F-15C	y		91-0321	F-15E	r
	86-0164	F-15C	y		91-0324	F-15E	r
	86-0165	F-15C	y	[493rd FS]	91-0326	F-15E	r

Type			Notes
91-0329	F-15E	bl	
91-0330	F-15E	r	
91-0331	F-15E	r	
91-0332	F-15E	bl	
91-0334	F-15E	r	
91-0335	F-15E	r	
91-0601	F-15E	r	
91-0602	F-15E	r	
91-0603	F-15E	r	
91-0604	F-15E	r	
91-0605	F-15E	bl	
92-0364	F-15E	r	
96-0201	F-15E	bl	
96-0202	F-15E	bl	
96-0204	F-15E	bl	
96-0205	F-15E	bl	
97-0217	F-15E	bl	
97-0218	F-15E	m	[48th FW]
97-0219	F-15E	bl	
97-0220	F-15E	bl	
97-0221	F-15E	bl	[492nd FS]
97-0222	F-15E	bl	
98-0131	F-15E	bl	
98-0132	F-15E	bl	
98-0133	F-15E	bl	
98-0134	F-15E	bl	
98-0135	F-15E	bl	

Sikorsky MH-53M
21st SOS/352nd SOG, RAF Mildenhall
01630 (FY70)
14994 (FY67)
31649 (FY73)
31652 (FY73)
95784 (FY69)
95795 (FY69)

Type			Notes
95796 (FY69)			

Lockheed C-130 Hercules
352nd SOG, RAF Mildenhall:
  7th SOS* & 67th SOS,

37814	(FY63)	C-130E
61699	(FY86)	MC-130H*
70023	(FY87)	MC-130H*
80193	(FY88)	MC-130H*
80194	(FY88)	MC-130H*
90280	(FY89)	MC-130H*
95825	(FY69)	MC-130P
95826	(FY69)	MC-130P
95828	(FY69)	MC-130P
95831	(FY69)	MC-130P
95832	(FY69)	MC-130P

Boeing KC-135R
Stratotanker
351st ARS/100th ARW,
  RAF Mildenhall [D] (r/w/bl)

00313	(FY60)
00351	(FY60)
14830	(FY64)
14835	(FY64)
23505	(FY62)
23538	(FY62)
23541	(FY62)
23551	(FY62)
23561	(FY62)
38871	(FY63)
38879	(FY63)
38884	(FY63)
72605	(FY57)
80124	(FY58)
80128	(FY58)
91459	(FY59)

UK-based US Navy Aircraft

Beech UC-12M Super King Air
Naval Air Facility, Mildenhall
3836 (163836)
3843 (163843)

European-based USAF Aircraft

These aircraft are normally based in Western Europe with the USAFE. They are shown in numerical order of type designation, with individual aircraft in serial number order as carried on the aircraft. Fiscal year (FY) details are also provided if necessary. The unit allocation and operating bases are given for most aircraft.

Notes	Type			Notes	Type		
	McDonnell Douglas				88-0444	AV pr	
	C-9A Nightingale				88-0446	AV pr	
	86th AW, Ramstein, Germany:				88-0491	AV pr	
	76th AS				88-0525	AV pr	
	FY71				88-0526	AV gn	
	10876				88-0529	AV pr	
					88-0532	AV gn	
	Fairchild A-10A Thunderbolt II				88-0535	AV gn	
	SP: 52nd FW, Spangdahlem,				88-0541	AV pr	
	Germany: 81st FS black/yellow				89-2001	AV m	[31st FW]
	80-0281	bk	[81st FS]		89-2009	AV gn	
	81-0948	bk			89-2011	AV pr	
	81-0951	bk			89-2016	AV gn	[16th AF]
	81-0952	m	[52nd FW]		89-2018	AV gn	
	81-0954	bk			89-2023	AV gn	
	81-0956	bk			89-2024	AV gn	
	81-0962	bk			89-2026	AV gn	
	81-0963	bk			89-2029	AV pr	
	81-0966	bk			89-2030	AV gn	
	81-0976	bk			89-2035	AV gn	[555th FS]
	81-0978	bk			89-2038	AV gn	
	81-0980	bk			89-2039	AV gn	
	81-0983	bk			89-2041	AV gn	
	81-0984	bk			89-2044	AV gn	
	81-0985	bk			89-2046	AV pr	
	81-0988	bk			89-2047	AV pr	
	81-0991	bk			89-2049	AV pr	[USAFE]
	81-0992	m	[52nd OG]		89-2057	AV pr	
	82-0649	bk			89-2068	AV gn	
	82-0650	bk			89-2102	AV gn	
	82-0654	bk			89-2118	AV pr	
	82-0656	bk			89-2137	AV pr	[31st OG]
					89-2178*	AV pr	
	Beech C-12D				90-0709	AV pr	
	US Embassy Flight, Budapest,				90-0772	AV gn	
	Hungary				90-0773	AV gn	
	FY83				90-0777*	AV pr	
	30495				90-0795*	AV gn	
					90-0796*	AV pr	
	Lockheed (GD) F-16C/F-16D*				90-0800*	AV gn	
	AV: 31st FW, Aviano, Italy:				90-0813	SP r	
	510th FS purple/white				90-0818	SP r	
	555th FS green/yellow				90-0827	SP r	
	SP: 52nd FW, Spangdahlem,				90-0828	SP r	
	Germany:				90-0829	SP r	[22nd FS]
	22nd FS red/white				90-0831	SP r	
	23rd FS blue/white				90-0833	SP r	
	87-0350	AV gn			90-0843*	SP r	
	87-0351	AV m	[31st OSS]		90-0846*	SP bl	
	87-0355	AV pr			91-0336	SP r	
	87-0359	AV gn			91-0337	SP r	
	88-0413	AV pr	[510th FS]		91-0338	SP r	
	88-0425	AV gn	[16th AF]		91-0339	SP r	[22nd FS]
	88-0435	AV gn			91-0340	SP r	
	88-0443	AV pr			91-0341	SP r	

Type		Notes
91-0342	SP *r*	
91-0343	SP *r*	
91-0344	SP *r*	
91-0351	SP *r*	
91-0352	SP *m*	[52nd FW]
91-0391	SP *r*	
91-0402	SP *bl*	
91-0403	SP *bl*	
91-0405	SP *bl*	
91-0406	SP *bl*	
91-0407	SP *bl*	
91-0408	SP *r*	
91-0409	SP *bl*	
91-0410	SP *bl*	
91-0412	SP *bl*	
91-0414	SP *bl*	
91-0416	SP *bl*	[52nd OG]
91-0417	SP *bl*	
91-0418	SP *bl*	
91-0419	SP *bl*	
91-0420	SP *bl*	
91-0421	SP *bl*	
91-0464*	SP *r*	
91-0472*	SP *bl*	
91-0474*	SP *bl*	
91-0481*	SP *bl*	
92-3915	SP *bl*	
92-3918	SP *bl*	
96-0080	SP *bl*	[23rd FS]
96-0081	SP *bl*	
96-0082	SP *m*	[52nd FW]
96-0083	SP *bl*	

Grumman C-20H Gulfstream IV
76th AS/86th AW, Ramstein,
 Germany
FY90
00300
FY92
20375

Gates C-21A Learjet
76th AS/86th AW, Ramstein,
 Germany
FY84
40068
40081

Type		Notes
40082		
40083		
40084		
40085		
40086		
40087		
40108		
40109		
40110		
40111		
40112		

**Gulfstream Aerospace C-37A
Gulfstream V**
309th AS/86th AW, Chievres,
 Belgium
FY01
10076

Sikorsky HH-60G Blackhawk
56th RQS/85th Wing, Keflavik,
 Iceland [IS]

26109	(FY88)	
26205	(FY89)	
26206	(FY89)	
26208	(FY89)	
26212	(FY89)	

Lockheed C-130E Hercules
37th AS/86th AW, Ramstein,
 Germany [RS] *(bl/w)*

01260	(FY70)	
01264	(FY70)	
01271	(FY70)	
01274	(FY70)	[86th AW]
10935	(FY68)	
10943	(FY68)	[86th OG]
17681	(FY64)	
37865	(FY63)	
37879	(FY63)	
37885	(FY63)	
37887	(FY63)	
40499	(FY64)	
40502	(FY64)	
40527	(FY64)	

European-based US Navy Aircraft

Notes	Type			Notes	Type		
	Lockheed P-3 Orion				3842	(163842)	Rota
	CinCUSNFE						
	NAF Sigonella, Italy;				**Fairchild C-26D**		
	NAF Keflavik, Iceland;				NAF Naples, Italy;		
	VQ-2, NAF Rota, Spain				NAF Sigonella, Italy		
	150495	UP-3A	NAF Keflavik		900528	Sigonella	
	150496	VP-3A	CinCUSNFE		900530	Sigonella	
	156519	[21] EP-3E	VQ-2		900531	Naples	
	156525	[525] P-3C	VQ-2		910502	Naples	
	156529	[24] EP-3E	VQ-2				
	157316	[23] EP-3E	VQ-2		**Sikorsky MH-53E Sea Stallion**		
	157325	[25] EP-3E	VQ-2		HC-4, NAF Sigonella, Italy		
	157326	[22] EP-3E	VQ-2		162504	[HC-40]	
	159884	[884] P-3C	VQ-2		162505	[HC-47]	
	159886	[09] P-3C	VQ-2		162514	[HC-50]	
	161000	[000] P-3C	VQ-2		162516	[HC-00]	
	161002	P-3C	VQ-2		163053	[HC-44]	
	161121	[15] P-3C	VQ-2		163055	[HC-45]	
					163057	[HC-41]	
	Beech UC-12M Super King Air				163065	[HC-43]	
	NAF Rota, Spain				163068	[HC-42]	
	3839	(163839)	Rota		164864	[HC-48]	

European-based US Army Aircraft

Notes	Type			Notes	Type		
	Bell UH-1H Iroquois				1st Military Intelligence Btn,		
	LANDSOUTHEAST, Cigli, Turkey;				Wiesbaden;		
	7th Army Training Center, Grafenwöhr;				'B' Co, 1st Btn, 214th Avn Reg't,		
	Combat Manoeuvre Training Centre,				Wiesbaden		
	Hohenfels;				*FY84*		
	6th Avn Co, Vicenza, Italy				40153	C-12U	1st MIB
	FY68				40156	C-12U	B/1-214th Avn
	16341	LANDSOUTHEAST			40157	C-12U	E/1-214th Avn
	16662	LANDSOUTHEAST			40158	C-12U	B/1-214th Avn
	FY72				40160	C-12U	E/1-214th Avn
	21569	CMTC			40161	C-12U	B/1-214th Avn
	21632	CMTC			40162	C-12U	B/1-214th Avn
	21636	CMTC			40163	C-12U	B/1-214th Avn
	FY73				40165	C-12U	B/1-214th Avn
	21668	CMTC			40180	C-12U	B/1-214th Avn
	21725	7th ATC			*FY94*		
	21786	CMTC			40315	C-12R	A/2-228th Avn
	21806	LANDSOUTHEAST			40316	C-12R	A/2-228th Avn
	21824	7th ATC			40318	C-12R	A/2-228th Avn
	FY74				40319	C-12R	A/2-228th Avn
	22318	6th Avn Co			*FY85*		
	22330	CMTC			50147	RC-12K	1st MIB
	22355	CMTC			50148	RC-12K	1st MIB
	22370	CMTC			50149	RC-12K	1st MIB
	22410	CMTC			50150	RC-12K	1st MIB
	22448	CMTC			50152	RC-12K	1st MIB
	22465	CMTC			50153	RC-12K	1st MIB
	22504	7th ATC			50155	RC-12K	1st MIB
	Beech C-12 Super King Air				**Beech C-12J**		
	'A' Co, 2nd Btn, 228th Avn Reg't,				HQ/USEUCOM, Stuttgart		
	Heidelberg;				*FY86*		
	HQ/USEUCOM, Stuttgart;				60079		
	'E' Co, 1st Btn, 214th Avn Reg't,						
	Det 1 Vicenza, Italy;						

Type	Notes		Type		Notes
Cessna UC-35A Citation V			40175	1-1st Cav	
214th Avn Reg't, Wiesbaden			40176	1-4th Cav	
FY95			40178	1-1st Cav	
50123			40179	1-1st Cav	
50124			40180	1-1st Cav	
FY97			*FY89*		
70101			90114	1-1st Cav	
70102			90116	1-1st Cav	
70105			90117	1-1st Cav	
FY99					
90102			**Sikorsky H-60 Black Hawk**		
			2nd Btn, 1st Avn Reg't, Ansbach;		
Boeing-Vertol CH-47D Chinook			45th Medical Co, Ansbach;		
'F' Co, 158th Avn Reg't Giebelstadt			'B' Co, 5th Btn, 158th Avn Reg't,		
FY87			Aviano;		
70072			'A' Co, 127th Divisional Avn		
70073			Support Btn, Bad Kreuznach;		
FY88			357th Avn Det/SHAPE, Chievres;		
80098			'B' Co, 70th Transportation Reg't,		
80099			Coleman Barracks;		
80100			214th Avn Reg't, Coleman Barracks;		
80101			'A' Co, 3rd Btn, 158th Avn Reg't,		
80102			Giebelstadt;		
80103			'B' Co, 3rd Btn, 158th Avn Reg't,		
80104			Giebelstadt;		
80106			'A' Co, 5th Btn, 158th Avn Reg't,		
FY89			Giebelstadt;		
90139			'C' Co, 5th Btn, 158th Avn Reg't,		
90140			Giebelstadt;		
90141			2nd Btn, 501st Avn Reg't, Hanau;		
90142			'B' Co, 7th Btn, 159th AVIM, Illesheim;		
90143			236th Medical Co (HA), Landstuhl;		
90144			6th Avn Co, Vicenza, Italy;		
90145			159th Medical Co, Wiesbaden		
			FY82		
Bell OH-58D(I) Kiowa Warrior			23675	UH-60A	45th Med Co
1st Btn, 1st Cavalry Reg't, Budingen;			23692	UH-60A	A/3-158th Avn
1st Btn, 4th Cavalry Reg't, Schweinfurt			23693	UH-60A	45th Med Co
FY90			23729	UH-60A	45th Med Co
00348	1-1st Cav		23735	UH-60A	236th Med Co
00371	1-1st Cav		23737	UH-60A	236th Med Co
00373	1-4th Cav		23738	UH-60A	159th Med Co
FY91			23745	UH-60A	236th Med Co
10540	1-1st Cav		23750	UH-60A	159th Med Co
10544	1-1st Cav		23751	UH-60A	159th Med Co
10564	1-1st Cav		23752	UH-60A	236th Med Co
FY92			23753	UH-60A	159th Med Co
20520	1-1st Cav		23754	UH-60A	45th Med Co
20529	1-1st Cav		23755	UH-60A	236th Med Co
20545	1-1st Cav		23756	UH-60A	159th Med Co
FY93			23757	UH-60A	214th Avn
30971	1-4th Cav		*FY83*		
30996	1-4th Cav		23854	UH-60A	A/5-158th Avn
30998	1-4th Cav		23855	UH-60A	214th Avn
31002	1-4th Cav		23868	UH-60A	214th Avn
31005	1-4th Cav		23869	UH-60A	214th Avn
31006	1-4th Cav		*FY84*		
31007	1-4th Cav		23951	UH-60A	45th Med Co
31008	1-4th Cav		23970	UH-60A	C/5-158th Avn
FY94			23975	UH-60A	C/5-158th Avn
40149	1-4th Cav		24019	EH-60A	2-1st Avn
40150	1-4th Cav		*FY85*		
40151	1-4th Cav		24391	UH-60A	45th Med Co
40152	1-1st Cav		24467	EH-60A	2-1st Avn
40153	1-4th Cav		24475	EH-60A	2-1st Avn
40154	1-4th Cav		24478	EH-60A	2-1st Avn
40174	1-4th Cav				

US Army Europe

Notes	Type			Notes	Type		
	FY86				26086	UH-60A	236th Med Co
	24498	UH-60A	2-501st Avn		*FY89*		
	24530	UH-60A	2-501st Avn		26138	UH-60A	159th Med Co
	24531	UH-60A	45th Med Co		26142	UH-60A	B/7-159th AVIM
	24532	UH-60A	45th Med Co		26145	UH-60A	B/5-158th Avn
	24538	UH-60A	214th Avn		26146	UH-60A	159th Med Co
	24550	UH-60A	236th Med Co		26151	UH-60A	159th Med Co
	24552	UH-60A	159th Med Co		26153	UH-60A	B/5-158th Avn
	24554	UH-60A	C/5-158th Avn		26164	UH-60A	C/5-158th Avn
	24555	UH-60A			26165	UH-60A	214th Avn
	24566	EH-60C	2-501st Avn		*FY95*		
	FY87				26621	UH-60L	2-1st Avn
	24579	UH-60A	A/5-158th Avn		26628	UH-60L	2-1st Avn
	24581	UH-60A	159th Med Co		26629	UH-60L	2-1st Avn
	24583	UH-60A	357th Avn Det		26630	UH-60L	2-1st Avn
	24584	UH-60A	357th Avn Det		26631	UH-60L	2-1st Avn
	24589	UH-60A	214th Avn		26632	UH-60L	2-1st Avn
	24621	UH-60A	214th Avn		26633	UH-60L	2-1st Avn
	24628	UH-60A	159th Med Co		26635	UH-60L	2-1st Avn
	24634	UH-60A	159th Med Co		26636	UH-60L	2-1st Avn
	24642	UH-60A	214th Avn		26637	UH-60L	2-1st Avn
	24644	UH-60A	45th Med Co		26638	UH-60L	2-1st Avn
	24645	UH-60A	45th Med Co		26639	UH-60L	2-1st Avn
	24647	UH-60A	214th Avn		26640	UH-60L	2-1st Avn
	24650	UH-60A			26641	UH-60L	B/3-158th Avn
	24656	UH-60C	159th Med Co		26642	UH-60L	B/3-158th Avn
	24660	EH-60C	2-501st Avn		26643	UH-60L	B/3-158th Avn
	24664	EH-60A	2-501st Avn		26644	UH-60L	2-1st Avn
	26001	UH-60A	45th Med Co		26645	UH-60L	B/3-158th Avn
	26002	UH-60A	159th Med Co		26646	UH-60L	2-1st Avn
	26003	UH-60A	B/5-158th Avn		26647	UH-60L	2-1st Avn
	26004	UH-60A	45th Med Co		26648	UH-60L	2-1st Avn
	FY88				26649	UH-60L	B/3-158th Avn
	26019	UH-60A	214th Avn		26650	UH-60L	B/3-158th Avn
	26020	UH-60A	236th Med Co		26651	UH-60L	A/3-158th Avn
	26021	UH-60A	B/5-158th Avn		26652	UH-60L	A/3-158th Avn
	26023	UH-60A	236th Med Co		26653	UH-60L	A/3-158th Avn
	26025	UH-60A	214th Avn		26654	UH-60L	A/3-158th Avn
	26026	UH-60A	B/5-158th Avn		26655	UH-60L	A/3-158th Avn
	26027	UH-60A	214th Avn		*FY96*		
	26028	UH-60A	C/5-158th Avn		26674	UH-60L	B/3-158th Avn
	26031	UH-60A	236th Med Co		26675	UH-60L	B/3-158th Avn
	26034	UH-60A	159th Med Co		26676	UH-60L	B/3-158th Avn
	26037	UH-60A	B/7-159th AVIM		26677	UH-60L	B/3-158th Avn
	26038	UH-60A	A/5-158th Avn		26678	UH-60L	B/3-158th Avn
	26039	UH-60A	45th Med Co		26679	UH-60L	B/3-158th Avn
	26040	UH-60A	236th Med Co		26680	UH-60L	B/3-158th Avn
	26041	UH-60A	A/5-158th Avn		26681	UH-60L	B/3-158th Avn
	26042	UH-60A	A/5-158th Avn		26682	UH-60L	B/3-158th Avn
	26045	UH-60A	45th Med Co		26683	UH-60L	A/3-158th Avn
	26050	UH-60A	159th Med Co		26684	UH-60L	A/3-158th Avn
	26051	UH-60A	A/5-158th Avn		26685	UH-60L	A/3-158th Avn
	26052	UH-60A	B/5-158th Avn		26686	UH-60L	A/3-158th Avn
	26053	UH-60A	A/5-158th Avn		26687	UH-60L	A/3-158th Avn
	26054	UH-60A	236th Med Co		26688	UH-60L	A/3-158th Avn
	26055	UH-60A	236th Med Co		26689	UH-60L	A/3-158th Avn
	26056	UH-60A	A/5-158th Avn		26690	UH-60L	A/3-158th Avn
	26058	UH-60A	159th Med Co		26691	UH-60L	A/3-158th Avn
	26063	UH-60A	B/5-158th Avn		26692	UH-60L	A/3-158th Avn
	26067	UH-60A	B/5-158th Avn		*FY97*		
	26068	UH-60A	236th Med Co		26762	UH-60L	2-501st Avn
	26072	UH-60A	236th Med Co		26763	UH-60L	2-501st Avn
	26075	UH-60A	159th Med Co		26764	UH-60L	2-501st Avn
	26077	UH-60A	C/5-158th Avn		26765	UH-60L	2-501st Avn
	26080	UH-60A	236th Med Co		26766	UH-60L	2-501st Avn
	26085	UH-60A	236th Med Co		26767	UH-60L	2-501st Avn

Type			Notes
FY98			
26795	UH-60L	2-501st Avn	
26796	UH-60L	2-501st Avn	
26797	UH-60L	2-501st Avn	
26798	UH-60L	2-501st Avn	
26799	UH-60L	2-501st Avn	
26800	UH-60L	2-501st Avn	
26801	UH-60L	2-501st Avn	
26802	UH-60L	2-501st Avn	
26813	UH-60L	2-501st Avn	
26814	UH-60L	2-501st Avn	
FY01			
26878	UH-60L	B/3-158th Avn	
26880	UH-60L	B/3-158th Avn	
26884	UH-60L	B/3-158th Avn	
26885	UH-60L	B/3-158th Avn	
26886	UH-60L	B/3-158th Avn	
26889	UH-60L	B/3-158th Avn	
FY02			
26970	UH-60L	B/3-158th Avn	
FY03			
26992	UH-60L	B/3-158th Avn	

MDH AH-64 Apache
1st Btn, 1st Avn Reg't, Ansbach;
1st Btn, 501st Avn Reg't, Hanau;
2nd Btn, 6th Cavalry Reg't, Illesheim;
6th Btn, 6th Cavalry Reg't, Illesheim

AH-64A

Type		Notes
FY86		
68940	2-6th Cav	
68942	2-6th Cav	
68943	2-6th Cav	
68946	2-6th Cav	
68948	2-6th Cav	
68951	2-6th Cav	
68952	2-6th Cav	
68955	2-6th Cav	
68956	2-6th Cav	
68957	2-6th Cav	
68959	2-6th Cav	
68960	2-6th Cav	
68961	2-6th Cav	
68981	2-6th Cav	
69026	2-6th Cav	
69030	2-6th Cav	
69032	2-6th Cav	
69037	2-6th Cav	
69041	1-501st Avn	
69048	2-6th Cav	
FY87		
70410	1-501st Avn	
70412	1-1st Avn	
70413	1-1st Avn	
70415	1-501st Avn	
70417	1-1st Avn	
70418	1-501st Avn	
70420	1-1st Avn	
70428	1-1st Avn	

Type		Notes
70432	1-1st Avn	
70436	1-1st Avn	
70437	1-1st Avn	
70438	1-501st Avn	
70439	1-1st Avn	
70440	1-501st Avn	
70442	1-1st Avn	
70443	2-6th Cav	
70444	1-501st Avn	
70445	1-501st Avn	
70446	1-501st Avn	
70447	1-501st Avn	
70449	1-501st Avn	
70451	1-501st Avn	
70454	1-501st Avn	
70455	1-501st Avn	
70457	1-1st Avn	
70470	1-1st Avn	
70471	1-1st Avn	
70474	1-1st Avn	
70475	1-1st Avn	
70476	1-1st Avn	
70477	1-1st Avn	
70478	1-1st Avn	
70481	1-1st Avn	
70487	1-501st Avn	
70496	1-501st Avn	
70503	2-6th Cav	
70504	1-501st Avn	
70505	1-501st Avn	
70506	1-501st Avn	
FY88		
80197	1-501st Avn	
80198	1-501st Avn	
AH-64D		
FY00		
05175	6-6th Cav	
05199	6-6th Cav	
05200	6-6th Cav	
05204	6-6th Cav	
05205	6-6th Cav	
05206	6-6th Cav	
05207	6-6th Cav	
05208	6-6th Cav	
05209	6-6th Cav	
05210	6-6th Cav	
05211	6-6th Cav	
05212	6-6th Cav	
05213	6-6th Cav	
05214	6-6th Cav	
05215	6-6th Cav	
05217	6-6th Cav	
05218	6-6th Cav	
05220	6-6th Cav	
05225	6-6th Cav	
05226	6-6th Cav	
05231	6-6th Cav	
05232	6-6th Cav	

US-based USAF Aircraft

The following aircraft are normally based in the USA but are likely to be seen visiting the UK from time to time. The presentation is in numerical order of the type, commencing with the B-1B and concluding with the C-141. The aircraft are listed in numerical progression by the serial actually carried externally. Fiscal year information is provided, together with details of mark variations and in some cases operating units. Where base-code letter information is carried on the aircraft's tails, this is detailed with the squadron/base data; for example the 7th Wing's B-1B 60105 carries the letters DY on its tail, thus identifying the Wing's home base as Dyess AFB, Texas.

Notes	Type			Notes	Type		
	Rockwell B-1B Lancer				60108	7th BW	bl/w
	7th BW, Dyess AFB, Texas [DY]:				60109	7th BW	r
	9th BS (bk), 13th BS (r)				60110	7th BW	bl/w
	& 28th BS (bl/w);				60111	28th BW	bk/or
	28th BW, Ellsworth AFB,				60112	7th BW	bk
	South Dakota [EL]:				60113	28th BW	bk/y
	13th BS (bl/br), 37th BS (bk/y)				60115	28th BW	bk/or
	& 77th BS (bk/or);				60116	28th BW	
	419th FLTS/412th TW, Edwards AFB,				60117	7th BW	bl/w
	California [ED]				60118	28th BW	
	FY84				60119	7th BW	bl/w
	40049	412th TW			60120	7th BW	bk
	FY85				60121	28th BW	bk/y
	50059				60122	7th BW	r
	50060	7th BW	bk		60123	7th BW	bl/w
	50061				60124	7th BW	
	50064	7th BW	r		60125	28th BW	bk/or
	50065	7th BW	bl/w		60126	7th BW	bl/w
	50066	28th BW	bk/or		60127		
	50068	412th TW			60129	28th BW	bk/or
	50069	7th BW			60130	7th BW	bl/w
	50072	28th BW	bk/y		60132	7th BW	bl/w
	50073	7th BW	bk		60133	7th BW	bl/w
	50074	7th BW	r		60134	28th BW	
	50075	28th BW	bk/or		60135	7th BW	bl/w
	50077	28th BW	bk/or		60136	7th BW	bl/w
	50079	28th BW	bk/or		60137	7th BW	r
	50080	7th BW	bl/w		60138	28th BW	bk/y
	50081	28th BW	bk/y		60139	28th BW	bk/y
	50083	28th BW	bk/y		60140	7th BW	bk
	50084	28th BW	bk/or				
	50085	28th BW	bk/y				
	50087	28th BW	bk/y		**Northrop B-2 Spirit**		
	50088				419th FLTS/412th TW, Edwards AFB,		
	50089	28th BW	bk/y		California [ED];		
	50090	28th BW	bk/or		509th BW, Whiteman AFB,		
	50091	28th BW	bk/y		Missouri [WM]:		
	FY86				325th BS, 393rd BS & 715th BS		
	60093	28th BW	bk/or		(Names are given where known.		
	60094	28th BW	bk/or		Each begins *Spirit of ...*)		
	60095				*FY90*		
	60098	7th BW	bl/w		00040	509th BW	*Alaska*
	60099	28th BW	bk/or		00041	509th BW	*Hawaii*
	60100	7th BW	r		*FY92*		
	60101	7th BW	bl/w		20700	509th BW	*Florida*
	60102	28th BW	bk/or		*FY82*		
	60103	7th BW	bk		21066	509th BW	*America*
	60104	28th BW	bk/y		21067	509th BW	*Arizona*
	60105	7th BW	bl/w		21068	412th TW	*New York*
	60107				21069	509th BW	*Indiana*
					21070	Northrop	*Ohio*

Type			Notes
21071	509th BW	*Mississippi*	
FY93			
31085	509th BW	*Oklahoma*	
31086	509th BW	*Kitty Hawk*	
31087	509th BW	*Pennsylvania*	
31088	509th BW	*Louisiana*	
FY88			
80328	509th BW	*Texas*	
80329	509th BW	*Missouri*	
80330	509th BW	*California*	
80331	509th BW	*South Carolina*	
80332	509th BW	*Washington*	
FY89			
90127	509th BW	*Kansas*	
90128	509th BW	*Nebraska*	
90129	509th BW	*Georgia*	

Boeing E-3 Sentry
552nd ACW, Tinker AFB,
  Oklahoma [OK]:
  960th AACS *(w)*, 963rd AACS *(bk)*,
  964th AACS *(r)*, 965th AACS *(y)*
  & 966th AACS *(bl)*;
961st AACS/18th Wg, Kadena AB,
  Japan [ZZ] *(or)*;
962nd AACS/3rd Wg, Elmendorf AFB,
  Alaska [AK] *(gn)*;

Type		Notes	
FY80			
00137	E-3C	bk	
00138	E-3C	y	
00139	E-3C	bk	
FY81			
10004	E-3C	bk	
10005	E-3C	bk	
FY71			
11407	E-3B	w	
11408	E-3B	w	
FY82			
20006	E-3C	y	
20007	E-3C	w	
FY83			
30008	E-3C	bk	
30009	E-3C	bk	
FY73			
31674	JE-3C	Boeing	
31675	E-3B	r	
FY75			
50556	E-3B	w	
50557	E-3B	w	
50558	E-3B	or	
50559	E-3B	bk	
50560	E-3B	y	
FY76			
61604	E-3B	r	
61605	E-3B	gn	
61606	E-3B	gn	
61607	E-3B	bl	
FY77			
70351	E-3B	w	
70352	E-3B	r	
70353	E-3B	y	
70355	E-3B	gn	
70356	E-3B	y	
FY78			
80576	E-3B	r	
80577	E-3B	r	

Type			Notes
80578	E-3B	*or*	
FY79			
90001	E-3B	*r*	
90002	E-3B	*y*	
90003	E-3B	*bl*	

Boeing E-4B
1st ACCS/55th Wg, Offutt AFB,
  Nebraska [OF]

31676	(FY73)		
31677	(FY73)		
40787	(FY74)		
50125	(FY75)		

Lockheed C-5 Galaxy
60th AMW, Travis AFB, California:
  21st AS *(bk/gd)* & 22nd AS *(bk/bl)*;
56th AS/97th AMW, Altus AFB,
  Oklahoma *(r/y)*;
137th AS/105th AW, Stewart AFB,
  New York *(bl)*;
68th AS/433rd AW AFRC, Kelly AFB,
  Texas;
436th AW, Dover AFB, Delaware:
  3rd AS *(y/r)* & 9th AS *(y/bl)*;
337th AS/439th AW AFRC, Westover
  ARB, Massachusetts *(bl/r)*

Type			Notes
FY70			
00445	C-5A	433rd AW	
00446	C-5A	433rd AW	
00447	C-5A	436th AW	y
00448	C-5A	439th AW	bl/r
00449	C-5A	60th AMW	bk/gd
00450	C-5A	97th AMW	r/y
00451	C-5A	60th AMW	
00452	C-5A	97th AMW	r/y
00453	C-5A	436th AW	y
00454	C-5A	97th AMW	r/y
00455	C-5A	97th AMW	r/y
00456	C-5A	60th AMW	bk/gd
00457	C-5A	60th AMW	bk/gd
00459	C-5A	60th AMW	bk/gd
00460	C-5A	105th AW	bl
00461	C-5A	436th AW	y
00462	C-5A	97th AMW	r/y
00463	C-5A	436th AW	y
00464	C-5A	60th AMW	bk/bl
00465	C-5A	97th AMW	r/y
00466	C-5A	436th AW	
00467	C-5A	436th AW	y
FY83			
31285	C-5B	436th AW	y/r
FY84			
40059	C-5B	436th AW	
40060	C-5B	60th AMW	bk/bl
40061	C-5B	436th AW	y
40062	C-5B	60th AMW	bk/gd
FY85			
50001	C-5B	436th AW	m
50002	C-5B	60th AMW	bk/bl
50003	C-5B	436th AW	y
50004	C-5B	60th AMW	bk/bl
50005	C-5B	436th AW	y
50006	C-5B	60th AMW	bk/gd
50007	C-5B	436th AW	y/bl
50008	C-5B	60th AMW	bk/gd

Notes	Type				Notes	Type			
	50009	C-5B	436th AW	y		80225	C-5A	439th AW	bl/r
	50010	C-5B	60th AMW	bk/gd		80226	C-5A	105th AW	bl
	FY86					*FY69*			
	60011	C-5B	436th AW	y/bl		90001	C-5A	60th AMW	bk/gd
	60012	C-5B	60th AMW	bk/bl		90002	C-5A	433rd AW	
	60013	C-5B	436th AW	y		90003	C-5A	439th AW	bl/r
	60014	C-5B	60th AMW	bk/bl		90005	C-5A	439th AW	bl/r
	60015	C-5B	436th AW	y/r		90006	C-5A	433rd AW	
	60016	C-5B	60th AMW	bk/bl		90007	C-5A	433rd AW	
	60017	C-5B	436th AW	y		90008	C-5A	105th AW	bl
	60018	C-5B	60th AMW	bk/gd		90009	C-5A	105th AW	bl
	60019	C-5B	436th AW	y		90010	C-5A	60th AMW	bk/bl
	60020	C-5B	436th AW	y		90011	C-5A	439th AW	bl/r
	60021	C-5B	60th AMW	bk/gd		90012	C-5A	105th AW	bl
	60022	C-5B	60th AMW	bk/bl		90013	C-5A	439th AW	bl/r
	60023	C-5B	436th AW	y		90014	C-5A	60th AMW	
	60024	C-5B	60th AMW	bk/bl		90015	C-5A	105th AW	bl
	60025	C-5B	436th AW	y		90016	C-5A	433rd AW	
	60026	C-5B	60th AMW	bk/gd		90017	C-5A	439th AW	bl/r
	FY66					90018	C-5A	436th AW	
	68304	C-5A	439th AW	bl/r		90019	C-5A	439th AW	bl/r
	68305	C-5A	433rd AW			90020	C-5A	439th AW	bl/r
	68306	C-5A	433rd AW			90021	C-5A	105th AW	bl
	68307	C-5A	433rd AW			90022	C-5A	439th AW	bl/r
	FY87					90023	C-5A	60th AMW	bk/bl
	70027	C-5B	436th AW	y/bl		90024	C-5A	436th AW	y
	70028	C-5B	60th AMW	bk/bl		90025	C-5A	97th AMW	r/y
	70029	C-5B	436th AW	y		90026	C-5A	60th AMW	bk/bl
	70030	C-5B	60th AMW	bk/bl		90027	C-5A	436th AW	y
	70031	C-5B	436th AW	y					
	70032	C-5B	60th AMW	bk/bl		**Boeing E-8 J-STARS**			
	70033	C-5B	436th AW	y		116th ACW, Robins AFB,			
	70034	C-5B	60th AMW	bk/gd		Georgia [WR]:			
	70035	C-5B	436th AW	y		12th ACCS *(gn)*, 16th ACCS *(bk)*,			
	70036	C-5B	60th AMW	bk/gd		128th ACS/Georgia ANG *(r)*			
	70037	C-5B	436th AW	y		& 330th CTS *(y)*;			
	70038	C-5B	60th AMW	bk/bl		Grumman, Melbourne, Florida			
	70039	C-5B	436th AW	y		*FY00*			
	70040	C-5B	60th AMW	bk/gd		02000	E-8C	116th ACW	
	70041	C-5B	436th AW	y		*FY90*			
	70042	C-5B	60th AMW	bk/gd		00175	E-8A	Grumman	
	70043	C-5B	436th AW	y/bl		*FY92*			
	70044	C-5B	60th AMW	bk/gd		23289	E-8C	116th ACW	m
	70045	C-5B	436th AW	y		23290	E-8C	116th ACW	bk
	FY67					*FY93*			
	70167	C-5A	439th AW	bl/r		30597	E-8C	116th ACW	gn
	70168	C-5A	433rd AW			31097	E-8C	116th ACW	gn
	70169	C-5A	105th AW	bl		*FY94*			
	70170	C-5A	105th AW	bl		40284	E-8C	116th ACW	gn
	70171	C-5A	433rd AW			40285	E-8C	116th ACW	bk
	70173	C-5A	105th AW	bl		*FY95*			
	70174	C-5A	105th AW	bl		50121	E-8C	116th ACW	bk
	FY68					50122	E-8C	116th ACW	r
	80211	C-5A	439th AW	bl/r		*FY96*			
	80212	C-5A	105th AW	bl		60042	E-8C	116th ACW	bk
	80213	C-5C	60th AMW	bk/bl		60043	E-8C	116th ACW	
	80214	C-5A	436th AW			*FY86*			
	80215	C-5A	439th AW	bl/r		60416	TE-8A	116th ACW	y
	80216	C-5C	60th AMW	bk/gd		60417	TE-8A	116th ACW	y
	80217	C-5A	97th AMW	r/y		*FY97*			
	80219	C-5A	439th AW	bl/r		70100	E-8C	116th ACW	gn
	80220	C-5A	433rd AW			70200	E-8C	116th ACW	bk
	80221	C-5A	433rd AW			70201	E-8C	116th ACW	bk
	80222	C-5A	439th AW	bl/r		*FY99*			
	80223	C-5A	433rd AW			90006	E-8C	116th ACW	gn
	80224	C-5A	105th AW	bl					

Type			Notes	Type			Notes
McDonnell Douglas				70118	60th AMW	bk/bl	
C-9 Nightingale				70119	60th AMW	bk/r	
86th AW, Ramstein, Germany:				70120	305th AMW	bl	
76th AS;				70121	305th AMW	bl	
99th AS/89th AW, Andrews AFB,				70122	305th AMW	bl/r	
Maryland;				70123	305th AMW	bl	
FY71				70124	305th AMW	bl/r	
10876	C-9A	76th AS		*FY79*			
FY73				90433	305th AMW	bl	
31681	C-9C	89th AW		90434	305th AMW	bl/r	
31682	C-9C	89th AW		91710	305th AMW	bl/r	
31683	C-9C	89th AW		91711	305th AMW	bl	
				91712	305th AMW	bl/r	
McDonnell Douglas				91713	305th AMW	bl	
KC-10A Extender				91946	60th AMW	bk/bl	
60th AMW, Travis AFB, California:				91947	305th AMW	bl	
6th ARS *(bk/bl)* & 9th ARS *(bk/r)*;				91948	60th AMW	bk/bl	
305th AMW, McGuire AFB,				91949	305th AMW	bl/r	
New Jersey:				91950	60th AMW	bk/bl	
2nd ARS *(bl/r)* & 32nd ARS *(bl)*				91951	60th AMW	bk/bl	
FY82							
20191	60th AMW	bk/bl		**McDonnell Douglas**			
20192	60th AMW	bk/r		**C-17 Globemaster III**			
20193	60th AMW	bk/bl		62nd AW, McChord AFB, Washington:			
FY83				4th AS, 7th AS,8th AS & 10th AS;			
30075	60th AMW	bk/r		58th AS/97th AMW, Altus AFB,			
30076	60th AMW	bk/bl		Oklahoma *(r/y)*;			
30077	60th AMW	bk/r		172nd AW Jackson IAP, Mississippi			
30078	60th AMW	bk/bl		ANG:			
30079	305th AMW	bl/r		183rd AS *(bl/gd)*			
30080	60th AMW	bk/bl		417th FLTS/412th TW, Edwards AFB,			
30081	305th AMW	bl		California [ED];			
30082	305th AMW	bl		437th AW, Charleston AFB,			
FY84				South Carolina *(y/bl)*:			
40185	60th AMW	bk/bl		14th AS, 15th AS,			
40186	305th AMW	bl/r		16th AS & 17th AS			
40187	60th AMW	bk/bl		*FY00*			
40188	305th AMW	bl/r		00171	C-17A	62nd AW	
40189	305th AMW	bl		00172	C-17A	62nd AW	
40190	305th AMW	bl/r		00173	C-17A	62nd AW	
40191	60th AMW	bk/bl		00174	C-17A	62nd AW	
40192	305th AMW	bl/r		00175	C-17A	62nd AW	
FY85				00176	C-17A	437th AW	y/bl
50027	305th AMW	bl/r		00177	C-17A	437th AW	y/bl
50028	305th AMW	bl/r		00178	C-17A	62nd AW	
50029	60th AMW	bk/r		00179	C-17A	62nd AW	
50030	305th AMW	bl/r		00180	C-17A	62nd AW	
50031	305th AMW	bl/r		00181	C-17A	62nd AW	
50032	305th AMW	bl/r		00182	C-17A	62nd AW	
50033	305th AMW	bl		00183	C-17A	62nd AW	
50034	305th AMW	bl/r		00184	C-17A	62nd AW	
FY86				00185	C-17A	62nd AW	
60027	305th AMW	bl		*FY90*			
60028	305th AMW	bl/r		00532	C-17A	437th AW	y/bl
60029	60th AMW	bk/r		00533	C-17A	97th AMW	r/y
60030	305th AMW	bl/r		00534	C-17A	437th AW	y/bl
60031	60th AMW	bk/r		00535	C-17A	97th AMW	r/y
60032	60th AMW	bk/r		*FY01*			
60033	60th AMW	bk/r		10186	C-17A	62nd AW	
60034	60th AMW	bk/r		10187	C-17A	62nd AW	
60035	305th AMW	bl		10188	C-17A	437th AW	y/bl
60036	305th AMW	bl		10189	C-17A	437th AW	y/bl
60037	60th AMW	bk/r		10190	C-17A	437th AW	y/bl
60038	60th AMW	bk/r		10191	C-17A	437th AW	y/bl
FY87				10192	C-17A	437th AW	y/bl
70117	60th AMW	bk/r		10193	C-17A	437th AW	y/bl

Notes	Type				Notes	Type			
	10194	C-17A	437th AW	y/bl		FY97			
	10195	C-17A	437th AW	y/bl		70041	C-17A	437th AW	y/bl
	10196	C-17A	437th AW	y/bl		70042	C-17A	437th AW	y/bl
	10197	C-17A	437th AW	y/bl		70043	C-17A	437th AW	y/bl
	FY02					70044	C-17A	437th AW	y/bl
	21098	C-17A	437th AW	y/bl		70045	C-17A	437th AW	y/bl
	21099	C-17A	437th AW	y/bl		70046	C-17A	437th AW	y/bl
	21100	C-17A	437th AW	y/bl		70047	C-17A	437th AW	y/bl
	21101	C-17A	437th AW	y/bl		70048	C-17A	437th AW	y/bl
	21102	C-17A	437th AW	y/bl		FY98			
	21103	C-17A	62nd AW			80049	C-17A	62nd AW	
	21104	C-17A	62nd AW			80050	C-17A	62nd AW	
	21105	C-17A	62nd AW			80051	C-17A	62nd AW	
	21106	C-17A	62nd AW			80052	C-17A	62nd AW	
	21107	C-17A	62nd AW			80053	C-17A	62nd AW	
	21108	C-17A	62nd AW			80054	C-17A	62nd AW	
	21109	C-17A	62nd AW			80055	C-17A	62nd AW	
	21110	C-17A	62nd AW			80056	C-17A	62nd AW	
	21110	C-17A	62nd AW			80057	C-17A	62nd AW	
	21112	C-17A	172nd AW			FY88			
	21113	C-17A	62nd AW			80265	C-17A	62nd AW	
	21114					80266	C-17A	97th AMW	r/y
	21115					FY99			
	FY92					90058	C-17A	62nd AW	
	23291	C-17A	62nd AW			90059	C-17A	62nd AW	
	23292	C-17A	437th AW	y/bl		90060	C-17A	62nd AW	
	23293	C-17A	62nd AW			90061	C-17A	62nd AW	
	23294	C-17A	97th AMW	r/y		90062	C-17A	62nd AW	
	FY93					90063	C-17A	62nd AW	
	30599	C-17A	97th AMW	r/y		90064	C-17A	62nd AW	
	30600	C-17A	62nd AW			90165	C-17A	62nd AW	
	30601	C-17A	437th AW	y/bl		90166	C-17A	62nd AW	
	30602	C-17A	97th AMW			90167	C-17A	62nd AW	
	30603	C-17A	437th AW	y/bl		90168	C-17A	62nd AW	
	30604	C-17A	437th AW	y/bl		90169	C-17A	62nd AW	
	FY03					90170	C-17A	62nd AW	
	31116					FY89			
	31117					91189	C-17A	437th AW	y/bl
	31118					91190	C-17A	437th AW	y/bl
	31119					91191	C-17A	437th AW	y/bl
	31120					91192	C-17A	437th AW	y/bl
	FY94								

Notes	Type			
	40065	C-17A	97th AMW	y/bl
	40066	C-17A	437th AW	y/bl
	40067	C-17A	437th AW	y/bl
	40068	C-17A	437th AW	y/bl
	40069	C-17A	437th AW	y/bl
	40070	C-17A	437th AW	y/bl
	FY95			
	50102	C-17A	437th AW	y/bl
	50103	C-17A	437th AW	y/bl
	50104	C-17A	62nd AW	
	50105	C-17A	437th AW	y/bl
	50106	C-17A	437th AW	y/bl
	50107	C-17A	437th AW	y/bl
	FY96			
	60001	C-17A	437th AW	y/bl
	60002	C-17A	437th AW	y/bl
	60003	C-17A	437th AW	y/bl
	60004	C-17A	437th AW	y/bl
	60005	C-17A	437th AW	y/bl
	60006	C-17A	437th AW	y/bl
	60007	C-17A	437th AW	y/bl
	60008	C-17A	437th AW	y/bl
	FY87			
	70025	C-17A	412th TW	

Boeing TC-18E

552nd ACW, Tinker AFB,
Oklahoma [OK]:
966th AACS (bl)

FY81	
10893	
10898	

Grumman C-20 Gulfstream III/IV

89th AW, Andrews AFB, Maryland:
99th AS;
OSAC/PAT, US Army, Andrews AFB,
Maryland;
Pacific Flight Detachment,
Hickam AFB, Hawaii

C-20A Gulfstream III

FY83	
30500	89th AW
30501	89th AW

C-20B Gulfstream III

FY86	
60201	89th AW
60202	89th AW
60203	89th AW
60204	89th AW

Type		Notes
60206	89th AW	
60403	89th AW	
C-20C Gulfstream III		
FY85		
50049	89th AW	
50050	89th AW	
C-20E Gulfstream III		
FY87		
70139	Pacific Flt Det	
70140	OSAC/PAT	
C-20F Gulfstream IV		
FY91		
10108	OSAC/PAT	

Boeing C-22B
201st AS/113th FW, DC ANG,
  Andrews AFB, Maryland
FY83
34615
34616

Boeing VC-25A
89th AW, Andrews AFB, Maryland
FY82
28000
FY92
29000

Boeing C-32A
1st AS/89th AW, Andrews AFB,
  Maryland
FY98
80001
80002
FY99
90003
90004

**Gulfstream Aerospace C-37A
Gulfstream V**
6th AMW, MacDill AFB, Florida:
  310th AS;
15th ABW, Hickam AFB, Hawaii:
  65th AS;
89th AW, Andrews AFB, Maryland:
  99th AS;
OSAC/PAT, US Army, Andrews AFB,
  Maryland

FY01	
10028	6th AMW
10029	6th AMW
10030	6th AMW
10065	15th ABW
FY02	
21863	OSAC/PAT
FY97	
70049	OSAC/PAT
70400	89th AW
70401	89th AW
FY99	
90402	89th AW
90404	89th AW

IAI C-38A Astra
201st AS/113th FW, DC ANG,
  Andrews AFB, Maryland

Type			Notes
FY94			
41569			
41570			

Boeing C-40
15th ABW, Hickam AFB, Hawaii:
  65th AS;
89th AW, Andrews AFB, Maryland:
  1st AS;
201st AS/113th FW, DC ANG,
  Andrews AFB, Maryland

FY01		
10005	C-40B	89th AW
10015	C-40B	15th ABW
10040	C-40B	89th AW
FY02		
20201	C-40C	201st AS
20202	C-40C	201st AS
20203	C-40C	
20204	C-40C	

Boeing T-43A
562nd FTS/12th FTW, Randolph
  AFB, Texas [RA] *(bk/y)*
FY71
11403
11404
11405
FY72
20288
FY73
31150
31151
31152
31153
31154
31156

Boeing B-52H Stratofortress
2nd BW, Barksdale AFB,
  Louisiana [LA]:
  11th BS *(gd)*, 20th BS *(bl)*
  & 96th BS *(r)*;
23rd BS/5th BW, Minot AFB,
  North Dakota [MT] *(r/y)*;
93rd BS/917th Wg AFRC,
  Barksdale AFB,
  Louisiana [BD] *(y/bl)*;
419th FLTS/412th TW Edwards AFB,
  California [ED]

FY60		
00001	2nd BW	bl
00002	2nd BW	gd
00003	93rd BS	y/bl
00004	5th BW	r/y
00005	5th BW	r/y
00007	5th BW	r/y
00008	2nd BW	r
00009	5th BW	r/y
00010	2nd BW	r
00011	2nd BW	gd
00012	2nd BW	r
00013	2nd BW	r
00014	2nd BW	bl
00015	5th BW	r/y
00016	2nd BW	r

B-52 – F-117

Notes	Type			Notes	Type		
	00017	2nd BW	gd		10024	2nd BW	r
	00018	5th BW	r/y		10027	5th BW	r/y
	00019	2nd BW	r		10028	2nd BW	gd
	00020	2nd BW	bl		10029	93rd BS	y/bl
	00022	2nd BW	r		10031	2nd BW	gd
	00023	5th BW	r/y		10032	93rd BS	y/bl
	00024	5th BW	r/y		10034	5th BW	r/y
	00025	2nd BW	bl		10035	5th BW	r/y
	00026	5th BW	r/y		10036	2nd BW	gd
	00028	2nd BW	r		10038	2nd BW	gd
	00029	5th BW	r/y		10039	2nd BW	gd
	00030	2nd BW	bl		10040	5th BW	r/y
	00031	2nd BW	bl					
	00032	2nd BW	gd		**Lockheed F-117A Nighthawk**			
	00033	5th BW	r/y		49th FW, Holloman AFB,			
	00034	5th BW	r/y		New Mexico [HO]:			
	00035	2nd BW	gd		8th FS (y) & 9th FS (r);			
	00036	419th FLTS			53rd Wg, Nellis AFB,			
	00037	2nd BW	r		Nevada [OT] (gy/w);			
	00038	2nd BW	gd		445th FLTS/412th TW, Edwards AFB,			
	00041	93rd BS	y/bl		California [ED]			
	00042	93rd BS	y/bl		79-783	(79-10783)	ED	
	00043	2nd BW	bl		79-784	(79-10784)	ED	
	00044	5th BW	r/y		80-786	(80-0786)	HO	r
	00045	93rd BS	y/bl		80-787	(80-0787)	HO	y
	00046	2nd BW	bl		80-788	(80-0788)	HO	
	00047	5th BW	r/y		80-789	(80-0789)	HO	r
	00048	2nd BW	gd		80-790	(80-0790)	HO	r
	00049	2nd BW	bl		80-791	(80-0791)	HO	y
	00050	412th TW			81-794	(81-10794)	HO	r
	00051	5th BW	r/y		81-795	(81-10795)	HO	y
	00052	2nd BW	r		81-796	(81-10796)	HO	r [48th OG]
	00053	2nd BW	r		81-797	(81-10797)	HO	r
	00054	2nd BW	r		81-798	(81-10798)	HO	r [49th FW]
	00055	5th BW	r/y		82-799	(82-0799)	HO	r
	00056	5th BW	r/y		82-800	(82-0800)	HO	y [8th FS]
	00057	2nd BW	gd		82-801	(82-0801)	HO	
	00058	2nd BW	gd		82-802	(82-0802)	HO	y
	00059	2nd BW	r		82-803	(82-0803)	HO	y
	00060	5th BW	r/y		82-804	(82-0804)	HO	y
	00061	2nd BW	gd		82-805	(82-0805)	HO	r
	00062	2nd BW	bl		83-807	(83-0807)	HO	
	FY61				83-808	(83-0808)	HO	
	10001	5th BW	r/y		84-809	(84-0809)	HO	r [9th FS]
	10002	2nd BW	bl		84-810	(84-0810)	HO	r
	10003	2nd BW	gd		84-811	(84-0811)	HO	r
	10004	2nd BW	bl		84-812	(84-0812)	HO	
	10005	5th BW	r/y		84-824	(84-0824)	HO	r
	10006	2nd BW	gd		84-825	(84-0825)	HO	y
	10007	5th BW	r/y		84-826	(84-0826)	HO	r
	10008	93rd BS	y/bl		84-827	(84-0827)	HO	y
	10009	2nd BW	r		84-828	(84-0828)	HO	r
	10010	2nd BW	bl		85-813	(85-0813)	HO	r
	10011	2nd BW	gd		85-814	(85-0814)	HO	r
	10012	2nd BW	gd		85-816	(85-0816)	HO	y [49th FW]
	10013	2nd BW	r		85-817	(85-0817)	HO	y
	10014	5th BW	r/y		85-818	(85-0818)	HO	y
	10015	2nd BW	gd		85-819	(85-0819)	HO	y [49th FW]
	10016	2nd BW	r		85-820	(85-0820)	HO	r
	10017	93rd BS	y/bl		85-829	(85-0829)	HO	y
	10018	5th BW	r/y		85-830	(85-0830)	HO	r
	10019	2nd BW	r		85-831	(85-0831)	ED	
	10020	2nd BW	r		85-832	(85-0832)	HO	y
	10021	93rd BS	y/bl		85-833	(85-0833)	HO	r
	10022	93rd BS	y/bl		85-834	(85-0834)	HO	y
	10023	2nd BW	bl		85-835	(85-0835)	OT	gy/w

Type	Notes
85-836 (85-0836) HO *r*	
86-821 (86-0821) HO *r*	
86-822 (86-0822) HO	
86-823 (86-0823) HO *r*	
86-837 (86-0837) HO *y*	
86-838 (86-0838) HO *y*	
86-839 (86-0839) HO *y*	
86-840 (86-0840) HO *r*	
88-841 (88-0841) HO *r* [9th FS]	
88-842 (88-0842) HO *y*	
88-843 (88-0843) HO *y*	

Lockheed C-130 Hercules

1st SOS/353rd SOG, Kadena AB, Japan;

3rd Wg, Elmendorf AFB, Alaska [AK]: 517th AS (*w*);

4th SOS/16th SOW, Hurlburt Field, Florida;

7th SOS/352nd SOG, RAF Mildenhall, UK;

8th SOS/16th SOW, Duke Field, Florida;

9th SOS/16th OG, Eglin AFB, Florida;

15th SOS/16th SOW, Hurlburt Field, Florida;

16th SOS/16th SOW, Hurlburt Field, Florida;

17th SOS/353rd SOG, Kadena AB, Japan;

37th AS/86th AW, Ramstein AB, Germany [RS] *(bl/w)*;

39th RQS/920th RQW AFRC, Patrick AFB, Florida [FL];

41st ECS/55th Wg, Davis-Monthan AFB, Arizona [DM] *(bl)*;

43rd AW, Pope AFB, North Carolina [FT]:
2nd AS (*gn/bl*) & 41st AS (gn/or);

43rd ECS/55th Wg, Davis-Monthan AFB, Arizona [DM] *(r)*;

53rd WRS/403rd AW AFRC, Keesler AFB, Missouri;

58th SOW, Kirtland AFB, New Mexico: 550th SOS;

67th SOS/352nd SOG, RAF Mildenhall, UK;

71st RQS/347th Wg, Moody AFB, Georgia [MY] *(bl)*;

79th RQS/55th Wg, Davis Monthan AFB, Arizona;

95th AS/440th AW AFRC, General Mitchell ARS, Wisconsin *(w/r)*;

96th AS/934th AW AFRC, Minneapolis/St Paul, Minnesota *(pr)*;

102nd RQS/106th RQW, Suffolk Field, New York ANG [LI];

105th AS/118th AW, Nashville, Tennessee ANG *(r)*;

109th AS/133rd AW, Minneapolis/ St Paul, Minnesota ANG [MN] *(gn/bl)*;

115th AS/146th AW, Channel Island ANGS, California [CI] *(gn)*;

122nd FS/159th FW, NAS New Orleans, Louisiana ANG [JZ];

129th RQS/129th RQW, Moffet Field, California ANG [CA] *(bl)*;

130th AS/130th AW, Yeager Int'l Airport, Charleston West Virginia ANG [WV] *(pr/y)*;

135th AS/175yh Wg, Martin State Airport, Maryland ANG [MD] *(bk/y)*;

139th AS/109th AW, Schenectady, New York ANG [NY];

142nd AS/166th AW, New Castle County Airport, Delaware ANG [DE] *(bl)*;

143rd AS/143rd AW, Quonset, Rhode Island ANG [RI] *(r)*;

144th AS/176th CW, Kulis ANGB, Alaska ANG *(bk/y)*;

154th TS/189th AW, Little Rock, Arkansas ANG *(r)*;

156th AS/145th AW, Charlotte, North Carolina ANG [NC] *(bl)*;

157th FS/169th FW, McEntire ANGS, South Carolina ANG [SC];

158th AS/165th AW, Savannah, Georgia ANG *(r)*;

159th FS/125th FW, Jacksonville, Florida ANG;

164th AS/179th AW, Mansfield, Ohio ANG [OH] *(bl)*;

165th AS/123rd AW, Standiford Field, Kentucky ANG [KY];

167th AS/167th AW, Martinsburg, West Virginia ANG [WV] *(r)*;

169th AS/182nd AW, Peoria, Illinois ANG [IL];

171st AS/191st AW, Selfridge ANGB, Michigan ANG *(y/bk)*;

180th AS/139th AW, Rosencrans Memorial Airport, Missouri ANG [XP] *(y)*;

181st AS/136th AW, NAS Dallas, Texas ANG *(bl/w)*;

185th AS/137th AW, Will Rogers World Airport, Oklahoma ANG [OK] *(bl)*;

187th AS/153rd AW, Cheyenne, Wyoming ANG [WY];

189th AS/124th Wg, Boise, Idaho ANG [ID];

192nd AS/152nd AW, Reno, Nevada ANG [NV] *(w)*;

193rd SOS/193rd SOW, Harrisburg, Pennsylvania ANG [PA];

198th AS/156th AW, San Juan, Puerto Rico ANG;

204th AS/154th Wg, Hickam AFB, Hawaii ANG [HH];

210th RQS/176th CW, Kulis ANGB, Alaska ANG [AK];

314th AW, Little Rock AFB, Arkansas: 48th AS, 53rd AS (*bk*) & 62nd AS *(bl)*;

317th AG, Dyess AFB, Texas: 39th AS (*r*) & 40th AS *(bl)*;

327th AS/913th AW AFRC, NAS Willow Grove, Pennsylvania *(bk)*;

Notes	Type				Notes	Type			
	328th AS/914th AW AFRC,					FY90			
	Niagara Falls, New York [NF] *(bl)*;					01791	C-130H	164th AS	*bl*
	357th AS/908th AW AFRC,					01792	C-130H	164th AS	*bl*
	Maxwell AFB, Alabama *(bl)*;					01793	C-130H	164th AS	*bl*
	374th AW, Yokota AB, Japan [YJ]:					01794	C-130H	164th AS	*bl*
	36th AS *(r)*;					01795	C-130H	164th AS	*bl*
	412th TW Edwards AFB, California:					01796	C-130H	164th AS	*bl*
	452nd FLTS [ED];					01797	C-130H	164th AS	*bl*
	463rd AG Little Rock AFB, Arkansas					01798	C-130H	164th AS	*bl*
	[LK]:					FY00			
	50th AS *(r)* & 61st AS *(gn)*;					01934	EC-130J	LMTAS	
	645th Materiel Sqn, Palmdale,					FY90			
	California [D4];					02103	HC-130N	210th RQS	
	700th AS/94th AW AFRC,					09107	C-130H	757th AS	*bl*
	Dobbins ARB, Georgia [DB] *(bl)*;					09108	C-130H	757th AS	*bl*
	711th SOS/919th SOW AFRC,					FY81			
	Duke Field, Florida;					10626	C-130H	700th AS	*bl*
	731st AS/302nd AW AFRC, Peterson					10627	C-130H	700th AS	*bl*
	AFB, Colorado *(pr/w)*;					10628	C-130H	700th AS	*bl*
	757th AS/910th AW AFRC,					10629	C-130H	700th AS	*bl*
	Youngstown ARS, Ohio [YO] *(bl)*;					10630	C-130H	700th AS	*bl*
	758th AS/911th AW AFRC,					10631	C-130H	700th AS	*bl*
	Pittsburgh ARS, Pennsylvania *(bk/y)*;					FY68			
	773rd AS/910th AW AFRC,					10935	C-130E	37th AS	*bl/w*
	Youngstown ARS, Ohio [YO] *(r)*;					10939	C-130E	43rd AW	*gn/bl*
	815th AS/403rd AW AFRC,					10941	C-130E	43rd AW	*gn/bl*
	Keesler AFB, Missouri [KT] *(r)*;					10943	C-130E	37th AS	*bl/w*
	LMTAS, Marietta, Georgia					10948	C-130E	463rd AG	*gn*
	FY90					FY91			
	00162	MC-130H	15th SOS			11231	C-130H	165th AS	
	00163	AC-130U	4th SOS			11232	C-130H	165th AS	
	00164	AC-130U	4th SOS			11233	C-130H	165th AS	
	00165	AC-130U	4th SOS			11234	C-130H	165th AS	
	00166	AC-130U	4th SOS			11235	C-130H	165th AS	
	00167	AC-130U	4th SOS			11236	C-130H	165th AS	
	FY80					11237	C-130H	165th AS	
	00320	C-130H	158th AS	*r*		11238	C-130H	165th AS	
	00321	C-130H	158th AS	*r*		11239	C-130H	165th AS	
	00322	C-130H	158th AS	*r*		FY01			
	00323	C-130H	158th AS	*r*		11461	CC-130J	115th AS	*gn*
	00324	C-130H	158th AS	*r*		11462	CC-130J	115th AS	*gn*
	00325	C-130H	158th AS	*r*		FY91			
	00326	C-130H	158th AS	*r*		11651	C-130H	165th AS	
	00332	C-130H	158th AS	*r*		11652	C-130H	165th AS	
	FY90					11653	C-130H	165th AS	
	01057	C-130H	204th AS			FY61			
	01058	C-130H	204th AS			12358	C-130E	171st AS	*y/bk*
	FY70					12359	C-130E	115th AS	*gn*
	01259	C-130E	43rd AW	*gn/bl*		12367	C-130E	115th AS	*gn*
	01260	C-130E	37th AS	*bl/w*		12369	C-130E	198th AS	
	01261	C-130E	43rd AW	*gn/bl*		12370	C-130E	171st AS	*y/bk*
	01262	C-130E	43rd AW	*gn/or*		12372	C-130E	115th AS	*gn*
	01263	C-130E	43rd AW	*gn/or*		FY64			
	01264	C-130E	37th AS	*bl/w*		14852	HC-130P	71st RQS	*bl*
	01265	C-130E	43rd AW	*gn/bl*		14853	HC-130P	71st RQS	*bl*
	01266	C-130E	43rd AW	*gn/bl*		14854	MC-130P	9th SOS	
	01267	C-130E	43rd AW	*gn/or*		14855	HC-130P	39th RQS	*y*
	01268	C-130E	43rd AW	*gn/bl*		14858	MC-130P	58th SOW	
	01270	C-130E	43rd AW	*gn/bl*		14859	C-130E	16th SOW	
	01271	C-130E	37th AS	*bl/w*		14860	HC-130P	39th RQS	
	01272	C-130E	43rd AW	*gn/bl*		14861	WC-130H	53rd WRS	
	01273	C-130E	43rd AW	*gn/bl*		14862	EC-130H	645th MS	
	01274	C-130E	37th AS	*bl/w*		14863	HC-130P	71st RQS	*bl*
	01275	C-130E	43rd AW	*gn/bl*		14864	HC-130P	39th RQS	
	01276	C-130E	43rd AW	*gn/bl*		14865	HC-130P	71st RQS	*bl*
						14866	WC-130H	53rd WRS	

Type			Notes		Type			Notes
17681	C-130E	37th AS	bl/w		21810	C-130E	314th AW	bl
FY91					21811	C-130E	115th AS	gn
19141	C-130H	773rd AS	r		21816	C-130E	314th AW	bl
19142	C-130H	773rd AS	r		21817	C-130E	189th AS	
19143	C-130H	773rd AS	r		21818	HC-130P	79th RQS	
19144	C-130H	773rd AS	r		21820	C-130E	171st AS	y/bk
FY82					21823	C-130E	96th AS	pr
20054	C-130H	144th AS	bk/y		21824	C-130E	154th TS	r
20055	C-130H	144th AS	bk/y		21826	C-130E	115th AS	gn
20056	C-130H	144th AS	bk/y		21829	C-130E	171st AS	y/bk
20057	C-130H	144th AS	bk/y		21832	HC-130P	79th RQS	
20058	C-130H	144th AS	bk/y		21833	C-130E	115th AS	gn
20059	C-130H	144th AS	bk/y		21834	C-130E	374th AW	r
20060	C-130H	144th AS	bk/y		21835	C-130E	96th AS	pr
20061	C-130H	144th AS	bk/y		21836	HC-130P	79th RQS	
FY92					21837	C-130E	189th AS	
20253	AC-130U	4th SOS			21839	C-130E	96th AS	pr
20547	C-130H	463rd AG	r		21842	C-130E	171st AS	y/bk
20548	C-130H	463rd AG	r		21843	MC-130E	711th SOS	
20549	C-130H	463rd AG	r		21844	C-130E	96th AS	pr
20550	C-130H	463rd AG	r		21846	C-130E	189th AS	
20551	C-130H	463rd AG	r		21847	C-130E	96th AS	pr
20552	C-130H	463rd AG	r		21848	C-130E	96th AS	pr
20553	C-130H	463rd AG	r		21849	C-130E	463rd AG	gn
20554	C-130H	463rd AG	r		21850	C-130E	314th AW	bk
21094	LC-130H	139th AS			21851	C-130E	115th AS	gn
21095	LC-130H	139th AS			21852	C-130E	96th AS	pr
FY72					21855	C-130E	374th AW	r
21288	C-130E	374th AW	r		21856	C-130E	143rd AS	r
21289	C-130E	374th AW	r		21857	EC-130E	43rd ECS	r
21290	C-130E	374th AW	r		21858	C-130E	171st AS	y/bk
21291	C-130E	314th AW	bk		21859	C-130E	122nd FS	
21292	C-130E	463rd AG	gn		21862	C-130E	115th AS	gn
21293	C-130E	463rd AG	gn		21863	HC-130P		
21294	C-130E	463rd AG	gn		21864	C-130E	189th AS	
21295	C-130E	314th AW	bl		*FY92*			
21296	C-130E	314th AW	bk		23021	C-130H	773rd AS	r
21299	C-130E	374th AW	r		23022	C-130H	773rd AS	r
FY92					23023	C-130H	773rd AS	r
21451	C-130H	156th AS	bl		23024	C-130H	773rd AS	r
21452	C-130H	156th AS	bl		23281	C-130H	328th AS	bl
21453	C-130H	156th AS	bl		23282	C-130H	328th AS	bl
21454	C-130H	156th AS	bl		23283	C-130H	328th AS	bl
21531	C-130H	187th AS			23284	C-130H	328th AS	bl
21532	C-130H	187th AS			23285	C-130H	328th AS	bl
21533	C-130H	187th AS			23286	C-130H	328th AS	bl
21534	C-130H	187th AS			23287	C-130H	328th AS	bl
21535	C-130H	187th AS			23288	C-130H	328th AS	bl
21536	C-130H	187th AS			*FY83*			
21537	C-130H	187th AS			30486	C-130H	139th AS	
21538	C-130H	187th AS			30487	C-130H	139th AS	
FY62					30488	C-130H	139th AS	
21784	C-130E	154th TS	r		30489	C-130H	139th AS	
21786	C-130E	189th AS			30490	LC-130H	139th AS	
21787	C-130E	154th TS	r		30491	LC-130H	139th AS	
21788	C-130E	154th TS	r		30492	LC-130H	139th AS	
21789	C-130E	314th AW	bk		30493	LC-130H	139th AS	
21791	EC-130E	41st ECS	bl		*FY93*			
21792	C-130E	463rd AG	gn		31036	C-130H	463rd AG	r
21793	C-130E	115th AS	gn		31037	C-130H	463rd AG	r
21798	C-130E	314th AW	bk		31038	C-130H	463rd AG	r
21799	C-130E	115th AS	gn		31039	C-130H	463rd AG	r
21801	C-130E	115th AS	gn		31040	C-130H	463rd AG	r
21804	C-130E	154th TS	r		31041	C-130H	463rd AG	r
21806	C-130E	96th AS	pr		31096	LC-130H	139th AS	
21808	C-130E	314th AW	bk					

C-130

Notes	Type				Notes	Type			
	FY83					37819	C-130E	374th AW	r
	31212	MC-130H	15th SOS			37821	C-130E	374th AW	r
	FY93					37823	C-130E	327th AS	bk
	31455	C-130H	156th AS	bl		37824	C-130E	143rd AS	r
	31456	C-130H	156th AS	bl		37825	C-130E	169th AS	
	31457	C-130H	156th AS	bl		37826	C-130E	327th AS	bk
	31458	C-130H	156th AS	bl		37828	EC-130E	193rd SOS	
	31459	C-130H	156th AS	bl		37829	C-130E	463rd AG	gn
	31561	C-130H	156th AS	bl		37830	C-130E	314th AW	bk
	31562	C-130H	156th AS	bl		37831	C-130E	115th AS	gn
	31563	C-130H	156th AS	bl		37832	C-130E	327th AS	bk
	FY73					37833	C-130E	327th AS	bk
	31580	EC-130H	43rd ECS	r		37834	C-130E	327th AS	bk
	31581	EC-130H	43rd ECS	r		37835	C-130E	314th AW	bk
	31582	C-130H	317th AG	r		37837	C-130E	374th AW	r
	31583	EC-130H	43rd ECS	r		37838	C-130E	314th AW	bl
	31584	EC-130H	43rd ECS	r		37839	C-130E	463rd AG	gn
	31585	EC-130H	41st ECS	bl		37840	C-130E	143rd AS	r
	31586	EC-130H	41st ECS	bl		37841	C-130E	198th AS	
	31587	EC-130H	41st ECS	bl		37842	C-130E	39th RQS	y
	31588	EC-130H	41st ECS	bl		37845	C-130E	463rd AG	
	31590	EC-130H	43rd ECS	r		37846	C-130E	314th AW	
	31592	EC-130H	41st ECS	bl		37847	C-130E	154th TS	r
	31594	EC-130H	41st ECS	bl		37848	C-130E	327th AS	bk
	31595	EC-130H	43rd ECS	r		37849	C-130E	314th AW	bl
	31597	C-130H	317th AG	r		37850	C-130E	374th AW	r
	31598	C-130H	317th AG	r		37851	C-130E	198th AS	
	FY93					37852	C-130E	463rd AG	gn
	32041	C-130H	204th AS			37853	C-130E	327th AS	bk
	32042	C-130H	204th AS			37856	C-130E	463rd AG	gn
	32104	HC-130N	210th RQS			37857	C-130E	463rd AG	gn
	32105	HC-130N	210th RQS			37858	C-130E	169th AS	
	32106	HC-130N	210th RQS			37859	C-130E	143rd AS	r
	37311	C-130H	731st AS	pr/w		37860	C-130E	314th AW	bl
	37312	C-130H	731st AS	pr/w		37861	C-130E	129th RQS	bl
	37313	C-130H	731st AS	pr/w		37864	C-130E	314th AW	bl
	37314	C-130H	731st AS	pr/w		37865	C-130E	37th AS	bl/w
	FY63					37866	C-130E	314th AW	bk
	37764	C-130E	463rd AG	gn		37867	C-130E	327th AS	bk
	37765	C-130E	314th AW	bl		37868	C-130E	143rd AS	r
	37767	C-130E	314th AW	bl		37871	C-130E	374th AW	r
	37768	C-130E	314th AW	bl		37872	C-130E	169th AS	
	37769	C-130E	327th AS	bk		37874	C-130E	314th AW	bk
	37770	C-130E	96th AS	pr		37876	C-130E	463rd AG	gn
	37776	C-130E	327th AS	bk		37877	C-130E	169th AS	
	37781	C-130E	463rd AG	gn		37879	C-130E	37th AS	bl/w
	37782	C-130E	143rd AS	r		37880	C-130E	314th AW	bl
	37784	C-130E	314th AW	bl		37882	C-130E	314th AW	bk
	37785	MC-130E	711th SOS			37883	C-130E	327th AS	bk
	37786	C-130E	171st AS	y/bk		37884	C-130E	463rd AG	gn
	37790	C-130E	374th AW	r		37885	C-130E	37th AS	bl/w
	37791	C-130E	314th AW	bl		37887	C-130E	37th AS	bl/w
	37792	C-130E	169th AS			37888	C-130E	463rd AG	gn
	37796	C-130E	314th AW	bk		37889	C-130E	143rd AS	r
	37799	C-130E	314th AW	bl		37890	C-130E	314th AW	bl
	37800	C-130E	169th AS			37892	C-130E	327th AS	bk
	37804	C-130E	314th AW	bl		37893	C-130E	314th AW	bk
	37808	C-130E	463rd AG	gn		37894	C-130E	463rd AG	gn
	37809	C-130E	463rd AG	gn		37895	C-130E	171st AS	y/bk
	37811	C-130E	143rd AS	r		37896	C-130E	314th AW	bk
	37812	C-130E	169th AS			37897	C-130E	169th AS	or
	37814	C-130E	67th SOS			37898	C-130E	16th SOW	
	37815	C-130E	193rd SOS			37899	C-130E	314th AW	bl
	37816	C-130E	193rd SOS			39810	C-130E	71st RQS	bl
	37817	C-130E	463rd AG	gn		39812	C-130E	314th AW	bk
	37818	C-130E	169th AS			39813	C-130E	171st AS	y/bk

Type			Notes		Type			Notes
39814	C-130E	314th AW	bl		41670	C-130H	317th AG	r
39815	C-130E	198th AS			41671	C-130H	317th AG	bl
39816	EC-130E	193rd SOS			41673	C-130H	317th AG	bl
39817	EC-130E	193rd SOS			41674	C-130H	317th AG	r
FY84					41675	C-130H	317th AG	r
40204	C-130H	700th AS	bl		41676	C-130H	3rd Wg	m
40205	C-130H	700th AS	bl		41677	C-130H	317th AG	bl
40206	C-130H	142nd AS	bl		41679	C-130H	317th AG	bl
40207	C-130H	142nd AS	bl		41680	C-130H	317th AG	r
40208	C-130H	142nd AS	bl		41682	C-130H	3rd Wg	w
40209	C-130H	142nd AS	bl		41684	C-130H	3rd Wg	w
40210	C-130H	142nd AS	bl		41685	C-130H	3rd Wg	w
40211	C-130H	142nd AS	bl		41687	C-130H	317th AG	r
40212	C-130H	142nd AS	bl		41688	C-130H	317th AG	bl
40213	C-130H	142nd AS	bl		41689	C-130H	317th AG	bl
40476	MC-130H	15th SOS			41690	C-130H	3rd Wg	w
FY64					41691	C-130H	317th AG	r
40495	C-130E	43rd AW	gn/or		41692	C-130H	3rd Wg	w
40496	C-130E	43rd AW	gn/bl		42061	C-130H	317th AG	r
40498	C-130E	43rd AW	gn/bl		42062	C-130H	3rd Wg	w
40499	C-130E	37th AS	bl/w		42063	C-130H	317th AG	bl
40502	C-130E	37th AS	bl/w		42065	C-130H	317th AG	bl
40504	C-130E	43rd AW	gn/bl		42066	C-130H	3rd Wg	w
40510	C-130E	198th AS			42067	C-130H	317th AG	r
40512	C-130E	154th TS	r		42069	C-130H	317th AG	r
40515	C-130E	198th AS			42070	C-130H	3rd Wg	w
40517	C-130E	43rd AW	gn/bl		42071	C-130H	3rd Wg	w
40518	C-130E	463rd AG	gn		42072	C-130H	317th AG	bl
40519	C-130E	314th AW	bl		42130	C-130H	317th AG	r
40520	C-130E	157th FS			42131	C-130H	3rd Wg	w
40521	C-130E	159th FS			42132	C-130H	317th AG	r
40523	MC-130E	8th SOS			42133	C-130H	3rd Wg	w
40525	C-130E	43rd AW	gn/bl		42134	C-130H	317th AG	r
40526	C-130E	154th TS	r		*FY94*			
40527	C-130E	37th AS	bl/w		46701	C-130H	167th AS	r
40529	C-130E	43rd AW	gn/or		46702	C-130H	167th AS	r
40531	C-130E	43rd AW	gn/bl		46703	C-130H	167th AS	r
40537	C-130E	43rd AW	gn/or		46704	C-130H	167th AS	r
40538	C-130E	314th AW	bk		46705	C-130H	167th AS	r
40539	C-130E	43rd AW	gn/or		46706	C-130H	167th AS	r
40540	C-130E	43rd AW	gn/bl		46707	C-130H	167th AS	r
40541	C-130E	314th AW	bk		46708	C-130H	167th AS	r
40544	C-130E	198th AS			47310	C-130H	731st AS	pr/w
40551	MC-130E	711th SOS			47315	C-130H	731st AS	pr/w
40555	MC-130E	711th SOS			47316	C-130H	731st AS	pr/w
40559	MC-130E	711th SOS			47317	C-130H	731st AS	pr/w
40561	MC-130E	711th SOS			47318	C-130H	731st AS	pr/w
40562	MC-130E	711th SOS			47319	C-130H	731st AS	pr/w
40565	MC-130E	711th SOS			47320	C-130H	731st AS	pr/w
40566	MC-130E	8th SOS			47321	C-130H	731st AS	pr/w
40567	MC-130E	8th SOS			48151	C-130J	815th AS	r
40568	MC-130E	8th SOS			48152	C-130J	815th AS	r
40569	C-130E	314th AW	bl		*FY85*			
40571	MC-130E	711th SOS			50011	MC-130E	15th SOS	
40572	MC-130E	8th SOS			50012	MC-130E	15th SOS	
FY74					50035	C-130	357th AS	bl
41658	C-130H	3rd Wg	w		50036	C-130	357th AS	bl
41659	C-130H	3rd Wg	w		50037	C-130	357th AS	bl
41660	C-130H	3rd Wg	w		50038	C-130	357th AS	bl
41661	C-130H	3rd Wg	w		50039	C-130	357th AS	bl
41663	C-130H	317th AG	bl		50040	C-130	357th AS	bl
41664	C-130H	3rd Wg	w		50041	C-130	357th AS	bl
41665	C-130H	317th AG	bl		50042	C-130	357th AS	bl
41666	C-130H	317th AG	bl		*FY65*			
41667	C-130H	317th AG	r		50962	EC-130H	43rd ECS	r
41668	C-130H	3rd Wg	w		50963	WC-130H	53rd WRS	
41669	C-130H	317th AG	bl					

C-130

Notes	Type				Notes	Type			
	50964	HC-130P	79th RQS			61004	C-130H	109th AS	gn/bl
	50966	WC-130H	53rd WRS			61005	C-130H	109th AS	gn/bl
	50967	WC-130H	53rd WRS			61006	C-130H	109th AS	gn/bl
	50968	WC-130H	53rd WRS			61007	C-130H	109th AS	gn/bl
	50970	HC-130P	39th RQS			61008	C-130H	109th AS	gn/bl
	50971	MC-130P	58th SOW			*FY86*			
	50973	HC-130P	71st RQS	bl		61391	C-130H	180th AS	y
	50974	HC-130P	102nd RQS			61392	C-130H	180th AS	y
	50975	MC-130P	58th SOW			61393	C-130H	180th AS	y
	50976	HC-130P	39th RQS			61394	C-130H	180th AS	y
	50977	WC-130H	53rd WRS			61395	C-130H	180th AS	y
	50978	HC-130P	102nd RQS			61396	C-130H	180th AS	y
	50979	NC-130H	412th TW			61397	C-130H	180th AS	y
	50980	WC-130H	53rd WRS			61398	C-130H	180th AS	y
	50981	HC-130P	71st RQS	bl		61699	MC-130H	7th SOS	
	50982	HC-130P	71st RQS	bl		*FY76*			
	50983	MC-130P	71st RQS	bl		63300	LC-130R	139th AS	
	50984	WC-130H	53rd WRS			63302	LC-130R	139th AS	
	50985	WC-130H	53rd WRS			*FY96*			
	50986	HC-130P	71st RQS	bl		65300	WC-130J	53rd WRS	
	50987	HC-130P	71st RQS	bl		65301	WC-130J	53rd WRS	
	50988	HC-130P	71st RQS	bl		65302	WC-130J	53rd WRS	
	50989	EC-130H	41st ECS	bl		67322	C-130H	731st AS	pr/w
	50991	MC-130P	9th SOS			67323	C-130H	731st AS	pr/w
	50992	MC-130P	17th SOS			67324	C-130H	731st AS	pr/w
	50993	MC-130P	17th SOS			67325	C-130H	731st AS	pr/w
	50994	MC-130P	17th SOS			68153	C-130J	815th AS	r
	FY95					68154	C-130J	815th AS	r
	51001	C-130H	109th AS	gn/bl		*FY87*			
	51002	C-130H	109th AS	gn/bl		70023	MC-130H	7th SOS	
	FY85					70024	MC-130H	15th SOS	
	51361	C-130H	181st AS	bl/w		70125	MC-130H	58th SOW	
	51362	C-130H	181st AS	bl/w		70126	MC-130H	58th SOW	
	51363	C-130H	181st AS	bl/w		70127	MC-130H	58th SOW	
	51364	C-130H	181st AS	bl/w		70128	AC-130U	4th SOS	
	51365	C-130H	181st AS	bl/w		*FY97*			
	51366	C-130H	181st AS	bl/w		71351	C-130J	135th AS	bk/y
	51367	C-130H	181st AS	bl/w		71352	C-130J	135th AS	bk/y
	51368	C-130H	181st AS	bl/w		71353	C-130J	135th AS	bk/y
	FY95					71354	C-130J	135th AS	bk/y
	56709	C-130H	167th AS	r		71931	EC-130J	193rd SOS	
	56710	C-130H	167th AS	r		75303	WC-130J	53rd WRS	
	56711	C-130H	167th AS	r		75304	WC-130J	53rd WRS	
	56712	C-130H	167th AS	r		75305	WC-130J	53rd WRS	
	FY66					75306	WC-130J	53rd WRS	
	60212	HC-130P	129th RQS	bl		*FY87*			
	60216	HC-130P	129th RQS	bl		79281	C-130H	95th AS	w/r
	60217	MC-130P	9th SOS			79282	C-130H	95th AS	w/r
	60219	HC-130P	129th RQS	bl		79283	C-130H	95th AS	w/r
	60220	MC-130P	17th SOS			79284	C-130H	700th AS	bl
	60221	HC-130P	129th RQS	bl		79285	C-130H	95th AS	w/r
	60222	HC-130P	102nd RQS			79286	C-130H	357th AS	bl
	60223	MC-130P	9th SOS			79287	C-130H	95th AS	w/r
	60224	HC-130P	79th RQS			79288	C-130H	758th AS	bk/y
	60225	MC-130P	9th SOS			*FY88*			
	FY86					80191	MC-130H	1st SOS	
	60410	C-130H	758th AS	bk/y		80192	MC-130H	1st SOS	
	60411	C-130H	758th AS	bk/y		80193	MC-130H	7th SOS	
	60412	C-130H	758th AS	bk/y		80194	MC-130H	7th SOS	
	60413	C-130H	758th AS	bk/y		80195	MC-130H	1st SOS	
	60414	C-130H	758th AS	bk/y		80264	MC-130H	1st SOS	
	60415	C-130H	758th AS	bk/y		*FY78*			
	60418	C-130H	758th AS	bk/y		80806	C-130H	185th AS	bl
	60419	C-130H	758th AS	bk/y		80807	C-130H	185th AS	bl
	FY96					80808	C-130H	185th AS	bl
	61003	C-130H	109th AS	gn/bl		80809	C-130H	185th AS	bl

Type			Notes
80810	C-130H	185th AS	bl
80811	C-130H	185th AS	bl
80812	C-130H	185th AS	bl
80813	C-130H	185th AS	bl
FY88			
81301	C-130H	130th AS	pr/y
81302	C-130H	130th AS	pr/y
81303	C-130H	130th AS	pr/y
81304	C-130H	130th AS	pr/y
81305	C-130H	130th AS	pr/y
81306	C-130H	130th AS	pr/y
81307	C-130H	130th AS	pr/y
81308	C-130H	130th AS	pr/y
FY98			
81355	C-130J	135th AS	bk/y
81356	C-130J	135th AS	bk/y
81357	C-130J	135th AS	bk/y
81358	C-130J	135th AS	bk/y
FY88			
81803	MC-130H	1st SOS	
FY98			
81932	EC-130J	LMTAS	
FY88			
82101	HC-130N	102nd RQS	
82102	HC-130N	102nd RQS	
84401	C-130H	95th AS	w/r
84402	C-130H	95th AS	w/r
84403	C-130H	95th AS	w/r
84404	C-130H	95th AS	w/r
84405	C-130H	95th AS	w/r
84406	C-130H	95th AS	w/r
84407	C-130H	95th AS	w/r
FY98			
85307	WC-130J	53rd WRS	
85308	WC-130J	53rd WRS	
FY89			
90280	MC-130H	7th SOS	
90281	MC-130H	15th SOS	
90282	MC-130H	15th SOS	
90283	MC-130H	15th SOS	
FY79			
90473	C-130H	192nd AS	w
90474	C-130H	192nd AS	w
90475	C-130H	192nd AS	w
90476	C-130H	192nd AS	w
90477	C-130H	192nd AS	w
90478	C-130H	192nd AS	w
90479	C-130H	192nd AS	w
90480	C-130H	192nd AS	w
FY89			
90509	AC-130U	4th SOS	
90510	AC-130U	4th SOS	
90511	AC-130U	4th SOS	
90512	AC-130U	4th SOS	
90513	AC-130U	4th SOS	
90514	AC-130U	4th SOS	
91051	C-130H	105th AS	r
91052	C-130H	105th AS	r
91053	C-130H	105th AS	r
91054	C-130H	105th AS	r
91055	C-130H	204th AS	
91056	AC-130U		
91181	C-130H	105th AS	r
91182	C-130H	105th AS	r
91183	C-130H	105th AS	r
91184	C-130H	105th AS	r

Type			Notes
91185	C-130H	105th AS	r
91186	C-130H	105th AS	r
91187	C-130H	105th AS	r
91188	C-130H	105th AS	r
FY99			
91431	CC-130J	143rd AS	r
91432	CC-130J	143rd AS	r
91433	CC-130J	143rd AS	r
91933	EC-130J	LMTAS	
95309	WC-130J	53rd WRS	
FY69			
95819	MC-130P	9th SOS	
95820	MC-130P	9th SOS	
95821	MC-130P	58th SOW	
95822	MC-130P	9th SOS	
95823	MC-130P		
95825	MC-130P	67th SOS	
95826	MC-130P	67th SOS	
95827	MC-130P	9th SOS	
95828	MC-130P	67th SOS	
95829	HC-130N	39th RQS	
95830	HC-130N	39th RQS	
95831	MC-130P	67th SOS	
95832	MC-130P	67th SOS	
95833	HC-130N	39th RQS	
96568	AC-130H	16th SOS	
96569	AC-130H	16th SOS	
96570	AC-130H	16th SOS	
96572	AC-130H	16th SOS	
96573	AC-130H	16th SOS	
96574	AC-130H	16th SOS	
96575	AC-130H	16th SOS	
96577	AC-130H	16th SOS	
96580	C-130E	43rd AW	gn/or
FY89			
99101	C-130H	757th AS	bl
99102	C-130H	757th AS	bl
99103	C-130H	757th AS	bl
99104	C-130H	757th AS	bl
99105	C-130H	757th AS	bl
99106	C-130H	757th AS	bl

Boeing C-135/C-137

6th AMW, MacDill AFB, Florida:
  91st ARS *(y/bl)*;
15th ABW, Hickam AFB, Hawaii:
  65th AS;
18th Wg, Kadena AB, Japan [ZZ]:
  909th ARS *(w)*;
19th ARG, Robins AFB, Georgia:
  99th ARS *(y/bl)*;
22nd ARW, McConnell AFB, Kansas:
  344th ARS *(y/bk)*, 349th ARS *(y/bl)*
  350th ARS *(y/r)* & 384th ARS *(y/pr)*;
55th Wg, Offutt AFB, Nebraska [OF]:
  38th RS *(gn)* & 45th RS *(bk)*;
88th ABW, Wright-Patterson AFB, Ohio;
92nd ARW, Fairchild AFB,
  Washington:
  92nd ARS *(bk)*, 93rd ARS *(bl)*,
  96th ARS *(gn)* & 97th ARS *(y)*;
97th AMW, Altus AFB, Oklahoma:
  55th ARS *(y/r)*;
100th ARW, RAF Mildenhall, UK [D]:
  351st ARS *(r/w/bl)*;

Notes	Type
	106th ARS/117th ARW, Birmingham, Alabama ANG *(w/r)*;
	108th ARS/126th ARW, Scott AFB, Illinois ANG *(w/bl)*;
	108th ARW, McGuire AFB, New Jersey ANG:
	141st ARS *(bk/y)* & 150th ARS *(bl)*;
	116th ARS/141st ARW, Fairchild AFB, Washington ANG *(gn/w)*;
	117th ARS/190th ARW, Forbes Field, Kansas ANG *(bl/y)*;
	121st ARW, Rickenbacker ANGB, Ohio ANG:
	145th ARS & 166th ARS *(bl)*;
	126th ARS/128th ARW, Mitchell Field, Wisconsin ANG *(w/bl)*;
	127th ARS/184th ARW, McConnell AFB, Kansas ANG;
	132nd ARS/101st ARW, Bangor, Maine ANG *(w/gn)*;
	133rd ARS/157th ARW, Pease ANGB, New Hampshire ANG *(bl)*;
	136th ARS/107th ARW, Niagara Falls, New York ANG *(bl)*;
	151st ARS/134th ARW, Knoxville, Tennessee ANG *(w/or)*;
	153rd ARS/186th ARW, Meridian, Mississippi ANG *(bk/gd)*;
	168th ARS/168th ARW, Eielson AFB, Alaska ANG *(bl/y)*;
	171st ARW, Greater Pittsburgh, Pennsylvania ANG:
	146th ARS *(y/bk)* & 147th ARS *(bk/y)*;
	173rd ARS/155th ARW, Lincoln, Nebraska ANG *(r/w)*;
	174th ARS/185th ARW, Sioux City, Iowa ANG *(y/bk)*;
	191st ARS/151st ARW, Salt Lake City, Utah ANG *(bl/bk)*;
	196th ARS/163rd ARW, March ARB, California ANG *(bl/w)*;
	197th ARS/161st ARW, Phoenix, Arizona ANG;
	203rd ARS/154th Wg, Hickam AFB, Hawaii ANG [HH] *(y/bk)*;
	319th ARW, Grand Forks AFB, North Dakota:
	905th ARS *(bl)*, 906th ARS *(y)*, 911th ARS *(r)* & 912th ARS *(w)*;
	366th Wg, Mountain Home AFB, Idaho [MO]: 22nd ARS *(y/gn)*;
	412th TW, Edwards AFB, California [ED]: 452nd FLTS *(bl)*;
	434th ARW AFRC, Grissom AFB, Indiana: 72nd ARS *(bl)* & 74th ARS *(r/w)*;
	452nd AMW AFRC, March ARB, California: 336th ARS *(y)*;
	459th ARW, AFRC Andrews AFB, Maryland: 756th ARS *(y/bk)*;
	507th ARW AFRC, Tinker AFB, Oklahoma: 465th ARS *(bl/y)*;
	645th Materiel Sqn, Greenville, Texas;
	916th ARW AFRC, Seymour Johnson AFB, North Carolina: 77th ARS *(gn)*;

Notes	Type
	927th ARW AFRC, Selfridge ANGB, Michigan: 63rd ARS *(pr/w)*;
	939th ARW, AFRC, Portland, Oregon: 64th ARS;
	940th ARW AFRC, McClellan AFB, California: 314th ARS *(or/bk)*
FY60	
00313	KC-135R 100th ARW *r/w/bl*
00314	KC-135R 434th ARW *r/w*
00315	KC-135R 126th ARS *w/bl*
00316	KC-135E 116th ARS *gn/w*
00318	KC-135R 203rd ARS *y/bk*
00319	KC-135R 22nd ARW
00320	KC-135R 319th ARW *w*
00321	KC-135R 97th AMW *y/r*
00322	KC-135R 434th ARW *bl*
00323	KC-135R 319th ARW *bl*
00324	KC-135R 319th ARW
00327	KC-135E 191st ARS *bl/bk*
00328	KC-135R 97th AMW *y/r*
00329	KC-135R 203rd ARS *y/bk*
00331	KC-135R 18th Wg *w*
00332	KC-135R 6th AMW *y/bl*
00333	KC-135R 92nd AMW *gn*
00334	KC-135R 168th ARS *bl/y*
00335	KC-135T 22nd ARW *y*
00336	KC-135T 92nd ARW *gn*
00337	KC-135T 92nd ARW *m*
00339	KC-135T 92nd ARW *bl*
00341	KC-135R 121st ARW *bl*
00342	KC-135T 319th ARW *y*
00343	KC-135T 19th ARG *y/bl*
00344	KC-135T 319th ARW *r*
00345	KC-135T 18th Wg *w*
00346	KC-135T 92nd ARW *bk*
00347	KC-135R 121st ARW *bl*
00348	KC-135R 319th ARW *r*
00349	KC-135R 916th ARW *gn*
00350	KC-135R 97th AMW *y/r*
00351	KC-135R 100th ARW *r/w/bl*
00353	KC-135R 22nd ARW
00355	KC-135R 319th ARW *y*
00356	KC-135R 22nd ARW *y/bl*
00357	KC-135R 22nd ARW *y*
00358	KC-135R 136th ARS *bl*
00359	KC-135R 434th ARW *r/w*
00360	KC-135R 22nd ARW *y*
00362	KC-135R 22nd ARW *y*
00363	KC-135R 434th ARW *bl*
00364	KC-135R 434th ARW *r/w*
00365	KC-135R 127th ARS
00366	KC-135R 19th ARG *y/bl*
00367	KC-135R 121st ARW *bl*
00372	C-135E 412th TW *bl*
FY61	
10264	KC-135R 121st ARW *bl*
10266	KC-135R 173rd ARS *r/w*
10267	KC-135R 92nd ARW *y*
10268	KC-135E 940th ARW *or/bk*
10270	KC-135E 927th ARW *pr/w*
10271	KC-135E 927th ARW *pr/w*
10272	KC-135R 434th ARW *r/w*
10275	KC-135R 18th Wg *w*
10276	KC-135R 173rd ARS *r/w*
10277	KC-135R 127th ARS
10280	KC-135R 452nd AMW *y*

Type			Notes	Type			Notes
10281	KC-135E	197th ARS		23503	KC-135R	939th ARW	
10284	KC-135R	319th ARW	bl	23504	KC-135R	319th ARW	y
10288	KC-135R	92nd ARW	bk	23505	KC-135R	100th ARW	r/w/bl
10290	KC-135R	203rd ARS	y/bk	23506	KC-135R	133rd ARS	bl
10292	KC-135R	22nd ARW	y	23507	KC-135R	92nd ARW	
10293	KC-135R	22nd ARW	y/r	23508	KC-135R	19th ARG	y/bl
10294	KC-135R	19th ARG	y/bl	23509	KC-135R	916th ARW	gn
10295	KC-135R	319th ARW	bl	23510	KC-135R	434th ARW	r/w
10298	KC-135R	126th ARS	w/bl	23511	KC-135R	121st ARW	bl
10299	KC-135R	319th ARW	bl	23512	KC-135R	126th ARS	w/bl
10300	KC-135R	319th ARW		23513	KC-135R	366th Wg	y/gn
10302	KC-135R			23514	KC-135R	203rd ARS	y/bk
10303	KC-135E	940th ARW	or/bk	23515	KC-135R	133rd ARS	bl
10304	KC-135R	92nd ARW	y	23516	KC-135R	22nd ARW	
10305	KC-135R	6th AMW	y/bl	23517	KC-135R	22nd ARW	
10306	KC-135R	319th ARW	bl	23518	KC-135R	434th ARW	bl
10307	KC-135R	434th ARW	r/w	23519	KC-135R	22nd ARW	
10308	KC-135R	97th AMW	y/r	23520	KC-135R	319th ARW	y
10309	KC-135R	126th ARS	w/bl	23521	KC-135R	434th ARW	r/w
10310	KC-135R	133rd ARS	bl	23523	KC-135R	19th ARG	y/bl
10311	KC-135R	22nd ARW	y	23524	KC-135R	106th ARS	w/r
10312	KC-135R	319th ARW	r	23526	KC-135R	173rd ARS	r/w
10313	KC-135R	916th ARW	gn	23527	KC-135E	108th ARW	bl
10314	KC-135R	22nd ARW	y	23528	KC-135R	22nd ARW	
10315	KC-135R	319th ARW		23529	KC-135R	319th ARW	w
10317	KC-135R	6th AMW	y/bl	23530	KC-135R	434th ARW	bl
10318	KC-135R	319th ARW	bl	23531	KC-135R	121st ARW	bl
10320	KC-135R	412th TW	bl	23533	KC-135R	319th ARW	bl
10321	KC-135R	18th Wg	w	23534	KC-135R	19th ARG	y/bl
10323	KC-135R	319th ARW	bl	23537	KC-135R	22nd ARW	
10324	KC-135R	452nd AMW	y	23538	KC-135R	100th ARW	r/w/bl
10330	EC-135E	412th TW	bl	23540	KC-135R	22nd ARW	
12662	RC-135S	55th Wg	bk	23541	KC-135R	100th ARW	r/w/bl
12663	RC-135S	55th Wg	bk	23542	KC-135R	916th ARW	gn
12666	NC-135W	645th MS		23543	KC-135R	434th ARW	bl
12669	C-135C	412th TW	bl	23544	KC-135R	19th ARG	y/bl
12670	OC-135B	55th Wg		23545	KC-135R	22nd ARW	
12672	OC-135B	55th Wg		23546	KC-135R	22nd ARW	y
FY64				23547	KC-135R	133rd ARS	bl
14828	KC-135R	97th AMW	y/r	23548	KC-135R	319th ARW	y
14829	KC-135R			23549	KC-135R	319th ARW	r
14830	KC-135R	100th ARW	r/w/bl	23550	KC-135R	22nd ARW	
14831	KC-135R	22nd ARW		23551	KC-135R	100th ARW	r/w/bl
14832	KC-135R	203rd ARS	y/bk	23552	KC-135R	319th ARW	r
14833	KC-135R	22nd ARW		23553	KC-135R	97th AMW	y/r
14834	KC-135R	434th ARW	r/w	23554	KC-135R	19th ARG	y/bl
14835	KC-135R	100th ARW	r/w/bl	23556	KC-135R	916th ARW	gn
14836	KC-135R	6th AMW	y/bl	23557	KC-135R	319th ARW	y
14837	KC-135R	22nd ARW		23558	KC-135R	22nd ARW	y
14838	KC-135R			23559	KC-135R	22nd ARW	y
14839	KC-135R	136th ARS	bl	23561	KC-135R	100th ARW	r/w/bl
14840	KC-135R	121st ARW	bl	23562	KC-135R	319th ARW	w
14841	RC-135V	55th Wg	gn	23564	KC-135R	22nd ARW	
14842	RC-135V	55th Wg	gn	23565	KC-135R	22nd ARW	
14843	RC-135V	55th Wg	gn	23566	KC-135E	153rd ARS	bk/gd
14844	RC-135V	55th Wg	gn	23568	KC-135R	100th ARW	r/w/bl
14845	RC-135V	55th Wg	gn	23569	KC-135R	19th ARG	y/bl
14846	RC-135V	55th Wg	gn	23571	KC-135R	168th ARS	bl/y
14847	RC-135U	55th Wg	gn	23572	KC-135R	127th ARS	
14848	RC-135V	55th Wg	gn	23573	KC-135R	92nd ARW	
14849	RC-135U	55th Wg	gn	23575	KC-135R	22nd ARW	
FY62				23576	KC-135R	133rd ARS	bl
23498	KC-135R	319th ARW	y	23577	KC-135R	916th ARW	gn
23499	KC-135R	22nd ARW	y	23578	KC-135R	22nd ARW	
23500	KC-135R	126th ARS	w/bl	23580	KC-135R	22nd ARW	
23502	KC-135R	18th Wg	w	23582	WC-135C	55th Wg	bk

Notes	Type				Notes	Type			
	24125	RC-135W	55th Wg	gn		38039	KC-135R	507th ARW	bl/y
	24126	C-135B	108th ARW	bk/y		38040	KC-135R	6th AMW	y/bl
	24127	RC-135W	55th Wg			38041	KC-135R	434th ARW	bl
	24128	RC-135S	55th Wg			38043	KC-135R	168th ARS	bl/y
	24129	TC-135W	55th Wg	gn		38044	KC-135R	22nd ARW	
	24130	RC-135W	55th Wg	gn		38045	KC-135R	319th ARW	
	24131	RC-135W	55th Wg	gn		38050	NKC-135B	412th TW	bl
	24132	RC-135W	55th Wg	gn		38058	KC-135D	117th ARS	bl/y
	24133	TC-135S	55th Wg	bk		38059	KC-135D	117th ARS	bl/y
	24134	RC-135W	55th Wg	gn		38060	KC-135D	117th ARS	bl/y
	24135	RC-135W	55th Wg	gn		38061	KC-135D	117th ARS	bl/y
	24138	RC-135W	55th Wg	gn		38871	KC-135R	100th ARW	r/w/bl
	24139	RC-135W	55th Wg	gn		38872	KC-135R	136th ARS	bl
	FY63					38873	KC-135R	319th ARW	y
	37976	KC-135R	6th AMW	y/bl		38874	KC-135R	22nd ARW	
	37977	KC-135R	97th AMW	y/r		38875	KC-135R	127th ARS	
	37978	KC-135R	92nd ARW	bk		38876	KC-135R	168th ARS	bl/y
	37979	KC-135R	22nd ARW			38877	KC-135R	97th AMW	y/r
	37980	KC-135R				38878	KC-135R	97th AMW	y/r
	37981	KC-135R	136th ARS	bl		38879	KC-135R	100th ARW	r/w/bl
	37982	KC-135R	22nd ARW			38880	KC-135R	507th ARW	bl/y
	37984	KC-135R	106th ARS	w/r		38881	KC-135R	97th AMW	y/r
	37985	KC-135R	507th ARW	bl/y		38883	KC-135R	319th ARW	w
	37987	KC-135R	97th AMW	y/r		38884	KC-135R	100th ARW	r/w/bl
	37988	KC-135R	173rd ARS	r/w		38885	KC-135R	18th Wg	w
	37991	KC-135R	173rd ARS	r/w		38886	KC-135R	319th ARW	w
	37992	KC-135R	121st ARW	bl		38887	KC-135R	22nd ARW	
	37993	KC-135R	121st ARW	m		38888	KC-135R	97th AMW	y/r
	37995	KC-135R	22nd ARW	y/bl		39792	RC-135V	55th Wg	gn
	37996	KC-135R	434th ARW	bl		*FY55*			
	37997	KC-135R	319th ARW	bl		53132	NKC-135E	412th TW	bl
	37999	KC-135R	97th AMW	y/r		53135	NKC-135E	412th TW	bl
	38000	KC-135R	22nd ARW			53141	KC-135E	174th ARS	y/bk
	38002	KC-135R	22nd ARW			53143	KC-135E	197th ARS	
	38003	KC-135R	18th Wg	w		53145	KC-135E	940th ARW	or/bk
	38004	KC-135R	127th ARS			53146	KC-135E	108th ARW	bk/y
	38006	KC-135R	97th AMW	y/r		*FY56*			
	38007	KC-135R	106th ARS	w/r		63593	KC-135E	108th ARW	bk/y
	38008	KC-135R				63604	KC-135E	116th ARS	gn/w
	38011	KC-135R	92nd ARW	y		63606	KC-135E	132nd ARS	w/gn
	38012	KC-135R	319th ARW	r		63607	KC-135E	151st ARS	w/or
	38013	KC-135R	121st ARW	bl		63609	KC-135E	151st ARS	w/or
	38014	KC-135R	319th ARW	bl		63611	KC-135E	171st ARW	y/bk
	38015	KC-135R	168th ARS	bl/y		63612	KC-135E	171st ARW	y/bk
	38017	KC-135R	92nd ARW	bk		63622	KC-135E	132nd ARS	w/gn
	38018	KC-135R	173rd ARS	r/w		63626	KC-135E	171st ARW	y/bk
	38019	KC-135R	97th AMW	y/r		63630	KC-135E	171st ARW	y/bk
	38020	KC-135R	97th AMW	y/r		63631	KC-135E	191st ARS	bl/bk
	38021	KC-135R	92nd ARW			63638	KC-135E	197th ARS	
	38022	KC-135R	22nd ARW	m		63640	KC-135E	132nd ARS	w/gn
	38023	KC-135R	97th AMW	y/r		63641	KC-135E	117th ARS	bl/y
	38024	KC-135R	452nd AMW	y		63643	KC-135E	151st ARS	w/or
	38025	KC-135R				63648	KC-135E	171st ARW	y/bk
	38026	KC-135R	319th ARW	y		63650	KC-135E	116th ARS	gn/w
	38027	KC-135R	92nd ARW	gn		63654	KC-135E	132nd ARS	w/gn
	38028	KC-135R	168th ARS	bl/y		*FY57*			
	38029	KC-135R	126th ARS	w/bl		71418	KC-135R	153rd ARS	bk/gd
	38030	KC-135R	203rd ARS	y/bk		71419	KC-135R	19th ARG	y/bl
	38031	KC-135R	92nd ARW	y		71421	KC-135E	116th ARS	gn/w
	38032	KC-135R	434th ARW	bl		71422	KC-135E	927th ARW	pr/w
	38033	KC-135R	97th AMW	y/r		71423	KC-135E	171st ARW	bk/y
	38034	KC-135R	97th AMW	y/r		71425	KC-135E	151st ARS	w/or
	38035	KC-135R	106th ARS	w/r		71426	KC-135E	197th ARS	
	38036	KC-135R	136th ARS	bl		71427	KC-135E	127th ARS	
	38037	KC-135R	97th AMW	y/r		71428	KC-135R	196th ARS	bl/w
	38038	KC-135R	133rd ARS	bl		71429	KC-135E	117th ARS	bl/y

Type			Notes	Type			Notes
71430	KC-135R	133rd ARS	bl	71512	KC-135R	452nd AMW	y
71431	KC-135E	108th ARW	bk/y	71514	KC-135R	126th ARS	w/bl
71432	KC-135R	106th ARS	w/r	72589	C-135E	412th TW	bl
71433	KC-135E	197th ARS		72593	KC-135R	121st ARW	bl
71434	KC-135E	116th ARS	gn/w	72594	KC-135E	108th ARS	w/bl
71435	KC-135R	18th Wg	w	72595	KC-135R	171st ARW	bk/y
71436	KC-135R	196th ARS	bl/w	72597	KC-135R	153rd ARS	bk/gd
71437	KC-135R	916th ARW	gn	72598	KC-135R	452nd AMW	y
71438	KC-135R	939th ARW		72599	KC-135R	916th ARW	gn
71439	KC-135R	319th ARW	bl	72600	KC-135E	116th ARS	gn/w
71440	KC-135R	319th ARW	r	72601	KC-135E	151st ARS	w/or
71441	KC-135E	108th ARS	w/bl	72602	KC-135E	108th ARS	bl
71443	KC-135E	132nd ARS	w/gn	72603	KC-135R	452nd AMW	y
71445	KC-135E	108th ARW	bk/y	72604	KC-135E	171st ARW	y/bk
71447	KC-135R	171st ARW	y/bk	72605	KC-135R	100th ARW	r/w/bl
71448	KC-135E	132nd ARS	w/gn	72606	KC-135E	108th ARW	bl
71450	KC-135E	132nd ARS	w/gn	72607	KC-135R	171st ARW	bk/y
71451	KC-135R	196th ARS	bl/w	72608	KC-135E	171st ARW	bk/y
71452	KC-135R	197th ARS		FY58			
71453	KC-135R	106th ARS	w/r	80001	KC-135R	319th ARW	w
71454	KC-135R	319th ARW		80003	KC-135E	108th ARS	w/bl
71455	KC-135R	151st ARS	w/or	80004	KC-135R	153rd ARS	bk/gd
71456	KC-135R	319th ARW	y	80005	KC-135E	117th ARS	bl/y
71458	KC-135E	108th ARS	w/bl	80006	KC-135E	191st ARS	bl/bk
71459	KC-135R	196th ARS	bl/w	80008	KC-135R	133rd ARS	bl
71460	KC-135R	117th ARS	bl/y	80009	KC-135R	126th ARS	w/bl
71461	KC-135R	173rd ARS	r/w	80010	KC-135R	153rd ARS	bk/gd
71462	KC-135R	121st ARW	bl	80011	KC-135R	22nd ARW	y/bl
71463	KC-135R	117th ARS	bl/y	80012	KC-135E	191st ARS	bl/bk
71464	KC-135E	108th ARW	bk/y	80013	KC-135E	927th ARW	pr/w
71465	KC-135E	151st ARS	w/or	80014	KC-135R	117th ARS	bl/y
71468	KC-135R	452nd AMW	y	80015	KC-135R	939th ARW	
71469	KC-135R	121st ARW	bl	80016	KC-135R	92nd ARW	y
71471	KC-135E	132nd ARS	w/gn	80017	KC-135E	171st ARW	y/bk
71472	KC-135R	434th ARW	bl	80018	KC-135R	22nd ARW	y
71473	KC-135R	19th ARG	y/bl	80020	KC-135E	171st ARW	y/bk
71474	KC-135R	18th Wg	w	80021	KC-135R	127th ARS	
71475	KC-135E	197th ARS		80023	KC-135E	136th ARS	bl
71479	KC-135E	452nd AMW	y	80024	KC-135E	171st ARW	y/bk
71480	KC-135E	108th ARS	w/bl	80027	KC-135R	319th ARW	y
71482	KC-135E	108th ARS	w/bl	80030	KC-135R	106th ARS	w/r
71483	KC-135R	92nd ARW		80032	KC-135E	108th ARW	bl
71484	KC-135E	197th ARS		80034	KC-135R	6th AMW	y/bl
71485	KC-135E	151st ARS	w/or	80035	KC-135R	22nd ARW	y
71486	KC-135R	18th Wg	w	80036	KC-135R	6th AMW	y/bl
71487	KC-135R	434th ARW	bl	80037	KC-135E	171st ARW	bk/y
71488	KC-135R	97th AMW	y/r	80038	KC-135R	916th ARW	gn
71491	KC-135E	132nd ARS	w/gn	80040	KC-135E	108th ARW	bl
71492	KC-135E	151st ARS	w/or	80041	KC-135R	927th ARW	pr/w
71493	KC-135R	97th AMW	y/r	80042	KC-135T	22nd ARW	
71494	KC-135E	108th ARS	w/bl	80043	KC-135E	191st ARS	bl/bk
71495	KC-135E	197th ARS		80044	KC-135E	108th ARW	bk/y
71496	KC-135E	197th ARS		80045	KC-135T	92nd ARW	bl
71497	KC-135E	191st ARS	bl/bk	80046	KC-135T	92nd ARW	bl
71499	KC-135R	319th ARW	r	80047	KC-135T	19th ARG	y/bl
71501	KC-135E	116th ARS	gn/w	80049	KC-135T	92nd ARW	y
71502	KC-135R	97th AMW	y/r	80050	KC-135T	92nd ARW	bk
71503	KC-135E	151st ARS	w/or	80051	KC-135R	507th ARW	bl/y
71504	KC-135E	927th ARW	pr/w	80052	KC-135R	452nd AMW	y
71505	KC-135E	132nd ARS	w/gn	80053	KC-135E	927th ARW	pr/w
71506	KC-135R	6th AMW	y/bl	80054	KC-135T	18th Wg	w
71507	KC-135E	108th ARW	bk/y	80055	KC-135T	18th Wg	w
71508	KC-135E	203rd ARS	y/bk	80056	KC-135R	153rd ARS	bk/gd
71509	KC-135E	171st ARW	bk/y	80057	KC-135E	108th ARS	w/bl
71510	KC-135E	191st ARS	bl/bk	80058	KC-135R	939th ARW	
71511	KC-135E	940th ARW	or/bk	80059	KC-135R	153rd ARS	bk/gd

C-135

Notes	Type				Notes	Type			
	80060	KC-135T	18th Wg	w		FY59			
	80061	KC-135T	319th ARW	r		91444	KC-135R	121st ARW	bl
	80062	KC-135T	18th Wg	w		91445	KC-135E	116th ARS	gn/w
	80063	KC-135R	507th ARW	bl/y		91446	KC-135R	153rd ARS	bk/gd
	80064	KC-135E	940th ARW	or/bk		91447	KC-135E	927th ARW	pr/w
	80065	KC-135T	22nd ARW			91448	KC-135R	196th ARS	bl/w
	80066	KC-135R	507th ARW	bl/y		91450	KC-135R	196th ARS	bl/w
	80067	KC-135E	108th ARS	w/bl		91451	KC-135E	927th ARW	pr/w
	80068	KC-135E	108th ARS	w/bl		91453	KC-135R	121st ARW	bl
	80069	KC-135T	92nd ARW	bk		91455	KC-135R	153rd ARS	bk/gd
	80071	KC-135T	22nd ARW	y/bk		91456	KC-135E	108th ARW	bk/y
	80072	KC-135T	18th Wg	w		91457	KC-135E	171st ARW	bk/y
	80073	KC-135R	106th ARS	w/r		91458	KC-135R	121st ARW	bl
	80074	KC-135T	92nd ARW			91459	KC-135R	100th ARW	r/w/bl
	80075	KC-135R	434th ARW	bl		91460	KC-135T	92nd ARW	gn
	80076	KC-135R	434th ARW	r/w		91461	KC-135R	168th ARS	bl/y
	80077	KC-135T	92nd ARW	bk		91462	KC-135T	319th ARW	bl
	80078	KC-135E	108th ARW	bl		91463	KC-135E	173rd ARS	r/w
	80079	KC-135R	507th ARW	bl/y		91464	KC-135T	92nd ARW	bk
	80080	KC-135E	191st ARS	bl/bk		91466	KC-135R	136th ARS	bl
	80082	KC-135E	174th ARS	y/bk		91467	KC-135T	92nd ARW	bl
	80083	KC-135E	121st ARW	bl		91468	KC-135T	92nd ARW	bl
	80084	KC-135T	92nd ARW	bl		91469	KC-135R	756th ARS	y/bk
	80085	KC-135R	319th ARW	w		91470	KC-135T	92nd ARW	y
	80086	KC-135T	92nd ARW	gn		91471	KC-135T	92nd ARW	y
	80087	KC-135E	108th ARW	bl		91472	KC-135R	203rd ARS	y/bk
	80088	KC-135T	18th Wg	w		91473	KC-135E	191st ARS	bl/bk
	80089	KC-135T	319th ARW	w		91474	KC-135T	92nd ARW	bk
	80090	KC-135E	940th ARW	or/bk		91475	KC-135R	97th AMW	y/r
	80092	KC-135R	133rd ARS	bl		91476	KC-135R	319th ARW	r
	80093	KC-135R	319th ARW	r		91477	KC-135E	927th ARW	pr/w
	80094	KC-135T	92nd ARW	bk		91478	KC-135R	153rd ARS	bk/gd
	80095	KC-135T	319th ARW	w		91479	KC-135E	171st ARW	y/bk
	80096	KC-135E	940th ARW	or/bk		91480	KC-135T	92nd ARW	gn
	80098	KC-135R	133rd ARS	bl		91482	KC-135R	319th ARW	
	80099	KC-135T	92nd ARW	bl		91483	KC-135R	121st ARW	bl
	80100	KC-135R	18th Wg	w		91484	KC-135E	171st ARW	bk/y
	80102	KC-135R	939th ARW			91485	KC-135E	108th ARW	bl
	80103	KC-135T	92nd ARW	gn		91486	KC-135R	22nd ARW	y
	80104	KC-135R	136th ARS	bl		91487	KC-135E	108th ARS	w/bl
	80106	KC-135R	106th ARS	w/r		91488	KC-135R	18th Wg	w
	80107	KC-135E	191st ARS	bl/bk		91489	KC-135E	191st ARS	bl/bk
	80108	KC-135E	940th ARW	or/bk		91490	KC-135T	92nd ARW	bk
	80109	KC-135R	153rd ARS	bk/gd		91492	KC-135R	97th AMW	y/r
	80111	KC-135E	108th ARW	bk/y		91493	KC-135E	132nd ARS	w/gn
	80112	KC-135T	92nd ARW	y		91495	KC-135R	173rd ARS	r/w
	80113	KC-135R	97th AMW	y/r		91496	KC-135E	171st ARW	y/bk
	80114	KC-135R	92nd ARW	bl		91497	KC-135E	108th ARW	bl
	80115	KC-135E	108th ARW	bl		91498	KC-135R	127th ARS	
	80116	KC-135R	197th ARS			91499	KC-135R	196th ARS	bl/w
	80117	KC-135T	92nd ARW	bl		91500	KC-135R	18th Wg	w
	80118	KC-135R	92nd ARW	gn		91501	KC-135R	6th AMW	y/bl
	80119	KC-135R	92nd ARW			91502	KC-135R	319th ARW	y
	80120	KC-135R	6th AMW	y/bl		91503	KC-135E	108th ARW	bk/y
	80121	KC-135R	507th ARW	bl/y		91504	KC-135T	92nd ARW	bk
	80122	KC-135R	168th ARS	bl/y		91505	KC-135R	196th ARS	bl/w
	80123	KC-135R	18th Wg	w		91506	KC-135R	116th ARS	gn/w
	80124	KC-135R	100th ARW	r/w/bl		91507	KC-135R	19th ARG	y/bl
	80125	KC-135T	92nd ARW	bl		91508	KC-135R	92nd ARW	y
	80126	KC-135R	22nd ARW	y		91509	KC-135R	196th ARS	bl/w
	80128	KC-135R	100th ARW	r/w/bl		91510	KC-135T	319th ARW	r
	80129	KC-135T	92nd ARW	bl		91511	KC-135R	22nd ARW	
	80130	KC-135R	126th ARS	w/bl		91512	KC-135T	18th Wg	w
	FY88					91513	KC-135T	92nd ARW	bl
	86005	EC-137D	88th ABW			91515	KC-135R	319th ARW	r
	86008	EC-137D	88th ABW			91516	KC-135R	196th ARS	bl/w

Type			Notes
91517	KC-135R	97th AMW	y/r
91519	KC-135E	171st ARW	y/bk
91520	KC-135T	92nd ARW	gn
91521	KC-135R	168th ARS	bl/y
91522	KC-135R	136th ARS	bl
91523	KC-135T	92nd ARW	bk

Lockheed C-141 Starlifter
164th AW, Memphis, Tennessee ANG:
   155th AS *(r)*;
172nd AW, Jackson Int'l Airport,
   Mississippi ANG:
   183rd AS *(bl/gd)*;
305th AMW, McGuire AFB,
   New Jersey *(bl)*:
   6th AS, 13th AS & 18th AS;
445th AW AFRC, Wright-Patterson
   AFB, Ohio *(si)*:
   89th AS & 356th AS;
452nd AMW AFRC, March ARB,
   California *(or/y)*:
   729th AS & 730th AS;
C-141B/C-141C*
FY63

38084*	452nd AMW	or/y
FY64		
40614*	172nd AW	bl/gd
40619	305th AMW	bl
40620*	445th AW	si
40627*	164th AW	r
40633	305th AMW	bl
40637*		
40640*	164th AW	r
40645*	445th AW	si
FY65		
50225*	452nd AMW	or/y
50226*		

Type			Notes
50229*	452nd AMW	or/y	
50237*	445th AW	si	
50248*	452nd AMW	or/y	
50249*	445th AW	si	
50250*	445th AW	si	
50261*	445th AW	si	
59412*	445th AW	si	
59414*	452nd AMW	or/y	
FY66			
60132*	445th AW	si	
60147	305th AMW	bl	
60151*	452nd AMW	or/y	
60152*	452nd AMW	or/y	
60157*	164th AW	r	
60164*	164th AW	r	
60169	305th AMW	bl	
60174*			
60177*	445th AW	si	
60181*	452nd AMW	or/y	
60183	305th AMW	bl	
60185*	164th AW	r	
60190*	172nd AW	bl/gd	
60193*	452nd AMW	or/y	
67944	305th AMW	bl	
67947	305th AMW	bl	
67950*	445th AW	si	
67953*	445th AW	si	
67954*	445th AW	si	
67955	305th AMW	bl	
67957*	452nd AMW	or/y	
67959*	445th AW	si	
FY67			
70012	305th AMW	bl	
70019	305th AMW	bl	
70021*	164th AW	r	
70029*	164th AW	r	
70031*	445th AW	si	
70166*	445th AW	si	

Boeing KC-10A 30076 flown by the 60th AMW from Travis AFB. *PRM*

Mighty C-17A Globemaster I 50102 flown by 437th AW from its base at Charleston, South Carolina. *PRM*

Lockheed P-3 Orion

CinCLANT/VP-30, NAS Jacksonville, Florida;
CinCPAC/ETD, MCBH Kaneohe Bay, Hawaii;
CinCUSNFE, NAF Sigonella, Italy;
CNO/VP-30, NAS Jacksonville, Florida;
NAF Keflavik, Iceland;
NASC-FS, Point Mugu, California;
Navy Research Lab, Patuxent River, Maryland;
USNTPS, NAS Point Mugu, California;
VP-1, NAS Whidbey Island, Washington [YB];
VP-4, MCBH Kaneohe Bay, Hawaii [YD];
VP-5, NAS Jacksonville, Florida [LA];
VP-8, NAS Brunswick, Maine [LC];
VP-9, MCBH Kaneohe Bay, Hawaii [PD];
VP-10, NAS Brunswick, Maine [LD];
VP-16, NAS Jacksonville, Florida [LF];
VP-26, NAS Brunswick, Maine [LK];
VP-30, NAS Jacksonville, Florida [LL];
VP-40, NAS Whidbey Island, Washington [QE];
VP-45, NAS Jacksonville, Florida [LN];
VP-46, NAS Whidbey Island, Washington [RC];
VP-47, MCBH Kaneohe Bay, Hawaii [RD];
VP-62, NAS Jacksonville, Florida [LT];
VP-64, NAS Willow Grove, Pennsylvania [LU];
VP-65, NAS Point Mugu, California [PG];
VP-66, NAS Willow Grove, Pennsylvania [LV];
VP-69, NAS Whidbey Island, Washington [PJ];
VP-92, NAS Brunswick, Maine [LY];
VP-94, NAS New Orleans, Louisiana [PZ];
VPU-1, NAS Brunswick, Maine;
VPU-2, MCBH Kaneohe Bay, Hawaii;
VQ-1, NAS Whidbey Island, Washington [PR];
VQ-2, NAF Rota, Spain;
VX-1, NAS Patuxent River, Maryland;
VX-20, Patuxent River, Maryland;
VX-30, NAS Point Mugu, California

Serial	Code	Type	Unit
148889		UP-3A	USNTPS
149674	[674]	NP-3D	NRL
149675		VP-3A	CinCPAC
149676		VP-3A	CNO
150495		UP-3A	NAF Keflavik
150496		VP-3A	CinCUSNFE
150499	[337]	NP-3D	VX-30
150511		VP-3A	CinCLANT
150515		VP-3A	CNO
150521	[341]	NP-3D	VX-30
150522	[340]	NP-3D	VX-30
150524	[335]	NP-3D	VX-30
150526		UP-3A	VQ-1
152141	[408]	P-3A	VP-1
152150	[150]	NP-3D	VX-20
152165	[404]	P-3A	VP-1
152739		NP-3B	LMAS
153442	[442]	NP-3D	NRL
153443	[443]	NP-3D	USNTPS
153450	[2]	P-3B	VPU-1
154587	[587]	NP-3D	NRL
154589	[589]	NP-3D	NRL
156507	[PR-507]	EP-3E	VQ-1
156509	[LC-509]	P-3C	VP-8
156510	[LL-510]	P-3C	VP-30
156514	[PR-33]	EP-3E	VQ-1
156515	[LY-515]	P-3C	VP-92
156516	[516]	P-3C	VP-45
156517	[PR-34]	EP-3E	VQ-1
156518	[LL-518]	P-3C	VP-30
156519	[21]	EP-3E	VQ-2
156520	[520]	P-3C	VP-45
156521	[PG-521]	P-3C	VP-65
156522	[YD-522]	P-3C	VP-4
156523	[LL-523]	P-3C	VP-30
156525	[525]	P-3C	VQ-2
156527	[PG-527]	P-3C	VP-65
156528	[PR-36]	EP-3E	VQ-1
156529	[24]	EP-3E	VQ-2
156530	[LL-530]	P-3C	VP-30
157310	[310]	P-3C	VP-16
157311	[LA-311]	P-3C	VP-5
157312	[PG-312]	P-3C	VP-65
157313	[LN-313]	P-3C	VP-45
157314	[314]	P-3C	VP-26
157315	[LC-315]	P-3C	VP-8
157316	[23]	EP-3E	VQ-2
157317	[YB-317]	P-3C	VP-92
157318	[PR-318]	EP-3E	VQ-1
157319	[LL-319]	P-3C	VP-30
157321	[321]	P-3C	VP-8
157322	[RC-322]	P-3C	VP-46
157323	[PG-323]	P-3C	VP-65
157324	[YD-324]	P-3C	VP-4
157325	[25]	EP-3E	VQ-2
157326	[22]	EP-3E	VQ-2
157327	[LC-327]	P-3C	VP-8
157328	[LL-328]	P-3C	VP-30
157329	[LY-329]	P-3C	VP-92
157330	[330]	P-3C	VP-1
157331	[LL-331]	P-3C	VP-30
158204	[204]	P-3C	VX-20
158205	[YB-205]	P-3C	VP-1
158206		P-3C	VPU-1
158207	[207]	P-3C	VP-26
158208	[YD-208]	P-3C	VP-4
158209	[PD-209]	P-3C	VP-9
158210		P-3C	VP-5
158211	[211]	P-3C	VP-40
158212	[PD-212]	P-3C	VP-9
158214	[LL-214]	P-3C	VP-30
158215	[215]	P-3C	VP-30
158216	[216]	P-3C	VP-46
158218	[RD-218]	P-3C	VP-47
158219	[LA-219]	P-3C	VP-5
158220	[YD-220]	P-3C	VP-4
158221	[RC-221]	P-3C	VP-46
158222	[YD-222]	P-3C	VP-4
158223	[YD-223]	P-3C	VP-4
158224	[LA-224]	P-3C	VP-5
158225	[RD-225]	P-3C	VP-47
158226	[PJ-226]	P-3C	VP-69
158227	[227]	NP-3D	NRL
158563	[LL-563]	P-3C	VP-30
158564	[564]	P-3C	VP-16
158565	[565]	P-3C	VP-92
158566	[LF-566]	P-3C	VP-16
158567	[567]	P-3C	VP-16
158568	[LD-568]	P-3C	VP-10
158569	[569]	P-3C	VP-45
158570	[JA-01]	P-3C	VX-1
158571	[LC-571]	P-3C	VP-8

158572	[572]	P-3C	VP-45	160767	[LV-767]	P-3C	VP-66
158573	[LC-573]	P-3C	VP-8	160768	[PR-51]	P-3C	VQ-1
158574		P-3C	NASC-FS	160769	[LD-769]	P-3C	VP-10
158912	[912]	P-3C	VX-20	160770	[770]	P-3C	VP-10
158913	[LA-913]	P-3C	VP-5	160999	[LL-999]	P-3C	VP-30
158914	[YD-914]	P-3C	VP-4	161000	[000]	P-3C	VQ-2
158915	[915]	P-3C	VP-40	161001	[LU-001]	P-3C	VP-64
158916	[LL-37]	P-3C	VP-30	161002		P-3C	VQ-2
158917	[LK-917]	P-3C	VP-26	161003	[PD-003]	P-3C	VP-9
158918	[PD-918]	P-3C	VP-9	161004	[LK-004]	P-3C	VP-26
158919	[919]	P-3C	VP-16	161005	[JA-07]	P-3C	VX-1
158920	[LA-920]	P-3C	VP-5	161006	[006]	P-3C	VP-8
158921	[YD-921]	P-3C	VP-4	161007	[PJ-007]	P-3C	VP-69
158922	[PD-922]	P-3C	VP-9	161008	[LL-008]	P-3C	VP-30
158923	[923]	P-3C	VP-4	161009		P-3C	VP-5
158924	[924]	P-3C	VP-16	161010	[LL-010]	P-3C	VP-30
158925	[LK-925]	P-3C	VP-26	161011	[011]	P-3C	VP-16
158926	[LK-926]	P-3C	VP-26	161012	[YD-012]	P-3C	VP-4
158927	[927]	P-3C	VP-16	161013	[LT-013]	P-3C	VP-62
158929	[LC-929]	P-3C	VP-8	161014	[LV-014]	P-3C	VP-66
158931	[LA-931]	P-3C	VP-5	161121	[121]	P-3C	VP-45
158932	[LF-932]	P-3C	VP-16	161122	[226]	P-3C	VPU-1
158933	[933]	P-3C	VP-26	161123	[LU-123]	P-3C	VP-64
158934	[YB-934]	P-3C	VP-1	161124	[LF-124]	P-3C	VP-16
158935	[LL-935]	P-3C	VP-30	161125	[LV-125]	P-3C	VP-66
159318	[LA-318]	P-3C	VP-5	161126	[PR-50]	P-3C	VQ-1
159319	[RD-319]	P-3C	VP-47	161127	[LU-127]	P-3C	VP-64
159320	[LD-320]	P-3C	VP-10	161128	[128]	P-3C	VP-5
159321	[QE-321]	P-3C	VP-40	161129	[LV-129]	P-3C	VP-66
159322	[LD-322]	P-3C	VP-10	161130	[YB-130]	P-3C	VP-1
159323	[RC-323]	P-3C	VP-46	161131	[LU-131]	P-3C	VP-64
159324	[324]	P-3C	VP-40	161132	[YD-132]	P-3C	VP-4
159326	[YD-326]	P-3C	VP-4	161329	[LU-329]	P-3C	VP-64
159327	[327]	P-3C	VP-9	161330	[LL-330]	P-3C	VP-30
159328	[YB-328]	P-3C	VP-1	161331	[LY-331]	P-3C	VP-92
159329	[RD-329]	P-3C	VP-47	161332	[PG-332]	P-3C	VP-65
159503	[LA-503]	P-3C	VP-5	161333	[PZ-333]	P-3C	VP-94
159504		P-3C	VPU-2	161334	[PZ-334]	P-3C	VP-94
159506	[568]	P-3C	VPU-1	161335	[PZ-335]	P-3C	VP-94
159507	[RD-507]	P-3C	VP-47	161336	[LY-336]	P-3C	VP-92
159512	[512]	P-3C	VP-16	161337	[PZ-337]	P-3C	VP-94
159513	[LL-513]	P-3C	VP-30	161338	[LA-338]	P-3C	VP-5
159514	[LL-514]	P-3C	VP-30	161339	[339]	P-3C	VP-9
159884	[884]	P-3C	VQ-2	161340	[340]	P-3C	VP-45
159885	[PD-885]	P-3C	VP-9	161404	[LL-404]	P-3C	VP-30
159886	[09]	P-3C	VQ-2	161405	[405]	P-3C	VP-40
159887		P-3C	NASC-FS	161406		P-3C	VP-40
159889	[04]	P-3C	VX-1	161407	[PG-407]	P-3C	VP-65
159894	[LL-894]	P-3C	VP-30	161408	[LV-408]	P-3C	VP-66
160283	[RD-283]	P-3C	VP-47	161409	[LV-409]	P-3C	VP-66
160284	[LL-284]	P-3C	VP-30	161411	[LL-411]	P-3C	VP-30
160286	[LD-286]	P-3C	VP-10	161412	[LU-412]	P-3C	VP-64
160287	[LC-287]	P-3C	VP-8	161413	[LL-413]	P-3C	VP-30
160288		P-3C	NASC-FS	161414	[LA-414]	P-3C	VP-5
160290	[290]	P-3C	VX-20	161415	[LL-415]	P-3C	VP-30
160291	[JA-05]	P-3C	VX-1	161585	[LY-585]	P-3C	VP-92
160292	[292]	P-3C	VPU-2	161586	[LL-586]	P-3C	VP-30
160293		P-3C	VP-4	161587	[YD-587]	P-3C	VP-4
160610	[PD-610]	P-3C	VP-9	161588	[LL-588]	P-3C	VP-30
160611	[LU-611]	P-3C	VP-64	161589	[589]	P-3C	VP-9
160612	[YB-612]	P-3C	VP-1	161590	[LL-590]	P-3C	VP-30
160761	[YD-761]	P-3C	VP-4	161591	[PZ-591]	P-3C	VP-94
160762		P-3C	VPU-2	161592	[PZ-592]	P-3C	VP-94
160763	[LT-763]	P-3C	VP-62	161593	[LL-593]	P-3C	VP-30
160764	[YJ-764]	P-3C	VP-4	161594	[LL-594]	P-3C	VP-30
160765	[765]	P-3C	VP-26	161595	[LV-595]	P-3C	VP-66
160766	[766]	P-3C	VPU-2	161596	[LL-596]	P-3C	VP-30

161763	[763]	P-3C	VP-47
161764	[YD-764]	P-3C	VP-4
161765	[LK-765]	P-3C	VP-26
161766	[PJ-766]	P-3C	VP-69
161767	[767]	P-3C	VP-9
162314	[314]	P-3C	VP-46
162315	[315]	P-3C	VP-46
162316	[316]	P-3C	VP-16
162317	[YB-317]	P-3C	VP-1
162318	[PJ-318]	P-3C	VP-69
162770	[PJ-770]	P-3C	VP-69
162771	[YD-771]	P-3C	VP-4
162772	[YB-772]	P-3C	VP-1
162773	[773]	P-3C	VP-40
162774	[774]	P-3C	VX-20
162775	[775]	P-3C	VP-47
162776	[776]	P-3C	VP-8
162777	[PD-777]	P-3C	VP-9
162778	[LK-778]	P-3C	VP-26
162998	[998]	P-3C	VP-40
162999	[PJ-999]	P-3C	VP-69
163000	[000]	P-3C	VP-45
163001	[LT-001]	P-3C	VP-62
163002	[PG-002]	P-3C	VP-65
163003	[PJ-003]	P-3C	VP-69
163004	[PG-004]	P-3C	VP-65
163006	[006]	P-3C	VP-45
163289	[YB-289]	P-3C	VP-1
163290	[290]	P-3C	VP-40
163291	[LT-291]	P-3C	VP-62
163292	[LF-292]	P-3C	VP-16
163293	[LF-293]	P-3C	VP-16
163294	[LY-294]	P-3C	VP-92
163295	[LY-295]	P-3C	VP-92

Boeing E-6 Mercury

Boeing, McConnell AFB, Kansas;
VQ-3 & VQ-4, SCW-1, Tinker AFB, Oklahoma

162782	E-6B	VQ-4
162783	E-6B	VQ-3
162784	E-6B	VQ-3
163918	E-6B	VQ-3
163919	E-6B	VQ-3
163920	E-6B	VQ-3
164386	E-6A	VQ-3
164387	E-6B	VQ-3
164388	E-6A	VQ-4
164404	E-6B	VQ-4
164405	E-6A	VQ-4
164406	E-6B	VQ-3
164407	E-6A	VQ-4
164408	E-6A	VQ-4
164409	E-6B	VQ-4
164410	E-6A	VQ-4

McDonnell Douglas C-9B Skytrain II/DC-9-32*

VMR-1, Cherry Point MCAS, North Carolina;
VR-46, Atlanta, Georgia [JS];
VR-52, Willow Grove NAS, Pennsylvania [JT];
VR-56, Norfolk NAS, Virginia [JU];
VR-57, North Island NAS, California [RX];
VR-61, Whidbey Island NAS, Washington [RS];

159113	[RX]	VR-57
159114	[RX]	VR-57
159115	[RX]	VR-57
159116	[RX]	VR-57
159117	[JU]	VR-56
159118	[JU]	VR-56
159119	[JU]	VR-56
159120	[JU]	VR-56
160046		VMR-1
160047		VMR-1
160048	[JT]	VR-52
160049	[JT]	VR-52
160050	[JT]	VR-52
160051	[JT]	VR-52
161266	[JS]	VR-46
161529	[JS]	VR-46
161530	[JS]	VR-46
162753	[JT]	VR-52
162754	[RS]	VR-61
163036*	[JS]	VR-46
164605*	[RS]	VR-61
164606*	[RS]	VR-61
164607*	[RS]	VR-61
164608*	[RS]	VR-61

Grumman C-20D Gulfstream III/ C-20G Gulfstream IV*

VR-1, NAF Washington, Maryland;
VR-48, NAF Washington, Maryland [JR];
VR-51, MCBH Kaneohe Bay, Hawaii [RG]

163691		VR-1
163692		VR-1
165093*	[JR]	VR-48
165094*	[JR]	VR-48
165151*	[RG]	VR-51
165152*	[RG]	VR-51
165153*		

Gulfstream Aerospace C-37A Gulfstream V

VR-1, NAF Washington, Maryland;

166375	VR-1
166376	
166377	
166378	
166379	

Boeing C-40A Clipper

VR-58, Jacksonville NAS, Florida [JV];
VR-59, NAS Fort Worth JRB, Texas [RY]

165829	[JV]	VR-58
165830	[RY]	VR-59
165831	[RY]	VR-59
165832	[JV]	VR-58
165833	[RY]	VR-59
165834	[JV]	VR-58
165835		Boeing
165836		Boeing

Lockheed C-130 Hercules

VR-53, NAF Washington, Maryland [AX];
VR-54, New Orleans NAS, Louisiana [CW];
VR-55, NAS Point Mugu, California [RU];
VR-62, Brunswick NAS, Maine [JW];
VMGR-152, Futenma MCAS, Japan [QD];
VMGR-234, NAS Fort Worth, Texas [QH];
VMGR-252, Cherry Point MCAS,
     North Carolina [BH];
VMGRT-253, Cherry Point MCAS,
     North Carolina [GR];
VMGR-352, MCAS Miramar, California [QB];
VMGR-452, Stewart Field, New York [NY];
VX-20, Patuxent River, Maryland

147572	[QB]	KC-130F	VMGR-352

147573	[QD]	KC-130F	VMGR-152	163023	[QH]	KC-130T	VMGR-234
148246	[GR]	KC-130F	VMGRT-253	163310	[QH]	KC-130T	VMGR-234
148247	[QB]	KC-130F	VMGR-352	163311	[NY]	KC-130T	VMGR-452
148248	[QD]	KC-130F	VMGR-152	163591	[NY]	KC-130T	VMGR-452
148249	[GR]	KC-130F	VMGRT-253	163592	[NY]	KC-130T	VMGR-452
148891	[BH]	KC-130F	VMGR-252	164105	[NY]	KC-130T	VMGR-452
148893	[QD]	KC-130F	VMGR-152	164106	[NY]	KC-130T	VMGR-452
148894	[GR]	KC-130F	VMGRT-253	164180	[NY]	KC-130T	VMGR-452
148896	[BH]	KC-130F	VMGR-252	164181	[NY]	KC-130T	VMGR-452
148897	[BH]	KC-130F	VMGR-252	164441	[NY]	KC-130T	VMGR-452
148898	[BH]	KC-130F	VMGR-252	164442	[NY]	KC-130T	VMGR-452
148899	[BH]	KC-130F	VMGR-252	164597	[NY]	KC-130T-30	VMGR-452
149788	[BH]	KC-130F	VMGR-252	164598	[QH]	KC-130T-30	VMGR-234
149789	[BH]	KC-130F	VMGR-252	164762	[CW]	C-130T	VR-54
149791	[BH]	KC-130F	VMGR-252	164763		C-130T	*Blue Angels*
149792	[QB]	KC-130F	VMGR-352	164993	[CW]	C-130T	VR-54
149795	[QB]	KC-130F	VMGR-352	164994	[AX]	C-130T	VR-53
149796	[QB]	KC-130F	VMGR-352	164995	[AX]	C-130T	VR-53
149798	[QB]	KC-130F	VMGR-352	164996	[AX]	C-130T	VR-53
149799	[QD]	KC-130F	VMGR-152	164997	[AX]	C-130T	VR-53
149800	[QB]	KC-130F	VMGR-352	164998	[AX]	C-130T	VR-53
149803	[GR]	KC-130F	VMGRT-253	164999	[QH]	KC-130T	VMGR-234
149806		KC-130F	VX-20	165000	[QH]	KC-130T	VMGR-234
149807	[QD]	KC-130F	VMGR-152	165158	[CW]	C-130T	VR-54
149808	[BH]	KC-130F	VMGR-252	165159	[CW]	C-130T	VR-54
149811	[BH]	KC-130F	VMGR-252	165160	[CW]	C-130T	VR-54
149812	[QD]	KC-130F	VMGR-152	165161	[RU]	C-130T	VR-55
149815	[QB]	KC-130F	VMGR-352	165162	[QH]	KC-130T	VMGR-234
149816	[QD]	KC-130F	VMGR-152	165163	[QH]	KC-130T	VMGR-234
150684	[GR]	KC-130F	VMGRT-253	165313	[JW]	C-130T	VR-62
150686	[BH]	KC-130F	VMGR-252	165314	[JW]	C-130T	VR-62
150689	[QB]	KC-130F	VMGR-352	165315	[NY]	KC-130T	VMGR-452
150690	[QD]	KC-130F	VMGR-152	165316	[NY]	KC-130T	VMGR-452
160013	[QD]	KC-130R	VMGR-152	165348	[JW]	C-130T	VR-62
160014	[QD]	KC-130R	VMGR-152	165349	[JW]	C-130T	VR-62
160015	[QB]	KC-130R	VMGR-352	165350	[RU]	C-130T	VR-55
160016	[QB]	KC-130R	VMGR-352	165351	[RU]	C-130T	VR-55
160017	[QB]	KC-130R	VMGR-352	165352	[NY]	KC-130T	VMGR-452
160018	[QD]	KC-130R	VMGR-152	165353	[NY]	KC-130T	VMGR-452
160019	[QD]	KC-130R	VMGR-152	165378	[RU]	C-130T	VR-55
160020	[QD]	KC-130R	VMGR-152	165379	[RU]	C-130T	VR-55
160022	[QB]	KC-130R	VMGR-352	165735	[BH]	KC-130J	VMGR-252
160240	[QB]	KC-130R	VMGR-352	165736	[BH]	KC-130J	VMGR-252
160625	[BH]	KC-130R	VMGR-252	165737	[BH]	KC-130J	VMGR-252
160626	[BH]	KC-130R	VMGR-252	165738	[BH]	KC-130J	VMGR-252
160627	[BH]	KC-130R	VMGR-252	165739	[BH]	KC-130J	VMGR-252
160628	[QB]	KC-130R	VMGR-352	165809	[BH]	KC-130J	VMGR-252
162308	[QH]	KC-130T	VMGR-234	165810	[BH]	KC-130J	VMGR-252
162309	[QH]	KC-130T	VMGR-234	165957	[BH]	KC-130J	VMGR-252
162310	[QH]	KC-130T	VMGR-234	166380	[BH]	KC-130J	VMGR-252
162311	[QH]	KC-130T	VMGR-234	166381	[BH]	KC-130J	VMGR-252
162785	[QH]	KC-130T	VMGR-234	166382	[BH]	KC-130J	VMGR-252
162786	[QH]	KC-130T	VMGR-234	166472		KC-130J	
163022	[QH]	KC-130T	VMGR-234	166473		KC-130J	

US-based US Coast Guard Aircraft

Gulfstream Aerospace
C-37A Gulfstream V
USCG, Washington DC
01

Grumman Gulfstream IV
USCG, Washington DC
02

Lockheed C-130 Hercules
USCGS Barbers Point, Hawaii;
USCGS Clearwater, Florida;
USCGS Elizabeth City,
   North Carolina;
USCGS Kodiak, Alaska;
USCGS Sacramento, California

1500	HC-130H	Elizabeth City
1501	HC-130H	Elizabeth City
1502	HC-130H	Elizabeth City
1503	HC-130H	Elizabeth City
1504	HC-130H	Elizabeth City
1603	HC-130H	Elizabeth City
1700	HC-130H	Sacramento
1701	HC-130H	Clearwater
1702	HC-130H	Kodiak
1703	HC-130H	Barbers Point
1704	HC-130H	Sacramento
1705	HC-130H	Barbers Point
1706	HC-130H	Clearwater
1707	HC-130H	Kodiak
1708	HC-130H	Clearwater
1709	HC-130H	Kodiak
1710	HC-130H	Kodiak
1711	HC-130H	Clearwater
1712	HC-130H	Clearwater
1713	HC-130H	Clearwater
1714	HC-130H	Barbers Point
1715	HC-130H	Kodiak
1716	HC-130H	Sacramento
1717	HC-130H	Clearwater
1718	HC-130H	Sacramento
1719	HC-130H	Clearwater
1720	HC-130H	Clearwater
1790	HC-130H	Clearwater
2001	HC-130J	Elizabeth City
2002	HC-130J	Elizabeth City
2003	HC-130J	Elizabeth City
2004	HC-130J	Elizabeth City

Aircraft in US Government or Military Services with Civil Registrations

BAe 125-800A (C-29A)
Federal Aviation Administration, Oklahoma

N94	(88-0269)
N95	(88-0270)
N96	(88-0271)
N97	(88-0272)
N98	(88-0273)
N99	(88-0274)

Gates Learjet 35A
Phoenix Aviation/Flight International/
   US Navy, Naples

N20DK
N50FN
N88JA
N118FN
N710GS

Angular, dark, stealthy shape of an F-117A Nighthawk. *PRM*

219

Military Aviation Sites on the Internet

The list below is not intended to be a complete list of military aviation sites on the Internet. The sites listed cover Museums, Locations, Air Forces, Companies and Organisations that are mentioned elsewhere in 'Military Aircraft Markings'. Sites listed are in English or contain sufficient English to be reasonably easily understood. Each site address is believed to be correct at the time of going to press. Additions are welcome via e-mail to hjcurtis@ntlworld.com. An up to date copy of this list is to be found at http://homepage.ntlworld.com/hjcurtis/mam.html.

Name of site	Internet Dial (all prefixed 'http://')
No 1 Sqn	www.raf-cott.demon.co.uk/1sqn.html
No 2 Sqn	www.rafmarham.co.uk/organisation/2squadron/2squadron.htm
No 4 Regiment Army Air Corps	www.4regimentaac.co.uk/
No 4 Sqn	www.raf-cott.demon.co.uk/4sqn.html
No 6 Flt	www.shawbury.raf.mod.uk/6fltaac.htm
No 6 Sqn	www.raf.mod.uk/rafcoltishall/squadrons/6Sqn.htm
No 7 Sqn	www.rafodiham.co.uk/structure/squadrons/7sqn/7sqn.htm
No 8 Sqn	www.users.globalnet.co.uk/~8sqnwad/
No 9 Sqn	www.rafmarham.co.uk/organisation/9squadron/9sqn_front.htm
No 10 Sqn	www.raf.mod.uk/rafbrizenorton/10squadron.html
No 12 Sqn	www.rafmod.uk/raflossiemouth/sqn/pages/12.htm
No 13 Sqn	www.rafmarham.co.uk/organisation/13squadron/13squadron.htm
No 14 Sqn	www.raf.mod.uk/raflossiemouth/sqn/pages/14.htm
No 15 Sqn	www.xvsquadron.com
No 16(R) Sqn	www.raf.mod.uk/rafcoltishall/squadrons/16Sqn.htm
No 18 Sqn	www.rafodiham.co.uk/structure/squadrons/18sqn/18sqn.htm
No 19(R) Sqn	www.rafvalley.org/Flying/19Sqn/19Sqnindex.htm
No 20(R) Sqn	www.raf.mod.uk/rafwittering/sqn20.htm
No 23 Sqn	www.users.globalnet.co.uk/~23sqnwad/
No 24 Sqn	www.lyneham.raf.mod.uk/24sqn/xxiv.htm
No 27 Sqn	www.rafodiham.co.uk/structure/squadrons/27sqn/27sqn.htm
No 31 Sqn	www.rafmarham.co.uk/organisation/31squadron/31sqn.htm
No 39(1 PRU) Sqn	www.rafmarham.co.uk/organisation/39squadron/39squadron2.htm
No 41 Sqn	www.raf.mod.uk/rafcoltishall/squadrons/41Sqn.htm
No 42(R) Sqn	www.kinloss-raf.co.uk//42sqnintro.html
No 45(R) Sqn	www.cranwell.raf.mod.uk/3fts/45sqn/45sqn.htm
No 51 Sqn	website.lineone.net/~redgoose/
No 54 Sqn	www.raf.mod.uk/rafcoltishall/squadrons/54Sqn.htm
No 55(R) Sqn	www.cranwell.raf.mod.uk/3fts/55sqn/55sqn.htm
No 70 Sqn	70sqn.tripod.com/
No 99 Sqn	www.raf.mod.uk/rafbrizenorton/99squadron.html
No 101 Sqn	www.raf.mod.uk/rafbrizenorton/101squadron.html
No 120 Sqn	www.kinloss-raf.co.uk//120sqnintro.htm
No 201 Sqn	www.kinloss-raf.co.uk//201sqnintro.html
No 206 Sqn	www.kinloss.raf.mod.uk/opswing/ops206.htm
No 216 Sqn	www.raf.mod.uk/rafbrizenorton/216squadron.html
No 617 Sqn	www.raf.mod.uk/raflossiemouth/sqn/pages/617.htm
Aberdeen, Dundee and St Andrews UAS	dialspace.dial.pipex.com/town/way/gba87/adstauas/
The Army Air Corps	www.army.mod.uk/armyaircorps/info.htm
Blue Eagles Home Page	www.deltaweb.co.uk/eagles/
Cambridge University Air Squadron	www.srcf.ucam.org/cuas/
Defence Helicopter Flying School	www.shawbury.raf.mod.uk/dhfs.htm
East Midlands UAS	www.emuas.dial.pipex.com/
Fleet Air Arm	www.royal-navy.mod.uk/static/pages/145.html
JFACTSU	www.raf.mod.uk/jfactsu/
Liverpool University Air Squadron	www.sn63.dial.pipex.com/
Manchester & Salford Universities Air Sqn	www.masuas.dial.pipex.com/
Ministry of Defence	www.mod.uk/

Name of site	Internet Dial (all prefixed 'http://')
Northumbrian UAS	www.dur.ac.uk/nuas/
Oxford University Air Sqn	users.ox.ac.uk/~ouairsqn/
QinetiQ	www.qinetiq.com/
RAF Benson	www.raf.mod.uk/rafbenson/index.htm
RAF Boulmer	www.rafboulmer.co.uk/
RAF Brize Norton	www.raf.mod.uk/rafbrizenorton/
RAF Church Fenton (unofficial)	www.rafchurchfenton.org.uk/
RAF College Cranwell	www.cranwell.raf.mod.uk/
RAF Cosford	www.raf.mod.uk/cosford/
RAF Kinloss	www.kinloss.raf.mod.uk/
RAF Leuchars	www.leuchars.raf.mod.uk/
RAF Lossiemouth	www.raf.mod.uk/raflossiemouth/
RAF Lyneham	www.lyneham.raf.mod.uk/
RAF Marham	www.rafmarham.co.uk/
RAF Northolt	www.rafnortholt.com/
RAF Northolt (unofficial)	www.fly.to/Northolt/
RAF Odiham	www.rafodiham.co.uk/
RAF Shawbury	www.shawbury.raf.mod.uk/
RAF Valley	www.rafvalley.org/
RAF Waddington	www.raf-waddington.com/
RAF Wittering	www.raf.mod.uk/rafwittering/
Red Arrows	www.raf.mod.uk/reds/redhome.html
Royal Air Force	www.raf.mod.uk/
Royal Auxiliary Air Force	www.rauxaf.mod.uk/
SAOEU	www.saoeu.org/
University of London Air Sqn	www.raf.mod.uk/ulas
Yorkshire UAS	www.yuas.dial.pipex.com/

MILITARY SITES – US

Air Combat Command	www.acc.af.mil/
Air Force Reserve Command	www.afrc.af.mil/
Air National Guard	www.ang.af.mil/
Aviano Air Base	www.aviano.af.mil/
Liberty Wing Home Page (48th FW)	www.lakenheath.af.mil/
NASA	www.nasa.gov/
Ramstein Air Base	www.ramstein.af.mil/home.html
Spangdahlem Air Base	www.spangdahlem.af.mil/
USAF	www.af.mil/
USAF Europe	www.usafe.af.mil/
USAF World Wide Web Sites	www.af.mil/sites/
US Army	www.army.mil/
US Marine Corps	www.usmc.mil/
US Navy	www.navy.mil/
US Navy Patrol Squadrons (unofficial)	www.vpnavy.com/

MILITARY SITES – ELSEWHERE

Armée de l'Air	www.defense.gouv.fr/air/
Aeronautica Militare	www.aeronautica.difesa.it
Austrian Armed Forces (in German)	www.bmlv.gv.at
Belgian Air Force	www.mil.be/aircomp/index.asp?LAN=E
Canadian Forces	www.forces.ca/
Finnish Defence Force	www.mil.fi/english/
Forca Aerea Portuguesa	www.emfa.pt/
Frecce Tricolori	users.iol.it/gromeo/
German Marine	www.deutschemarine.de/
Greek Air Force	www.haf.gr/gea_uk/frame.htm
Irish Air Corps	www.military.ie/aircorps/index.html
Israeli Defence Force/Air Force	www.idf.il/
Luftforsvaret	www.mil.no/
Luftwaffe	www.luftwaffe.de/
NATO	www.nato.int/
Royal Australian Air Force	www.defence.gov.au/RAAF/
Royal Danish Air Force (in Danish)	www.ftk.dk/
Royal Netherlands AF	www.mindef.nl/english/rnlaf1.htm
Royal New Zealand AF	www.airforce.mil.nz/
Singapore Air Force	www.mindef.gov.sg/rsaf/
South African AF Site (unofficial)	www.saairforce.co.za/
Spanish Air Force	www.aire.org/
Swedish Air Force	www.mil.se/
Swedish Military Aviation (unofficial)	www.canit.se/%7Egriffon/aviation/
Swiss Armed Forces	www.vbs.admin.ch/internet/e/armee/
Turkish General Staff (Armed Forces)	www.tsk.mil.tr/

Military Aviation Internet

AIRCRAFT & AERO ENGINE MANUFACTURERS

BAE Systems	www.baesystems.com/
Bell Helicopter Textron	www.bellhelicopter.textron.com/index.html
Boeing	www.boeing.com/
Bombardier	www.bombardier.com/
Britten-Norman	www.britten-norman.com/
CFM International	www.cfm56.com/
Dassault	www.dassault-aviation.com/
EADS	www.eads.net/
Embraer	www.embraer.com/
General Electric	www.ge.com/
Gulfstream Aerospace	www.gulfstream.com/
Kaman Aerospace	www.kaman.com/
Lockheed Martin	www.lockheedmartin.com/
Lockheed Martin Aeronautics	www.lmaeronautics.com/palmdale/index.html
Raytheon	www.raytheon.com/rac/
Rolls-Royce	www.rolls-royce.com/
SAAB	www.saab.se/
Sikorsky	www.sikorsky.com/
Westland	www.whl.co.uk/

UK AVIATION MUSEUMS

Aeroventure	www.aeroventure.org.uk/
Aviation Museums in Great Britain	www.rdg.ac.uk/AcaDepts/sn/wsn1/dept/av/gb.html
Bournemouth Aviation Museum	www.aviation-museum.co.uk/
Brooklands Museum	www.brooklandsmuseum.com/
City of Norwich Aviation Museum	www.cnam.co.uk/
de Havilland Aircraft Heritage Centre	www.hertsmuseums.org.uk/dehavilland/index.htm
Dumfries & Galloway Aviation Museum	www.dgam.co.uk/
Fleet Air Arm Museum	www.fleetairarm.com/
Gatwick Aviation Museum	www.gatwick-aviation-museum.co.uk/
The Helicopter Museum	www.helicoptermuseum.co.uk/
Imperial War Museum, Duxford	www.iwm.org.uk/duxford/
Imperial War Museum, Duxford (unofficial)	dspace.dial.pipex.com/town/square/rcy85/
The Jet Age Museum	www.jetagemuseum.org/
Lincs Aviation Heritage Centre	freespace.virgin.net/nick.tasker/ekirkby.htm
Midland Air Museum	www.midlandairmuseum.org.uk/
Museum of Army Flying	www.flying-museum.org.uk/
Museum of Berkshire Aviation	fly.to/MuseumofBerkshireAviation/
Museum of Flight, East Fortune	www.nms.ac.uk/flight/main.htm
Museum of Science & Industry, Manchester	www.msim.org.uk/
Newark Air Museum	www.newarkairmuseum.co.uk/
North East Aircraft Museum	www.neam.co.uk/
RAF Manston Spitfire & Hurricane Memorial	www.spitfire-museum.com/
RAF Museum, Hendon	www.rafmuseum.org.uk/
Science Museum, South Kensington	www.sciencemuseum.org.uk/
Yorkshire Air Museum, Elvington	www.yorkshireairmuseum.co.uk

AVIATION SOCIETIES

Air Britain	www.air-britain.com/
Air North	www.airnorth.demon.co.uk/
Cleveland Aviation Society	homepage.ntlworld.com/phillip.charlton/ cashome.html
East London Aviation Society	www.westrowops.co.uk/newsletter/elas.htm
Friends of Leeming Aviation Group	www.screamin-leeming.co.uk/
Gilze-Rijen Aviation Society	www.gras-spotters.nl/
Royal Aeronautical Society	www.raes.org.uk/
St Athan Aviation Group	www.westrowops.co.uk/newsletter/stamu.htm
Scottish Air News	www.scottishairnews.co.uk/
Scramble (Dutch Aviation Society)	www.scramble.nl/
Solent Aviation Society	www.solent-aviation-society.co.uk/
Spitfire Society	www.spitfiresociety.demon.co.uk/
The Aviation Society Manchester	www.tasmanchester.com/
Ulster Aviation Society	www.d-n-a.net/users/dnetrAzQ/
Wolverhampton Aviation Group	www.wolverhamptonag.fsnet.co.uk/

OPERATORS OF HISTORIC AIRCRAFT

The Aircraft Restoration Company	www.arc-duxford.co.uk/
Battle of Britain Memorial Flight	www.bbmf.co.uk/
Catalina Online	www.catalina.org.uk/
De Havilland Aviation	www.dehavilland.net/
Delta Jets	www.deltajets.ik.com/
Hunter Flying Club	www.hunterflyingclub.co.uk/

Name of site	Internet Dial (all prefixed 'http://')
Kennet Aircraft	www.airplane.demon.co.uk/
Old Flying Machine Company	www.ofmc.co.uk/
The Fighter Collection	www.fighter-collection.com/
The Real Aeroplane Company	www.realaero.com/
The Shuttleworth Collection	www.shuttleworth.org/
The Vulcan Operating Company	www.tvoc.co.uk/

SITES RELATING TO SPECIFIC TYPES OF MILITARY AIRCRAFT

The 655 Maintenance & Preservation Society	www.jetman.dircon.co.uk/xm655/
The Avro Shackleton Page	www.home.aone.net.au/shack_one/
B-24 Liberator	www.b24bestweb.com/
EE Canberra	www.bywat.co.uk/
English Electric Lightning - Vertical Reality	www.aviation-picture-hangar.co.uk/Lightning.html
The Eurofighter site	www.eurofighter.org/
The ex FRADU Canberra Site	www.fradu-hunters.co.uk/canberra/
The ex FRADU Hunter Site	www.fradu-hunters.co.uk/
F-4 Phantom II Society	www.f4phantom.com/
F-16: The Complete Reference	www.f-16.net/
F-86 Web Page	f-86.tripod.com/
F-105 Thunderchief	www.geocities.com/Pentagon/7002/
The Gripen	www.gripen.com/
K5083 - Home Page (Hawker Hurricane)	www3.mistral.co.uk/k5083/
Lockheed C-130 Hercules	hometown.aol.com/SamC130/
Lockheed SR-71 Blackbird	www.wvi.com/~lelandh/sr-71~1.htm
The MiG-21 Page	www.topedge.com/panels/aircraft/sites/kraft/mig.htm
P-3 Orion Research Group	home.wxs.nl/~p3orin/
P-51 Mustang	www.p51.mustangsmustangs.com/
Scramble on the Web - SAAB Viggen Database	www.scramble.nl/viggen.htm
Thunder & Lightnings (Postwar British Aircraft)	www.thunder-and-lightnings.co.uk/
UK Apache Resource Centre	www.ukapache.com/
Vulcan 558 Club	www.vulcan558club.demon.co.uk/
Vulcan Restoration Trust	www.XL426.com

MISCELLANEOUS

Aerodata	www.aerodata.biz/
Aeroflight	www.netlink.co.uk/users/aeroflt/
The AirNet Web Site	fly.to/AirNet/
The AirNet Web Site: Aviation Mailing Lists	homepage.ntlworld.com/hjcurtis/lists.html
Air-Scene UK	www.f4aviation.co.uk
Chinese Military Aviation	www.concentric.net/~Jetfight/
Joseph F. Baugher's US Military Serials Site	home.att.net/%7Ejbaugher/
Military Aircraft Database	www.csd.uwo.ca/~pettypi/elevon/gustin_military/
Military Aviation	www.crakehal.demon.co.uk/aviation/aviation.htm
Military Aviation Review/MAP	www.mar.co.uk/
Pacific Aviation Database Organisation	www.gfiapac.co.uk/
Polish Aviation Site	aviation.pol.pl/
Russian Aviation Page	aeroweb.lucia.it/~agretch/RAP.html
Scramble on the Web - Air Show Reports	www.scramble.nl/airshows.htm
The Spotter's Nest	www.spotters.it/
Target Lock Military Aviation E-zine	http://www.targetlock.org.uk/
UK Military Aircraft Serials Resource Centre	www.serials.com/
UK Military Spotting	www.thunder-and-lightnings.co.uk/spotting/

Maryland ANG C-130J Hercules 81355 of the 135th AS rapidly disgorging a load of crates. *PRM*

Boeing C-135C 12669 flown by the 412th TW from Edwards AFB, California. *PRM*